QMW Library
KU-627-412
23 1164063 3

REVOLT OR REVOLUTION

AUSTRALIA
The Law Book Company
Brisbane . Sydney . Melbourne . Perth

CANADA
Carswell
Ottowa . Toronto . Calgary . Montreal . Vancouver

AGENTS
Steimatzky's Agency Ltd., Tel Aviv;
N.M. Tripathi (Private) Ltd., Bombay;
Eastern Law House (Private) Ltd., Calcutta;
M.P.P. House, Bangalore;
Universal Book Traders, Delhi
Aditya Books, Delhi;
Macmillan Shuppan KK, Tokyo;
Pakistan Law House, Karachi, Lahore.

REVOLT OR REVOLUTION

The Constitutional Boundaries of the European Community

DIARMUID ROSSA PHELAN

Barrister,
Jean Monnet Lecturer in European Law,
Trinity College, Dublin

DUBLIN
ROUND HALL SWEET & MAXWELL
1997

Published in 1997 by
Round Hall Sweet & Maxwell
Brehon House, 4 Upper Ormond Quay,
Dublin 7.

Typeset by
Carrigboy Typesetting, Durrus, Co. Cork.

Printed by
Hartnolls, Bodmin, Cornwall.

ISBN 1-899738-24-X

A catalogue record for this book
is available from the British Library.

This book is dedicated to my grandmother
Anne Fortune, R.I.P.

ACKNOWLEDGEMENTS

This book is a Ph.D. thesis defended in May 1995 in the European University Institute in Florence, and somewhat amended. Thanks are due to many.

I owe a particular debt to those who have been involved in the development of this Ph.D. thesis: Professor Francis Snyder of the European University Institute as supervisor for his constant supervision, encouragement, inspiration, and help, Professor John Finnis of University College, Oxford, Professor Bernard Rudden of Brasenose College, Oxford, and Professor Gunther Teubner, of the London School of Economics (formerly of the European University Institute) for their guidance and Professor Christian Joerges of the University of Bremen for his encouragement.

To those who examined the work, Mr Justice John Murray of the Court of Justice of the European Communities (Chairman of the Board), Professor William Binchy of Trinity College Dublin, Professor Yves Mény of the Robert Schuman Centre at the European University Institute, Professor Francis Snyder, and Professor Bernard Rudden.

To my parents.

To those who have encouraged me in the study of European Community law and in the development of perspectives, principally Professor Stefan Riesenfeld of the University of California at Berkeley, Professor Richard Buxbaum of that University, and Dr John Handoll.

To those who have read and commented on parts of the work, Mr Justice Donal Barrington of the Supreme Court (formerly of the Court of First Instance of the European Communities), Anthony Collins, barrister, Gráinne de Burca of Somerville College Oxford, Professor Barry Fitzpatrick of the University of Ulster, Mr Justice Roderick O'Hanlon, formerly of the High Court, Mr Justice Brian Walsh of the European Court of Human Rights, Anthony Whelan, *référendaire* at the Court of Justice of the European Communities, Dr Simon Whittaker of St. John's College Oxford and Mr Gerry Whyte of Trinity College Dublin.

To the institutions to which I have been attached in the course of this work: the European University Institute, Brasenose College Oxford, Hertford College Oxford, Trinity College Dublin, the Law Library, and the law firm of Hughes Hubbard & Reed and there in particular to Mr John M. Townsend. To the Court of Justice of the European Communities and in particular to Mr Justice Murray, Paul Nihoul, Michel Struys, Pierre Roseren, and Anthony Collins, Nicole Charpentier, Mark Ronayne and John O'Sullivan.

To the sources of funding: the Department of Education, the European University Institute, Hertford College, Brasenose College, the *Fondation Robert Schuman*, the Arts and Social Sciences Benefaction Fund, the Provost's Academic Development Fund, the Moran Fund, and the Court of Justice of the European Communities.

To all those in the European University Institute milieu for their stimulus, with apologies for omissions, including Zenon Bankowski, Thomas Bourke, David Coen, Jason Coppel, Professor Stuart Holland, Kees Kuilwijk, Tom Lawton, Miguel Poaires Maduro, Declan Murphy, Síofra O'Leary, Aidan O'Neill, Sol Picotto, Wolf Sauter, John Stanton-Ife, and Professor Eric Stein (University of Michigan).

To Isabelle Krauss.

To the research assistants who assisted in the editing of this work: Philip Rahn, Killian Kearney, and Susan Lanigan.

Thanks are also due to Round Hall Sweet & Maxwell and in particular, Alison Caldwell, Thérèse Carrick, Julietta Clancy who prepared the index, Bart Daly, Michael Diviney, Catherine Dolan who prepared the tables, and Paul Power for their encouragement, work and expertise in publishing a Ph.D. as a book. Various parts of the manuscript and related publications have been in circulation since 1992, and some parts are published in altered form in the (1992) *Modern Law Review*, the (1993) *Irish Law Times*, and the (1994) *Dublin University Law Journal* and thanks are due to those journals for permission to retain the altered parts here.

The argument opens on a number of fronts, national and Community, simultaneously. It is published in the entirety in the hope that the risks inherent in attempting the first co-ordinated assaults on these fronts will be outweighed by its attempted contribution to the development of later thinking on the constitutional problems posed by integration. An effort has been made within the time and space to incorporate brief answers to some of the commentators on earlier versions who have come to my attention to date, and to take into account some changes in the law since thesis submission, although there may be omissions.

The author is responsible for the contents.

D.R.P.

Easter Monday, 1996

TABLE OF CONTENTS

Page

Acknowledgements vii
Detailed Table of Contents xiii
Table of Treaties, Protocols and Declarations of the European Communities .. xxv
Table of Legislation of the European Communities xxx
Table of Treaties and International Instruments xxxii
Table of National Legislation xxxiv
Chronological Table of Cases before the Court of Justice of the European Communities xlii
Alphabetical Table of Cases before the Court of Justice of the European Communities xlix
Table of Opinions of the Court of Justice of the European Communities and Table of Cases before the Court the First Instance lvi
Table of the Permanent Court of International Justice and the International Court of Justice and Table of Cases before the European Court of Human Rights lvii
Table of National Cases lviii

PART I **INTRODUCTION** 1

Chapter 1 Method and Summary of Argument 3

PART II **EUROPEAN COMMUNITY LAW** 19

Chapter 2 Perceptions of European Community Law 21
Chapter 3 In General 26
Chapter 4 Origin 29
Chapter 5 Competences 32
Chapter 6 The Status of Public International Law Treaties in European Community Law 38
Chapter 7 The Status of General Public International Law Rules, Principles, and Principles of Interpretation 46
Chapter 8 Rights to Individuals 62
Chapter 9 Citizenship 141
Chapter 10 Treaty as Constitution 144
Chapter 11 Amendability 148
Chapter 12 Jurisdiction for Conflicts 159
Chapter 13 European Community Law as a Federal Legal Order ... 160

Part III **French Constitutional Law** 163

Chapter 14 A Legal Constitution with the Possibility of Inter-Order conflicts with European Community Law 165
Chapter 15 The History of the Ratification of the Treaty on European Union 186
Chapter 16 Sovereignty 190
Chapter 17 Denunciation and Reversibility 217
Chapter 18 French Constitutional Law Interpretation of European Community Law in the Ratification of the Treaty on European Union 222
Chapter 19 The Condition of Reciprocity 236
Chapter 20 Internal Conflict and Reservations of Interpretation 237
Chapter 21 The Substance of the Essential Conditions for Exercise of National Sovereignty 240
Annex 255
Chapter 22 The Conseil d' État and The Cour de Cassation 255

Part IV **Irish Constitutional Law** 271

Chapter 23 Legitimation of Irish Constitutional Law 273
Chapter 24 Concepts of Irish Constitutional Law 303
Chapter 25 The Constitutionalisation of Irish Law 313
Chapter 26 Public International Law in Irish Constitutional Law 323
Chapter 27 European Community Law in Irish Constitutional Law 328
Chapter 28 Coping with Conflicts 356
Chapter 29 Limits on Amendment 358
Conclusion 368

Part V **Conflicts** 369

Chapter 30 National Constitutional Law Natural Right versus European Community Law Right 371
Chapter 31 Different Interpretations of Similarly Named Right . . 401
Chapter 32 National Constitutional Law Policy versus European Community Policy/Right/Principle 404

Part VI **Future Direction** 411

Chapter 33 Available Directions 413
Chapter 34 The Proposed Direction 417

Chapter 35 How to Take the Proposed Direction 420
Chapter 36 Support within European Community Law for the Proposed Direction 421
Chapter 37 Resistance Within European Community Law to the Proposed Direction 429

Bibliography 433

Index 453

DETAILED TABLE OF CONTENTS

Page

PART I: INTRODUCTION

1. METHOD AND SUMMARY OF ARGUMENT 3

1–1 – 1–8 3–7
1–9 SUMMARY OF ARGUMENT 10
1–9 I. European Community Law 11
1–9 III. National Law 13
1–9 IV. Conflicts 14
1–9 V. Future Directions 16

PART II: EUROPEAN COMMUNITY LAW

INTRODUCTION 19

2. PERCEPTIONS OF EUROPEAN COMMUNITY LAW 21

2–1 Public International Law Perception 21
2–2 National Law Perception 22
2–3 European Community Law Perception 22

3. IN GENERAL 26

3–1 Public International Law Perception 26
3–2 European Community Law Perception 28

4. ORIGIN 29

4–1 Public International Law Perception 29
4–2 European Community Law Perception 31

5. COMPETENCES 32

5–1 Public International Law Perception 32
5–2 European Community Law Perception 33
Competence to Conclude Public International Law Treaties 35
5–3 Public International Law Perception 35
5–4 European Community Law Perception 35

6. THE STATUS OF PUBLIC INTERNATIONAL LAW TREATIES IN EUROPEAN COMMUNITY LAW 38

6–1 38
6–2 Public International Law Perception 38
6–3 European Community Law Perception 38
6–4 The Treaty Establishing the European Community and Treaties with Third States 39
6–5 Secondary Law ("*Droit dérivé*") and Treaties 41
Member State Responsibility in Public International Law for Acts of the European Community 42
6–6 Public International Law Perception 42
6–7 European Community Law Perception 45
The Court of Justice and Decisions of International Tribunals ... 45
6–8 Public International Law Perception 45
6–9 European Community Law Perception 45

7. THE STATUS OF GENERAL PUBLIC INTERNATIONAL LAW RULES, PRINCIPLES, AND PRINCIPLES OF INTERPRETATION 46

Rules and Principles of Public International Law in General 46
7–1 46
7–2 Public International Law Perception 46
7–3 European Community Law Perception 46
Pacta Sunt Servanda 47
7–4 European Community Law Perception 47
7–5 Public International Law Perception 47
Reciprocity 47
7–6 Public International Law Perception 47
7–7 European Community Law Perception 48
7–8 Public International Law Perception 49
Exhaustion of Domestic Remedies 50
7–9 Public International Law Perception 50
7–10 European Community Law Perception 51
7–11 Obligation in the Result – Non-Transformation of Regulations 51
7–12 Public International Law Perception 52
7–13 European Community Law Perception 52
Public International Law Influence in Interpretation 57
7–14 European Community Law Perception 57
7–15 Public International Law Perception 59
Public International Law as Quarry for Unwritten European Community Law Rule 60
7–16 European Community Law Perception 60
7–17 Public International Law Perception 61

8. RIGHTS TO INDIVIDUALS ... 62

8–1 Introduction ... 62
8–2 European Community Law Perception ... 62
8–3 Public International Law Perception ... 63
Individual Rights ... 63
8–4 Public International Law Perception ... 63
8–5 European Community Law Perception ... 64
Case 26/62 *Van Gend en Loos* ... 65
8–6 *Introduction* ... 65
8–7 *Jurisdiction: A Tale Foretold* ... 66
8–8 *Nature of the Treaties – Rejection of the Public International Law Contractual Model* ... 67
8–9 *Public International Law Note* ... 68
8–10 *Interpretation of Article 12 (EEC)* ... 68
8–11 *Nature of the Treaties – Rejection of International Responsibility* ... 69
8–12 *Article 177 (EEC) – A Ground for Individual Rights* ... 69
8–13 *Public International Law Note* ... 71
8–14 *The General Result – the Nature of the Legal Order, Sovereignty, and Legal Heritage* ... 71
8–15 *"New Legal Order of International Law"* ... 71
8–16 *Sovereignty* ... 72
8–17 *Public International Law Note* ... 73
8–18 *Sovereignty (Continued)* ... 74
8–19 *"Independently of the Legislation of Member States"* ... 75
8–20 *Legal Heritage/Patrimony* ... 75
8–21 *Effectiveness and Uniformity* ... 75
8–22 *Uniformity* ... 75
8–23 *Effectiveness* ... 77
8–24 *The Basis of the Decision* ... 77
8–25 *The Demands Placed on National Law* ... 78
The Development and Expansion of *Van Gend en Loos* ... 79
8–26 *The Expansion of the Field of its Effect* ... 79
8–27 *Tests* ... 79
8–28 *Treaty Provisions* ... 81
8–29 *International Treaties* ... 83
8–30 *Regulations* ... 84
8–31 *Directives* ... 85
8–32 *Decisions* ... 88
8–33 *Remedy in Damages* ... 88
8–34 *Direct Effect as a Doctrine Independent of its Original Legitimation* ... 91
8–35 *The Development of the Depth of its Penetration* ... 92
8–36 *European Community Law as Source of National Judicial Power and Duty* ... 92

8–37 *European Community Law Constrains National Judicial Power* ... 96
8–38 *European Community Law Conditions National Judicial Power* ... 97
Supremacy ... 98
8–39 Public International Law Perception ... 98
8–40 European Community Law Perception ... 100
Case 6/64 *Costa v. ENEL* ... 102
8–41 *Background to the Article 177 Reference* ... 102
8–42 *Admissibility and the Structure of Argument* ... 104
8–43 *The Role of the Court of Justice: Interpreter or Applier of European Community law?* ... 105
8–44 *Validity of National Law* ... 105
8–45 *Application of European Community Law* ... *106*
The Basis for Supremacy ... 107
8–46 *The Text of the Judgment* ... 107
8–47 *Rejection of Public International Law* ... 108
8–48 *Integration and Spirit* ... 109
8–49 *Sovereignty* ... 110
8–50 *Uniformity and Effectiveness:*
Executive Uniformity ... 111
8–51 *Objectives* ... 112
8–52 *Provisions of the Treaty* ... 113
8–53 *Summary* ... 114
The Development and Expansion of Case 6/64 *Costa v. ENEL* 114
8–54 *Supremacy over National Law of Whatever Nature* ... 114
8–55 *No Power to Strike Down a Conflicting National Law* ... 116
8–56 *Requiring Abrogation of Conflicting National Law* ... 117
8–57 *Preemption* ... 118
8–58 Case 106/77 *Simmenthal* ... 119
Fundamental Rights ... 120
8–59 Public International Law Perception ... 120
8–60 European Community Law Perception ... 120
8–61 Extension of European Community Law's Jurisdiction and Demands ... 121
Basis of the Extension ... 123
8–62 *Fundamental Rights as General Principles* ... 123
8–63 *Textual Basis for General Principles* ... 124
Jurisprudential Basis for Fundamental Rights ... 126
8–64 *No Jurisprudential Basis for Fundamental Rights* ... 126
8–65 *Jurisprudential Basis for Fundamental Rights* ... 128
8–66 *Sources of Fundamental Rights Independent from Jurisprudential Basis* ... 132
8–67 *International Sources of Fundamental Rights Helps Reference Back to Treaty Basis* ... 136

8–68 *Basis of Jurisdictional Extension* 136
8–69 Fundamental Rights Currently Included 203

9. CITIZENSHIP 141

9–1 Public International Law Perception 141
9–2 European Community Law Perception 141

10. TREATY AS CONSTITUTION 144

10–1 Public International Law Perception 144
10–2 European Community Law Perception 145

11. AMENDABILITY 148

11–1 Importance 148
11–2 Preliminaries 148
General Rules 149
11–3 Public International Law Perception 149
11–4 European Community Law Perception 150
11–5 Unanimity 151
Unilateral change 152
11–6 Public International Law Perception 152
11–7 European Community Law Perception 152
Institutional Involvement and Procedural Limits to the Member States' Powers of Amendment 153
11–8 European Community Law Perception 153
11–9 Public International Law Perception 154
Substantive Limits 154
11–10 Public International Law Perception 154
11–11 European Community Law Perception 155

12. JURISDICTION FOR CONFLICTS 159

13. EUROPEAN COMMUNITY LAW AS A FEDERAL LEGAL ORDER 160

13–1 Public International Law Perception 160
13–2 European Community Law Perception 160

PART III: FRENCH CONSTITUTIONAL LAW

INTRODUCTION 163

14. A LEGAL CONSTITUTION WITH THE POSSIBILITY OF INTER-ORDER CONFLICTS WITH EUROPEAN COMMUNITY LAW 165

14–1 Introduction . . . 165
The *Conseil Constitutionnel* . . . 167
14–2 Background . . . 167
14–3 Authority . . . 170
14–4 The *Conseil Constitutionnel's* Control of the French Constitutional Legal Order . . . 172
14–5 *Article 54 – Control of International Treaties, Agreements, and Council Directives* . . . 173
14–6 *Control of* Lois . . . 176
14–7 *Article 61.2 – Constitutional Control of* Lois . . . 176
14–8 *Article 46.5 and 61.1 – Constitutional Control of Organic* Lois . . . 181
14–9 *Articles 58 and 59 - Electoral Jurisdiction Control of Compatibility of Promulgated Lois with Treaties* . . 182
14–10 *Control of Executive Measures* . . . 183
14–11 *Articles 58 and 59* . . . 183
14–12 *Article 61.2 and Article 38* . . . 183
14–13 *Article 37* . . . 184
14–14 Conclusion . . . 185

15. THE HISTORY OF THE RATIFICATION OF THE TREATY ON EUROPEAN UNION . . . 186

16. SOVEREIGNTY . . . 190

16–1 Summary . . . 190
16–2 History of the Principle of Sovereignty . . . 190
16–3 Constitutional Basis of Public International Law . . . 195
16–4 The Concepts Involved in the French Constitutional Law Perception of European Community Law . . . 198
16–5 The Distinction Between the Limitation and Transfer of Sovereignty . . . 199
16–6 The Inalienability of Sovereignty . . . 204
16–7 The Controlling Norm of the Essential Conditions for the Exercise of National Sovereignty . . . 204
The Limits on Amendment under the Constitution of 1958 . . . 206
16–8 *Limits to Amendment on the face of the Constitution and Decisions of the* Conseil Constitutionnel . . . 206
16–9 *Limits to Amendment Implicit in the Controlling Norm of the Essential Conditions for the Exercise of National Sovereignty* . . . 209
16–10 The Limits to Recognition of the Legal Effects of National Sovereignty as Political Concept or Fact . . . 212
16–11 Conclusion . . . 216

17. DENUNCIATION AND REVERSIBILITY 217

17–1 217
Constitutional Law 217
17–2 The Treaty on European Union 217
17–3 Future Treaties 218
17–4 The Relevance of the Public International Law of Treaties . . 219

18. FRENCH CONSTITUTIONAL LAW INTERPRETATION OF EUROPEAN COMMUNITY LAW IN THE RATIFICATION OF THE TREATY ON EUROPEAN UNION

18–1 222
18–2 The *Conseil Constitutionnel's* Interpretation of the European Community 223
18–3 The European Parliament 224
18–4 Union Citizenship 224
18–5 The Right to Vote in European Parliament Elections . . . 225
18–6 Voting in Council 226
18–7 The Interpretation in the Debates 226
18–8 Article 88-1: The European Communities and the European Union 228
18–9 Article 88-2: Economic and Monetary Union and Control of External Frontiers 229
18–10 Article 88-3: Elections 231
18–11 Article 88-4: Resolutions 233
18–12 Conclusion 235

19. THE CONDITION OF RECIPROCITY 236

20. INTERNAL CONFLICT AND RESERVATIONS OF INTERPRETATION 237

20–1 237
20–2 Internal Conflicts in the Constitution 237
20–3 Effect of Reservations of Interpretation 238

21. THE SUBSTANCE OF THE ESSENTIAL CONDITIONS FOR EXERCISE OF NATIONAL SOVEREIGNTY 240

21–1 240
21–2 Assuring the Guarantee of the Rights and Liberties of Citizens 240
21–3 As a Competence 240
21–4 Sources of the Rights and Liberties of Citizens 243
21–5 *Formal Sources* 244

21–6 *Material Sources* 244
21–7 *Nature and Legitimation of French Constitutional Law Fundamental Rights* 245
21–8 *Foundation of Constitution and End of Polity* 245
21–9 *Non-Positivist Nature of Rights and Freedoms* 246
21–10 *God* 246
21–11 *Recognition, not Creation* 247
21–12 *Natural Rights* 247
21–13 *Rights of Foreigners* 247
21–14 *Rights and Freedoms Understood in a Framework of Interdependent Concepts* 248
21–15 Summary 250
21–16 Assuring Respect for the Institutions of the Republic . . . 250
21–17 Assuring the Continuation of the Life of the Nation 251
21–18 Summary 253

CONCLUSION 254

Annex to Part II
22. THE *CONSEIL D'ÉTAT* AND THE *COUR DE CASSATION* 255

22–1 255
22–2 The *Conseil d'État* 256
22–3 Application of public international law treaties 256
22–4 Control of Lois 257
22–5 Control of *Règlements* 261
22–6 Conflict between the *Conseil d'État's* Interpretation of Direct Effect and Supremacy of European Community Law and European Community Law's Self-Interpretation 262
22–7 The *Cour de Cassation* 265
22–8 Conclusion 269

PART IV: IRISH CONSTITUTIONAL LAW

INTRODUCTION 271

23. LEGITIMATION OF IRISH CONSTITUTIONAL LAW 273

23–1 273
Natural Law based on Reason: Reconstructing the Doctrine 273
23–2 A Fundamental Conflict 273
23–3 The Text of the Constitution 275
23–4 Jurisprudence 276
23–5 The Role of Reason 277

23–6 Natural Law based on Theology/Religion: Debunking the Myth 280
23–7 Unenumerated Personal Rights Resulting from the Nature of the State 290
23–8 Fundamental Rights based on a Contract between State and Citizens 290
23–9 Unenumerated Personal Rights resulting from Judges' Ideas of Changing Concepts of Prudence, Justice and Charity 292
23–10 Waiver of Constitutional Rights may not be Possible 298
23–11 Resolution of Internal Constitutional Conflicts 299

24. CONCEPTS OF IRISH CONSTITUTIONAL LAW 303

24–1 303
24–2 Sovereignty of the State 303
24–3 Sovereignty of the People 306
24–4 The Common Good 307
24–5 Society 310

25. THE CONSTITUTIONALISATION OF IRISH LAW 313

25–1 313
25–2 How Conflicts can Occur Jurisdictionally 313
25–3 The Extension of Constitutional Justice into Administrative Law and Contract Law 314
25–4 The Extension of Constitutional Rights into Private Relations 317
25–5 *Locus Standi* in Proceedings against Public and Private Parties 319
25–6 Against Private Parties 319
25–7 Against the State 320
25–8 The Provision of Remedies 320
25–9 The Relaxation of Procedural Requirements 321

26. PUBLIC INTERNATIONAL LAW IN IRISH CONSTITUTIONAL LAW 323

26–1 323
26–2 Dualism 323
26–3 General Principles of Public International Law 323

27. EUROPEAN COMMUNITY LAW IN IRISH CONSTITUTIONAL LAW 328

27–1 328

27–2 History of Membership 328
The Amendment of National Law to Preempt Conflicts 329
27–3 Constitutional Amendments 329
27–4 Statutory Amendments 332
27–5 Article 29.4.3 and Article 29.4.4: Membership 334
27–6 Article 29.4.5 338
27–7 Article 29.4.5 [a] 339
27–8 Article 29.4.5 [b] 349
27–9 Why Conflicts Can Occur 352

28. COPING WITH CONFLICTS 356

29. LIMITS ON AMENDMENT 358

29–1 The Problematic 358
29–2 The Provision on Amendment 359
29–3 Manner 360
29–4 "Provision" 360
29–5 Self-Amendment 361
29–6 Popular Sovereignty and its Natural Law Limits in Irish Constitutional Law 361
29–7 Irish Constitutional Natural Law 365

CONCLUSION 368

PART V: CONFLICTS

INTRODUCTION 369

30. NATIONAL CONSTITUTIONAL LAW NATURAL RIGHT VERSUS EUROPEAN COMMUNITY LAW RIGHT 371

30–1 371
30–2 Irish Constitutional Law Natural Right versus European Community Law Right 372
30–3 The Background 374
The Scope of the European Community Law on Services 376
30–4 *Perspective of Irish Constitutional Law* 376
30–5 *Perspective of European Community Law* 377
30–6 *European Community Law Characterisation of Irish Constitutional Law Fundamental Right* 378
30–7 *European Community Law Demands on National Law* 379
30–8 *Extension of European Community Law on Services* 381
Contrasting Legitimations 383
30–9 *Contrasting Objectives* 383

30–10 *Contrasting Views of What Is Fundamental* 384
30–11 *The Extension of European Community Law Demands on National Law by Reference to Fundamentals* 385
30–12 Conflict of Fundamentals 388
30–13 National Constitutional Law Fundamental Rights as Derogations from European Community law Economic Principle 392

31. DIFFERENT INTERPRETATIONS OF A SIMILARLY NAMED RIGHT 401

31–1 401
31–2 French Constitutional Law versus European Community Law 402
31–3 Irish Constitutional Law versus European Community Law 402

32. NATIONAL CONSTITUTIONAL LAW POLICY VERSUS EUROPEAN COMMUNITY POLICY/RIGHT/PRINCIPLE .. 404

32–1 404
32–2 Irish Constitutional Law versus European Community law .. 404
32–3 French Constitutional Law versus European Community Law 407

CONCLUSION 407

PART VI: FUTURE DIRECTIONS

THE PROBLEM 411

33. AVAILABLE DIRECTIONS 413

33–1 413
33–2 Direction One 413
33–3 Direction Two 414
33–4 Direction Three 414
33–5 Direction Four 415

34. THE PROPOSED DIRECTION 417

35. HOW TO TAKE THE PROPOSED DIRECTION 420

36. SUPPORT WITHIN EUROPEAN COMMUNITY LAW FOR THE PROPOSED DIRECTION 421

36–1 421

36–2 Disuniformity 421
36–3 Further Support from within European Community Law . . 424

37. RESISTANCE WITHIN EUROPEAN COMMUNITY LAW TO THE PROPOSED DIRECTION 429

CONCLUSION 430

Bibliography 433

Index 453

TABLE OF TREATIES, PROTOCOLS AND DECLARATIONS OF THE EUROPEAN COMMUNITIES

Treaty establishing the European Economic Community, later the European Community (EEC or EC)

Preamble 67, 126, 155, 426
Part Three 33, 388
Title III 142
Art. 2 .... 149, 338, 381, 384
Art. 3b 33, 37, 149, 161, 162, 422, 428
Art. 4 154
Art. 5 .... 36, 47, 89, 96, 98, **117–118**, 124, 161, 424
(2) 108
Art. 6 126
Art. 7 ((EEC) now Art. 6 (EC)) 58, 81, 108, 114
Art. 8(1) 8, 122
Art. 8a 375, 384
Art. 8a(1) 122, 142
Art. 8b(1) 142, 232, 233
Art. 8b(2) 142
Art. 8c 142
Art. 8d 142
Art. 8–8e 142
Art. 12 .... 48, 65, 66, 68–69, 75, 80
Art. 30 .... 138, 264, 386, 387, 397
Art. 31 387
Art 36 .... 138, 387, 422
Arts. 30 and 36 84
Art. 37 264
Arts. 48 to 66 386
Art. 48 .... 81, 117, 117, 137
(1) 64
(2) 81
(3) 137, 383, 392, 395
(a) to (d) 64
Art. 49 64
Art. 52 .... 64, 267
Art. 54 .... 34, 219
Art. 56 .... 263, 392, 394, 422
Art. 57 (2) 34

Art. 59 .... 81, 375, 381, 381, 382, 383, 388, 392, 394, 400
Art. 60 .... 375, 377, 378, 381
Art. 60(d) 377
Art 66 .... 392, 394, 422
Art. 73f 422
Art. 73g 422
Art. 75 (1) (a) 36
Arts. 85 to 90 65
Art. 85 .... 64, 64, 65
Art. 86 64
Art. 87 .... 64, 64
Art. 88 .... 64, 65
Art. 89 (2) 65
Art. 92 (3)(b) 401
Art. 95 .... 93, 94, 265, 266
Art. 100a 37
(4) 422
Art. 100c 226, 231
(5) 231
Art. 102a 384
Art. 109i(1) 422
Art. 109j 422
Art. 113(3) 35
Art. 115 422
Art. 119 .... 81, 82, 83, 139, 423
Art. 128 .... **425**
Art. 129 372
Art. 129a (1)(b) 387
Art. 130m 35
Art. 130r(4) 35
Art. 130u(2) 125
Art. 130y 35
Art. 135 35–36
Art. 138(3) **175**,
Art. 164 .... 41, **124**, 127, 146, 156, 157, 346, 351, 416
Art. 165 24
Art. 168 24
Art. 169 .... 57, 58, 68, 77, 103, 104, 106, 115, 118, 159, 347, 348, 381, 384, 426
Art. 170 .... 58, 68, 77, 103, 104, 236, 347, 381, 384
Art. 171 .... 24, 159, 348
(2) 381, 385
Art. 172 .... 24, 31

Art. 173 . . . . 8, 24, 31, 64, 124, 145, 154, 155
Art. 177 . . . . 15, 24, 40, 42, 51, 51, 54, 57, 58, 59, 65, 66, 69, 70, 71, 76, 78, 85, 88, 90, 93, 96, 97, 101, 102, 104, 104, 104, 105, 106, 108, 115, 128, 129, 141, 159, 181, 255, 257, 264, 267, 268, 339, **340, 341**, 343, 347, 349, 351, 352, 354, 356, 371, 375, 383, 389, 393, 405, 424
Art. 182 347
Art. 185 98
Art. 186 98
Art. 187 24
Art. 189 . . . . 52, 57, 67, 70, 80, **84, 85**, 86, 108, 113, 262, 349
Art. 210 35
Art. 215 125
Art. 219 . . . . 24, 220, 221
Art. 220 161
Art. 222 403
Art. 227 (1) 259
Art. 228 . . . . 35, 39, 40, 41, 42
(2) 37
(5) 41, 151
(6) 39, 40
(7) 39, 41, 45
Art. 229 35
Art. 231 35
Art. 234 . . . . 72, 422
Art. 235 . . . . 34, 37, 147, 149, 162, 338, 386
Art. 236(now replaced by Art. N of the EU Treaty) 39, 150
Art. 238 . . . . 35, 156, 157
Art. 239 . . . . 151, 155, 372
Art. 240 . . . . 148, 219
Protocol (No. B) 24

Treaty establishing the European Union (EU)

Title II 333
Title III 333
Title IV 333
Tilte V 346
Title VI 346
Title VII 333
Preamble 121–122, 126, 155, 409
Art. A 151, 155, 425
Art. B 151, 155, 338
Art. D 153

Art. F 241
(1) 425
(2) 125, 225, 241, 385, 395
(3) 162
Art. G (38) 125, 372
Art. L 125, 126, 241, 333, 425
Art. J.1(2) 125
Art. K.1 385
Art. K.2(1) 125
Art. M 333
Art. N (Replaces Art. 236 of the E.C.) 39, 149, 151, 329
(1) **150**, 155
(2) 151, 155
Art. P 333
Art. Q 148, 219
Art. R 236

European Social Charter

Art. 4(4) 257

Treaty establishing the European Coal and Steel Community (ECSC Treaty)

Art. 31 127
Art. 87 24
Art. 95 149
Art. 96 150
Art. 97 148

Treaty establishing the European Atomic Energy Community (Euratom or EAEC)

Art. 203 149
Art. 204 150
Art. 208 148

Single European Act (SEA)

Title III 310, 329, 335, 336
Preamble 121, 126, 136, 380
Art. 1 384
Art. 3(1) 143
Art. 6 153
Art. 31 126

Treaty concerning the Accession of Denmark, Ireland, Norway and the United Kingdom

Art. 2 54
Art. 152 54

Protocols

Protocol (No. 2) concerning Article 117 of the Treaty establishing the European Community (the "Barber Protocol") 423
Protocol (No. 10) on the Transition to the Third Stage of Economic and Monetary union 155
Protocol (No. 14) on Social Policy 151
Protocol (No.17) Annexed to the Treaty on the European Union and to the Treaties Establishing the European Communities 373, 385

Declarations

Declaration on Citizenship of the Union
Art. 4 75
Declaration on Cooperation in the Fields of Justice and Home Affairs 75
Declaration of the High Contracting Parties to the Treaty on European Union (signed at Maastricht on the 7th Day of February 1992) 373
Declaration by the European Parliament of Fundamental Rights and Freedoms [1989] O.J. C120/51 387
Declaration on Human Rights by the European Council (29 June 1991) [1991] European Community Bull. 6 Annex V 122
Joint Declaration of 1977 [1977] O.J. C103/1 121
Declaration (No. 13) (EU) on the Role of National Parliaments in the European Union 233
Solemn Declaration of Stuttgart of 19 June 1983
s.2.5 384

TABLE OF LEGISLATION OF THE EUROPEAN COMMUNITIES

Regulations

Council Regulation 1612/68 on the Freedom of Movement of Workers and their Families [1968] O.J. L257/2 .... 380, 405
art. 8 395
Council Regulation 1111/77 of 17 May 1977 laying down common provisions for isoglucose [1977] O.J. L134/4 178

Directives

64/221/EEC : Council Directive of 25 February 1964 on the co-ordination of special measures concerning the movement and residence of foreign nationals which are justified on grounds of public policy, public security or public health [1964] O.J. L056/850
Art. 3 395
(1) 85, 263
68/151/EEC : First Council Directive of 9 March 1968 on co-ordination of safeguards which, for the protection of the interests of members and others, are required by Member States of companies within the meaning of the second paragraph of Article 58 of the Treaty, with a view to making such safegaurds equivalent throughout the Community [1968] O.J. L065/8
Art. 11 87
76/207/EEC : Council Directive of 9 February 1976 on the implementation of the principle of equal treatment for men and women as regards access to employment, vocational training and promotion, and working conditions [1976] O.J. L039/40
Art. 5(1) 86
80/987/EEC : Council Directive of 20 October 1980 on the approximation of the laws of the Member States relating to the protection of employees in the event of the insolvency of their employer [1980] O.J. L283/23 88
93/109/EC : Council Directive of 6 December 1993 laying down detailed arrangements for the exercise of the right to vote and to stand as a candidate in municipal elections by citizens of the Union residing in a Member State of which they are not nationals [1993] O.J. L329/34 142

94/80/EC : Council Directive of 19 December 1994 laying down detailed arrangements for the exercise of the right to vote and to stand as a candidate in municipal elections by citizens of the Union residing in a Member State of which they are not nationals [1994] O.J. L368/38 142

Decisions

Council Decision 76/787 [1976] O.J. L278/1 143

Written Questions of the European Parliament and Replies

No. 27, J.O. 2161/64, 11 August 1964 114
E–246/95 Single European Currency [1995] O.J. C230/7 155
E–337/95 forced sale of property in Ireland [1995] O.J. C190/8 .. 403
E–1381/95 Production of information on the European Union in Irish [1995] O.J. C230/38 404
E–2043/93 on fundamental rights of the European Union Citizens [1995] O.J. C311/30–31 385

TABLE OF TREATIES AND INTERNATIONAL INSTRUMENTS

Charter of the United Nations

Preamble 68, 126
Art. 1 126
Art. 2 126
(2) 47
(7) **418–419**
Art. 5 47
Art. 92 426

Statute of the International Court of Justice

Art. 9 426
Art. 36(2) 323
Art. 38(1) **61**
Art. 42 220

Vienna Convention on the Law of Treaties 1969

Art. 4 27
Art. 5 .... 27, 38, 149, 150
Art. 27 .... **98**, 99
Art. 31 .... **59**, 150, 384
(1) 59
(3) 59
Art. 39 149
Art. 40(1) 149, 150
Art. 46 .... **98**, 99
Art. 54 152
Art. 56 152
Art. 57 152
Art. 59 152
Art. 62 220

Vienna Convention on the Law of Treaties between States and International Organisations and between International Organisations 1986

Preamble 35, 152
Art. 5 .... 27, 38

Art. 46 41
Art. 74 45

Geneva Convention of 18 July 1951 180

Art. 33 180

Schengen Treaty 196, 202, 218–219, 221, 249, 407

Art. 2 242,

European Convention on the Protection of Human Rights and Fundamental Freedoms

Preamble **120**
Art. 1 43
Art. 6 44
(1) 257
Art. 7 124
Art. 8 .... 380, 394
Art. 9 394
Art. 10 .... 373, 394
Art. 10(1) 387
Art. 10(2) 388
Art. 11 394
Art. 34.4 324
Art. 65 218
First Protocol
Art. 3 182

TABLE OF NATIONAL LEGISLATION

IRELAND

Constitution of 1922 .... 303, 358, 365
Art. 4 405

Constitution of 1937 .... 271, 358
Preamble 250, **283**, 361, 365, **383–384**, 390
Art. 1 .... 310, 311, 365
Art. 3 376
Art. 5 .... 303, 304, 305, 306, **330**, 365
Art. 6 .... 283, 308, 310, 325, 330, 364
Art. 8 .... **404**, 405
Art 8.1 .... 283, 404
Art.8.3 .... 404, 405
Art.9 291
Art. 15 350
Art. 15.2 331
Art. 15.2.1 .... 324, 344
Art. 16.1 300
Art. 25.5.4 283
Art. 25.5.6 404
Art. 26 .... 313, 327
Art. 26.3 327
Art. 26.3.1 272
Art. 26.4 327
Art. 28 304
Art. 28.2 .... 304, 331
Art. 28.3 338
Art. 28.3.3 313
Art. 29 323
Art. 29.1 .... **323**
Art. 29.2 323
Art. 29.3 .... **324**, 325, 326, 327, 353
Art. 29.4 .... 304, 327, 334, 350, 354, 363, 399
Art. 29.4.1 .... 331, 353
Art. 29.4.2 310,
Art. 29.4.3 .... 299, 326, 328, 329, **334**, 335, 336, 351, 352, 352
Art. 29.4.4 .... **335**
Art. 29.4.5 .... 274, 299, 326, 334, **338**, 339 *et seq*, 361, 404

Art. 29.4.5 339–352
Art. 29.5.2 .... 305, 320
Art. 29.6 .... **323**, 324, 324, 325, 351
Arts. 33–37 313
Arts. 34 to 38 331
Art. 34 351
Art. 34.3.1 331
Art. 34.3.2 .... 313, 339
Art. 34.3.3 .... 313, 327, 327, 338, 341
Art. 34.4.3 .... 331, 341
Art. 34.5.1 353
Art. 38.2 288
Arts. 40 to 44 .... 291, 377
Art.40 .... 298, 395
Art. 40.1 .... 275, 291, 314, 321, 405
Art. 40.2 377
Art. 40.3 .... 276, 291, 315, 354
Art. 40.3.1 .... 275, 320
Art. 40.3.2 .... 291, 301, 342
Art. 40.3.3 .... 287, 319, 372, 373, 375, **377**, 385, 398, 423
Art. 40.4.1 275
Art. 40.6.1.i 291, 309
Art. 40.6.1.ii 291
Art. 40.6.1.iii 291
Art. 41 .... 276, 292, 298, 321, 390
Art. 41.1.1 .... 275, 311
Art. 41.1.2 292
Art. 41.5 .... 275, 309
Art. 42 .... 276, 298, 390
Art. 42.1 275
Art. 42.5 292
Art. 43 .... 276, 342, 343, 390
Art. 43.1.1 .... 275, 402
Art. 43.2.2 .... 309, 402
Art. 44 .... 299, 300
Art. 44.1 .... **289**
Art. 44.2 .... **289**, 290, 300
Art. 44.2.2 299
Art. 44.3 .... **289**, 342
Art. 44.3.3 299
Art. 45 312
Art. 45.2 .... **309**
Art. 45.2.iv 312
Art. 46 .... 328, **359**, 361, 365

Art. 46.1 .... 360, 362, 365
Art. 46.2 362
Art. 46.5 .... 328, 362
Art. 47 .... **359–360**, 361, 365
Art. 47.1 362

Statutes

Parliament of the United Kingdom of Great Britain and Ireland

Indecent Advertisements Act 1889 (52 & 53 Vict., c. 18)
s.3 377
Offences Against the Person Act 1861 (24 & 25 Vict., c. 100)
ss. 58 and 59 377

Acts of the Oireachtas

Censorship of Publications Acts 1929–1967
s.16 377
Censorship of Publictions Act 1929 (No. 21)
s.17 377
Central Bank Act 1942 (No. 22)
s.6(1) 312
Eleventh Amendment of the Constitution Act 1992 329
European Communities Act, 1972 (No.27) 326, 327, 328, 331, 332, 333, 334, 337, 339, 350, 351, 352, 406
s.1 333
s.2 .... **333**, 341, 345, 347, 350
s.3(2) 339, 343, 344
European Communities (Amendment) Act 1986 (No. 37) ... 329, 335
European Communities (Amendment) Act 1992 (No. 24) 333
Executive Authority (External Relations) Act 1936 (No. 58) 310
Health (Family Planning) Act 1979 (No. 20)
s.10(b) 377
s.12(1) 377
s.12(2) 377
Offences against the State (Amendment) Act 1940 (No. 2) 324
Regulation of Information (Services Outside the State for Termination of Pregnancies) Act 1995 (No.5) 377
s.6 373
Republic of Ireland Act 1948 (No. 22) 310
Shops (Hours of Trading) Act 1938 (No. 3)
s.25 299
Tenth Amendment of the Constitution Act 1987 .... 329, 362
Thirteenth Amendment to the Constitution Act 1992 301

FRANCE

French Constitutions

Declaration of the Rights of Man and of the Citizen 1789 .... 163, 165, 193, 223, 238, 242, 244, 246, 247, 248
Preamble 246
Art. 2 .... 191, **246**, 247, 254, 402
Art. 3 .... 190, 223, 232
Art. 4 .... 192, 247, **248**
Art. 5 .... **248**
Art. 6 192
Art. 10 248
Art. 11 249
Art. 16 .... **245**
Art. 17 .... 237, 248
Arts. 17 and 18 .... **191**

First Written Constitution of 3 September 1791 .... 190, 247
Preamble 246, 247
Article 249

Constitution of Year VIII 208

Constitutional Act of 24 June 1793 .... 246, 247, 248
Preamble 246, 247
Art. 1 247
Art. 6 247
Articles 7 to 10 191
Art. 7 .... **191**

Declaration of the Rights and Duties of Man and Citizen of the Constitution of 1795 247

Constitution of 1814
Preamble 191

Constitution of the Second Republic 1848 191

Consitution of the Second Empire 1852 191
Art. 1 .... **191**
Art. 5 191

Constitution of the Fourth Republic 1946 . . . . 186, 192, 223
Preamble 193, 196, 199, 220, 223, 238, 238, 242, 244, 245, 247
para. 4 . . . . 202, 238
para. 14 183
Title IV 195
Art. 3 . . . . **193**
Art. 8 170
Art. 26 196
Art. 27 223
Art. 28 218
Art. 95 . . . . **208**

Constitution of the Fifth Republic 1958 . . . . . . 166, 167, 168, 192, 193, 194, 195, 198, 199, 206, 208, 209, 212, 213, 216, 218, 223, 226, 244, 246, 250, 251, 261, 331
Preamble 184, 193, 195, 220, 244, 247, 250
para. 14 and 15 195
Title VI 195, 196
Title XIV 189, 217
Title XV 178, 180, 181, 237
Art. 2 . . . . **193**
Art. 3 . . . . **193**, 198, 206, 207, 214, 223, 230, 232, 237, 252
Art. 4 . . . . **194**, 369
Art. 7 . . . . **207**
Art. 11 . . . . 178, 188, 192, **193**, 208
Art. 16 . . . . 170, 207
Art. 20 234
Art. 24 . . . . 232, 251
Art. 25 182
Art. 26 236
Art. 34 . . . . 167, 168, 178, 207, 230, 234, 238, 243, 245
Art. 34.3 184
Art. 34.5 184
Art. 37 . . . . 171, 173, **184**, 234
Art. 37.2 184
Art. 38 . . . . 183, 258
Art. 41 170
Art. 45 . . . . 187, 188
Art. 46.5 . . . . 181, 182
Art. 49 234
Art. 50 234
Art. 52 . . . . 175, 186, 234
Arts. 52 to 55 196
Art. 53 . . . . 175, 186, 188, **196**, 223, 243

Art. 53–1 196
para. 1 197
para. 2 197
Art. 54 .... 171, **173**, 174, 175, 177, 178, 182, 186, 186, 188, 195, 196, 200, 201, 207, 219, 227, 230, 259
Art. 55 .... 175, 178, 180, 181, 183, 196, 200, 236, 256, 258, 260, 262, 265, 266, 267, 268
Art. 56 169
Art. 57 169
Art. 58 .... 170, 182, 183
Art. 59 .... 170, 182, 183, 259
Art. 60 .... 170, 177
Art. 61 .... 171, 173, 179, 183, 266
Art. 61.1 .... 181, 182
Art. 61.2 .... 173, 174, **176**, 177, 178, 179, 180, 182, 183, 188, 202, 210, 213, 242
Art. 61.3 181
Art. 62 .... 171, 172, 181, 239, 255, 268, 269
Art. 66 .... 184, 245, 268
Art. 72 .... 232, 251
Art. 74 234
Art. 88–1 to 88–4 179
Art. 88–4 369
Art. 88–1 .... 181, 203, 205, 224, 228, 229, 230, 237, 239
Art. 88–2 .... 181, 206, 229, 230, 231, 231, 236, 237
Art. 88–3 .... 182, 204, 205, 206, 225, 229, 230, 232, 233, 236, 237
Art. 88–4 235,
Art. 89 .... 186, 187, 192, 197, 202, 205, 208
Art. 89–2 178
Art. 89–4 .... 207, 233, 235
Art. 89–5 .... 207, **208**, 251

Legislation

Lois

Constitutional *lois* of 24 and 25 February and 16 July 1875 191
Constitutional *loi* of 25 February 1875
Art. 2 191
Constitutional *loi* of 14 August 1884
Art. 2 208
Constitutional *loi* of 3 June 1958 268
Constitutional *loi* No. 74–904 of 29 October 1974, J.O. 11035, 30 October 1974 176
Loi No. 90–385 235

Constitutional *loi* No. 92–554 of 25 June 1992, J.O. p. 8406 ... 173, 196
Art. 2 ... 173, 211
Constitutional *loi* No. 93–1526 of 25 November 1993, J.O. p. 16296 ... 197
Constitutional *loi* No. 95–880 of 4 August 1995 ... 192, 198
Proposed constitutional *loi on the status of Corsica* ... 193, 252,
Art. 3 ... 193

Ordonnances
Ordonnance of the French Committee of National Liberation of 3 June 1944 on the Provisional Government of the French Republic ... 215
Ordonnance of the Provisional Government of the French Republic of 9 August 1944 on the re-establishment of republican legality on the continental territory ... 208, 215
Art. 1 ... **215**
Art. 2 ... **215**
Art. 8 ... 215
Art. 9 ... 215
Ordonnance No. 58/1067 of 7 November 1958 ... 169
Art. 3 ... 169
Art. 7 ... 169, 170
Ordonnance No. 58/1100 of 17 November 1958 on the functioning of the parliamentary assemblies ... 235

UNITED KINGDOM

Abortion Act 1967 (c. 87)
s.1(1) ... 379
Commonwealth of Australia Constitution Act 1900 (63 & 64 Vict., c.12) ... 417
European Communities Act 1972 ... 334
Art. 2(1) ... 116
s.3(1) ... 334
Shop Act 1950 (14 Geo. 6, c. 28)
s.47 ... 397

SPAIN

Constitution
Art. 3.9.1 ... 312
Civil Code
Art. 1275 ... 87

UNITED STATES

Constitution
Art. IV
Sec.4 208
Art. V 151
Art. VI
Sec.2 .... **101**

GREECE

Constitution
Art. 21 312
Art. 108(2) 157

GERMANY

Constitution 389
Art. 6(1) 312
Art. 12 388
Art. 14 388

AUSTRALIA

Constitution
Article 106 417
Commonwealth of Australia Constitution Act 1900
(63 & 64 Vict., c.12) 417

CHRONOLOGICAL TABLE OF CASES BEFORE THE COURT OF JUSTICE OF THE EUROPEAN COMMUNITIES

Case 5/55, ASSIDER v. High Authority of the ECSC [1954–1956] E.C.R. 135 46

Case 8/55, Fédération Charbonnière de Belgique v. High Authority of the ECSC [1954–1956] E.C.R. 292 .... 25, 61, 145

Case 18/57, Nold KG v. High Authority [1959] E.C.R. 41 ...... 127, 133

Case 1/58, Stork & Co. v. High Authority [1959] E.C.R. 17 .... 126, 127, 128

Joined Cases 36–38 & 40/59, Präsident Ruhrkolen-Verkaufsgesellschaft, Geitling Ruhrkoolen-Verkaufsgesellschaft, Mausegatt Ruhrkohlen-Verkaufsgesellscaft and I. Nold KG v. High Authority [1960] E.C.R. 423 .... 127, 128, 133

Case 6/60, Humblet v. Belgium [1960] E.C.R. 559 .... 73, 105, 106, 117

Case 13/61, De Geus v. Bosch GmbH [1962] E.C.R. 45; [1962] C.M.L.R. 1 .... 51, 64, 66

Case 26/62, Van Gend en Loos v. Nederlandse Aministratie der Belastingen [1963] E.C.R. 1; [1963] C.M.L.R. 105 .... 26, 54, 55, 58, 59, 64, 65 *et seq*, 102, 103, 104, 108 *et seq*, 116, 117, 120, 128, 131, 146, 264, 330, 333, 353, 374, 383, 384, 427, 428

Joined Cases 90 & 91/63, Commission v. Luxembourg and Belgium [1964] E.C.R. 625; [1965] C.M.L.R. 58 ...... 23, 48, 50, 71

Case 6/64, Costa v. ENEL [1964] E.C.R. 585;[1964] C.M.L.R. 425 .... 31, 48, 54, 67, 78, 89, 92, 101, 102 *et seq*, 117, 128, 130, 131, 132, 155, 156, 174, 263, 266, 374, 384, 428, 430

Case 57/65, Lütticke GmbH v. Hauptzollamt Saarlouis [1966] E.C.R. 205;[1971] C.M.L.R. 674 .... 92, 93

Case 28/67, Molkerei-Zentrale Westfalen/Lippe GmbH v. Hauptzollamt Paderborn[1968] E.C.R. 143; [1968] C.M.L.R. 187 .... 71, 75, 92, 104, 119

Case 14/68, Wilhelm v. Bundeskartellamt [1969] E.C.R. 1; [1969] C.M.L.R. 100 118

Case 29/69, Stauder v. City of Ulm [1969] E.C.R. 419; [1970] C.M.L.R. 112 .... 121, 129,

Case 41/69, ACF Chemiefarma v. Commission [1970] E.C.R. 661 ... 129

Case 45/69, Boehringer Mannheim GmbH v. Commission [1970] E.C.R. 769 129

Case 77/69, Commission v. Belgium [1970] E.C.R. 237; [1974] 1 C.M.L.R. 203 .... 115, 348

Case 9/70, Grad v. Finanzant Traunstein [1970] E.C.R. 825; [1971] C.M.L.R. 1 88
Case 11/70, Internationale Handelsgesellscaft v. Einfuhr- und Vorratsstelle fur Getreide[1970] E.C.R. 1125; [1972] C.M.L.R. 255 .... 121, 130, 132, 134, 227, 374, 380, 429
Case 22/70, Commission v. Council [1971] E.C.R. 263 153
Case 48/71, Commission v. Italy [1972] E.C.R. 527; [1972] C.M.L.R. 699 115
Joined Cases 21–24/72, International Fruit Co. NV v. Produktschap voor Groenten en Fruit (No. 3).[1972] E.C.R. 1219; [1975] 2 C.M.L.R. 1 .... 41, 42, 141
Case 39/72, Commission v. Italy [1973] E.C.R. 101; [1973] C.M.L.R. 439 .... 53, 415
Case 4/73, Nold v. Commission [1974] E.C.R. 491; [1974] 2 C.M.L.R. 338 .... 123, 127, 131, 133, 134, 135, 136, 249, 379, 380, 385, 388, 389, 390, 421
Case 7/73, Nold [1974] E.C.R. 491 139
Case 34/73, Variola v. Amministrazione Italiana delle Finanze [1973] E.C.R. 981 .... 53, 54
Case 146/73, Rheinmuhhlen-Dusseldorf v. Einfuhr-und Vorratsstelle Getreide [1974] E.C.R. 139; [1974] 1 C.M.L.R. 523 352
Case 167/73, Commission v. France [1974] E.C.R. 359; [1974] 2 C.M.L.R. 216 .... 54, 117, 426
Case 181/73, Haegeman v. Belgium [1974] E.C.R. 449; [1975] 1 C. M..L.R. 515 .... 39, 40
Case 8/74, Procureur du Roi v. Dassonville [1974] E.C.R. 837; [1974] 2 C.M.L.R. 436 381
Case 33/74, Van Binsbergen v. Bestuur van de Bedrijfsvereniging voor de Metaalnijverheid [1974] E.C.R. 1299; [1975] 1 C.M.L.R. 298 382
Case 36/74, Walrave and Koch v. Association Union Cycliste Internationale [1974] E.C.R. 1405; [1975] 1 C.M.L.R. 320 .. 81, 86, 87
Case 41/74, Van Duyn v. Home Office [1974] E.C.R. 1337; [1975] 1 C.M.L.R. 1 .... 85, 137, 383, 392, 393
Case 74/74, CNTA v. Commission [1975] E.C.R. 533; [1977] 1 C.M.L.R. 171 .... 123, 132
Case 11/75, Mazzali v. Ferrovia del Renon [1976] E.C.R. 657 70
Case 36/75, Rutili v. Minister of the Interior [1975] E.C.R. 1219; [1976] 1 C.M.L.R. 140 .... 122, 137, 264, 392, 393, 394, 395, 407
Case 43/75, Defrenne v. SABENA (No.2) [1976] E.C.R. 455; [1976] 2 C.M.L.R. 98 .... 49, 81, 82, 83, 86, 121, 139, 153, 383
Case 52/75, Commission v. Italy [1976] E.C.R. 277; [1976] 2 C.M.L.R. 320 .... 72, 115

Case 87/75, Bresciani v. Ammistrazione Italiana delle Finanze [1976] E.C.R. 129; [1976] 2 C.M.L.R. 62 .... 83, 84
Case 118/75, The State v. Watson and Belmann [1976] E.C.R. 1185; [1976] 2 C.M.L.R. 552 386
Case 7/76, IRCA v. Amministrazione delle Finanze dello Stato [1976] E.C.R. 1213 .... 132, 222, 379, 428
Case 30/77, R. v. Bouchereau [1977] E.C.R. 1999; [1977] 2 C.M.L.R. 800 393
Case 106/77, Amministrazione delle Finanze dello Stato v. Simmenthal SpA [1978] E.C.R. 629; [1978] 3 C.M.L.R. 263 .... 51, 70, 92, 97, 103, 106, 116, 119–120, 174, 263
Case 15/78, Société Générale Alsacienne de Banque v. Koestler [1978] E.C.R. 1971; [1979] 1 C.M.L.R. 89 381
Case 120/78, Rewe-Zentral AG v. Bundesmonopolverwaltung für Branntwein [1979] E.C.R. 649; [1979] 3 C.M.L.R. 494 ..... 381, 382
Case 148/78, Pubblico Ministero v.Ratti [1979] E.C.R. 1629; [1980] 1 C.M.L.R. 96 80
Case 232/78, Commission v. France [1979] E.C.R. 2729; [1980] 1 C.M.L.R. 418 49
Joined Cases 41, 121 & 796/79, Testa v.Bundesanstalt für Arbeit Nürnberg [1980] E.C.R. 1979; [1981] 2 C.M.L.R. 552 139
Case 44/79, Hauer v. Land Rheinland-Pfalz [1979] E.C.R. 3727; [1980] 3 C.M.L.R. 42 .... 132, 134, 136, 139, 380, 388, 389, 390, 396, 401, 421
Case 52/79, Procureur du Roi v. DeBauve [1980] E.C.R. 833; [1981] 2 C.M.L.R. 362 381
Case 62/79, Coditel v. Ciné Vog Films [1980] E.C.R. 881; [1981] 2 C.M.L.R. 362 382
Case 104/79, Foglia v. Novello (No.1) [1980] E.C.R. 745; [1981] 1 C.M.L.R. 45 104
Case 155/79, AM & S Europe v. Commission [1982] E.C.R. 1575; [1982] 2 C.M.L.R. 264 .... 134, 140, 380
Case 66/80, SpA International Chemical Corporation v. Amministrazione delle Finanze dello Stato [1981] E.C.R. 1191; [1983] 2 C.M.L.R. 593 75
Case 158/80, Rewe Handelsgesllschaft Nord mbH and Rewe Markt Steffen v. Hauptzollamt Kiel [1981] E.C.R. 1805; [1982] 1 C.M.L.R. 449 96
Case 270/80, Polydor and RSO v. Harlequin Record Shops and Simons Records [1982] E.C.R. 329;[1982] 1 C.M.L.R. 677 84
Case 279/80, Webb [1981] E.C.R. 3305; [1982] 1 C.M.L.R. 719 .. 382, 392
Case 77/81, Zuckerfabrik Franken GmbH v. Germany [1982] E.C.R. 681 .... 122, 138
Case 104/81, Hauptzollamt Mainz v. Kupferberg & Cie. [1982] E.C.R. 3641; [1983] 1 C.M.L.R. 1 .... 84, 91, 92

Joined Cases 115 & 116/81, Rezguia Adoui and Cornuaille v. Belgian State and City of Liège; [1982] E.C.R. 1665; [1982] 3 C.M.L.R. 631 393
Case 283/81, CILFIT v. Ministro della Sanit [1982] E.C.R. 3415; [1983] 1 C.M.L.R. 472 .... 59, 267, 341, 346, 424
Case 267–269/81, Amministrazione delle Finanze dello Statov. SPI [1983] E.C.R. 801 60
Case 286/81, Oosthoek's Uitgeversmaatschappij v. The Netherlands [1982] E.C.R. 4575 386
Case 199/82, Amministrazione delle Finanze dello Stato v. San Giorgio [1983] E.C.R. 3595 51
Case 286/82 and 26/83, Luisi and Carbone v. Ministero del Tesoro [1984] E.C.R. 377; [1995] 3 C.M.L.R. 52 .... 377, 378, 386
Case 14/83, Von Colson and Kamann [1984] E.C.R. 1891 87
Case 63/83, R. v. Kirk [1984] E.C.R. 2689 124
Case C–69/93 and C–258/93 Punto Casa and PPV [1994] E.C.R. I–2355 397
Case 133/83, R. v. Thomas Scott & Sons Bakers Ltd [1984] E.C.R. 2863; [1985] 1 C.M.L.R. 188 272
Case 293/83, Gravier v. City of Liège [1985] E.C.R. 606; [1985] 3 C.M.L.R. 1 .... 34, 58
Case 294/83, Partie écologiste "Les Verts" v. European Parliament [1986] E.C.R. 1339; [1987] 2 C.M.L.R. 343 .... 31, 145
Case 60/84, Cinéthèque v. Fédération Nationale des Cinémas Français [1985] E.C.R. 2605; [1986] 1 C.M.L.R. 365 138
Case 152/84, Marshall v. Southampton and South West Hampshire Area Health Authority (Teaching) [1986] E.C.R. 723; [1986] 1 C.M.L.R. 688 86,
Case 222/84, Johnston v. Chief Constable of the Royal Ulster Constabulary [1986] E.C.R. 1651; [1986] 3 C.M.L.R. 240 ... 135, 139
Joined Cases 133–136/85, Walter Rau Lebensmittelwerke v. BALM [1987] E.C.R. 22 139,
Case 234/85, Staatsanwalt Freiburg v. Keller [1986] E.C.R. 2897; [1987] 1 C.M.L.R 875 139
Case 314/85, Foto Frost v. Hauptzollamt Lübeck-Ost [1987] E.C.R. 4199; [1988] 3 C.M.L.R. 57 .... 96, 97
Case 286/85, McDermott and Cotter [1987] E.C.R. 1453; [1987] 2 C.M.L.R. 607 .... 348, 369–370
Case 12/86, Demirel v. Stadt Schwäbisch Gmünd [1987] E.C.R. 3719; [1989] 1 C.M.L.R. 421 .... 40, 79
Joined Cases 31 & 35/86, Levantina Agricola Industrial SA (LAISA) and CPC Espana v. Council [1988] E.C.R. 2285; [1988] 2 C.M.L.R 420 .... 145, 154, 155
Case 104/86, Commission v. Italy [1988] E.C.R. 1799; [1989] 3 C.M.L.R 25 54

Case 120/86, Mulder v. The Netherlands [1988] E.C.R. 2321; [1989] 2 C.M.L.R. 1 123
Case 249/86, Commission v. Germany [1989] E.C.R. 1263; [1990] 3 C.M.L.R. 540 380
Case 22/87, Commission v. Italy [1989] E.C.R. 143 89
Case 46/87 & 227/88, Hoechst v. Commission [1989] E.C.R. 2859 ... 139
Case 85/87, Dow Benelux v. Commission [1989] E.C.R. 3137 139
Joined Cases 97–99/87, Dow Chemical Ibérica v. Commission [1989] E.C.R. 3165 .... 139 140
Case 186/87, Cowan v. Tresor Public [1990] 2 C.M.L.R. 613 386
Case 193/87, Maurissen and Union Syndicate v. Court of Auditors [1989] E.C.R. 1045 145
Case 302/87, Parliament v. Council (Comitology) [1988] E.C.R. 5615 .... 96, 145
Case 379/87, Groener v. Minister for Education [1989] E.C.R. 3967 .... 392, 405–406
Case 5/88, Wachauf v. Bundesamt für Ernahrung und Fortwirtschaft [1989] E.C.R. 2609 .... 122, 136, 138, 389, 401
Case 70/88, European Parliament v. E.C. Council (Chernobyl) [1990] E.C.R. I–2041; [1992] 1 C.M.L.R. 91 .... 96, 145
Case 100/88, Oyowe and Traore v. Commission [1989] E.C.R. 4285 140
Joined Cases C–143/88 and C–92/89, Zuckerfabrik Süderdithmarschen and Zuckerfabrik Soest v. Hauptzollamt Itzehoe and Hauptzollamt Paderborn [1991] E.C.R. I–415 .. 97, 120
Case 145/88, Torfaen Borough Council v. B. & Q. plc [1989] E.C.R. 3851; [1990] 1 C.M.L.R. 337 .... 397, 398
Case 306/88, Rochdale Borough Council v. Anders [1992] E.C.R. I–6457 397
Case 362/88, GB–INNO–BM v. Confédération du Commerce Luxembourgeois [1990] 1 E.C.R. 667 386
Joined Cases C–100 & 101/89, Kaefer and Procacci v. France [1990] E.C.R. I–4647 .... 72, 88, 91
Case C–106/89, Marleasing v. La Comercial Internacional de Alimentación [1990] E.C.R. 4135; [1992] 1 C.M.L.R. 305 ..... 87, 418, 423
Case C–146/89, Commission v. United Kingdom [1991] E.C.R. I–3533 .... 40, 49, 72, 92
Case C–154/89, Commission v. France [1981] E.C.R. I–659 382
Case C–180/89, Commission v. Italy [1991] E.C.R. I–709 ...... 382, 392
Case C–188/89, Foster v. British Gas plc [1990] I–3313; [1990] 2 C.M.L.R. 833 87
Case C–192/89, Sevince v. Staatssecretaris van Justitie [1990] E.C.R. I–3461; [1992] 2 C.M.L.R. 57 .... 84, 91

Case C–198/89, Commission v. Greece [1991] E.C.R. 727 ..... 382, 392
Case C–213/89, R. v. Secretary of State for Transport ex parte Factorame Ltd. [1990] E.C.R. I–2433; [1990] 3 C.M.L.R. 1 ... 90, 115
Case C–260/89, Elliniki Radiophonia Tileorassi – Anonimi Etairia (ERT–Ae) v. Dimotiki Etairia Pliroforissis (DEP) [1991] E.C.R. I–2925 .... 122, 135, 136, 137, 138, 140, 394
Case C–312/89, Conforama (Société Internationale de Distribution d'Équipements Familiaux) v. Union Départementale des Syndicats CGT [1990] E.C.R. I–997 398
Case C–332/89, Criminal proceedings against Marchandise and others [1991] E.C.R. I–1027 398
Case C–353/89, Commission v. Netherlands [1991] E.C.R. I–4069 ... 400
Case C–377/89, McDermott and Cotter v. Minister for Social Welfare [1991] E.C.R. I–1155 .... 348, 369–370
Joined Cases C–6 & C–9/90, Francovich and Bonifaci v. Italy [1991] E.C.R. I–5357; [1993] 2 C.M.L.R. 66 .... 75, 87–88, 89–90,
Case C–18/90, ONEM v. Bahia Kziber [1991] E.C.R. I–119 84
Case C–62/90, Commission v. Germany [1992] E.C.R. I–2575 .. 123, 140
Case C–76/90, Sager v. Société Dennemeyer [1991] E.C.R. I–4221; 3 C.M.L.R. 639 .... 382, 387
Case C–159/90, Society for the Protection of the Unborn Child v. Grogan and others[1991] E.C.R. I–4685; [1991] 3 C.M.L.R. 849 .... 122, 138, 341, 374, 375, 376, 377–378, 379, 380, 381, 382, 385, 386, 387, 390, 392, 393, 394, 396, 397–397, 408, 421
Case C–208/90, Emmott v. Minister for Social Welfare [1991] E.C.R. I–4269; [1991] 3 C.M.L.R. 894 348
Case C–304/90, Reading Borough Council v. Payless DIY Ltd [1992] E.C.R. I–6493 397
Case C–369/90, Micheletti v. Delagacion del Gobierno en Cantabria [1992] E.C.R. I–4239 .... 34, 142
Case C–168/91, Konstantinidis v. Stadt Altensteig-Standesamt [1993] E.C.R. I–1191; [1993] 1 C.M.L.R. 401 137
Case C–169/91, Council of the City of Stoke-on-Trent and Norwich City Council v. B & Q Plc [1992] E.C.R. I–6635 397
Case C–219/91, Criminal proceedings against Ter Voort [1992] E.C.R. I–5485 140
Case C–237/91, Kazim Kus v. Landeshauptstadt Wiesbaden [1992] E.C.R. I–6781; [1993] 2 C.M.L.R. 887 84
Joined Cases C–267 & 268/91, Criminal proceedings against Keck and Mithourard [1993] E.C.R. I–6079; [1995] 1 C.M.L.R. 101 ... 386, 397
Case C–271/91, Marshall v. Southampton and South West Hampshire Area Health Authority (No. 2) [1993] E.C.R. I–4367 86

Case C–314/91, Weber v. Parliament [1993] E.C.R. I–1093 145
Case C–91/92, Faccini Dori v. Recreb [1994] E.C.R. I–3315 86
Joined Cases C–46 & C–48/93, Brasserie du Pêcheur SA v. Germany; R v. Secretary for Transport, ex parte Factorame [1996] E.C.R. I–1029; [1996] 1 C.M.L.R. 889; [1996] All E.R. (E.C.) 301 90
Case C–58/93 Zoubir Yousfi v. Belgium [1994] E.C.R. I–353 84
Case C–312/93 Peterbroeck v. Belgium [1995] E.C.R. I–4599 .. 96, 257
Case C–280/93, Germany v. Council [1994] E.C.R. I–4973 98
Case C–316/93, Vaneetveld v. Le Foyer SA [1994] E.C.R. I–763; [1994] 2 C.M.L.R. 852 86
Case–392/93, R. v. the Treasury, ex parte British Telecommunications [1996] E.C.R. I–1631 91
Joined Cases C–418–421/93, C–460–464/93, C–9–11/94, C–14–15/94, C–23–24/94, and C–232/94, Semeraro Caso Uno v. Sindaco del Commune di Eurbuso [1996] E.C.R. I–2975 397
Joined Cases C–422 & 424/93, Erasun et al. v. Instituto National de Empleo, [1995] E.C.R. I–1567 104
Joined Cases C–430–431/93, Van Schijindel and Van Veen [1995] E.C.R. I–4705; [1996] 1 C.M.L.R. 801; [1996] All E.R. (E.C.) 259 ..... 92, 95, 96, 257
Case C–466/93, Atlanta Fruchthandelsgesellschaft mbh e. a. v. Bundesamt für Ernährund und Forstwirtschaft [1995] E.C.R. I–3799 .... 92, 97, 98, 120, 401, 425, 426
Case C–2/94, Accession by the Community to the European Convention for the Protection of Fundamental Rights and Freedoms [1996] E.C.R. I–1759 123
Joined Cases C–178–179 & 188–190/94, Dillenkofer v. Germany (8 October 1996) 91
Case C–5/94, R v. Minister for Agriculture, Fisheries and Food ex parte Hedley Lomas (Ireland) Ltd [1996] E.C.R. I–2553 90
Case C–25/94, Commission v. Council [1996] E.C.R. I–1469 32

ALPHABETICAL TABLE OF CASES BEFORE THE COURT OF JUSTICE OF THE EUROPEAN COMMUNITIES

Accession by the Community to the European Convention for the Protection of Fundamental Rights and Freedoms [1996] E.C.R. I–1759 123
ACF Chemiefarma v. Commission [1970] E.C.R. 661 129
AM & S Europe v. Commission [1982] E.C.R. 1575; [1982] 2 C.M.L.R. 264 .... 134, 140, 380
Amministrazione delle Finanze dello Stato v. SPI [1983] E.C.R. 801 60
Amministrazione delle Finanze dello Stato v. San Giorgio [1983] E.C.R. 3595 51
Amministrazione delle Finanze dello Stato v. Simmenthal [1978] E.C.R. 629;[1978] 3 C.M.L.R. 263 .... 51, 70, 92, 97, 103, 106, 116, 119–120, 174, 263
ASSIDER v. High Authority of the ECSC [1954–1956] E.C.R. 135 ... 46
Atlanta Fruchthandelsgesellschaft mbH e.a. v. Bundesamt für Ernährund und Forstwirtschaft [1995] E.C.R. I–3799 ..... 97, 98, 120, 401, 425, 426

Boehringer Mannheim v. Commission [1970] E.C.R. 769 129
Brasserie du Pêcheur SA v. Germany and R. v. Secretary of Transport *ex parte* Fractortame Ltd. and others [1996] 1 C.M.L.R. 889; [1996] E.C.R. I–1029;[1996] All E.R. (E.C.) 301 90
Bresciani v. Ammistrazione Italiana delle Finanze [1976] E.C.R. 129; [1976] 2 C.M.L.R. 62 .... 83, 84

CILFIT v. Ministro della Sanità [1982] E.C.R. 3415; [1983] 1 C.M.L.R. 472 .... 59, 267, 341, 346, 424
Cinéthèque v. Fédération Nationale des Cinémas Français [1985] E.C.R. 2605; [1986] 1 C.M.L.R. 365; [1986] 1 C.M.L.R. 365 ... 138
CNTA v. Commission [1975] E.C.R. 533; [1977] 1 C.M.L.R. 171 .... 123, 132
Coditel v. Cine Vog Films [1980] E.C.R. 881; [1981] 2 C.M.L.R. 362 382
Commission v. Netherlands [1991] E.C.R. I–4069 400
Commission v. Belgium [1970] E.C.R. 237; [1974] 1 C.M.L.R. 203 .... 115, 348

Commission v. Council [1996] E.C.R. I–1469 32
Commission v. Council [1971] E.C.R. 263 53
Commission v. France [1974] E.C.R. 359; [1974]
2 C.M.L.R. 216 .... 54, 117, 426
Commission v. France [1979] E.C.R. 2729; [1980] 1 C.M.L.R. 418 .. 49
Commission v. France [1981] E.C.R. I–659 382
Commission v. Germany [1992] E.C.R. I–2575 .... 123, 140
Commission v. Germany [1989] E.C.R. 1263;
[1990] 3 C.M.L.R. 540 380
Commission v. Greece [1991] E.C.R. 727 .... 382, 392
Commission v. Italy [1972] E.C.R. 527; [1972] C.M.L.R. 699 115
Commission v. Italy [1973] E.C.R. 101; [1973] C.M.L.R. 439 ... 53, 415
Commission v. Italy [1976] E.C.R. 277; [1976] 2 C.M.L.R. 320 ... 72, 115
Commission v. Italy [1988] E.C.R. 1799; [1989] 3 C.M.L.R 25 54
Commission v. Italy [1989] E.C.R. 143 89
Commission v. Italy [1991] E.C.R. 709 .... 382, 392
Commission v. Luxembourg and Belgium [1964] E.C.R.
625; [1965] C.M.L.R. 58 .... 23, 48, 50, 71
Commission v. United Kingdom [1991] E.C.R. I–3533 ... 40, 49, 72, 92
Conforama (Société Internationale de Distribution d'Équipements
Familiaux) v. Union Départementale des Syndicats CGT
[1990] E.C.R. I–997 398
Costa v. ENEL [1964] E.C.R. 585;[1964] C.M.L.R. 425 .... 31, 48,
54, 67, 78, 89, 92, 101, 102 *et seq*, 117, 128, 130, 131, 132, 155,
156, 174, 263, 266, 374, 384, 428, 430
Council of the City of Stoke-on-Trent and Norwich City Council
v. B & Q Plc [1992] E.C.R. I–6635 397
Cowan v. Tresor Public [1990] 2 C.M.L.R. 613 386

Defrenne v. SABENA (No.2) [1976] E.C.R. 455;
[1976] 2 C.M.L.R. 98 .... 49, 81, 82, 83, 86, 121, 139, 153, 383
De Gues v. Bosch GmbH [1962] E.C.R. 45;
[1962] C.M.L.R. 1 .... 51, 64, 66
Demirel v. Stadt Schwäbisch Gmünd [1987] E.C.R. 3719;
[1989] 1 C.M.L.R. 421 .... 40, 79
Dillenkofer v. Germany (October 1996) 91
Dow Benelux v. Commission [1989] E.C.R. 3137 139
Dow Chemical Iberica v. Commission [1989] E.C.R. 3165 .... 139, 140

Elliniki Radiophonia Tileorassi – Anonimi Etairia (ERT–Ae) v. Dimotiki
Etairia Pliroforissis (DEP) [1991] E.C.R. I–2925 .... 122, 135,
136, 137, 138, 140, 394

Emmott v. Minister for Social Welfare [1991] E.C.R. I–4269; [1991] 3 C.M.L.R. 894 348
Erasun et al. v. Instituto National de Empleo, [1995] E.C.R. I–1567 104
European Parliament v. E.C. Council (Chernobyl) [1990] E.C.R. I–2041; [1992] 1 C.M.L.R. 91 . . . . 96, 145
European Parliament v. E.C. Council (Comitology) [1988] E.C.R. 5615 . . . . 96, 145

Faccini Dori v. Recreb [1994] E.C.R. I–3315 86
Fédération Charbonnière de Belgique v. High Authority of the ECSC [1954–1956] E.C.R. 245 . . . . 25, 61, 145
Foglia v. Novello [1980] E.C.R. 745 104
Foster v. British Gas [1990] I–3313; [1990] 2 C.M.L.R. 833 87
Foto Frost v. Hauptzollamt Lübeck-Ost [1987] E.C.R. 4199; [1988] 3 C.M.L.R. 57 . . . . 96, 97
Francovich and Bonifaci v. Italy [1991] E.C.R. I–5357 . . 75, 87–88, 89–90,

GB–INNO–BM v. Confédération du Commerce Luxembourgeois [1990] 1 E.C.R. 667 386
Germany v. Council [1994] E.C.R. I–4973 98
Grad v. Finanzant Traunstein [1970] E.C.R. 825; [1971] C.M.L.R. 1 88
Gravier v. City of Liège [1985] E.C.R. 606; [1985] 3 C.M.L.R. 1 . . . . 34, 58
Groener v. Minister for Education [1989] E.C.R. 3967 . . . 392, 405–406

Haegeman v. Belgium [1974] E.C.R. 449; [1975] 1 C.M.L.R. 515 . . 39, 40
Hauer v. Land Rheinland-Pfalz [1979] E.C.R. 3727; [1980] 3 C.M.L.R. 42 . . . . 132, 134, 136, 139, 380, 388, 389, 390, 396, 401, 421
Hauptzollamt Mainz v. Kupferberg & Cie. [1982] E.C.R. 3641; [1983] 1 C.M.L.R. 1 . . . . 84, 91
Hoechst v. Commission [1989] E.C.R. 2859 139
Humblet v. Belgium [1960] E.C.R. 559 . . . . 73, 105, 106, 117

International Fruit Company NV v. Produktschap voor Groenten en Fruit (No.3) [1972] E.C.R. 1219; [1975] 2 C.M.L.R. 1 . . . . 41, 42, 141
Internationale Handelsgesellscaft v. EVFG [1970] E.C.R. 1125; [1972] C.M.L.R. 255 . . . . 121, 130, 132, 134, 227, 374, 380, 429
IRCA v. Amministrazione delle Finanze dello Stato [1976] E.C.R. 1213 . . . . 132, 222, 379, 428

Johnston v. Chief Constable of the Royal Ulster Constabulary [1986] E.C.R. 1651; [1986] 3 C.M.L.R. 240 . . . . 135, 139

Kaefer and Procacci v. France [1990] E.C.R. 1–4647 .... 72, 88, 91
Kazim Kus v. Landeshauptstadt Wiesbaden [1992] E.C.R. I–6781; [1993] 2 C.M.L.R. 887 84
Keck and Mithourard, Criminal proceedings against, [1993] E.C.R. I–6079 .... 386, 397
Konstantinidis v. Stadt Altensteig-Standesamt [1993] E.C.R. I–1191; [1993] 1 C.M.L.R. 401 137

Levantina Agricola Industrial SA (LAISA) and CPC Espana v. Council [1988] E.C.R. 2285; [1988] 2 C.M.L.R 420 .... 145, 154, 155
Luisi and Carbone v. Ministero del Tesoro [1984] E.C.R. 377; [1995] 3 C.M.L.R. 52 .... 377, 378, 386,
Lütticke v. Hauptzollamt Saarlouis [1966] E.C.R. 205; [1971] C.M.L.R. 674 .... 92, 93

Marchandise and others, Criminal proceedings against, [1991] E.C.R. I–1027 398
Marleasing v. La Comercial Internacional de Alimentación [1990] E.C.R. I–4135 .... 87, 418, 423
Marshall v. Southampton and South West Hampshire Area Health Authority (Teaching) [1986] E.C.R. 723; [1986] 1 C.M.L.R. 688 .. 86
Marshall v. Southampton and South West Hampshire Area Health Authority (No. 2) [1993] E.C.R. I–4367 86
Maurissen and Union Syndicate v. Court of Auditors [1989] E.C.R. 1045 145
Mazzali v. Ferrovia del Renon [1976] E.C.R. 657 70
McDermott and Cotter v. Minister for Social Welfare [1987] E.C.R. 1453; [1987] 2 C.M.L.R. 607; [1991] E.C.R I–1155 ... 348, 369–370
Micheletti v. Delagacion del Gobierno en Cantabria [1992] E.C.R. I–4239 .... 34, 142
Molkerei-Zentrale Westfalen/Lippe GmbH v. Hauptzollamt Paderborn [1968] E.C.R. 143; [1968] C.M.L.R. 187 ...... 71, 75, 92, 104, 119
Mulder v. The Netherlands [1988] E.C.R. 2321; [1989] 2 C.M.L.R. 1 123

Nold [1974] E.C.R. 491 139
Nold v. Commission [1974] E.C.R. 491; [1974] 2 C.M.L.R. 338 ..... 123, 127, 131, 133, 134, 135, 136, 249, 379, 380, 385, 388, 389, 390, 421
Nold v. High Authority [1959] E.C.R. 41 .... 127, 133

ONEM v. Bahia Kziber [1991] E.C.R. I–119 84
Oosthoek's Uitgeversmaatschappij v. The Netherlands [1982] E.C.R. 4575 386
Oyowe and Traore v. Commission [1989] E.C.R. 4285 140

Partie écologiste "Les Verts" v. European Parliament [1986] E.C.R. 1339; [1987] 2 C.M.L.R. 343 .... 31, 145
Peterbroeck v. Belgium [1995] E.C.R. I–4599 .... 96, 257
Polydor and RSO v. Harlequin Record Shops and Simons Records [1982] E.C.R. 329; [1982] 1 C.M.L.R. 677 84
Président Ruhrkolen-Verkaufsgesellschaft, Geitling Ruhrkoolen-Verkaufsgesellschaft, Mausegatt Ruhrkohlen-Verkaufsgesellscaft and I. Nold KG v. High Authority v. High Authority [1960] E.C.R. 423 .... 127, 128, 133
Procureur du Roi v. Dassonville [1974] E.C.R. 837; [1974] 2 C.M.L.R. 436 381
Procureur du Roi v. DeBauve [1980] E.C.R. 833; [1981] 2 C.M.L.R. 362 381
Pubblico Ministero v.Ratti [1979] E.C.R. 1629; [1980] 1C.M.L.R. 96 80
Punto Casa and PPV [1994] E.C.R. I–2355 397

R. v. Bouchereau [1977] E.C.R. 1999; [1977] 2 C.M.L.R. 800 393
R. v. Kirk [1984] E.C.R. 2689 124
R v. Minister for Agriculture, Fisheries and Food ex parte Hedley Lomas (Ireland) Ltd [1996] E.C.R. I–2553 90
R. v. Secretary of State for Transport ex parte Factorama Ltd. [1990] E.C.R. I–2433; [1990] 3 C.M.L.R. 1 .... 90, 115
R. v. the Treasury, ex parte British Telecommunications [1996] E.C.R. I–1631 91
R. v. Thomas Scott & Sons Bakers Ltd [1984] E.C.R. 2863; [1985] 1 C.M.L.R. 188 272
Reading Borough Council v. Payless DIY Ltd [1992] E.C.R. I–6493 ... 397
Rewe v. Bundesmonopolverwaltung für Branntwein [1979] E.C.R. 649; [1979] 3 C.M.L.R. 494 .... 381, 382
Rewe Handelsgesllschaft Nord mbH and Rewe Markt Steffen v. Hauptzollamt Kiel [1981] E.C.R. 1805; [1982] 1 C.M.L.R. 449 .. 96
Rezguia Adoui and Cornuaille v. Belgian State and City of Liege [1982] E.C.R. 1665; [1982] 3 C.M.L.R. 631 393
Rheinmuhhlen-Dusseldorf v. Einfuhr-und Vorratsstelle Getreide [1974] E.C.R. 139; [1974] 1 C.M.L.R. 523 352
Rochdale Borough Council v. Anders [1992] E.C.R. I–6457 397
Rutili v. Minister of the Interior [1975] E.C.R. 1219; [1976] 1 C.M.L.R. 140 ..... 122, 137, 264, 392, 393, 394, 395, 407

S.Z. Sevince v. Staatssecretaris van Justitie [1990] E.C.R. I–3461; [1992] 2 C.M.L.R. 57 .... 84, 91
Sager v. Société Dennemeyer [1991] E.C.R. I–4221; 3 C.M.L.R. 639 .... 382, 387

Semeraro Caso Uno v. Sindaco del Commune di Erbuso [1996] E.C.R. I–2975 397
Société Générale Alsacienne de Banque v. Koestler [1978] E.C.R. 1971; [1979] 1 C.M.L.R. 89 381
Society for the Protection of Unborn Children v. Grogan and others [1991] E.C.R. I–4685; [1991] 3 C.M.L.R. 849 122, 138, 341, 374, 375, 376, 377–378, 379, 380, 381, 382, 385, 386, 387, 390, 392, 393, 394, 396, 397–397, 408, 421
SpA International Chemical Corporation v. Amministrazione delle Finanze dello Stato [1981] E.C.R. 1191; [1983] 2 C.M.L.R. 593 .. 75
Staatsanwalt Freiburg v. Keller [1986] E.C.R. 2897; [1987] 1 C.M.L.R 875 139
Stauder v. City of Ulm [1969] E.C.R. 419; [1970] C.M.L.R. 112 ... 121, 129
Stork v. High Authority [1959] E.C.R. 17 .... 126, 127, 128

Ter Voort, Criminal proceedings against, [1992] E.C.R. I–5485 ... 140
Testa v. Bundesanstalt für Arbeit Nürnberg [1980] E.C.R. 1979; [1981] 2 C.M.L.R. 552 139
The State v. Watson and Belmann [1976] E.C.R. 1185; [1976] 2 C.M.L.R. 552 386
Torfaen Borough Council v. B & Q plc [1989] E.C.R. 3851; [1990] 1 C.M.L.R. 337 .... 397, 398

Van Binsbergen v. Bestuur van de Bedrijfsvereniging voor de Metaalnijverheid [1974] E.C.R. 1299; [1975] 1 C.M.L.R. 298 382
Van Duyn v. Home Office [1974] E.C.R. 1337 ... 85, 137, 383, 392, 393
Van Gend en Loos v. Nederlandse Aministratie der Belastingen [1963] E.C.R. 1; [1963] C.M.L.R. 105 .... 26, 54, 55, 58, 59, 64, 65 *et seq*, 102, 103, 104, 108 *et seq*, 116, 117, 120, 128, 131, 146, 264, 330, 333, 353, 374, 383, 384, 427, 428
Van Schijindel and Van Veen [1995] E.C.R. I–4705 .... 95, 96, 257
Vaneetveld v. Le Foyer SA [1994] E.C.R. I–763; [1994] 2 C.M.L.R. 852 86
Variola v. Amministrazione Italiana delle Finanze [1973] E.C.R. 981 .... 53, 54
Von Colson and Kamann [1984] E.C.R. 1891 87

Wachauf v. Bundesamt für Ernährung und Forstwirtschaft [1989] E.C.R. 2609 .... 122, 136, 138, 389, 401
Walrave and Koch v. Association Union Cycliste Internationale [1974] E.C.R. 1405; [1975] 1 C.M.L.R. 320 .... 81, 86, 87
Walter Rau Lebensmittelwerke v. BALM [1987] E.C.R. 22 139
Webb [1981] E.C.R. 3305; [1982] 1 C.M.L.R. 719 .... 382, 392
Weber v. Parliament [1993] E.C.R. I–1093 145

Wilhelm v. Bundeskartellamt [1969] E.C.R. 1; [1969] C.M.L.R. 100 118

Zoubir Yousfi v. Belgium [1994] E.C.R. I–353 84
Zuckerfabrik Franken GmbH v. Germany [1982] E.C.R. 681 . . 122, 138
Zuckerfabrik Suderdithmarschen and Zuckerfabrik Soest v. Hauptzollamt Itzehoe and Hauptzollamt Paderborn [1991] E.C.R. I–415 . . . . 97, 120

TABLE OF OPINIONS OF THE COURT OF JUSTICE OF THE EUROPEAN COMMUNITIES

Opinion 1/76, Re the Laying-up Fund for Inland Waterway Vessels [1977] E.C.R. 741 .... 36, 424
Opinion 1/91, Re the Draft Agreement between the Community and EEA countries [1991] E.C.R. I–6079 .... 24, 39, 45, 62, 71, 72, 78, 84, 125, 145, 156, 162, 351, 374, 384, 428, 429, 431
Opinion 2/91, Convention 170 of the International Labour Organisation [1993] E.C.R. I–1061 .... 35, 36
Opinion 1/92, Draft Agreement between the Community and the EFTA countries on a European Economic Area [1992] E.C.R. I–2821 .... 24, 40
Opinion 2/92, Re Third Reissued Decision of the OECD on National Treatment [1995] E.C.R. I–521 37
Opinion 1/94, Re the Uruguay Round Agreements [1995] 1 C.M.L.R. 205 .... 33, 34, 37, 40
Opinion 2/94, Accession by the Community to the European Convention for the Protection of Human Rights and Fundamental Freedoms (March 28, 1996) [1996] E.C.R. I–759 .... 33, 37, 40, 149, 157, 162, 222, 338, 428
Opinion 3/94, Re the Framework on Bananas (13 December 1995) 40

TABLE OF CASES BEFORE THE COURT OF FIRST INSTANCE

Case T–30/91, Solvay SA v. Commission, [1995] E.C.R. II–1775 ... 139
Case T–36/91, ICI v. Commission, [1995] E.C.R. II–1847 139
Joined Cases T–244 & T–486/93, TWD Textilwerke Deggendorf GmbH v. Commission [1995] E.C.R. II–2265 33
Joined Cases T–466, 469, 473, 474 and 477/93, O'Dwyer v. Council [1995] E.C.R. II–2071 402
Case T–584/93, Roujansky v. Council [1994] E.C.R. II–587 ... 154, 155

TABLE OF THE PERMANENT COURT OF INTERNATIONAL JUSTICE AND THE INTERNATIONAL COURT OF JUSTICE

Advisory Opinion of the International Court of Justice – Namibia case [1971] International Court of Justice Reports 16 27
Advisory Opinion of the Permanent Court of International Justice, Greek – Bulgarian Communities, 31 July 1930, Series A/B No. 37 99
Advisory Opinion of the Permanent Court of International Justice, Jurisdiction of the Courts of Danzig, 3 March, Series A/B No. 283/ Series B No. 15 63
Polish Upper Silesia, Treatment of Polish Nationals Permanent Court of International Justice, 25 May 1926, Series A No. 7 99
Switzerland v. USA ("International") (preliminary objections), International Court of Justice, 21 March 1959, International Law Reports, Vol. 27, at 475 50

TABLE OF CASES BEFORE THE EUROPEAN COURT OF HUMAN RIGHTS

Beaumartin v. France, 24 November 1994, Series A, No. 296–B 257
Confederation Francaise Democratique du Travail v. The European Communities, the Member States of the European Communities Collectively and the Member States of the European Communities Individually [1979] 2 C.M.L.R. 229 (decision of 10 July 1978) .. 43, 44
D. v. Belgium [1987] 2 C.M.L.R. 57 43
Norris v. Ireland, Series A, No. 142 (1991) 13 E.H.R.R. 186 100
Open Door Counselling Ltd. and Dublin Well Woman Centre Ltd and Others v. Ireland, (Report of the Commission, 7 March 1991) (1992) 14 E.H.R.R. 131 .... 378, 395, 400
Open Door Counselling and Dublin Well Woman v. Ireland (1993) 15 E.H.R.R. 244 373

TABLE OF NATIONAL CASES

IRELAND

Application of Woods [1970] I.R. 154 324
Article 26 and the Housing (Private Rented Dwellings) Bill, 1981, Re [1983] I.R. 181 327
Article 26 and the Regulation of Information (Services Outside the State for Termination of Pregnancies) Bill, 1995, Re [1995] 1 I.R. 1, [1995] 2 I.L.R.M. 81 .... 276, 282, 287, 293, 294, 295, 306, 361, 376
Attorney General v. X [1992] 1 I.R. 1; [1992] I.L.R.M. 401 .... 282, 287, 293, 294, 297, 299, 300, 301, 314, 354, 376, 390, 393, 398, 399, 400, 427
Attorney General v. Paperlink Ltd. [1984] I.L.R.M. 373 ..... 309, 312,
Attorney General (S.P.U.C.) v. Open-Door Counselling [1987] I.L.R.M. 477; [1988] I.R. 593 ...... 318, 319, 375, 377, 397
Boland v. An Taoiseach [1974] I.R. 338 305
Byrne v. Ireland [1972] I.R. 241 .... 304, 306, 311, 320, 364
Cahill v. Sutton [1980] I.R. 269 .... 319, 320
Campus Oil Ltd v. Minister for Industry and Energy (No. 1) [1983] I.R. 82 .... 341, 351
Cityview Press Ltd. v. An Chomhairle Oiliúna [1980] I.R. 381 344
Clover Meats v. Minister for Agriculture (1992) 1 *Irish Journal of European Law* 162 331
Condon v. Minister for Agriculture (1993) 2 *Irish Journal of European Law* 151 .... 314, 342
Conroy v. Attorney General [1965] I.R. 411 288
Cotter and McDermott v. the Minister for Social Welfare, unreported, High Court, May 13, 1985; unreported, High Court, June 10, 1988 ([1990] 2 C.M.L.R. 141); unreported, Supreme Court, July 27, 1989; unreported, Supreme Court, June 6, 1991 ... 369–370
Crotty v. An Taoiseach [1987] I.L.R.M. 400; [1987] I.R. 713 ...... 304, 305, 310, 314, 320, 321, 329, 332, 335, 337, 338, 347, 353, 360, 366, 376
De Búrca v. Attorney General [1976] I.R. 38 314
Delap v. An tAire Dlí agus Cirt, Éire agus an Ard Aighne, unreported, High Court, O'Hanlon J., July 13, 1990 404
Desmond v. Glackin [1992] I.L.R.M. 490; [1993] 3 I.R. 1 ..... 324, 326
Doyle v. An Taoiseach [1986] I.L.R.M. 693 .... 341, 351
Draper v. Attorney General (High Ct.), *Irish Times*, November 25, 1986 286

E. v. E. [1982] I.L.R.M. 497 324
E.R. v. J.R. [1981] I.L.R.M. 125 289
East Donegal co-operative [1970] I.R. 317 343
Educational Company v. Fitzpatrick [1961] I.R. 323 . . . . 317, 375
F. v. F. [1994] I.L.R.M. 401 . . . . 281, 288, 292, 293
Fajujonu v. Minister for Justice [1990] 2 I.R. 151 292
Finn v. Attorney General [1983] I.R. 154 291
G. v. An Bord Uchtála [1980] I.R. 32 . . . . 277, 279, 298, 377, 390
Garda Devine v. Fitzgerald [1986] I.L.T.R. 228 272
Glover v. BLN [1973] I.R. 388 316
Government of Canada v. Employment Appeals Tribunal [1992] I.L.R. M. 325 325
Greene v. Minister for Agriculture [1990] 2 I.R. 17 . . . . . . 292, 342, 369
Haughey, Re Pádraig, [1971] I.R. 217 . . . . 315, 316
Irish Family Planning Association v. Ryan [1979] I.R. 295 287
Kennedy v. Ireland [1987] I.R. 587 . . . . 291, 312
Kerry Co-Operative Creameries v. An Bord Bainne [1991] I.L.R.M. 851 312
Landers v. Attorney General (1975) 109 I.L.T.R. 1 . . . . 309, 312
Lawlor v. Minister for Agriculture [1990] 1 I.R. 356; [1988] I.L.R.M. 400 . . . . 342, 402
McGee v. Attorney General [1974] I.R. 284 . . . . 275, 276, 277, 278, 281, 287, 288, 292, 294, 297, 308, 312, 362, 377, 390
McGimpsey v. Ireland [1990] 1 I.R. 110 323
McKenna v. An Taoiseach [1995] 2 I.R. 10 306
McKinley v. Minister for Defence and Others [1992] 2 I.R. 333 321
McMahon v. Attorney General [1972] I.R. 69 300
Meagher v. Minister for Agriculture [1994] 1 I.R. 329 (High Ct.); 344 (Sup. Ct.) 314, 339, 340, 343, 344, 369
Meskell v. Coras Iompar Éireann [1973] I.R. 121 . . . . 318, 321
Moore v. Attorney General [1935] I.R. 472 358
Murphy v. P.M.P.A. Insurance Co [1978] I.L.R.M. 725 277
Murphy v. The Turf Club [1989] I.R. 171 316
Murray v. Ireland [1985] I.R. 532 . . . . 275, 301
Murtagh Properties v. Cleary [1972] I.R. 330 312
Nestor v. Murphy [1979] I.R. 326 345
Norris v. Attorney General [1984] I.R. 36 . . . . 283, 284, 285, 286, 324, 356
Northants County Council v. A.B.F. [1982] I.L.R.M. 164 277
Northampton County Council v. A.B.F. and M.B.F. [1982] I.L.R.M. 164 291
O'B v. S [1984] I.R. 316 324
O'Domhnaill v. Merrick [1985] I.L.R.M. 40 326
O'Foghludha v. McClean [1934] I.R. 469 405

O'Láighléis, Re [1960] I.R. 93 .... 318, 324, 325
O'Murchú v. Cláraitheor na gCuideachtaí, unreported, High court, O'Hanlon J., June 20, 1988 405
O'Neill v. Beaumont Hospital Board [1990] I.L.R.M. 419 .... 315, 316
O'Neill v. Iarnród Eireann [1991] I.L.R.M. 129 316
O'Reilly v. Limerick Corporation [1989] I.L.R.M. 181 .... 291, 292
P.H. v. John Murphy & Sons Ltd [1987] I.R. 621 292
People (Attorney General) v. Ballins [1964] Ir. Jur. Rep. 14 286
People (Director of Public Prosecutions) v. Shaw [1982] I.R. 1 .... 300, 301, 354
People (Director of Public Prosecutions) v. O'Shea [1982] I.R. 384 345
Pigs and Bacon Commission v. McCarron, unreported, Costello J., High Court, June 30, 1978 330
Quinn's Supermarket v. Attorney General [1972] I.R. 1 ... 283, 299, 300
Rogers v. I.T.& G.W.U. [1987] I.L.R.M. 51 312
Ryan v. Attorney General [1965] I.R. 294 ...... 276, 290, 298, 381, 395
Ryan v. V.I.P. Taxi Co-operative, unreported, High Court, Lardner J., January 10, 1989; *The Irish Times*, April 10, 1989 ..... 314, 316, 317
S.P.U.C. v. Coogan [1990] I.L.R.M. 70 319
S.P.U.C. v. Grogan [1989] I.R. 753; [1990] I.L.R.M. 350 .... 338, 340, 341, 345, 349, 354, 398
S.P.U.C. v. Grogan [1990] 1 C.M.L.R. 688 .... 397, 398
Stát (MacFhearraigh) v. MacGamhna, Cathaoirleach An Bhínse Achomhairc Fostsíochta, unreported, High Court, O'Hanlon J., June 1, 1983 404
State (Burke) v. Lennon [1940] I.R. 136 276
State (D.P.P.) v. Walsh [1981] I.R. 412 326
State (Gallagher, Shatter & Co) v. De Valera (No. 2) [1987] I.R. 55; [1987] I.L.R.M. 555 (High Ct.) 322
State (Healy) v. Donoghue [1976] I.R. 325 .... 277, 293, 364, 390
State (Nicolaou) v. An Bord Uchtála [1966] I.R. 567 ...... 276, 291, 298
State (Quinn) v. Ryan [1965] I.R. 70 .... 289, 297
State (Ryan) v. Lennon [1935] I.R. 170 .... 276, 358, 365
State (Sumers Jennings) v. Furlong [1966] I.R. 184 325
T.M. and A.M. v. An Bord Uchtála [1983] I.L.R.M. 577 292
Tormey v. Ireland [1985] I.R. 289 .... 299, 345
Ussher v. Ussher [1912] 2 I.R. 445 286
Ward of Court, Re a [1995] 2 I.L.R.M. 401 283, 285, 289, 290, 293, 298, 302, 308
Webb v. Ireland [1988] I.R. 353 .... 303, 304, 306, 308, 311, 365

FRANCE

Decisions of the Conseil Constitutionnel

58–42/191, 5 May 1959, Rec. p.215, *A.N.. Algerie (fifteenth electoral ward)* 182
59–2 DC, 17, 18, 24 June 1959, Rec. p. 58, *Standing Orders of the National Assembly* 234, 238
62–18 L, 16 January 1962, Rec. p.31, *loi on agricultural policy* 171
62–20 DC, 6 November 1962, Rec. p.27; *Direct amendment on popular election of the President.* (*See* Rudden, *A Source-Book on French Law* (Oxford, 1991), p.55 . . . . 178, 208, 213, 244
66–7 FNR, 21 December 1966, Rec. p.37, *Indemnification of French Repatriates* 234
70–39 DC, 19 June 1970, Rec. p.15, *Budgetary and Merger Treaties* 173, 186, 201, 205, 230, 231, 236, 260
71–44 DC, 16 July 1971, Rec. p.29, *Freedom of Association* 240, 244
73–80 L, 28 November 1973, Rec. p.45, *Contraventions* . . . 169, 184, 257
74–54 DC, 15 January 1975, Rec. p.19, *Abortion loi* 179, 180, 240, 245, 259, 266
76–73 DC, 28 December 1976, Rec. p.41, *Examination of the loi on Finances for 1977* 234
76–71 DC, 30 December 1976, Rec. p.15;, *European Community Council Decision for direct elections to European Parliament.* (*See* Rudden, *A Source-Book on French Law* (Oxford, 1991) pp. 58–60) 175, 186, 199, 224
76–75 DC, 12 January 1977, Rec. p.33; *On Police Search Powers.* (B. Rudden, *A Source-Book on French Law* (Oxford, 1991) pp.65–66) 244
77–58 DC, 23 July 1975, Rec. p.16; *Juge unique, juge inique.* (*See* (1976) *Actualités Juridiques* 44) 176, 242
77–90 DC, 30 December 1977, Rec. p.44, *On the Finance Rectification loi of 1977* 178, 260
78–93 DC, 29 April 1978, Rec. p.23, *Amendment of the Statutes of the International Monetary Fund* 178
78–102 DC, 17 January 1979, Rec. p.26, *The Seventh Plan* 234
78–93 DC, 29 April 1978, Rec. p.23, *Amendment of the Statutes of the International Monetary Fund* 178
79–10 FNR, 26 April 1979, Rec. p.55, *Amendments creating permanent parliamentary committees on energy conservation* 170
80–116 DC, 17 July 1980, Rec. p.36, *Franco-German Convention on Judicial Cooperation* 178
80–127 DC, 19 and 20 January 1981, Rec. p.15, *loi reinforcing security and protecting the freedom of persons* 249

81–132 DC, 16 January 1982, Rec. p.18; *On nationalisation*, (*See* Rudden, *A Source-book on French Law* (Oxford, 1991) pp.67–71) 169, 211, 237, 248
82–146 DC, 18 November 1982, Rec. p.48, *The Electoral Loi* 177
84–181 DC, 10 and 11 October 1984, Rec. p.73, *Press Pluralism* 249
85–155 DC, 22 May 1985, Rec. p.15, *Protocol on the abolition of the death penalty* 202
85–187 DC, 25 January 1985, Rec. p.34, *On the loi on the state of emergency in New Caledonia and dependencies* 174, 177
85–188 DC, 22 May 1985, Rec. p.15, *Protocol on the abolition of the death penalty* 201, 218, 240
86–207 DC, 25–6 June 1986, Rec. p.61, *De-nationalisation loi* 184, 211, 260
86–210 DC, 29 July 1986, Rec. p.110, *loi reforming the legal regime for the press* 249
86–216 DC, 3 September 1986, Rec. p.135, *loi on the conditions of entry and stay of foreigners in France* 179, 180
86–224 DC, 23 January 1987, Rec. p.8, *Competition council* 183
88–242 DC, 17 January 1989, Rec. p.15, *International Labour Convention No. 159* 178
88–244 DC, 20 July 1988, Rec. p.119; *The Renault Ten I* (*See* Rudden *A Source-Book on French Law* (Oxford, 1991) pp.67–71) . . . 169, 172, 250
88–1082/1117, 21 October 1988, Rec. p–183, *A.N., Val-d'Oise (fifth electoral ward)* 182, 259
89–258 DC, 8 July 1989, Rec. p.48; *Renault Ten II.* (*See* Rudden, *A Source-Book on French Law* (Oxford 1991) pp.80–81) 169, 172
91–290 DC, 9 May 1991, Rec. p.50; *Loi on the status of Corsica.* (*See* West *et al.*, *The French Legal System* (London: Fourmat Publishing, 1992) pp. 194–195, ... 193, 227, 252
91–293 DC, 23 July 1991, Rec. p.77; *Loi granting European Community nationals access to public employment* (*See* (1991) *Revue de Droit Public* 1514) 179, 201
91–294 DC, 25 July 1991, Rec. p.91; *Schengen Treaty.* (*See* (1991) *Revue de Droit Public* 1517) 179, 196, 202, 205, 219, 221, 242, 248, 249, 407
92–307 DC, 25 February 1992, Rec. p.48, *Foreigners in transit zones* 177, 178, 238
92–308 DC, 9 April 1992, Rec. p.55; *TEU No.1.* (*See* (1992) 28 *Revue Trimestrielle du Droit Europeen 418*) 169, 170, 174, 186, 200, 203, 205, 212, 220, 223, 224, 227, 229, 230, 231, 232, 233, 239, 241, 251, 268, 371
92–312 DC, 2 September 1992, Rec. p.76; *TEU No.2* (*See* (1992) *Revue de Droit Public* 1610) 172, 182, 188, 205, 206, 209, 213, 229, 230, 231, 232, 237, 239, 251

92–313 DC, 23 September 1992, Rec. p.94; *TEU No.3.* (*See* (1992) *Revue de Droit Public* 1618) 177, 178, 188, 213
92–314 DC, 17 December 1992, Rec. p.126, *Standing Orders of the National Assembly* 235
92–315 DC, 12 January 1993, Rec. p.9, *Standing Orders of the Senate Assembly* 235
93–318 DC, 30 June 1993, Rec. p.153, *Franco-Mongolian Investment Treaty* 178
93–319 DC, 30 June 1993, Rec. p.155, *International Labour Convention No. 139* 178
93–324 DC, 3 August 1993, Rec. p.208, *Statute of the Bank of France* 179, 181, 231, 236
93–325 DC, 13 August 1993, Rec. p.224; *On the Control of Immigration.* (*See* (1993) *La Semaine Juridique (Textes)* 373) 168, 180, 196, 239, 248
93–331 DC, 13 January 1994, Rec. p. 17, *Renewing General Councils* . . . 168
94–343/344 DC, 27 July 1994, Rec. p.100; [1995] Rec. Dalloz Sirey 237, *lois on respect for the human body and biotechnology* 168, 169, 372
94–345 DC, :29 July 1994, JO 2 August 1994; [1994] Rec. Dalloz Sirey (Textes) 379, *Loi on the use of the french language* 12

Decisions of the Conseil d'État

Jabin-Dudognon, 1 July 1938, Rec. Lebon p.607 256
Bourgin, 10 January 1958, Rec. Lebon p.25.
Syndicat des propriétaires de forêts de chênes-lièges d'Algérie, 7 February 1958, Rec. Lebon p.74 261
Syndicat général des ingénieurs-conseils, 26 June 1959, Rec. Lebon p.394; [1959] Recueil Dalloz Sirey 202 261
Secrétaire d'État aux P.T.T. c. Eurard, 5 October 1960, Rec. Lebon p. 566.
Fédération nationale des syndicats de police, 24 November 1961, Rec. Lebon p.658 258
Syndicat Général des Fabricants des Semoules de France, 1 March 1968, Rec. Lebon p.149; (See (1968) 24 *Actualité Juridique, Droit Administratif* 238) 258, 266
Confédération française démocratique du travail et confédération générale du travail, 3 February 1978, Rec. Lebon p.47 257
Klaus Croissant, 7 July 1978, Rec. Lebon p.292 258
Cohn-Bendit, 22 December 1978, Rec p.524 . . . . 263, 264
Ministre du budget c. Valton e.a., 20 April 1984, Rec. Lebon p.148 . . . 257
Subrini, 11 July 1984, Rec. Lebon p.259 257
Confédération nationale des Sociétés de protection des animaux, 28 September 1984, Rec. Lebon p.481 262
Fédération française des sociétés de protection de la nature, 7 December 1984, Rec. Lebon p.410 262

Zakine, 13 December 1985, Rec. Lebon p.515 264
S.A. Établissements Outters, 20 December 1985, Rec. Lebon p.382; (*See* (1986) *Revue française de droit administratif* 513) 171
Rassemblement des opposants à la chasse, 7 October 1988, Rec. Lebon p. 335 261
Alitalia, 3 February 1989, Rec. Lebon p.44 264
Nicolo, 20 October 1989, Rec. Lebon p.190; (See (1989) *Revue française de droit administratif* 823) 256, 258, 259, 260, 261, 262, 267
Donyon, 23 February 1990, Rec. Lebon p.773 257
Groupe d'information et de soutien des travailleurs immigrés, 29 June 1990, Rec. Lebon p.171 256
Ministère de l'Agriculture c. Société coopérative agricole "Coop 2000", 27 July 1990, Rec. Lebon p.226 264
Boisdet, 24 September 1990, Rec. Lebon p.251 260
Société Arizona Tobacco Products and Philip Morris France, 28 February 1992, Rec. Lebon p.78 .... 260, 263, 264
SA Rothmans International France and SA Philip Morris France, 28 February 1992, Rec. Lebon p.80 .... 260, 263, 264
Préfet de la Gironde c. Mahmedi, 18 December 1992, Rec. Lebon p.446 218
Compagnie Générale des Eaux, 23 July 1993, Rec. Lebon p.225; [1994] 2 C.M.L.R. 373 264
Association Greenpeace France, 29 September 1995 218

Decisions of the Cour de Cassation

Sanchez c. Consorts Gozland, 22 December 1931, (1931) Rec. Sirey 257 265
Administration des Douanes c. Sociétés 'Cafés Jacques Vabre', 24 May 1975, [1975] Rec. Dalloz Sirey 505 .... 265, 266
Von *Kempis v. Epoux Geldof*, 15 December 1975, [1976] Rec. Dalloz Sirey 33 267
Fox, Bumbury et consorts c. Duc de Richmond [1839] Rec. Dalloz Sirey I.257 265
The Republic v. Weckerle (Criminal Chamber) 15 February 1994, [1995] 1 C.M.L.R. 49 267
CPAM de Seine et Marne c. Ponnau, 13 April 1994, (1994) La Semaine Juridique (Jurisprudence) S.2286 265

Cour d'Appel de Paris

Johansson v. Institut National de la Propriété Industrielle, 16 December 1992, [1994] 1 C.M.L.R. 269 268

Tribunal des Conflits

Compagnie des Eaux et de L'Ozone c. SA Établissements Vetillard, 12 January 1987, Rec. Lebon p.442; (See (1987) *Revue française de droit administratif* 284) 171

Tribunal Adminisratif, Papeete

Knolle v. France [1994] 2 C.M.L.R. 779 91

GERMANY

Brunner v. The European Union Treaty [1994] 1 C.M.L.R. 57 . . 162, 338
Internationale Handelsgesellschaft v. EVGF ("Solange No. I") [1974] 2 C.M.L.R. 540 133
Wünsche Handelsgesellscaft v. EVGF ("Solange No. II"): [1987] 3 C.M.L.R. 225 . . . . 133, 211

UNITED KINGDOM

Mendip District Council v. B & Q plc [1991] 1 C.M.L.R. 113 397
Stoke-on-Trent City Council v. B & Q plc. [1991] 2 W.L.R. 43 397
W.H. Smith Do-it-All Ltd and Payless DIY Ltd v. Peterborough City Council [1990] 2 C.M.L.R. 577 000

UNITED STATES

Pacific States Telephone & Telegraph Co. v. Oregon 223 U.S. 118 (1912) 208
McCulloch v. Maryland 17 U.S. (4 Wheat.) 316 34
State v. McHorse 85 N.M. 753, 517 P.2d 75 118

PART I

INTRODUCTION

1. METHOD AND SUMMARY OF ARGUMENT

1–1 The method and the argument in this work are intertwined.

This work concentrates on a coherent explanation of European Community law and national law as they are in their constitutional relationships with each other and of the different sets of higher rules or principles to which they conform. The focus is on how the three legal orders of public international law, European Community law, and national law (more particularly, national constitutional law),[1] by legal provisions, decisions, and other authoritative sources, describe themselves internally, their relations with the other orders and, so far as necessary to describe their relations with the other orders, those other orders. Wider perspectives are not considered,[2] whether they be questions of justification in the sense of evaluation[3] by, or soundness in respect of, any extra-order principles or values, comparative federalist perspectives,[4] or legal theories.[5] This "order approach" is an extension in the context of relations between legal orders of the internal approach to law, and is humbler than considering the other perspectives listed but has the advantage of trying to avoid the debates which surround perspectives of justification, the mutually

---

1 What is stated for national constitutional law (or national law) is claimed to be correct only as a matter of Irish constitutional law (or Irish law) and French constitutional law (or French law), although this may often also be true for the constitutional legal orders of other Member States. An effort has been made to translate everything into English.

2 The approach is "formalist", rather than "realist" in the sense of considering law and legal doctrine as just one component of a policy making enterprise – R. W. Gordon, "Critical Legal Histories" (1984) Stanford Law Review 57 at p. 67. Not to adopt a realist approach is not to deny the value of such an approach. Snyder may well be correct that "European Community law . . . calls out to be understood by means of a political economy of law, or from an interdisciplinary, contextual or critical perspective": F. Snyder, *New Directions in European Community Law,* (Law in Context series) (London: Weidenfeld and Nicolson, 1991) p. 9. However the goals of this work are themselves largely formal, which makes a formal approach suitable.

3 For example, H. Rasmussen, *On Law and Policy in the European Court of Justice* (Martinus Nijhoff, 1986).

4 For example, K. Lenaerts, *Le Juge et la Constitution aux États-Unis d'Amérique et dans l'Ordre Juridique Européen,* (Bruxelles: Bruylant, 1988). An approach which compares European Community law with the law of an established federal nation runs the risk (avoided in the cited example) of approaching European Community law with a federal slant. As Lord Mackenzie Stuart has pointed out: "One can eliminate any comparison on the constitutional or institutional plane . . . The authors of the [United States] constitution shared a common approach to the problems of government deriving not only from the philosophies of the Enlightenment but also from their shared theology ..." – "Problems of the European Community Transatlantic Parallels" (1987) 36 *International and comparative Law Quarterly* 184.

5 For example, J. Bengoetxea, *The Legal Reasoning of the European Court of Justice* (Oxford: Clarendon Press, 1993).

disputed positions of federalists and states' rightists, and legal theories. The order approach is concerned with questions of legitimation of the legal orders in the sense of the process or action of rendering, verifying or declaring a rule to be in conformity with the sets of rules which constitute the legal orders. It is an attempt to find the most neutral approach to the identification and consideration of the problems treated in this work. It is not a reaction to perceived dominant ideologies in adjudication (a worthwhile undertaking), but an analysis of the legal reactions of integrating orders. The approach is to try to describe so far as is possible the law as is, and not as it ought to be or as it would be if viewed through the varying lenses of wider perspectives.

Unfortunately, lawyers seem to differ just as much over what the law is as over what the law ought to be. One can but try.

1–2 Any systematic reconstruction and description of constitutional law and its legitimation in the light of a particular problem may be controversial. The likelihood of controversy is increased where the problem is the conflict between national constitutional law and European Community law, because both European Community law and academic writings thereon tend to be relatively politicised (and the same is true to a lesser extent for national constitutional law). A stalking cat must be belled[6] at the outset. The trusty empire-building principle of divide and rule might lurk behind professed legal differences about how national constitutional law can cope with European Community law. Lawyers who believe that it is justified that the demands of European Community law be met by Irish constitutional law or French constitutional law (for example because they are unhappy with the current state of Irish constitutional law or French constitutional law, or because their principal concern is promoting integration) stand to benefit from confusion over what constitutes Irish constitutional law or French constitutional law and from clarity of European Community law claims.

1–3 In terms of certainty of position on the conflicts arising between European Community law and national constitutional law, European Community law is in a favourable position because it has been created and moulded with these issues in mind, in stark contrast to national constitutional law. The reconstruction of national constitutional law is therefore likely to be more controversial than the reconstruction of European Community law. However, there is sufficient room within European Community law to suggest a future direction for European Community law which develops from European Community law as is.

1–4 The attempt to reconstruct internally the law of competing legal orders rather than to approach them on the basis of a uniform questionnaire (for example: Who has the competence to decide the scope of competences? What is the list of fundamental rights protected? etc.) leads to complexity in

---

[6] To use Kelly's phrase – J. Fanagan (ed.), *Belling the Cats: Selected Speeches and Articles of John Kelly* (Dublin: Moytura Press / Fine Gael, 1992).

detail and variation of presentation to correspond to the way each order thinks,[7] but also hopefully to strength because the reconstruction must be refuted internally. The style and layout of the Parts are determined by the order under analysis and so differ from one Part to the next. The alternative would be to impose an artificial similarity in headings, etc., which would do violence to differences in the orders. Ireland and France are the only national legal orders examined, on the principle that it is better to attempt to analyse two orders thoroughly than 15 orders superficially. The reasons why these orders were chosen, apart from this author's limited competence, are given at the start of those Chapters. The term "national constitutional law" purports to embrace all national orders, but is supported in this work by the analysis of French and Irish law only. The term "national law" embraces both national constitutional law and other national law.

1–5 Consistent terminology in European Community law matters is difficult given the continuing amendments and indeed liable to distract from the thrust of the thesis. The focus of this work is the European Community, formerly the European Economic Community. Often in the text the terms "European Community" or "Community" could be inclusive of the European Coal and Steel Community and the European Atomic Energy Community. Treaty articles are cited with the reference (EC) for the Treaty establishing the European Community, and (EEC) for that treaty prior to the Treaty on European Union, (EU) for that treaty, (ECSC) for the Treaty establishing the European Coal and Steel Community, and (Euratom) for the Treaty establishing the European Atomic Energy Community. Reference to articles is to their present form unless otherwise appears, for example when examining case law which predates amendments. The European Union, which has no legal personality and which created intergovernmental arrangements in separate titles on Justice and Home Affairs and Common Foreign and Security Policy, is not focussed on. Provisions of the Treaty on the European Union over which the Court of Justice of the European Communities has jurisdiction are important. There are doubtless inconsistencies in the use of terminology but this should not distract from the thesis.

1–6 An order approach may sound banal but it has not been systematically employed in the study of the nature of European Community law[8] and its interaction with public international law and, of more interest to this work, national constitutional law.[9] Perhaps this is partly because European

[7] The idea of a legal order thinking is drawn from G. Teubner, "How the Law Thinks: Toward a Constructivist Epistemology of Law" (1989) 23 *Law and Society Review* 727.

[8] An order approach is not unknown in a consideration of the constitutional problems of formerly colonised emerging states; the difference in perception of British law and Irish law over amendments to the Constitution of Saorstát Éireann were an important part of the legal background in Ireland prior to the enactment of the 1937 Constitution.

[9] The first attempt since is the excellent commentary by G. Hogan and A. Whelan, *Ireland and the European Union: Constitutional and Statutory Texts and Commentary* (London: Sweet

Community law commentators tend to situate themselves in, and argue from (and most often for), the European Community law perspective. How European Community law describes its basis is not the same description which would be given to that basis by public international law or national law. Even if the European Community law self-description and the national law description of European Community law were the same, and this work argues that they are not,[10] that would not mean that national law necessarily acceded to the demands of European Community law: national law could reject the demands of European Community law.

1–7 Where descriptions differ, it is not the description given by the order with whose perspective the commentator identifies which is the correct[11]

& Maxwell, 1995) Chap. 1. However the authors slip into an external perspective in the effort to smooth over the possibility of conflicts when taking issue with some of the points made in this work. They are correct that the order approach encompasses the possibility that "differing legal orders can make differently legitimated claims to regulate the same subject matter, each justified in its own terms" (p. 11) (an effort is made in this work to leave the term "justified" for external critical or evaluative perspectives) but overlook the necessity to locate each claim within a legal order's perception or clearly outside it, and to understand this work as doing so unless it otherwise makes clear (for example when fears are raised for the observance by judges of the rule of law). Thus the authors "find unconvincing, that the Community legal order must evolve into a federal state with a single source of legitimacy, or relapse into public international law", a statement attributed as "implicit" to this author, rather than to this author's understanding of the present possibilities open to European Community law as a matter of public international law. As a matter of European Community law, such a statement would be inaccurate, and it is difficult to see why national law must have a view on that, although a particular national legal order might.

[10] Hogan and Whelan, *op. cit.*, appear to consider that it is paradoxical that the Community legal order is a federal legal order within its field of action, and that the national constitutional order remains the supreme source of authority within its territory of both national and Community competence (p. 10). This author, for the reasons developed in this work, thinks both those claims are accurate. However this is not a paradoxical situation, since the premises of each legal order do not lead to self-contradiction (what is paradoxical is that European Community law claims to be independent from public international law – See below, Part II, Chap. 4, para. 4–1 "Origin – Public International Law Perception"). Rather, they lead to mutual contradiction: conflict. Again, this author agrees "that legal orders may accommodate (or conflict) each other on different bases, each consistent with its own paradigm" (*ibid.* p. 11) as a possibility for legal orders, but this does not mean that such a situation is consistent with the requirements of European Community law. The authors continue that the Court of Justice has never claimed that the Community legal order has entirely subsumed the national legal order (p. 11) (this author is a stranger to such a claim; it is curious that the authors later speak of the national legal order as "subsisting" – p. 13) and state "there is nothing to support that, as in the case of public international law, Community law cannot be fully accommodated in terms different from but not in practical terms inconsistent with its own by national constitutional legal orders." It is not clear in which perspective this statement is located. If it is a statement of the European Community law position, then it profoundly misconceives the concept of integration. This point is considered in detail below in Part II, Chap. 7, para. 7–13 "Obligation in the Result – Non-transformation of Regulations European Community Law Perception".

[11] That is, where the commentator assumes the description to be correct from all points

description in any general or external sense. The description by the order with which the commentator identifies may be important, especially for consequences within that order, and may be correct, in the sense of accurate, within the terms of that order. But that is all it is. The description is not dispositive of which of the descriptions of differing orders is correct. (To attempt to decide that, a commentator would need both an external perspective (that is, one outside the order), and to do battle with competing external perspectives.) In the context of a plurality of interacting legal orders, the order approach aids the development of the perspective from "what is the law" to the perspective "what is the law in each order" and then to "how does each order see the other". There is a problem on the borders of the order approach because the disputable nature of the definition of intra-order doctrinal terms leads into problems of definition of the theoretical terms.[12]

The application of this method to the reconstruction and analysis of laws establishes the propositions set out in paragraph 1–9, "Summary of Argument", there are constitutional boundaries in European Community law and more particularly in national constitutional law, to the process of European integration which have now been reached and which cannot be crossed without revolt or revolution. From that point future work can build on the theoretical and political implications of the status quo and the future directions.[13]

1–8 All this must, at this stage, seem a little abstract. The approach is best illustrated by the diagrams on page 9, below.

There are five points to be made about the diagrams.

1. Diagram 1 illustrates how the order approach avoids the hierarchical conceptualisation often foisted on studies of this nature, which could be represented as in diagram 2. Such a conceptualisation helps to predetermine

---

of view, or independently of any point of view, or does not even consider the question of from which point of view he assumes the description to be correct.

Even Hogan and Whelan, *op. cit.*, occasionally slip into the European Community law perception in place of what they perceive to be the neutral perception, for example when they speak of the unlikelihood, as a matter of Irish constitutional law, that there would have to be a constitutional amendment if there were European Community law alterations in the procedure for the achievement of Economic and Monetary Union "given the considerable transfer of national monetary sovereignty already agreed to" (p. 40). This does not represent the Irish constitutional law position which does not speak in such terms at all (nor does French constitutional law).

[12] This problem is not fully resolved in this work. "Now our treatment of this science will be adequate if it achieves that amount of precision which belongs to its subject matter. The same exactness must not be expected in all departments of philosophy alike . . . it is the mark of an educated mind to expect that amount of exactness which the nature of the particular subject admits."

Aristotle, *Nichomachean Ethics* I.iii 1–4 (Loeb Classical Library, Harvard University Press, 1934, translated by H. Rackham).

[13] For a start, see D.R. Phelan, "Two Hats, One Wig, No Halo" (1995) 45 Doctrine and Life 130. C. Joerges is correct when he asserts: "The tension between legal integration

issues. There is no hierarchy in the order approach. The answer to hierarchical questions would depend on the order in which the answerer (for example, a judge) situates himself. So, for example, a national judge in a dualist order might look at a conflict of norms as in diagram 3, or as in diagram 4, whereas a Community judge might look at it as in diagram 5, and there are other variants possible. While judges may have to view the orders in a hierarchy, observers do not have to locate themselves in a single view.

2. The order approach shows that there are at least three possible answers (one from each order) to any single question. Of course, there are as many possible answers as there are internally defensible arguments supporting an answer from any of the perspectives. But there are at least three. And each of these three answers, although they may diametrically conflict in reasoning or result, will be legitimate or correct in the sense of the order proposing it.

3. Because national legal orders differ, there are really as many possible diagrams as Member States. Because public international law and European Community law remain the same, diagram 6 is a more accurate representation and there are at least seventeen possible answers.

4. The diagrams have the advantage of putting the individual in the centre, where the individual is in this study as the holder of rights and obligations. It is true that the individual may be found also in the European Community circle (for example, directly before the Court of Justice pursuant to an Article 173 challenge) or in the public international law circle (for example, before the European Court of Human Rights), but in general the individual is before national tribunals. Even to hold the rights pertaining to European citizenship after the Treaty on European Union, an individual must first be recognised as a citizen in national law (Article 8(1) (EC)).

5. Whilst European Community law combines a public international law origin with a tendency to transform itself into federal law, the diagrams make clear that European Community law differs from both.

These are two spectres haunting the legal orders of Europe: revolt and revolution.

---

and national legal systems implies tension not only between European and national law but between supranational regimes and national democracies as well . . . " (p. 35) and "neither is European economic law and its impact on national legal systems simply theoretically neutral." (p. 31). "European Economic Law, the Nation-State and the Maastricht Treaty" in R. Dehousse (ed.), *Europe after Maastricht: An Ever Closer Union?* (Munich: Beck, Law Books in Europe, 1994) p. 29.

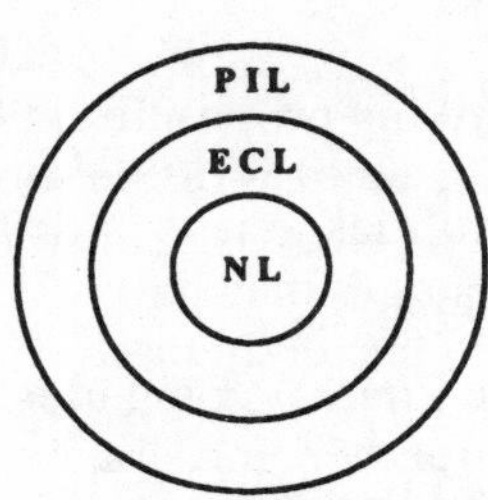

Diagram 1

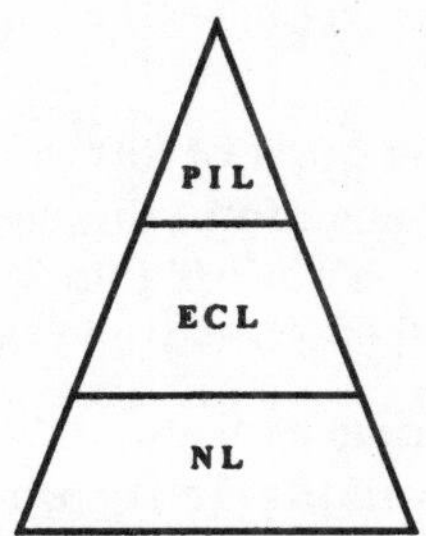

Diagram 2

Diagram 3

Diagram 4

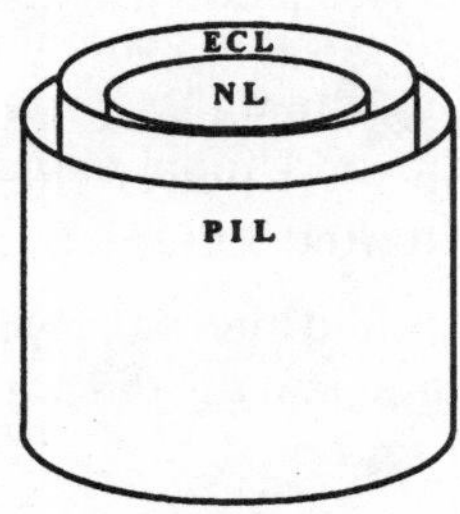

Diagram 5

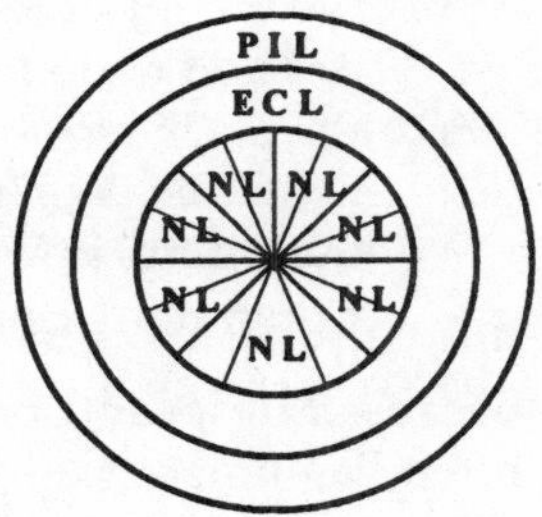

Diagram 6

KEY

PIL = public international law
ECL = European Community law
NL = national law

SUMMARY OF ARGUMENT

1–9 The point of this work is to establish the following propositions through the application of the method set out above to the analysis of the substance of European Community law, French constitutional law, Irish constitutional law and, to a lesser extent, public international law.

I. National constitutional law is at breaking point. There is going to be either a revolution in law where consistent legitimation becomes impossible or a revolt of national constitutional authorities, the focal case being courts, to avoid a revolution:

A. because of the demands placed on national law by European Community law.

1. in degree of integration; and
2. in breadth of European Community law competence.

B. because there is a gap between:

1. how European Community law views its status in and demands on national courts:
   (a) European Community law can be asserted before national courts because of European Community law;
   (b) national courts are under a European Community law obligation to give effect to European Community law;
2. and how national courts view these same demands:
   (a) the validity of European Community law in national law is dependent on national law;
   (b) the duty of national courts is ultimately to uphold the Constitution which creates them and gives them what power they have, including power to uphold to a limited extent European Community law.

C. because European Community law and national law are based on different legitimacies:

1. European Community law is based on the attainment of the objective of European integration.
2. National law is based on the fundamental commitments of sovereignty and a constitutional version of natural law and natural rights based on reason.

D. because there are limits to how far national law can be amended without a legal revolution, that is, a discontinuity in the legitimation of law.

European Community Law

I. Proposition I holds true even though European Community law has its historical origin in international treaties.

A. The historical origin of European Community law in treaties, and its continuing amendment by treaties, suggests the following:

1. European Community law demands on national courts and national law would not be such as to threaten a revolution;
2. there would not be such a gap between how European Community law and national law view their interrelations;
3. there would be no problem in amending European Community law.

B. However, European Community law is an autonomous legal order.

1. Public international law accepts that European Community law is an autonomous system of law, but maintains that European Community law is public international law, more particularly, a subset of the law of international organisations.
2. Even if European Community law could qualify as public international law, European Community law rejects this.

II. There are two aspects to European Community law as an autonomous legal order: a new *sui generis* system; a legal order *ex proprio vigore.*

A. European Community law is a new legal system, a *sui generis* legal system.

1. European Community law's substantive rules and institutions distinguish it from both public international law (whence it originated) and national law (into which it is integrated).
2. It is not clear what *sui generis* (of its own type) legal system means. This is probably part of the attraction of the terms. It appears to mean not public international law, without stating the plunge to the law of a federation.
3. It is not possible, according to public international law, for there to be a third type of order.
4. A third type of order may be possible, according to national law, depending on the view of national law, but in any event European Community law is not viewed by national law as European Community law views itself.

B. European Community law is a legal order *ex proprio vigore*, with autonomous validity.

1. The validity of European Community law is not dependent on public international law.
2. The autonomous validity of European Community law as a legal order was created by the Court of Justice. The normative root of the order is an act of will by that court.

3. European Community law remains autonomous when integrated into national law.
4. This autonomous validity is not simply a characteristic under the rubric of "*sui generis*".
   (a) The autonomous validity of European Community law appears to be grounded in many of the same characteristics which make European Community law *sui generis.*
   (b) However the autonomy of European Community law goes beyond the idea of system.

C. The idea of European Community law as *ex proprio vigore* is not clear.

1. It means that the agreement of the Member States is no longer the root of title of European Community law.
2. It means that their intention as expressed by the Treaty is not so important.
3. As a development it has occurred on the back of progress in other *sui generis* characteristics, such as:
   (a) the progressive development of constitutional doctrines such as direct effect and supremacy;
   (b) the broadening of European Community competences;
   (c) the strengthening of European Community institutions *vis-à-vis* the Member States.
4. It implies a break between the actual origin of primary positive European Community law in the treaties establishing the European Communities and the legitimation of European Community law.
5. It is established as a fundamental constitutional tenet of European Community law by a legitimation based on the attainment of objectives, the supreme objective (the objective of the attainment of lesser objectives) being an ill-defined political and economic, but predominantly legal "European unity".
6. This legitimation of European Community law grounds the development by the Court of Justice of European Community law rules, doctrines, and principles of constitutional importance.
7. The idea of European Community law as a new legal order, as opposed to a new legal system, is one of long standing in European Community law; the contrast between the concepts of order and system supports the claim to a hierarchic system *ex proprio vigore.*

D. One of the aspects of European Community law as an autonomous constitutional order legitimated ultimately by reference to the attainment of the objective of "European unity" is the possible limits to how the Member States can change European Community law, that is, limits to the amendability of European Community law.

1. The Member States are no longer the masters of European Community law in certain fundamental areas. The Member States agreed as a

matter of public international law or at least of European Community law to transfer sovereignty to the institutions to achieve integration. The transfers and integration have progressed to the stage where the Member States cannot interfere with certain legal structures which promote "European unity".

2. The limits to how far European Community law can be amended may mean that the Member States cannot amend European Community law to avoid a revolution in national law without causing a revolution in European Community law.
   (a) But there is sufficient support in European Community law for amendment without revolution which amendment will avoid revolt or revolution in national constitutional law.
   (b) Or a revolution in European Community law or national law is unavoidable, unless national courts revolted against the demands of European Community law and refused to apply such European Community law as would cause a revolution in national law. This would result in the Member State being in breach of its European Community obligations.
   (c) Since national law is not applied in European Community courts there is no possibility of the Court of Justice revolting against the claims of national constitutional law.
   (d) There is not sufficient support in national constitutional law for amendment without revolution which amendment would satisfy European Community law claims.

National Law

III. Proposition I is supported by four fundamental national law propositions on the relationship of national law to European Community law.

A. National law restricts its recognition of the present and future claims of European Community law.

1. European Community law is in force in national law ultimately because of national law.
2. There are limits to the force of law of European Community law when it conflicts with national constitutional law, and in particular with national constitutional fundamental commitments.
3. The national constitutional law description of European Community law conflicts with European Community law's self-description.
4. According to national law, the State can withdraw from the European Community.

B. The fundamental commitments of national constitutional law are likely to come into conflict in courts with European Community law.

1. Both legal orders make claims in the same areas.
2. National constitutional law has constitutionalised national law.
3. National constitutional law is not merely a specialised branch of public law, but the foundation for national law.
4. Jurisdictionally, national constitutional law can be enforced in the national legal order through the courts, where and when European Community law can be enforced.

C. The legitimation of national constitutional law contrasts with that of European Community law, and depends on:

1. as a *sine qua non*, the protection and promotion of fundamental commitments to the human person and to the place of the person in relation to the State adjusted according to concepts of society and the common good;
2. a national constitutional law version of natural law which limits the acts of the sovereign which can have the authority of law;
3. for its origin and provisions, the sovereignty of the People, who are the ultimate legislator and in a sense the representative of the Nation.

D. The possibility of revision of national constitutional law to resolve conflicts with European Community law is limited.

1. Revision to comply in full with the demands of European Community law would call into question the coherence and legitimation of national constitutional law and hence of national law and would result in a break in that legitimation and consequently in a legal revolution.
2. In order to avoid a legal revolution and to uphold the rule of law, national courts (the focal case, or other organs of government) may revolt against European Community law demands.

Conflicts

IV. Whether or not European Community law is *ex proprio vigore*, there is conflict between national and European Community legal orders.

A. This conflict is not avoided by the assertion that the Member States agreed to the demands of European Community law.

1. Even if the Member States agreed as a matter of fact, which is denied, to the extent of European Community law demands, European Community law cannot legitimate its claims on the basis of agreement and consent as a matter of public international law when it refuses to consider itself as public international law and on occasion disregards the will of the Member States expressed as treaty law.
2. The Member States did not bring national law into line with such agreement, and the discord of national law with European Community law claims poses a problem for the integration of European Community law into national law.

B. The conflict between orders will result in conflicts between courts because of:

1. the jurisdictional rules of both national constitutional law and European Community law (particularly Article 177 (EC));
2. the constitutionalisation of the national legal order which means that the validity of national law depends on its conformity to national constitutional law against which it can be tested and the substance of national law is influenced by national constitutional law;
3. the extent of the overlap between the claims of European Community law and national law in respect of the same or different aspects of many justiciable actions.

C. There may be conflict irrespective of the similarity or difference in status within each order of the conflicting claims, which claims:

1. may be fundamental commitments in both orders, such as a national constitutional law natural right and a fundamental but different European Community law right necessary to achieve European Community objectives.
2. may be differently interpreted rights with the same name.
3. may be a national law rule based on a national constitutional law policy and a European Community law policy, right, or principle.
4. The European Community law claim may be both of minor importance to European Community law and of secondary formal status such as a Commission Regulation implementing a Council Regulation, yet spark a conflict because the claim is automatically fitted into European Community constitutional structures such as direct effect and supremacy.

D. The conflict may be between claims which are fundamental commitments in both European Community and national legal orders, which conflict:

1. may pose the dilemma of revolt or revolution simultaneously in both a national legal order and the European Community legal order.
2. is rooted, as well as in different substantive claims, in different legitimations of law in the European Community and national legal orders.
3. cannot be avoided by the present techniques employed in European Community law.
   (a) Derogations are restricted in scope to accord with the attainment of European Community law objectives.
   (b) The protection of fundamental rights in European Community law does not avoid all conflicts with human rights which are fundamental commitments in national constitutional law.

Future Directions

V. There are three principal directions in which the relationship of European Community law with national constitutional law can develop.

A. Continuation along current lines, which would mean:
   1. revolt in national constitutional law, or
   2. revolution in national constitutional law.

B. Reform of European Community law to solve the revolt or revolution dilemma, by the adoption of a European Community law rule that the integration of European Community law into national law is limited to the extent necessary to avoid a legal revolution in national law.

   1. The extent to which such limitation is necessary is to be finally determined by national constitutional law authorities such as constitutional courts in accordance with the essential commitments of the national legal order, not by the Court of Justice in judgments or by the Member States in ad hoc Protocols.
   2. If there are no limits to how European Community law can be amended, then this adaptation could come either as treaty amendment or as jurisprudential change. There is already sufficient basis in European Community law for such jurisprudential change:
      (a) the resulting lack of uniformity is not fatal to the coherence of European Community law because there are plenty of examples of disuniformity in European Community law;
      (b) there are other supporting strands of European Community law, such as the preservation of the national identity of the Member States;
      (c) integration requires the instruments of national court cooperation and observance of the rule of law.
   3. If there are limits to how far European Community law can be changed, then this amendment or jurisprudential development does not fall within them.
   4. If this amendment does fall within limits to how far European Community law can be changed, then European Community law has gone so far that it cannot adapt to allow national law to avoid a revolution, or national courts to avoid a prolonged revolt.
      (a) This is itself an important result.
      (b) It means that not only can the Member States not recover transferred sovereignty, but also that the European Community and its institutions lack the sovereignty to grant away sovereignty, whilst European Community law paradoxically claims that this is exactly what the Member States have done.
      (c) A choice must be made between revolution in European Community law and national law.

C. A new European Community law constitution which would remove conflict but would cause:

   1. Revolution in national constitutional law.
   2. Perhaps, but not necessarily, revolution in European Community law.

VI. With any direction other than V.B there is a profound attack on:

1. the rule of law;
2. the sense of judicial duty to uphold the law;
3. the authority of law;
4. the type of legitimation which grounds national constitutional law.

Part II

EUROPEAN COMMUNITY LAW

INTRODUCTION

An order analysis of European Community law establishes the following constitutional characteristics of European Community law:

1. European Community law is an autonomous legal order, both *sui generis* and *ex proprio vigore*;
2. European Community law is separated from public international law;
3. this autonomy results from act(s) of will by the Court of Justice;
4. European Community law makes demands on national law, and these demands hold good for all European Community law, primary and secondary;
5. European Community law has a particular legitimation by reference to the integration of Europe and the establishment of a federal legal order;
6. there are possible limits to its amendment.

There are four points to note about the approach taken in this Part. First, the attention paid to the legitimation of European Community law developments given by the European Court of Justice is not for the purpose of criticising its reasoning (which would imply an external standpoint), but to show what the legitimation is and how it helps to establish the above propositions. Secondly, the focus is on legal structure, not on the content of laws. Thirdly, the material which establishes these propositions largely overlaps, so the Part is not divided into chapters corresponding to these characteristics. Fourthly, from the mass of possible constitutional issues, this work concentrates on those directly connected to individual rights both because these are central to the nature of European Community law and because it is here that conflicts are most likely to occur jurisdictionally.

2. PERCEPTIONS OF EUROPEAN COMMUNITY LAW

Public International Law Perception

2–1 The public international law perception of European Community law must be examined to some degree to understand the *sui generis* nature of European Community law and its *ex proprio vigore* claims because it helps show how European Community law's perception of itself and its autonomy from public international law is different to the public international law perception. This difference is despite what might have been presumed from the historical treaty origin of European Community law, namely that the public international law perception would have influenced how European Community law perceived itself. The independence of European Community law from public international law is one of its most salient constitutional characteristics because it implies *inter alia* that "constitution" in European Community law terms is to be understood not as the constitution of an international organisation but as the constitution of an entity tending towards a federal State.

Furthermore, should European Community law cease to be valid in public international law, it may cease to be valid in national law.[1] However, European Community law ceasing to be valid in public international law is different from European Community law ceasing to be public international law. In the latter case, European Community law may have become the constitution of a federal State accepted by national law and recognised by public international law.

Public international law's perception has also a subsidiary importance in this work for three reasons: it may influence how national law perceives European Community law; in case of conflict between European Community law rule and public international law rule, public international law's version of European Community law may be important before a national judge; and in case of conflict between national constitutional law and European Community law, a national judge may be influenced by public international law's view of European Community law in interpreting how national constitutional law views European Community law.

---

1 "If, by reason of its annulment or its lapse into nullity, this agreement loses its international validity, the applicability of its provisions in the internal legal order of the Member States will cease immediately."

M. Waelbroeck, "Contributions à l'étude de la nature juridique des Communautés Européennes", in *Problèmes de Droit des Gens: Mélanges offerts à Henri Rolin* (Paris: Editions A. Pedone, 1964), p. 506.

National Law Perception

2–2 This is dealt with in detail below in Parts III and IV. Therefore only a few comments are made here.

There was no question but that European Community, law had an origin autonomous from national law. The view that public international law is merely an extension of national law into the area of foreign affairs has long been disfavoured. European Community law was established by public international law treaty. The Court of Justice in its conversion of European Community law wished to distance European Community law from public international law and integrate European Community law as far as possible into national law without losing its nature in national law as European Community law. This autonomy from national law has some limitation when it comes to demanding a revolution in national law, because to convert itself from public international law and to develop its constitutional doctrines of individual rights and fundamental rights, European Community law became to an extent dependent on national law (transfers viewed from national law).[2]

The most important point about national law's perception of European Community law is that European Community law may be asserted before national courts as a matter first of national law, not European Community law.[3] European Community law is therefore dependent on national law and is not autonomous from it in the sense of being autonomously in force in national law or before national courts (though there may be exceptions to this in national legal orders not examined in this work, for example in Belgium and Luxembourg).

Indeed it is not clear that the description *sui generis* given to European Community law had anything other than a psychological effect on national tribunals (which is difficult to assess), because to the extent that their treatment of European Community law differs from that accorded to public international law, this difference may stem both from national law provisions which are more favourable to European Community law than public international law, and from the differences recognised in public international law between European Community law and other types of public international law (for example, "soft" law).

European Community Law Perception

2–3 Whether or not the public international law perception that European Community law can be understood in terms of public international law is

---

[2] See on "Further Support from Within European Community Law" below, Part VI, para. 36–20.

[3] Of course, only European Community law which European Community law considers to be capable of assertion before national courts is likely to be capable of assertion according to national law.

correct,[4] the most important point is that European Community law rejects public international law as an explanation. This rejection itself could be analysed as a legal revolution, breaking from the old order and at the same time founding the new. Even if European Community law is "wrong" from a public international law perception, this is nonetheless a rejection, and European Community law does not base itself in or on public international law. Therefore whilst Wyatt may be correct as a matter of public international law or of reason when, under a section entitled "The Court's denial that Community law is international law", he states as regards the reciprocity case[5] that "[t]he Court's misapprehension as to the applicable rules of international law would seem to diminish the significance of the rejection of international legal reasoning, and its resort to the 'new legal order' as an alternative basis",[6] and whilst the indignation of lawyers for public international law[7] is understandable, as a matter of European Community law the rejection of public international law is no less definite.

There are many constitutional features of European Community law which could be analysed to show how they distance European Community law from public international law and the European Community from an international organisation,[8] such as the system of self-financing, the institutions (including the future European Central Bank) and the federal principle of subsidiarity. Something is said about the European Parliament in the context of citizenship.[9]

---

4 *e.g.* W.G. van der Meersch, "L'Ordre juridique des Communautés Européennes et le Droit international" (1975) 148 (V) *Recueil des Cours de l'Académie de Droit International* 1; B. de Witte, "Retour à *Costa* – La primauté du droit communautaire à la lumière du droit international" (1984) *Revue Trimestrielle de Droit Européen* 425; D. Wyatt, "New Legal Order or Old?" (1982) European Law Review 147; D. Wyatt and A. Dashwood, *Wyatt and Dashwood's European Community Law* (London: Sweet & Maxwell, 1993); C. Leben, "À propos de la nature juridique des Communautés Européennes" (1991) *Droits – Revue française de théorie juridique* 61; Boulouis, "Le droit des Communautés Européennes dans ses rapports avec le droit international général" (1992) Vol. 235 (IV) *Recueil des Cours* 19. These authors are sometimes referred to in the text as "public international lawyers" to capture the sense of exposition of a different perception of the nature of European Community law. However, the authors are also renowned European Community lawyers who are describing European Community law as they perceive it and some of their writings do not place European Community law in a public international law perspective. Placing their views in the perspective of another order is not to assert that their views are less accurate than those of "European Community lawyers". Rather, it is because their perception is not the dominant perception within European Community law. The authors collectively might better be termed "internationalists" rather than public international lawyers, but this would be to import a political dimension which this work tries to eschew.

5 Joined Cases 90 & 91/63 [1964] E.C.R. 625. See below, Chap. 7, para. 7–6, "Reciprocity".

6 D. Wyatt (1982) *op. cit.* above, n.4, at p. 160.

7 *e.g.* Pellet, Lectures during the Academy of European Law at the European University Institute, Florence, July 1994, forthcoming in "Collected Courses of the Academy of European Law".

8 See below, Chap. 13, para. 13–2, "European Community Law as a Federal Legal Order – European Community Law Perception".

9 See below, Chap. 9, para. 9–2, "Citizenship – European Community Law Perception".

However the analysis focuses on the Court of Justice's constitutionalisation of European Community law both because of its importance in this regard and because of the focus of this thesis on conflicts which might occur before and between courts as the authoritative interpreters of legal orders, according to those legal orders. Something therefore needs to be said about the Court of Justice.

The Court of Justice is at once the most federalising institution in the European Community and the most international in form.[10] Its judgments are binding and may be enforced (Article 187 (EC)); it may be given unlimited jurisdiction as regards penalties provided for by Regulations (Article 172 (EC)); and the Treaty on European Union gave it the power to impose fines for failures by the Member States in their Community obligations (Article 171 (EC)). Member States are prohibited from having recourse to external means to resolve justiciable disputes (Article 219 (EC), Article 87 (ECSC), Article 192 (Euratom)). Furthermore, individuals have the right to challenge directly the validity of Community acts via Article 173, paragraph 4 (EC). (The fact that individuals have some direct access to the Court of Justice is not that unusual for an international tribunal – for example, the European Court of Human Rights.)

There is no system of Community courts like the federal courts in the United States. What is extraordinary about the Court of Justice as an institution is both the European Community law it has created, and the nature of the institutional role it has created for itself, by virtue of its position within European Community law as its authoritative interpreter, its development of a judicial policy to complement the Article 177 (EC) preliminary reference procedure, and (mostly through this procedure) its success in securing the effective application of European Community law by national courts. In these regards the Court of Justice has made itself quite unlike an international tribunal. It regards the binding nature of its decisions as a *sine qua non* of the Community order, an aspect of it which perhaps cannot be changed.[11] The Court cannot give (and the Treaty perhaps cannot be amended to change this) an interpretative opinion to help solve a dispute on the interpretation of law in the European Economic Area – it must give a binding decision.[12]

How the Court of Justice looked at itself was summed up very early in a European Coal and Steel Community case by Advocate-General Lagrange where he replied to the argument that the Court of Justice should follow the practice of international courts such as the International Court of Justice and

---

[10] Articles 165 to 168 (EC) and also Protocol (No. B) on the Statute of the Court of Justice of the European Community annexed to the Treaty establishing the European Community.

[11] Opinion 1/91 [1991] E.C.R. I-6079; Opinion 1/92 [1992] E.C.R. I-2821. See below, Chap. 11, particularly para. 11-10.

[12] Opinion 1/92 [1992] E.C.R. I-2821, para. 34.

interpret the powers of the European Coal and Steel Community High Authority strictly because they originated in an international treaty:

> "it could be objected that our Court is not an international court but the court of a Community created by six states on a model which is more closely related to a federal than to an international organisation and although the Treaty which the Court has the task of applying was concluded in the form of an international treaty and although it unquestionably is one, it is nevertheless, from a material point of view, the charter of a community, since the rules of law which derive from it constitute *the internal law of the community*."[13]

[13] Case 8/55 *Fédération Charbonnière de Belgique* [1954 to 1956] E.C.R. 245 at 277, original emphasis.

3. IN GENERAL

Public International Law Perception

3–1 European Community law is the law of an international organisation. The relations between the Member States remain governed by treaties which, whatever their particularity, remain in the public international law sphere.[1] This approach has been succinctly summarised:

> "'By creating a Community of unlimited duration, having its own institutions, its own personality, its own legal capacity and capacity of representation on the international plane and, more particularly, real power stemming from a limitation of sovereignty or a transfer of powers from the States to the Community'[2] the signatories of the European treaties did not innovate."[3]

Although unlike European Community law the functional idea of transferring competences to an international organisation normally has the long-term goal of cooperation rather than integration, the goal of integration in the European Community to which competences have been massively transferred is not sufficient to eradicate European Community law from public international law.

Public international lawyers concede that European Community law is original or of a particular character within the law of international organisations, either because of particular innovations or because it innovates by grouping so many legal developments together into one system. One commentator points to the following characteristics as distinguishing European Community law: the treaty amendment procedures; the methods and procedures for interpretation and the procedures for rulings of the Court of Justice; the autonomy of the system of legislation; the competence of the Commission to supervise the application of the Treaty and to sue Member States; direct effect and individual rights; and a court which is supreme interpreter, the judgments of which are binding, and which considers the distribution of competences and the validity of laws.[4]

---

1 There is a parallel between the insistence that European Community law remains public international law, and the insistence that European integration can only be explained by general theories of international relations and does not need a *sui generis* theory. For the latter proposition see A. Moravcsik, "Preferences and Power in the European Community: a Liberal Intergovernmentalist Approach" (1993) 31 *Journal of Common Market Studies* 473.

2 Case 26/62 *Van Gend en Loos v. Nederlandse Aministratie der Belastingen* [1963] E.C.R. 1.

3 B. de Witte, "Retour à *Costa* – La primauté du droit communautaire à la lumière du droit international" (1984) *Revue Trimestrielle de Droit Européen* 425 at p. 447.

4 W.G. van der Meersch, "L'Ordre juridique des Communautés Européenes et le Droit international" (1975) 148 (V) *Recueil des Cours de l'Académie de Droit International*, at p. 17.

The word "autonomy" does not pose a problem to European Community law remaining within public international law because of the meaning public international law gives the term as a specific body of law. All international organisations develop a body of law which is specific to them and is in this sense autonomous from public international law. This does not stop this body of autonomous law being dependent ultimately on public international law. That is not to say that each rule of an international organisation falls to be tested in its operation against every rule of public international law. Far from it, since public international law itself recognises that the rules of international organisations derogate. Article 5 of the first and second Vienna Convention on the Law of Treaties[5] provides that whilst the Conventions apply to the constituent treaties of international organisations and to any treaty adopted within the organisation, that is "without prejudice to any relevant rules of the organization." However the first Convention was not in force until 1980, and does not apply retroactively according to its Article 4. The second Convention is not yet in force and it also does not apply retroactively. As against that, the first Convention is to some extent declaratory of existing public international law,[6] although this is a more problematical assertion as regards the second Convention.

One commentator has considered that European Community law innovates in being a sort of combination legal system – part public international law, part national law.[7] Another has described European Community law as an example of an intermediate system – a system which exists between public international law and national law and tends to approach one or the other – displaying a degree of interiorisation.[8] Although such descriptions may assist in coming to grips with a *sui generis* system, they do not encompass (indeed these commentators reject) the notion of autonomy to which European Community law lays claim, which includes a legitimation independent of public international law of a body of law *ex proprio vigore.*

The effect of taking a broad view of public international law is to preempt European Community law from removing itself from public international law (perhaps even to steal European Community law's thunder) and thereby from depriving itself of a sustainable legitimation.

---

5 Convention of 29 May 1969 on the law of treaties (entered into force on 27 January 1980 following the deposit of the thirty-fifth instrument of ratification or accession), and Convention of 21 March 1986 on the law of treaties between States and international organisations and between international organisations (not yet in force).

6 See, *e.g.* the Advisory Opinion of the International Court of Justice in the *Namibia* Case [1971] International Court of Justice Reports 16 at 47.

7 J. Boulouis, "Le droit des Communautés Européennes dans ses rapports avec le droit international général" (1992) Vol. 235 (IV) *Recueil des Cours* 19 at p. 23 and p. 49.

8 P. Reuter, "Les recours de la Cour de Justice des Communautés Européennes à des principes généraux de droit" in *Problémes de Droit des Gens: Mélanges offerts à Henri Rolin* (Paris: Editions A. Pedone, 1964) p. 283.

European Community Law Perception

3–2 European Community law firmly distinguishes itself from being public international law as a *sui generis* legal order. Before considering various characteristics of European Community law which distinguish itself (always according to European Community law itself) from public international law, it is worth noting the descriptions of a few commentators.

One authoritative commentator (then a judge of the Court of Justice) who may be described as "integrationist" who takes a generous attitude to European Community law, and what public international law would regard as a restrictive attitude to public international law, stated that the point of his book *The Law of Integration* [9] was to convince the reader of "a qualitative difference between this 'law of integration' now being born and the so-called classical international legal order". Pescatore considered that the European Community system "differs in every respect from the characteristic ingredients of the relationships governed by traditional international law".[10] The most important difference was that European Community law had unification as its objective. It is a supranational system, by its nature different to public international law "since it originates in questioning a fundamental concept of the international legal order, namely that of sovereignty".[11]

Allowing public international law or national law to penetrate the autonomy of European Community law "would introduce an element of disintegration into a law whose fundamental object rests in the integration which is constitutionally required."[12] In addition to an apparent root conflict with European Community law's integrative or federal ambitions, penetration by public international law would give rise to obstacles to integration in, *inter alia,* the following constitutional characteristics in European Community law considered in this Part: the scope of competences; the status of public international treaties, rules, and principles, and principles of interpretation, the sources used as quarries for European Community unwritten law; the doctrines of rights to individuals, direct effect, and supremacy; the concept of citizenship; the transformation of the constituent treaties into a constitution of an entity approaching a federation; the restriction of amendments and the federalisation of the legal order in general.

---

9 P. Pescatore, Preface, *The Law of Integration: the Emergence of a New Phenomenon in International Relations, Based on the Experience of the European Communities* (Leiden: Sitjhoff, 1974).

10 *ibid.* p. 48.

11 *ibid.* p. 49.

12 W.G. Van der Meersch (1975) *op. cit.* above, n.4, p. 213.

4. ORIGIN

Public International Law Perception

4–1 It is an undeniable fact that European Community law has its historical origin in treaties. The importance of this has been forcefully stated in doctrine:

> "It is scarcely debatable that, by its formal sources whether it is a question of the treaties instituting the Communities, unilateral acts of its institutions, or agreements concluded by the Community, Community law remains international law."[1]

The nature of the constituent act determines its juridical nature: treaty implies international organisation; constitution as distinct from constitutive treaty implies a form of federal state. The Member States as subjects of public international law were the enactors of the written law basis of the European Communities: the Treaties establishing the Communities. Even if the structures, content and scope of European Community law resemble more closely federal law than public international law, this does not mean that the validity of European Community law ceases to be dependent on the Treaties and public international law.[2] The public international law nature of European Community law remains a *sine qua non* of its validity. It is a paradox that European Community law claims to be independent of public international law.[3] States are subject to European Community law only because of their consent, and there, sovereignty finds a fundamental guarantee to which Member States may always appeal.[4]

However, the statement that the nature of the constituent act determines its juridical nature needs some qualification. Historical origin is not necessarily determinative of the present nature of European Community law: "The sole fact that the constitutive acts of the Communities might be international treaties does not allow the prejudgment of the nature of the organisations which are their progeny."[5] It can happen that treaties lose their public international law nature and become the constitution of a new state:

> "Fusion of two or more States into one is hardly conceivable without the deliberate collective action of the States concerned. It will, therefore, almost

---

1 J. Boulouis, "Le droit des Communautés Européennes dans ses rapports avec le droit international général" (1992) Vol. 235 IV *Recueil des Cours* 19 at p. 23.

2 M. Walbroeck, "Contributions à l'étude de la nature juridique des Communautés Européennes" in *Problémes de Droit des Gens: Mélanges offerts à Henri Rolin* (Paris: Editions A. Pedone, 1964) p. 508.

3 Boulouis (1992) *op. cit.* above, n.1, p 22.

4 *ibid.* p. 79.

5 W.G. van der Meersch, "L'Ordre juridique des Communautés Européenes et le Droit international" (1975) 148 (V) *Recueil des Cours de l'Académie de Droit International* at p. 45.

> always be the outcome of an international juridical act, accomplished with a view to uniting the separate entities and will thus constitute a direct creation by law. The law which governs the agreement is clearly the law of nations, but here we are confronted with a transmutation in the opposite direction from international into constitutional law. By the very fact of the entering into effect of the agreement concerned this loses its original legal nature and is simultaneously and automatically transformed into an instrument which is incorporated as an integral part into the constitutional law of the new State.
>
> Such a fusion need not, however, necessarily destroy the whole international legal personality of the fusing States since their uniting may have had as its object the establishment of a federal State which reserves a certain amount of freedom to act in the international field to its component members. In such a case the fusing States ('in the sense of international law', according to some theorists) lose their former individual status of fully fledged members of the international legal order, remaining in that order with only a limited personality and a limited freedom to act and being, for the rest, downgraded to mere 'States in the sense of public law', i.e., in the light of the general theory of the State, no longer States in any real sense at all."[6]

The favourite example in European Community law secondary literature is the German Empire, created in 1870–1871 by means of international treaties. However Verzijl gives other examples[7]: the abortive United Arab Republic formed from Egypt and Syria in 1958, and the Republic of Tanzania formed on 23 April 1964 from the union of Tanganyika and Zanzibar.

Therefore public international law can originate historically legal orders which are not public international law. However the examples given by Verzijl were deliberate once-off bilateral acts whose sole purpose was to effect the fusion of two states to form a new state, very different acts to those forming the European Communities.[8]

One of the tests for identifying this mysterious process of transformation is whether the rules of revision of the treaty constitution have changed, and specifically whether there are limits to possible changes and whether the requirement of unanimity has been retained.[9]

---

6 J.H.W. Verzijl, *International Law in Historical Perspective – Part II: International Persons* (Leiden: Sijthoff, 1969) pp. 92–93.

7 *ibid.* p. 93. The other examples are not based on international instruments.

8 There are also cases where states make treaties guaranteeing the sovereignty of states or recognising limited sovereignty of constituent parts of a state, for example the treaties at Münster and Osnabrück on 30 January and 24 October 1648 concluding the Peace of Westphalia, which guaranteed the independence of Switzerland and the territorial sovereignty of the German princes. Such cases are further removed from the acts constituting the European Communities than the examples given in the text because the Peace of Westphalia was disintegrative (of the Holy Roman Empire) rather than integrative, and because it recognised in law what happened in fact rather than trying to make fact follow law. See A.M. De Zayas, "Westphalia, Peace of (1648)" in R. Bernhardt (ed.), *Encyclopedia of Public International Law* (Amsterdam – New York – Oxford: North Holland, 1984) Vol. 7, p. 536.

9 See below Chap. 11, "Amendability.".

European Community Law Perception

4–2 The Court of Justice early on contrasted the Treaty establishing the European Economic Community with "ordinary international treaties".[10] The most radical approach to the nature of European Community law is to hold it to be not only *sui generis* but also a system of law *ex proprio vigore*: although European Community law may owe its forms and substance in large part to both public international law and national law, it owes its validity to neither. Kakouris has stated that the Treaty,

> "is in force by itself in an autonomous fashion and constitutes the primary source of validity of the whole Community legal order, exactly like the Constitutions of Member States constitute the primary source of their legal orders. That was not clear during the first years of the existence of the Community, but it is now."[11]

One of the aims of this Part is to establish that European Community law's detachment from public international law not only as a legal system but also as a legal order encompasses both the content and character of law and also its legitimation, by which European Community law rules derive normatively from European Community law bases and only historically from public international law. For its root of legitimation European Community law has relied on the achievement of its goals – economic and political but also legal – and on the future as well as present factual entity "Europe" it is helping to bring into being. The intention of the Member States, which is expressed in the Treaty articles as well as in the Preamble and objectives of the Community is ignored at crucial junctures and replaced by the "spirit" of the Treaty.[12] This is established by the cases analysed in this chapter, although other instances could be given. For example, when the Court of Justice created an additional head of jurisdiction under Article 173 (EEC) to allow acts of the European Parliament to be challenged (thus raising the status of the acts of the Parliament and *ipso facto* of the Parliament itself),[13] Advocate-General (now judge) Mancini stated that:

> "the obligation to observe the law takes precedence over the strict terms of the written law. Whenever required in the interests of judicial protection, the Court is prepared to correct or complete rules which limit its powers in the name of the principle which defines its mission."[14]

---

10 Case 6/64 *Costa v. ENEL* [1964] E.C.R. 585 at 593.

11 C.N. Kakouris, "La rélation de l'ordre juridique communautaire avec les ordres juridiques des États membres (Quelques réflexions parfois peu conformistes)" (1987) in C-D Ehlermann *et. al., Du droit international au droit de l'intégration, Liber Amicorum Pierre Pescatore* (Baden-Baden: Nomos 1987) p. 331.

12 Apart from the analysis in this chapter, see also T.C. Hartley, "The European Court, Judicial Objectivity and the Constitution of the European Union" (1996) 112 L.Q.R. 95.

13 Case 294/83 *Parti écologiste "Les Verts" v. European Parliament* [1986] E.C.R. 1339.

14 *ibid.* at 1350. The Advocate-General does not expand further on this mission. This passage has been called "[p]ossibly the most revealing statement concerning the ECJ's [Court of Justice's] attitude to the actual language used in the texts which it has to construe . . . ": P. Neill, "The European Court of Justice: a Case Study in Judicial Activism" (Oxford: Manuscript, 23 January 1995).

5. COMPETENCES

Public International Law Perception

5–1 European Community law is the most developed example of the law of international organisations because it groups together innovations in public international law to a massive extent. But this is a matter of quantity of law and techniques: the quality of the law as a specific subset of public international law does not change. There may come a point where competences and techniques become so massed that the quantity becomes quality in that they represent the competences of a State. To public international law the creation of a State can be to a large degree a historical event in the sense of an actual occurrence: "to which international law attaches *a posteriori* certain legal effects, and which consequently belongs to the theoretical category of 'juridical facts'."[1] There must be as a matter of juridical fact a population,[2] a territory, and a political authority supreme internally and entitled to represent the people and territory externally.[3] But for that to happen the quantity of competences would have to encompass the external and military affairs of the Member States, and deprive them of the power of unanimous revision. As above, this has not happened. The massing of competences has also brought about a degree of solidarity in fact, but this has not yet reached the stage of creating a stable community and political authority within the sense of the juridical facts which public international law requires to be established. The transfer of competences as a feature of the Community appears to have been accepted by public international law, at least to some degree, although not as a feature exclusive to the Community.[4]

---

1 J.H.W. Verzijl, *International Law in Historical Perspective – Part II: International Persons* (Leiden: Sijthoff, 1969) p. 63.

2 The Montevideo Convention refers to "a permanent population" which connotes "a stable community" – I. Brownlie, *Principles of Public International Law* (4th ed.: Oxford: Clarendon Press, 1990) p. 73.

3 Verzijl (1969) *op. cit.* above, n.1, p. 62.

4 The Member States negotiated in the Food and Agriculture Organisation, a subsidiary organ of the United Nations, for the admission to membership of the European Community. The Constitution of the FAO was amended to provide for the admission of "a regional organisation constituted by sovereign States . . . to which its Member States have transferred competence" (Art. II.4). See Case C–25/94 *Commission v. Council* [1996] E.C.R.I.–1469. The fact that the European Community was not named but rather was covered in a category indicates that the Member States of FAO considered that other international organisations could qualify. The use of the word "Constitution" for the basic document of the FAO indicates that the word does not mean in public international law the basic document of an entity tending towards federation. See further Chap. 10, para. 10–1, "Treaty as Constitution – Public International Law Perception".

European Community Law Perception

5–2 European Community law sees the Community as having competences not simply because of international treaties for the time being in force but because national sovereignty has been transferred to the institutions. This partly explains the European Community law perception of the Community as being more than an international organisation without worrying about fulfilling the public international law criteria for statehood. However there is no express statement of transfer as distinct from an enumeration of competences, let alone sovereignty, in the Treaties establishing the European Communities. The use of such phrases has been established by case law and doctrine. It appears to have been accepted by the Member States at least for the purposes of their negotiations on the accession of the Community to the Food and Agriculture Organisation.[5] Nor are there any rules in the Treaties establishing the Communities directly expressed to be on the division of powers between the Community and the Member States,[6] save Article 3b (EC) paragraph one which states that: "The Community shall act within the limits of the powers conferred upon it by this Treaty and of the objectives assigned to it therein." This has been referred to as the basis of the institutional system of the Community to be respected in the internal and the external action of the Community.[7]

The competences of the Community which are expressly stated in the Treaty establishing the European Community are very wide-ranging. Part Three of that treaty has 17 Titles, each concerned with separate Community policies and conferring on the Community competences in their regard.[8]

---

5 *ibid.*

6 The popularity of the phrase is itself relatively new – for example, as regards powers to deal with Third States, Opinion 1/94 *Re the Uruguay Round Agreements* [1995] 1 C.M.L.R. 205, para. 24 ("division of international powers between the Member States and the Community"), and, as regards the division of internal powers within the Community, Joined Cases T–244 & T–486/93 *TWD Textilwerke Deggendorf GmbH v. Commission* [1995] E.C.R. II–2265.

7 Opinion 2/94, *Accession by the Community to the European Convention for the Protection of Human Rights and Fundamental Freedoms,* [1996] E.C.R. I–1759, paras. 23, 24, and 30.

8 In regard to the exercise of those competences a former judge of the Court of Justice thought that there should be minimum interference with the market because the market was politically neutral, and therefore the maximum possible sovereignty would be left to the Member States – P. Ver Loren Van Themaat, "Some Preliminary Observations on the Intergovernmental Conferences: the Relations between the Concepts of a Common Market, a Monetary Union, an Economic Union, a Political Union, and Sovereignty" (1991) 28 *Common Market Law Review* 291. But this interesting suggestion simply cedes sovereignty to the market or, more accurately, cedes control to the market of those matters which have formerly been controlled by the sovereign to the extent the sovereign considered beneficial. The suggestion appears to rest on a presumption both about the proper degree of government control of the market and, presuming that the author intended whatever control there was, or the abolition of control, to be organised on the Community level, on a presumption of the proper division of the powers of control between the Member States and the Community.

Furthermore, the Court of Justice adopts as correct an extremely broad[9] construction of the Community's manifold competences both internal[10] and external[11] beyond that provided for in the text of the Treaties establishing the Communities despite the existence of Article 235 (EC). Even where the Member States have retained competence, it must be exercised in accordance with European Community law and not jeopardise the attainment of Community objectives, upon which it may impinge.[12] Although the Court of Justice sees the objectives of the Treaty establishing the European Community as a reason for acknowledging Community competence in diverse areas to attain those objectives, it appears not to see the competence as limited to that necessary to attain the objective to which it relates. In Opinion 1/94 *Re the Uruguay Round Agreements* the Court held:

> Although the only objective expressly mentioned in the chapters on the right of establishment and on freedom to provide services is the attainment of those freedoms for nationals of the Member States of the Community, it does not follow that the Community institutions are prohibited from using the powers conferred on them in that field in order to specify the treatment which is to be accorded to nationals of non-member countries.[13]

The Court appears in the next sentence to legitimate this extension by reference to Member State practice: "Numerous acts adopted by the Council on the basis of Articles 54 and 57(2) of the Treaty – but not mentioned by it – contain provisions in that regard." However earlier on in the same opinion the Court held: "the Court has consistently held that a mere practice of the Council cannot derogate from the rules laid down in the Treaty . . . "[14]

The constitutional structures within which the Community exercises its competences are examined below in regard to individual rights. The extent of penetration and demands on national law to which this gives rise are examined in Part V. The tension (although not necessarily an inconsistency) in the approach of the Court of Justice in arriving at a vision of the Treaty as

---

9 Compare the implied powers doctrine of United States constitutional law which was summed up early on by Marshall C.J.: "Let the end be legitimate, let it be within the scope of the constitution, and all means which are plainly adapted to that end, which are not prohibited, but consist with the letter and spirit of the constitution, are constitutional" – *McCulloch v. Maryland* 17 U.S. (4 Wheat.) 316 at 421. The United States Supreme Court's insistence on consistency with the letter as well as the spirit is if anything more literal than the approach of the Court of Justice.

10 *e.g.* Case 293/83 *Gravier v. City of Liège* [1985] E.C.R. 606.

11 See the next para., "Competence to Conclude Public International Law Treaties".

12 *e.g.* Case C–369/90 *Micheletti v. Delagacion del Gobierno en Cantabria* [1992] E.C.R. I–4239.

13 [1995] 1 C.M.L.R. 205, para. 90.

14 Para. 52 (citation omitted). The sentence continued " . . . and cannot, therefore, create a precedent binding on Community institutions with regard to the correct legal basis." The principle, however, is the same. Indeed legal basis is a question related to that posed on the scope of chapters of the Treaties. The chapters at issue in para. 90 were on the right to establishment and the freedom to provide services. The legal basis in question in para. 52 was that for agreements on transport.

a constitution of a federal legal order,[15] by applying a teleological technique on the grounds that it is interpreting a public international law treaty, supports the importance of objectives in the legitimation of European Community law.

Competence to Conclude Public International Law Treaties

Public International Law Perception

5–3 In the public international law perception, "[t]he existence of legal personality does not of itself support a power to make treaties, and everything depends on the terms of the constituent instrument of the organisation."[16] The terms of the Treaty establishing the European Community are very limited on the power of the European Community to conclude treaties, and European Community law has gone far beyond those terms. Whilst it is true that the Preamble to the Second Vienna Convention provides: "[n]oting that international organisations possess the capacity to conclude treaties which is necessary for the exercise of their functions and the fulfillment of their purpose" it is unlikely that this statement could be called declaratory of customary public international law. Further, as a general rule[17] international organisations allow only states to be members, and consequently the European Community could not be a party to a convention concluded by the members of such an organisation within its framework.[18]

European Community Law Perception

5–4 The European Community (but not the European Union) has legal personality (Article 210 (EC)). The European Community has treaty-making powers with Third States and international organisations which are expressly granted in Article 113(3) (EC) on the Common Commercial Policy, Article 238 (EC) on association agreements, Article 130m (research and technology) and Article 130r(4) (environment) inserted originally by the Single European Act, and in Article 130y (development cooperation) inserted by the Treaty on European Union. There is an almost express grant of power in Articles 229 to 231 (EC) on maintaining all appropriate relations with the organs of the United Nations, the General Agreement on Tariffs and Trade, the Council of Europe, and the Organisation for Economic Cooperation and Developement. There is no other express grant of power.[19] Article 228 (EC) provides a special

---

[15] See below Chap. 13, "European Community Law as a Federal Legal Order".

[16] I. Brownlie (1990) *op. cit.* above, n.2, pp. 684–685.

[17] One exception is the FAO.

[18] For example, Convention 170 of the International Labour Organisation – Opinion 2/91 [1993] Rec. I–1061.

[19] The Community also has competence under Part Four (EC) "Association of the Overseas Countries and Territories" which provides in Article 135 for the conclusion of agreements

procedure for the adoption of such international treaties, which are obviously creations and part of public international law.

The Court of Justice has held that the Community may have competence to enter into treaties even where this is not provided for in the Treaty establishing the European Community, if such a power can be deduced from the system of the Treaty as well as its substantive provisions and the acts of the institutions.[20] The Court of Justice held that where the Community has adopted common rules, the Member States, *ipso facto*, no longer have the right to make treaties with Third States in that field. There does not appear to be a bar in public international law to Member States making treaties. The Court of Justice concluded that "the system of measures internal to the Community cannot be separated from that of external relations." Following Opinion 1/76 *Re the Laying-up Fund for Inland Waterway Vessels*[21] one could have attempted a summation of the doctrine of implied powers on which this interpretation of the external powers of the Community is based as this: wherever the Community has internal powers, it also has parallel external powers necessary to achieve the objective of the implied powers; until the Community has exercised its powers, internal or implied external, the Member States retain concurrent competence; thereafter, the Community has exclusive competence.

However after Opinion 2/91 *Re Convention No. 170 of the International Labour Organisation*[22] it appeared that, as a result of the Article 5 (EC) obligation to secure the objectives of the Treaty establishing the European Community, the Community might have implied exclusive external powers even where it had not exercised (express) internal powers.[23] This was the case even though the Community was incapable "in the present state of international law" to conclude the treaty[24] as the International Labour Organisation did not allow the European Economic Community to be a member. The Court of Justice held that in such a situation the obligation of tight cooperation between the Member States and the Community institutions, which results from the

---

on free movement of workers with the unanimous approval of the Member States. However such agreements are not treaties because of the status of the overseas countries and territories.

Article 75(1)(a) (EC) refers to the adoption by the Council of "common rules applicable to international transport to and from the territory of a Member State." This reference has helped ground an implied treaty making power – Case 22/70 *Commission v. Council* ("*ERTA*") [1971] E.C.R. 263. However it refers expressly to common rules only, that is, common to the Member States, although they may be applicable to transport entering from Third States.

20 Case 22/70 *Commission v. Council* ("*ERTA*") above, n.19; see also Opinion 1/92 [1992] E.C.R. I–2845, para. 40.

21 [1977] E.C.R. 741.

22 [1993] Rec. I–1061; the Convention is on the safety in the use of chemical products at work.

23 *ibid.* paras. 10 and 18. As regards the Convention at issue, the Court found that competence to conclude it was shared.

24 *ibid.* para. 37 of the Opinion.

requirement of unity in international representation of the Community (mentioned in the Treaty establishing the European Coal and Steel Community and transferred by analogy to the European Economic Community) is all the more stringent.[25] This opinion is an example of the Court of Justice evolving without a Treaty basis other than a reference to securing Treaty objectives European Community law directly contrary to the public international law conception of the Community.

The doctrine of implied external competence has been developed further by the Court of Justice in Opinion 1/94 *Re the Uruguay Round Treaties*.[26] The Community has implied exclusive external competences on the basis of parallel internal competences, despite the facts that the internal competences have not been exercised and that there is no Treaty provision conferring power on the institutions to negotiate with Third States in the area of competence, if the internal competences can only be exercised effectively at the same time as external competences.[27] Otherwise, internal competence gives rise to exclusive external competence only when it is exercised. Once the internal competence is partially exercised, the Member States retain competence only so far as that competence cannot affect the internal rules adopted.[28] Articles 100a and 235 (EC) and the objectives of the Treaty cannot by themselves ground exclusive competence.[29] The extent to which they can ground joint external competence remains unclear.

There are limits to the Community's external competence as to its internal competence in accordance with the principle of conferred powers in Article 3b(1) (EC).[30]

There is a possibility that the Council can exercise the implied, as well as the express (Article 228(2) (EC)), treaty-making powers of the Community without unanimity,[31] which if accurate moves the Community closer to federation.

---

25 *ibid.* paras. 36 and 37 of the Opinion.

26 [1995] 1 C.M.L.R. 205. See also Opinion 2/92 *Third Revised Decision of the OECD on National Treatment* [1995] E.C.R. I–521.

27 *ibid.* paras. 86, 89 and 100.

28 *ibid.* para. 96.

29 *ibid.* paras. 87 to 89.

30 Opinion 2/94 *Accession by the Community to the European Convention for the Protection of Human Rights and Fundamental Freedoms*, [1996] E.C.R. I–1759, paras. 23–30.

31 H.G. Schermers, "Case note on Opinion 1/91 and Opinion 1/92" (1992) 29 *Common Market Law Review* 991.

6. THE STATUS OF PUBLIC INTERNATIONAL LAW TREATIES IN EUROPEAN COMMUNITY LAW

6–1 This section is concerned with the status and effect in European Community law of treaties entered into by the European Community (solely, or jointly with the Member States) or binding upon it (by virtue of the principle of substitution) and, to a lesser extent, with the status and effect of such treaties in national law by virtue of European Community law. This constitutional issue is of concern here because it involves the relations between public international law, European Community law, and national law, and the sovereignty of the European Community and the Member States as understood in those orders, and because such treaties are capable of giving rise to rights in individuals which may either conflict with directly effective European Community law rights before national courts or, more likely, be made directly effective by virtue of European Community law and conflict with national law.

Public International Law Perception

6–2 Public international law does not appear to take a position on the status of international treaties in the laws of international organisations bound by them. Article 5 of the first and second Vienna Convention has been considered,[1] and the entry into force and non-retroactivity of those Conventions has been mentioned. Even if the rules in Article 5 applied in public international law at the time of many of European Community law's constitutional developments, the Article is close to public international law withdrawing from this area. To say that European Community law is consistent in this regard with public international law therefore does not mean much.

European Community Law Perception

6–3 European Community law in developing its constitutional law on this issue has not relied on Article 5 of the Vienna Conventions.

The most important point concerns the status of such treaties with the Treaty establishing the European Community: if the European Community enters into a treaty which is incompatible with the Treaty establishing the European Community, it is not yet clear whether the Court of Justice will

---

1 See above, para. 3–1.

apply the Treaty establishing the European Community over the conflicting treaty.[2] This would support the idea of the Treaty establishing the European Community as constitution: a constitution against which the validity or at least the applicability of international treaties falls to be tested; a constitution which cannot be modified by collateral treaty.

European Community law is a monist system in that treaties to which it is a party become part of its internal law without a further act of the Community legislature, and the treaties enter at a normative level above *droit dérivé* but probably below the Treaty establishing the European Community.

Although Article 228(7) (EC) provides that agreements concluded according to the procedure in Article 228 "shall be binding on the institutions of the Community and on Member States", there is no provision on the status of such agreements in European Community law.[3] The judicial recognition of the status of such agreements as "an integral part of Community law" without a provision in the Treaty establishing the European Community to that effect makes European Community law more monist than most so-called monist national legal orders, which depend on a provision of national law to refer out to and import in public international law.[4]

The Treaty Establishing the European Community and Treaties with Third States

6–4 There is a procedure for judicial review of the compatibility of a proposed agreement with the Treaty. According to Article 228(6) (EC) the Council, Commission or a Member State may obtain the opinion of the Court of Justice as to whether an envisaged treaty is compatible with the Treaty establishing the European Community. If the Court of Justice decides it is incompatible, the envisaged treaty can enter into force only after amending the Treaty establishing the European Community to remove the European Community law incompatibility with the draft treaty, by way of the procedure provided,[5] or by changing the envisaged treaty to remove its incompatibility. The Court of Justice has held proposed treaties incompatible with the Treaty establishing the European Community, for example the Draft Agreement establishing a European laying-up fund for inland waterway vessels in Opinion 1/76[6] because the Draft Agreement called into question the power of the institutions in the field of international transport.[7] The incompatibility need not be with a provision of the Treaty establishing the European Community, but can be with

---

2 See below, para. 6–4.
3 Case 181/73 *Haegeman v. Belgium* [1974] E.C.R. 449.
4 *e.g.* below, para. 16–3, "Constitutional Basis of Public International Law".
5 Formerly Article 236 (EC), now Article N (EU).
6 [1977] E.C.R. 741.
7 See also Opinion 1/91 [1991] E.C.R. I–6079.

a constitutional aspect of the Community. For example a proposed international treaty will be incompatible with the Treaty establishing the European Community if it denatures the function of the Court of Justice as it is conceived of in the Treaty.[8] This Article 228(6) procedure is of constitutional importance. As developed by the Court of Justice it may also be used to test the respective competences of the Community and the Member States to negotiate and conclude a treaty even after the Community has signed the treaty provided that the Community's consent to be bound has not been finally expressed.[9]

The European Court of Justice has not pronounced conclusively on the question of whether international treaties which bind the Community and to which it is a party are subordinate in European Community law to the Treaty establishing the European Community. The Court has jurisdiction over this question.[10] Although Article 228 (EC) cannot be used to raise a question over the compatibility of a ratified treaty with the Treaty establishing the European Community, the Court of Justice retains jurisdiction over the validity of the instrument of ratification (usually a Council Decision).[11] By an attack on the validity of the instrument of ratification the Court of Justice could refuse to apply an incompatible treaty.[12] This does not mean that the Court pronounces on the validity of the treaty as such.

---

8 Opinion 1/92 [1992] E.C.R. I–2821, 2843 para. 32.

9 Opinion 1/94 [1995] 1 C.M.L.R. 205.

10 In Case 181/73 *Haegeman v. Belgium* [1974] E.C.R. 449 at 459–460, the Court held, on an Article 177 (EEC) reference from a Belgian tribunal on the interpretation of an Association Agreement with Greece (then a Third State), that as soon as the agreement with the Third State enters into force, its provisions become "an integral part of Community law" and, as any other act of a Community institution, the agreement would be subject to the jurisdiction of the Court. The same approach applies to mixed agreements – those entered into with a Third State both by the Communities and the Member States individually – since the Court of Justice views these as acts of Community institutions and therefore also an "integral part of the Community legal system" – Case 12/86 *Demirel v. Stadt Schwäbisch Gmünd* [1987] E.C.R. 3719.

11 Opinion 3/94 *Re the Framework Agreement on Bananas* of 13 December 1995, para. 22. There are statements earlier in the opinion which suggest that once a treaty has been concluded its force cannot be denied in European Community law – paras. 12 and 13. See also Opinion 2/94 of 28 March 1996, paras. 12 and 13.

12 Some support might also be gleaned from the superiority of the constituent treaties over rules of public international law. In Case C–146/89 *Commission v. United Kingdom* [1991] E.C.R. I–3533 at 3559, para. 23, Advocate-General Lenz stated, in the context of the fisheries limits dispute between the United Kingdom (relying, *inter alia,* on the London Convention 1964) and the European Community on the use of ambulatory or fixed-line baselines:

> "the question immediately arises whether and to what extent there has been a modification of concepts of public international law pursuant to the Community law in which they are embedded, in particular because Community law 'constitutes a new legal order of international law' [citing *Van Gend en Loos*] which, in the relations between the Member States, has clear precedence over obligations arising under public international law [citing Joined Cases 180 & 266/80 [1981] E.C.R. 2997]."

In that case it was held that the Act of Accession and Community secondary legislation had modified the obligations of the Member States.

However a direct pronouncement on this issue of the status of ratified international treaties *vis-à-vis* the Treaty establishing the European Community depends on how the Court would view the Treaty establishing the European Community as Constitution. In Hartley's view, it is unlikely that a treaty within Community competence could be applied in European Community law if it directly conflicted with a provision of the constitutive treaties.[13] This interpretation is backed up by the implied prohibition in Article 228(5) (EC) of the indirect amendment of the Treaty establishing the European Community by international agreement of the Council.

The Court of Justice has further held that where there is an incompatibility with Article 164 (EEC) and more generally with the very foundations of the Community, there are restrictions on the power of the Member States to amend the Treaty establishing the European Community.[14]

As regards the effect in public international law of the invalidity in European Community law of a treaty:

> "the Community would be able to invoke [in public international law] the invalidity as against a non-Member State party only if the violation of its internal rules was 'manifest and concerned a rule of fundamental importance.' [citing Article 46 of the 1986 Vienna Convention on the Law of Treaties] Otherwise, an agreement held internally invalid would continue in effect as an international obligation."[15]

The incidents of the treaty in public international law (valid – must be implemented) and European Community law (invalid – cannot be implemented) would therefore be in conflict unless the exceptional case of manifest violation of internal rule of fundamental importance was established (which exception is provided for in public international law).

Secondary Law ("*Droit dérivé*") and Treaties.

6–5 However as regards treaties which are compatible with the Treaty establishing the European Community, European Community law adopts a monist approach according to which such treaties take precedence over acts of the institutions, including secondary law. Such treaties appear to take precedence by virtue of their own nature as treaties. Article 228(7) (EC) provides another reason: it provides that agreements concluded pursuant to Article 228 shall bind the institutions. In Joined Cases 21–24/72 *International Fruit*[16] the Court of Justice held that the Court's jurisdiction to rule on the validity of acts of

---

[13] T.C. Hartley, *The Foundations of European Community Law* (3rd ed., Oxford: Clarendon Press, 1994) p. 187.

[14] Opinion 1/91 – see below, Chap. 11, "Amendability".

[15] E. Stein, "External Relations of the European Community: Structure and Process" in *Collected Courses of the Academy of European Law* (Dordrecht: Martinus Nijhoff, 1991) 115 at p. 164.

[16] [1972] E.C.R. 1219.

the institutions pursuant to Article 177 (EEC) extended to all grounds capable of invalidating such acts. Without offering a further reason, the Court of Justice held that one such ground was "a rule of international law"[17] which phrase, standing by itself, appears to mean any rule of international law which binds the Community. However, the Court of Justice goes on to talk of provisions of international law, and so appears to limit the principle to treaties binding the Community.[18] In that case Advocate-General Mayras expressly stated the view that where a directly effective agreement conflicted with a Community act, the act will be invalid if it was subsequent to the agreement.[19]

The Court of Justice decided that, before the invalidity of an act of a Community institution can be relied on before a national court, the provision of international law must be capable of conferring rights on "citizens of the Community" which they can invoke before courts (in other words, the provisions must have direct effect in the sense of individual rights).[20] This is to be contrasted with the other possibilities, implicitly rejected: that "citizens of the Community" could rely on the international obligation as a shield to the enforcement of secondary Community law (in *International Fruit*, restrictions in Regulations), on the ground that the measure is invalid because adopted contrary to international obligations; or that "citizens of the Community" could have relied directly on the institutions' breach of European Community law obligations, namely Article 228 (EC).

Member State Responsibility in Public International Law for Acts of the European Community

Public International Law Perception

6–6 The Community is bound by its treaties with Third States as a matter of public international law, and Member States are directly bound also if the treaty is a mixed agreement. Member States would be subsidiarly liable in public international law for treaties concluded by the Communities because they acted through the Communities.[21] But it is not yet clear whether the international responsibility of Member States would be directly engaged because they acted through the Communities. If their international responsibility was not engaged then, from the public international law perception, this would be a step towards federation. The answer to this question sheds light on the public international law perception of the Communities. However

[17] *ibid.* at para. 6.
[18] *ibid.* at para. 8.
[19] *ibid.* at 1233–1234.
[20] *ibid.* at para. 8.
[21] E. Stein, *op. cit.* above, n.15, at p. 167.

public international law appears to be moving to the position that the absence of direct Member State responsibility could be provided for as part of the law of international organisations, and therefore that the absence of Member State responsibility would not mean a federation.

So far as the approach of the European Commission of Human Rights to the European Community is an indicator of the public international law position, the fact that this Commission's approach is not tailored to the European Communities but applies to other international organisations indicates that the European Communities are treated like other international organisations.

The European Commission of Human Rights has held that Member States who are signatories to the Convention for the Protection of Human Rights and Fundamental Freedoms and have accepted the right of individual petition cannot be liable for their participation as states in the decisions of the Council of the European Communities.[22] (There was no jurisdiction *ratione personae* over the European Communities because they were not parties to the Convention.) This holding supports the proposition that the Member States are not subsidiarly liable in public international law for the acts of the Communities, subject to two limitations in the decision itself. First, the Commission emphasised that the act impugned was an act of a European Community organ bearing on the composition of another European Community organ and thus the effects of the act were within the internal framework of the European Communities.[23] Therefore the decision does not cover acts with external effects. Secondly, the decision is confined to accountability before the European Commission of Human Rights, not public international law in general. The decision turned on the construction of the meaning of "jurisdiction" within Article 1 of the Convention, holding that a Member State's acts within the Council were not acts of jurisdiction. However this holding indicates an approach to the nature of the Council which approximates that of European Community law.[24]

In Case 11055/84 *D. v. Belgium*[25] the European Commission of Human Rights held that it had no jurisdiction *ratione personae* over Belgium because Belgium was not responsible for the failure to provide domestic jurisdiction to review the acts of the European School because it was an international organisation (the European School was set up by an international convention of 12 April 1957) established on its territory. Implicitly, the European Commission also decided that Belgium was not responsible, as a contracting state to convention

---

22 Case 8030/77 *Confédération Francaise Démocratique du Travail v. The European Communities, the Member States of the European Communities Collectively and the Member States of the European Communities Individually* [1979] 2 C.M.L.R. 229 (decision of 10 July 1978).

23 *ibid.* at 233, para. 2.

24 This is supported by the identification by the Commission of the Member States' collective activities through the Council as acts of an institution of the European Community, and as nothing else.

25 [1987] 2 C.M.L.R. 57.

setting up the European School, for the alleged breach of the Convention by that organisation, and furthermore that Belgium did not breach the Convention by setting up with other states an organisation which (allegedly) breached the Convention.

In Case 13258/87 *M. & Co. v. Germany*[26] the applicant sued Germany for breach of Article 6 of the Convention for executing a judgment of the Court of Justice of the European Communities and thereby giving effect to the violations by that Court of Article 6. For the purposes here there are two important points. First, the Commission called the European Community an international organisation and dealt with it as such, albeit one to which there had been a "transfer of powers". Secondly, the Commission held that Member States are responsible for all acts of their domestic organs[27] regardless of whether the act is a consequence of domestic law or of the necessity to comply with international obligations. The Commission refused to hold that the German authorities were acting as quasi-Community agents. The Commission recited the standard public international law position, quoting from an earlier case: "if a State contracts treaty obligations and subsequently concludes another international agreement which disables it from performing its obligations under the first treaty it will be answerable for any resulting breach of its obligations under the earlier treaty".[28] The Commission held that provided fundamental rights received protection equivalent to that under the Convention there was no bar to powers being transferred to such an organisation.[29] The Commission found that this was the case in the European Community, and further that the Court of Justice had respected Article 6.[30] This case stands for the proposition that the Member States are liable for acts outside of the European Community institutions for acts implementing their European Community law obligations. (It also suggests that in such cases the Commission will look into the institutions' observance of the protection of fundamental rights for the purposes of

---

26 [1990] 64 *Decisions and Reports of the European Commission of Human Rights* 138 (decision of 9 February 1990 on the admissibility of the application).

27 *cf.* the absence of Member State responsibility for acts of institutions of an international organisation – Case 8030/77 *Confédération Française Démocratique du Travail v. the European Communities, the Member States of the European Communities Collectively and the Member States of the European Communities Individually* [1979] 2 C.M.L.R. 229 (decision of 10 July 1978).

28 Above, n.26, at 145.

29 The next step is unclear: the Commission held that it would be against the idea of transfer of powers to an international organisation to hold Member States responsible for examining each case before issuing a writ of execution where Article 6 was respected in the original judgment.

30 Above, n.26, at 146. This is unclear. The Commission appeared to be dealing with the complaint that Germany had violated the Convention only by transferring powers, not by the act of execution (which was part of the applicant's case). The Commission concluded:

> "The Commission has also taken into consideration that it would be contrary to the very idea of transferring powers to an international organisation to hold the member States responsible for examining, in each individual case before issuing a writ of execution for a judgement of the European Court of Justice, whether Article 6 of the Convention was respected in the underlying proceedings."

assessing the Member State's liability for an implementing act, whilst at the same time suggesting a position akin to that of the German courts in not intervening in each case if in general there are guarantees in European Community law analogous to those under the Convention.) The Commission held the application inadmissible *ratione materiae.*

The question of Member State responsibility for treaties concluded by international organisations with Third States was expressly reserved by Article 74 of the second Vienna Convention, the reason for the reservation being that the public international law of international organisations was not crystallised to the extent necessary to resolve it.[31]

European Community Law Perception

6–7 Member States are also directly bound in European Community law by treaties concluded by the European Community virtue of Article 228(7) (EC).[32]

The Court of Justice and Decisions of International Tribunals

Public International Law Perception

6–8 Decisions of international tribunals are binding.[33]

European Community Law Perception

6–9 If a treaty between the European Community and a Third Party provided for an international tribunal[34] to settle disputes between the European Community and the Third Party then the decisions of that tribunal would bind the Court of Justice in its interpretation of that treaty.[35] However it appears from the same judgment that European Community law is contrary to public international law because the Court of Justice would not uphold the compatibility with the Treaty establishing the European Community of, or indeed allow the Treaty establishing the European Community to be amended to accommodate, such a treaty where it would put the foundations of European Community law in doubt.[36]

---

[31] E. Stein, *op. cit.* above, n.15 at p. 167.

[32] But there appears to be an exception where treaties are concluded in areas where disuniformity is provided for by European Community law, such as in monetary policy. Member States outside of Economic and Monetary Union could not be bound by those provisions of the treaties which concern Economic and Monetary Union – C.-D. Ehlermann, "Increased Differentiation or Stronger Uniformity", E.U.I. Working Paper Robert Schuman Centre No. 95/21 (EUI: Florence, 1995) pp. 29–30.

[33] This may give rise to future problems with the new dispute resolution apparatus of the World Trade Organisation.

[34] The international tribunal could not be the International Court of Justice because under Article 34(1) of its present Statute only States have *locus standi.*

[35] Opinion 1/91 on the EC–EEA Agreement [1991] E.C.R. I–6079, paras. 39 and 40.

[36] *ibid.*

7. THE STATUS OF GENERAL PUBLIC INTERNATIONAL LAW RULES, PRINCIPLES, AND PRINCIPLES OF INTERPRETATION

7–1 There is considerable overlap between rules, principles, and principles of interpretation, of public international law. Which is which depends partly on what one means by "rule" as distinct from "principle", how one wishes to describe or state the rule or principle, and to what use the rule/principle might be put. It is not necessary for the purposes of this work to develop a scheme for this. The purposes of these sections are to expound European Community law's rejection of public international law and its development as a *sui generis ex proprio vigore* legal order.

Rules and Principles of Public International Law in General

Public International Law Perception

7–2 These are binding.

European Community Law Perception

7–3 From the start, the Court of Justice has made reference to principles of public international law but it did not consider them as public international law principles as much as general principles which are valid in every legal order.[1] Thus Advocate-General Lagrange in Case 5/55 *Assider v. High Authority of the ECSC*[2] in considering the principles applying to an application for interpretation of the meaning or scope of a judgment of the Court of Justice, analysed both national law and international law side by side and concluded that there were not "any valid reasons for the Court to depart from those generally recognised principles".[3]

---

1 P. Reuter, "Les recours de la Cour de Justice des Communautés Européennes à des principes généraux de droit" (1964) *Problèmes de Droit des Gens: Mélanges offerts à Henri Rolin* 263 at p. 281.

2 [1954–1956] E.C.R. 135 at 147–149.

3 *ibid.* at 149 – leaving open the possibility for the Court of Justice to so depart if there was a European Community law reason to do so.

Pacta Sunt Servanda

European Community Law Perception

7–4 The Court of Justice has not considered itself limited by rules of public international law. Considering the most fundamental, *pacta sunt servanda* and the obligation of good faith fulfillment of international obligations, the President of the Court of Justice has written extra-curially on its relation to Article 5 (EC). This article contains the general obligation on Member States to ensure fulfillment of obligations of the Treaty establishing the European Community, to facilitate the achievement of the Community's tasks, and to abstain from any measure which jeopardises the Treaty objectives. The President wrote:

> "Article 5 has taken on, in the jurisprudence of the Court, an importance which overtakes by far that of the principle of *pacta sunt servanda* in international law and which approaches the principle of federal law which, in German constitutional law, is called *Bundestreue.*"[4]

Public International Law Perception

7–5 However, from a public international law perception, there is nothing radical about Article 5 (EC). It appears to be no more than a summation of Article 2 paragraphs 2 ("All Members, in order to ensure to all of them the rights and benefits resulting from membership, shall fulfil in good faith the obligations assumed by them in accordance with the present Charter") and 5 ("All Members shall give the United Nations every assistance in any action it takes in accordance with the present Charter . . . ") of the Charter of the United Nations, which is an international organisation. Indeed, these two provisions impose an obligation which is somewhat more positive than the more restrictive negative obligation imposed by Article 5 (EC).

Reciprocity

Public International Law Perception

7–6 This public international law principle, which is closely connected to the basic idea of a treaty being a creation of mutual consent, like a contract between international legal persons, is expressed in many forms, such as *inadimplenti non est adimplendum.* In public international law contracting states can seek to avoid their obligations to a defaulting state. This perception is considered further at paragraph 7–8, below.

---

4 O. Due, "Article 5 du traité CEE. Une disposition de caractère fédéral" in *Collected Courses of the Academy of European Law* (Dordrecht: Martinus Nijhoff, 1991), p. 35.

European Community Law Perception

7–7 The Court of Justice appeared to rely partly on the principle of reciprocity in Case 6/64, *Costa v. ENEL*[5] to establish the doctrine of supremacy. The Court of Justice stated:

> "The integration into the laws of each Member State of provisions which derive from the Community, and more generally the terms and the spirit of the Treaty, make it impossible for the States, as a corollary, to accord precedence to a unilateral and subsequent measure over a legal system accepted by them on the basis of reciprocity."[6]

However, reliance on reciprocity is only one of three grounds stated in this sentence,[7] the first being the integration of European Community law into national law and the second the terms and spirit of the Treaty. If supremacy had been stated in a Treaty Article (it is asserted nowhere in the Treaties), then the Court of Justice could simply have stated *pacta sunt servanda* and reciprocity and Italy would clearly have been in breach of its obligations. But to ground the European Community law doctrine of supremacy, the focus has to be on integration and the spirituality of the Court of Justice

That said, the Court of Justice acknowledged in Case 6/64 *Costa* that European Community law was accepted by the Member States on the basis of reciprocity. But when this got in the way of integration its effect (where there was no reciprocity, there would be no obligation) was denied.[8] In Joined Cases 90 & 91/63 *Commission v. Luxembourg and Belgium*[9] the defendants argued that because the Commission had failed to submit proposals in the area of milk levies despite a Council resolution requesting them to do so within a time limit, the Community could not now seek to compel the defendants, by suing them for Article 12 (EEC) (elimination of customs duties) infringement, to withdraw measures which should have been adopted through the Community framework had the Community acted in time. The Court of Justice devoted four paragraphs to dismissing[10] the defence of reciprocity which the defendants claimed was recognised by international law to the effect that a party harmed by the unexecuted obligations of the other party had the right not to execute his own obligations and thus the Commission had lost its power to sue them for treaty violation. The Court held that:

---

5 [1964] E.C.R. 585.

6 *ibid.* at 593–594.

7 Furthermore, there were other grounds stated in the rest of the judgment, the presence of which further dilutes the importance of the public international law principle – see below, para. 8–41,"Case 6/64 *Costa v. ENEL*".

8 As indeed in Case 6/64 *Costa* the statement that European Community law was a "new legal order of *international* law" in Case 26/62 *Van Gend en Loos* [1963] E.C.R. 1 was changed to "own legal order" in *Costa* in order to establish a non-international law doctrine of supremacy and "new legal order" thereafter – see below, para. 8–6, "Case 26/62 *Van Gend en Loos*" and para. 8–4, "Case 6/64 *Costa v. ENEL*".

9 [1964] E.C.R. 625.

10 *ibid.* at 631–632.

- this link between the obligations of European Community law subjects could not be recognised in European Community law;
- the treaty was not limited to creating reciprocal obligations but established a "new legal order" which regulated the powers, rights and obligations of its subjects as well as the procedures to declare and sanction violations;
- this new legal order therefore implied a prohibition of self-help by the Member States;
- therefore the inexecution of obligations by Community institutions could not dispense the defendants from their obligations.

The Court of Justice has also rejected the proposition that a default by one Member State suspends the reciprocal obligations of other Member States[11] to accord European Community law rights either to nationals of another Member State or to their own nationals.[12]

The Court based its rejection of the rule or principle of reciprocity on the basis that European Community law was a new legal order. A point from the European Community law perception and a point from the public international law perception may be made in that regard.

First, the rights and obligations of individuals in the new legal order could not be made dependent on the notion of reciprocity as then or now understood in public international law without accepting the importance in European Community law of the nationality of the holder of the rights, which is contrary to the European Community law goal of integration (nationality is important in considering whether a European Community law right arises at all – for example in reverse discrimination cases – but this differs from the suspension of an acknowledged right for lack of reciprocity in fulfillment of European Community law obligations).

Public International Law Perception

7–8 Secondly, Wyatt suggests,[13] the result "is perfectly consistent with the public international law basis of the Community legal system". The International Court

---

11 Case 232/78 *Commission v. France* [1979] E.C.R. 2729 at 2739, para. 9, where the Court held that Member States may pursue their grievances as regards the failure of another Member State to fulfil its obligations by taking action through the Council, Commission, or Court: "A Member State cannot under any circumstances unilaterally adopt, on its own authority, corrective measures . . . "; Case C–146/89 *Commission v. United Kingdom* [1991] E.C.R. I–3533 at 3580, para. 47: "Under the legal order established by the Treaty, the implementation of Community law by Member States cannot be made subject to a condition of reciprocity. Articles 169 and 170 of the Treaty provide suitable means of redress when dealing with the failure by Member States to fulfil their obligations under the Treaty".

12 Case 43/75 *Defrenne v. SABENA* [1976] E.C.R. 455 at 472, para. 14.

13 D. Wyatt and A. Dashwood, *Wyatt and Dashwood's European Community Law*, (London: Sweet & Maxwell, 1993) p. 55; D. Wyatt, "New Legal Order or Old?" (1982) *European Law Review* 147 at p. 160.

of Justice has affirmed the principle that the provision of procedures to provide a remedy for the breach of an international obligation may oust the customary public international law right of self-help.[14] One may add that this should apply *a fortiori* in a multilateral treaty establishing an international organisation.

However, what is more important than the argument that European Community law could have relied on public international law to achieve the same result (although the decision of the International Court of Justice which Wyatt cites came some 17 years after the Court of Justice in Cases 90 & 91/63 *Commission v. Luxembourg and Belgium*), is that it did not, and instead chose to rely on the assertion of European Community law as a new legal order.

Exhaustion of Domestic Remedies

Public International Law Perception

7–9 Generally in public international law an individual must first exhaust domestic remedies before the public international law responsibility of the defaulting state can be assessed by an international tribunal:

> "The rule according to which local remedies must be exhausted before international proceedings may be instituted is a well established rule of customary international law; the rule has been generally observed in cases in which a State has adopted the cause of its national whose rights are claimed to have been disregarded in another State in violation of international law. Before resort may be had to an international court in such a situation it has been considered necessary that the State where the violation occurred should have an opportunity to redress it by its own means, within the framework of its own domestic legal system. *A fortiori*, the rule must be observed when domestic proceedings are pending, and when the two actions . . . [in national and international court] are designed to obtain the same result".[15]

Part of the reason for this rule is to give the State the opportunity to right the wrong and therefore to avoid every incident of infringement of a public international law right ending up before an international tribunal. In the *Interhandel* case the Swiss action was held inadmissible by the International Court of Justice because proceedings were still in train in the United States, even though the United States had already expropriated property belonging to a Swiss national, and so domestic remedies were not exhausted.

A well-known example of the necessity to exhaust domestic remedies is the procedure for enforcing the European Convention on Human Rights and Fundamental Freedoms.

---

[14] "Hostages" (1980) International Court of Justice Reports 3 at 28, para. 83.

[15] *Switzerland v. USA* ("*Interhandel*") (preliminary objections) 21 March 1959, International Law Reports, Vol. 27, at 475. See also L. Weber, "Interhandel Case" in R. Bernhardt, (ed.), *Encyclopedia of Public International Law* (Amsterdam – New York: Holland, 1981) Vol. 2 p. 136.

European Community Law Perception

7–10 The Court of Justice rejected this rule in an early case on the interpretation of the Protocol on the Privileges and Immunities of the Treaty establishing the European Coal and Steel Community[16] in a judgment which logically applied to all three Communities. In considering the question the Court of Justice first stated that the problem had to be examined "in the light of the scheme of the Treaty and the rules of law generally accepted in the Member States",[17] not in the light of public international law. The Court of Justice appeared to reason that because it was not acting as a court of appeal from the national courts there was no need to exhaust domestic remedies.[18] This reason would also apply to other international tribunals. The Court of Justice therefore looked to national law and European Community law and pointedly not to public international law to reject the public international law rule. This approach was confirmed in European Economic Community law in Case 13/61 *De Geus v. Bosch*[19] where the Court rejected the argument that a preliminary ruling could not be given unless the ruling of the national court had the force of *res judicata*. The Court held that the Treaty made the jurisdiction of the Court dependent solely on the evidence of a request for a preliminary ruling within the meaning of Article 177 (EEC). This decision was supported by the text of Article 177 (EEC) itself, but it is important that the basis given in Case 6/60 *Humblet v. Belgium*, which predated Case 13/61 *De Geus v. Bosch*, was not dependent on the text of that Article.

In Case 199/82, *San Giorgio* the Court stated more clearly that the right to make a reference to the Court by virtue of Article 177 (EEC) belonged to all national jurisdictions, whatever the stage of the proceeding in the national jurisdiction and the nature of the decision which that jurisdiction was called on to give.[20]

Article 177 (EC), both in its express terms as a pre-judgment remedy, and in its interpretation and development by the Court of Justice, distances European Community law from public international law.

Obligation in the Result – Non-Transformation of Regulations

7–11 The issue of obligation in the result in the wider context of European Community law rights to individuals is considered separately.[21]

---

16 Case 6/60 *Humblet v. Belgium* [1960] E.C.R. 559.

17 *ibid.* at 571.

18 *ibid.* at 572.

19 [1962] E.C.R. 45 at 49–50.

20 Case 199/82 *Amministrazione delle Finanze dello Stato v. San Giorgio* [1983] E.C.R. 3595; see also, in the context of direct effect and supremacy, below, para. 8–58, Case 106/77 *Simmenthal*: [1978] E.C.R. 629 holding that there cannot be even a "temporary impediment" to the full effectiveness of Community law which would have been caused by a reference, necessary under national law, to the Italian Constitutional Court.

21 See below, Chap. 8, "Rights to Individuals".

Public International Law Perception

7–12 Public international law works on the basis that international obligations bind States in the result. At least three aspects of this basis have been rejected in European Community law. One aspect of this, the exhaustion of local remedies, has been considered above. A second aspect, which distinguishes public international law external supremacy from European Community law internal supremacy, will be considered below. Related to this second aspect is a third – direct applicability.

The idea of direct applicability was not unknown to public international law – for example the regulations of the former Danube Commissioners applied directly to sailors without intervention by the riparian states.[22] However in public international law direct applicability depends not only on the treaty in question but also on whether the national law is monist or dualist.

European Community Law Perception

7–13 European Community law distinguishes itself from public international law by Article 189 (EC) according to which all Member States agree that Regulations shall be directly applicable. This is an innovation on the face of the Treaty establishing the European Community. There is a distinction between implementation, permissible if required, and transformation into national law either by re-enacting the substance of the law or making its normative force dependent on national law, which it is not.

The Court of Justice has relied on this innovation to increase legal integration. Whilst innovative, Article 189 (EC) does not have on its face the importance that the Court of Justice has given it. The fact that contracting parties agreed to something not previously agreed to irrespective of the monist or dualist nature of the contracting parties' national law does not mean (in the perception of public international law) a departure from public international law, but a development in it, nor does it mean that national jurisdictions would recognise its effect. But the Court of Justice has relied on this provision to distance itself from public international law and to develop integration, in three ways.

First, a Member State failure to recognise the direct applicability of a Regulation does not give rise only to that Member State's international responsibility but also to a European Community law duty on national courts, irrespective of whether their process of ratification has imposed a similar obligation in national law to disapply conflicting national law.

Secondly, whilst Member States might recognise direct applicability at European Community law level, this would not mean they could not use implementing law if they were to be bound in any event only in the result, and not also in the form. But it was held to be contrary to European Community law for Member States to transform regulations into national law. The

---

[22] The European Commission for the Danube was founded in 1851.

judgments Case 39/72 *Commission v. Italy*[23] and Case 34/73, *Variola v. Amministrazione italiana delle finanze*[24] show the peculiar nature of direct applicability because they illustrate in the context of regulations the general point that European Community law rights before national courts result, according to European Community law, purely as a matter of European Community law. This does not mean that Member States can keep on their books laws which conflict with European Community law without breaching their European Community law obligations. Nor does it mean that the normative force of the European Community law right necessarily derives exclusively from European Community law. The European Community law right may require implementation; if so, there is no European Community law problem with reliance on the implementing legislation; but a European Community law right may not require implementation, in which case reliance on national provisions for normative force is contrary to European Community law. This point arises most clearly in the context of Regulations. It is illegal in European Community law to interpose national law between the Community source of the right (the Regulation[25]) and the individual. In Case 39/72 *Commission v. Italy*[26] the Court held contrary to European Community law the reproduction of Regulations in a decree on the ground that this brought into doubt the legal nature of the Regulations (and their date of entry into force). The Court held that Regulations come into force solely by virtue of their publication, stating that:

> "all methods of implementation are contrary to the Treaty which would have the result of creating an obstacle to the direct effect of Community Regulations and of jeopardising their simultaneous and uniform application in the whole of the Community."

The manner, not just the delay, of Italy's implementation was held to constitute a default.

In Case 34/73 *Variola* the Court made the point even clearer:

> "The direct applicability of a Regulation means that its entry into force and its application in favour of or against those subject to it are independent of any measure of reception into national law."[27]

The Court appears to make a concession to the role of national law in its next sentence where it stated that the Member States are obliged not to obstruct direct applicability by virtue of the obligations arising from the Treaty and "assumed on ratification". However this reference to ratification cannot be interpreted as an acknowledgement that direct applicability depends on what Member States did to their national system in order to be able to ratify, since

---

23 [1973] E.C.R. 101.
24 [1973] E.C.R. 981.
25 This depends on the Regulation, however, because some Regulations require detailed implementation.
26 [1973] E.C.R. 101 at 113–114.
27 [1973] E.C.R. 981 at 990.

ratification in accordance with a Member State's constitutional requirements does not require that the Member State has adapted its national law to accord with the European Community obligations (including the Treaty of Accession[28]), for example by implementing Directives. Ratification requires confirmation of the authority of the signatories to bind their States to membership. To ground its judgment in Case 34/73 *Variola* the Court relied on uniformity:

> "Strict compliance with this obligation is an indispensable condition of simultaneous and uniform application of Community Regulations throughout the Community."

The Court was also concerned by the possibility that national implementing legislation would conceal the European Community law origin of the rule and therefore reduce the likelihood of Article 177 (EEC) references.[29] A reduction does not appear to have occurred in references concerning national law implementing a Directive.

In Case 104/86 *Commission v. Italy*[30] Italy argued that the Commission's application that the failure to abrogate a national law which was contrary to European Community law,

> "would lead in fact to a negation of the direct applicability of Community rules and would reintroduce the idea that the implementation of directly applicable rules of Community law may be affected only by adopting domestic legislation."[31]

The Court of Justice held that Italy had failed in its European Community law obligations. As the Advocate-General pointed out, the direct effect of Community law does not exempt a Member State from bringing its legislation into line with substantive European Community law rules.[32] Nor would an administrative order not to apply the national law suffice.[33]

The statement that European Community law rights before national courts depend as a matter of European Community law for their normative force purely on European Community law has been doubted by Hogan and Whelan.[34] De Witte goes so far as to assert that the ground the Court of Justice advanced in Case 26/62 *Van Gend en Loos* and Case 6/64 *Costa v. ENEL* of the limitation of sovereignty was an invitation to national courts "to make use, if necessary, of their constitutions' integration clause for furthering the application of EC law."[35] Hogan and Whelan indicate, correctly, that there is a difference

---

[28] See *e.g.* the Treaty concerning the Accession of Denmark, Ireland, Norway and the United Kingdom, Articles 2 and 152.

[29] [1973] E.C.R. 981 at 991, para. 11.

[30] [1988] E.C.R. 1799 at 1803, para. 16.

[31] *ibid.* at 1803, para. 16.

[32] *ibid.* at 1811.

[33] Case 167/73 *Commission v. France* [1974] E.C.R. 359. See below para. 8–56, "Requiring Abrogation of Conflicting National Law".

[34] G. Hogan and A. Whelan, *Ireland and the European Union: Constitutional and Statutory Texts and Commentary* (London: Sweet & Maxwell, 1995), p. 11.

[35] B. de Witte, "Sovereignty and European Integration: The Weight of Legal Tradition" (1995) *Maastricht Journal of European and Comparative Law* 145 at pp. 155–156.

between "dressing up directly applicable European Community law measures as national law, without any attribution of source (thus disguising not only the nature of the rights but also, quite possibly the avenues available for their enforcement in the event of denial), and giving full effect to European Community law, acknowledged as such, in a national legal order by virtue of a national provision authorising such effect." However this difference does not make the second method compatible with European Community law (so far as directly applicable provisions, for example Regulations as distinct from Directives which are absorbed into national law when properly transposed, are concerned) – although it might be argued that it should or ought to be compatible with the European project properly conceived. The authors continue: "It is nowhere indicated that Community law is thereby a species of national law rather than an autonomous legal order, although its force in the national legal order may be (from the national point of view) dependent on national law." But this fails to differentiate between public international law and European Community law. The point is that European Community law requires its force to be dependent on European Community law, not national law, and the duty to uphold that law to be dependent on European Community law also.[36] For example, the Court in Case 26/62 *Van Gend en Loos* said that European Community law rights were independent from national law for their force. Grounding provisions of national law deny this directness. At root, the authors are arguing that European Community law obliges in the (effective) result only: "there is nothing [in European Community law] to support that, as in the case of public international law, European Community law cannot be fully accommodated on terms different from but not in practical terms inconsistent with its own by national constitutional legal orders."

This argument succinctly summarises the received wisdom and there is force to that analysis. The position is abstract and ambiguous. Nonetheless, it is not enough for European Community law that national courts vindicate national law rights that copy, even perfectly were it possible, European Community law rights. The point remains that according to European Community law it is a European Community law right, not a national law right, and a European Community law duty, not a national law duty, to uphold that European Community law right. It is a matter of European Community law how a European Community law right is upheld before a national court (it is, of course, according to national law, a matter of national law). A mirror image is not integration. While a mirror image does not of itself bring into question the autonomy of European Community law as a legal order, for example autonomous from public international law, it does bring into question the autonomous validity of European Community law before national courts. European Community law becomes a quarry from which the statement of the right may be derived, but not the normative force. The bindingness is

---

36 See below, Chap. 8, "Rights to Individuals".

reduced to the obligation to go to the quarry and ensure the statement is derived and further (and here European Community law would in any event arguably differ from public international law, as the authors agree) that national law grants it immediate normative force.

Not only would such a mirror image argument be contrary to the structure of integration, it also disguises what European Community law considers to be the true origin of the right. This is why the cases where the Court of Justice focuses on the confusion caused are also relevant. It could be argued that European Community law should not require the right to be acknowledged as a European Community law right if it was perfectly mirrored in national law, without confusion as to enforcement or scope, but without acknowledgement of the quarry origin of the statement of the right. But this is contrary to what European Community law does require. Nor would European Community law be likely to reverse its position on this point, not only because of its constitutional structures but also because the executive uniformity of European Community law rights in fact might be jeopardised by relying on national law to mirror that protection as the requirements, for example procedural requirements, for the protection of the right develop. Furthermore, a mirror image does not make European Community law supreme over national law, it makes European Community law national law (albeit because it is European Community law).

The concept of integration is clarified by a comparison of the approach in the Case 26/62 *Van Gend en Loos* line of authority with Case C–106/89 *Marleasing*.[37] Precisely because Directives are not capable as a matter of European Community law of giving rise directly to obligations on individuals, the Court of Justice placed the national court under an obligation to interpret national law to protect the European Community law right. In that case there was the rider "so far as possible". If the Court were to remove that rider for directly effective obligations, that would not be an accurate account of how, according to European Community law, European Community law rights derived from Treaty articles and regulations are to be protected.

The concept of integration is also clarified by the direct contrast made by the Court of Justice in Opinion 1/91 between recognition of the principles of direct effect and supremacy and national grounding provisions:

> "without recognising the principles of direct effect and primacy which that case-law necessarily entails, the Contracting Parties undertake merely to introduce into their respective legal orders a statutory provision to the effect that EEA rules are to prevail over contrary legislative provisions."[38]

The authors may well be correct, as an external policy statement, that it would be "foolhardy for Community law to require the suppression of national acts of reception which are the means by which its claims are given effect in

---

[37] [1990] E.C.R. I–4135.

[38] Opinion 1/91 on the Draft Agreement between the Community and EEA countries [1991] ECR I–6079 at 6103, para. 27.

the national legal orders". The existence of, for example, grounding national constitutional provisions have not been challenged. It may also, as a statement of how European Community law might develop, be "unnecessary" for European Community law to require their suppression. Even in the state of European Community law at the moment, this author could argue that the achievement of some of the political objectives of the Community recognised as central in European Community law would be more likely to be achieved if such provisions were not suppressed. However it remains the case that their existence is incompatible with European Community law, even though, in terms of policy, they may not be a target and the Court of Justice may for the moment content itself in restating the exclusively European Community law basis for the right, the duty to uphold the right, and the requirements of effective upholding. It is unlikely that the Commission will sue a Member State under Article 169 (EC) because a national judge has relied on national grounding provisions, or that the Court of Justice will point this out unasked in an Article 177 (EC) reference (the Court simply refuses to acknowledge that such grounding provisions have relevance, without going to the logical conclusion of pointing out not only are they otiose but that they obscure the origin of the right and place national law in a state of proclaimed disobedience). The incompatibility of national courts relying on national law and jurisdiction for the enforcement of a European Community law right is one element of the state of constitutional disobedience that exists in national law and national courts, the other being the limits to the recognition of European Community law in national law, the difference between the national law perception of European Community law and European Community law's self-perception, the possibility of unilateral denouncement and withdrawal, and the limits on amendment to incorporate European Community law's claims.

The third way in which the Court of Justice has relied on Article 189 (EC) to distance European Community law from public international law was in establishing the supremacy of European Community law,[39] although direct applicability does not necessarily require this.

Public International Law Influence in Interpretation

European Community Law Perception

7–14 This work does not focus on the development of European Community law constitutional doctrines and the legitimation of Community law by the Court of Justice as interpretation, but rather as law-determination and reasoning. Therefore, interpretation and interpretive methods, as separate subjects of study, are considered only briefly here. This distinction is in part

---

[39] See below, para. 8–52, on the "Provisions of the Treaty".

semantic and in part one of emphasis. Throughout this thesis examples are given of the extraordinary reliance the Court of Justice places on achieving what it considers to be the objectives of European integration. Whereas the Court in interpreting the Treaty establishing the European Coal and Steel Community started out protecting the rights of Member States in conformity with the principle that restrictions on these rights are to be narrowly interpreted,[40] and that exceptions to obligations are to be broadly interpreted, it very quickly reversed itself (in Case 26/62 *Van Gend en Loos*[41] the Court did not even refer to the Netherlands' argument[42] that Article 177 (EEC) should be restrictively construed because a broad interpretation would diminish the protection of the State via Articles 169 and 170 (EEC)) and arrived at the stage where it included as objectives to Community competences objectives which the Treaty did not specify, on the grounds that the objectives were not strangers to those competences: in Case 292/83 *Gravier v. City of Liège*[43] the Court held that although education policy was not included within the Community spheres of competences it was "not unconnected with Community law".[44] Vocational training was "likely to promote the free movement of persons"[45] and therefore fell within the scope of the Treaty. (In this judgment the Court reversed the rational order of analysis. Before considering if the matter (vocational training) fell within Community competence, the Court held that there existed discrimination prohibited by Article 7 ((E.E.C.), now Article 6 (EC)) if it did fall within Community competence.)[46]

According to Reuter, the Court of Justice did not interpret the Treaties as Treaties because "the judge would be confined to a restrictive interpretation of the States' obligations as a function of the fundamental principle of sovereignty, and it would even seem doubtful whether [the judge] could fill gaps".[47] In comparison, by taking the "internal law" line the Court would be tempted to exclude general principles of international law and could not refuse to rule on the pretext of *lacunae*: "it could even conduct its interpretation of the constitutive charters with much more suppleness".[48] The Court has almost exclusive recourse to the object and end of a provision as a function of the progressive building of the Community legal order.[49] This will be seen below

---

40 J. Boulouis, "Le droit des Communautés Européennes dans ses rapports avec le droit international général" (1992) Vol. 235 (IV) *Recueil des Cours* 19 at p. 44.

41 [1963] E.C.R. 1.

42 *ibid.* at 9.

43 [1985] E.C.R. 606.

44 *ibid.* at 612, para. 19.

45 *ibid.* at 613, para. 24.

46 See J. Handoll, "State Definition and Free Movement of Workers" (1987) D.U.L.J. 73 (N.S.).

47 P. Reuter, "Les recours de la Cour de Justice des Communautés à des principes généraux de droit" in *Problèmes de Droit des Gens: Mélanges offerts à Henri Rolin* (Paris: Editions A. Pedone, 1964), pp. 280–281.

48 *ibid.*

49 J. Boulouis, (1992) *op. cit.* above, n.40, at p. 44.

in the development of the doctrine of individual rights, but it can be pointed out here that although the Court has used the existence of the Article 177 procedure as a reason for grounding decisions of constitutional importance such as Case 26/62 *Van Gend en Loos* it has nonetheless read limits into that Article which do not exist in the text on the ground that the ensuring of uniformity, which is the objective of that Article, does not require the referral of certain questions.[50]

The Court of Justice rejects another public international law principle, that of the liberty of forms, in interpreting the amendment provisions of the Treaty establishing the European Community (now contained in the Treaty on European Union).[51]

Public International Law Perception

7–15 Treaties establishing international organisations invariably articulate goals for the organisation and then proceed to specify the machinery by which the goals will be achieved.[52] This is logical. Such treaties do not provide that, in the absence of the intergovernmental or internal legislative machinery functioning to the satisfaction of the court of the organisation or aggrieved individuals, the court will step into the place of that machinery to legislate, as distinct from providing that the court will have an invokable jurisdiction to declare failures or require compliance. Article 31 of the first Vienna Convention provides for the interpretation of treaties. This Article largely codifies existing public international law. Article 31(1) provides the general rules:

> "A Treaty shall be interpreted in good faith and in accordance with the ordinary meaning to be given to the terms of the Treaty in their context and in the light of its object and purpose."

"Ordinary meaning" is to be highlighted. The text is presumed to be "the authentic expression of the intention of the parties".[53] The "context" does not mean the general background to a treaty to be defined by a court, but:

> "(a) any agreement relating to the treaty which was made between all the parties in connection with the conclusion of the treaty;
>
> (b) any instrument which was made by one or more parties in connection with the conclusion of the treaty and accepted by the other parties as an instrument related to the treaty."[54]

Furthermore, according to Article 31(3), the following are to be taken into account:

> "(a) any subsequent agreement between the parties regarding the interpretation of the treaty or the application of its provisions;

---

[50] Case 283/81 *CILFIT* [1982] E.C.R. 3415 at 3428, para. 7.

[51] See below, Chap. 11, "Amendability".

[52] J. S. Gibson, *International Organisations, Constitutional Law, and Human Rights* (New York: Praeger, 1991) p. 61.

[53] Report of the International Law Commission, reproduced in (1967) 61 *American Journal of International Law* 248 at p. 354.

[54] Article 31(2).

(b) any subsequent practice in the application of the treaty which establishes the agreement of the parties regarding its interpretation;
(c) any relevant rules of international law applicable in the relations between the parties."

This would include, *inter alia*, the Luxemburg Compromise, the practice of the Member States (including their practice in the conclusion of international treaties and the practice of providing exceptions for a Member State in an area sensitive to it – for example, by way of Protocol), interpretative Declarations, and any other treaties which the Member States may conclude between themselves. Yet these have not been taken into account by the Court of Justice, which takes as its context the transformation of Europe in terms of both what has been achieved in that transformation and the Court of Justice's vision of what is to be achieved. The Court of Justice is guided certainly by "the spirit of the Treaties", but not its words, ancillary agreements and instruments, interpretative agreements, subsequent practice, or relevant rules of public international law.

Wyatt argues that there is a general move in international law away from interpretative practices which were the product of ad hoc tribunals set up to interpret bilateral treaties.[55] One might point out, however, that the Court has relied on object and purpose to avoid the ordinary meaning of the Treaty's terms, not to explain them, and has even relied on policy according with spirit to avoid the implications of the text, intention, and object of certain Articles.[56] Even if there has been a general move in international law, it can to some degree be explained by public international law trying to catch up with the interpretative techniques of European Community law expounded by the Court of Justice.[57]

Public International Law as Quarry for Unwritten European Community Law Rule

European Community Law Perception

7–16 The above paragraph demonstrates how European Community law rejects the proposition that certain important public international law rules apply in European Community law because they are public international law

---

[55] D. Wyatt, "New Legal Order or Old?" (1982) European Law Review 147 at p. 148.

[56] In addition to the examples given in this work, see T.C. Hartley's critique of Cases 267–269/81 *SPI* [1983] E.C.R. 801 on the scope of Article 177 (EEC) in *The Foundations of European Community Law, Clarendon Law Series* (Oxford: Oxford University Press, 1988) at pp. 252–253, and p. 286, and T.C. Hartley, "The European Court, Judicial Objectivity and the Constitution of the European Union" (1996) 112 L.Q.R. 95.

[57] A. Whelan has commented pithily on this sentence: the phenomenon represents Eisenberg inverted – one cannot know the effect of the thing observed on the observer.

rules. This section considers the different matter of which sources of law the Community judge quarries from to find the rules and principles necessary to fill in lacunae in the European Community treaties. Here is put in question not the normative status of public international law norms but whether public international law has exercised as large a substantive influence on the content of European Community law as might have been expected in a treaty-based system of law. This question is therefore distinct from the influence on the nature of European Community law, but comes back to that so far as one can point to content to explain nature.

From very early on it was made clear that public international law would serve as a secondary and subsidiary source to national law.[58] Thus an Advocate-General stated early on that, as regards the sources of the internal law of a Community – the European Coal and Steel Community (which he stated more closely resembled a federal than an international organisation):

> "there is obviously nothing to prevent them being sought, where appropriate, in international law, but normally and in most cases they will be found rather in the internal law of the various Member States".[59]

Where public international law is used, the rules or principles are usually adopted if they are common to any legal system, not because they are specific to public international law. This is the case with the European Convention on Human Rights and Fundamental Freedoms. The Court of Justice referred to this as a source of European Community law human rights principles, but also to the laws of the Member States. So even when public international law is referred to, it is not thereby possible to chalk up a point for the public international law argument.

Public International Law Perception

7–17 The sources of law used as a quarry by international law tribunals (to be distinguished from the International Court of Justice itself, which these sources bind directly) have been set out in Article 38(1) of the Statute of the International Court of Justice as:

(i) international conventions expressly recognised by the contesting states;
(ii) international custom as evidence of a general practice accepted as law;
(iii) general principles of law recognised by civilised nations;
(iv) judicial decisions and the teachings of the most qualified publicists.

These sources are not those on which the Court of Justice regularly relies.[60]

---

58 J. Boulouis, (1992) *op. cit.* above, n.40, at pp. 45–46.

59 Advocate-General Lagrange, Case 8/55 *Fédération Charbonnière de Belgique v. High Authority of the ECSC* [1954–1956] E.C.R. 245.

60 One notable exception not developed by the Court until the 1970s is the European Convention on Human Rights and Fundamental Freedoms.

8. RIGHTS TO INDIVIDUALS

Introduction

8–1 By rights to individuals is meant the European Community law modification of the position (primarily before national courts) of persons subject to national law, making them subjects also of European Community law. This chapter combines the doctrine of direct effect, supremacy, and the development of fundamental rights protection. The development of rights to individuals in European Community law:

- is central to establishing the autonomy of European Community law from public international law;
- illustrates in terms of jurisdiction and legal structures the demands placed on national law[1];
- best illustrates in the context of the integration of European Community law into national law the legitimation of European Community law and the use and meaning of core constitutional concepts (*e.g.* sovereignty, efficacy, uniformity, the overriding importance of objectives and the place given to the spirit of the Treaty);
- illustrates how a new legal order was established by act(s) of will by a court, causing a break from the public international law origin of European Community law and founding the legitimation for a new order, which break, if entire, could be analysed itself as a legal revolution.

The constitutional importance of making individuals, and not just the Member Sates, subjects of European Community law, to the extent done by European Community law, is obvious, as is the importance of the insistence that these European Community law rights, including fundamental rights developed by the Court of Justice, override national law of whatever nature. The grounds given for the progressive establishment of these doctrines point to the basis and nature of European Community law.

European Community Law Perception

8–2 The doctrines of direct effect and supremacy of European Community law have been held to be "the essential characteristics of the Community legal order".[2]

---

1 Specific examples are considered below in Part V.
2 Opinion 1/91, para. 11 – a legal order which is there described in constitutional and sovereign terms: see below, para. 10–2.

In literature the doctrines have been referred to as "the twin pillars of the Community legal system".[3]

Public International Law Perception

8–3 According to public international law, these doctrines are two of the central qualities the presence of which does not remove European Community law from public international law.[4]

Individual Rights

Public International Law Perception

8–4 This is a public international law doctrine. The Permanent Court of International Justice had held as early as 1928 that the Danzig-Polish Treaty of 22 October 1921 concerning railway officials was directly applicable between the Polish Railways Administration and the Danzig officials who had passed into the permanent service of that Administration, and that the treaty created rights directly enforceable before the Danzig courts. The Permanent Court of International Justice stated that,

> "the very object of an international agreement, according to the intention of the contracting Parties, may be the adoption by the Parties of some definite rules creating individual rights and obligations enforceable by the national courts . . . The intention of the Parties, which is to be ascertained from the contents of the Agreement, taking into consideration the manner in which the Agreement has been applied, is decisive."[5]

The Permanent Court of International Justice concluded that the treaty "should not be construed in a manner which would make the applicability of the provisions of the [treaty] depend on their incorporation into a Polish Regulation".[6]

The potential of public international law treaties to create individual rights is upheld by public international lawyers.[7] As a matter of practice, "it is indeed common for international treaties to provide for the regulation of the rights of individuals vis-à-vis the State".[8]

Considering the text of the Treaty establishing the European Economic Community in order to determine the intent of the sovereign states who

---

[3] D. Wyatt and A. Dashwood, *Wyatt and Dashwood's European Community Law,* (London: Sweet & Maxwell, 1993) p. 54.

[4] D. Wyatt, "New Legal Order or Old?" (1982) *European Law Review* 147 at p. 148.

[5] Advisory Opinion of the Permanent Court of International Justice, *Jurisdiction of the Courts of Danzig,* 3 March 1928, Series A/B No. 283/Series B No. 15, pp. 17–18.

[6] *ibid.* at p. 20.

[7] *e.g.* van der Meersch, Leben, Wyatt, and Boulouis.

[8] D. Wyatt (1982) *op. cit.* above, n.4, at 148.

created it, obligations are placed on Member States. Looking at the text, there are no obligations imposed directly on individuals. There appears to be a possible exception to this with competition rules: Article 85 (EC) prohibits certain agreements and declares them to be void; Article 86 (EC) prohibits undertakings from abusing their dominant position. But Article 87 (EC) makes clear that effect is to be given to these principles by the Council within three years of entry into force of the Treaty. Until then, the obligation is clearly placed on Member States.[9]

Nor are there any substantive rights granted directly to individuals by the text of the Treaties before the Treaty on European Union. The closest to an exception to this are the right of establishment[10] and the right to free movement for work purposes.[11] But as regards the right to free movement for work purposes, Article 48(1) (EC) and Article 49 (EC) makes clear that it is the Member State's obligation to secure these rights, and only then not until the end of the transitional period. As regards the right of establishment, this is announced in the second paragraph of the Article after the obligation is placed on the Member States.

Furthermore, the jurisdiction of the Court is mostly limited to disputes amongst Member States and institutions. There is no general right of action for individuals although there is a very limited right of action under Article 173 paragraph 4 (EC).

European Community Law Perception

8–5 European Community law does not rely on the public international law doctrine of individual rights in developing its own constitutional version. Before looking closely at Case 26/62 *Van Gend en Loos*, it should be noted that it was not the first case raising the direct effect issue. This came a year earlier[12] when the Court of Appeal of the Hague asked whether Article 85 (EEC) had the effect of rendering void a prohibition on exports in an agency agreement concluded between the Bosch company and each of its sales agencies. The Court held that, until the entry into force of the implementing regulations envisaged by Article 87 (EEC),[13] agreements prohibited under Article 85 (EEC) could not be declared automatically void for that reason unless the

---

9 Article 88 (EC).

10 More precisely, the right to take up and pursue activities as self-employed persons and to set up and manage undertakings in a Member State under the same conditions as that Member State's nationals – Article 52 (EC).

11 More precisely, the right to accept offers of employment, to move for this purpose, to stay for this purpose under the same conditions as the host Member State's own nationals, and to remain there after employment subject to Community implementing legislation (Article 48(3)(a) to (d) (EC)).

12 Case 13/61 *Bosch* [1962] E.C.R. 45.

13 Article 87 had in fact entered into force at the time of the Advocate-General's opinion, *ibid.* at 64.

Member States' authorities (acting under Article 88 (EEC)) or the Commission (acting under Article 89(2) (EEC)) had so declared. In so deciding the Court did not reply directly to the contention of the respondents that Article 85 (EEC) was incapable of direct applicability to individuals. However Advocate-General Lagrange did address the question in responding to the point of view of the Rotterdam Court (where the action was initiated) that the anti-cartel provisions could not have direct applicability until the Common Market had been made a reality by implementing legislation. The Advocate-General, in a statement which identifies in the particular context of competition law part of the approach of European Community law to attaining objectives, considered that the application of Articles 85 to 90 (EEC) was not merely a way in which the Common Market would function but rather one of the most important factors in its gradual establishment. In short, direct applicability was important in achieving the goal sought.

Case 26/62 *Van Gend en Loos*

Introduction

8–6 For the reasons to be given below, Case 26/62 *Van Gend en Loos* was a critical point of separation between public international law and European Community law and in the establishment of the constitutional characteristics set out in the Introduction to this Part. A lot of attention is given here to Case 26/62 *Van Gend en Loos*. The reason why the reasoning of the Court of Justice, or absence thereof, is examined in some detail is not to criticise it from an external standpoint but to help establish the characteristics of European Community law set out in the Introduction to this Part.

Since the Treaty provisions were addressed to Member States, what was an undertaking to do if confronted with an apparent failure by a Member State to honour its obligations? In the early 1960s the trading activities of a Dutch importing undertaking called Van Gend en Loos fell foul of an increase by the Dutch government of customs duties on certain products which may have been contrary to Article 12 (EEC) which imposed a stand-still obligation on Member States. Van Gend en Loos raised the issue of non compliance by the Netherlands with its Treaty obligations before a Dutch tax court in an action to annul a decision of the Netherlands Inland Revenue Administration. The tax court in turn made a reference under Article 177 (EEC) to the Court of Justice concerning the interpretation of Article 12 (EEC): did this Article confer individual rights on nationals of Member States and specifically on the undertaking concerned which they could seek to enforce before national courts notwithstanding that the provision in question was clearly addressed to Member States?[14] The obvious answer to this question was no. The three

---

[14] Case 26/62 *Van Gend en Loos v. Nederlandse Administratie der Belastingen* [1963] E.C.R. 1.

governments who presented written observations to the Court (the Netherlands, Belgium and Germany) and Advocate-General Roemer so concluded (although the Advocate-General thought that the Court had jurisdiction). The Court answered yes.

Jurisdiction: A Tale Foretold

8–7 The most fundamental difference was over jurisdiction. The Netherlands, Belgium and Germany argued that the Court of Justice had no jurisdiction under Article 177 (EEC) to answer the question since the result before the national judge depended on the resolution of an internal constitutional problem: which law of ratification should be given preference (the provision allegedly conflicting with Article 12 (EEC) had its origin in another international treaty (a Benelux protocol) and was ratified by national law subsequent to the Treaty of Rome). Therefore the ruling of the Court of Justice would be irrelevant. The Member States were not stubbornly missing the point; rather, they were not conceding the argument.

The Advocate-General conceded: "It was impossible to clarify exhaustively the real legal effects of an international agreement on the nationals of a Member State without having regard to the constitutional law of that Member State"[15] but thought that the Court had jurisdiction if it limited itself to the intended effects of the Treaty, and not their actual effects. The Advocate-General therefore accepted the crucial distinction between obligation in the result and executive uniformity (a concept developed below).

The Court went further, grounding its jurisdiction in ambiguous reasons: it was not asked about national law but about Article 12 (EEC) "within the context of Community law *and* with reference to its effect on individuals" (emphasis added). "With reference to its effect on individuals" relates to the effect before national courts which the Advocate-General had conceded was a matter of national law. Therefore even at this stage of the judgment the Court has implicitly established two doctrines. First, the effect on individuals depends on European Community law, not on national law. The reality that this is false, from the point of view of national law, will not be contemplated by European Community law. This judgment is in contrast to Case 13/61 *Bosch*[16] where the Court held admissible an Article 177 (EEC) reference from a court whose ruling was under appeal and therefore not *res judicata*, by distinguishing European Community law and national law as two legal orders. The argument against admissibility in Bosch rested, according to the Court of Justice, on "a failure to appreciate that the municipal law of any Member State, whose court requests a preliminary ruling from this Court, and Community law constitute two separate and distinct legal orders". Secondly, the effect of

---

[15] *ibid.* at 18–19.
[16] [1962] E.C.R. 45 at 49–50.

European Community law is not international responsibility but that a judge must disapply national law. This second point predicts Case 6/64 *Costa v. ENEL*.[17]

Nature of the Treaties – Rejection of the Public International Law Contractual Model

8–8 The Advocate-General stated that European Community law "does not just consist of contractual relations between a number of States considered as subjects of the law of nations", basing the difference primarily on the presence of institutions and their ability to take measures directly creating rights and duties on Member States, their authorities, and citizens (citing, *inter alia*, Article 189 (EEC)).

The Court, however, based its rejection of the contractual model of public international law treaty relations on the objective of establishing a Common Market. The Court stated: "The objective of the Treaty establishing the European Economic Community, which is to establish a Common Market, the functioning of which is of direct concern to interested parties in the Community, implies that this Treaty is more than an agreement which merely creates mutual obligations between the contracting states."[18]

As to the other grounds offered in support of this conclusion, first, the direct concern to individuals of the functioning of the Common Market is not a reason for the conclusion that the Treaty is different because the reason presumes the answer to the question of whether individual rights occur (any other interpretation of this phrase relying on a non-legal meaning of "direct concern" would imply that "ordinary international treaties" are not of "direct concern" to individuals, which is not necessarily true).

Secondly, the Court refers both to the Preamble's reference not only to governments but also to peoples, and to the establishment of institutions (special reference was made to "the European Parliament and the Economic and Social Committee"). However, in the language of the judgment, these grounds "confirmed", and therefore did not establish, the Court's conclusion. The importance of the institutions has been supported by doctrine. Pescatore also puts the institutions central to his efforts to distinguish European Community law from public international law.[19] But the reliance by the Court of Justice on the institutions came whilst these are still in the form of the institutions of an international organisation, for example before the development of majority voting in the Council or the conversion of the Assembly to the European Parliament, before the European Central Bank was mooted. The present shape of the institutions cannot provide support for the Court's arguments particularly where its formation was assisted by the propositions which the Court established with the help of this argument.

---

17 [1964] E.C.R. 585.

18 Case 26/62 *Van Gend en Loos* [1963] E.C.R. 1 at 12.

19 P. Pescatore, The Law of Integration – Emergence of a new phenomenon in international relations based on the experience of the European Communities, (Leiden: Sitjhoff, 1974) n.65.

8–9 *Public International Law Note* The reasons advanced for the rejection of the public international law contractual model are insufficient. As regards the reference to peoples, the Preamble to the Charter of the United Nations also refers to peoples, and yet the United Nations remains an intergovernmental organisation. Indeed, the Preamble to the Charter is much less intergovernmental in character than that of the Treaty establishing the European Community. It reads "We the peoples of the United Nations determined [sets out the goals and actions of the UN] . . . have resolved to combine our efforts to accomplish these aims. Accordingly, our respective Governments . . . do hereby establish . . . the United Nations." As regards objectives, the objectives of the United Nations appear to be much more closely concerned with the individual, certainly compared with the Treaty establishing the European Economic Community at the time of *Van Gend en Loos.* These include fundamental human rights, dignity and worth of the human person, the equal rights of men and women, social progress and better standards of life, and economic and social advancement of all peoples.

Interpretation of Article 12 (EEC)

8–10 The Netherlands argued that this was to be established by the intention of the parties and the wording of the provision, and in fact the wording made the intention perfectly clear: "Member States shall refrain from introducing between themselves any new customs duties on imports or exports or any charges having equivalent effect . . .". The Advocate-General had, in considering the question admissible, already stated the importance of intention in deciding that the Court of Justice's answer had to be limited to establishing the authors' intended meaning of the provision.[20] To establish this he made "an examination of the system of the Treaty taken as a whole, upon the wording, the content and the context of the provision to be interpreted".[21] He carefully went through many Treaty articles, looking at their wording, material content and context, and the necessity for implementing provisions. He was in no doubt that Article 12 (EEC) imposed a direct obligation on the Member States, enforceable by Articles 169 (EEC) and 170 (EEC), but equally that it did not give rise to individual rights.

The Court's method of interpretation was also to look at three points, of which two concorded with those of the Advocate-General (although the Court's analysis of these points was more perfunctory). These two were the general scheme of the Treaty and the wording of the provisions. But where the Advocate-General had introduced the intention of the Member States the Court introduced the spirit of the Treaty: "To ascertain whether the provisions of an international treaty extend so far in their effects it is necessary to

---

[20] Case 26/62 *Van Gend en Loos* [1963] E.C.R. 1 at 19.
[21] *ibid.* at 24.

consider the spirit, the general scheme and the wording of those provisions."[22] Spirituality will be returned to in considering Pescatore's analysis of the case.[23] The word "intended" surfaces only in the conclusion, where no active subject is ascribed to it: "Community law therefore not only imposes obligations on individuals but is also intended to confer upon them rights . . .".[24]

Nature of the Treaties – Rejection of International Responsibility

8–11 This is a point which will be reconsidered in the context of supremacy. The Advocate-General, in examining the scheme of the Treaty to find the intent of the Member States in Article 12 (EEC), considered that it was "within the framework of supranational law that ways of dealing with breaches of the Treaty have been devised",[25] and that was through suing the Member State before the Court (Articles 169 and 170 (EEC)). (By "supranational" the Advocate-General appears to mean no more than the law of an international organisation.) The three governments who submitted observations also considered this to be the case.

The Court, however, held that the fact that a defaulting Member State could be brought directly before it did not preclude the possibility of pleading infringements before the national courts.[26] But this is a conclusion, not a reason. The Advocate-General offered Articles 169 and 170 (EEC) as a reason why infringements should not be pleaded before national courts to establish individual rights. As well as its holding, the Court's reasons, coming in the next two paragraphs, also presuppose the answer to the question: Articles 169 and 170 (EEC) would be ineffective supervision of Member States for the protection of individual rights. The concept of effectiveness is discussed below.

Article 177 (EEC) – A Ground for Individual Rights

8–12 The intervening Member States and the Advocate-General concentrated on Article 177 (EEC) only in the context of admissibility. They did not see it as relevant to the question whether Article 12 (EEC) should have direct effect. The Advocate-General cited it as an example of a provision which was intended to be incorporated into national law and to supplement it.[27]

The Court, however, gave it prominence, holding:

> "the task assigned to the Court of Justice under Article 177, the object of which is to secure uniform interpretation of the Treaty by national courts and tribunals, confirms that the states have acknowledged that Community law has

---

22 *ibid.* at 12.
23 See below, para. 8–24, on Case 26/62 *Van Gend en Loos*: "The Basis of the Decision".
24 Case 26/62 *Van Gend en Loos* [1963] E.C.R. 1 at 12.
25 *ibid.* at 21.
26 *ibid.* at 13.
27 *ibid.* at 20.

> an authority which can be invoked by their nationals before those courts and tribunals."[28]

This is the only Article cited by the Court in support of its general result. The Article refers to a mechanism only. As a reason, it is not sufficient to establish that Treaty articles may give rise to individual rights invocable, as a matter of European Community law, before the national courts, and completely insufficient for the general conclusion on the nature of the European Community legal order. A national court of a Member State may decide that a ruling is "necessary for it to give judgement" as a matter of national law, or indeed on its interpretation of European Community law. This does not support the conclusion by the Court of Justice that European Community law gives rise to individual rights before all national courts because a ruling must be necessary as a matter of European Community law. Article 177 (EEC) does not show what sources of European Community law could be invoked – it could have been confined to Regulations which pursuant to Article 189 (EEC) were directly applicable (the Court makes no mention of Article 189 (EEC) in its judgment). Nor does Article 177 (EEC) show by whom and for what purpose European Community law may be invoked – for example by a Member State being sued in its own courts as a defence to a challenge based on national law to the legality of an act (for example a statute or an executive action) to show that the act was required by international obligations. Article 177 (EEC) would not be rendered nugatory in the absence of direct effect: in Case 11/75 *Mazzali v. Ferrovia del Renon*[29] the Court of Justice answered a preliminary reference on the interpretation of European Community law which was not directly effective.

The structure of this part of the judgment is that the objective of the Treaty determines its nature.[30] This was confirmed by the Preamble and the establishment of institutions. In addition, the Article 177 (EEC) pitch was made. "The conclusion to be drawn from this" included the existence of individual rights. Article 177 (EEC) was thus a confirmation of the nature of the treaty as more than an agreement creating mutual obligations, and a confirmation and reason for the general result of the decision.[31]

---

28 *ibid.* at 12.

29 [1976] E.C.R. 657 at 665.

30 See above, para. 8–8, "The Nature of the Treaties – Rejection of the Public International Law Contractual Model".

31 This interpretation is supported by Case 106/77 *Amministrazione delle Finanze dello Stato v. Simmenthal* [1978] E.C.R. 629 at 643–644 where the Court summarised its doctrines of direct effect, supremacy and preemption on the basis of the effectiveness of European Community law and the foundations of the Community (para. 18), and referred to Article 177 (EEC) and the necessity that the Article be effective as giving rise to the same conclusion (para. 19). Therefore the conclusion is established on other grounds and Article 177 (EEC) is not a necessary ground for the holding in Case 26/62 *Van Gend en Loos*: according to the Court it is at best a secondary and independent ground.

8–13 *Public International Law Note* The public international law perception of the importance of Article 177 (EEC) has been succinctly stated:

> "the EEC Treaty with its procedure for the preliminary ruling, certainly broke new ground. That is not to say, however, that the obligations imposed by the EEC Treaty and the Acts made thereunder are anything other than obligations in international law, which are capable of rationalisation, analysis and development, in such terms."[32]

The General Result – the Nature of the Legal Order, Sovereignty, and Legal Heritage

8–14 Having referred to the objective of the Treaty ("which is to establish a Common Market") making the Treaty more than one of mutual obligations, as confirmed by the Preamble and the existence of the institutions, and to the task of the Court under Article 177 (EEC), the Court held:

> "The conclusion to be drawn from this is that the Community constitutes a new legal order of international law for the benefit of which the states have limited their sovereign rights, albeit within limited fields, and the subjects of which comprise not only Member States but also their nationals. Independently of the legislation of Member States, Community law therefore not only imposes obligations on individuals, but is intended also to confer upon them rights which become part of their legal heritage."[33]

There are several points here.

8–15 *"New Legal Order of International Law"* After this judgment, international law is never mentioned again. Often when this passage is quoted, it is done so *à la Animal Farm*[34]: "a new legal order 'for the benefit of which . . .'".[35] The Court, for its part, puts it like this: "As the Court of Justice has consistently held, the Community treaties established a new legal order for the benefit of which . . . (see, in particular, the judgment in Case 26/62 *Van Gend en Loos*)".[36] The phrase "new legal order" has been recited in other cases also, for example in Joined Cases 90 & 91/63 *Commission v. Luxembourg and Belgium*[37] where the Court refused on this ground to accept the defence that the Commission's failure in its obligations suspended the Member States' reciprocal obligations; in Case 28/67 *Molkerei-Zentrale Westfalen*[38] where the

---

[32] D. Wyatt (1992) *op. cit.* above, n.4, at p. 149.

[33] Case 26/62 *Van Gend en Loos* [1963] E.C.R. 1 at 12.

[34] A novel by George Orwell where the rules of the new polity are written down and publicised but mutate and disappear over time without explanation.

[35] See, *e.g.* P. Pescatore (1974) *op. cit.* above, n.19, where this form of quotation is used to support his argument that European Community law was autonomous from public international law.

[36] Opinion 1/91 [1991] E.C.R. I–6079, para. 21.

[37] [1964] E.C.R. 625 at 631; see above, para. 7–6, "Reciprocity – European Community Law Perception".

[38] [1968] E.C.R. 143 at 154; see below, para. 8–35, "The Development and Expansion of *Van Gend en Loos* – The Development of the Depth of its Penetration".

Court refused to accept domestic problems as a defense to the direct effect of Treaty articles; in Case 52/75 *Commission v. Italy*[39] where the Court refused to accept as a defence to the non-implementation of a directive that the other Member States had not reciprocated because they too had not implemented, and in Opinion 1/91.[40] Even when an Advocate-General, exceptionally, used the original phrase "new legal order of international law", he stated that European Community law takes clear precedence over public international law.[41]

One can comment with hindsight that Case 26/62 *Van Gend en Loos* appears to predict this transformation by the tensions inherent in the phrase used. The idea of European Community law as both new, as distinct from an example of the law of international organisations which already existed, and an order, as distinct from a system, predicted the removal of "international" which happened in a matter of months.

As the doctrine of individual rights has developed, the Court has also recognised that "ordinary" public international law treaties can give rise to individual rights by virtue of the fact that they are binding on the Community. This illustrates how European Community law doctrines may assume a life of their own to some extent independent from the reasons originally offered to ground them. In Joined Cases C–100 & 101/89 *Kaefer and Procacci*,[42] Advocate-General Mischo stated that the Court "has gone on to acknowledge that rights enuring to the benefit of individuals may also arise from certain obligations imposed on Member States by an agreement which does not establish a new legal order."

8–16 *Sovereignty* Neither the intervening states nor the Advocate-General mention sovereignty, presumably because they did not think that sovereignty was in issue. The Treaty makes no mention of transfers, let alone transfers of sovereignty. Where the Treaty goes further than a simple statement of the powers and functions of the institutions it is to refer to a "conferring of powers" (Article 234 paragraph 3 (EC)).

The Court of Justice held that the Member States have "limited their sovereign rights". It did not say "transfer".

But the Court virtually said this in Case 26/62 *Van Gend en Loos* because when referring to the institutions as one of its grounds, it states that they are "endowed with sovereign rights". If the institutions have got sovereign rights, and the Member States have limited their sovereign rights, the necessary implication may be that there has been a transfer.[43]

---

39 [1976] E.C.R. 277 at 284, para. 11.

40 [1991] E.C.R. I–6079; see below, para. 10–2, "Treaty as Constitution – European Community Law Perception".

41 See Case C–146/89 *Commission v. United Kingdom* [1991] E.C.R. I–3533, Opinion of Advocate-General Lenz at 3559, para. 23.

42 [1990] E.C.R I–4647 at 4663, para. 41; see below, para. 8–34, "Direct Effect of a Doctrine Independent of its Original Legitimation".

43 Another case where the transfer of sovereignty is implied by the reasoning, and not

Sovereignty had been mentioned by the Court before Case 26/62 *Van Gend en Loos*. In Case 6/60 *Humblet v. Belgium*[44] the Court stated:

> "Taken as a whole, the three Treaties in this respect share common ground in that they withdraw the remuneration paid to officials of the Community from the Member States' sovereignty in tax matters."

This was not a necessary statement to reach the conclusion in the case that the Protocol on the Privileges and Immunities of the Treaty establishing the European Coal and Steel Community prohibited a Member State from taxing an official. But not much more can be drawn from this earlier case on this issue, save that the Court was already thinking in terms of sovereignty.

Doctrine has pointed out from early on that the notion of limitation of sovereignty, on its own, would give rise to disuniformity:

> "In contrast to simple limitations, which leave subsisting national partitions, the transfers institute a common competence which results from the partial fusion of national competence. That is why one speaks of a Community."[45]

As van der Meersch has put it, the notion of the limitation of sovereign powers to which Case 26/62 *Van Gend en Loos* refers is insufficient to characterise European Community law:

> "it is necessary to add that these limitations cannot leave subsisting partitions in the heart of the Community; they are, without doubt, the result of a transfer or of an attribution of powers and of competence by the contracting States to the Community."[46]

8–17 *Public International Law Note* Public international lawyers like van der Meersch who consider that there has been a transfer refer to a transfer of competence or powers, not of sovereignty. Although the public international law position differs with European Community law (see below), this does not mean that it accords with national constitutional law. For example, van der Meersch goes on to state that this delegation of powers and competence is not one which could be temporary. Furthermore, it is a delegation of power, not the exercise of a power which would make the States seem to remain the controllers of the game.[47] The notion of such a delegation is in contrast to national constitutional law.[48] It is interesting to note the predisposition of

---

only by the result, of a decision is Opinion 1/91 *Re the Draft Agreement on the European Economic Area* [1991] E.C.R. I–6079 where the Court contrasted the European Economic Area, which "provides for no transfer of sovereign rights" with the European Community. The Court cites its own statement on sovereign rights from Case 26/62 *Van Gend en Loos*.

44 [1960] E.C.R. 559 at 577.

45 P. Reuter, writing about the Treaty establishing the European Coal and Steel Community, *La Communauté du charbon et de l'acier* (Paris: 1953) p. 139, quoted by W.G. van der Meersch, "L'Ordre juridique des Communautés Européennes et le Droit international" (1975) 148 (V) *Recueil des Cours de l'Académie de Droit International* 1 at p. 197.

46 Van der Meersch (1975) *op. cit.* above, n.45, at p. 197.

47 *ibid.* at p. 198.

48 See below, Parts III and IV on French and Irish Constitutional Law respectively.

doctrine to raise the spectre of war when they affirm the fixity of the transfer.[49] Whatever a lawyer's perspective, the use of such examples raises suspicion.

8–18 *Sovereignty (Continued)* The public international law view is to be compared with, for example, Pescatore: "The law of integration relies on a premise quite unknown to so-called 'classical' international law: that of the divisibility of sovereignty."[50] According to Pescatore, the issue of sovereignty is one of the premises of European Community law (and is not accepted by public international law), and the distinction drawn between transfer of competence and transfer of sovereignty is,

> "merely a euphemism, a mask placed on reality for the 'transfers of competence' here in question are concerned with the exercise of the fundamental and vital functions of the State . . .
>
> . . . these concepts of limited, shared, transferred sovereignty, or pooling, are more than theoretical visions, more than simple *a posteriori* explanations. They are operative legal concepts."[51]

He explains what he means by this last sentence: both the Court of Justice and national courts make substantial use of these concepts in grounding their judgments, in other words they have direct importance in the legitimation of decisions within these legal orders. Although Pescatore admits that the "*principe de l'attribution des competences* has visibly inspired the Community system", it is "counterbalanced by a complex of factors which provide a way of escape from the rigidity and lack of coherence resulting from the analytical method of the Treaties".[52] The first of these is the idea of a progressive evolution of Community activities, a "state of mind . . . rich in possibilities for development".[53] Louis states that the "basis of the Community legal order is . . . the transfer of sovereignty"[54] and sees no importance in the Court's choice of words: "No significance may be attached to the fact that the Court referred to sovereignty only being 'limited', not 'transferred'".[55]

The interpretation of the Government of Denmark of the extent of the constitutional demands of European Community law after the negative referendum result on the Treaty on European Union is of note. Denmark negotiated a "Decision of the Heads of State or Government, Meeting within

---

49 *e.g.* Van der Meersch (1975) *op. cit.* above, n.45, at pp. 196 *et seq.*.

50 P. Pescatore, The Law of Integration – Emergence of a new phenomenon in international relations based on the experience of the European Communities, (Leiden: Sitjhoff, 1974). The Title to Chapter II of his book is "Refashioning of Sovereignties"; see also above, para. 3–2, "In General – European Community Law Perception".

51 *ibid.* pp. 31–32.

52 *ibid.* p. 38.

53 *ibid.* p. 39.

54 J.V. Louis, *The Community Legal Order, The European Perspectives Series,* Ed. Commission of the European Communities (Brussels: Office for Official Publications of the European Communities, 1990) p. 11.

55 *ibid.* p. 12.

the European Council, concerning Certain Problems raised by Denmark on the Treaty on European Union".[56] To accompany this Decision Denmark made "Unilateral Declarations of Denmark to be Associated to the Danish Act of Ratification of the Treaty on European Union and of which the 11 other Member States will take Cognizance", in which it refers to extensions of Community competence in the spheres of citizenship and justice and home affairs involving a "transfer of sovereignty".[57]

8–19 *"Independently of the Legislation of Member States"* This rejects the possibility that the assertion of European Community law rights depends on national law. This is extremely important, as it moves away both from public international law and from national law perceptions and indicates an order *ex proprio vigore*. It also predicts supremacy, since if the European Community law rights exist independently of national legislation, the implication is that national legislation cannot touch them. This holding combined with the others in the decision, makes *Van Gend en Loos* the foundation of the Community legal order.

8–20 *Legal Heritage/Patrimony* This obscure phrase does not appear to have any independent worth in Community law doctrine. It has been occasionally referred to since Case 26/62 *Van Gend en Loos* where that judgment has been cited, without further explanation.[58] It appears to be drawn from an important concept of French civil law which refers to the extent of an individual's legal rights (for example, a right to sue may pass on death to the executor of the deceased's estate if that right forms part of the deceased's *patrimoine juridique*). The idea of patrimony seems to import an idea of ownership of rights, so that Member States' refusal to recognise such rights amounts not so much to a failure to provide as to a deprivation.

Effectiveness and Uniformity

8–21 These two concepts often come together because disuniformity weakens the effectiveness of a Community-wide rule, and effectiveness in European Community law doctrine implies uniformity. They are not highly developed in this case[59] but there are important points to be made about them here.

8–22 *Uniformity* The Advocate-General considered that the doctrine of direct effect applied to Article 12 (EEC) would bring about disuniformity,

---

56 Annex 1 to the Conclusions of the Presidency, Edinburgh Council 11 and 12 December 1992, [1992] O.J. C 348/1.

57 Declaration on Citizenship of the Union, Article 4; Declaration on Cooperation in the Fields of Justice and Home Affairs.

58 Case 28/67 *Molkerei-Zentrale* [1968] E.C.R. 143 at 152, and Joined Cases C–6 & 9/90 *Francovich and Bonifaci v. Italy* [1991] E.C.R. I–5357 at 5413, para. 31.

59 The Court has subsequently stated that "uniform application of Community law is imperative" – Case 68/80 *SpA International Chemical Corporation* [1981] E.C.R. 1215.

not uniformity, in the application of Community law. This was because "[T]he position of the constitutional laws of the Member States, above all with regard to the determination of the relationship between supranational or international law and subsequent national legislation, is far from uniform".[60] The Advocate-General made the important connection between intent, constitutional disparities, direct effect and uniformity:

> "The authors of the Treaty were faced with this situation in the field of constitutional law when they ratified the legal texts of the Community. Having regard to this situation it is in my opinion doubtful whether the authors, when dealing with a provision of such importance to customs law, intended to produce the consequences of an uneven development of the law involved in the principle of direct application, consequences which do not accord with an essential aim of the Community."[61]

The four main obstacles to uniformity which the authors of the Treaty would have confronted still confront European Community law and cause problems in the wake of Case 26/62 *Van Gend en Loos*:

- First, the reach of the principles varies between Member States depending on whether European Community law is recognised in national courts by virtue of national or European Community law. If the former (for example, Ireland, France, the United Kingdom, Germany, and Italy) then ipso facto national law does not conform to European Community law; if the latter (for example, the Netherlands, Belgium, and Luxembourg) then European Community law is recognised by virtue of its nature as public international law, albeit a specific version of same, which is not in conformity with European Community law's federalist ambitions.
- Secondly, national constitutional law in the Member States varies in the jurisdictions it confers on inferior tribunals to disapply a law enacted after ratification of the European Community Treaties which conflicts with European Community law.
- Thirdly, national rules or judicial practices on the use of Article 177 (EEC) can affect the application of European Community law.
- Fourthly, and only now coming into its own as the centre of concern in the Court's jurisprudence, the diversity between available remedies will cause disuniformity in executive effect of European Community law.

Uniformity also comes up implicitly in the concept of transfers of sovereignty and the nature of the legal order – as considered above – in order to avoid "national partitioning". It is a central point of this work that national partitionings are inevitable unless a legal revolution occurs and that certain national partitioning can be recognised as legitimate by European Community law.[62]

---

[60] Case 26/62 *Van Gend en Loos* [1963] E.C.R. 1 at 23.
[61] *ibid.* at 24.
[62] See below, Part VI, "Future Directions".

8–23 *Effectiveness* This has been mentioned above as a reason put forward for the rejection of the argument that Articles 169 and 170 point against the direct effect of provisions which impose an obligation on Member States: it was asserted that effectiveness is not a reason to reject that argument.

Pescatore, in an article dealing with direct effect and analysing Case 26/62 *Van Gend en Loos*, stresses the importance of the notion of *effet utile* for European Community law, and states: "If it is not operative, it is not a rule of law. The task of lawyers is therefore not to thwart the effects of legal rules, but to help in putting them into operation".[63] If one takes the order approach one can see that it is simply incorrect that if a rule of law in one order is not operative in another that it is not a rule of law. This assertion of incorrectness is not made for the purposes of criticism, but to explain that this is not a normal legal test for legal validity, certainly in the context of the law of international organisations. It is a political test for a political goal.

However the importance Pescatore ascribes to "*effet utile*" as well as the use of effectiveness by the Court, does make sense, as does the use of uniformity despite the Advocate-General's point, if one suppresses the lawyer's innate rejection of illogical argument. The next paragraph attempts to explain the sense.

The Basis of the Decision

8–24 The reasons offered by the Court for its general conclusion do not add up. The judgment makes sense, however, because it is based, as the Court itself states, on the securing of an objective[64]: "the Common Market". As Pescatore states,

> "The Court did not follow the course which was thus suggested to it with great authority. The important thing is to see what are the motives underlying this decision. The reasoning of the Court shows that the judges had '*une certaine idée de l'Europe*' of their own, and that it is this idea which has been decisive and not arguments based on the legal technicalities of the matter."[65]

The judgment flows from the desire to attain the objective: "the Common Market". It is an act of will by the Court, free from the will of the Member States and the text of the law. This "Common Market" is a political end to which the legal concepts of institutions, sovereignty, a legal order distinct from public international law, individual rights, efficacy, uniformity, and the concept of

---

63 P. Pescatore, "The Doctrine of 'Direct Effect': An Infant Disease of Community Law" (1983) 18 *European Law Review* 155.

64 The importance of objectives for the development of European Community law is focussed on here as regards individual rights, but it pervades all areas of European Community law – see, for example, J. O'Reilly, "Judicial Review and the Common Fisheries Policy in Community Law" (1992) in D. Curtin and D. O'Keeffe (eds.), *Constitutional Adjudication in European Community and National Law: Essays for the Hon. Mr. Justice T.F. O'Higgins* (Dublin: Butterworths, 1992).

65 P. Pescatore (1983) above, n.63, at 157.

supremacy implied in the decision on admissibility and to be developed in Case 6/64 *Costa*, are a means. It is also a legal end in which all these concepts are both means and ends – means because they secure the end and ends because they are the legal shape of that end, if not its content (which consists of all the substantive rules).

Although it is clear from the Treaty that the Member States aspired to attain that objective at least for the purpose of the often grandiloquent preambles in treaties, it is equally clear that they intended to attain it themselves through the Council, assisted by the Commission, and not that the Court would attain it for them. The very vagueness of the objective which was indicative of Member State control has given scope to Court of Justice control. From this judgment on, the intention of the Member States is marginal. The removal of the Member States acting together as the sovereign will, behind European Community law is crucial: the passage quoted states: "Community law . . . is intended also to confer upon [individuals] rights . . . "

Thus the use of, for example, the concept of effectiveness can be understood. Of course it does not ground individual rights, but once the doctrine of individual rights was decided upon as a step to securing the objective, then these rights needed to be effectively protected for individuals to be effective to secure that objective, the Common Market.

Thus the implicit concern for uniformity. As the Advocate-General pointed out, the general conclusion of individuals as subjects of Community law was likely to cause disuniformity, but the Court did not want uniformity of European Community law as such, it wanted to secure "*une certaine idée de l'Europe*", here summarised as "the Common Market" (later, in Opinion 1/91, as "European Unity"), and consequently the uniformity of European Community law of a nature which would secure that objective.

The Demands Placed on National Law

8–25 The concepts of European Community law sovereignty, a legal order distinct from public international law, individuals as subjects of European Community law as well as states, rights, efficacy, uniformity, the implied concept of supremacy, and the insistence on spiritual interpretation all run up against national conceptions. That there was going to be a national constitutional law problem was already clear from this case, and was pointed out both by the Advocate-General and the intervening Member States. But more than that, the idea of individual rights and the use of Article 177 (EEC) to police them means that the problems become problems in legal orders, in that the conflicts occur not across the divide of a negotiating table but in a court which must decide which right to uphold.

The Development and Expansion of *Van Gend en Loos*

The Expansion of the Field of its Effect

8–26 Had the judicial discovery of individual rights remained exceptional the doctrine would have had less constitutional significance (sheer volume, whilst not establishing the constitutional significance of individual rights, adds to it), much less practical effect, and fewer possibilities for conflict with national law. But, in general, the Court has so expanded this area despite the wording of European Community law provisions that direct effect is presumed to be the rule rather than the exception:

> "under Community law it is automatically assumed that the Contracting Parties intended to confer rights on individuals by means of the Treaties and the only requirement for direct applicability is that the rules in question be precise and complete . . .".[66]

8–27 *Tests* The Court in Case 26/62 *Van Gend en Loos* indicated one of the basic problems confronting the development of the doctrine of individual rights. Since the Treaty does not grant any expressly, when can they be judged to arise?

> "These rights arise not only where they are expressly granted by the Treaty, but also by reason of obligations which the Treaty imposes in a clearly defined way upon individuals as well as upon the Member States and upon the institutions of the Community."

The Court, in developing the doctrine of individual rights, has had to define the limits of how and when rights can be deduced from obligations imposed for the most part on Member States. This problem has been at the root of an evolving jurisprudence and of an enormous body of secondary literature.

The derivation of individual rights from texts which speak primarily of Member States' obligations raises four questions:

- First, what is the test to establish whether a provision of Community law confers rights on individuals?
- Secondly, to which Community law sources may this test be applied? That is, which formal sources are capable of giving rise to rights in individuals?
- Thirdly, once the individual right is established, can the right be asserted against individuals or is the right confined to being a corollary of the express obligation on the Member State? The answer to this question reaffirms that the right can be asserted both on the ground that the Member State cannot be allowed to plead its own failure to implement its Community

---

66 Advocate-General Darmon, Case 12/86 *Demirel v. Stadt Schwäbisch Gmünd* [1987] E.C.R. 3719 at 3742, para. 18, contrasting the more cautious approach to the direct effect of provisions of international "mixed" treaties.

obligations as a defense to the right those obligations sought to create,[67] and also on the broader grounds of the attainment of Community objectives and the efficacy of legal provisions.

- Fourthly, if the right is not simply a corollary of the obligation on a Member State and can be asserted to some extent against other individuals, is the assertion of rights by individuals against other individuals circumscribed by the principle of legal certainty which forbids the imposition by judicial declaration of obligations on individuals who cannot be expected to have known about them?

The answer to the first question is straightforward and applies irrespective of the formal source of Community law. The test was laid down in Case 26/62 *Van Gend en Loos* itself.[68] The prohibition in Article 12 (EEC) against the introduction of further tariff barriers gave rise to individual rights because (a) the article's wording contained an unconditional prohibition imposing a negative obligation, and (b) the obligation was not qualified by a reservation, which reservation would have made the implementation of the obligation conditional upon positive legislative state action.

> "The wording of Article 12 contains a clear and unconditional prohibition which is not a positive but a negative obligation. This obligation, moreover, is not qualified by any reservation on the part of states which would make its implementation conditional upon a positive legislative measure enacted under national law. The very nature of this prohibition makes it adapted to produce direct effects in the legal relationship between Member States and their subjects."[69]

These requirements have been softened to the requirements that the provisions be clear, precise, and unconditional as the core of the test for direct effect which may be applied to any source of binding European Community law. On the application of this test in Case 26/62 *Van Gend en Loos*, Article 12 (EEC) was held to confer rights to individuals against Member States.

However, no mention was made of rights of individuals against other individuals, which is the substance of questions three and four. Here are considered five of the principal sources of Community law – the Treaty establishing the European Community, international treaties, Regulations, Directives, and Decisions. Some of the answers to these questions vary depending on the source (the second question above) and the answer always depends on the wording and objective of the provision itself. The Court bases its

---

67 This was suggested as a ground for the direct effect of directives, along with the grounds of the bindingness ascribed to Directives in Article 189 and the necessity to make Directives effective, in Case 148/78 *Ratti* [1979] E.C.R. 1629 at 1642: a Member State "may not rely, as against individuals, on its own failure to perform the obligations which the directive entails".

68 [1963] E.C.R. 1.

69 *ibid.* at 13.

jurisprudential development of the doctrine on securing the objectives of the Treaty and the efficacy of provisions designed to achieve those objectives.

Treaty Provisions

8–28 Case 26/62 *Van Gend en Loos* had settled the general question of whether Treaty provisions could give rise to individual rights. The question of horizontal direct effect establishing individual obligations was squarely decided in Case 36/74 *Walrave v. Union Cycliste Internationale.*[70] There the Court had to decide whether two Dutch pacemakers had the Community law right, capable of assertion against an international organisation with its headquarters in Geneva and against the Dutch and Spanish (Spain was not a member of the European Economic Community at this time) cycling associations, to avoid the discrimination on grounds of nationality imposed by their rules. These were rules private to an umbrella organisation for sporting associations; the rules were not the result of state action. Under these rules the pacemaker had to be of the same nationality as the racer. The Dutch cyclists pleaded that these rules were incompatible with, *inter alia,* Article 7 (EEC) (now Article 6 (EC)) (the general prohibition of discrimination on the grounds of nationality within the scope of the Treaty), Article 48 (2) (EEC) (prohibition of discrimination on the grounds of nationality between workers as regards conditions of employment), and Article 59 (EEC) (abolition of restrictions on the freedom to provide services). Accepting that the prohibition of discrimination on the grounds of nationality in these areas fulfil the Case 26/62 *Van Gend en Loos* criteria for giving rise to rights against the state, the question remains whether they impose obligations upon individuals. The Court held that these provisions gave effect to the general rule of non-discrimination based on nationality, which rule covered all works and services:

> "the exact nature of the legal relationship under which such services are performed is of no importance . . .
>
> . . .
>
> Prohibition of such discrimination does not only apply to the action of public authorities but extends likewise to rules of any other nature aimed at regulating in a collective manner gainful employment and the provision of services."[71]

The bases for thus generalising the obligation not to discriminate on the grounds of nationality were threefold:

- First, it was necessary to attain the treaty objective of abolition of obstacles to the free movement of persons and the free provision of services.

---

[70] [1974] E.C.R. 1405. There is some argument that this decision is confined to the acts of quasi-legislative bodies. However, as Professor Barry Fitzpatrick has pointed out, it would be odd if Article 119 (EEC) should create, post Case 43/75 *Defrenne v. SABENA* [1976] E.C.R. 455, complete horizontal direct effect but Article 48 (EC) should be restricted to imposing obligations on such types of body only.

[71] *ibid.* at 1417, 1418.

- Secondly, limiting the prohibition to the acts of public authorities would lead to inequality of the application of working conditions from the point of view of the worker, since working conditions may equally be imposed by private arrangements such as contract as well as by public regulation. However, this argument has not been accepted as a basis for holding that another source of Community law, Directives, are capable of giving rise to rights which individuals can assert against other individuals (in other words, Directives do not impose obligations on individuals). Furthermore, the judgment applied only to the collective regulation of employment and not to private contracts.
- Thirdly, although the Treaty provisions provide for the abolition of barriers by the State, this does not limit the general nature of the provisions on the abolition of discrimination which make no distinction on the source of the restrictions to be abolished (although it does point out that it is Member States who should abolish them).

The second and third bases have not been required in later cases which leave the attainment of objectives as the sole basis for this extension of the direct effect of articles of the constituent treaties to relations between individuals.

The extension of the direct effect of Treaty provisions to relations between individuals and the legal bases of such extension were spectacularly confirmed in Case 43/75 *Defrenne v. SABENA*.[72] In this case a Belgian air hostess asserted the right to compensation for discriminatory pay against the company employing her. The Treaty provision invoked by the air hostess before the Labour Court in Brussels was Article 119, which provides: "Each Member State shall . . . ensure and subsequently maintain the application of the principle that men and women should receive equal pay for equal work." Like almost all Treaty provisions, this is an obligation imposed on its face on states, not individuals. Accepting that it fulfills the *Van Gend en Loos* test for direct effect of individual rights against the state, what was the basis for extending these rights and the correlative obligation to private relationships? The Court gave three bases:

- First, the application of the principle of equal pay

> "forms part of the social objectives of the Community, which is not merely an economic union, but is at the same time intended, by common action, to ensure social progress and seek the constant improvement of the living and working conditions of their peoples . . . [and] forms part of the foundations of the Community."

---

72 [1976] E.C.R. 455. See B. Rudden, *Basic Community Cases* (Oxford: 1987), p. 135 where it is pointed out that Article 119 (EEC) is the first example of an Article in the Treaty establishing the European Economic Community without an intrinsic cross-border element being found to be directly effecting and imposing a positive obligation.

This is an important expansion of what the Court takes to be the objectives of the Treaty from the economic to the social.[73]

- Secondly, the effectiveness of the provision, and by implication the attainment of a social objective of the Community, cannot be affected by the failure of the Member States to fulfil the obligation it imposes on them[74];
- Thirdly, undertakings established in Member States which Member States had implemented their obligations would be placed on an unequal competitive footing in the Common Market,[75] and thus conflict with the objective of the Common Market.

This ruling clearly had implications for the respect of the principle of legal certainty and for the correlated right of undertakings to legitimate expectations as to the content of the law. The judgment itself acknowledges in the quotation above that the attainment of objectives is intended to be by common action and therefore by implication not by judicial fiat. The governments of Ireland and the United Kingdom pointed out that the decision would result in claims dating back to the time when the individual right arose (which was the end of the transition period for Article 119). The Court held that: "important considerations of legal certainty affecting all the interests involved, both public and private, make it impossible in principle to reopen the question as regards the past."[76]

8–29 *International Treaties* International treaties between the European Community and Third States may give rise to rights in individuals which these may assert both before the Community courts and before national tribunals.[77] Whether or not a treaty does give rise to such rights is a matter of interpretation of the particular treaty in question. Thus the Court of Justice held[78] that "Community 'citizens'"[79] had the right to rely on the Yaoundé Convention in order to challenge the imposition of a national duty, having regard to the spirit and general scheme of the Convention and its provisions.[80] Because such a treaty is an integral part of Community law, the Court of Justice is the authoritative interpreter of it so far as the Member States and the Community institutions are concerned. The reason for the possible direct applicability of treaties is that the Member States must fulfil their obligation to the Community by ensuring respect for commitments arising from an agreement.

---

73 *Defrenne v. SABENA* [1976] E.C.R. 455 at 472.
74 *ibid.* at 575.
75 *ibid.* at 472.
76 *ibid.* at 481.
77 See above, Chap. 6, "Status of Public International Law Treaties in European Community Law".
78 Case 87/75 *Bresciani v. Ammistrazione Italiana delle Finanze* [1976] E.C.R. 129.
79 *ibid.* para. 15.
80 *ibid.* para. 16.

The effect of these commitments could not be allowed to vary according to who was responsible for applying them – the Community or the Member States, or different Member States.[81] However the similarity of the wording of a treaty between the Community and a Third State with directly effective wording of the provisions of the Treaty establishing the European Economic Community is not enough in itself to guarantee the direct applicability of the provision, because the purpose of the treaty is also relevant.[82] In summary, the commitments must be uniformly and effectively observed – two of the most habitual grounds for Court of Justice judgments of constitutional importance.

Provisions of several treaties have been held to give rise to individual rights.[83] Not only may provisions of treaties give rise to individual European Community law rights, but also secondary law made thereunder, such as decisions of the Council of the EEC–Turkey Association, if they satisfy the same criteria as apply to international treaties.[84] No reason was given for this decision, which is considered further under the section "Direct Effect as a Doctrine Independent from its Original Legitimation".

8–30 *Regulations* Article 189 paragraph 2 provides: "A regulation shall have general application. It shall be binding in its entirety and directly applicable in all Member States." Given this wording, the Court had no trouble in slotting

---

81 Case 104/81 *Kupferberg* [1982] E.C.R. 3641 at 3662.

82 In Case 270/80 *Polydor v. Harlequin Record Shops* [1982] E.C.R. 329 the Court of Justice held that provisions of the free trade agreement between the European Economic Community and the Portuguese Republic which paralleled Articles 30 and 36 (EEC) on the free movement of goods did not allow an importer of goods from Portugal to defend a claim for breach of copyright with the defence that the protection of individual and commercial property did not justify in the case law of the Court the restriction on the free movement of goods by the partitioning of markets, because the purpose of the agreement between the European Economic Community and Portugal was to establish a free trade area (at 347, para. 10) whereas the purpose of the Treaty establishing the European Economic Community was "to create a single market reproducing as closely as possible the conditions of a domestic market" (at 349, para. 18).

Interestingly, it is implicit in the judgment that the concepts of the construction of Europe and European unity appear to differ, because the overall objective of the agreement between the European Economic Community and Portugal was to contribute "to the work of constructing Europe" (at 347, para. 10) whereas the overall objective of the Treaty establishing the European Economic Community is European unity (Opinion 1/91 [1991] E.C.R. I–6079), and the Court held that the purpose of the two agreements differed, unless European Unity became the objective some time after 1980.

83 *e.g.* the Yaoundé Convention in Case 87/75 *Bresciani v. Ammistrazione Italiana delle Finanze* [1976] E.C.R. 129; the EEC–Portuguese Association Agreement in Case 104/81 *Kupferberg* [1982] E.C.R. 3641; the EEC–Morocco Co-operation Agreement of 1976 in Case C–18/90 *ONEM v. Bahia Kziber* [1991] E.C.R. I–119 and in Case C–58/93 *Zoubir Yousfi v. Belgium* [1994] E.C.R. I–1353; the EEC–Turkey Association Agreement in Case C–192/89 *S.Z. Sevince v. Staatssecretaris van Justitie* [1990] E.C.R. I–3461 and in Case C–237/91 *Kazim Kus v. Landeshauptstadt Wiesbaden* [1992] E.C.R. I–6781.

84 Case C–192/89 *S.Z. Sevince v. Staatssecretaris van Justitie* [1990] E.C.R. I–3461 at 3502, para. 15.

Regulations into its framework of individual rights.[85] It has been already noted[86] that the wording of Article 189 paragraph 2 did not of itself determine that individual rights resulting from Regulations would impose on national courts a European Community law duty to uphold them or that these individual rights could not be implemented by national law.

However, the issues of whether any particular provision of a Regulation can give rise to an individual right where such is not declared on the face of the text is a matter for the interpretation of the provision in the light of the tests for indirect effect originally laid down in Case 26/62 *Van Gend en Loos*. Similarly, Regulations may expressly create rights and obligations between individuals. If not done expressly, then it is a matter once again of interpretation.

8–31 *Directives* Article 189 paragraph 3 (EC) provides: "A directive shall be binding, as to the result to be achieved, upon each Member State to which it is addressed, but shall leave to the national authorities the choice and form of methods." In contrast to Regulations, Directives therefore seem to impose obligations on states alone and so it was widely believed that Directives gave rise exclusively to rights and obligations between the institutions and the Member States. The Court dispelled this assumption in Case 41/74 *Van Duyn v. Home Office*.[87] In that case a Dutch woman was refused leave by the Home Office to enter the United Kingdom for the purpose of employment with the Church of Scientology on the grounds that the activities of that organisation were socially harmful. She asserted the right before the English High Court to have this public policy decision taken exclusively on the ground of her personal conduct, basing this right in a provision of a Directive which required the State to ensure this.[88] The United Kingdom argued that Directives could not give rise to individual rights because of the clear distinction between Directives and Regulations.

Despite the wording of Article 189 paragraph 2 (EC), the Court held that Directives were capable of direct effects, basing its judgment on two grounds[89]:

- First, it would weaken the effectiveness of a Directive, whose obligatoriness is acknowledged by Article 189 (EEC), if individuals could not rely on it before national courts.

- Secondly, Article 177 (EEC) empowers national courts to refer to the Court questions on the interpretation of all Community acts without distinction, which implies that Directives, as Community acts, can be invoked before the national courts.

---

85 See, *e.g.* Case 43/71 *Politi v. Italian Ministry of Finance* [1971] E.C.R. 1039 at 1048.
86 See para. 7–10 above, "Obligation in the Result – Non-Transformation of Regulations".
87 [1974] E.C.R. 1337.
88 Article 3(1) of Council Directive 64/221 of 25 February 1964.
89 [1974] E.C.R. 1337 at 1348.

The question of whether a particular provision created individual rights was held once again to be a question of interpretation of "the nature, general scheme and wording of the provision in question." The result was that the Directive "confers on individuals rights which are enforceable by them in the courts of a Member State and which the national courts must protect."[90]

Directives cannot give rise to rights and obligations between individuals. This limitation to Directives was maintained in Case 152/84 *Marshall.*[91] In that case Marshall asserted a Community law right to equality of treatment for men and women in dismissals. A Council Directive guaranteed this principle.[92] She asserted this right against her employer, an English Health Authority, who had dismissed her because she had exceeded the retirement age for women, which was earlier than that for men. Once it was established that the provision of the Directive was sufficiently clear and unconditional to give rise to rights of individuals against the state, Marshall still had to overcome the United Kingdom objection that Directives cannot impose obligations on individuals or on a Member State *qua* employer, that is a Member State acting in a private capacity. The Court held:

> "according to Article 189 of the EEC Treaty, the binding nature of a directive, which constitutes the basis for the possibility of relying on the directive before a national court, exists only in relation to 'each Member State to which it is addressed'. It follows that a directive may not in itself impose obligations on an individual and that a provision of a directive may not be relied upon as such against such a person."[93]

However the argument of the United Kingdom that the State acting in private law could avoid its Community obligations was forcefully rejected by the Court, which held that the capacity in which the State acted was irrelevant.

The resulting inequality for individuals employed in the private sector has been tackled by the Court of Justice in three ways. (The equality arguments for extending the direct effect of treaty provisions to the relations of individuals *inter se* in Case 36/74 *Walrave*[94] – otherwise employees in the private sector would be at a disadvantage in working conditions – and in Case 43/75 *Defrenne*[95] – failure to extend obligations to private parties would put undertakings in a Member State which had complied with its Community commitments by imposing the obligation on undertakings through implementing national law at a competitive disadvantage – were not accepted as a ground in Case

---

90 *ibid.* at 1349, para. 15.

91 [1986] E.C.R. 723, confirmed in Case C–91/92 *Faccini Dori v. Recreb* [1994] E.C.R. I–3315 despite the Opinion of Advocate-General Lenz in that case and two earlier opinions of Advocates-General in Case C–271/91 *Marshall v. Southampton and South West Hampshire Area Health Authority* [1993] E.C.R. I–4367 (Van Gerven) and Case C–316/93 *Vaneetveld* [1994] E.C.R. I–763 (Jacobs).

92 Article 5(1) of Council Directive 76/207.

93 Case 152/84 *Marshall* [1986] E.C.R. 723 at 749.

94 Case 36/74 [1974] E.C.R. 1405.

95 Case 43/75 [1976] E.C.R. 455.

152/84 *Marshall*[96] for either restricting the imposition of obligations derived from a Directive to a Member State acting in a public capacity or for expanding it to encompass all individuals.)

- First, the Court has adopted a very broad definition of "Member State" for the purposes of casting the net of Community obligations as wide as possible (and thereby increasing the catch of European Community rights). (Case C–188/89 *Foster v. British Gas*[97]: "a body, whatever its legal form, which has been made responsible, pursuant to a measure adopted by the state, for providing a public service under the control of the state and which has for that purpose special powers beyond those which result from the normal rules applicable in relations between individuals . . .")
- Secondly, the Court has held that the European Community obligation on national courts to ensure compliance with a Directive entails interpretation, as far as is possible, of national law in the light of the Directive's wording and purpose.

  In Case C–196/89 *Marleasing*[98] a Spanish company sought the annulment of the contract of association of another company which had been created by a third debtor company for the sole purpose of removing its assets beyond the reach of creditors. The plaintiff based its action on general principles of the Spanish Civil Code, particularly Article 1275 under which a contract is of no effect when its cause is contrary to law or morality. The defendant mounted a European Community law defence claiming that a Council Directive laid down exclusively the situations where a Company could be annulled.[99] The Court held that the national court must interpret its national law so as to preclude a declaration of nullity on grounds other than those in the Council Directive.[100] The implication of the decision is that contradicting national law cannot be used by an individual against another individual where the national law conflicts with a Directive.
- Thirdly, the Court of Justice created a remedy in damages for individuals who suffer damage as a result of a Member State's failure to transpose a Directive into national law in Joined Cases C 6 & 9/90 *Francovich and*

---

96 Case 152/84 [1986] E.C.R. 723.
97 Case C–188/89 [1990] E.C.R. I–3313 at 3348.
98 Case C–196/89 [1990] E.C.R. I–4135; the Court of Justice first specified this obligation in Case 14/83 *Von Colson and Kamann* [1984] E.C.R. 1891. The case in the text is a better example: whereas in Case 106/89 *Marleasing* the conflict between the Directive and the Spanish law was direct, in Case 14/83 *Von Colson* the German Government asserted before the Court of Justice that the national law left sufficient scope for the national court to interpret it in accordance with the Directive.
99 Article 11 of Council Directive 68/151.
100 Case C–196/89 *Marleasing* [1990] E.C.R. I–4135 at 4160–4161.

Bonifaci v. Italy.[101] This remedy protects rights against others than the state which rights a Member State should have protected by implementation but failed to do so. However the remedy is not confined to the denial of rights resulting from the non-implementation of Directives and so is considered separately.[102]

8–32 *Decisions* In Case 9/70 *Grad v. Finanzamt Traunstein*[103] the Court considered the question of whether Decisions, which are binding in their entirety on those addressed, could be invoked by all those who have an interest in the fulfillment of the obligation which the Decision imposes.[104] The Court refused to treat the source separately but fitted it directly into the Case 26/62 *Van Gend en Loos* framework, holding that because Article 177 (EEC) allows a national court to refer questions concerning the validity of all acts of the institutions, individuals may invoke such acts before national courts if it satisfies the tests for direct effects.[105]

In Joined Cases C–100 & 101/89 *Kaefer and Procacci v. France*[106] the Court expanded the field of individual rights to include European Community nationals claiming before a French Polynesian administrative court (which the Court of Justice held to be an integral part of the French judicial system) the right to stay in French Polynesia. This claim was based on an article in a Council Decision on the association of the overseas countries and territories with the European Economic Community. France and the Commission argued that the relevant article of the Decision imposed an obligation only as to the result to be achieved since it was subject to a condition of reciprocity, and therefore did not fulfil the tests for direct effect. However the Court held that this condition did not leave discretion to the Member States but only required them to decide whether or not it was satisfied.[107]

8–33 *Remedy in Damages*[107a] This important step for individual rights in Community law was taken in Joined Cases C–6 & 9/90 *Francovich and Bonifaci v. Italy.*[108] This concerned a Directive establishing a minimum protection for employees of an insolvent employer, specifically the repayment of unpaid remuneration.[109] The Member States were to organise under national law funds

---

101 Joined Cases C–6 & 9/90 [1991] E.C.R. I–5357.
102 See below, para. 8–33, "Remedy in Damages".
103 [1970] E.C.R. 825.
104 *ibid.* at 837, para. 5.
105 *ibid.* at 837, para. 7; at 838, para. 9.
106 [1990] E.C.R. I–4647.
107 *ibid.* at I–2673–2674.
107a This is analysed in more detail in B.A. Rudden and D.R. Phelan, *Basic Community Cases* (2nd ed., 1997).
108 [1991] E.C.R. I–5357. The constitutional importance of this decision has been recognised, *e.g.* M. Ross, "Beyond *Francovich*" (1993) 56 *Modern Law Review* 55.
109 Council Directive 80/987.

for this purpose. The plaintiff individuals were owed salary from an insolvent employer and sued Italy in the national courts for damages for failure to implement the Directive (Italy's failure had already been definitely established in Case 22/87 *Commission v. Italy*[110]).

Despite the absence of any textual foundation, the Court held that it was a principle of Community law that Member States must compensate damage caused to individuals by violations of Community law imputed to them. It based this principle on three grounds:

- First, the Treaty establishing the European Economic Community creates its own legal order whose subjects are not only States but also their nationals on whom it imposes obligations and grants rights, citing Case 26/62 *Van Gend en Loos* and Case 6/64 *Costa v. ENEL.*
- Secondly, the full effect of Community norms must be guaranteed.

  On the basis of these two grounds, the Court declared the principle to be "inherent in the scheme of the Treaty".[111] This ground of inherence is therefore by way of support for the obligation deduced from general principles.
- Thirdly, Article 5 (EEC) imposes on Member States the general obligation to take all measures to ensure the carrying out of its Treaty obligations, and this must be interpreted to include the duty to repair the illegal consequences of a violation of Community law.

The conditions for the application of the principle of the obligation to provide compensation are threefold[112]:

- First, the result prescribed by the directive must involve the creation of individual rights.
- Secondly, the content of these rights must be identifiable from the provisions of the Directive. (This is different from the test for direct effect, where the obligation, as distinct from the rights, must be clear and unconditional.)
- Thirdly, there must be a causal link between the Member State's failure in its Community obligation and the damage caused.

Three further points arise from this case.

- First, the Court held that the provisions in the Directive were not sufficiently clear to give rise to individual rights invocable against the state (because it was not clear that the state was the obligor). The Joined Cases

---

110 [1989] E.C.R. 143.
111 Joined Cases C–6 & 9/90 *Francovich and Bonifaci v. Italy* [1991] E.C.R. I–5357 at 5414.
112 *ibid.* at I–5415.

C–6 & 9/90 *Francovich*[113] remedy therefore extends the protection of individual rights where there is no horizontal effect of directives.[114]

- Secondly, even if a remedy, in Joined Cases C–6 & 9/90 *Francovich* damages against the state, is alien to national law, national courts must make it available regardless.[115] This last point has been further elucidated.
- Thirdly, the Joined Cases C–6 & 9/90 *Francovich* remedy extends beyond non-implemented Directives to damage caused to an individual for Member State failure to comply with the requirements of European Community law. This last point has been further elucidated in Joined Cases C–46 & 48/93 *Brasserie du Pêcheur SA v. Germany* and *R. v. Secretary of Transport ex parte Factortame Ltd. and others*,[116] where the Court of Justice found that Member States are obliged to make good damage caused by breaches of Community law attributable to the State even where the national legislature was responsible for the breach. Where the national legislature was acting in a field in which it has wide discretion, the breach must be sufficiently serious, although it cannot be made dependent on fault. Reparation must be commensurate with the loss. This remedy applies in any case where there is a breach of a rule of Community law, not just a Directive, intended to confer rights on individuals, the rights are identifiable, and there is a causal link between the breach and the damage suffered. The Court of Justice stated clearly that the purpose of the direct effect of individual rights was to secure supremacy: "The purpose of ['the right of individuals to rely on the directly effective provisions of the Treaty before national courts'] is to ensure that the provisions of Community law prevail over national provisions."[117] The Court of Justice reiterated "the fundamental requirement of the Community legal order that Community law be uniformly applied"[118] in holding that the obligation to repair damage cannot depend on domestic rules on the division of powers between constitutional authorities.[118a]

---

113 [1991] E.C.R. I–5357.

114 See above, para. 8–31, "Directives".

115 This general principle was forcefully stated in Case C–213/89 *Factortame* [1990] E.C.R. I–2433 (grant of an interim injunction suspending the application of national law pending the outcome of a Court of Justice Article 177 (EEC) decision on its compatibility with Community law).

116 [1996] E.C.R. I–1029. Prior to this decision, Advocate-General Léger was of the opinion that there was State liability for the acts of a national administration in implementing European Community law in Case C–5/94 *R. v. Minister for Agriculture, Fisheries and Food ex parte Hedley Lomas (Ireland) Ltd.* [1996] E.C.R. I–2553, 2556, and in Joined Cases C–46 & 48/93 *Brasserie du Pêcheur SA v. Germany* and *R. v. Secretary of Transport ex parte Factortame Ltd. and others* itself. Advocate-General Tesauro was of the opinion that there was state liability for a national legislature's failure to abrogate laws contrary to articles of the Treaty establishing the European Economic Community, and for a national legislature's misuse of its discretion in implementing European Community law.

117 Joined Cases C–46 & 48/93, above, n.116 at para. 20.

118 *ibid.* at para. 33.

118a The remedy has been further developed in Case C–392/93 *R. v. the Treasury, ex parte*

Direct Effect as a Doctrine Independent of its Original Legitimation

8–34 In Joined Cases C–100 & 101/89 *Kaefer and Procacci v. France*[119] the United Kingdom argued on the basis of Case 26/62 *Van Gend en Loos* that the direct effect of Community law rested upon the purpose of the Treaty establishing the European Economic Community to secure economic integration in a common market, and consequently did not extend to a Council Decision on the association of overseas countries and territories taken pursuant to Part Four of the Treaty establishing the European Economic Community on the association of overseas countries and territories which has the different purpose of furthering the interests of the inhabitants in those countries and territories to lead them to development.[120] This argument therefore went straight to the legal basis of direct effect which the Court offered in Case 26/62 *Van Gend en Loos.*[121] The Court rejected the argument giving two reasons: first, the Court had already held that provisions in agreements between the Community and third countries could have direct effect[122]; secondly, that it was "settled case-law" that provisions of a Council Decision could produce direct effect if they satisfied the tests. This response implies that the doctrine of direct effect has acquired a legitimacy in the edifice of European Community law independent of its original foundation.[123] It is a good example of where the legal means to the political goal of economic integration becomes itself an end, and where the legal and political goals blur into each other.

Professor Snyder[124] has considered this issue in the context of the direct effect of Association Agreements where "the specific normative instrument from which the provisions are drawn is not oriented towards economic integration". Snyder correctly considers that this implies that economic and legal integration do not proceed in tandem but that legal integration can proceed more rapidly than economic integration. One may add that legal integration can proceed in ways whose orientation – no longer solely economic – is far from clear, and cannot even be considered to be political integration between Member States because an associated state is by definition not a Member State.

British Telecommunications [1996] E.C.R. I–1631 and Joined Cases C–178–179 & 188–190/94 *Dillenkofer* (8 October 1996).

119 [1990] E.C.R. I–4647.

120 *ibid.* at 4673, para. 24.

121 See above, para. 8–24, "The Basis of the Decision".

122 Case 104/81 *Hauptzollamt Mainz v. Kupferberg & Cie* [1982] E.C.R. 3641.

123 In Case C–192/89 *S.Z. Sevince v. Staatssecretaris van Justitie* [1990] E.C.R. I–3461 at 3476 Advocate-General Darmon took the position that once a text belonged to the Community legal order it was in principle capable of direct effect. The French Administrative Court of Papeete has accepted the ruling in *Kaefer. Knolle v. France* [1994] 2 C.M.L.R. 779 at 780.

124 F. Snyder, "Droit, Symboles et Politique Méditerranéenne: Réflexions sur Quelques Décisions Récentes de la Cour de Justice Européenne" (1994) in Jacques Bourrinet, *La Méditarrané Espace de Cooperation – en l'honneur de Maurice Flory* (Paris: Economica, 1994) 303 at pp. 308–309.

The rationale for the extension of the doctrine of direct effect to international treaties is the avoidance of embarrassment to the Community if Member States fail to implement an agreement concluded by the Community with a Third State.[125] This is a very different rationale to that given in the first place for direct effect.

The Development of the Depth of its Penetration

8–35 This development is explored more generally below.[126] However it is worth mentioning four cases here which focus clearly on the problems of direct effect before national courts which are not immediately linked to conflicting national law, but rather to the source of constraints and conditions on national judicial power.[127]

8–36 *European Community Law as Source of National Judicial Power and Duty* Just as Case 26/62 *Van Gend en Loos* predicted Case 6/64 *Costa*, so did Case 28/67 *Molkerei* predict Case 106/77 *Simmenthal*. The German Federal Finance Court ("Bundesfinanzhof") asked the Court of Justice to reconsider its ruling in Case 57/65 *Lütticke v. Hauptzollamt Saarlouis*[128] that parts of Article 95 (EEC) on the prohibition of discriminatory internal taxation were directly effective, which ruling gave rise to widespread, major, and complicated effects within the German tax system and the judicial supervision thereof. In replying to the Federal Finance Court, the Court of Justice first summarised its ruling in Case 26/62 *Van Gend en Loos* and then reiterated that the Article was capable of producing direct effects: "The fact that this article describes the Member States as being subject to the obligation of non-discrimination does not imply that individuals cannot directly benefit from it."[129] In summarising Case 26/62 *Van Gend en Loos*, the Court dropped the qualifying "of international law" after "new legal order",[130] thus reinforcing the autonomy of European Community law from public international law. In later cases, the Court has even dropped the "new".[131]

---

125 Case 104/81 *Kupferberg* [1982] E.C.R. 3641 at 3662. See also T.C. Hartley, *The Foundations of European Community Law* (Oxford: Clarendon Press, 2nd ed. 1994) pp. 229 –230.

126 See above, paras. 8–39 *et. seq.*, "Supremacy" and below, Part V, "Conflicts".

127 Case 28/67 *Molkerei-Zentrale Westfalen v. Hauptzollamt Paderborn* [1968] E.C.R. 143; Joined Cases C–430 & 431/93 *Van Schijndel v. Stichting Pensioenfonds voor Fysiotherapeuten* and *Van Veen v. Stichting Pensioenfonds voor Fysiotherapeuten*, [1995] E.C.R. I–4705; Case C–466/93, *Atlanta Fruchthandelsgesellschaft mbH e.a. v. Bundesamt für Ernährund und Forstwirtschaft* [1995] E.C.R. I–3799.

128 [1966] E.C.R. 205.

129 Case 28/67 *Molkerei – Zentrale Westfalen v. Hauptzollamt Paderborn* [1968] E.C.R. 143 at 153; see also Case 57/65 *Lütticke* [1966] E.C.R. 205 at 210.

130 Case 28/67 *Molkerei – Zentrale Westfalen v. Hauptzollamt Paderborn* [1968] E.C.R. 143 at 152.

131 See *e.g.* Case C–146/89 *Commission v. United Kingdom* [1991] E.C.R. I–3533 at 3580, para. 47: the phrase used is "the legal order established by the Treaty".

The Federal Finance Court had pointed out that national courts would be obliged to place the individual in the same position as if the Member State had already fulfilled the obligations imposed upon it by Article 95 (EEC), whereas the Community could merely require the implementation of those obligations. In other words, courts cannot take as done what ought to be done according to European Community law. This is a correct reading of the text of the Treaty establishing the European Economic Community and accords with the public international law approach to international responsibility. However the Court replied that "It is not possible to base an argument – contrary to the interpretation of Article 95 as it follows from the judgment in Case 57/65 *Lütticke v. Hauptzollamt Saarlouis* – on a comparison of the rights conferred by this provision on individuals, on the one hand, and the powers conferred on the Community institutions, on the other."[132] This stands the argument on its head, since the point is that the right must result from the exercise of the powers conferred. The Court's rejection of this basic point reaffirms, in the face of national court resistance, the autonomy of European Community law from what the Member States intended by international treaty. In the next sentence, the Court pointed the way to conflicts between the European Community and national legal orders: "Every time a rule of Community law confers rights on individuals, those rights, without prejudice to the methods of recourse made available by the Treaty, may be safeguarded by proceedings brought before the competent national courts."

The Court continues: "In fact proceedings by an individual are intended to protect individual rights in a specific case, whilst intervention by the Community authorities has as its object the general and uniform observance of Community law." Not only does this description of the different procedures once more presume the result of individual rights, but it contradicts Case 26/62 *Van Gend en Loos*, where the Court held that individuals had a role in the supervision of the Member States' European Community law obligations,[133] and contradicts many of the judgments considered above where uniformity was pivotal in deciding whether an individual right had to be upheld by the referring national court. Even more spectacularly, this description, reinforced in the next sentence ("It thus appears that the guarantees given to individuals under the Treaty to safeguard their individual rights and the powers granted to the Community institutions with regard to the observance by the States of their obligations have different objects, aims and effects and a parallel may not be drawn between them") is flatly contradicted on the next page of the Reports:

> "Resort by the national courts to Article 177 makes it possible for the Court to ensure a uniform interpretation of the Treaty and is capable of bringing about its identical application."[134]

---

132 [1968] E.C.R. at 153.

133 [1963] E.C.R. 1 at 13.

134 Case 28/67 [1968] E.C.R. 143 at 154. That there should be such contradiction in the judgments of the Court of Justice is not so surprising when one remembers the obligation on the judges to reach a collegiate decision.

As regards the specific issue of the powers of national courts, the Federal Finance Court pointed out that the finance courts did not have the power under German fiscal law to take decisions whose effects extended beyond the case in question and that it was not their proper task "to make good by thousands of separate decisions provisions of tax law which have not been passed."[135] It must be clarified that this point goes to the power of the national courts themselves,[136] not to a conflict with a substantive national law right or obligation, and only indirectly to the question of whether a provision of European Community law gives rise to individual rights.[137] This is important because the Court handles this argument in a distinctive way:

> "These arguments as a whole, which are based on rules of national law, cannot prevail over the rules of law laid down by the Treaty. It is clear from the fundamental principles of the Treaty and the objectives which it is intended to attain that those provisions, so far as by their nature they are capable of doing so, enter into national legal systems without the assistance of any national measure. The complexity of given situations in a State cannot alter the legal nature of a directly applicable Community provision, especially as the Community rule must be applied with the same force in all Member States.
>
> In particular, the prohibition laid down by Article 95 would lose the effect which it derives from the Treaty if the force of this provision depended on national implementing measures not provided for in the Treaty and without which the prohibition itself would have no effect."

There are several important points in this answer.

First, the Court answers in terms of supremacy a question which goes to the nature of the individual rights: the right prevails not only over conflicting provisions of national law, but also conflicting absences of provisions in national law, creating the power to enforce the right which arises before whatever national court in which it is raised. From this case on, the doctrines of individual rights and supremacy are completely intertwined. European Community law rights create the power for their own enforcement, as distinct from solely being supreme over conflicting rules. If a national constitutional law court was to hold that it was incapable under the national constitution to uphold a European Community law right which conflicted with an essential commitment of national constitutional law, then the

---

135 *ibid.* at 154.

136 J.-V. Louis, and A. Alen, "La Constitution et la Participation à la Communauté Européenne" (1994) 27 *Revue Belge de droit international* 81, have stated that "the European Community . . . is founded on the 'principle of indifference' as to that which concerns the institutional structure of the Member States."

137 The Federal Finance Court was not alone with this problem of competence: the *Conseil d'État* refused to apply European Community law over a posterior statute until 1989 on a similar ground – see below, paras. 22–2 *et seq.*, "The *Conseil d'État*". This problem of the competence of the national judge is acute in France, Italy, and Germany: F. Hervouet, "Politique Jurisprudentielle de la Cour de Justice et des Juridictions Nationales: Réception du Droit Communautaire par le Droit Interne" (1992) *Revue de Droit Public* 1257.

European Community law answer is clear: the court is empowered to do so by European Community law. This case, as early as 1968, points to a new source of national judicial power which can be relied on by national courts in the event of a legal revolution. Where a national court cannot reconcile the application of European Community law with national law in a case outside the limits of national law's accommodation of European Community law, the national court cannot derive the power to apply European Community law from national law, but could rely (as a possibility although it would cause a legal revolution) on European Community law for that power.[138] The claims of European Community law can be at the same time the cause of a legal revolution and a point of repair for the establishment of a new order.

Secondly, European Community law denies that the assertibility of the European Community law right is linked to provision in national law for the observance of European Community law. There is here a basic conflict in constitutional structures both with national constitutional law and with public international law. With national constitutional law in the case of dualist systems, this conflict is clear. With public international law there is a basic difference between international responsibility on the one hand, and the direct obligation on and power conferred to the national judge to uphold the European Community law right on the other hand. If national law interposes itself between European Community law and this power and obligation to reach the same result then this may have consequences for the national court perception of European Community law, but the European Community law perception is that the national law interposition is at best irrelevant – the obligation and power are directly conferred – and contrary to European Community law if the interposition infringes that obligation and power, and is in any event in a state of permanent constitutional disobedience.[139]

Thirdly, the reason given for why this autonomous nature of European Community law cannot be altered is because of the requirements of uniformity and effectiveness.

Fourthly, the bases for this nature of European Community law – in a word, integrative – are "the fundamental principles of the Treaty and the objectives which it is intended to obtain". "Fundamental principles" are not described. It is a rabbit in the hat: the fundamental principle is that European Community law is integrative, that it be integrated, which is the legal counterpart to the fundamental objective, integration.

Joined Cases C–430 & 431/93 *Van Schijndel* and *Van Veen*[140] establishes a European Community law duty and power of a national court where there is

---

138 D.R. Phelan, "Two Hats, One Wig, No Halo" (1995) 45 *Doctrine & Life* 130.

139 As to which, although with the focus on how the individual and not the tribunal perceives the European Community law right, see above, para. 7–11 *et seq.*, "Obligation in the Result – Non-Transformation of Regulations".

140 [1995] E.C.R. I–4705.

a national law power in respect of national law, but not otherwise, to raise of its own motion an issue of European Community law. This duty is reduced to a permissive power where it would oblige national courts to go beyond the ambit of the dispute set out by the parties.[141]

8–37 *European Community Law Constrains National Judicial Power* In Case 314/85 *Foto Frost v. Hauptzollamt Lübeck-Ost*[142] the Court of Justice held that national courts do not have the power to decide on the validity of European Community measures, even pending an appeal to a higher national court which could be obliged to make an Article 177 (EEC) reference to the Court of Justice. This decision is important here for three reasons: first, it restricts both the national court national law power and the national court European Community law power to decide on the validity of the rules it applies[143]; secondly, it increases the likelihood of conflicts in the same action between national and Community courts; and thirdly, it provides a good example of the requirement of uniformity overriding the text of the Treaty establishing the European Economic Community.

Advocate-General Mancini admitted that on the wording of Article 177 (EEC) there was "a syllogism of undeniable persuasive force"[144]: indent (b) of the first paragraph puts questions of interpretation and validity on the same footing, and paragraphs two and three allow court to make references

---

141 The limitation on the duty is justified by the European Community law principle that it is for the parties to take the initiative, which principle reflects conceptions prevailing in most Member States as to the relation between the State and the individual, safeguards the rights of the defence, and ensures the avoidance of improper delays – para. 21 of the decision. In the case of C–312/93 *Peterbroeck* [1995] E.C.R. I–4599 the same question was posed against a different factual backdrop. The Court of Justice phrased its response in terms of the European Community law precluding the application of a domestic procedural rule which prevents a national court from raising the question *ex officio*, and not directly in terms of the power of the national court. The decision, when coupled with the duty on national courts to uphold European Community law, implies that national courts have the power to raise a point of European Community law *ex officio*, but is not clear on whether there is a corresponding duty. Joined Cases C–430 & 431/93 *Van Schijndel* and *Van Veen* is clearer on this point. Article 5 (EC) was the sole article cited in support of these decisions.

These decisions are not compatible with Case 158/80 *Rewe v. Hauptzollamt Kiel* [1981] E.C.R. 1805 where the Court of Justice held that European Community law does not create new procedures or remedies which could be availed of before national courts. The Court of Justice has developed its case law away from this position over the last 15 years. For a starker example of the Court of Justice overturning previous decisions, see Case C–70/88 *Parliament v. Council* (*Chernobyl*) [1990] E.C.R. I–2041 and Case 302/87 *Parliament v. Council* (*Comitology*) [1988] E.C.R. 5615.

142 [1987] E.C.R. 4199.

143 The extent to which national courts have this power depends on the court and the rule. Some national courts had taken the view that they had jurisdiction to consider the validity in a particular case of a rule, or of the application of a rule, of European Community law – see the Opinion of Advocate-General Mancini.

144 Case 314/85 *Foto Frost* [1987] E.C.R. 4199 at 4215.

on such questions but oblige only the court of final appeal in the case. It follows that lower courts, and arguably (although the Advocate-General does not accept this) the court of final appeal at least prior to the answer to the reference, have jurisdiction to decide the validity of the application of a rule in a particular case. The Advocate-General then considers that the Member States must not have meant what they said: "the 'elliptical' wording of Article 177 is attributable to a singular but not impossible oversight".[145] The Court of Justice appeared to have accepted that on the wording of the text national courts had this power, because it had suggested that "a provision should be included [in the Treaty] to prohibit national courts from treating a Community act as invalid".[146]

Nonetheless, the Court of Justice held that national courts not only had no European Community law power to decide on validity, but that they were prohibited from declaring European Community law measures invalid, because of the risk to the principle of the uniform application of European Community law, which "would be liable to place in jeopardy the very unity of the Community legal order and detract from the fundamental requirement of legal certainty".[147]

8–38 *European Community Law Conditions National Judicial Power* National courts do have power to suspend temporarily the application of a European Community rule, which power cannot be based on national law,[148] but from European Community law,[149] which power is subject to European Community law conditions. This power was clarified in Case C–466/93 *Atlanta Fruchthandelsgesellschaft mbH e.a. v. Bundesamt für Ernährund und Forstwirtschaft*,[150] which arose out of a banana controversy where the Frankfurt am Main Administrative Court had serious doubts on the validity of a European Community Regulation and not only suspended its application but also ordered the German administrative authorities to grant the applicant fruit importer licences contrary to the Regulation, considering that it was compelled to do so by virtue of the principle of judicial protection contained in the German Basic law, pending the Court of Justice's determination of the validity of the measure. The Administrative Court referred two sets of questions to the Court of Justice, the first on its power to make the interim orders controlling the legal relations of the parties in the case, and the second on the validity of the

---

145 *ibid.* at 4218.

146 [1975] 9 E.C.R. Bull. Supp. 20–21, quoted by Advocate-General Mancini at p. 4217.

147 Case 314/85 *Foto Frost* [1987] E.C.R. 4199 at 4231, para. 15.

148 See below, para. 8–58, "Case 106/77 *Simmenthal*". In that case the duty, found to be incompatible with European Community law, was pursuant to a ruling of the Constitutional Court that national courts refer such matters to it.

149 Joined Cases C–143/88 and C–92/89 *Zuckerfabrik Süderdithmarschen* and *Zuckerfabrik Soest* [1991] E.C.R. I–415.

150 [1995] E.C.R. I–3799.

Regulation.[151] The Court of Justice held that as a result of a litigant's right in European Community law to judicial protection, national courts had a European Community law power to make such interim orders, but that these powers were circumscribed by various European Community law conditions. The identity of all these conditions is not the important point in this context. What is central is that the Court of Justice balanced, on the back of a European Community law right acknowledged in response to a serious threat of disobedience from a German court, the European Community law powers and duties of national courts in applying and suspending the application of European Community law. One of the conditions is that the national court takes duly into account the interest of the Community and recognises that it is a matter for the Court of Justice to decide how this interest is to be balanced against the general national interests of Member States. Another condition and duty which the Court of Justice deemed necessary to spell out is that the national court respects the decisions of the Community courts on the validity of the measure. This level of control of national jurisdictions' powers and duties characterises a federal/state court relationship. The Court of Justice evolves these rules with no support in the Treaty establishing the European Community other than a reference to Article 5 (EC)[152] and an argument by analogy based on the Court of Justice's own powers to make interim orders.[153]

Supremacy

Public International Law Perception

8–39 Article 27 of the Vienna Convention on the Law of Treaties[154] provides:

> "*Internal law and observance of treaties*
>
> A party may not invoke provisions of its internal law as justification for its failure to perform a treaty. This rule is without prejudice to article 46."

Article 46 provides:

> "*Provisions of internal law regarding competence to conclude treaties*
>
> 1. A State may not invoke the fact that its consent to be bound by a treaty has been expressed in violation of a provision of its internal law regarding competence to conclude treaties as invalidating its consent unless that violation was manifest and concerned a rule of its internal law of fundamental importance.
>
> 2. A violation is manifest if it would be objectively evident to any State conducting itself in the matter in accordance with normal practice and good faith."

---

[151] Subsequent to the reference but prior to its decision the Court of Justice upheld the validity of the Regulation in a direct action brought by Germany – Case C–280/93 *Germany v. Council* [1994] E.C.R. I–4973. The Court of Justice upheld the validity of the Regulation again in Case C–466/93 *Atlanta ibid.* in response to the German Court's question.

[152] Above, n.150, para. 46.

[153] Articles 185 and 186 (EC) – above, n.150, paras. 27 and 39.

[154] Entered into force on the 27 January 1980.

All the Member States are parties to this Vienna Convention. Therefore they are covered by Article 27, and Article 46 does not provide an exception in the case of the European Community treaties because these are expressed not to come into force until they are ratified in accordance with domestic constitutional requirements. This reduces the risk of manifest violation, and it is accepted in this work that there has been to date no objectively evident manifest violation within the terms of Article 46 in the conclusion by the Member States of the Treaties establishing the European Communities and the treaties amending same.

It is apparent from Article 27 that public international law does not regard itself as supreme over national law, rather that national law cannot provide a defense in public international law to the international responsibility of a contracting party to a treaty. Article 27 codified the existing law. The Permanent Court of International Justice in its Advisory Opinion in the *Greek – Bulgarian Communities* case[155] held:

> "From the standpoint of International Law and of the Court which is its organ, municipal laws are merely facts which express the will and constitute the activities of States, in the same manner as do legal decisions or administrative measures. The Court is certainly not called upon to interpret the Polish law as such; but there is nothing to prevent the Court's giving judgement on the question whether or not, in applying that law, Poland is acting in conformity with its obligations towards Germany under the Geneva Convention."[156]

In this public international law sense of supremacy, an international judge cannot admit of a conflict between national law and public international law as having any legal consequence in public international law. This "uninvokability" of national law extends to national constitutional law, as the Permanent Court of International Justice held in *Polish Upper Silesia, Treatment of Polish Nationals*[157]:

> "according to generally accepted principles, a State cannot rely, as against another State, on the provisions of the latter's Constitution, but only on international law and international obligations duly accepted, on the other hand and conversely, a State cannot adduce as against another State its own Constitution with a view to evading obligations incumbent upon it under international law or treaties in force."

It is to be noted that this non–reliance on national constitutional law cuts both ways: it implies that European Community law (so far as it is public international law) cannot rely on national constitutional law to support its claims.

The public international law principle of primacy of international law imposes on a state the general obligation to conform its legal order to the international provisions to which it is bound, but a state has latitude in the

---

155 31 July 1930 Series A/B No. 37 and in the *Polish Upper Silesia* Case "Chorzow Factory", 25 May 1926, Series A No. 7.

156 *ibid.* at p. 19.

157 Series A/B No. 44, p. 24.

choice of means of conforming.[158] In general, monist states adopt public international law, whilst dualist states transform it. Such states, for example France, do not necessarily recognise the adopted public international law as supreme over national constitutional law. This is also the case with European Community law.[159] In dualist states, for example Ireland, the question of the place of the public international law rule in the hierarchy of internal norms disappears, strictly speaking, since the public international law rule acquires the status of the instrument of transformation.[160]

When the rules of implementation fail in a concrete case for whatever reason to effect conformity of national law with the public international law rule, there is a violation of public international law which may be sanctioned by the international responsibility of the state, provided in the case of an individual right that there has been exhaustion of effective domestic remedies.[161] The potentiality for conflict must be actualised: a conflict between a public international law rule and a national law rule which has not yet been applied does not give rise to a public international law illegality.[162] Pursuant to Article 6 of the Codification of State Responsibility proposed by the International Law Commission, an act of a state organ is considered as an act of the state for the purposes of engaging international responsibility. Consequently, what public international law demands is a supremacy in application, failure for which engages the state's international responsibility. The international judge may then declare the illegality of the result, but not the nullity of the measure:

> "The Permanent Court of International Justice has ... in no case ever expressly condemned the abusive application of national law. It has always limited itself to stating in such a case that the application of the national law had as a consequence the violation of a rule of the law of peoples."[163]

The national law may continue to override public international law in the domestic system and be applied by state organs until rectified by the internal rule-modifying process, for example by legislation or constitutional amendment.

European Community Law Perception

8–40 This is analysed in depth below. Three preliminary remarks are to be made here.

---

158 The following summary of the Public International Law perspective on supremacy draws on B. de Witte, "Retour à *Costa* – La primauté du droit communautaire à la lumière du droit international" (1984) *Revue Trimestrielle de Droit Européen* 425, section II.

159 See above, para. 6–4, "The Treaty Establishing the European Community and Treaties with Third States".

160 At best. The instrument of transformation, for example a statute, could not confer a status superior to statute, although it could specify an inferior status.

161 See above paras. 7–9 *et seq.*, "Exhaustion of Domestic Remedies".

162 Unless the threat of application of the national law rule is an actuality prohibited by a public international law rule *e.g. Norris v. Ireland* Series A, No. 142 (1991) 13 E.H.R.R. 186.

163 P. Guggenheim, *Traité de droit international publique* (Geneva, 1967) p. 66.

First, there is no provision in the Treaty for the supremacy of European Community law over national law. This can be compared to Article VI [2] of the Constitution of the United States:

> "This Constitution, and the Laws of the United States which shall be made in Pursuance thereof; and all Treaties made, or which shall be made, under the Authority of the United States, shall be the supreme Law of the Land; and the Judges in every State shall be bound thereby, any Thing in the Constitution or Laws of any State to the Contrary notwithstanding."

Secondly, some commentators[164] have considered that European Community law supremacy, whereby the Court of Justice concerns itself not only with the interpretation but also the application of European Community law by putting an obligation directly on the national judge to disapply national law in favour of conflicting European Community law, can be explained within public international law because of Article 177 (EC). This is a provision of an international treaty agreed between the Member States which effects Community Court intervention before the result of a denial of a European Community law right. Three arguments can be made in reply to this claim: the existence of a procedure is not sufficient basis for the general result; Article 177 (EEC) is not the basis of Case 6/64 *Costa v. ENEL*; and European Community law does not rely on public international law at all in order to establish its supremacy – indeed it expressly distances itself from it.

Thirdly, the insistence by the Court of Justice on the specificity of European Community law has allowed, it is often asserted,[165] dualist countries (Italy, Germany, the United Kingdom, Ireland, and Denmark) to accept direct effect and supremacy whilst maintaining their traditional attitude to public international law. The thesis here is that this is not accurate, since dualist countries have not accepted the doctrine of supremacy as European Community law sees it, and indeed cannot unless they cease to be dualist at least as regards European Community law, nor has European Community law avoided all conflict with monist countries, France being the example studied.[166]

---

[164] *e.g.* D. Wyatt (1982) *op. cit.* above, n.4; B. De Witte "Retour à *Costa* La primauté du droit communautaire à la lumière du droit international" (1984) *Revue Trimestrielle de Droit Européen* 425 at pp. 431–433.

[165] *e.g.* by P. Pescatore (1974) *op. cit.* above, n.19.

[166] However it may well be true as a tactical matter that the specificity of European Community law has helped the avoidance of conflicts, since national court's acceptance of European Community law does not mean acceptance of public international law, either as a matter of European Community law or as an unavoidable inference. The inference is avoidable because national law may perceive European Community law differently to public international law, at least for some purposes, since, for example, national law may specifically refer to international organisations or to European Community law in a way different to public international law in general.

Case 6/64 *Costa v. ENEL*[167]

Background to the Article 177 Reference

8–41 Mr Costa, "a litigious Milanese attorney",[168] did not want to pay his electricity bill of an amount equivalent (then) to $3.08. He claimed before the *Giudice Conciliatore* in Milan that he did not have to because the law nationalising the electricity industry was contrary to the Articles of the Treaty establishing the European Economic Community and the Italian Constitution. The *Giudice Conciliatore* made references to both the Court of Justice and the Constitutional Court ("*Corte Costituzionale*").

The Constitutional Court ruled in a judgment dated 24 February–7 March 1964[169] that because the Treaty establishing the European Economic Community was ratified in Italy by ordinary law[170] and because nationalisation was brought about by ordinary law, the question before the *Giudice Conciliatore* was to be resolved simply by the application of the usual rule *lex posterior derogat priori.* Therefore the question of a possible infringement of the Treaty as a consequence of the domestic nationalising law went only to the international responsibility of the State, and consequently the Article 177 (EEC) reference was pointless.

Advocate-General Lagrange saw that this put in issue "the constitutional relations between the European Economic Community and its Member States"[171] and would have "disastrous consequences"[172] for the future of the Common Market.

The problem here was already implicitly answered in Case 26/62 *Van Gend en Loos,* which was even more radical a judgment than it is given credit for. There are four important points here:

- First, Case 6/64 *Costa* did not "have to happen" in the sense usually asserted, which is that if Case 6/64 *Costa* had not happened Case 26/62 *Van Gend en Loos* would become meaningless because individual European Community law rights would not be enforced and the individual would be left without a remedy, and European Community law would not be applied uniformly (and therefore Case 6/64 *Costa* was a logical extension of Case 26/62 *Van Gend en Loos* and that is sufficient basis). In reply to this it is to be agreed that without Case 6/64 *Costa* the effect of Case 26/62 *Van Gend en Loos* would have been lessened. But without Case 6/64 *Costa* the European Community law right would still exist, just as a right under the European Convention of Human Rights and Fundamental Freedoms still exists even

167 Case 6/64 [1964] E.C.R. 585.
168 E. Stein, "Toward Supremacy of Treaty – Constitution by Judicial Fiat in the European Economic Community" (1965) 48 *Rivista di Diritto Internazionale* 3 at p. 4.
169 The decision of the Court of Justice was on July 15, 1964.
170 Case 6/64 *Costa v. ENEL* [1964] E.C.R. 585 at 605.
171 *ibid.* at 600.
172 *ibid.* at 605.

when it is denied. It might not be uniformly applied until, for example, Italy and any other Member State which denied the right changed its law *sua sponte* or following a declaration by the Court of Justice in an action brought by the Commission pursuant to Article 169 (EC) or by a Member State pursuant to Article 170 (EC). This ought to result in uniformity, at least in theory. So Case 6/64 *Costa* did not "have to" happen as a matter of usual legal reasoning.

- Secondly, Case 6/64 *Costa* did not have to happen because two wrongs do not make a right. If Case 26/62 *Van Gend en Loos* was going to cause disuniformity, then that deprives that decision of one of its supporting reasons, rather than providing a supporting reason for another decision.

- Thirdly, Case 6/64 *Costa* did have to happen as a matter of securing the goals as set out in Case 26/62 *Van Gend en Loos*, and so as a matter of the European Community legal reasoning which Case 26/62 *Van Gend en Loos* championed. The uniformity the Court is looking for is not theoretical, but actual and in application, because the goal of the Common Market is both a goal for the shape of the legal order and a goal for the shape of the markets and polities of Europe, a common market which will exist and a law which will exist autonomously from all other legal orders, yet be effective through their agencies. However these reasons for the "had to happen", which were indeed those given by the Court itself, are the same as for many other cases – the securing of objectives and uniformity.

- Fourthly, Case 6/64 *Costa* did have to happen because it was predicted by the doctrinal innovation which is special to Case 26/62 *Van Gend en Loos*. This is the holding that European Community law rights both arose and had to be enforced before national courts independently of national law. Case 6/64 *Costa* made clear the denial of the effect of the *lex posterior*. But Case 26/62 *Van Gend en Loos* had already established, if not made clear, the denial of the necessity of the *lex anterior*, and the duty on national courts to give effect to European Community law rights. Therefore, as far as European Community law was concerned, the *lex posterior* could derogate from the *lex anterior* without affecting the European Community law right.

It has been commented that the real message behind Case 106/77 *Simmenthal*, the case taken as the clearest exposition of the doctrines of direct effect and supremacy, was "that 'direct' application (and indeed 'direct' effects) means what it says: provided the machinery exists to give domestic effect to the Community Treaties, then rights and obligations flowing directly from those Treaties or legislation made under them are no concern of national law and are not affected by it".[173] But this is in fact a restriction of the prin-

---

[173] J. Usher, "Current Survey: Legal Order of the Communities: *Simmenthal*" (1978) *European Law Review* 214 at p. 217.

ciple established in Case 26/62 *Van Gend en Loos* that existing national "machinery" can be used to enforce European Community law rights pursuant to European Community law, and as Case 28/67 *Molkerei-Zentrale Westfalen* made clear, pursuant to a European Community law power and authority. The fact that "the Court failed to specify that these rights must prevail over conflicting national legislation"[174] does not indicate judicial reluctance. In Case 26/62 *Van Gend en Loos* the Court established the constitutional structure of European Community law which provides for both supremacy over any national law, not only subsequent legislation but also national constitutional law.

Admissibility and the Structure of Argument

8–42 On the basis of the judgment of the Constitutional Court, Italy objected to the admissibility of the Article 177 (EEC) reference, and submitted that an examination of an infringement by a Member State of its Community obligations through its domestic law had to take place via Articles 169 and 170 (EEC). The Court treated Italy's submissions on admissibility as three: inadmissibility because the intention was to get a ruling on the validity of national law, inadmissibility because the ruling was unnecessary, and inadmissibility because the national court had to apply national law.

These three submissions are all based on a public international law view of supremacy and international responsibility and go to the effect of the Court's ruling under Article 177 (EEC).

The Court dismissed the second submission by simply holding that it could not second-guess the referring court. This was a straightforward tactical move on the Court's part which was part of its evolution of judicial policy. It simply reversed this holding when it became inexpedient.[175] Although this work does not focus on judicial policy, and so the rejection of the other two submissions are the focus of this subsection, the fact that the Court rejected Italy's legal argument on policy grounds is support for the importance of securing objectives as both the Court's basis for decisions and its *modus operandi*.

It is important to point out here that if the Court had adopted the Wyatt/De Witte/public international law/internationalist Article 177 (EEC) approach, the Court would have decided the case by boot strapping. Italy said that

---

174 E. Stein, "Toward Supremacy of Treaty – Constitution by Judicial Fiat in the European Economic Community" (1965) 48 *Rivista di Diritto Internazionale* 3 at p. 11.

175 In Case 104/79 *Foglia v. Novello* [1980] E.C.R. 745, the Court of Justice held that it would not entertain a reference in the context of a collusive action. In Joined Cases C–422–424/93, *Erasun et al. v. Instituto Nacional de Empleo* [1995] E.C.R. I–1567, the Court of Justice held that it is for the Court, in order to confirm its own jurisdiction, to examine the conditions in which the case has been referred to it by the national court. The problems which may be entailed in the exercise of the power of appraisal of whether to make a reference by the national court, and the relations which the national court maintains with the Court of Justice within the framework of Article 177 (EC), are governed exclusively by European Community law.

because of the relationship of national law to European Community law the answers to the questions can have no meaning within this procedure, so the questions are inadmissible. The Court would have had to reply that because of this procedure, coming before the national court has decided, the constitutional relationship between national law and European Community law is such that the answers are relevant and therefore the questions via this procedure are admissible. Internationalists could say that this is not incompatible with public international law because it is based upon a provision in an international treaty agreed between States which specifies an unusual, although not unheard of,[176] procedure which allows the international jurisdiction to pronounce before the result and which has as its consequence a different effect on national law.

However, the structure of the Court's judgment is different and indeed more rational: because of the constitutional relationship between European Community law and national law, the answers are relevant because the national judge must disapply national law, and consequently the questions are admissible. The Court, not only in the reasons it gives for its constitutional doctrine, but also in the structure of its argument, distances itself from public international law. The Court reached this result by establishing the constitutional developments for which Case 6/64 *Costa* is famous, all under the analytical heading in the decision "On the application of Article 177".

The Role of the Court of Justice: Interpreter or Applier of European Community law?

8–43 The Court rejected Italy's first submission – that the reference was inadmissible because the intention was to get a ruling on the validity of national law – holding:

> "This provision gives the Court no jurisdiction either to apply the Treaty to a specific case or to decide upon the validity of a provision of domestic law in relation to the Treaty, as it would be possible for it to do under Article 169".[177]

There are two points here.

8–44 *Validity of National Law* First, the Court considers that it cannot decide on the validity of national law because its role under Article 177 (EEC) is to give an interpretation of Community law. In the earlier case of Case 6/60 *Humblet*, the Court had considered the basis and extent of the Court's jurisdiction under the equivalent Treaty establishing the European Coal and Steel Community provision, holding:

> "the Court has no jurisdiction to annul legislative or administrative measures of one of the Member States.

---

[176] Opinion of the Permanent Court of International Justice on the *Competence of the Courts of Danzig* (1928) Reports Series B, no. 15.

[177] Case 6/64 *Costa v. ENEL* [1964] E.C.R. 585 at 592–593.

> The Treaty establishing the European Coal and Steel Community is based on the principle of a strict separation of the powers of the Community institutions and those of the authorities of the Member States.
>
> Community law does not grant to the institutions of the Community the right to annul legislative or administrative measures adopted by a Member State."[178]

What is an extraordinary assertion of jurisdiction in Case 6/64 *Costa* is that the Court of Justice considers that it can decide on the validity of national law at all, stating it would be possible in an Article 169 (EEC) action. The assertion has never been followed up by the Court and it has never held a national law invalid.[179] This jurisdiction is in sharp contrast to holding that national law is no defence, or that its application is an illegality. The jurisdiction to hold a law, as distinct from its enforcement, to be invalid, tends to imply the jurisdiction to hold it void as a result of its invalidity. By asserting a jurisdiction to consider the validity of national law, the Court is therefore distancing European Community law radically from public international law. The Court suggested the same jurisdiction in Case 106/77 *Simmenthal*[180] holding that European Community law precluded the valid adoption of new legislative measures to the extent of their incompatibility with European Community law. If the legislative measure could not be validly adopted, the implication is that once adopted it would be invalid.

8–45 *Application of European Community Law* Secondly, although the Court does not apply the law in a preliminary reference, it is very much concerned with how the law is applied, not just with what the law is. Although the Court does not decide in an Article 177 (EC) reference on either the validity of the national law or who wins or loses the action in national court, it does concern itself with more than mere interpretation – it concerns itself with how the national court applies the Treaty, because it imposes a duty directly on national courts ("national courts must") to apply directly effective European Community law rights in preference to their national law.

This is a major difference to public international law and results in direct stress in national law. That there exists a stress to national law is clear, and this will be explored in Parts III to V.

The difference to public international law cannot merely be explained, as Wyatt indicates,[181] by the timing of the intervention by the Court of Justice to make the ruling. Certainly, the timing is important, but the Court could just declare that European Community law means such and such and the Member State is obliged not to conflict in the result required by this mean-

---

178 Case 6/60 *Humblet* [1960] E.C.R. 559 at 568.

179 Vaughan denies that the Court has such a jurisdiction at all: D. Vaughan (ed.), *Law of the European Communities* (London: Butterworths, 1990) 2/60, Issue 2.

180 See below, para. 8–58, Case 106/77 *Simmenthal*.

181 D. Wyatt (1982) *op. cit.* above, n.4.

ing. The fact that an act of a State organ, such as a national court, gives rise to international responsibility (Article 6 of the International Law Commission's proposed code on state responsibility for internationally wrongful acts) does not mean that the organs of State have a public international law duty. The public international law duty falls on the Member State as a subject of public international law. The rejection of this fundamental tenet of public international law by the Court of Justice is a constitutional rejection of the governing of the relation between Member States by public international law (that is, by European Community law as a category of public international law).

It is often asserted that the Court of Justice does not mind how, in terms of restructuring or ignoring national law, the national courts arrive at the correct application of European Community law. This is constitutionally different from the more limited position where the Court of Justice would not mind how the national courts reached a result which accorded with European Community law.

The Basis for Supremacy

8–46 *The Text of the Judgment* It is in rejecting Italy's third submission – inadmissibility because the national court had to apply national law – that the Court sets out its argument for internal or European Community law supremacy, relying on the interrelated concepts of integration, spirit of the Treaty, uniformity, objectives, transfers, sovereignty and nature of European Community law, and rejecting both external or public international law supremacy and public international law as the basis of European Community law supremacy. Although the analysis made here does not follow the judgment blow for blow, it may be helpful to the reader to set out the following passages, with numbering added.

"1. By contrast with ordinary international treaties, the EEC Treaty has created its own legal system which, on the entry into force of the Treaty, became an integral part of the legal systems of the Member States and which their courts are bound to apply.
2. By creating a Community of unlimited duration, having its own institutions, its own personality, its own legal capacity and a capacity of representation on the international plane and, more particularly, real powers stemming from a limitation of sovereignty or a transfer of powers from the States to the Community, the Member States have limited their sovereign rights, albeit within limited fields, and have thus created a body of law which binds both their nationals and themselves.
3. The integration into the laws of each Member State of provisions which derive from the Community, and more generally the terms and the spirit of the Treaty, make it impossible for the States, as a corollary, to accord precedence to a unilateral and subsequent measure over a legal system accepted by them on a basis of reciprocity. Such a measure cannot therefore be inconsistent with that legal system. The executive force of a Community law cannot vary from one State to another in deference to subsequent

domestic laws, without jeopardising the attainment of the objectives of the Treaty set out in Article 5(2) and giving rise to the discrimination prohibited by Article 7 [now Article 6 (EC)].

4. The obligations undertaken under the Treaty establishing the Community would not be unconditional, but merely contingent, if they could be called in question by subsequent legislative acts of the signatories . . . .
5. The precedence of Community law is confirmed by Article 189, whereby a regulation 'shall be binding' and 'directly applicable in all Member States'. This provision, which is subject to no reservation, would be quite meaningless if a State could unilaterally nullify its effects by means of a legislative measure which could prevail over Community law.
6. It follows from all these observations that the law stemming from the Treaty, an independent source of law, could not, because of its special and original nature, be overridden by domestic legal provisions, however framed, without being deprived of its character as Community law and without the legal basis of the Community itself being called into question.
7. The transfer by the States from their domestic legal system to the Community legal system of the rights and obligations arising under the Treaty carries with it a permanent limitation of their sovereign rights, against which a subsequent unilateral act incompatible with the concept of the Community cannot prevail. Consequently Article 177 is to be applied regardless of any domestic law, whenever questions relating to the interpretation of the Treaty arise."[182]

Professor Rudden has remarked:

> "Thus the Court affirms that Community law is like Frankenstein's monster: independent of its creator, imbued with a life of its own, supreme throughout the States' territories, and immune from attack by their laws and constitutions."[183]

8–47 *Rejection of Public International Law* The Court of Justice rejects public international law not just by implication and in the result, but explicitly in paragraph (1), by contrasting the Treaty establishing the European Economic Community with "ordinary international treaties". But the Court goes further in its explicit rejection than in Case 26/62 *Van Gend en Loos*: by replacing the Case 26/62 *Van Gend en Loos* formulation ("new legal order of international law") with "own legal order" the Court implies that not only is European Community law not "ordinary" public international law, it is not public international law at all. According to De Witte this is a "flagrant contradiction" with its former judgment to let it be known that European Community law has broken from its mooring with public international law, the full articulation of which was left to doctrine.[184] This doctrinal articulation was achieved in no small part by judges writing extra-curially and being cited by Advocates-General. This reformulation is reinforced by the Court

---

182 Case 6/64 *Costa v. ENEL* [1964] E.C.R. 585 at 593–594.
183 B. Rudden, *Basic Community Cases* (Oxford: Clarendon Press, 1987) p. 52.
184 B. de Witte (1984) *op. cit.* above, n.164 at p. 445–446.

basing its judgment on the "special and original nature" of European Community law (paragraph (6)) despite the fact that it is law "stemming from the Treaty". The description of the Treaty as "an independent source of law" therefore seems to imply independence not only from national law but also from public international law, not in historical origin but in normative order.

If European Community law is overridden by domestic law before a domestic Court, this deprives it of its character of European Community law and calls the basis of the Community into question (paragraph (6)), which is not the case for public international law. This threat to the basis of the Community was also highlighted by the Advocate-General.[185]

The Court does make oblique reference to the principles of *pacta sunt servanda* and reciprocity in paragraph (3). Suffice to add here[186] that the Member States could equally well have accepted a legal system which had external or international supremacy on the basis of reciprocity. Their signing of the treaties on the basis of reciprocity does not ground this judgment. To this can be added the later rejection of the principle of reciprocity by the Court.[187]

8–48 *Integration and Spirit* The threat of calling the basis of the Community into question is because, in contrast to public international law, the European Community legal order is an "integral part" of Member States' "legal systems" (paragraph (1)). There are five points here:

1. The contrast between the use of the word "order" and "system" implies that European Community law is at the peak of the pyramid of norms in the legal order applying in national courts. This does not mean that European Community law claims that the normativity of purely domestic laws does not derive independently from European Community law. However the contrast conveys the idea that European Community law applying in the national order does so because of the European Community law pyramid of norms.

2. The contrast also reinforces European Community law's separation from public international law. European Community law is not a mere subsystem in the public international legal order; it constitutes its own legal order.

3. The assertion that the integration of European Community law depends on the entry into force of the Treaties rather than on national law states in broader terms the central thesis of Case 26/62 *Van Gend en Loos.*

4. Integration of European Community law means also a direct duty on national courts to apply that law.

---

185 Costa 6/64 *Costa v. ENEL* [1964] E.C.R. 585 at 606.
186 See above, paras. 7–4 and 7–5, "*Pacta Sunt Servanda*".
187 See above, paras. 7–6 *et seq.* "Reciprocity".

5. The autonomy of European Community law is reinforced because the concept of integration appears to be based largely on an act of will by the Court. The Court does highlight some characteristics of the European Community legal order in paragraph (2), although it is not clear whether these are offered as reasons for integration or not. These characteristics have a meaning particular to European Community law: institutions, legal personality, and legal capacity in European Community law and in public international law and subjects both State and individuals. These characteristics not only *per se* reinforce the autonomy of European Community law, they are relied on, as is the case here, by the Court in its construction of constitutional doctrines on the autonomy and nature of European Community law.

The Court relies directly on integration and the spirit of the Treaty in paragraph (3) to establish as a corollary the proposition of European Community law supremacy. As a corollary, that proposition flows from integration and spirit without the need for further proof (which is fortunate).

8–49 *Sovereignty* The other characteristic mentioned in paragraph (2) is sovereignty. The use by the Court of Justice of this concept develops beyond its use in Case 26/62 *Van Gend en Loos.* The Court refers to sovereignty in paragraphs (2) and (7). First, the Court refers to transfers from the States, not just a limitation in national legal orders and an endowment of the institutions, which would be more compatible with public international law because the endowment of public international law powers could arguably arise by virtue of Member States' treaty action in public international law, and limitations by action in national law during ratification. The idea of transfer (the Court uses every phraseology but "transfer of sovereignty") appears rationally to ground integration in the sense that integration is the return effect of the exercise of the Community's sovereign powers and not the effect of national law recognising to varying extent European Community law. But such an argument does not cover the constituent treaty which established the transfers and created the European Economic Community.

De Witte asserts in his ground-breaking analysis[188] that the transfer of competences has a very tenuous link with European Community law supremacy[189] because the transfer of competences operated by a treaty is not opposable against signatory States except so far as the treaty is endowed with supremacy, and therefore the Court is putting the cart before the horse.[190] But this argument does not appear to hold up so well for secondary European Community law. Whilst it is generally accurate that to create judicially European Community constitutional law by putting the cart ("Europe") before the horse

188 B. de Witte (1984) *op. cit.* above, n.164.

189 *ibid.* at p. 442.

190 *ibid.* at p. 438, para. 1.

(European Community law) is the Court's *modus operandi* – moved by "the spirit of the Treaties" in a particular *séance*, it envisions the objectives of Europe and develops law to reach them – the supremacy of secondary European Community law, counter-intuitively, has a better claim to supremacy than the Treaty if it can be viewed as the exercise of transferred competence. However there is a more fundamental problem with taking issue with Case 6/64 *Costa*: Case 26/62 *Van Gend en Loos* denied the need for a *lex anterior* and established that a European Community law duty operated directly on the national courts to enforce European Community law rights, and it logically follows that a conflict between a national law right and a European Community law right results not in the invalidity of the national law but in the national court duty to uphold the European Community law right. The point to which one must return is not Case 6/64 *Costa* but Case 26/62 *Van Gend en Loos*.

The Court also states, without further explanation or reasoning, that the transfer results in a permanent limitation of Member States' sovereignty. This could conceivably have importance for amendment of the Treaty.

8–50 *Uniformity and Effectiveness: Executive Uniformity* In the third sentence of paragraph (3) the Court relies also on the necessity for uniformity in executive force to attain the objectives of the Treaty as a ground for the doctrine of supremacy. This is important because it shows the following: that the nature of uniformity with which the Court is concerned is not mere theoretical uniformity but uniformity conceptually, indeed organically, linked to effectiveness; that the securing of objectives is dependent on such uniformity; and that objectives, effectiveness, and uniformity combined can form a legitimation for the evolution of constitutional doctrine.[191] This notion of uniformity in execution does not accord with the reality which is that European Community law is not applied everywhere in the same way for many reasons.[192]

The then President of the Commission of the European Economic Community gave the Commission's opinion on this case: without supremacy "to acknowledge the supremacy of Community law would be no more than a courteous gesture, carrying no obligations. In reality the Member States could do what they liked".[193] The President also pointed to the political importance of the concept of uniformity underpinning the constitutional doctrine:

---

[191] The following point, although outside the European Community law perspective, ought to mentioned here and is returned to in Part VI "Future Directions". The achievement of executive uniformity of European Community law through constitutional doctrine and a judicial policy developed by the Court of Justice, aided by the Commission, and national courts is extraordinary because the Community has no executive. Although those who are political partisans of deeper integration consider this to be solely the result of courageous and innovative jurisprudence, the achievement depends on the developed sense of the rule of law in national courts.

[192] See below, Parts III, IV and VI.

[193] English translation from European Community Bull. 10–11 August 1964, quoted in E. Stein "Uniformity and Diversity in a Divided Power System: the United States'

> "a unified solution valid for the whole Community must be provided for the order of precedence here mentioned. Any attempt to solve the order of precedence differently to accord with the idiosyncrasies of the Member States, their constitution and political structure, runs counter to the unifying character of European integration, and thus to the fundamental principles of our Community. The Commission thinks it particularly important to note this fact."[194]

Pescatore has commented that the dual concepts of purpose and European Community law as system have meant that the Court, by invoking the principle of *effet utile*, has been able to arrive at "constructive decisions concerning the definition of the competence and powers of the Community".[195] Pescatore makes clear in the following sentences that "constructive" means providing the means of attainment of a union.

8–51 *Objectives* This reasoning – that constitutional conclusions flow from the objectives of integration and, partly as means and partly as definition of legal integration, from the uniformity and efficacy of Community law – is illustrated also by the Advocate-General, who states that "[f]or encroachment on the part of national authorities, *there must also be a sanction*",[196] and deduces from this "must", which is really an "ought", that there is in European Community law a sanction: national courts have a duty to disapply conflicting law. (The same reasoning at an even more general level is provided by Pescatore: the case law of the Court of Justice expresses "with ever increasing clarity" that "the vision of the objectives [of Europe] must be accompanied by a corresponding reality of powers".[197]) The Advocate-General also highlights more explicitly the link between integration and objectives:

> "the system of the Common Market is based upon the creation of a legal system separate from that of the Member States, but nevertheless intimately and even organically tied to it in such a way that the mutual and constant respect for the respective jurisdictions of the Community and national bodies is one of the fundamental conditions of a proper functioning of the system instituted by the Treaty and, consequently, of the realization of the aims of the Community."[198]

As considered above, in paragraph (6) the Court relies on the "special and original nature" of European Community law to establish European Community law supremacy, which is itself a conclusion from objectives via the observations on integration, spirit, and uniformity.

Experience" (1986) *Washington Law Review* 1081, n.66. The opinion implies a low opinion of the efficacy of public international law, as well as a low opinion of the Member States. "In reality the Member States could do what they liked" anyway, unless by "Member States" is meant the executive branch of governments only. But even these could "do what they liked" if not for respect for the rule of law.

194 *ibid.*

195 P. Pescatore (1974) *op. cit.* above, n.19, at p. 41.

196 Case 6/64 *Costa v. ENEL* [1964] E.C.R. 585 at 603 (original emphasis).

197 P. Pescatore (1974) *op. cit.* above, n.19, at p. 42.

198 Case 6/64 *Costa v. ENEL* [1964] E.C.R. 585 at 605–606.

De Witte considers that there is a second logic in Case 6/64 *Costa*: the Court deduces the specific nature of Community law from the necessity to assure internal supremacy.[199] Putting this point of view in terms of objectives, one could say that the reasons are decided upon after the objective and result of internal supremacy has been selected, in order to reach that objective and result.

8–52 *Provisions of the Treaty* The Court mentions also the provisions of the Treaty establishing the European Economic Community in the first sentence of paragraph (3) without specifying which provisions. As stated above, there is no provision, unlike in a federal constitution, on this issue. Specific provisions are mentioned in paragraphs (4) and (5). Suffice to say, in regard to paragraph (4), that there is nothing unusual in unconditional obligations in public international law treaties being contingent for their execution on national law.

As regards Article 189 (EEC) (which the Court refers to only for confirmation) and direct applicability, three points can be made on the marginal nature of this textual argument. First, the provision would not be meaningless: secondary legal instruments would just not be as effective without supremacy. Second, the Article 189 (EEC) argument is expressed to apply only to Regulations and to no other formal source of European Community law rights (this case concerned articles of the Treaty establishing the European Economic Community), and would actually offer a ground for withholding supremacy from European Community law rights which arise directly from Directives, whereas the potential of Directives to result in rights either against the State or against third parties has been established and expanded, and has given rise to the Joined Cases C–6 & 9/90 *Francovich* remedy. Third, if one accepts the Court's interpretation of Article 189 (EEC) on the direct applicability of Regulations, this interpretation runs opposite to the result in Case 26/62 *Van Gend en Loos* (direct effect and individual rights derived from Treaty provisions) on which the Court is building: since direct applicability is only mentioned in regard to Regulations, it may be concluded that European Community law was only to be directly applied when the Council had decided to act, interpret and implement a part of the Treaty framework by this type of instrument.

The point here is that Article 189 (EEC) provides little or no textual basis for the supremacy doctrine. However, direct applicability (in its broader constitutional form as expounded in Case 26/62 *Van Gend en Loos*[200] and not in a form dependent on Regulations or Article 189) is an important argument for European Community law supremacy, as the analysis of *Van Gend en Loos*

---

199 B. de Witte (1984) *op. cit.* above, n.164, at p. 445.
200 [1963] E.C.R. 1.

has hopefully made clear, because it denies the necessity for any grounding national law.

The Court also throws in the possibility of discrimination prohibited by Article 7 (EEC) (paragraph (3)). But this is not a ground because if there were such discrimination, this would constitute a breach of the Treaty, and give rise to the international liability of the State.

Summary

8–53 The constitutional doctrines brought to the fore so strikingly in Case 6/64 *Costa* by the legal background to that case were established in Case 26/62 *Van Gend en Loos.* With that reservation, Case 6/64 *Costa* is brilliantly summarised by Stein in an article published as early as 1965:

> "The judgement in the *Costa* case may be interpreted as holding that Community law (that is, the treaty and the regulations) is superior to national law, including national constitutions, not only in the Community legal order but also in the national legal orders and that the supremacy rule is directly and immediately applicable by national courts, and any contrary national provisions regarding ordinary treaties notwithstanding. If this is the correct interpretation, it is perhaps the first time in history that a court established by an international treaty has asserted its power to determine with effect not only in the 'international' (or Community) legal order but also in national law, the hierarchical value of the very norm to which it owes its existence. If one accepts the new doctrinal basis suggested above, the Court could be said to have dealt with the Community treaty as if it were a constitution rather than a treaty and in effect *to have rejected the public international law rationale for its power.*"[201]

It should be noted that the Council of Ministers gave their political backing to the Case 6/64 *Costa* decision, acknowledging the "political importance of a faithful application of Community law in the member States for the establishment of the Common Market and more generally for the realization of the objectives of the European treaties."[202]

The Development and Expansion of *Costa v. ENEL*

Supremacy over National Law of Whatever Nature

8–54 The cases of the Court of Justice which deal directly with the primacy of European Community law over national constitutional law have considerable shock value for national lawyers, sometimes initiate or necessitate

---

201 E. Stein, "Toward Supremacy of Treaty – Constitution by Judicial Fiat in the European Economic Community" (1965) 48 *Rivista di Diritto Internazionale* 3 at p. 24. Stein goes on to compare Case 6/64 *Costa* to a U.S. Supreme Court decision where that court replaced an international law rationale for a doctrine with a new one drawn from the "constitutional underpinnings" of the federation.

202 Reply to written question No. 27, J.O. 2161/64, 11 August 1964.

national constitutional law change, and provide a focus point for considerable constitutional soul-searching. But these cases do not constitute a doctrinal advance for European Community law, although their acceptance in national constitutional law may constitute a significant success for the Court's judicial policy and an advance in the factual executive uniformity of European Community law. As stated above, the doctrinal development took place in Case 26/62 *Van Gend en Loos* with the denial of the relevance of national law and the imposition of a direct duty on national tribunals and was reinforced by Case 6/64 *Costa*. The Court actually stated in Case 6/64 *Costa* that European Community law (specifically, Article 177 (EEC)) was to be applied regardless of "*any* domestic law" (emphasis added), although admittedly it is not certain whether this phrase means "any legislation whatever" or "national law of any nature".

This issue is reconsidered below in paragraphs 8–59 *et seq.* and particularly in Part VI, where there is an analysis of a conflict between a written European Community law right as interpreted in the light of unwritten European Community law and a national constitutional law fundamental right as interpreted in the light of national constitutional natural law.

Outside of the area of fundamental rights the Court first pronounced directly on these issues in Article 169 (EEC) proceedings. The judgments are interesting because the Court refused, as is usual for a public international law tribunal, to countenance national constitutional law as a defence to a Member State failure in its Treaty obligations, holding that the State is liable for a failure of any of its institutions, judicial, legislative, etc.[203] However, at the same time and in contrast to public international law, the Court in Article 169 (EEC) proceedings imposes a direct duty on the State's institutions to apply the conflicting European Community law rule.[204]

A good example of a decision which falls squarely within long-established jurisprudence having shock value is Case C–213/89 *Factortame*.[205] In that case the conflict was between the effectiveness of European Community law rights and an old common law rule of constitutional importance to the effect that an interim injunction could not be granted against the Crown,[206] more particularly to suspend an Act of Parliament because of the sovereignty of Parliament and the separation of powers. This common law rule was supported in the case by the common law principle of statutory interpretation that an Act of Parliament was in conformity with European Community law

---

203 Case 77/69 *Commission v. Belgium* [1970] E.C.R. 237 at 243, para. 15; Case 48/71 *Commission v. Italy* [1972] E.C.R. 527 at 535, para. 9; Case 52/75 *Commission v. Italy* [1976] E.C.R. 277 at 285, para. 14.

204 See below, para. 8–56.

205 [1990] E.C.R. I–2433.

206 The Court of Justice did not specify the issue if injunctions were to be a requirement of European Community law: what was required was effective interim relief, which is more general and does not necessarily imply an injunction. This point has been made by Professor A. Barav, in a series of lectures at Oxford University, 1996.

until a decision on its incompatibility was given. The problem was similar, *mutatis mutandis*, to the Italian problem in Case 106/77 *Simmenthal*.[207] The judgment of the Court of Justice was distinctive because 16 of its 23 paragraphs were taken up with setting out carefully the English legal and factual position, and only seven to disposing of the case by relying directly on Case 106/77 *Simmenthal* (paragraphs 18 and 20) and the necessity to ensure the full effectiveness of European Community law (paragraph 21). The House of Lords decision[208] subsequently does not at all subscribe to the Court of Justice's doctrinal viewpoint since it maintains a strict dualist approach: European Community law is in force by virtue of Article 2(1) of the United Kingdom's European Communities Act 1972. However the House of Lords reached a position which will avoid immediate conflicts because it made clear that the doctrine of implied repeal had no application to the 1972 Act, but that a conflicting statute was to be read as if it incorporated a clause stating that it was to be without prejudice to the directly enforceable rights of nationals of any Member State of the European Economic Community. This was even though the purpose of the conflicting statute was precisely to deny European Community law rights of Spanish fishermen. The case is "surely a landmark in [the British] constitutional system",[209] but it was waiting to happen since Case 26/62 *Van Gend en Loos*.

No Power to Strike Down a Conflicting National Law

8–55 Although there is a duty to repeal, and not just a duty to disapply, a conflicting national law rule, unlike the Supreme Court of the United States the Court of Justice asserts no power to strike down the conflicting national law rule.[210] But this does not affect the application of Community law and its uniformity and effect because the national judge has a direct (that is independently from national law) European Community law obligation to apply the European Community rule.

The absence of this power is wholly consistent with the approach of the Court of Justice, although the description of European Community law as integrated into national law implies that one of the rules – European Community law or national law – must be invalid. The description "integration" is misleading in this context. As a statement of the national law perception, it is more correct to say either that European Community law is in force by transformation, or as public international law by virtue of recognition in national constitutional law. As a statement of the European Community law perception, it is more correct to say that European Community law is integrated into the duty of national authorities, judicial, legislative, and administrative, to uphold the law.

207 Case 106/77 [1978] E.C.R. 629.

208 [1990] 2 A.C. 85.

209 D. Wyatt and A. Dashwood (1993) *op. cit.* above, n.3, p. 58.

210 This has been considered in part above in para. 8–44, "Role of the Court of Justice – Validity of National Law".

There is no reason, on this interpretation, why a national law rule cannot be disapplied where it conflicts with European Community law, and applied where it does not, or why, if the European Community law rule is repealed or changed, the national law rule cannot be reapplied in situations where its application was suspended by the national judge.

Requiring Abrogation of Conflicting National Law

8–56 The requirement imposed by the Court of Justice that national authorities invalidate or abrogate national rules is different to the invalidation or abrogation of national rules by the Court of Justice. The latter has been considered above, the former is considered here.

This obligation of rescission was stated arguably as early as Case 6/60 *Humblet* (on the law of the European Coal and Steel Community) where the ground given appeared to be national law:

> "This obligation is evident from the Treaty and from the Protocol [with which the national tax measure conflicted] which have the force of law in the Member States *following their ratification* and which take precedence over national law."[211]

Although Case 6/60 *Humblet* does not appear to depart radically from public international law, the development in thinking post-Case 26/62 *Van Gend en Loos* does and is clearly illustrated in Case 167/73 *Commission v. France*.[212] The Court of Justice held that a Member State had failed in its Community obligations under Article 48 (EEC) and the applicable Regulation in not abrogating a law which, although contrary to European Community law, was not applied. In such a situation there was no concrete denial of an individual's European Community law right. The Court considered that the uncertainty for those subject to the law created by the maintenance in force of the national legislative provision constituted an obstacle albeit a secondary obstacle, to the equality of access to employment,[213] despite the direction by the French government to the relevant authorities that nationals of Member States be treated as French nationals.[214] Rather, the internal legal order of the Member State was in a state incompatible with the European Community law constitutional principle of internal supremacy. The Court of Justice relied on Article 5 (EEC) because there is no supremacy clause as such. Article 5 provides:

> "Member States shall take all appropriate measures, whether general or particular, to ensure fulfillment of the obligations arising out of this Treaty or

---

211 Case 6/60 *Humblet v. Belgium* [1960] E.C.R. 559 at 569 (emphasis added).

212 [1974] E.C.R. 359. See also above, paras. 7–11 *et seq.*, "Obligation in the Result – Non-Transformation of Regulations.

213 [1974] E.C.R. 359 at 372–373.

214 However the uncertainty in this case was not any greater than the uncertainty where there is an actualised conflict between national law and European Community law and the potential for the denial of a European Community law right, but in cases like Case 6/64 *Costa v. ENEL* the Court of Justice does not declare that the national law must be abrogated, as distinct from disapplied.

> resulting from action taken by the institutions of the Community. They shall facilitate the achievement of the Community's tasks.
>
> They shall abstain from any measure which could jeopardise the attainment of the objectives of this Treaty."

This Article does not give any indication as to why a non-applied national law should not remain on the books.[215] Such a law could be contrary to the Member States' obligations or the general objectives of the Treaty only if these included a constitutional structure which aimed further than a result in compliance with European Community law, further than ensuring executive uniformity and thereby attainment of the Treaty objectives, to a constitutional situation with a tendency to federation, and in which in its current form the Member States are perpetually in a state of constitutional disobedience.

In general, the ruling of the Court of Justice in an Article 169 (EC) action is

> "a prohibition having the full force of law in the competent national authorities against applying a national rule recognized as incompatible with the Treaty and, if circumstances so require, an obligation on them to take all appropriate measures to enable Community law to be fully applied."[216]

Preemption

8–57 This federal doctrine[217] goes to the power of the national legislature, which it disempowers, and has no application in public international law since a State may adopt whatever national laws it likes, subject always to the declaration of the international responsibility of the State should such laws lead to results in conflict with the State's public international law obligations. However the Court moved quickly to establish such a doctrine in European Community law. In Case 14/68 *Wilhelm v. Bundeskartellamt*[218] the Court, grounding its judgment on executive uniformity, attainment of Treaty objectives, integration, European Community law as its own legal order, and the character of European Community law, held that:

> "It would be contrary to the nature of such a system to allow Member States to introduce or to retain measures capable of prejudicing the practical effectiveness of the Treaty."

---

215 There may be many reasons apart from political entropy for a Member State to want to keep a non-applied national law on the books, such as the application of that law to categories of persons not covered by the conflicting European Community law, *e.g.* those not holding Union citizenship.

216 Case 48/71 *Commission v. Italy* [1972] E.C.R. 527, para. 7; see also Joined Cases C 6 & 9/90 *Procureur de la Republique v. Waterkeyn* [1982] E.C.R. 4337 dealing particularly with the obligation of courts to "draw the necessary inferences" of a finding of incompatibility of national law with European Community law.

217 The doctrine of federal preemption in the United States has an additional aspect not found in European Community law because of the absence of federal jurisdiction, where state courts are prohibited from asserting jurisdiction where federal law occupies the field: *State v. McHorse* 85 N.M. 753, 517 P. 2d 75.

218 [1969] E.C.R. 1 at 14, para. 6.

The nature of the European Community legal order is therefore federal in this respect.

Case 106/77 *Simmenthal*[219]

8–58 This case neatly summarises the doctrines of direct effect, supremacy, and preemption and clarifies the national court's European Community law power and duty.[220] In Case 106/77 *Simmenthal* there was a conflict between competing rules of European Community law and national law, a conflict between legislative competences because both the European Community institutions and the Italian legislature had acted in the same area, and a clash between national and Community court jurisdictions. The Italian legal context is well described by Usher.[221] Suffice to state here that the Italian Constitutional Court had held that only it had the power to set aside a law posterior to the ratification law which conflicted with European Community law, which it would do on the grounds of unconstitutionality. A lower Italian Court asked in a preliminary reference whether pursuant to European Community law it was to disregard the law immediately. The Court of Justice held:

> "in accordance with the principle of the precedence of Community law, the relationship between provisions of the Treaty and directly applicable measures of the institutions on the one hand and the national law of the Member States on the other is such that those provisions and measures not only by their entry into force render automatically inapplicable any conflicting provision of current national law but – in so far as they are an integral part of, and take precedence in, the legal order applicable in the territory of each of the Member States – also preclude the valid adoption of new national legislative measures to the extent to which they would be incompatible with Community provisions."[222]

The Court of Justice goes on to consider that any other solution would imperil effectiveness of European Community law and the very foundations of the Community.[223] It then states its solution in terms of the power of the national court (which power is conferred by European Community law):

> "Accordingly any provision of a national legal system and any legislative, administrative or judicial practice which might impair the effectiveness of Community law by withholding from the national court having jurisdiction to apply such law the power to do everything necessary at the moment of its application to

---

219 Case 106/77 [1978] E.C.R. 629.

220 This question of power was first squarely addressed in Case 28/67 *Molkerei-Zentrale Westfalen* [1968] E.C.R. 143. See above para. 8–35.

221 J. Usher, "Current Survey: Legal Order of the Communities: *Simmenthal*" (1978) *European Law Review* 214.

222 Case 106/77 *Amministrazione delle Finanze dello Stato v. Simmenthal* [1978] E.C.R. 629 at 643, para. 17.

223 *ibid.* at 643, para. 18, the Court holds that any recognition of any legal effect of any national law which was incompatible with Community law would be a "denial of the obligations undertaken unconditionally and irrevocably by the Member States pursuant to the Treaty and would thus imperil the very foundations of the Community".

> set aside national legislative provisions which might prevent Community rules from having full force and effect are incompatible with those requirements which are the very essence of Community law."[224]

This incompatibility exists even if the threat to the full effectiveness of European Community law is "only temporary".[225]

Fundamental Rights

Public International Law Perception

8–59 There was no mention of fundamental rights in the Treaties establishing the European Communities, therefore there was no competence to consider them, save so far as they formed part of the general principles of public international law or *ius cogens*. But European Community law did not rely on these grounds to establish its fundamental rights jurisdiction. (Neither did it rely on national constitutional law.) The Treaty is to be contrasted with the European Convention for the Protection of Human Rights and Fundamental Freedoms, which sees human rights protection as a method for the achievement of the aim of the Council of Europe.[226]

European Community Law Perception

8–60 European Community law supremacy in the sphere of fundamental rights is worth a separate treatment from the establishment of the doctrines of individual rights and primacy, because:

- the development of this doctrine, six years after Case 26/62 *Van Gend en Loos*, is of separate constitutional importance, marking another leap along the road to legal federation in the rejection of public international law and in the establishment of European Community law's *sui generis* and *ex proprio vigore* characteristics[227];

---

224 *ibid.* at 644, para. 22.

225 *ibid.* at para. 23. Only temporary because the Constitutional Court would decide on the constitutionality of the conflicting Italian law. This holding has been refined, or reversed, by Joined Cases 143/88 and C–92/89 *Zuckerfabrik Süderdithmarschen* and *Zuckerfabrik Soest* [1991] E.C.R. I–415 and Case C–466/93 *Atlanta Fruchthandelsgesellschaft mbH e.a. v. Bundesamt für Ernährund und Forstwirtschaft* [1995] E.C.R. I–3761. See para. 8–38, above.

226 The Preamble provides:

> "Considering that the aim of the Council of Europe is the achievement of greater unity between its members and that one of the methods by which that aim is to be pursued is the maintenance and further realisation of human rights and fundamental freedoms."

227 According to a former president of the Court of Justice, the Court's fundamental rights jurisdiction has enabled it "to exercise a full judicial review comparable to that carried out by the Constitutional Court of a Federal State." – O. Due, "A Constitutional Court for the European Communities" in D. Curtin and D. O'Keeffee (eds.),

- the reasons given for the jurisprudential development of this doctrine, and the fact that it was developed by the Court of Justice without textual support of the Treaty establishing the European Economic Community, are important for ascertaining the legitimation of European Community law;
- European Community law fundamental rights extend to overruling any national law rule within an area of Community competence, and so they constitute a European Community law demand on national law.

Extension of European Community Law's Jurisdiction and Demands

8–61 The doctrine of European Community law fundamental rights has developed in several stages, which may be divided into six.[228]

First, no one foresaw initially the need for such a doctrine, probably for two reasons. First and most important, there was nothing in the Treaties to indicate that there could be a jurisdictional conflict between national courts and the Court of Justice over the application in national courts of the national constitution. As stated above, there were no Treaty articles founding the doctrines of supremacy or direct effect. Second, it may have appeared early on that the nature of the European Community was limited and could not give rise to problems of fundamental rights.

Secondly, the doctrine of fundamental rights then developed jurisprudentially when the absence of such a doctrine jeopardised the application of European Community law in national courts where such application was contrary to national fundamental rights protection.[229] This jurisprudential development appeared to be politically endorsed by the three other institutions in their Joint Declaration of 1977.[230] However the President of the Council signed the Helsinki Final Act on the basis of the Community competence in the field of commercial policy.[231] In the Preamble to the Single European Act, the Member States stated their determination to promote democracy on the basis of fundamental rights.[232] In the Preamble to the Treaty on

---

Constitutional Adjudication in European Community and National Law: Essays for the Hon. Mr. Justice T.F. O'Higgins (Dublin: Butterworth Ireland, 1992) p. 3 at 8.

228 For a different division, see F.G. Jacobs, "The Protection of Human Rights in the Member States of the European Community: the Impact on the Case Law of the Court" in J. O'Reilly (ed.) *Human Rights and Constitutional Law: Essays in Honour of Brian Walsh* (Dublin: Round Hall Press, 1992) p. 25.

229 Case 29/69 *Stauder v. City of Ulm* [1969] E.C.R. 419; Case 11/70 *Internationale Handelsgesellschaft* [1970] E.C.R. 1125. The protection of fundamental rights, once announced, perhaps mandated Case 43/75 *Defrenne v. SABENA* – see Rudden, *Basic Community Cases* (Oxford, 1987) p. 123.

230 [1977] O.J. C103/1.

231 D. Lasok and J.W. Bridge, *Law and Institutions of the European Community* (5th ed., Butterworths, 1991) p. 187.

232 For recitation of textual references to human rights see below, para. 8–63, "Textual Basis for General Principles".

European Union, the Member States confirmed their attachment to respect for human rights. There have been several political declarations, among them the Declaration on human rights by the European Council on 29 June 1991,[233] the Resolution on human rights, democracy, and development by the Council and the Member States meeting within the Council on 28 November 1991,[234] Conclusions on the Implementation of the Resolution on human rights, democracy, and development by the Council and the Member States on 18 November 1992, and the Statement by the European Union on human rights of 11 December 1993 on the occasion of the forty-fifth anniversary of the Universal Declaration of Human Rights.[235]

Thirdly, Member States' laws or executive actions fell to be disapplied and actions suspended in areas of Community competence where the rules or actions would be permissible derogations from substantive European Community law rules were there no conflict with European Community law fundamental rights.[236]

Fourthly, Member States' implementing rules must comply with the general principles of European Community law,[237] including fundamental rights.[238] This extension of European Community law control does not mean that it is contrary to European Community law for national law to control Member States' implementation of European Community law according to national fundamental rights, provided that the implementation taken by the Member State was not necessitated by European Community law obligations and the control does not otherwise jeopardise European Community law.

Fifthly, Member States' own fundamental rights which crossed an area of European Community competence fall to be tested against European Community fundamental rights, at least according to Advocate-General Van Gerven, who based himself squarely on established jurisprudence.[239]

Sixthly, fundamental rights were given Treaty protection, as distinct from jurisprudential development backed by political declaration, by the Treaty on European Union in two ways. First, a citizenship of the Union is established within the Treaty establishing the European Community (Article 8(1)) and brings with it what may be called European Community law fundamental rights, at least as regards the right to move and reside freely (Article 8a(1)) as well as the fundamental civic rights in elections[240]; secondly, the Union is to be bound

---

233 [1991] E.C. Bull. 6, Annex V.

234 [1991] E.C. Bull. 11, at 130, point 2.3.1.

235 [1992] E.C. Bull. 12, point 1.4.12.

236 Case 36/75 *Rutili v. Minister of the Interior* [1975] E.C.R. 1219 (concerning Article 48(3)); Case C–260/89 *Elliniki Radiophonia Tileorassi* [1991] E.C.R. I–2925 (the public policy proviso in Articles 66 and 56).

237 Case 77/81 *Zuckerfabrik* [1982] E.C.R. 681.

238 Case 5/88 *Wachauf* [1989] E.C.R. 2609.

239 Case 159/90 *Society for the Protection of Unborn Children v. Grogan* [1991] E.C.R. I–4685 (Opinion of Advocate–General Van Gerven).

240 See below, para. 9–2, "Citizenship – European Community Law Perception".

by fundamental rights (Article F(2) (EU)) but this Article is not cognisable by the Court of Justice (Article L (EU)) and to that extent does not form part of the European Community legal order.[241]

The future development of fundamental rights lies in two paths. First, they may become part of Community competence as such and any national rule conflicting must be disapplied, along the lines of the protection of constitutional rights in the United States. This has already happened with one right, the right to free movement of persons, but not as a matter of general doctrine. Secondly, the European Community may accede to the European Convention on Human Rights and Fundamental Freedoms and itself become bound by that Convention and judgments of the European Court of Human Rights,[242] although such accession could take place only after amendment to the European Convention[243] and to the Treaty establishing the European Community.[244]

Opinion 2/94 makes clear that the European Community has no human rights competence, express or implied, on which specific measures can be taken.

Basis of the Extension

Fundamental Rights as General Principles

8–62 The first point to be made about European Community law fundamental rights is that they are treated as general principles of European Community law. They concern the interpretation and application of other rules whose existence they presuppose. Since there was no statement of a fundamental rights competence or of fundamental rights, European Community law treated fundamental rights as principles, not as rules. There is no conceptual distinction in Community law between the textual source, juridical basis or role in the legal system of the various general principles recognised, for example between the principle of the protection of legitimate expectations as "a superior rule of law"[245] and the right to respect for private life.[246] The Court has declared "fundamental rights form an integral part of the general principles of law, the observance of which [the Court] ensures".[247] Thus to a large extent whether a certain rule is referred to as a general principle or as a fundamental

---

241 See further below, para. 8–63, "Textual Basis for General Principles".

242 On this proposition see K. Lenaerts, "Fundamental Rights to be Included in a Community Catalogue" (1991) 16 *European Law Review* 367.

243 Article 66(1) permits accession by members of the Council of Europe, membership of which is comprised of states only.

244 Opinion 2/94 *Accession by the Community to the European Convention for the Protection of Fundamental Rights and Freedoms* [1996] E.C.R. I–1759.

245 Case 74/74 *CNTA v. Commission* [1975] E.C.R. 533, para. 44. The Court has held a Regulation invalid to the extent that it denied the legitimate expectation of a dairy farmer – Case 120/86 *Mulder v. The Netherlands* [1988] E.C.R. 2321.

246 Case C–62/90 *Commission v. Germany* [1992] E.C.R. I–2575.

247 Case 4/73 *Nold v. Commission* [1974] E.C.R. 491 at 507.

right is largely a question of description, as is the categorisation of principles, for example of principles of the rule of law concerned with keeping the legal system in good legal order, principles of good administration, and the principle of equality.

This is illustrated by Case 63/83 *R. v. Kirk.*[248] Kirk was the master of a Danish fishing boat which had been intercepted by the British navy. He was prosecuted in English courts pursuant to a statutory order which was made during a gap in the Community organisation of fishery resources. A later Council Regulation purported to grant such orders retroactive validity. The Court held, first, that the statutory order had not been authorised under European Community law and, second, the Council Regulation could not validate the order *ex post facto.* The reason for this second holding neatly illustrates that the categorisation of general principles of European Community law is descriptive rather than determinative of normative hierarchy:

> "The principle that penal provisions may not have retroactive effect is one which is common to all the legal orders of the Member States and is enshrined in Article 7 of the European Convention for the Protection of Human Rights and Fundamental Freedoms as a fundamental right; it takes its place among the general principles of law whose observance is ensured by the Court of Justice."[249]

Textual Basis for General Principles

8–63 There are three provisions of the original Treaty in which the Court has been able to find the legal basis for giving the force of law to unwritten general principles of law:

- First and most important of these is Article 164 (EC):

  > "The Court of Justice shall ensure that in the interpretation and application of this Treaty the law is observed."

  Because of the counter-position of "the Treaty" and "the law", "the law" means more than just the provisions of the Treaty or the legislation thereunder. Article 164 (EC) is to European Community constitutional higher law doctrine what Article 5 (EC) is to European Community federal law doctrine.

- Secondly, Article 173 (EC) on the Court's jurisdiction provides that the Court may review the legality of the acts of Community institutions on the grounds of "lack of competence, infringement of an essential procedural requirement, infringement of this Treaty *or of any rule of law relating to its application,* or misuse of powers" (emphasis added). In this Article "rule of law" is poised as a separate ground independent of all the other possible grounds of illegality.

---

248 [1984] E.C.R. 2689.

249 *ibid.* at 2718.

- Thirdly, Article 215 (EC) provides that the non-contractual liability of the Community be governed by "the general principles common to the laws of the Member States", which phrase recognises a source of law outside of Community texts.

None of these provisions provides any hint that general principles include fundamental rights. The Court relied on none of these provisions for establishing the protection of fundamental rights. There is a further provision, Article 130u(2) (EC) inserted by Article G(38) (EU), which states that Community development cooperation policy shall contribute to the general objectives of respecting human rights and fundamental freedoms.

There is now explicit reference to general principles and fundamental rights in the Treaty on European Union. Article F(2) (EU) provides:

> "The Union shall respect fundamental rights, as guaranteed by the European Convention for the Protection of Human Rights and Fundamental Freedoms signed in Rome on 4 November 1950 and as they result from the constitutional traditions common to the Member States, as general principles of Community law."

There are three points here. First, the Article is not directly cognisable by the Court of Justice (Article L (EU)). Secondly, this Article summarises the jurisprudential development which had already taken place, and consequently taken place without textual support. Thirdly, important in this summary is that the rights are to be protected as Community law general principles, not as rights created by public international law or national constitutional law.

There are two further references to fundamental rights in the provisions of the Treaty on European Union which are not cognisable by the Court of Justice and are found in the intergovernmental Titles. Article J.1(2) (EU) states that the development and consolidation of respect for human rights and fundamental freedoms is an objective of the Common Foreign and Security Policy; Article K.2(1) (EU) states that the areas of common interest in cooperation in the fields of justice and home affairs shall be dealt with in compliance with the European Convention for the Protection of Human Rights and Fundamental Freedoms, the Convention relating the Status of Refugees of 28 July 1951, and the protection afforded by Member States to persons persecuted on political grounds. This is a reference to compliance with international obligations rather than general principles of European Community law. The Member States, acting as an intergovernmental body under this Title, would be bound in public international law without the Article K.2(1) (EU) obligation by the treaties which they had entered into singly.

There are also textual references in the Preambles to the constituent treaties[250]:

---

250 A good example of the importance of Preambles to the Court's development of Community law is given by Opinion 1/92 *Draft Treaty on the EEA* [1991] E.C.R. I–6079 at 6106.

- The Preamble to the Treaty establishing the European Community (and the European Community before it) states:

  "Intending to confirm the solidarity which binds Europe and the overseas countries and desiring to ensure the development of their prosperity, in accordance with the principles of the Charter of the United Nations."

  However this reference to the Charter of the United Nations is not strictly supportive, because the principles of the Charter (set out in its Article 2) concern the conduct of Member States between themselves, whereas human rights are referred to not as principles but rather in the Preamble and as one of the purposes of the United Nations (Article 1).

- The Preamble to the Single European Act declared that the signatories were

  "Determined to work together to promote democracy on the basis of the fundamental rights recognized in the constitutions and laws of the Member States, in the Convention for the Protection of Human Rights and Fundamental Freedoms and the European Social Charter, notably freedom, equality and social justice."

  However Article 31 (SEA) does not grant the Court of Justice jurisdiction to have recourse to this preamble.

- The Preamble to the Treaty on European Union has gone the farthest, declaring the signatories'

  "attachment to the principles of liberty, democracy and respect for human rights and fundamental freedoms and the rule of law".

  Article L (EU) appears to exclude direct recognition of Preamble as part of European Community law.

Community fundamental rights differ from other general principles of European Community law in that their substance is deduced not from European Community law texts but from external texts, unlike for example the general principle against discrimination on the grounds of nationality, which is grounded in Article 6 (EC), which Article comes in Part One of the Treaty establishing the European Community, which is entitled "Principles".

Jurisprudential Basis for Fundamental Rights

8–64 *No Jurisprudential Basis for Fundamental Rights* Consistently with a public international law approach to European Community law, the Court of Justice at first refused point blank on jurisdictional grounds to entertain arguments based on fundamental rights.

In Case 1/58 *Stork v. High Authority*[251] the applicant found his status as a wholesaler who buys directly from a producer to be threatened. The collieries in the Ruhr had formed themselves into joint selling agencies (one of whom

[251] [1959] E.C.R. 17.

was Geitling) during the reorganisation of the coal industry and adopted identical decisions that they would allow direct orders to be placed only by wholesalers with a specified, increased turnover. The joint selling agencies, being stalked by Stork in the German courts, requested and got authorisation from the High Authority for the decisions. That applicant then brought a direct action before the Court of Justice to annul this Decision granting authorisation.

The applicant claimed that the High Authority had "failed to respect certain fundamental rights which are protected under almost all the constitutions of the Member States and limit the area of application of the Treaty".[252] The applicant gave the German Basic Law ("*Grundgesetz*") as just one example of a Member State constitution protecting the right of the citizen to the free choice of his trade, occupation or profession. Advocate-General Lagrange did not refer to this argument and the Court rejected it shortly, categorising it as an argument for the assessment of the Decision of the High Authority according to national law. The Court held that its only function was to ensure in the interpretation and application of the Treaty, the law was observed (citing Article 31 (ECSC), which is the equivalent in the Treaty establishing the European Coal and Steel Community to Article 164 (EC)). Similarly, the High Authority was not empowered to examine a complaint that it had infringed provisions of German constitutional law[253] (although the applicant had not based his argument on German constitutional law exclusively, but rather on constitutional protection common in the Member States).

It should be noted that the same problem of setting quantitative criteria, and several of the same High Authority Decisions, were again litigated in the next case in the reports, Case 18/57[254] brought by I. Nold, KG, Kohlen-und Baustoffgrosshandlung, a limited partnership governed by German law, having its registered offices in Darmstadt.[255] The name is important. The applicant was a limited partnership whose right to receive direct supplies was "essential to the existence of the company".[256] Here the applicant was successful and secured the annulment of the Decisions on the limited ground of infringement of an essential procedural requirement – insufficient reasoning.

Case 40/59 of Joined Cases 36–38 & 40/59 *Geitling and I. Nold v. High Authority*,[257] was brought by I. Nold KG seeking the annulment of a Decision of the High Authority which replaced the previously annulled Decisions,

---

252 *ibid.* at 24.
253 *ibid.* at 26, para. 4(a).
254 Case 18/57 *Nold v. High Authority* [1959] E.C.R. 41.
255 A similarly named family firm recurs in Case 4/73 *Nold v. Commission* [1974] E.C.R. 491. See below, para. 8–66, "Sources of Fundamental Rights Independent from Jurisprudential Basis". There is a legal history waiting to be written on the fate of family-owned coal distributorship in the Ruhr.
256 Case 1/58 *Stork v. High Authority* [1959] E.C.R. 17 at 49.
257 [1960] E.C.R. 423.

reduced the quantitative restrictions somewhat, and offered more reasons. The applicant was successful again on the grounds of insufficient reasoning. In support of its right, in its capacity as previous first-hand trader, to continue to obtain direct supplies, the applicant relied on the *Grundgesetz* right to private property, as interpreted by the German courts. The applicant stressed the necessity of interpreting the provisions of the Treaty establishing the European Coal and Steel Community in a way which would not conflict with fundamental rights under national law.[258] The Court rejected this argument holding that it was not for the Court "to ensure that rules of internal law, even constitutional rules, enforced in one or other of the Member States are respected." Advocate-General Lagrange again did not consider the point.

8–65 *Jurisprudential Basis for Fundamental Rights* It is often pointed out that the Court of Justice did not accept arguments for the annulment of Community measures based on abuse of fundamental rights until the threat of revolt became immediate, and therefore before the threat to the uniform application of European Community law became real.[259] The jurisdiction involved in Case 1/58 *Stork* and Joined Cases 36–38 & 40/59 *Geitling* support this explanation. These cases were direct challenges to High Authority decisions, whereas *Stauder et alia* were Article 177 (EEC) references coming after Case 26/62 *Van Gend en Loos*. The success of Article 177 (EEC) as a procedure to enforce individual European Community law rights by virtue of a direct national court duty depended on avoiding confrontation with a higher national court duty. It must be remembered that while *Stork* and *Geitling* threatened the infringement without recourse to Community Court of what were claimed as fundamental constitutional rights, there was at that time, before Case 26/62 *Van Gend en Loos* and Case 6/64 *Costa*, no established obligation on national courts to disapply conflicting national law, so that the applicants could have sought national court protection.

The point here is not to criticise a court for developing a fundamental rights jurisdiction and jurisprudence on that basis, nor to criticise the legal order to which it contributes, but to show that by bootstrapping itself once more on its own objectives, as interpreted by the Court of Justice, European Community law reinforced its autonomy from public international law and at the same time made both a constitutional leap towards a federal legal order and further demands on national law. Given the marginalisation of fundamental states' rights of the Member States, who created the European Community, in the construction of the integrationist jurisprudential constitutional doctrines of European Community law, it is perhaps natural that human rights also would be dependent on the achievement of, but not one of, dynamic political objectives such as "European unity".

---

258 *ibid.* at 437.

259 See *e.g.* T.C. Hartley, *The Foundations of European Community Law* (Oxford: 2nd ed., Clarendon Law Series, 1988) pp. 132 *et seq.*

The first case mentioning fundamental rights directly was Case 29/69 *Stauder v. City of Ulm.*[260] The plaintiff in the main action believed that a Commission decision requiring him to reveal his name and address in order to benefit from an offer of inexpensive butter was an infringement of the fundamental rights enshrined in the Basic Law (*Grundgesetz*). He initiated two simultaneous actions in national law, one before the Administrative Court of Stuttgart (*Verwaltungsgericht Stuttgart*) and the second a constitutional complaint to the Federal Constitutional Court. Before the ruling of the Constitutional Court, the Administrative Court came to the conclusion that the legality of the Commission's decision was in doubt because of the fundamental rights protected at national law.[261] Consequently it made an Article 177 (EEC) reference asking whether the Commission Decision was compatible with the general principles of European Community law. The Court interpreted the decision as not requiring the identification of the beneficiary, and stated:

> "Interpreted in this way the provision at issue contains nothing capable of prejudicing the fundamental human rights enshrined in the general principles of Community law and protected by the Court."[262]

There was no reasoning offered for this reversal. It just arrived. Advocate-General Roemer distinguished the reference from the Administrative Court from a question asking for the decision on the compatibility of European Community law with national constitutional law. The Advocate-General accepted the test that general qualitative concepts of national constitutional law, in particular fundamental rights, must be ascertained by a comparative analysis and observed in making secondary law, because they form part of the general legal principles of unwritten European Community law. The Advocate-General did not explain why he accepted this.[263] The Commission also accepted that the protection guaranteed by fundamental rights is assured in part by unwritten European Community law derived from the general principles of law in force in Member States.[264] The pragmatic nature of this reversal is explained perhaps by the desire of the Court of Justice not so much to avoid all future conflict (probably impossible unless all the fundamental rights of all the Member States were protected) but rather to control the conflict institutionally by persuading the national courts at least to refer the conflict to the Court of Justice before finally deciding it. Once the Court of Justice secured jurisdiction of the conflict, it could decide on the implications of a particular case for the acceptance of direct effect and supremacy of European Community law.

---

260 [1969] E.C.R. 419. This case was quickly followed by the competition law cases Case 41/69 *ACF Chemiefarma v. Commission* [1970] E.C.R. 661 and Case 45/69 *Boehringer Mannheim v. Commission* [1970] E.C.R. 769.

261 This background is set out in the Opinion of Advocate-General Roemer, Case 29/69 *Stauder v. City of Ulm* [1969] E.C.R. 419 at 427.

262 *ibid.* at 425.

263 *ibid.* at 428.

264 *ibid.* at 422.

The first coherent statement of European Community law fundamental rights protection came in Case 11/70 *Internationale Handelsgesellschaft*,[265] where the *Verwaltungsgericht Frankfurt-am-Main* refused to accept the validity of part of the common organisation of the market in cereals. The German Court had held invalid provisions of a Council Regulation and a Commission Regulation providing for the forfeit of deposits attaching to export licenses because they ran contrary to principles of the German Basic Law, particularly proportionality, freedom of action, and economic liberty.[266] The Advocate-General, having pointed to "the danger of divergent if not contradictory case law developing in the Member States" declared that the one certain point was that "the argument which seduced the Frankfurt court must be rejected categorically". The place of the fundamental principles of national legal systems in European Community law was limited. Advocate-General Dutheillet de Lamothe stated[267]:

> "They contribute to forming that philosophical, political and legal sub-stratum common to the Member States from which through the case-law an unwritten Community law emerges, one of the essential aims of which is precisely to ensure the respect for the fundamental rights of the individual.
>
> In that sense, the fundamental principles of the national legal systems contribute to enabling Community law to find in itself the resources necessary for ensuring, where needed, respect for the fundamental rights which form the common heritage of the Member States."

The Court set out clearly that a national court testing the validity of secondary European Community law "would have an adverse effect on the uniformity and efficacy of Community law". In an important passage the Court continued:

> "In fact, the law stemming from the Treaty, an independent source of law, cannot because of its very nature be overridden by rules of national law, however framed, without being deprived of its character as Community law and without the legal basis of the Community itself being called in question. Therefore the validity of a Community measure or its effect within a Member State cannot be affected by allegations that it runs counter to either fundamental rights as formulated by the constitution of that State or the principles of a national constitutional structure."[268]

This reasoning is an application of the reasoning for the supremacy of European Community law applied to a threat not from a posterior national rule but from a fundamental right. The Advocate-General made express reference to Case 6/64 *Costa v. ENEL*.[269] If the Court treated European Community law like public international law there would be no problem: it is axiomatic as far as public international law is concerned that national law cannot affect

---

265 [1970] E.C.R. 1125.

266 *ibid.* at 1133, and Opinion of Advocate-General Dutheillet de Lamothe at 1146.

267 *ibid.* at 1146–1147.

268 *ibid.* at 1134, para. 3.

269 *ibid.* at 1146.

its validity before a public international law tribunal, whatever a national court might say. But the Court is saying here that if a national court refuses to apply a European Community law rule (on the grounds of fundamental rights) then this deprives the European Community law rule of its character and calls into question the legal basis of the Community. Therefore as a matter of European Community law it cannot be done. This is the rabbit in the hat Case 26/62 *Van Gend en Loos* – Case 6/64 *Costa v. ENEL* reasoning applied in this context.

The Court of Justice then looked for "any analogous guarantee inherent in Community law" to the German constitutional right. It does not explain why, but just states straight up in the next paragraph:

> "In fact, respect for fundamental rights forms an integral part of the general principles of law protected by the Court of Justice. The protection of such rights, whilst inspired by the constitutional traditions common to the Member States, must be ensured within the structure and objectives of the Community."[270]

The phrase "in fact" is revealing: because there were no grounds in law, the fact of this judgment becomes the legal basis for the jurisdiction of the Court of Justice. Because there is no extra reason given to ground the respect for fundamental rights in European Community law other than the reasons given in the previous paragraph of the judgment for the European Community law prohibition on national courts from suspending the application of European Community law on the grounds of national constitutional law rights, the conclusion is that in order to defend (1) the uniformity of European Community law, (2) the efficacy of European Community law, (3) the character of European Community law, (4) the legal basis of the Community, it had simply become practically necessary to respect fundamental rights. Therefore the Court founds a fundamental rights jurisdiction by an act of will legitimated by the necessity to preserve in execution these constitutional integrationist doctrines. The Court of Justice held that the Community measures were appropriate to ensuring the common organisation of the market and therefore a justifiable restriction on fundamental rights.

Advocate-General Trabucchi appeared to suggest a basis for the protection of fundamental rights by the Court of Justice in Case 4/73 *Nold v. Commission*[271]: they are principles *quarum causa omne ius constitutum est.* The Advocate-General refers to such principles being found in ancient law and in the codes of the nineteenth century, and now formally proclaimed in modern constitutions. But the Court of Justice does not adopt such an approach, which would have put the protection of fundamental rights on the basis that all systems of law recognised such universal principles. The Court of Justice preferred to maintain the inspirational link with the Constitutions of the Member State, with the result that some commentators were of the opinion even as late as 1988

---

270 *ibid.* at 1134, para. 4.
271 [1974] E.C.R. 491 at 514.

that the Court of Justice would accept as a general principle of European Community law a principle which is constitutionally protected in only one Member State.[272]

8–66 *Sources of Fundamental Rights Independent from Jurisprudential Basis* The "inspiration" drawn from common constitutional traditions, mentioned for the first time in Case 11/70 *Internationale Handelsgesellschaft*, is not a reason for protecting human rights, but a means for deciding the content of the rights to be protected. This is an important distinction.

The source of common constitutional traditions would be a reason for the protection of fundamental rights only if the Court of Justice adopted the reasoning of Advocate-General Warner in Case 7/76 *IRCA v. Amministrazione delle Finanze dello Stato*.[273] In that case the applicant claimed *inter alia* that a Commission Regulation providing for the retroactive calculation of a monetary compensation amount was invalid because retroactivity was contrary to general principles common to all Member States. Neither the Court of Justice nor the parties analysed the question as one of fundamental rights but Advocate-General Warner, in advising the Court of Justice to hold the Regulation invalid (the Court of Justice upheld it) as contrary to the principle that Community institutions may not legislate retroactively to defeat legitimate expectations[274] advocated a refinement in the approach of the Court of Justice to the protection of fundamental rights. This "refinement" is extremely important because the Court has not adopted it, and impliedly rejected it:

> "a fundamental right recognized and protected by the Constitution of any Member State must be recognized and protected also in Community law. The reason lies in the fact that, as has so often been held by the Court,[275] Community law owes its very existence to a partial transfer of sovereignty by each of the Member States to the Community. No Member State can, in my opinion, be held to have included in that transfer power for the Community to legislate in infringement of rights protected by its own Constitution. To hold otherwise would involve attributing to a Member State the capacity, when ratifying the Treaty, to flout its own Constitution, which seems to me impossible."[276]

The rejection of this proposition, made clear in Case 44/79 *Hauer v. Land Rheinland-Pfalz*,[277] goes to the core of the Court's approach to European Community law. The transfer of sovereignty was not the fundamental support for *Costa*: that was a certain idea of Europe and the necessity of achieving executive uniformity in the application of European Community law as

---

272 T.C. Hartley, *The Foundations of European Community Law* (Oxford: 2nd ed. Clarendon Law Series, 1988) p. 136.

273 [1976] E.C.R. 1213.

274 Citing Case 74/74 *CNTA v. Commission* [1975] E.C.R. 533.

275 See *e.g.* Case 6/64 *Costa v. ENEL* [1964] E.C.R. 593, at para. 2 of the text quoted in para. 8–46 above.

276 Case 7/76 *IRCA* [1976] E.C.R. 1213 at 1237.

277 [1979] E.C.R. 3727.

a means for achieving that objective. So far as the transfer of sovereignty idea makes European Community law dependent on national constitutional law, the Court rejects it just as it rejects public international law[278] where that would affect the autonomy of European Community law.

The analysis has jumped chronologically ahead of the development of the Court's jurisprudence. The Advocate-General was suggesting a refinement on the Court's approach after Case 4/73 *Nold v. Commission.*[279] That case was brought by J. Nold, KG, Kohlen- und Baustoffgrosshandlung, a limited partnership governed by German law, having its registered offices in Darmstadt.[280] The applicant brought a direct action for the annulment of a Commission Decision authorising the Ruhr coal selling agency (there was only one at this stage) to make direct supply subject to massive purchase requirements greatly exceeding Nold's annual sales in the sector and therefore withdrawing its status as direct wholesaler, and putting the business which it had carried on for more than a hundred years in dire jeopardy. Nold argued that the Decision violated his rights to property, personality, and freedom of economic action, protected by the Member States' constitutions and "received" into European Community law.[281] I. Nold had the same arguments rejected in Joined Cases 36–38 and 40/59 *Geitling and I. Nold v. High Authority.*[282]

The Court, without elucidating why fundamental rights formed "an integral part"[283] of the general principles of European Community law, stated that:

> "the Court is bound to draw inspiration from constitutional traditions common to the Member States and it cannot therefore uphold measures which are incompatible with fundamental rights recognized and protected by the Constitutions of those States."

This appeared to indicate that the Court was bound to hold invalid any European Community law conflicting with a fundamental right protected by just one Member State. This may have been the impression it was supposed to give; in any event it succeeded in persuading the German Federal Constitutional Court, which relied expressly on that passage when it withdrew from conflict with the Court of Justice, holding that so long as the Court protected fundamental rights equivalent to those protected under the Basic Law, it would not interfere.[284] This almost wilful determination on behalf of a constitutional court to interpret European Community law contrary to its

---

278 This rejection is stated here as a general proposition, not to suggest that it is contrary to public international law for a state to act contrary to its constitution.

279 [1974] E.C.R. 491.

280 A similarly named family firm brought Case 18/57 *Nold v. High Authority* [1959] E.C.R. 41. See above, para. 8–64, "No Jurisprudential Basis for Fundamental Rights".

281 Case 4/73 *Nold v. Commission* [1974] E.C.R. 491 at 501.

282 [1960] E.C.R. 423.

283 Case 4/73 *Nold v. Commission* [1974] E.C.R. 491 at 507, para. 13.

284 *Wunsche Handelsgesellschaft* ("*Solange II*") [1987] 3 C.M.L.R. 225 at 260, para. 38, reversing its position in *Internationale Handelsgesellschaft v. EVGF* ("*Solange I*") [1974] 2 C.M.L.R. 540 at 549.

development by the Court of Justice to accord with its constitutional requirements is indicative of the gap existing between national and European Community law.

For the Court of Justice had made clear quite quickly after Case 4/73 *Nold* that the fundamental rights common to the Member States did not bind the Court, and hence were not the basis of those rights or their protection in European Community law, although they might provide a quarry for the production of European Community law fundamental rights. The importance of the fundamental rights of national constitutional law was inspiration, not basis. In *Hauer* the Court held:

> "14. As the Court declared in [Case 11/70, *Internationale Handelsgesellschaft*], the question of a possible infringement of fundamental rights by a measure of the Community institutions can only be judged in the light of Community law itself. The introduction of special criteria for assessment stemming from the legislation or constitutional law of a particular Member State, by damaging the substantive unity and efficacy of Community law, would inevitably lead to the destruction of the unity of the Common Market and the jeopardizing of the cohesion of the Community.
>
> 15. The Court also emphasized in the judgement cited, and later in [*Nold*], that fundamental rights form an integral part of the general principles of the law, the observance of which it ensures; that in safeguarding those rights, the Court is bound to draw inspiration from constitutional traditions common to the Member States, so that measures which are incompatible with the fundamental rights recognized by the constitutions of those States are unacceptable in the Community; and that, similarly, international treaties for the protection of human rights on which the Member States have collaborated or of which they are signatories, can supply guidelines which should be followed within the framework of Community law . . . ".[285]

The Court here makes clear, first, that there can be no reliance on the fundamental rights of a particular Member State to avoid application of a Community act because of uniformity and efficacy of European Community law. Secondly, that fundamental rights not just recognised by one Member State but common to the Member States (the contrast suggests common to all Member States) provide inspiration, nothing more. Otherwise the Court could have left the second half of the relevant sentence stand on its own without the first half, as "[m]easures which are incompatible with the fundamental rights recognized by the constitutions of the Member States are unacceptable". Further, the Court considers international treaties on which Member States have merely collaborated but not signed to be a source of equal status to national constitutional law fundamental rights.[286] In any event, treaties supply

---

285 Case 44/79 *Hauer v. Land Rheinland-Pfalz* [1979] E.C.R. 3727 at 3744–3745.

286 The strongest judicial statement of the importance of principles and concepts common to the Member States as a source of European Community law is Case 155/79 *AM&S Europe v. Commission* [1982] E.C.R. 1575, para. 18 where the Court holds that it "must take into account" these principles and concepts.

only guidelines. This judgment is a definite rejection of Advocate-General Warner's approach to European Community law fundamental rights in Case 7/76 *IRCA*.[287]

That this is the correct interpretation of these two paragraphs is borne out by the approach of the Court of Justice to the problem before it. The Court appears to embark on what can only be a futile search for a common meaning to the right to property and the restrictions allowed thereto. Since these rights are determined by national legal orders and the European Convention on Human Rights and Fundamental Freedoms, it is not possible to see how they could have the same meaning unless every one of these orders were the same, which of course they are not.[288] The Court turns first to the European Convention and only then, because the Convention does not provide "a sufficiently precise answer"[289] to the "indications provided by the constitutional rules and practices of the nine Member States", citing only three of these.[290] With the development of this fundamental rights jurisdiction, the European Convention for the Protection of Human Rights and Fundamental Freedoms has become the first source among equals.[291]

Furthermore, in Case 4/73 *Nold v. Commission*,[292] the Court had made clear that fundamental rights had meaning in European Community law only so far as they were fitted into the Community framework. Thus the Court found that the protection of rights such as property and free exercise of a trade are "subject always to limitations laid down in accordance with the public interest".[293] Whilst this is an uncontroversial proposition in the abstract, in this context the finding means that these rights may be limited in European Community law according to the Community conception of the public interest. This is clearly not the same as protecting a right subject to a national conception of the public interest and a national conception of how it limits the fundamental right. The Court continued:

> "Within the Community legal order it likewise seems legitimate that these rights should, if necessary, be subject to certain limits justified by the overall objectives pursued by the Community, on condition that the substance of these rights is left untouched."[294]

---

287 [1976] E.C.R. 1213: see above.

288 See below Part V, Chap. 31, "Different Interpretations of a Similarly Named Right".

289 [1976] E.C.R. 1213 at 3746, para. 19.

290 *ibid.* para. 20.

291 Joint Declaration of 5 April 1977, referred to in Case 222/84 *Johnston v. Chief Constable of the Royal Ulster Constabulary* [1986] E.C.R. 1663 at 1682, para. 18; Case C–260/89 *ERT* [1991] E.C.R. I–2925 at 2963, para. 41; Article F(2) (EU). The European Convention partly fulfills the role of a domestic bill of rights in some jurisdictions, such as Luxembourg and increasingly in Belgium.

292 [1974] E.C.R. 491.

293 *ibid.* at 508, para. 14.

294 *ibid.*

This clearly puts fundamental rights in the Community framework and subject to the objectives of the Community. This approach was strengthened in Case 5/88 *Wachauf*[295] where the Court added the concept of social function as a limitation, which implies a notion of European society.

8–67 *International Sources of Fundamental Rights Helps Reference Back to Treaty Basis* International treaties for the protection of human rights on which the Member States have collaborated or of which they are signatories are also a quarry from which the Court can unearth fundamental rights. This was first established in Case 4/73 *Nold v. Commission*,[296] confirmed in Case 44/79 *Hauer v. Land Rheinland-Pfalz*,[297] with the European Convention for the Protection of Human Rights and Fundamental Freedoms accorded special importance.[298]

This has an importance for several reasons:

- Extra demands are placed on national law by the incorporation, in areas of Community competence, of obligations on Member States such as are contained in the European Convention for the Protection of Human Rights and Fundamental Freedoms.
- As above, it supports the rejection of the argument made by the Advocate-General on the jurisprudential basis of European Community law fundamental rights protection.
- It provides a way back to the Preamble to the Single European Act, the Preamble to the Treaty on European Union, and to Article F(2) (EU). However because it is no more than a way back, these preambles and articles do not supply direct textual support.

8–68 *Basis of Jurisdictional Extension* We have seen that the basis for fundamental rights protection in European Community law is jurisprudential in origin and is the attainment of the objective of integration through the preservation of the primacy of and executive uniformity in application of European Community law. This subsection considers whether this objective of integration also formed the basis for the extension of this jurisdiction which makes increasing demands on the national legal order. This extension has been summarised above.[299]

One extension was that Member States' executive actions were to be suspended and rules disapplied in areas of Community competence where the rules or actions would be permissible derogations from substantive European

---

295 [1989] E.C.R. 2609 at 2639, para. 18.
296 [1974] E.C.R. 491 at 507, para. 13.
297 [1979] E.C.R. 3727 at 3745.
298 Case C–260/89 *ERT* [1991] E.C.R. I–2925, para. 41.
299 See above, para. 8–61, "Extension of European Community Law's Jurisdiction and Demands".

Community law rules were there no conflict with European Community law fundamental rights.[300] In Case 36/75 *Rutili* the Court used several rights in the European Convention for the Protection of Human Rights and Fundamental Freedoms to support its restriction of France's attempt to derogate on the grounds of public policy pursuant to Article 48(3) (EC). The Court held that the derogation must:

> "be interpreted strictly, so that its scope cannot be determined unilaterally by each Member State without being subject to control by the institutions of the Community."[301]

Unilateral determination would clearly have adverse effects for the uniformity of European Community law and the securing of its objectives, one of which is the free movement of workers in Article 48 (EC). Consequently the Court decided that it had jurisdiction to determine whether France's action was in response to what it would consider to be "a genuine and sufficiently serious threat to public policy"[302] to "limit the discretionary power of Member States".[303] This jurisdictional point had been made in Case 41/74 *Van Duyn*.[304] This approach, as Advocate-General Mayras pointed out in Case 36/75 *Rutili*, "corresponds to the need for uniform application of European Community law and implies that an attempt is being made to define the meaning of the concept according to that requirement." The extension in Case 36/75 *Rutili* was to the control of Member State action within a derogation to a fundamental freedom.[304a] The Court of Justice held that Member State action which infringed rights protected in the European Convention for the Protection of Human Rights and Fundamental Freedoms could not be tolerated unless the action was necessary to protect national security or public safety as those interests are understood "in a democratic society".[305] Why the Court of Justice could draw on the European Convention for the Protection of Human Rights and Fundamental Freedoms here was not explained, unless the explanation lies in its employment as a technique to restrict Member States' disuniformity-causing discretion. Advocate-General Mayras did not refer to the European Convention for the Protection of Human Rights and Fundamental Freedoms but relied instead on the rule of equal treatment on the grounds of nationality.

---

300 Case 36/75 *Rutili v. Minister of the Interior* [1975] E.C.R. 1219 (concerning Article 48(3)); Case C–260/89 *Elliniki Radiophonia Tileorassi* [1991] E.C.R. I–2925 (the public policy proviso in Articles 56 and 66).

301 Case 36/75, *Rutili* [1975] E.C.R. 1219 at 1231, para. 27.

302 *ibid.* at 1231, para. 28.

303 *ibid.* at 1236, para. 2 of the ruling.

304 [1974] E.C.R. 1337.

304a Another example of potential control of Member State action, this time German laws, where there is interference with the economic rights of a migrant worker, is Case C–168/91 *Konstantinidis v. Stadt Altensteig* [1993] E.C.R. I–1191.

305 Case 36/75, *Rutili* [1975] E.C.R. 1219 at 1232, para. 32.

The Court of Justice reaffirmed its approach in Case C–260/89 *ERT*[306]:

> "the national rules can fall under the exceptions provided for by the combined provisions of Articles 56 and 66 only if they are compatible with the fundamental rights the observance of which is ensured by the Court."[307]

The Court of Justice left the appraisal of this up to the national court.[308]

Another extension is that Member States' implementing rules must comply with the general principles of European Community law,[309] including fundamental rights.[310] In Case 77/81 *Zuckerfabrik* the Court simply stated without introduction that it had to consider whether national implementing rules were compatible with "superior rules of Community law",[311] in that case the principles of legal certainty and proportionality. In Case 5/88 *Wachauf*[312] the Court held that since the requirement of the protection of fundamental rights is also binding on the Member States when they implement Community rules, the Member States must, as far as possible, apply those rules in accordance with those requirements. "As far as possible" here means within the boundaries of the discretion accorded by the Community rules. The Court is not allowing the Member States to change the rules to accord with fundamental rights. Any change in the Community rules could only come from the institutions – for example from the Court in an action challenging their validity.

A further extension is that Member States' own fundamental rights which cross an area of Community competence fall to be tested against European Community fundamental rights, at least according to Advocate-General Van Gerven, who based himself squarely on established jurisprudence.[313]

These jurisdictional extensions demonstrate the demands placed on the legal order, and how the achievement of the objectives of the Community and the requirement of executive uniformity remain the foundation for constitutional advancement. The jurisdiction has changed from one where the Court declared itself willing to hold secondary European Community law invalid in order to avoid national constitutional courts doing so, and causing consequent disuniformity, to include a jurisdiction where the Court will hold

---

306 The approach was also present in Case 60/84 *Cinéthèque v. Fédération Nationale des Cinémas Français* [1985] E.C.R. 2605. However the exception allowed to the scope of Article 30 justified by mandatory requirements of the public interest was not deemed to be subject to this approach, while the Article 36 derogations were.

307 Case C–260/89 [1991] E.C.R. I–2925 at 2964, para. 43.

308 *ibid.* 2964, para. 44. Advocate-General Lenz had been of the opinion that the European Convention for the Protection of Human Rights and Fundamental Freedoms was almost certainly irrelevant to the case (at 2949, para. 51).

309 Case 77/81 *Zuckerfabrik* [1982] E.C.R. 681.

310 Case 5/88 *Wachauf* [1989] E.C.R. 2609.

311 [1982] E.C.R. 681 at 695, para. 22.

312 [1989] E.C.R. 2609.

313 Case C–159/90 *Society for the Protection of the Unborn Child v. Grogan* [1991] E.C.R. I–4685 (Opinion of Advocate-General Van Gerven). This case and the extension of jurisdiction to which it pointed are considered in detail in Part V, paras. 30–2 *et seq.*, "Conflicts".

inapplicable national laws within areas of Community competence,[314] in order to avoid disuniformity in application of Community rules and to restrict Member States' derogations from textually based European Community law principles such as the free movement of workers which is one of the objectives of the Community.

Fundamental Rights Currently Included

8–69 The following non-exhaustive list indicates the scope of the jurisprudence of the Court in protecting fundamental rights,[315] which right may result in demands on the national legal order as well as limitations to the acts of the institutions of the European Communities. The Court has recognised

- the right to property[316];
- the right to freedom of work[317];
- the right to the free exercise of commerce[318];
- the right to professional activities[319];
- the right to non-discrimination on the ground of sex[320];
- the right of human persons to the non-violability of the dwelling[321];

---

314 This extension of the Court's fundamental rights jurisdiction was established as early as Case 43/75 *Defrenne v. SABENA* [1976] E.C.R. 455 but that case is limited in so far as the fundamental right there in issue was grounded in a Treaty provision – Article 119 (EC).

315 In addition to fundamental rights not covered in this list, there is a line of cases on fundamental general principles of European Community law which give rise to procedural rights, for example Case T–30/91 *Solvay SA v. Commission*, [1995] E.C.R. II–1775 and Case T–36/91 *ICI v. Commission*, [1995] E.C.R. II–1847, on the rights of the defence as a fundamental principle of European Community law encompassing the general principle of the equality of arms, which requires equal access to information and the disclosure of documents in competition investigations, and there is a line of cases which ground a right to a remedy before national courts for breach of a European Community law right, *e.g.* Case 222/84 *Johnston v. Chief Constable of the Royal Ulster Constabulary* [1986] E.C.R. 1651 at 1682 (strictly speaking, the right was recognised in this case by the interpretation of the applicable directive in the light of the general principle of the requirement of judicial control).

316 Case 44/79 *Hauer* [1979] E.C.R. 3727; Joined Cases 41, 121 & 796/79 *Testa* [1980] E.C.R. 1979.

317 Case 7/73 *Nold* [1974] E.C.R. 491.

318 *ibid.*

319 Joined Cases 133–136/85, *Walter Rau Lebensmittelwerke* [1987] E.C.R. 2289; Case 234/85 *Ministre Public de Fribourg v. Keller* [1986] E.C.R. 2897.

320 Case 43/75 *Defrenne v. SABENA* [1976] E.C.R. 455.

321 Joined Cases 46/87 & 227/88 *Hoechst* [1989] E.C.R. 2859 (D. Edward has hinted that the Court of Justice might have the competence to issue warrants – "Constitutional Rules of Community Law in EEC Competition Cases" in 1992 and *EEC/U.S. Competition and Trade Law* (Fordham Corporate Law Institute 1992); Case 85/87 *Dow Benelux* [1989] E.C.R. 3137; Joined Cases 97–99/87 *Dow Chemical Iberica* [1989] E.C.R. 3165.

- the right of a moral or legal person to have all government intervention in its private sphere of activity justified by a legal basis and be non-arbitrary and proportionate[322];
- the right to freedom of expression[323];
- the right to respect for private life[324];
- the right to medical secrecy[325];
- the right to legal professional privilege.[326]

322 Joined Cases 97–99/87 *Dow Chemical Iberica* [1989] E.C.R. 3165.
323 Case 100/88 *Oyowe and Traore v. Commission* [1989] E.C.R. 4285; Case C–260/89 *ERT* [1991] E.C.R. I–2925; Case C–219/91 *Ter Voort* [1992] E.C.R. I–5485.
324 Case C–62/90 *Commission v. Germany* [1992] E.C.R. I–2575.
325 *ibid.*
326 Case 155/79 *AM&S Europe v. Commission* [1982] E.C.R. 1575.

9. CITIZENSHIP

Public International Law Perception

9–1 Clearly the concept of citizenship forms no part of the law of international organisations, whose members are generally states, but never individuals. The concept expresses the notion of a polity, allegiance, and direct legitimating link between citizen and polity.

European Community Law Perception

9–2 The concept[1] was directly introduced into European Community law only by the Treaty on European Union and follows on from the constitutional developments in European Community law. The Court of Justice had referred before to "European 'citizens'", quoting from the phrase used by the referring court in an Article 177 (EEC) reference.[2] "Citizenship of the Union" is now Part Two of the Treaty establishing the European Community.

The acquisition of citizenship remains dependent on the holding of nationality of a Member State, and the Member States retain control over their nationality laws. This is a restriction on the concept – Member States still come first in the line between Union and individual. Declaration (No. 2) on nationality of a Member State, attached by the Treaty on European Union to the Treaty establishing the European Community, provides that "the question whether an individual possesses the nationality of a Member State shall be settled solely by reference to the national law of the Member State concerned." This is reinforced by the Decision of the Heads of State or Government, Meeting within the European Council, concerning Certain Problems Raised by Denmark on the Treaty on European Union. This is expressed by the European Council to be "fully compatible with the Treaty" and states in Section A that the provisions on citizenship

> "do not in any way take the place of national citizenship. The question whether an individual possesses the nationality of a Member State will be settled solely by reference to the national law of the Member State concerned."

The Birmingham Declaration provides that Union citizenship is introduced for national citizens "without in any way taking the place of their national

---

1 "I have met Italians, Russians, Spaniards, English, French: nowhere have I met *l'homme au général*" – Joseph de Maistre.

2 Joined Cases 21–24/72 *International Fruit* [1972] E.C.R. 1219, para. 8.

citizenship".[3] However the Court of Justice, prior to the Treaty on European Union, had made a major reservation on Member States' control over their nationality laws. In Case C–369/90 *Micheletti v. Delagacion del Gobierno en Cantabria*[4] it held that the definition of conditions governing the acquisition and loss of citizenship were matters which were in the competence of each Member State (this is the public international law rule[5]) but the competence must be exercised in accordance with European Community law.

The citizen is granted nine express rights by the Treaty on European Union (Article 8–8e (EC)): the right to move and the right to reside (Article 8a(1) (EC)), the right to vote and the right to stand as a candidate at municipal elections in the Member State in which the Union citizen resides but of which he is not a national (Article 8b(1)),[6] the right to vote and the right to stand in European Parliament elections (Article 8b(2)(EC),[7] the right to protection by diplomatic and consular authorities (Article 8c (EC)),[8] the right to petition the European Parliament (Article 8d (EC)), and the right to apply to the Ombudsman (Article 8d (EC)). As for the right to move and the right to reside, their direct effect is not expressed to be dependent to the adoption of further measures, although such measures may condition the rights and facilitate their exercise. The right to petition the European Parliament and the right to apply to the Ombudsman are not subject to any provision for further measures (although the right to apply to the Ombudsman was necessarily dependent on the appointment of an Ombudsman). The apparent intention that at least these four rights be directly effective is in stark contrast to the provisions of Part Three Title III "Free movement of persons, services and capital" of the Treaty establishing the European Community. However the necessity for the right to diplomatic representation to be implemented by the Member States themselves, not through measures of the institutions, highlights the limitations of the concept of citizenship.

Three of the nine express rights of citizenship – the right to vote, and the right to stand as a candidate in elections to the European Parliament in the Member State of the citizen's residence, and the right to petition the European Parliament – feed directly into the European Parliament. Therefore the

---

[3] Para. A(2).

[4] [1992] E.C.R. I–4239.

[5] This is in line with Article 1 of the Convention on Certain Questions relating to the Conflict of Nationality Laws, which provides: "It is for each State to determine under its own law who are its nationals." – see D. O'Keeffe, "Union Citizenship", *Legal Issues of the Maastricht Treaty* (D. O'Keeffe and P. M. Twomey eds., London: Wiley Chancery Law, 1994) p. 87 at pp. 91–92.

[6] Implemented by Council Directive 94/80 of 9 December 1994 [1994] O.J. L368.

[7] Implemented by Council Directive 93/109 of 6 December 1993 [1993] O.J. L329.

[8] This right had to be established by the Member States among themselves, not through the European Community institutions – Article 8c (EC) and Decision of the Representatives of the Governments of the Member States meeting within the Council of 19 December 1995 [1995] O.J. L314/73.

European Parliament can be viewed as exercising powers conferred on it directly by the citizens of Europe, bypassing the legitimation provided by the Treaties. The European Parliament got treaty recognition for that name from the Single European Act (Article 3(1)). It had been changed from a body drawn from the parliamentary institutions of the Member States to a directly-elected body in 1979 pursuant to a Council Decision in 1976.[9] Its powers were greatly increased by the Treaty on European Union. Now a directly-elected body with substantial powers over the budget, the admission of new members, and the election of the Commission and with a role in the legislative process and the amendment of the treaties, and whose members group in trans-national parties, it resembles a federal parliament elected by its citizens more than an international institution.

The sixth right is the right to petition the Ombudsman, established under the Treaty establishing the European Community as amended by the Treaty on European Union.

---

[9] Council Decision 76/787 [1976] O.J. L278/1.

10. TREATY AS CONSTITUTION

Public International Law Perception

10–1 Internationalists considering the position of European Community law in public international law consider that the description of the European Community treaties as constitutional, and of European Community law as an autonomous legal order, does not remove European Community law from a modern, evolved view of public international law.[1] The idea of referring to the laws of the European Community as being rooted in a constitution appears to be a notion of national public law but in fact has been in use in public international law since at least 1932.[2] The San Francisco Charter of 1947 establishing the United Nations Organisation has been described as "a true Constitution".[3] The basic organising text of the Food and Agriculture Organisation, a specialised agency of the United Nations, is called a constitution. The founding instrument of the Universal Postal Union is termed "Constitution". In fact the word "constitutional" begs the question: constitutional of what? The word is not specific to a type of legal system, such as the complete legal order of a nation state. Rather, each legal system will have a somewhat different style of constitution but that will not make it any the less constitutive of that system. Taking the European Community law constitution to be the provisions at the origin and serving as the basis for European Community law and its development, the existence of a European Community law constitution does not cut European Community law off from public international law.[4] The word could apply to all international organisations where there is normative generalisation, a large number of rules effectively applied, procedures for the elaboration and modification of law, and rules on the organisation and distribution of power.[5]

---

1 See *e.g.* van der Meersch, Boulouis, Leben, and Wyatt.

2 "Droit constitutionnel international" is the heading for the second part of G. Scelle's "Précis de droit des gens, principes et systematiques" (Paris, 1932).

3 W.G. van der Meersch, "L'Ordre juridique des Communautés Européennes et le Droit international" (1975) 148 (V) *Recueil des Cours de l'Académie de Droit International* at p. 21 quoting Virally.

4 J. Boulouis, "Le droit des Communautés Européennes dans ses rapports avec le droit international general" (1992) 235 (IV) *Recueil des Cours* 19 at p. 27.

5 Van der Meersch (1975) *op. cit.* above, n.3, at p. 22.

European Community Law Perception

10–2 The significance of the terms "constitution" and "constitutional" have to be seen in the context of other doctrinal developments, such as rights to individuals and the other aspects set out above of the relationship between European Community law and public international law. As Mancini has summarised, the Court "has sought to constitutionalise the Treaty, that is to fashion a constitutional framework for a federal type structure in Europe".[6] European Community law understands the term "constitution" in the sense of a federal, not an international, organisation. In particular, the term refers to the "quasi-constitutional status within the domestic legal orders" of European Community law: "the European Community Treaty and the Treaty on European Union form a complementary constitution for each of the Member States which, like their national constitution, structures their legal order."[7]

The use of the term by the Court of Justice indicates that what European Community law means by "constitution" approximates the constitution of a federal state.

The term was first used by Advocate-General Lagrange in Case 8/55 *Fédéchar.*[8] In Case 294/83 *Parti Ecologiste 'Les Verts' v. Parliament*[9] the Greens sought via Article 173 (EEC) a declaration that two decisions of the Bureau of the European Parliament concerning allocations of appropriations of the General Budget of the European Community and the use of such allocations to reimburse the European Parliament election expenses of political parties were void.[10] By far the most important use of the term to date was in Opinion 1/91.[11] In that Opinion the Court of Justice held that the objectives of the Treaty establishing the European Economic Community are economic integration, an internal market and economic and monetary union. The overriding objective of all the Community treaties is "to contribute together to making concrete progress towards European unity".[12] The Court continued that the provisions of the Treaty establishing the European Economic Community on free movement and competition, far from being an end in

---

6 F. Mancini, "The Making of a Constitution for Europe" (1989) *Common Market Law Review* 595 at 596. See also K. Lenaerts, "Fundamental Rights to be Included in a Community Catalogue" (1991) 16 *European Law Review* 367.

7 B. de Witte, "International Agreement or Constitution" in *The Treaty on European Union: Suggestions for Revision* ('s-Gravenhage: Asser Instituut, 1995) p. 1 at 13–14.

8 [1956] E.C.R. 245.

9 [1986] E.C.R. 1339.

10 Joined Cases 31 & 35/86 *Levantina Agricola Industrial SA (Laisa) and CPC Espana v. Council* [1988] E.C.R. 2285; Case 193/87 *Maurissen and Union Syndicale v. Court of Auditors* [1989] E.C.R. 1045; Case 302/87 *Parliament v. Council* [1988] E.C.R. 5615; Order Case 2/88 [1990] E.C.R. I–3365; Case 70/88 *Parliament v. Council* [1990] E.C.R. I–2041; Case C–314/91 *Weber v. Parliament* [1993] E.C.R. I–1093.

11 [1991] E.C.R. I–6079.

12 *ibid.* at para. 17.

themselves, are only means for attaining those objectives. This is a very useful statement of the constitutional importance of objectives, and an exposition of those objectives which the Court of Justice took as key (economic integration, an internal market and economic and monetary union).

The Opinion then continues with its exposition on the juridical nature of the Communities: "The context in which the objective of the [Draft EEA] agreement is situated also differs from that in which the Community aims are pursued." By context the Court is referring to the origin and nature of Community law, as is made clear by the two paragraphs immediately following. These are the best summary of the constitutional development of European Community law, made at the close of 1991:

> "The EEA is to be established on the basis of an international treaty which, essentially, merely creates rights and obligations as between the Contracting Parties and provides for no transfer of sovereign rights to the inter-governmental institutions which it sets up.
>
> In contrast, the EEC Treaty, albeit concluded in the form of an international agreement, none the less constitutes the constitutional charter of a Community based on the rule of law. As the Court of Justice has consistently held, the Community treaties established a new legal order for the benefit of which the States have limited their sovereign rights, in ever wider fields, and the subjects of which comprise not only Member States but also their nationals (see, in particular [Case 26/62 *Van Gend en Loos*]). The essential characteristics of the Community legal order which has thus been established are in particular its primacy over the law of the Member States and the direct effect of a whole series of provisions which are applicable to their nationals and to the Member States themselves."

In this Opinion, relying on Article 164 (EEC) and "the very foundations of the Community", the Court stated that there were substantive limits to amendment.[13] On the basis of this Opinion the idea of constitution in European Community law has to be understood as a concept

- distinguishing European Community law from the law of international organisations;
- dependent on the transfer of sovereign rights to the institutions;
- locked into the rule of law, and informed by a general idea of law, both concepts which have a meaning, developed by the Court of Justice, specific to the European Community legal order;
- constituting a new and developing legal order, the subjects of which constitute also the nationals of the Member States, which is directly effective in and takes primacy over the law of the Member States;

---

[13] Analysed in more detail in Chap. 11, "Amendability".

- resistant in some essential attributes to change by the Member States[14];
- designed to secure the objectives of the European Community, and being one of those objectives itself.

[14] See further below, Chap. 11. But not necessarily incapable of change. In Opinion 2/94 *Accession by the Community to the European Convention for Human Rights and Fundamental Freedoms* [1996] E.C.R. I–1759, the Court of Justice held:

> "Such a modification of the system for the protection of human rights in the Community, with equally fundamental institutional implications for the Community and for the Member States, would be of constitutional significance and would therefore be such as to go beyond the scope of Article 235. It could be brought about only by way of Treaty amendment."

11. AMENDABILITY

Importance

11–1 The question of amendment of European Community law is of great importance:

- to the public international law perception of the nature of European Community law. It is only when the Member States have been refused the powers of amendment that the constitutive treaties could be considered as acts escaping from public international law and founding an autonomous legal order.[1]
- for revolt and revolution, because if European Community law cannot bend on the points which would bring such to a head, then there is the spectre of intransigent orders integrated into one another and in internal and external normative conflicts.

Preliminaries

11–2 Before analysing the amendability of European Community law further, there are two preliminaries.

1. The main importance of the articles expressing the treaties to be concluded for an unlimited period[2] is the exclusion of the possibility of automatic expiry. These articles do not determine the answers to the questions considered here.[3]
2. The Treaty provisions on amendment must be distinguished from the general provisions allowing the Council, acting unanimously on a proposal from the Commission and after consulting the European Parliament, to

---

[1] See also W.G. van der Meersch, "L'Ordre juridique des Communautés Européenes et le Droit international" (1975) 148 (V) *Recueil des Cours de l'Académie de Droit International,* 45.

[2] Article Q (EU), Article 240 (EC), Article 208 (Euratom); *cf.* Article 97 (ECSC): 50 years from entry into force.

[3] One author has expressed the opinion that "the word 'unlimited' was chosen deliberately in preference to the more usual expression in constitutions or treaties without a fixed term, 'indefinite'. The authors of the EEC and Euratom Treaties wished to signify thereby the irrevocability of their commitment." Louis, *The Community Legal Order* from the European Perspectives Series (Brussels: Office for Official Publication of the European Communities, 1990) p. 74.

take appropriate measures.[4] Such measures are limited to those necessary to attain existing Treaty objectives where the necessary powers have not been transferred to the European Community. There is no requirement that the measures be ratified in accordance with the constitutional requirements of the Member States. Given the scope of the Treaty objectives, these are very important provisions. However, the Court of Justice has held that Article 235 (EC) cannot be used to effect constitutional change, for which Article N (EU) provides the procedure. The institutions are limited by the Article 3b (EC) principle of acting within conferred powers.[5]

This position is not quite reached in European Community law so far as the objectives remain a control but if one recalls that the tasks of the European Community set out in Article 2 (EC) encompass raising the quality of life and promoting social cohesion, then one might consider that the position is close to being reached in fact (and increasingly in law).[6] However, objectives such as a common defence are stated to be Union, not European Community, objectives, and therefore if measures are to be taken by the institutions where the necessary powers have not already been transferred, amendment of the Treaties pursuant to Article N (EU) is necessary.

General Rules

Public International Law Perception

11–3 Article 5 of the first Vienna Convention provides that it applies to any treaty which is the constituent instrument of an international organisation and to any treaties adopted within it without prejudice to any relevant rules of the organisation. Article 39 of that Convention provides: "A treaty may be amended by agreement between the parties. The rules laid down in [the Part on the Conclusion and Entry into Force of Treaties] apply except in so far as the treaty may otherwise provide." Article 40(1) specifies that the general international law rules on the procedures for amendment of multilateral treaties only apply if the Treaty does not otherwise specify. The Convention also provides that for any treaty (which presumably includes a treaty within an international organisation amending same) the consent of the States to be bound is necessary. This may be expressed "by signature, exchange of instru-

---

4 Article 235 (EC), Article 95 (ECSC) (no need to consult the European Parliament), Article 203 (Euratom).

5 Opinion 2/94 *Accession by the Community to the European Convention for Human Rights and Fundamental Freedoms* [1996] E.C.R. I-1759.

6 See above, para. 5–2, "Competences – European Community Law Perception".

ments constituting a treaty, ratification, acceptance, approval or accession, or by any other means if so agreed".[7]

On the basis of the let-out in Article 5 it does not appear that restricting the amendability of a constituent treaty of an international organisation on the basis of rules contained in that treaty are contrary to public international law. But, as has been mentioned before, Article 5 amounts to a partial public international law retreat from direct control. However the common provisions to the European Communities and European Union treaties do not specify limits to amendability so it is difficult for Article 40(1) to have application, and consequently for limits to amendability to be sustainable in public international law by virtue of Article 5. Furthermore, Article 31, which is more in the nature of a codification of existing public international law, provides some counterweight to such a permissive interpretation, as do other principles of public international law such as the sovereignty of States, consent, and the fundamental rule of *pacta sunt servanda* (although this cuts both ways, there is the additional principle of *posterior lex derogat*) which indicate that there cannot be limits if all the original parties consent.[8]

European Community Law Perception

11–4 The procedures for amendment were formerly laid down in the various treaties in Article 236 (EC), Article 96 (ECSC), and Article 204 (EURATOM), but these articles have since been repealed and replaced by Article N.1 (EU), which is substantially the same except that it provides for consultation with the European Central Bank. Article N provides:

> "1. The government of any Member State or the Commission may submit to the Council proposals for the amendment of the Treaties on which the Union is founded.
>
> If the Council, after consulting the European Parliament and, where appropriate, the Commission, delivers an opinion in favour of calling a conference of representatives of the governments of the Member States, the conference shall be convened by the President of the Council for the purpose of determining by common accord the amendments to be made to those Treaties. The European Central Bank shall also be consulted in the case of institutional changes in the monetary area.
>
> The amendments shall enter into force after being ratified by all the Member States in accordance with their respective constitutional requirements."

---

7 Article 11.

8 See below, paras. 11–8 *et seq.*, on "Institutional Involvement and Procedural Limits to the Member States' Powers of Amendment".

Article 228 (5) (EC) provides:

> "When the Council envisages concluding an agreement which calls for amendments to this treaty, the amendments must first be adopted in accordance with the procedure laid down in Article N of the Treaty on European Union."

Five points fall to be made immediately on these provisions:

1. The power of amendment is unrestricted on the face of the text. This is in stark contrast to Article N(2) (EU) where the conference of representatives of the governments to be convened in 1996 must apparently consider revision of the Treaties "in accordance with" (not merely "in the light of") Articles A (on the foundation of the Union and its place in the process of an ever closer union) and B (on the objectives of the Union) of the Treaty on European Union which, without reproducing these articles here, appears to commit the conference to greater integration.
2. Amendment by the Council via international treaty is prohibited. However, the reference to the Council means that this provision does not cover an international treaty between the Member States.
3. The institutions play a major role in the process.
4. The final paragraph makes clear that amendment depends on consent, which consent is to be expressed by ratification.
5. Amendment requires unanimity.

Unanimity

11–5 Unanimity is still required by Article N (EU) according to which the amendment will not enter into force until it is ratified by all the Member States. However, the continued existence of this requirement, in contrast to a majority requirement, far from dispositive of the character – federal or public international law – of the rules on treaty change. Apart from the fact that it is merely one factor, the Protocol (No. 14) on social policy, which by virtue of Article 239 (EC) forms an integral part of that Treaty, provides for a whole policy to go ahead without the United Kingdom. However, the United Kingdom did consent to this amendment, so in strict terms the retention of unanimity for amendment means merely that the Member States unanimously agree to disagree on amendment.

A further point could be made by comparative example. In the United States, undoubtedly a federal order, the Constitution cannot be amended to deprive a State of its equal suffrage in the Senate without the consent of that State.[9]

---

9 Article V of the Constitution of the United States.

Finally, the fact that unanimity is required to change the treaty does not mean that European Community law accepts the unanimity of the Member States as sufficient. It does not, since involvement by the institutions of the European Union is required, quite apart from possible substantive limits.[10]

Unilateral Change

Public International Law Perception

11–6 Can a Member State unilaterally withdraw or abrogate or revise one of the constitutive treaties? No, on the application of the rules codified in the Vienna Conventions. If the treaty so provides, or with the consent of all the parties, a treaty may end or a party withdraw.[11] But there are special rules for when the treaty is silent.[12] In that case unilateral change is possible only if it was the intention of the parties or if a Member State's right to denounce the treaty can be deduced from the treaty. Such an intention or deduction would not be readily drawn from the Treaty by the Court of Justice, in deciding the effect of a withdrawal in European Community law.

However, the Member States are not as "locked in" to the European Community as this seems to suggest. The application of any treaty may be suspended in regard to one or all parties[13] or, according to Article 59 (first Convention), any treaty can be terminated if the parties so agree, and this termination can even be implied from a later treaty. The overriding principle of public international law in the law of treaties is that they are of a consensual nature[14] and this means that the contracting Member States remain the masters. To this must be added the rider: as long as the contracting Member States remain States in the eyes of public international law.

European Community Law Perception

11–7 The problem has never been posed in European Community law, although it has been threatened politically by France (under de Gaulle), England (from time to time), and Denmark (after the "No" vote to the Treaty on European Union ratification). It appears certain that unilateral change cannot be in accordance with European Community law.

---

10 See below, paras. 11–8 *et seq.*
11 Article 54 (first Convention).
12 Article 56 (first Convention).
13 Article 57 (first Convention).
14 Preamble (second Convention). There is an example of withdrawal of part of a Member State – Greenland. This was done by all Member States ratifying the treaty permitting it to withdraw.

Institutional Involvement and Procedural Limits to the Member States' Powers of Amendment

European Community Law Perception

11–8 The Member States must observe the procedures in the Treaty in order to effect its (multilateral and unanimous) revision.[15]

But the procedures may be viewed as facilitative and not obligatory, which means that an amendment not following the Treaty prescribed procedures would not be null.[16] There have been two precedents where the Treaty establishing the European Coal and Steel Community has been amended outside of the prescribed procedures, the Treaty amending the Treaty establishing the European Coal and Steel Community because of the Return of the Sarre to the Federal Republic of Germany,[17] and the Convention on Certain Institutions Common to the European Communities.[18] Furthermore, no procedure was engaged to amend the Treaties on the unification of Germany, this decision not to amend being taken outside of the Community institutional framework by the European Council. The European Council is a political meeting of the heads of state or government of the Member States. These meetings have occurred since March 1975 following a decision by the heads of state or government of the previous year. Although the European Council is mentioned in the Single European Act (Article 6) it is not a Community institution. The first attempt to tie it legally into the Community institutional framework is Article D (EU) (which provides that a report must be submitted to the European Parliament) which came after the decision not to amend the European Community treaties consequent upon German reunification. The importance of the change to the legal order caused by unification – the extension of its territory of application and its subjects (since individuals are subjects) – might be considered to necessitate amendment,[19] since both territory and subjects are important elements of the legal order.[20]

---

15 Case 43/75, *Defrenne v. SABENA* [1976] E.C.R. 455; see also Case 22/70 *Commission v. Council* [1971] E.C.R. 263.

16 M. Walbroeck, "Contributions à l'étude de la nature juridique des Communautés Européennes" *Problèmes de Droit des Gens: Mélanges offerts à Henri Rolin* (Paris: Éditions A. Pedone, 1964) p. 515; W.G. van der Meersch, "L'Ordre juridique des Communautés Européennes et le Droit international" (1975) (148) (V) *Recueil des Cours de l'Académie de Droit International* 49.

17 Signed on 27 October 1956.

18 Signed on 25 March 1957 (the same day as the signing of the Treaty establishing the European Economic Community).

19 However Germany had made Declarations on the reintegration of its national territory since 1952.

20 For this second proposition, see C.N. Kakouris, "La relation de l'ordre juridique communautaire avec les ordres juridiques des États membres (Quelques réflexions parfois peu conformistes)" in *Du droit international au droit de l'intégration*, (C–D Ehlermann *et al.* ed., Liber Amicorum Pierre Pescatore, 1987) p. 321.

These precedents support a facilitative interpretation. There is also doubt about the jurisdiction of the Court of Justice to consider the legality of amendments, at least pursuant to a direct challenge. In Case T–584/93 *Roujansky v. Council* [21] the Court of First Instance held that the Treaty on European Union was not an act of an institution within the meaning of Articles 4 and 173 (EC) and consequently it had no jurisdiction to review its provisions via an Article 173 (EC) challenge.[22]

Public International Law Perception

11–9 Even if the procedures are perceived to be obligatory, the treaties may still be amended unanimously outside of these procedures because basic public international law rules apply on account of the Treaties' international origin. The basic rule is *pacta sunt servanda*, and the law of treaties is based on the consent of those bound. The Member States, as subjects of international law, remain sovereign to make a modifying treaty. On the application of the "*principe de l'acte contraire*", a treaty may always be modified by a subsequent treaty concluded by common accord. This applies equally to the Treaties establishing the three Communities and to the Treaty on European Union.[23] Some commentators have claimed that this right to modify derives even from *ius cogens.*[24] The Member States thus remain in control of the treaties. This perception is reinforced by the two precedents of amendment of the Treaties without the involvement of the Community institutions.[25]

In any event, the preliminary procedure could itself be removed by amendment.[26]

Substantive Limits

Public International Law Perception

11–10 The arguments against procedural limits in the last paragraph apply *a fortiori* against the possibility of substantive limits.

It should be noted that there is a possibility of limits in public international law to what States can agree to do, or at least to what States would be

---

21 [1994] E.C.R. II–587.

22 See also Case 31/86 *LAISA v. Council* [1988] E.C.R. 2285.

23 See the commentators cited by R. Bieber, "Les limites matérielles et formelles à la révision des traités établissant la Communauté Européenne" (1993) 367 *Revue du Marché Commun et de l'Union Européenne* 343 at pp. 345–346.

24 See Bieber, *ibid.* fn. 15.

25 See above, para. 11–8.

26 W.G. van der Meersch "L'Ordre Juridique des Communautés Européennes et le Droit international" (1975) (148) (V) *Recueil des Cours de l'Académie de Droit International*, 50; *cf.* below, para. 11–11.

bound to even if they did agree. But these limits do not concern any conceivable amendment – they derive from *ius cogens* and concern, for example, an agreement to commit gross and systematic human rights abuses.

It has been asserted that the capability of a treaty to remain flexible and adaptable is a condition of its continuing validity.[27] This may imply that if the treaties imposed rigid limits (in the perception of public international law) on substantial revision, they may cease to become binding in public international law.

European Community Law Perception

11–11 As noted above, there appears to be no ground on the text of Article N(1) (EU) for restricting what can be amended in the Treaties. The Court has held that it lacks jurisdiction via Article 173 (EC) to review an amendment to the Treaties provided that the act is one of the Member States and not of the Council,[28] but the issue could arise before the Court in other ways. There are no articles in the Treaties expressed to be unamendable. However Article N(2) (EU) provides that the intergovernmental conference will review provisions in accordance with the objectives set out in Articles A and B (EU), which appears to constrain what the Member States can do at that conference. Furthermore, the Preambles (which are not provisions) to the Treaty on European Union and the Treaties establishing the European Community state the Member States' determination to move to "an ever closer union among the peoples of Europe" in which process the Treaty on European Union is expressly stated to be a stage (Article A (EU)). Substantive limits imposed by the text may be indicated also by Protocol (No. 10) on the transition to the third stage of economic and monetary union which declares "the irreversible character of the Community's movement to the third stage of economic and monetary union". Protocols form an integral part of the Treaty by virtue of Article 239 (EC). There is certainly support that this constitutes a limit at least on the intergovernmental conference, since one of the objectives in Article B (EU) is a single currency. Article N(2) (EU) interacts with Article B (EU). There appears to be support in the European Parliament for the opinion that the intergovernmental conference has no powers to challenge the provision for a single currency by the year 1999.[29]

However the existence of substantive limits to amendment has been asserted both by the Court of Justice and doctrine.[30] In *Costa v. ENEL* the Court of

---

27 W.G. van der Meersch, at 77 (citing Cavare, *Annuaire de la Commission*, II, (1969) p.212).

28 Case 31/86 *Laisa v. Council* [1988] E.C.R. 2285. See also Case T–584/93 *Roujansky v. Council* [1994] E.C.R. II–587.

29 Written Question E–246/95 [1995] O.J. C230/7. This may not represent the view of the European Parliament *qua* institution. In any event, the Council declared itself unaware of such an interpretation: *ibid.*

30 See, *e.g.* Curtin's opinion that there may be limits to amendments which "breach fundamental human rights as protected in the Community legal order or violate certain

Justice referred to the transfer of competences as creating a permanent limitation of sovereign rights.[31] A restrictive interpretation of this statement in the context of that case could limit the meaning of "permanent limitation" to deny each Member State the competence (as distinct from holding the exercise of the competence to be in breach of European Community law) to breach unilaterally its European Community law obligations by enacting conflicting national laws. However an even wider interpretation is possible: "permanent limitation" could mean an irreversible transfer.

As early as 1975 the Court of Justice suggested that "*[l]a sécurité juridique* supposes the irreversibility of transferred competences, which cannot be subjected to returns backwards without danger for the whole of the construction."[32]

The Court made its position clearest in Opinion 1/91.[33] This opinion on the draft agreement between the Community and the countries of the European Free Trade Association relating to the creation of the European Economic Area is by far the most important authority on the existence of substantive limits to amendments. The Court in that Opinion set out important aspects of its view of Treaty as Constitution.[34] The Court goes on to state that there are limits, effectively constitutional limits, to the Member States' power of amendment. The Court found that the draft agreement set up a system of courts which conflicted with the Court's Article 164 (EEC) obligation to ensure that in the interpretation and application of the Treaty, the law is observed, and with the very foundations of the Community.[35] It continued:

> "For the same reasons, an amendment of Article 238 in the way indicated by the Commission could not cure the incompatibility with Community law of the system of courts to be set up by the agreement."[36]

Therefore an amendment of a treaty article could not cure a fundamental constitutional conflict, even though the European Community law with which the treaty was conflicting was largely a judicial construction.[37]

---

constitutional principles with mandatory (and hence superior) status in the Community legal order such as the supremacy of Community law over all provisions of national law", in D. Curtin, "The Constitutional Structure of the Union: A Europe of Bits and Pieces" (1994) 30 *Common Market Law Review* 17 at p. 63. Hartley considers that the Court of Justice might arrogate to itself the jurisdiction to declare Treaty amendments void: T.C. Hartley, "The European Court, Judicial Objectivity and the Constitution of the European Union" (1996) 112 *Law Quarterly Review* 95 at p. 108.

31 [1964] E.C.R. 585. See above, paras. 8–41 *et seq.*, "Case 6/64 *Costa v. ENEL* – Sovereignty".

32 [1975] European Community Bull. Supp. *Suggestions de la Cour de Justice sur l'Union Européenne* 17 at p. 18.

33 [1991] E.C.R. I–6079.

34 See above, para. 10–2.

35 [1991] E.C.R. I–6079, at para. 72.

36 [1991] E.C.R. I–6112, at para. 72.

37 This appears to be the majority consensus on the meaning of the ruling – see, *e.g.* P. Neill, "The European Court of Justice: a Case Study in Judicial Activism" (Oxford: Manuscript, January 23, 1995), and B. de Witte, "International Agreement on European Law" in *The Treaty on European Union: Suggestions for Revision* ('s-Gravenhage: Asser Instituut, 1995) p. 18.

The import of the judgment of the Court is restricted for three reasons. First, this statement was to a high degree *obiter*. Secondly, the Court referred only to the amendment of a particular article. This leaves open the possibility that, for example, Article 164 (EC) could be amended.[38] Thirdly, the Court referred to amendment of Article 238 "in the way indicated by the Commission". Article 238 (EC) provides:

> "The Community may conclude with one or more States or international organizations agreements establishing an association involving reciprocal rights and obligations, common action and special procedures."[39]

The Commission indicated amending this article so that "special procedures" included the establishment of courts functionally integrated with the Court of Justice and guaranteeing the specific nature and integrity of European Community law.[40] But the Court of Justice held that the system of courts envisaged by the Agreement attacked the integrity of European Community law and therefore the amendment suggested could not cure the incompatibility. This leaves open as a possibility that a different amendment, of Article 238 (EC) or of other articles, might have cured the incompatibility.

In Opinion 2/94[41] some support may be found for the proposition that there are no limits to amendment, because the Court held:

> "Such a modification of the system for the protection of human rights in the Community, with equally fundamental institutional implications for the Community and for the Member States, would be of constitutional significance and would therefore be such as to go beyond the scope of Article 235. It could be brought about only by way of Treaty amendment."[42]

However, this may mean no more than the protection of fundamental rights as currently understood does not form part of the unamendable core of European Community law. Indeed the suggested amendment[43] to give the European Community a specific competence in human rights would advance European Community law toward a federal legal order.

---

38 The logic to arguments on self-reference and amendability is further explored in Parts III and IV. The idea of limits to "legal" amendment has to be distinguished from political reality. For example, the Greek Constitution of 1952 contained an Article 108 (2) stating that the monarchic character of the state was unamendable. Although this was not able to prevent the constituent power in 1975 from replacing this clause with a clause stating the republican form of the State to be unamendable, this does not mean that this amendment was legal within the terms of the Constitution of 1952.

39 At the time of judgment, Article 238 (EEC) read: ". . . States, a union of States or an international . . . ".

40 [1991] E.C.R. I–6079 at 6098. Belgium saw nothing against this proposal in principle. The United Kingdom thought that the phrase "common action and special procedures" already contained in Article 238 was sufficient as it stood.

41 Opinion 2/94 *Accession by the Community to the European Convention for Human Rights and Fundamental Freedoms*, 28 March 1996.

42 *ibid.* para. 35.

43 *ibid.* para. 27.

For a national constitutional order, the principle that the constituent power must respect certain fundamental rules and principles for an amendment to the constitution to be "legal" is not extraordinary. By asserting this proposition the Court makes clear that "constitution" in European Community law approximates a federal constitution. The proposition is not intrinsically foreign to a legal order where "*une certaine idée de l'Europe*" has been a fundamental referent in judicial constitutional development.

12. JURISDICTION FOR CONFLICTS

12–1 There is no difficulty in bringing conflicts between national law and European Community law before a Community court. These could arise under many of the heads of jurisdiction, in particular under Articles 169 to 171 (EC) and, for direct conflicts between courts with an interwoven jurisdiction in the same action, under Article 177 (EC).[1]

[1] See above, Chap. 8, "Rights to Individuals".

13. EUROPEAN COMMUNITY LAW AS A FEDERAL LEGAL ORDER

Public International Law Perception

13–1 It does not appear possible within this perception to escape from the choice between two mutually exclusive alternatives[1]: either the relations between the Member States are governed by treaties which, whatever their particularity, remain within public international law; or those relations are not governed by international law but by the internal law of a federation however loose.

This second alternative has not been reached, because the European Community does not satisfy the public international law criteria for statehood. The European Community has a population, a defined territory, and a government with centralised legislative and administrative functions in many areas. However the European Community government has not the power to decide on the scope of its competences, does not have competence in the area of defence, and in large part has to rely on the executive and judicial organs of the governments of the Member States in order to exercise its powers. Furthermore, the European Community is not independent from the Member States in that it does not have a nationality law of its own, nor can it conclude treaties in all areas.

Conversely, the Member States still probably satisfy the public international law conditions of statehood, although "it would be possible for a tribunal to hold that a state which had granted away piecemeal a high proportion of its legal powers had ceased to have a separate existence as a consequence."[2]

European Community Law Perception

13–2 In 1987 Judge Kakouris asserted that "from the purely legal point of view, the relationship Community – Member States is federal".[3] Since then the federal nature of European Community law has been strengthened by

---

1 C. Leben, "A propos de la nature juridique des Communautés Européennes" (1991) *Droits – Revue française de théorie juridique* 61 at p. 64.

2 I. Brownlie, *Principles of Public International Law*, (4th ed, Oxford: Clarendon Press, 1990) p. 79.

3 C.N. Kakouris, "La relation de l'ordre juridique communautaire avec les ordres juridiques des États membres (Quelques réflexions parfois peu conformistes)" (1987) in *Du droit international au droit de l'intégration*, (C–D Wesmann *et al.* ed., Liber Amicorum Pierre Pescatore) p. 344.

case law and the Treaty on European Union. The following federal characteristics or claims of European Community law which establish the characteristics set out in the Introduction to this Chapter can now be stated:

- the existence of sovereign institutions independent of intergovernmental control;
- the breadth and nature of community competences;
- the use of the institutions of the Member States as organs of Community government;
- the judicial development of Article 5 (EC)[4];
- the conclusion of conventions pursuant to Community policy (such as the Brussels Convention on the Mutual Recognition of Judgments in Civil and Commercial Matters, concluded pursuant to Article 220 (EC)), giving jurisdiction to the Court of Justice, and in this regard the existence in the wings of the Union pillar of Justice and Home Affairs;
- the constitutionally entrenched position of economic and monetary union;
- the territory of the Community corresponds to the territory of the Member States where European Community law applies;
- European Community law's rejection of the public international law basis of European Community law, despite its origin in treaties;
- European Community law's self-perception as an autonomous legal order which is both *sui generis* and *ex proprio vigore*;
- the self-financing of the Community;
- the doctrines of supremacy and direct effect;
- the position of the individual as a subject of European Community law, which in addition to the doctrines of supremacy and direct effect includes fundamental rights protection and citizenship;
- the development of the notion of the Treaties establishing the European Communities and the Treaty on European Union as the constitution of an entity tending toward a federation;
- the development of the role of the Court of Justice as constitutional court;
- the constitutional status of the federal principle of subsidiarity[5];

---

[4] See O. Due, "Article 5 du traité CEE. Une disposition de caractère fédéral", *Collected Courses of the Academy of European Law* (Dordrecht: Martinus Nijhoff, 1991).

[5] Article 3b (EC). Whatever the wisdom of making this principle justiciable – Lord MackenzieStuart, "Subsidiarity, A Busted Flush?" (1992) in *Constitutional Adjudication in European Community and National Law: Essays for the Hon. Mr Justice T.F. O'Higgins* (D. Curtin

- the resistance of the Constitution to change by the Member States;
- the question of whether the Community or the Member States has the competence to decide on the extent of competences is not clear: on the one hand, there is the expansive interpretation of the Community's internal and external competences, Article 235 (EC) in conjunction with this expansive interpretation and the wide and vague nature of the Community's objectives, the possible restraints on recovering transferred competences, Opinion 1/91, the disregard for the specific intentions of the Member States, and the reliance on objectives and the spirit of the treaty[6]; on the other hand, there is the wording and origin of the treaty, Article 3b(1) (EC) and Opinion 2/94;
- the exclusive or shared European Community competence in foreign affairs in areas corresponding to internal European Community policies, and the extension of Union competence into foreign affairs in defense matters coupled with the crossovers between Union competences and European Community competences in this area;
- the legitimation of constitutional developments by reference to securing dynamic goals which have themselves changed, from "the Common Market" to integration and "European unity", which are given a federalist interpretation.

---

and D. O'Keeffe eds., Dublin: Butterworth (Ireland), 1992) p. 19 – this has now been done. As to the different interpretations of the principle before the Treaty on European Union, see C. Onestini, "Whose subsidiarity?" (1993) IV (1) *Oxford International Review* 29.

6 Mention might also be made of the future importance of Article F(3) (EU): "The Union shall provide itself with the means necessary to attain its objectives and carry through its policies." This is not a provision of European Community law, being in that part of the Treaty on European Union excluded from the jurisdiction of the Court of Justice. A narrow reading of this Article was advocated by the Commission before the Federal German Constitutional Court in *Brunner v. The European Union Treaty* [1994] 1 C.M.L.R. 57 (which court also took a narrow view).

Part III

FRENCH CONSTITUTIONAL LAW

INTRODUCTION[1]

France is a particularly important country to study for several reasons. First, it is the national legal order which has most influenced the development of European Community law and the institution of the Court of Justice. Secondly, the legitimation of constitutional law presented by the revolutionary Declaration of the Rights of Man and of the Citizen (1789) has influenced the western notion of legitimation of law and the constitutional protection of fundamental rights.[2] Thirdly, the concept of national sovereignty is more to the fore than in Irish constitutional law. Fourthly, the relatively recent constitutionalisation of the national legal order and the division of jurisdictions between courts presents a challenge to the thesis that conflicts between national constitutional law and European Community law present the prospect of revolution in the legal order. Fifthly, the constitutional tension between French constitutional law and European Community law have not been focussed on to the same extent as the tensions between European Community law and, for example, German or Italian constitutional law; attention has been more focussed on the different status of European Community law in the different court systems of France and not on the problem of revolt or revolution.

The ratification of the Treaty on European Union does not mean that European Community law is incorporated into French law to the degree which the Court of Justice considers to be required by European Community law. This Part establishes the following:

1. French constitutional law has a restricted view of the present and future claims of European Community law. The French constitutional law descrip-

---

1 Citations to decisions of the *Conseil Constitutionnel* are given where possible from the *Recueil des décisions du Conseil constitutionnel*, represented by "Rec."; citations to decisions of the *Conseil d'État* are given where possible from the *Recueil des décisions du Conseil d'État*, represented by "Rec. Lebon", and prefixed with "decision of the *Conseil d'État*".

2 The former President of France, F. Mitterand, on the bicentenary of Bastille Day, stated that the French Declaration and the events of 1789 had reverberated around the world, a fact the world recognises – D. Pollard, "France's Conseil Constitutionnel – Not Yet a Constitutional Court?" (1988) XXIII *Irish Jurist* (N.S.) 2.

tion of European Community law conflicts with European Community law's self-description.

2. The fundamental commitments of French constitutional law are likely to come into conflict with European Community law.
3. Further European Community law inroads into French constitutional law may call into question both the coherence of French constitutional law and the legitimation of French law.
4. The possibility of revision of the Constitution to resolve these conflicts is limited.

The author is not a French lawyer. The above points, established by the following analysis of French consitutional law, are put forward with more tentativeness than the points in Irish constitutional law and European Community law. Insecurity is the price a comparativist pays when analysis leads in directions away from established doctrinal paths.

14. A LEGAL CONSTITUTION WITH THE POSSIBILITY OF INTER-ORDER CONFLICTS WITH EUROPEAN COMMUNITY LAW

> "[S]ince an agreement, at least on the principles, cannot be found between the two categories of jurisdictional orders (European Community and French), this is often because constitutional questions are in play. Since national, and especially constitutional, judges draw their competence from the Fundamental Law itself, this cannot but be for them the supreme norm from where they draw the legitimacy of their existence and of their decisions. They are thus necessarily led to refuse to compromise the constitutional rule and as a result are in great danger to enter in conflict with the Community legal order."[1]

Introduction

14–1 This section endeavours to establish that the French Constitution is legal, and not just political,[2] in the sense that it is the foundation of the legal order and the applicability and validity of other rules may be tested against it in courts. This constitutionalisation of French law means that European Community law's applicability is dependent on it being within the limits of the French constitutional law interpretation of European Community law. Another effect is that a discontinuity in the legitimation of French constitutional law would mean a legal revolution. In French constitutional law the protection of human rights is particularly important.[3]

It is more necessary in French constitutional law than in Irish constitutional law to address the place of constitutional control by courts (as distinct from the substantive content of French constitutional law) because, until comparatively

---

1 F. Hervouet, "Politique Jurisprudentielle de la Cour de Justice et des Juridictions Nationales: Réception du Droit Communautaire par le Droit Interne" (1992) *Revue de Droit Public* 1257 at p. 1292.

2 This is not to deny that study of "the law–politics dialectic that inheres in any regime of constitutional control" (F.L. Morton, "Judicial Review in France: A Comparative Analysis" (1988) 36 *American Journal of Comparative Law* 89 at p. 110) can be made of the *Conseil Constitutionnel*, but to assert that the *Conseil Constitutionnel* may be analysed also from the purely legal perspective as an intra-order Court which is the authoritative interpreter of a constitutionalised legal order.

3 Human rights are unquestionably also important politically: "Since [the Declaration of 1789] every new regime has felt obliged, on coming into power, to affirm its own legitimacy by declaring an adherence to the notion of human rights": West *et al.*, *The French Legal System, an introduction*, (London: Fourmat Publishing, 1992) p. 140.

recently, due to the rigid interpretation of the principle of the separation of powers as restricting constitutional review save in a restrictive sense following special procedures before the *Conseil Constitutionnel*, constitutional control by courts has not been a feature of the French legal order.[4] For most of the two hundred years of French constitutional law starting with the Revolution, France has had texts proclaiming fundamental rights of constitutional status without jurisdictional mechanisms to support them. As Rivero puts it, the responsibility of lawyers "far from negligible, consists in elaborating the instruments without which human rights, although officially proclaimed, would remain lost in the world of ideals instead of taking shape in the life of free communities."[5] Furthermore, as Professor Rudden has pointed out, the idea of the inherent powers of the judiciary which forms part of the common law, is alien to French law.[6]

The *Conseil Constitutionnel* is the supreme constitutional court. The observance of the administrative judiciary, whose supreme court is the *Conseil d'État*, and the regular judiciary, whose supreme court is the *Cour de Cassation*, of French constitutional law is not straightforward. The *Conseil Constitutionnel*, the *Conseil d'État*, and the *Cour de Cassation* all view European Community law differently. This Chapter focuses on the *Conseil Constitutionnel*. A brief consideration of the *Conseil d'État* and *Cour de Cassation* is annexed.[7]

Traditionally, the idea of a court with control of the legislature has been very unpopular in France. Since the cry of "down with the parliaments [courts]" in the French Revolution, interference with parliamentary sovereignty was perceived to be an attack on the politically legitimate order of representative democracy. However under the Constitution of 1958, as the control by the *Conseil Constitutionnel* and to a lesser extent by the other courts demonstrates, the Parliament and Executive must be kept within the limits of the powers given by the nation in the Constitution.[8] But the continuing influence of the doctrine of the separation of powers, as opposed to the checks and balances in Irish constitutional law, and the consequent division of the jurisdictions of public law (presided over by the *Conseil d'État*) and private and criminal law (presided over by the *Cour de Cassation*) and the absence of any procedural bridge between either of these jurisdictions and the *Conseil Constitutionnel*,

---

4 Even as late as 1986 a commentator stated: "A dispute burns across the landscape of French constitutional law regarding the juridical nature of the French constitutional 'Supreme Court', the *Conseil Constitutionnel*: is it a court": M.H. Davis, "The Law/Politics Distinction, the French Conseil Constitutionnel, and the U.S. Supreme Court" (1986) 34 *American Journal of Comparative Law* 45.

5 J. Rivero, "The Constitutional Protection of Human Rights in French Law" (1977) XII *Irish Jurist* 1 at p. 14, translated by A. Cras.

6 B. Rudden and L. Kahn-Freund, *A Source-Book on French Law* (Oxford: Clarendon Press, 1991) p. 144: "France shares with England the rule of law – it does not share the rule of the courts."

7 See below, Chap. 22, "The *Conseil d'État* and *Cour de Cassation*".

8 J. Bell, *French Constitutional Law* (Oxford: Clarendon Press, 1992) p. 56.

means that there are jurisdictional limits to the control of the courts, and indeed to how far French law can be said to constitute a unified legal order. The resulting jurisdictional situation is complex, in places uncertain. The process of constitutionalisation is partly because of the *Conseil Constitutionnel's* interpretation of the new constitutional order set up by the Constitution of 1958, partly because the direct grant of power in the Constitution to the executive involves the *Conseil d'État* in constitutional control, and not least because the problem of taking the constitutional claims of European Community law into account straddles all domestic jurisdictions.

The *Conseil Constitutionnel*

Background

14–2 "The *Conseil Constitutionnel* permits, for the first time in the history of the French Republic, the assurance of the effective supremacy of the constitution over the other legal norms."[9]

This was not obvious in 1958.[10] The *Conseil Constitutionnel* is one of a number of mechanisms under the Constitution of 1958 which ensure a strong executive by keeping Parliament within the domain of *loi* described in Article 34 (traditionally the Executive acted under the Parliament with the *Conseil d'État* controlling the exercise of its delegated functions). Whether the functions of the *Conseil Constitutionnel* were intended to be confined to policing the boundary between Parliament and the Executive may be disputed. Debré said that the *Conseil Constitutionnel* "subordinates the *loi,* that is the decisions of Parliament, to the higher law of the Constitution". Parliament not only lost powers to the executive, but also "lost capacity and esteem as . . . a defender of the citizen's rights and liberties".[11] For our purposes it is sufficient that the *Conseil Constitutionnel* controls *lois,* public international law agreements, and in some cases *règlements,* against constitutional criteria other than the separation of legislative and executive domains, and that this function of control is legitimated by the order which it interprets.

---

9 C. Debasch, and J.-M. Pontier, *Les Constitutions de la France,* (Paris: Dalloz, 2nd ed., 1989) p. 276.

10 Indeed much later Cappelletti was of the opinion that the *Conseil Constitutionnel* does not qualify to be described as a constitutional court – M. Cappelletti, *Judicial Review in the Contemporary World* (Indianopolis Bobbs-Merril Company, 1971).

11 D. Thomson, *Democracy in France since 1870* (Oxford: Oxford University Press, 5th ed., 1969), p. 273. *c.f.* J. Bell, *op. cit.* above, n.8, p. 228, who argues that the *Conseil Constitutionnel* arrogated to itself its functions of human rights protection and has continued since then to define its own role as something removed from its original conception in the Constitution of 1958.

The new relationship between the Parliament and the *Conseil Constitutionnel* under the Constitution of 1958 means that, first, the *Conseil Constitutionnel* is the ultimate guardian of constitutional rights but that, secondly, Parliament has retained part of its former position (of guardian of the rights and liberties of citizens as an aspect of its exercise of national sovereignty) in its control of the framework of *lois* within which those rights are exercised, in its margin of appreciation of the balance between state and individual interests, in its decisions on what the *Conseil Constitutionnel* considers to be disputed issues of fact,[12] and in its assessment of the common good.[13] Article 34 provides that "*Loi* shall fix the rules concerning: civic rights and the fundamental guarantees accorded to citizens for the exercise of public freedoms [*libertés publiques*]". As Nicholas puts it, the function of the *Conseil Constitutionnel* is to ensure that, although constitutional rights are exercised within the framework of *lois* which regulate them, the restrictions on their exercise do not call into question the existence of the right itself.[16] However there is no constitutional basis for the *Conseil Constitutionnel* to accord to European Community legislative organs a similar role or leeway in the exercise of their competences. Just as human rights may be balanced with other juridical concepts of constitutional value such as public order only within a complete political community with an intelligible commonwealth,[15] so may the framework *lois* within which these

---

12 In 94–343/344 DC, 27 July 1994, Rec. p. 100; (1995) Rec. Dalloz Sirey 237, *lois on respect for the human body and biotechnology*, the *Conseil Constitutionnel* decided, in respect of the decision of Parliament that the respect for every human being from the start of its life was not applicable to embryos which had never been implanted in the womb:

> "that it is not the function of the *Conseil Constitutionnel*, which does not enjoy a power of appreciation and of decision identical to that of Parliament, to put into question, in respect of the state of knowledge and techniques, the provisions thus adopted by the legislature."

13 Examples of the recognition by the *Conseil Constitutionnel* of the importance of the position of the Parliament are 93–331 DC, 13 January 1994, Rec. p. 17, *Renewing General Councils* where the *Conseil Constitutionnel*, in holding that it did not have a general power of appreciation and decision identical to that of Parliament, stated:

> "it is not up to [the *Conseil Constitutionnel*] to see if the objectives which the legislator has assigned itself can be attained by other ways so long as, as in the instant case, the means adopted by the *loi* are not manifestly inappropriate to these objectives",

and 93–325 DC, 13 August 1993, Rec. p. 224; (1993) *La Semaine Juridique (Textes)* 373, *On the Control of Immigration*, where the *Conseil Constitutionnel* held:

> "if the legislator can adopt in respect of foreigners specific provisions, it is its function to respect the liberties and fundamental rights of constitutional value acknowledged to all those who reside on the territory of the Republic; that if they must be reconciled with the safeguard of public order which constitutes an objective of constitutional value . . . ; that they must benefit from the exercise of jurisdictional protection assuring the guarantee of these rights and liberties",

which reaffirms not only that the Parliament in the first instance reconciles constitutional rights with more general objectives of constitutional value but that ultimately, as in this case, the *Conseil Constitutionnel* will control the balance, and the other jurisdictions will protect the rights in particular cases.

14 B. Nicholas, "Fundamental Rights and Judicial Review in France" [1978] *Public Law* 161.

15 See below, para. 21–14, "Rights and Freedoms Understood in a Framework of Interdependent Concepts".

rights are exercised and limited be established only by the Parliament – an institution of the Republic. Therefore constitutional control by the *Conseil Constitutionnel* of European Community law is not restrained by respect for the role of Parliament.[16]

Articles 56 and 57 (Constitution of 1958) set out the basics. The *Conseil Constitutionnel* comprises nine members whose mandate lasts for a non-renewable period of nine years, three members to be elected triennially. The presidents of the Republic, the National Assembly, and the Senate elect three members each. In addition, former presidents of the Republic are *ex officio* members (but in practice do not sit). The functions of membership are incompatible with being a minister or a member of Parliament. Other conditions are laid down by Organic *loi.*[17] Under Article 3 of that *ordonnance* (of the same status as an Organic *loi*) members of the *Conseil Constitutionnel* must swear an oath to exercise their functions impartially, to respect the Constitution, to keep secrecy and not take any public position or give advice on matters within the *Conseil Constitutionnel's* jurisdiction. The members of the *Conseil Constitutionnel* are almost all legally qualified, several being professors of law or drawn from the *Cour de Cassation* or the *Conseil d'État.* They are usually at the end of their political career and thus, coupled with the nine-year non-renewable term of office and their duties under Article 7 of the *ordonnance* ensuring their independence, have as much independence as a constitutional judge tenured for life. They are the "independent guardians of the constitutional tradition".[18] At the same time, the political background of the members means they are in touch with political and social concerns. Bell summarises: "Although standing within the political process, the *Conseil* aims to impose stable and fundamental values in a situation where opportunism and short-term considerations have a significant place in the motives of the principle actors."[19]

As a court, the *Conseil Constitutionnel* has demonstrated its willingness to cause upset in the criminal law system,[20] in European Community law matters,[21] and in particularly sensitive areas of domestic law and politics.[22]

---

16 There may be something of an exception of a class of conflicts (categorised below as case two conflicts – para. 14–4, "The *Conseil Constitutionnel's* Control of the French Constitutional Legal Order") where the Parliament enacts a *loi* which would be unconstitutional were it not required by a European Community measure, but that European Community measure is outside of French law's interpretation of European Community law.

17 *Ordonnance* No. 58/1067 of 7 November 1958.

18 Bell, (1992) *op. cit.* above, n.8, p. 34.

19 *ibid.* p. 40.

20 73–80 L, 28 November 1973, Rec. p. 45; [1973] Rec. Dalloz Sirey 237 at 269, *Contraventions*; see B. Nicholas, *op. cit.* above, n.14, at p. 92.

21 92–308 DC, 9 April 1992, Rec. p. 55; (1992) 28 *Revue Trimestrielle du Droit Européen* 418, *TEU No. 1.*

22 81–132 DC, 16 January 1982, Rec. p. 18, *On nationalisation.* 88–244 DC, 20 July 1988, Rec. p. 119; [1988] *L'Actualité Juridique, Droit Administratif* 752, *The Renault Ten I.* 89–258 DC, 8 July 1989, Rec. p. 48; in Rudden (1991) *op. cit.* above, n.6, pp. 80–81, *Renault Ten II.*

Authority

14–3 The political acceptance of the authority of the *Conseil Constitutionnel* was seen most clearly only after the signing of the Maastricht treaty on 7 February 1991. The *Conseil Constitutionnel's* constitutional law exposition set the terms of the debate not only on the Constitutional *loi* of 27 June 1992 but also on the whole question of ratification. Its decisions, quite apart from *TEU No. 1*,[23] were frequently referred to by members of parliament as authoritative expositions and decisions of constitutional issues.

The composition of the *Conseil Constitutionnel* is also important for its authority over political actors.

The political acceptance of the authority of the *Conseil Constitutionnel* is reinforced by its jurisdiction over several types of political dispute.[24]

First, Article 41 provides for the *Conseil Constitutionnel* to decide a dispute between Parliament and the Executive in the course of the legislative procedure[25] on whether or not a measure belongs in the domain of *loi*. Under this jurisdiction the *Conseil Constitutionnel* will consider only the division of functions between Parliament and the Executive, not other considerations of constitutionality.[26]

Secondly, Article 59 transferred from the two chambers of Parliament to the *Conseil Constitutionnel* jurisdiction to supervise parliamentary elections to avoid bias in the application of the election *lois*.[27]

Thirdly, under Article 60 the *Conseil Constitutionnel* supervises the regularity of referenda and proclaims the results.

Fourthly, under Article 16 the *Conseil Constitutionnel* gives non-binding advice to the President in the exercise of his emergency functions. This jurisdiction highlights by contrast the binding nature of the *Conseil Constitutionnel's* decisions in the exercise of its other jurisdictions. Article 16 further provides a role for the *Conseil Constitutionnel* when the Constitution can be effectively suspended by the President when "the institutions of the Republic, the independence of the Nation, the integrity of its territory or the maintenance of its international engagements are threatened in a serious and immediate way and the regular functioning of the constitutional public powers is interrupted." Finally, under Article 7 the *Conseil Constitutionnel* confirms the vacancy or incapacity of the President.

---

23 92–308 DC, Above, n.21.

24 The extent of the *Conseil Constitutionnel's* jurisdiction which touches directly on the constitutionalisation of the legal order is considered below, para. 14–4, "The *Conseil Constitutionnel's* control of the French Constitutional Legal Order.

25 As distinct from Article 37 control.

26 79–10 FNR, 26 April 1979, Rec. p. 55, *Amendments creating permanent parliamentary committees on energy conservation.*

27 Under Article 8 of the Constitution of 1946 the two chambers of Parliament were the judges of the eligibility of their members and the regularity of their election. See also below, para. 14–9, "Articles 58 and 59 – Electoral Jurisdiction Control of Compatibility of Promulgated *Lois* with Treaties".

In addition to political acceptance, the *Conseil Constitutionnel's* decisions are also increasingly accepted by the other court jurisdictions. In the *Conseil d'État* and the *Tribunal des conflits*, a decision of the *Conseil Constitutionnel* can be cited as a sufficient reason for a judgment.[28] In the *Cour de Cassation* the decisions of the *Conseil Constitutionnel* may often be the basis for the conclusions of the Advocate-General and provide the inspiration for the *Cour de Cassation's* decision without being cited as such in the body of the judgment.[29]

Constitutionally, the binding nature of the decisions of the *Conseil Constitutionnel* is clear. Under Article 54 a treaty which contains a provision contrary to the Constitution cannot be ratified before constitutional revision. As for the decisions under Article 61, their binding nature is covered by Article 62:

> "A provision declared unconstitutional cannot be promulgated or put into application.
>
> The decisions of the *Conseil Constitutionnel* are not susceptible to any appeal. They bind the public powers and all administrative and judicial authorities."

The binding nature of the decision of the *Conseil Constitutionnel* under Article 37 of the Constitution on the proper domain, *loi* or *réglementaire*, of measures was stated firmly in the decision *loi on agricultural policy*.[30] The *Conseil Constitutionnel* quoted the last paragraph of Article 62 and continued: "the authority of decisions envisaged by that provision attaches not only to their holding but also to those reasons which are the necessary support and constitute the very foundation of them." The *Conseil Constitutionnel* held that it would not pronounce on the proper domain of the measures in question because it was clear from its earlier decisions that it was *réglementaire*.[31] It was stated in the Senate report[32] that in the event of an eventual divergence in jurisprudence between the *Conseil Constitutionnel* and the Court of Justice "the French public powers cannot but bow to the French constitutional jurisdiction, whose decisions, in France, compel recognition by all, in conformity with Article 62 of the Constitution".

---

28 Decision of the *Conseil d'État, S.A. Établissements Outters*, 20 December 1985, Rec. Lebon p. 382; (1986) *Revue français de droit administratif* 513. Decision of the *Tribunal des conflits, Compagnie des Eaux et de l'Ozone c. S.A. Établissements Vetillard*, 12 January 1987, Rec. Lebon p. 442; (1987) *Revue français de droit administratif* 284.

29 J. Bell (1992) *op. cit.* above, n.8, p. 52.

30 62–18 L, 16 January 1962, Rec. p. 31.

31 This decision on the binding nature of decisions of the *Conseil Constitutionnel* is particularly strong because it was possible to argue, on a strict reading of the wording of Article 37 of the Constitution, that a reference to the *Conseil Constitutionnel* was necessary no matter how clear-cut a case it was, because a specific declaration by the *Conseil Constitutionnel* on the nature of the measure was necessary before the government could act.

32 Senate, *Rapport fait au nom de la commission des Lois constitutionelles, de législation, du suffrage universel, du Règlement et d'administration générale sur le projet de loi constitutionelle adoptée par l'Assemblée Nationale ajoutant à la Constitution un titre*: "Des Communautés européennes et de l'Union européenne", No. 2676 (Annexe), by J. Larché, 27 May 1992.

An example of the authority and independence of the *Conseil Constitutionnel* is its decision in a particularly sensitive labour matter, *Renault Ten II.*[33] The *Conseil Constitutionnel* rejected an amended *loi* which had not cured the defects of the original *loi* (the *Conseil Constitutionnel* indicated the unconstitutional defects of the *loi* in its decision *Renault Ten I*[34]), stating that the amended provision disregarded the authority which attaches in virtue of Article 62 of the Constitution to its earlier decision, and that therefore the provision was contrary to the Constitution. Also important is the bindingness of *Conseil Constitutionnel* decisions on itself – precedent. In *TEU No. 2*[35] the *Conseil Constitutionnel* reiterated that its authority attaches not only to the ruling but also to the reasons which constitute the necessary support and foundation of the ruling, and to the *chose jugée,*[36] to prevent the putting into doubt of provisions of the Treaty on European Union which had already been held constitutional as interpreted.

The *Conseil Constitutionnel's* Control of the French Constitutional Legal Order

14–4 Although the *Conseil Constitutionnel* has increased in jurisdiction, authority, and prestige, it remains limited compared to, for example, the Irish Supreme Court and High Court, the German Federal Constitutional Court, the Italian Constitutional Court, or the Supreme Court of the United States. The control exercised by the *Conseil Constitutionnel* is preventive and abstract. There is no jurisdictional bridge to the other systems of courts, and there appears to be no jurisdictional bridge to the Court of Justice because the *Conseil Constitutionnel* must rule within very strict time limits.

There now follows a consideration of the specific heads of jurisdiction set out in the Constitution of 1958 for the purpose of seeing how conflicts between French constitutional law and European Community law may be brought to a decision by the *Conseil Constitutionnel.* The same question is briefly considered in regard to the *Conseil d'État* and the *Cour de Cassation* in the annex to this chapter.

In considering the jurisdictional rules it may be helpful to keep in mind three of the principal types of case in which a conflict may occur between French constitutional law and European Community law within the current constitutional and treaty framework:

1. where a directly effective European Community measure or treaty is outside of the French constitutional law interpretation of European Community law and contrary to French constitutional law;

---

[33] 89–258 DC, 8 July 1989, Rec. p. 48; in B. Rudden and L. Kahn-Freund (1991) *op. cit.* above, n.6, pp. 80–81.

[34] 88–244 DC, 20 July 1988, Rec. p. 119; [1988] *L'Actualité Juridique, Droit Administratif* 752.

[35] 92–312 DC, 2 September 1992, Rec. p. 76; (1992) *Revue de Droit Public* 1610.

[36] The "thing judged"; the dispute in question.

2. where a domestic measure (*loi, réglement,*[37] or *décision*) would be unconstitutional were it not based on a European Community law measure but that European Community law measure is unconstitutional in the sense of case (1);

3. where a domestic measure is taken not on the basis of European Community law but to promote a constitutional principle (for example, the right to property) which conflicts with a European Community law rule which is outside the French constitutional law interpretation of European Community law.

Article 54 – Control of International Treaties, Agreements, and Council Directives

14–5 "Article 54. – If the *Conseil Constitutionnel*, seized by the President of the Republic, by the Prime Minister or by the president of either Assembly, or by sixty deputies or sixty senators, has declared that an international engagement includes a clause contrary to the Constitution, the authorisation to ratify or to approve it cannot take place until after the revision of the Constitution."[38]

As in the case of the Article 61.2 control of *lois*, the initiation of this procedure depends on political decision. Article 2 of constitutional *loi* of 25 June 1992 rewrote Article 54 in order to add 60 deputies or 60 senators to the categories of potential initiators of review. A similar extension by amendment to Article 61 proved enormously important for the development of the constitutional review of *lois* and for the status of the *Conseil Constitutionnel* as a constitutional court. The revised Article 54 may have similar importance for the control of French constitutional law conflicts with European Community law.

There are two ways to bring case one conflicts (where a directly applicable European Community measure or treaty is outside of the French constitutional law interpretation of European Community law and contrary to French constitutional law) within the Article 54 jurisdiction of the *Conseil Constitutionnel*. First, if another treaty amending a European Community treaty is signed, it can be referred.[39] Whilst the constitutionality of the new treaty falls to be controlled, it is not clear if this (re-)opens the question of the constitutionality of previously ratified treaties. This depends on whether or not the doctrine of the treaty screen[40] applies, under which the *Conseil Constitutionnel* is said to refuse to control the constitutionality of ratified international engagements by way of exception, that is, on the occasion of a reference of a posterior related treaty. Thus the new treaty could only be considered so far as it

---

37 A *règlement* is a legal measure of general application taken by the government in fields which do not have to be governed by *loi* – Article 37 of the Constitution of 1958.

38 As amended by Constitutional *loi* No. 92–554 of 25 June 1992, J.O. p. 8406, 26 June 1992.

39 70–39 DC, 19 June 1970, Rec. p. 15, *Budgetary and Merger Treaties.*

40 *"Traité écran".*

departed from the anterior treaty. In *TEU No. 1*[41] the *Conseil Constitutionnel* held:

> "Considering that it falls to the *Conseil Constitutionnel*, seized under the procedure instituted by Article 54 of the Constitution of a treaty which modifies or completes one or more international engagements already introduced into the internal legal order, to determine the reach of the treaty submitted to its examination in step with[42] international engagements which this treaty has as its object to modify or complete".

Favoreau considered that in this case the *Conseil Constitutionnel* forbade itself from considering the constitutionality of previously ratified treaties (that is, the Treaties establishing the European Communities and the Single European Act) on the occasion of the examination of a later treaty (the Treaty on European Union) submitted to its control[43] – in other words that the treaty screen applied. The point seems to turn on the interpretation of *en fonction de* ("in step with"). It may be, however, that this passage is more an implicit finding of the constitutionality of previous treaties than a bar on its jurisdiction to consider the question. Such an interpretation is supported by the fact that the *Conseil Constitutionnel* interpreted the nature of European Community law as a whole in a way clearly contrary to European Community law's self-interpretation[44] prior to the Treaty on European Union in, for example, Case 6/64 *Costa v. ENEL* or Case 106/77 *Simmenthal*.[45] It is further supported by the analogy which could be made to the *Conseil Constitutionnel's* jurisdiction to consider the constitutionality of promulgated *lois* incidental to the examination of an unpromulgated amending or modifying *loi*.[46] Therefore it is possibly excessive to interpret this paragraph of the *TEU No. 1*[47] decision as announcing the doctrine of the treaty screen as a jurisdictional rule.

Whatever the status of the treaty screen doctrine may be after *TEU No. 1*, what is more important is that this decision made clear that in the event of a further treaty the *Conseil Constitutionnel* has sufficient jurisdiction to consider the nature and import of European Community law, any conflicts of interpretation, and any substantive changes.

The second method of bringing case one conflicts within the Article 54 jurisdiction of the *Conseil Constitutionnel* is the referral of secondary European Community legislation. The *Conseil Constitutionnel* has interpreted its Article 54 jurisdiction as extending to the control of the constitutionality of legal

---

41 92–308 DC, 9 April 1992, Rec. p. 55; (1992) 28 *Revue Trimestrielle du Droit Européen* 418.

42 "*en fonction de*".

43 Larché Report, see above, n.32: Favoreau's comments are contained in the Report.

44 See Chap. 18 below, "French Constitutional Law Interpretation of European Community Law in the Ratification of the Treaty on European Union".

45 See above, para. 8–41, "Case 6/64 *Costa v. ENEL*" and Part II, para. 14–6, *et seq.*, "Case 106/77 *Simmenthal*".

46 85–187 DC, 25 January 1985, Rec. p. 34; see below, para. 14–7, on "Article 61.2 – Constitutional Control of *Lois*".

47 92–308 DC, 9 April 1992, Rec. p. 55; (1992) *Revue Trimestrielle du Droit Européen* 418.

commitments taken in the application of constituent treaties.[48] This method may be founded on the broadness of the term "international engagement" in Article 54 which differs from the words "treaty" and "agreement" used in the title to Title VI and in Articles 52, 53, and 55 thereunder, and may be broader than them. But the scope of this jurisdiction remains uncertain. To date, the *Conseil Constitutionnel* has controlled only one such measure, upholding the constitutionality of the Council Decision (EEC) on direct elections to the European Parliament on a referral by the President of the Republic.[49] The *Conseil Constitutionnel* held that no procedure of approval or ratification had to follow before the Decision took effect.[50]

Abraham considers that this decision may be limited to European Community measures which necessarily involve Parliament in implementation but not in ratification.[51] The Council Decision in question was an implementation of Article 138(3) (EEC), which makes it special. Article 138(3) (EEC) provided[52]:

> "The Assembly shall draw up proposals for elections by direct universal suffrage in accordance with a uniform procedure in all Member States.
> The Council shall, acting unanimously, lay down the appropriate provisions, which it shall recommend to Member States for adoption in accordance with their respective constitutional requirements."

In the light of this article, the Council Decision on direct elections may be distinguished from secondary European Community legislation by the apparently non-binding nature of the Decision ("recommend to Member States"), by the acknowledgement of the possible necessity of constitutional revision ("for adoption in accordance with their respective constitutional requirements"), by the requirement of unanimity, or by one or a combination of these points. However it could be argued that the decision of the *Conseil Constitutionnel* that no approval or ratification was necessary for such a Decision implies a fortiori that no approval or ratification is required for secondary legislation. With the possibility of references by 60 deputies or senators, the *Conseil Constitutionnel* may have the opportunity to clarify what Council measures can be referred under Article 54.

---

48 E. Zoller, *Droits des relations extérieures* (Paris: PUF, 1992), p. 270.

49 76–71 DC, 30 December 1976, Rec. p. 15; in B. Rudden and L. Kahn-Freund (1991) *op. cit.* above, n.6, pp. 58–60, *European Community Council Decision for direct elections to European Parliament.*

50 Despite the *Conseil Constitutionnel's* decision, the Parliament subsequently passed a *loi* (30 June 1977) "authorising the approval" of the Council Decision.

51 R. Abraham, *Droit international, droit communautaire et droit français*, P.E.S., (J. Généreux ed., Paris: Hachette, 1980) pp. 47–48.

52 Article 138(3) (EC) was amended by the Treaty on European Union and now provides:

> "The European Parliament shall draw up proposals for elections by direct universal suffrage in accordance with a uniform procedure in all Member States.
> The Council shall, acting unanimously after obtaining the assent of the European Parliament, which shall act by a majority of its component members, lay down the appropriate provisions, which it shall recommend to Member States for adoption in accordance with their respective constitutional requirements."

Control of Lois

14–6 The principal gap in the *Conseil Constitutionnel's* jurisdiction which, unlike the control of executive measures, is not remedied by complementary jurisdictions in other courts, remains the absence of control of *lois* after promulgation.[53] In its decision *Juge unique, juge inique*[54] the *Conseil Constitutionnel* held unconstitutional a *loi* affecting the principle of equality before the law in the proper administration of justice. This *loi* was merely the wider application of an earlier *loi* which was thus impliedly unconstitutional, but because it had been promulgated it remained valid unless repealed by Parliament. Thus there are difficulties in the *Conseil Constitutionnel* obtaining jurisdiction of a case two conflict involving a *loi* once that *loi* has been promulgated. The President of the Republic and the President of the *Conseil Constitutionnel* proposed that the ordinary courts should be allowed to refer the issue of the constitutionality of *lois* with regard to fundamental rights to the *Conseil Constitutionnel*. The proposed constitutional amendment was blocked by Parliament in 1990.[55] But similar proposals have recurred (and appear to have the support of some academic writing)[56] such as the proposal to expand the jurisdiction of the *Conseil Constitutionnel* by the introduction of an "*exception d'inconstitutionalité*" against *lois* already promulgated which could be contrary to fundamental rights. Under this proposal a reference could be made by the *Conseil d'État*, the *Cour de Cassation*, or any jurisdiction and the *Conseil Constitutionnel* would have power to abrogate the *loi*. The proposal got as far as two Constitutional *loi* Bills.[57] The problem is considered further below.

14–7 *Article 61.2 – Constitutional Control of* Lois Article 61.2 provides:

> "To the same ends [control of conformity with the Constitution], *lois* may be referred to the *Conseil constitutionnel*, before their promulgation, by the President of the Republic, the Prime Minister, the President of the National Assembly, the President of the Senate or sixty deputies or sixty senators."[58]

The amendment of this Article was very important in the history of the *Conseil Constitutionnel*; the widening of the categories of those who can make a reference to the *Conseil Constitutionnel* to include deputies and senators dramatically increased the number of references and encouraged the *Conseil*

---

[53] The jurisdictions of the *Conseil d'État* and *Cour de Cassation* are considered below in Chap. 22, "The *Conseil d'État* and the *Cour de Cassation*", as regards constitutional control of *lois* and *règlements* when reviewing compatibility with European Community law.

[54] 77–58 DC, 23 July 1975, Rec. p. 16; (1976) *Actualités Juridiques* 44, *Juge unique, juge inique*.

[55] J. Bell (1992) *op. cit.* above, n.8, p. 56.

[56] *e.g.* T.S. Renoux, "Le droit au recours juridictionnel" (1993) 3675 19 *La Semaine Juridique (Doctrine)* 211 at 212. See further Chap. 22, "The *Conseil d'État* and the *Cour de Cassation*".

[57] *La Semaine Juridique*, 31 March 1993, 1–3. For an earlier failed proposal, see D. Pollard, "France's *Conseil Constitutionnel* – Not Yet a Constitutional Court?" (1988) XXIII *Irish Jurist* 2 at pp. 34–36.

[58] As amended by the Constitutional *loi* No. 74–904 of 29 October 1974, J.O. 11035, 30 October 1974.

Constitutionnel to take a more activist approach to determination of constitutionality.[59] It was a key step in the recognition, indeed formation, of the *Conseil Constitutionnel* as a constitutional court and of the importance of French constitutional law in the functioning of the legal order.

However there are three principal constraints on the Article 61.2 jurisdiction.

First, like the control under Article 54, Article 61.2 is permissive; nothing mandates that a *loi* be referred.

Secondly, Article 61.2 refers only to the control of *lois* before promulgation, although this defect of the lack of control of promulgated *lois* in the *Conseil Constitutionnel's* jurisdiction has been partly remedied by the *Conseil Constitutionnel* in two ways. First, the *Conseil Constitutionnel* is nonetheless able to exercise some control over promulgated *lois*, incidental to its other jurisdictions. Thus if a conflict escapes review before promulgation, it may nonetheless still be brought before the *Conseil Constitutionnel*. The *Conseil Constitutionnel* has declared *obiter* that "the validity with respect to the Constitution of a promulgated *loi* may be properly contested on the occasion of an examination of the legislative provisions that amend it".[60] Secondly, the operation of this control does not depend on politicians (who did not refer the original *loi*) raising it. The *Conseil Constitutionnel* considers that it has power in general to raise constitutional questions *ex officio* – it is not limited in this regard to the questions raised by those who made the reference.[61] Furthermore, in its decision *Zones of Transit*,[62] the *Conseil Constitutionnel* considered that it has the power to consider provisions of *loi* other than those specified in the reference.

Thirdly, the *Conseil Constitutionnel* will consider only *lois* adopted by Parliament "not at all those which, adopted by the French people following a referendum controlled by the *Conseil Constitutionnel* under Article 60, constitute the direct expression of national sovereignty".[63] The people can

---

59 Vedel points out that "approximately one-tenth of the Members of the Assemblé Nationale and one-fifth of the Members of the Senate can refer a statute to the Constitutional Council after it is passed and before it is enacted. This represents an upheaval of considerable proportions. . . . In a nation whose political life is essentially bi-polarized, it is obvious that there will always be, for a statute of any importance, 60 *députés* or 60 *sénateurs* who will refer that statute to the Constitutional Council." – G. Vedel, "The Conseil Constitutionnel: Problems of Legitimization and Interpretation", in *Constitutional Justice under Old Constitutions* (E. Smith ed., The Hague: Kluwer Law International, 1995) p. 331.

60 85–187 DC, 25 January 1985, Rec. p. 34, *On the* loi *on the state of emergency in New Caledonia and dependencies.*

61 82–146 DC, 18 November 1982, Rec. p .48, *The Electoral* Loi. See also J. Bell, *French Constitutional Law* (Oxford: Clarendon Press, 1992) at p. 349.

62 92–307 DC, 25 February 1992, Rec. p. 48, *Foreigners in transit zones.*

63 92–313 DC, 23 September 1992, Rec. p. 94; (1992) *Revue de Droit Public* 1618 (1992), *TEU No. 3.*

enact a *loi* directly when it is submitted to them under Article 11 by President of the Republic (as in the case of the *loi* authorising the ratification of the Treaty on European Union), when a Constitutional *loi* is submitted under Article 89.2, and where a Constitutional *loi* is submitted directly without recourse to the constitutional procedures under Article 89.2.[64]

A case one conflict may arise under Article 61.2 because the *Conseil Constitutionnel* admits the referral of a *loi* Bill authorising the ratification of an international treaty or agreement (provided it is not a *loi* Bill adopted by the people pursuant to Article 11[65]). The control of constitutionality will include the application of Article 54 to decide the constitutionality of the international treaty or agreement itself.[66]

A case two conflict could arise in the consideration (at least before promulgation) of the constitutionality of a *loi* implementing a European Community obligation. The decision of the *Conseil Constitutionnel on the Finance Rectification* loi *of 1977*[67] appears to stand against this proposition. That *loi* regulated the means of recovery of the Community levy on isoglucose production set out in a Council Regulation.[68] The *Conseil Constitutionnel* held:

> "the repercussions of the division of competences thus operated between the Community institutions and the national authorities, in respect of as much the conditions of exercise of national sovereignty as the provisions of Article 34 of the Constitution on the correct scope of the domain of *loi*,[69] are only the consequence of international undertakings given by France which have entered into the field of Article 55 of the Constitution; that, in these circumstances, the provisions of the *loi* on financial rectification for 1977 submitted to the examination of the *Conseil Constitutionnel* are not contrary to any rule or any principle of constitutional value."

However, since that decision a new Title XV has been inserted into the Constitution which changes the solution likely to be offered by the *Conseil Constitutionnel*. This is considered further below in this Section. Furthermore, since that decision, implementing *lois* have been referred under Article 61.2,

---

64 62–20 DC, 6 November 1962, Rec. p. 27; B. Rudden and L. Kahn-Freund (1991) *op. cit.* above n.6, p. 55, "Direct amendment on popular election of the President".

65 92–313 DC, 23 September 1992, Rec. p. 94 (1992) *Revue de Droit Public* 1618 (1992), *TEU No. 3.*

66 78–93 DC, 29 April 1978, Rec. p. 23, *Amendment of the Statutes of the International Monetary Fund.* 80–116 DC, 17 July 1980, Rec. p. 36, *Franco-German Convention on Judicial Cooperation.* 88–242 DC, 17 January 1989, Rec. p. 15, *International Labour Convention No. 159.* 91–294 DC, 25 July 1991, Rec. p. 91; (1991) Recueil de Droit Public 1517, *Schengen Treaty.* 93–318 DC, 30 June 1993, Rec. p. 153, *Franco-Mongolian Investment Treaty.* 93–319 DC, 30 June 1993, Rec. p. 155, *International Labour Convention No. 139.*

67 77–90 DC, 30 December 1977, Rec. p. 44. See also 78–93 DC, 29 April 1978, Rec. p. 23, *Amendment of the Statutes of the International Monetary Fund*, where the *Conseil Constitutionnel* held that an amendment envisaged by the original international agreement entered into force by virtue of the ratification of the original agreement and the conformity of the amendment to it, without the need for authorisation under Article 53.

68 Council Regulation 1111/77 of 17 May 1977.

69 "*Jeu de régles de l'art. 34 de la Constitution relatives au domaine de la loi*".

for example the *loi* on the conditions for entry and stay of foreigners in France,[70] the *loi* granting European Community nationals access to public employment,[71] and the proposed Statute of the Bank of France.[72] During the Treaty on European Union debates Professor Favoreau pointed out that there are numerous provisions of European Community law which need to be transposed and which belong to the domain of *loi*.[73] This statement is supported by the Minister for European Affairs who, in replying to questions on the consequences of the Treaty on European Union on internal law stated that the application of the Treaty required the elaboration of numerous Community texts, for example the directive on visas, whose transposition into internal law would be according to habitual constitutional procedures. Parliament would thus have multiple opportunities to exercise its control on the consequences of the treaty.[74] It would be odd if the *Conseil Constitutionnel* would not consider the constitutionality of referred examples of this control and of the changing interpretation of the Treaty itself.

A case three conflict may arise by the referral of an ordinary *loi* which promotes a constitutional principle but which is contrary to European Community law. The legal structures in which such a conflict falls to be decided may have changed with the addition of Article 88–1 to 88–4. Prior to this addition the *Conseil Constitutionnel* would not control the compatibility of *lois* with treaties in the exercise of its Article 61.2 jurisdiction, which control is left up to other jurisdictions. This jurisprudence began with the *Conseil Constitutionnel's* refusal to review the compatibility of a *loi* permitting abortion with the right to life in the European Convention of Human Rights and Fundamental Freedoms.[75] In such cases it falls to "various organs of the State to supervise the application of these international conventions in the framework of their respective competences".[76] In that decision on the *loi*

---

[70] 86–216 DC, 3 September 1986, Rec. p. 135, Loi *on the conditions of entry and stay of foreigners in France.*

[71] 91–293 DC, 23 July 1991, Rec. p. 77, Loi *granting European Community nationals access to public employment.* The *Conseil Constitutionnel* held that the *loi* authorised access of citizens of Member States of the European Economic Community only to those jobs for which the attributions are severable from the exercise of sovereignty, and therefore there was no infringement of the conditions essential to the exercise of national sovereignty.

[72] 93–324 DC, 3 August 1993, Rec. p. 208, *Statute of the Bank of France.*

[73] National Assembly, *Rapport au nom de la commission des* lois *constitutionelles, de la legislation et de l'administration générale de la République sur le projet de loi constitutionelle (No. 2623) ajoutaut à la Constitution un titre*: "De l'Union européenne", No. 2676, registered 4 May 1992. (Gouzes' Report). See below, Chap. 15.

[74] Gouzes' Report, *ibid.* p. 47.

[75] 74–54 DC, 15 January 1975, Rec. p. 19, *Abortion loi.* The *Conseil Constitutionnel* has held also that it is not its responsibility under Art. 61 to assess the compliance of an international obligation (in that case the Schengen Treaty) with the rules and regulations of a particular treaty (the Treaty establishing the European Economic Community) – 91–294 DC, 25 July 1991, Rec. p. 91; (1991) *Revue de Droit Public* 1517, *Schengen Treaty.*

[76] 86–216 DC, 3 September 1986, Rec. p. 135, Loi *on the conditions of entry and stay of foreigners in France.*

concerning the conditions of entry and stay of foreigners in France, the *Conseil Constitutionnel* drew the attention of the "various organs" to the treaties it thought relevant.[77]

Importantly, however, the *Conseil Constitutionnel* made clear that it would hold unconstitutional a *loi* which directly attacked Article 55 of the Constitution by attempting to restrict its application (as distinct from a *loi* which was merely inconsistent with treaty obligations). The *loi* in question attempted to exclude from the application of its provisions only treaties regularly ratified and not denounced which was held to be an unconstitutional restriction on Article 55.[78] This line was developed further in *On the Control of Immigration*[79] where the *Conseil Constitutionnel* upheld the constitutionality of a section of the *Conseil Constitutionnel* which allowed for refusal of asylum qualified by respect of a specific article of a binding treaty[80] because it interpreted this legislative qualification as extending to all the provisions of that convention capable of being applied, holding that otherwise the *loi* would be contrary to Article 55 of the Constitution. This decision goes a long way by implication to reversing *Abortion loi*[81] although the immigration decision can be distinguished because the *loi* dealt with an area specially covered by treaty and made specific reference to the treaty in question.

In summary, if the *Abortion loi* line of jurisprudence remains controlling after the Constitutional *loi* of 25 June 1992, then the *Conseil Constitutionnel* will uphold a *loi* which is incompatible with European Community law thereby actualising a conflict, provided that the *loi* does not expressly exclude the application of European Community law, which application will be left to the decision of other jurisdictions.

However the new Title XV (Articles 88–1 to 88–3) gave constitutional status to participation in the European Community. It seems a logical consequence that the *Conseil Constitutionnel* has now to consider European Community law obligations as different to other public international law obligations as far as its Article 61.2 jurisdiction is concerned. This has implications for the three cases posited, and may have jurisdictional effects for cases two and three. In this regard, the new Title could mean two things. First, the *Conseil Constitutionnel* confines control to whether or not the *loi* directly attacks the statement of France's participation in the European Community in the Title – the same degree of control it exercises with regard to Article 55, leaving the control on incompatibility of *loi* and European Community law provisions to other jurisdictions. Secondly, the *Conseil Constitutionnel* considers whether the *loi* is

---

77 The Geneva Convention of 18 July 1951 and the New York Protocol of 31 January 1967.

78 86–216 DC, 3 September 1986, Rec. p. 135, Loi *on the conditions of entry and stay of foreigners in France.*

79 93–325 DC, 13 August 1993, Rec. p. 224; (1993) *La Semaine Juridique (Textes)* 373.

80 Article 33 of the Geneva Convention of 28 July 1951 as amended by the New York Protocol, 31 January 1967.

81 74–54 DC, 15 January 1975, Rec. p. 19.

consistent with the French constitutional law version of European Community law, and in so doing will be able to consider how far it accepts developments or insistence upon European Community law's self-interpretation.[82] No question of an Article 177 (EC) reference to the Court of Justice can arise (even if the *Conseil Constitutionnel* determined that it had jurisdiction to make such a reference) because of the stringent time limits on the *Conseil Constitutionnel's* decision-making. Article 61.3 requires the *Conseil Constitutionnel* to rule within a month from the reference or, if there is urgency, within eight days. It appears from *Statute of the Bank of France*[83] that the *Conseil Constitutionnel* will control the consistency of the *loi* with the French constitutional law version of European Community law. In that decision the *Conseil Constitutionnel* held that there was no ground to review the conformity of the *loi* with Article 88–1 and Article 88–2 of the Constitution and the stipulations of the Treaty on European Union because that Treaty, at the time of the decision, was not yet in force. Now that the Treaty is in force, the implication is that the *Conseil Constitutionnel* will review consistency of *lois* with it, although it would be possible to argue that the review in *Statute of the Bank of France* was confined to a *loi* which directly affected the provisions in Title XV (specifically, Article 88–2), in the same way as review is confined to a *loi* which directly affects Article 55. The decision of the *Conseil Constitutionnel*, without an Article 177 (EC) reference, would bind the other jurisdictions by virtue of Article 62. An interesting situation of potential conflicts would arise if another jurisdiction made a reference to the Court of Justice on a point where it differed with the *Conseil Constitutionnel*. Under Article 62 and in accordance with one of the assumptions made in the debate on the Treaty on European Union,[84] it appears that the jurisdiction would be bound by the *Conseil Constitutionnel's* interpretation.

14–8 *Article 46.5 and 61.1 – Constitutional Control of Organic* Lois

"Article 46. – [Describes procedural rules for the passing of an Organic *loi*] [paragraph 5] Organic *lois* cannot be promulgated until after the declaration by the *Conseil Constitutionnel* of their conformity with the Constitution.

Article 61.1. – Organic *lois*, before their promulgation, and the *réglements* of the Parliamentary assemblies, before they are brought into force, must be submitted to the *Conseil Constitutionnel*, who shall decide on their compatibility with the Constitution."

---

82 See below, para. 18–9, "Article 88–2: Economic and Monetary Union and Control of External Frontiers".

83 93–324 DC, 3 August 1993, Rec. p. 208.

84 In the event of an eventual divergence in jurisprudence between the *Conseil Constitutionnel* and the Court of Justice "the French public powers cannot but bow to the French constitutional jurisdiction, whose decisions, in France, compel recognition by all, in conformity with Article 62 of the Constitution." Larché's Report p. 52: see above, n.34.

These Articles strongly reinforce the *Conseil Constitutionnel's* role *vis-à-vis* the Parliament as supreme arbiter of constitutionality under the Constitution of 1958. These two Articles establish that Organic *lois* and the internal rules of the two Assemblies must be referred to the *Conseil Constitutionnel* where their constitutionality, in the wide sense, falls to be judged. The submission to the *Conseil Constitutionnel* is not permissive, as it is in Article 54 and Article 61.2, but mandatory. Organic *lois* are a special category of important *lois* which is required by the Constitution to regulate certain matters of direct constitutional significance, such as the rules governing the Assembly (Article 25). Organic *lois* are subject to a special regime of creation (Article 46) which makes it necessary to have greater political consensus on their content. Even with the special method of adoption by the Assemblies, the *Conseil Constitutionnel* remains the ultimate arbiter of their constitutionality.

The *Conseil Constitutionnel's* Article 61.1 jurisdiction may give rise to case three-type conflicts. It is unlikely there will be many European Community obligations necessitating Organic *lois* so the chance of case two conflict is slim.[85]

14–9 *Articles 58 and 59 – Electoral Jurisdiction Control of Compatibility of Promulgated* Lois *with Treaties* The *Conseil Constitutionnel* exercises control over the regularity of elections:

> "Article 58. – The *Conseil Constitutionnel* shall supervise the validity of the election of the President of the Republic.
>
> It shall investigate complaints, and declare the results of the ballot.
>
> Article 59. – The *Conseil Constitutionnel* shall rule, in the case of dispute, on the regularity of the election of deputies and senators."

This jurisdiction may give rise to case three conflicts (and perhaps case two conflicts concerning the election of senators). As an election court, the *Conseil Constitutionnel* does not have jurisdiction to consider the conformity with the Constitution of *lois* bearing on the elections which *lois* will necessarily be already promulgated and in force.[86] However, the *Conseil Constitutionnel* will consider under this jurisdiction the compatibility of a *loi* with ratified treaties. In *Val d'Oise (fifth electoral ward)*[87] the *Conseil Constitutionnel* tested the compatibility of the *loi* of 11 July 1981 on the determination of the method of scrutiny for the election of deputies to the National Assembly with Article 3 of the First Protocol to the European Convention for the Protection of Human

---

[85] However there may be some scope in the Organic *loi* required by Article 88–3 on the right to vote and the eligibility to elections, although the *Conseil Constitutionnel* has held in *TEU No. 2* 92–312 DC, 2 September 1992, Rec. p. 76; (1992) *Revue de Droit Public* 1610 that "the Organic *loi* will have to respect the prescriptions laid down at the Community level for the putting into place of the right [to vote and stand in municipal elections]".

[86] 58–42/191, 5 May 1959, Rec. p. 215, *A.N., Algerie (fifteenth electoral ward).*

[87] 88–1082/1117, 21 October 1988, Rec. p. 183, *A.N., Val-d'Oise (fifth electoral ward).*

Rights and Fundamental Freedoms, wherein the States pledge themselves to free elections with a secret ballot. At the same time, the *Conseil Constitutionnel* refused to test the constitutional conformity of the promulgated *loi*. Thus under Article 59 the *Conseil Constitutionnel* is willing to consider the compatibility of promulgated *lois* with treaties but not their constitutionality, whereas under Article 61 the *Conseil Constitutionnel* will consider the constitutionality of unpromulgated *lois* but there are problems in considering their compatibility with treaties.[88]

Control of Executive Measures

14–10 Normally, the control of executive measures falls to the *Conseil d'État*.[89] However it is inaccurate to overlook the *Conseil Constitutionnel's* control of executive measures which occur incidentally to certain of the *Conseil Constitutionnel's* jurisdictions. This control may give rise to a consideration by the *Conseil Constitutionnel* of conflicts between European Community law and French constitutional law. There are three possibilities.

14–11 *Articles 58 and 59* First, via Articles 58 and 59 the *Conseil Constitutionnel* will control, under the rubric of regularity, the compatibility of *règlements* and of executive action with treaties, as well as their compatibility with any relevant *loi*, thus giving rise to the possibility of a case three conflict (and possibly a case two conflict concerning the election of senators).

14–12 *Article 61.2 and Article 38* Secondly, under Article 61.2 by virtue of Article 38. Article 38 provides for the government to request Parliament for authorisation in the form of an Empowering *loi* to make *ordonnances* in the domain of *loi* in order to execute its program. Presumably this procedure could be used for the implementation of European Community law. These *ordonnances* enter into force on publication but lapse if they are not laid before Parliament within the time limit fixed by the Empowering *loi*. The *Conseil Constitutionnel* has held in *Competition Council*[90] that an *ordonnance* as a text

---

88 See above, paras. 14–6 *et seq.* "Control of *Lois*", and D. Rousseau, "Chronique de Jurisprudence Constitutionnelle 1992–1993" (1994) *Recueil de Droit Public* 103 at pp. 116–119, where the author considers the jurisprudence of the *Conseil Constitutionnel* to be floating between the position that the appreciation of the constitutionality of a *loi* cannot be made on the basis of international conventions and the position that the constitutional requirement of the superiority of treaties over *lois* (Article 55) and the principle *pacta sunt servanda* (para. 14 of the Preamble of the Constitution of 1946) are part of the *bloc de constitutionalité*.

89 The incompatibility of the approach of the *Conseil d'État* with the requirements of European Community law where individual executive decisions do not conform to Directives is considered below in para. 22–6, "Conflict between the *Conseil d'État's* Interpretation of Direct Effect and Supremacy of European Community Law and European Community Law's Self-Interpretation".

90 86–224 DC, 23 January 1987, Rec. p. 8.

of regulatory value remains outside the jurisdiction of the *Conseil Constitutionnel* until ratified by a *loi.* If a *loi* which expressly or impliedly ratifies the *ordonnance* is referred to the *Conseil Constitutionnel* then it falls to the *Conseil Constitutionnel* to state how far the *loi* ratifies the *ordonnance* and "if the provisions to which the ratification confers legislative value" are constitutional. The *Conseil Constitutionnel* has made clear in its decision *On the* loi *authorising the Government to de-nationalize*[91] that it will consider the contrariness of the *ordonnances* to France's international obligations as well as their constitutionality. This willingness to consider in regard to *ordonnances* both conformity with the Constitution and compatibility with international obligations within the exercise of the same instance of control contrasts with the problematic position in regard to *lois.*[92] This clearly presents scope for considering conflicts between European Community law and French constitutional law.

14–13 *Article 37* Thirdly, Article 37 allows the executive to amend, by *décret,* provisions of *loi* which are outside the proper domain of *loi* specified in Article 34.

> "Article 37. – Matters other than those which are within the province of *loi* have a regulatory [*réglementaire*] character.
> Texts of legislative form passed on these matters may be modified by *décrets* taken after the advice of the *Conseil d'État.* Those of these texts which were passed after the entry into force of the present Constitution cannot be modified by *décret* unless the *Conseil Constitutionnel* has declared that they have a regulatory character by virtue of the preceding paragraph."

A case two conflict may arise if the executive tried to implement European Community law in an area covered by *loi* which was outside the proper domain of *loi.* Such moves by the executive may be disputed hotly politically because, as Professor Gicquel has stated,[93] Parliament must be able to claim for itself the Community texts on which it must pronounce. In the exercise of its Article 37.2 jurisdiction the *Conseil Constitutionnel* has demonstrated its willingness to control possible *décrets* in this domain by strict reservations of interpretation. In *Contraventions,* the *Conseil Constitutionnel* held that provisions of the Rural Code were outside the domain of *loi* and so could be amended by *décret* but there were restrictions, amongst which was that penalties fixed by executive rules could not include the deprivation of liberty because of the combined effect of the Preamble (Constitution of 1958), Article 34.3 and Article 34.5, and Article 66.[94] This control could encompass conflicts between European Community law and constitutional law if certain measures touching on European Community law were amended by *décret* to conform properly with European Community law obligations, but the *décret* contained unconstitutional

---

91 86–207 DC, 25–6 June 1986, Rec. p. 61, *De-nationalisation* loi.
92 See above, para. 14–7, "Article 61.2 – Constitutional Control of *Lois*".
93 Reported in Larché's Report, above, n.34.
94 73–80 L, 28 November 1973, Rec. p. 45.

provisions going beyond the French constitutional interpretation of European Community law.

Conclusion

14–14 Despite the complexities of the jurisdictional rules and types of control exercisable by the *Conseil Constitutionnel,* conflicts between European Community law and French constitutional law are more readily subject to constitutional control than has been appreciated. The justiciability of French constitutional law is the basis for an intra-order mechanism, in addition to and integrated with the possibilities of legislative debate,[95] in which revolt by or revolution in French constitutional law can be established.

[95] See below, Chap. 15, "The History of the Ratification of the Treaty on European Union".

15. THE HISTORY OF THE RATIFICATION OF THE TREATY ON EUROPEAN UNION

15–1 For the first time in the history of the Fifth Republic[1] the full logic of the *Conseil Constitutionnel's* control of treaties pursuant to Article 54[2] had to be applied in the wake of the *Conseil Constitutionnel* decision *TEU No. 1,*[3] and Parliament deliberated on a Constitutional *loi* Bill prior to the ratification of the Treaty on European Union.

The procedural history of the ratification may be summarised as follows.[4] The Treaty was signed by the President's plenipotentiary in Maastricht on 7 February 1992 pursuant to Article 52 of the Constitution according to which the President of the Republic negotiates and ratifies treaties. The President referred the treaty to the *Conseil Constitutionnel* under Article 54 for a ruling on its constitutionality. The *Conseil Constitutionnel* had never before found that a treaty was contrary to the Constitution but in its decision of 9 April 1992[5] it held that the Treaty included clauses contrary to the Constitution. Therefore, according to Article 54, authorisation to ratify the Treaty (which needed to be in the form of a *loi* by virtue of Article 53) could be given only after revision of the Constitution. Article 89 provides for the procedure of revision, under which a Constitutional *loi* Bill must first be approved in identical terms by the National Assembly and the Senate. The Senate was thus on an equal footing with the National Assembly in this process of

---

1 The Treaties establishing the European Communities were ratified under the Constitution of 1946 (the Treaty establishing the European Economic Community by *loi* No. 57–880 of 2 August 1957 authorising the ratification of the Treaty and by the *décret* of publication No. 58–84 of 28 January 1958).

2 The *Conseil Constitutionnel* had previously found compatible with the Constitution the Treaty Establishing a Single Council and a Single Commission of the European Communities, the Decision of the Council of the European Communities of 21 April 1970 on the replacement of the contributions of the Member States with the Community's own resources (70–39 DC, 19 June 1970, Rec. p. 15, *Budgetary and Merger Treaties*), and the Decision of the Council of the European Communities of 20 September 1976 on the election of the Assembly of the Communities by direct universal suffrage (76–71 DC, 30 December 1976, Rec. p. 15, *European Community Council Decision for direct elections to European Parliament*). Therefore no constitutional amendment was necessary prior to the ratification of those treaties.

3 92–308 DC, 9 April 1992, Rec. p. 55, (1992) 28 *Revue Trimestrielle du Droit Européen* 418.

4 For a different summary see H. Cohen, "Member States Ratification Process of the Treaty on European Union: France" (1993) *European Law Review* 233.

5 92–308 DC, above, n.3, *TEU No. 1,* noted by J.-P. Jacqué, "Commentaire de la décision du Conseil Constitutionnel No. 92–308 DC du 9 Avril 1992" (1992) 28 *Revue Trimestrielle de Droit Européen* 251.

constitutional amendment and their input was equally important. Unlike the case of ordinary *lois* as provided in Article 45, there is no possibility under Article 89 for the government to demand, in the event of disagreement between the two houses of Parliament, the reunion of a mixed commission to solve the disagreement, and in the event of failure by the mixed commissions, to give the last word to the Assembly.

Pursuant to Article 89, on 22 April 1992 the President duly submitted to the National Assembly the Bill for a Constitutional *loi* adding to the Constitution a title "On European Union".[6] During the course of the legislative process in which hearings of renowned constitutional experts took place several reports of high quality were produced on the constitutional implications of the Treaty on European Union and, more generally, of the compatibility of the doctrine of sovereignty with the process of European integration. The interpretation of European Community law and French constitutional law in the debates is important within the order approach for three reasons. First, given the still restricted constitutional jurisdiction, conflicts between French constitutional and European Community legal orders can be sharpest in such debates. Secondly, the National Assembly is the legislative organ of government and has an elevated status in French constitutional law as the exerciser of popular sovereignty under the Constitution and as the body which determines the framework within which constitutional rights are exercised and regularly assesses what the common good requires. Thirdly, the debate was heavily influenced by the direct contributions of distinguished jurists. The first reading of the Bill in the National Assembly gave rise to parliamentary reports: the report by Deputy Gouzes in the name of the Commission for Constitutional *Lois*, Legislation, and the General Administration of the Republic (hereinafter Gouzes' Report[7]); two annexes to this report, one by Deputy Caro in the name of the Commission for Foreign Affairs (hereinafter Caro's Report[8]), and the other by Deputy Alphandêry in the name of the Commission of Finances, General Economy, and Plan (hereinafter Alphandêry's Report[9]); a supplemental report in the name of the Commission for Constitutional *Lois*, Legislation, and the General Administration of the Republic by Deputy Gouzes (hereinafter Gouzes' Supplemental Report[10]).

---

[6] National Assembly Document No. 2623, registered 22 April 1992.

[7] National Assembly, *Rapport au nom de la commission des lois constitutionnelles, de la législation et de l'administration générale de la République sur le projet de loi constitutionnelle (No. 2623) ajoutant à la Constitution un titre*: "De l'Union européene", No. 2676, registered 4 May 1992.

[8] National Assembly, *Observations et amendments présentés au nom de la commission des affaires étrangères, saisie pour avis*, No. 2676 (Annexe), by J.-M. Caro, 4 May 1992.

[9] National Assembly, *Observations et amendments présentés au nom de la commission des finances, de l'économie générale et du plan, saisie pour avis*, No. 2676 (Annexe), by E. Alphandêry, 4 May 1992.

[10] National Assembly, *Rapport supplémentaire au nom de la commission des lois constitutionnelles, de la législation et de l'administration générale de la République sur le projet de loi constitutionnelle*

The Bill was then debated, the amendments of the Commissions considered, and the amended Bill forwarded to the Senate.[11] Senator Larché made a report on 26 May 1992 in the name of the Commission of Constitutional *Lois*, Legislation, Universal Suffrage, Regulation, and General Administration (hereinafter Larché's Report[12]). After the Senate debate, the Bill as amended was resubmitted to the National Assembly on the 17 June 1992. A final report on the Bill as modified by the Senate was made by Deputy Gouzes in the name of the Commission for Constitutional *Lois*, Legislation, and the General Administration of the Republic (hereinafter Gouzes' Final Report).[13] After passage through the two houses it was adopted by them in Congress on 25 June 1992.[14]

One of the amendments in the Constitutional *loi* of 25 June 1992 extended the categories of persons capable of referring a matter to the *Conseil Constitutionnel* under Article 54 to include 60 deputies or senators ("seisin" is the word used in this Part to describe the state in which the *Conseil Constitutionnel* is *saisi* or "seised" of a dispute). Such a number promptly referred the Treaty once more under Article 54 to the *Conseil Constitutionnel*, claiming it remained unconstitutional despite the revision. The *Conseil Constitutionnel* upheld its constitutionality in a decision of 2 September 1992.[15] The President chose the method of referring the *loi* Bill,[16] which was required by Article 53 of the Constitution to authorise his ratification of the Treaty on European Union, to the people via Article 11 of the Constitution[17] who adopted it by referendum on 20 September 1992. A final reference to the *Conseil Constitutionnel* was sought to be made, this time under Article 61.2 on the constitutionality of the ratifying *loi* adopted by the people.[18] The *Conseil Constitutionnel* declared the reference inadmissible. On 24 September 1992 the Bill authorising ratification was passed and was officially promulgated by the President on 25 September 1994.

(No. 2623) ajoutant à la Constitution un titre: "De l'Union européene", No. 2684 by G. Gouzes, 11 May 1992.

11 Senate Document No. 334 of 13 May 1992.

12 Senate, *Rapport fait au nom de la commission des lois constitutionnelles, de législation, du suffrage universel, du règlement et d'administration générale sur le projet de loi constitutionnelle adoptée par l'Assemblée Nationale ajoutant à la Constitution un titre*: "Des Communautés européennes et de l'Union européenne", No. 2676 (Annexe), by J. Larché, 27 May 1992.

13 National Assembly, *Rapport au noms de la commission des lois constitutionnelles, de la législation et de l'administration générale de la Republique sur le projet de loi constitutionnelle, modifié par le Sénat, ajoutant à la Constitution un titre*: "De l'Union européenne", No. 2803 by G. Gouzes, 18 June 1992.

14 No. 92–554 of 25 June 1992, J.O. p. 8406, 26 June 1992.

15 92–312 DC, *TEU No. 2*, 2 September 1992, Rec. p. 76; (1992) *Revue de Droit Public* 1610.

16 The text of the Bill provided simply: "The ratification of the treaty concluded in Maastricht on 7–2–92 has been authorised."

17 The alternative to Article 11 was to authorise ratification by ordinary *loi* pursuant to Article 45 and Article 53.

18 92–313 DC, 23 September 1992, Rec. p. 94; (1992) *Revue de Droit Public* 1618, *TEU No. 3*.

The results of this process are that the Treaty on European Union has been ratified by the President of the Republic and the Constitution has been revised adding, *inter alia*, a new Title XIV entitled "On the European Communities and the European Union".

16. SOVEREIGNTY

Summary

16–1 The concept of sovereignty is the fulcrum of French constitutional legitimation. The concept is more to the forefront than in Irish constitutional law, understandably in a nation of such a long continuous history of unbroken sovereignty. The current positive law doctrine of sovereignty upheld by the majority consensus, as illustrated in the debates and *Conseil Constitutionnel* decisions surrounding the amendment of the Constitution and the ratification of the Treaty on European Union appears to be the following. Sovereignty is tied to the concept of nation and is inalienable and indivisible. The holder of sovereignty is the people. The people may delegate its exercise to institutions of the Republic. The republican form of government cannot be amended. Thus there is a division, as there is in all modern legal orders resting upon the concept of popular sovereignty, between the source and the regular organs of exercise of sovereignty. The exercise of sovereignty can be limited and corresponding competences transferred to an international organisation, subject to reciprocity. In the case of a transfer of competences involving the essential conditions for the exercise of national sovereignty a constitutional revision is necessary before the transfer can take place constitutionally. After constitutional revision and ratification, France has transferred to the European Community competences affecting the essential conditions for exercise of national sovereignty. But French constitutional law has restricted both the extent of the transfer of competences and its view of the scope of European Community law.[1]

History of the Principle of Sovereignty

16–2 The principle of sovereignty has been central to French constitutional history since the Revolution. Article 3 of the Declaration of the Rights of Man and of the Citizen of 26 August 1789 ("the Declaration") states: "The principle of all sovereignty resides essentially in the Nation. No body nor individual can exercise authority which does not emanate expressly from it." The Declaration was put at the head of the first written French Constitution, that of 3 September 1791. The Constitution provided for a constitutional monarchy, but it made clear, in Article 1, that "Sovereignty is one, indivisible, inalienable,

---

[1] See below Chap. 18, "French Constitutional Law Interpretation of European Community Law in the Ratification of the Treaty on European Union".

and imprescriptible. It belongs to the Nation; no section of the people, no individual, can attribute its exercise to himself". The title to Articles 7 to 10 of the Constitutional Act of 24 June 1793 is "On the sovereignty of the people". Article 7 provides: "The sovereign people is the universality of the French citizens." Articles 17 and 18 of the Declaration of the Rights and Duties of Man and of the Citizen, which headed the Constitution of Year III (the Girondin Constitution, which was never in force) provided: "17. Sovereignty resides essentially in the universality of the citizens. 18. No individual, no partial grouping of citizens can attribute sovereignty to itself." In Article 2 it provided "The universality of French citizens is the sovereign".

There was indirect reference to the popular source of power in the Constitution of Year VIII but the principle naturally did not feature prominently during the First Empire or the Restoration. However the Constitutional Senatorial Bill of 6 April 1814 declares in Article 1 that: "The French people call freely on the throne of Louis Stanislas Xavier of France". Charles X abdicated in 1830 after a popular uprising and the Charter of 1830, although not differing substantially from that of 1814, suppressed the Preamble of the Constitution of 1814 in which the King had granted the Constitution to his subjects. Rather, the Charter of 1830 declared a pact. Furthermore, the King was no longer the King of France but the King of the French. The Orleanist order rested on an ambiguity about the locus of sovereignty.

The Constitution of the Second Republic[2] returned to the notions of the Revolution in its first Article: "Sovereignty resides in the universality of the French citizens. It is inalienable and imprescriptible. No individual or fraction of the people can appropriate its exercise." Although the Second Republic was quickly succeeded by the Second Empire, popular sovereignty was maintained in principle, albeit not institutionally. The Constitution of the Second Empire of 14 January 1852 declared itself "made in virtue of the powers delegated by the French people to Louis-Napoléon Bonaparte by the vote of 20 and 21 December 1851". Bonaparte was to be the President of the Republic for a period of 10 years. Article 1 provided that "the Constitution recognises, confirms and guarantees the great principles which were proclaimed in 1789 and are the basis of the public law of the French." The contrast between principle and practice is illustrated by Article 5 under which: "The President is responsible before the French People, to which he has always the right to make appeal." In practice plebiscites were used to ratify decisions already made.

The Constitution of the Third Republic marks the ascendancy of the principle of popular sovereignty. The Constitution is composed of three constitutional *lois* of 24 and 25 February and 16 July 1875. Article 2 of the *loi* of 25 February provided that the head of State was to be referred to as the President of the Republic, which marked symbolically the changeover from

---

[2] 4 November 1848.

empire. The power of the Parliament was increased at the President's expense. Paradoxically, although the Constitution of the Third Republic returned to the principle of popular sovereignty, the Constitution does not expressly declare the basis of power. This became established as a matter of practice: Gambetta once declared to MacMahon: "When the country has spoken, it is necessary to submit or to resign"; after MacMahon's resignation, the subsequent President, Grévy, declared: "I will never enter into conflict with the national will expressed by its constitutional organs".[3]

It can be seen from these constitutional developments that, from the Revolution of 1789 until the end of World War II, the constitutional debate on sovereignty was focussed on the opposition between "supporters of national sovereignty oriented towards a strictly representative democracy opposed to those of a popular sovereignty implying a more direct democracy".[4] All were agreed on the principle that sovereignty was inalienable. Furthermore, "the principle of national sovereignty has always been closely linked to the idea of individual liberty".[5] The boundaries to the protection of human rights could only be determined by *lois* (Article 4, Declaration 1789), which were the expression of the general will (Article 6 of the Declaration). But Parliament could not have delegated away control over human rights to another organ because only Parliament could express the general will which was necessary for limitation of human rights, which general will (a concept not defined by positive law) could not be delegated. As will be seen below, when sovereignty shifted to popular sovereignty, human rights became a limitation on popular sovereignty.

Since the War, this debate on popular or representative sovereignty has been closed off by the Constitutions of 1946 and 1958. Principally, this appears to have been achieved: first, by running together the notions of nation and sovereignty into national sovereignty, thus reducing the number of elements from four (nation, sovereignty, people, and representative) to three (national sovereignty, people, and representative); and, secondly, by distinguishing the holder of sovereignty (the people) from its delegated exerciser (the organs established by the Constitution, including the assemblies convened in Congress under Article 89 as the constituent power or the people within the limits of the Article 11 referendum process[6]). The Constitution of the Fourth

---

3 C. Debasch and J.M. Pontier, *Les Constitutions de la France* (2nd ed., Paris: Dalloz, 1989), p. 188.

4 National Assembly, *Rapport au nom de la commission des lois constitutionelles, de la législation et de l'administration générale de la République sur le projet de loi constitutionelle (No. 2623) ajoutant à la Constitution un titre:* "De l'Union européenne", No. 2676, registered 4 May 1992 (Gouzes' Report) p. 10.

5 A. West *et al.*, *The French Legal System, An Introduction* (London: Fourmat Publishing, 1992).

6 The people, if the President so chooses, may play a part in the amendment of the Constitution by referendum under Article 89. They may also participate directly in government by referendum according to Article 11, which has been expanded by Constitutional *loi* No. 95–880 of 4 August 1995 extending the field of application of the

Republic[7] referred in its Preamble to the Declaration of 1789 and proclaimed in Article 3:

> "National Sovereignty belongs to the French people. No section of the people and no individual can appropriate its exercise. The people exercise it, in constitutional matters, by the vote of their representatives and by referendum. In all other matters, it is exercised by their deputies in the national Assembly, elected by universal, equal, direct and secret suffrage."

The Constitution of the Fifth Republic[8] states in the first sentence of its preamble the two connected fundamental commitments of French constitutional doctrine – national sovereignty and human rights: "The French people solemnly proclaim their attachment to Human Rights and to the principles of national sovereignty, such as they are defined by the Declaration of 1789, confirmed and completed by the preamble of the Constitution of 1946." The first title to the Constitution is "On Sovereignty". It provides in part as follows:

> "Article 2. – France is an indivisible, lay, democratic, and social Republic. . . .
> Its principle is: government of the people, by the people, and for the people.
>
> Article 3. – National sovereignty rests with the people, who exercise it by their representatives and by way of referendum.
> No section of the people nor any individual can appropriate its exercise. . . . "

This notion of the French people as the holders of sovereignty was affirmed in the decision of the *Conseil Constitutionnel on the* loi *on the status of Corsica*[9] where it held unconstitutional Article 1 of that *loi* which recognised "the Corsican people, component of the French people". The grounds were that "the legal concept of 'French people' has constitutional value"; Article 1 of the *loi* offended against Article 3 which designates the people as sovereign, against the Preamble to the Constitution of 1958 which postulates the unity of the "French people", and against Article 2 on the indivisibility of the Republic.

---

referendum, instituting a single ordinary parliamentary session, amending the regime of parliamentary immunity and abrogating the provisions on the [French] Community and transitory provisions (expansion shown in italics):

> "Article 11. – The President of the Republic, on the proposal of the government during sessions or on the joint proposal of the two Assemblies, published in the Official Journal, may submit to referendum any *loi* bill concerning the organisation of public powers, *reforms of the political or social economy of the nation and the public services which contribute to it,* approving a treaty of the [French] Community or authorising the ratification of a treaty which, without being contrary to the Constitution, will have effects on the functioning of the institutions.
>
> *When the referendum is organised on the proposal of the government, the government must, before each Assembly, make a declaration which is followed by a debate.*
>
> When the referendum is concluded by the adoption of a *loi* bill, the President of the Republic will promulgate the *loi in the fifteen days which follow the proclamation of the results of the consultation.*"

[7] 26 October 1946.

[8] 4 October 1958.

[9] 91–290 DC, 9 May 1991, Rec. p. 50; [1991] *Recueil Dalloz Sirey* 624; in West *et al.*, (1992) *op. cit.* above, n.3, pp. 194–195, "*Loi* on the status of Corsica".

The Constitution of 1958 also had another effect on the traditional distinction between people on the one hand and their representatives in Parliament on the other, an effect which arose not from its provisions on sovereignty but from its provisions on government. In order to ensure a strong executive for stability in government, the executive receives a direct grant of power from the people via the Constitution. Thus Parliament and executive are better seen as organs of sovereignty, not as its representatives, which organs must be kept within the limits laid down in the Constitution. This is reinforced by the status of national sovereignty as a principle which binds political parties.[10] This view of Parliament and Executive is important for making the Constitution legally binding on the organs of government, for the role of the *Conseil Constitutionnel* as a constitutional Court, and for the systematisation of constitutional notions, especially those related to sovereignty such as fundamental rights. As was stated in the course of the debates, "neither the significance, nor the bearing of the constitutional principle of sovereignty are susceptible to a unique interpretation."[11] The origin and exercise of sovereignty may be summarised in the present in the following way: the people are the holders of national sovereignty, which is a fundamental commitment of French constitutional law, but have delegated its exercise to the organs of government under the Constitution: Parliament, Executive, President, and Courts.

De Witte considers that the principle of national sovereignty in the Member States is an obstacle to integration; sovereignty means "the ultimate source of legal authority within a State".[12] De Witte does not claim that this definition is valid in a particular legal order, and points out that the intra-order meaning of sovereignty is often imprecise. This work, based on an analysis of French constitutional law and Irish constitutional law only, considers that sovereignty is the ultimate originator of positive law but that the validity or legal authority of positive law depends not only on its pedigree but also on compliance with national constitutional natural law, particularly the protection and promotion of fundamental human rights. De Witte's definition identifies a major conceptual problem for integration in the account of the exercise of power by supranational institutions without any direct control by States or by people. Without doubting that this is a problem, this work focusses on the anterior problem of revolt or revolution posed by the challenge of the internalisation into national law of European Community law's self-perception to the fundamental commitments of national constitutional law which comprise not only the principle of sovereignty but national constitutional natural law,

---

10 Article 4 of the Constitution of 1958 provides:

> "Parties and political groups contribute to the expression of suffrage. They may form and exercise their activity freely. They must respect the principles of national sovereignty and democracy."

11 Gouzes' Report, above n.4, p. 14.

12 B. De Witte, "Sovereignty and European Integration: The Weight of Legal Tradition" (1995) 2 *Maastricht Journal of European and Comparative Law* 145 at pp. 146–147.

the integrity of national constitutional law, and a national constitutional concept of the common good.

Constitutional Basis of Public International Law

16–3 The question posed squarely for the first time in the Treaty on European Union debates was not "what is the importance of sovereignty for the French Constitution?" nor "how is sovereignty distributed internally?" but "how can French sovereignty accommodate the normative demands of the European Community?" This is not simply a question of how far the public international law and national law descriptions of French sovereignty coincide or differ. The problem is that European Community law claims authority superior to that of incompatible *lois* and constitutional provisions and must be enforced directly in the French courts in a whole range of matters composing traditionally the very substance of national government.

The Constitution of 1958 refers in its Preamble to the Preamble of the Constitution of the Fourth Republic. It is in this preamble that French constitutional law first made the innovative step of recognising internally the constraints of a new type of public international law, the law of international institutions, on sovereignty. The Preamble provides in paragraphs 14 and 15:

> "The French Republic, faithful to its traditions, shall comply with the rules of public international law. It shall not undertake any war of conquest and shall never use its forces against the liberty of any people.
>
> Subject to reciprocity, France consents to the limitations of sovereignty necessary for the organisation and the defence of peace."[13]

Historically, the purpose of these provisions was to allow the participation of France in the diplomatic and military actions of the United Nations. These provisions permitted only limitations of sovereignty, not the transfer of sovereignty: and these were limited to those necessary for the organisation and defence of the peace. The *Conseil Constitutionnel*, in the exercise of its Article 54 jurisdiction on the compatibility of international agreements with the Constitution, did not build the legal structures for addressing this new and complex problem on these preambular provisions alone.

The Constitution of 1958 is the supreme positive norm of reference of validity of law for the French legal order.[14] There is no reference to public international law in its short Preamble except indirectly by reference to the

---

[13] Title IV of the Constitution (1946) provides for diplomatic treaties, but has been superseded by Title VI (Constitution of 1958) entitled "Treaties and International Agreements".

[14] Senate, *Rapport fait au nom de la commission des Lois constitutionelles, de législation, du suffrage universel, du règlement et d'administration générale sur le projet de loi constitutionelle adoptée par l'Assemblée Nationale ajoutant à la Constitution un titre*: "Des Communautés européennes et de l'Union européenne", No. 2676 (Annexe), by J. Larché, 27 May 1992. (Larché's Report) p. 10.

Preamble of the Constitution of 1946. Prior to the constitutional *loi* of 25 June 1992, there was no mention of the European Communities despite the fact that the Constitution was posterior to the Treaty of Rome (1957). However Title VI of the Constitution of 1958, entitled "Treaties and International Agreements" covers the relationship of the public international law of treaties to domestic law. It comprises Articles 52 to 55. International treaties and agreements signed by France are not automatically applicable in the domestic legal order. They must first be ratified. The authority and final decision rests ultimately with the President irrespective of whatever other enabling procedures are followed (such as, in the case of the Treaty on European Union, constitutional revision and an authorising *loi* enacted by referendum).

All European Community treaties fall within the categories of treaties set out in Article 53 and consequently need a *loi* to authorise their ratification.[15] Once ratified, Article 55 applies:

> "Regularly ratified or approved treaties or agreements have, from their publication, an authority superior to that of *lois* subject, for each agreement or treaty, to its application by the other party."

This Article is consistent with the shift begun in Article 26 of the Constitution of 1946 away from France's traditional dualist approach to public international law. By virtue of this Article international treaties do not need implementing legislation in order to be applied in preference to incompatible *lois*. The reservation of reciprocity makes clear that international treaties, whilst superior to *loi*, have a contingent character and do not form part of the domestic legal order. Article 55 combined with Article 54 make clear that public international law cannot attain in the French legal order authority superior to that of the Constitution. The conferral by Article 55 of supra-legislative status to duly ratified and promulgated treaties implies their infra-constitutional status.

The constitutional amendment which inserted an Article 53–1 specifies the infra-constitutional and contingent status of a category of public international law treaties in a way similar to the treatment of public international law treaties as a whole. That Article resulted indirectly from the Schengen treaty. Although the Schengen treaty was held not to be contrary to the Constitution,[16] the *loi* implementing this Convention[17] and the Dublin Convention was held contrary to the unwritten fundamental rights of foreigners.[18] That *loi* was promulgated

---

[15] Article 53 provides:

> "Peace treaties, commercial treaties, treaties relating to international organizations, those which commit the finances of the State, those relating to the status of persons, and those which involve transfer, exchange, or addition of territory may only be ratified or approved by a *loi*.
>
> They take effect only after they are ratified or approved. No transfer, exchange, or addition of territory is valid without the consent of the populations concerned."

[16] 91–294 DC, 25 July 1991, Rec. p. 91; (1991) *Revue de Droit Public* 1517, *Schengen Treaty*.

[17] 15 June 1990.

[18] 93–325 DC, 13 August 1993, Rec. p. 224; (1993) *La Semaine Juridique (Textes)* 373, *On the Control of Immigration.*

without the censured provisions, but subsequently, in order to avoid future incompatibilities, the Parliament in Congress adopted a Constitutional *loi* via Article 89 of the Constitution,[19] which added the new Article 53–1. The reservations in the first paragraph of this Article make clear the contingent nature of such treaties:

> "The Republic may conclude with European states which are bound by identical agreements to its agreements in the field of asylum and the protection of the rights of man and of fundamental freedoms, treaties determining their respective competences for the examination of requests for asylum which are presented to them."

The second paragraph of the Article expressly authorises the authorities to derogate unilaterally from such treaty obligations:

> "Nevertheless, even if the request does not enter into their competence by virtue of these treaties, the authorities of the Republic have always the right to grant asylum to any foreigner persecuted by reason of his action in favour of liberty or who solicits the protection of France for another reason."

The constitutional principle of superiority of constitutional law over public international law has been summarised by Abraham: "everything proceeds from the Constitution".[20] There is no distinction in principle in French law according to the type of public international law treaty, bilateral or multilateral, European Community or other. French constitutional law's non-recognition of the superiority of European Community law means that French constitutional law's interpretation (primarily and authoritatively by the *Conseil Constitutionnel*) of European Community law, which must take place in order to establish conformity, is in conflict with European Community law's self-interpretation (primarily and authoritatively by the Court of Justice).[21] European Community actions (laws, court decisions) taken pursuant to Treaties can be enforced in France only so far as these actions fit the limitations of interpretation of French constitutional law. In the event of future conflicts, the Constitution must be revised again (either directly or by revising its interpretation).

---

19 No. 93–1526 of 25 November 1993, J.O. p. 16296, 26 November 1993.

20 R. Abraham, *Droit international, droit communautaire et droit français*, P.E.S., (1st ed. with update, 1990, Paris: Hachette, 1989) pp. 35–36:

> " . . . in the internal order, *everything proceeds from the Constitution.* All the public authorities – whether they are legislative, administrative, or jurisdictional – hold their competences, and their very existence, directly or indirectly from the Constitution. All the legal rules applicable on the territory of the state proceed from the Constitution, either because they figure explicitly or implicitly in it, or because they are contained in the enacted acts following the procedures and conforming to the rules of competences provided for by the Constitution: international conventions, *lois*, and *règlements.*
>
> The supremacy of the Constitution in the internal legal order is thus (as long as international society is founded on the political fact of the sovereignty of States) a primary and incontrovertible truth."

21 See above, paras. 8–39 *et seq.*, "Supremacy".

The Concepts Involved in the French Constitutional Law Perception of European Community Law

16–4 The problems posed by European Community law for French constitutional law, and in particular in the revision of the Constitution and for future revisions, give rise to conceptual difficulties which make the coherent presentation of French constitutional law's cryptic and somewhat conflicting answers to these problems difficult. It is not surprising that there is difficulty as the problems are new. There are several core concepts, which are all interrelated but (apart from the first) will be dealt with in separate sections for the purpose of exposition.[22]

First, there is the distinction, which runs partly hidden through the other concepts, between sovereignty as it exists under the Constitution of 1958, as it is defined by the rules, organs and relations of government and the restrictions on their powers and by the role of government constituted as the constituent power (either as the President and the two houses of Parliament in Congress, or as the President, the two houses of Parliament, and the people in a referendum), and full national sovereignty as it exists in the people as a matter of fact and as a political concept recognised to some degree by French constitutional law. Article 3 of the Constitution of 1958[23] makes clear that the same intra-order concept of sovereignty covers the rules, organs, restrictions on, and relations, of government by the people's representatives, and the constituent power in the organs of government with or without popular consultation in a referendum. Consultation of the people is not necessary for the constituent function, and indeed the provisions on referendum can be amended by the constituent power acting without popular consultation.[24]

Related to this first distinction is the distinction between French constitutional law as it exists under the Constitution of 1958 (the sense in which the term is used in this work) and French constitutional law doctrine as it can exist independently of this particular Constitution but with some kind of latent historic continuing authority which is not quite intra-order but not external (in the sense of theory or comparative law) either. This doctrine represents the analyses of the constitutional foundations of the various French orders. Not being clearly intra-order, it comes in on the margins of this thesis. In this doctrine, there is also the concept of sovereignty of the nation, as distinct from sovereignty belonging to the people.[25] Sovereignty in all its meanings is limited in the lawfulness of its power by observance of funda-

---

[22] This process remains in this work one of identification and reconstruction of authority, not an attempt to clarify theoretically or make proposals from an external perspective. See above, Part I.

[23] Quoted above, para. 16–2, "History of the Principle of Sovereignty".

[24] Constitutional *loi* No. 95–880 of 4 August 1995, J.O. p. 11744, 5 August 1995.

[25] See below, paras. 21–2 *et seq.*, "Assuring the Continuation of the Life of the Nation".

mental rights and liberties, and possible by the idea of a republic or republican legality.[26]

Secondly, there is the distinction between the limitation and the transfer of sovereignty, which is tied to the French constitutional law view of the European Community as the destination of transferred competences, not transferred sovereignty, and to the French constitutional law view of itself as amended to restrict the essential conditions for the exercise of sovereignty under the Constitution of 1958.

Thirdly, there is the inalienability of sovereignty. Sovereignty under the Constitution of 1958 has not been alienated because the French constitutional law interpretation of European Community law is based at present on the transfer of competences. It is unlikely French constitutional law will allow for the alienation of sovereignty under the Constitution of 1958 – such would cause a revolution in law. It also appears that so far as French constitutional law recognises national sovereignty as a political concept and in the people as a fact, it regards such sovereignty as inalienable. Furthermore, this is the view of French constitutional doctrine beyond the Constitution of 1958.

Fourthly, there is the controlling norm tailored by the Conseil Constitutionnel to deal with the demands of the law of international organisations: the essential conditions for the exercise of national sovereignty. When these change, sovereignty as it exists under the Constitution of 1958 changes (as distinct from sovereignty as political concept or fact).

Fifthly, there are the limits to the amendability of French constitutional law. Some are deducible from the controlling norm of essential conditions for the exercise of national sovereignty, and some are specified in the Constitution itself.

Sixthly, there are the limits to what French constitutional law regards as the law creating power of national sovereignty as it exists as a political concept or fact. It is not surprising that there is a crossover between these limits and the limits under the Constitution 1958.

The Distinction Between the Limitation and Transfer of Sovereignty

16–5 The distinction between the limitation and transfer of sovereignty predates the use of the concepts of the restriction of essential conditions for the exercise of national sovereignty (which is related to the limitation of sovereignty) and the transfer of competences (related to the transfer of sovereignty).

The *Conseil Constitutionnel* relied on this distinction suggested in the Preamble to the Constitution of 1946 in its decision *European Community Council Decision for direct elections to the European Parliament.*[27] The Council Decision of

---

[26] This is discussed further in the following chapters and in Chap. 21, "The Substance of the Essential Conditions for Exercise of National Sovereignty".

[27] 76–71 DC, 30 December 1976, Rec. p. 15; in B. Rudden and L. Kahn-Freund, *A Source-Book on French Law* (Oxford: Clarendon Press, 1991) pp. 58–60.

20 September 1976 was referred by the President of the Republic under Article 54 of the Constitution of 1958. The *Conseil Constitutionnel* stated:

> "Considering that, whereas the preamble to the Constitution of 1946, confirmed by that of the Constitution of 1958, provides that, *subject to reciprocity*, France consents to *limitations* of sovereignty *necessary* to the organisation and the defense of the peace, no provision of a constitutional nature authorises a *transfer* of all or part of the national sovereignty to *any organisation whatever*." (Emphasis added.)

There are five restrictions in this one paragraph. The paragraph is not elucidated because the *Conseil Constitutionnel* found that universal direct election to the European Parliament was merely a different method of selecting the membership of an institution which drew its powers from the Treaties establishing the European Communities. Thus the Council Decision did not create a sovereignty or an institution incompatible with respect for national sovereignty (note that this term combining the concepts of nation and sovereignty is the one used in the judgment), nor did it undermine the Republic's institutions, notably the Parliament. This restrictive interpretation of European Community developments is characteristic of the *Conseil Constitutionnel's* approach.[28] If the *Conseil Constitutionnel* had considered the direct elections as the first step towards establishing a European sovereignty based on a European people, it would have had to explain the distinction between limitation and transfer of sovereignty. The distinction appears to have the merit from the perspective of French constitutional law of allowing the domestic order to regard as merely a limitation of sovereignty *that which* the European Community order regards as a transfer of sovereignty. But what is the *that which*?

Competences. Transfer of sovereignty as such is impermissible.[29] What is at stake then is the legal capacity to take measures which will be binding in the French legal order by virtue of the ratification of a treaty. The measures will be authoritative provided that the *Conseil Constitutionnel* allows a limitation such that an entity may exercise a competence in the place of France to make rules which will not be unconstitutional on the grounds of the nature of the competence exercised by that entity and provided that the rules on ratification or approval (Article 55) are complied with. Subsequently under Article 55 the measures made in the exercise of the transferred legal capacity have authority superior to *loi*. Thus the *Conseil Constitutionnel* has differentiated between the concept of sovereignty and of legal capacity (competence). Its

---

[28] The technique of controlling constitutionality through reservations of interpretation is considered below, in para. 20–3, "Effect of Reservations of Interpretation".

[29] This decision has been criticized by P. Oliver, "The French *Conseil Constitutionnel* and the Treaty of Maastricht" (1994) *International and Comparative Law Quarterly* 1 at p. 8. Oliver considers that the *Conseil Constitutionnel* in its decision *TEU No. 1* allowed for a transfer of sovereignty without constitutional amendment (*ibid.* at p. 16). This work maintains that it is clear only that competences may be transferred, and these cannot be transferred without amendment if the transfer affects any of the three controlling norms. (For their enumeration, see below, para. 16–7, "The Controlling Norm of the Essential Conditions for the Exercise of National Sovereignty".)

decision on the *European Community Council Decision for direct elections to the European Parliament* is indeed something of an aberration for not spelling this out. The *Conseil Constitutionnel* had considered the question earlier in *Budgetary and Merger Treaties*.[30] This treaty had been referred to the *Conseil Constitutionnel* under Article 54 by the prime minister. The *Conseil Constitutionnel* found that the treaty did not affect relations between states and the European Community, but between institutions within the European Community. Thus the Treaty did not affect "neither by its nature, nor by its importance, the essential conditions for exercise of national sovereignty." This formula interposes two barriers between the conflicting claims of a treaty and national sovereignty. The *Conseil Constitutionnel* thus analyses the Treaty as potentially affecting neither national sovereignty nor the exercise of national sovereignty but the conditions for exercise of national sovereignty. Further, the use of this test means that not only are treaties which entail a transfer of sovereignty unconstitutional, but treaties which entail a limitation of sovereignty may be unconstitutional also.

The *Conseil Constitutionnel* repeated this formulation and listed the essential conditions in *Protocol on the abolition of the death penalty*.[31] The President of the Republic referred this Protocol to the European Convention for the Protection of Human Rights and Fundamental Freedoms to the *Conseil Constitutionnel* under Article 54. The *Conseil Constitutionnel* held that because the Protocol did not outlaw the death penalty during times of war or threat thereof, its abolition in other circumstances was not incompatible with the duty of the State to assure the respect of the institutions of the Republic, the continuation of the life of the Nation, and the rights and liberties of citizens, and that therefore the Protocol was not unconstitutional because it did not attack essential conditions for exercise of national sovereignty and contained no clause contrary to a particular clause of the Constitution.[32]

The *Conseil Constitutionnel* repeated this formulation in the *Loi granting European Community nationals access to public employment*.[33] That *loi* permitted European Community nationals access to jobs in the public service, provided that the attributes of such jobs were separable from the exercise of sovereignty and the jobs did not involve any direct or indirect participation in the exercise of the prerogatives of the public power of the State. The *Conseil Constitutionnel*

---

30 70–39 DC, 19 June 1970, Rec. p. 15.

31 85–188 DC, 22 May 1985, Rec. p. 15.

32 This judicial reference to particular clauses of the Constitution is a reminder that it is not only conflicts with the essential conditions for exercise of national sovereignty which will ground a finding of the unconstitutionality of a treaty. The essential conditions for exercise of national sovereignty is only one of the constitutional norms used to control the compatibility of a treaty with the Constitution. Not all attacks on the constitutionality of the treaty will be classed as indirect attacks on the constitutional principle of sovereignty.

33 91–293 DC, 23 July 1991, Rec. p. 77; (1991) *Revue de Droit Public* 1514.

found that all attacks on essential conditions for exercise of national sovereignty were excluded by this proviso, and upheld the constitutionality of the *loi*. In this case the *loi* was referred under Article 61.2 by more than 60 senators which demonstrates that the test of the undermining of the essential conditions for exercise of national sovereignty is a test for constitutionality which can be employed by the *Conseil Constitutionnel* in the exercise of either its Article 61.2 or Article 54 jurisdiction, requiring or permitting it to decide on the constitutionality of the instrument referred.

In its decision of 25 July 1991 under Article 61.2 of the constitutionality of the *loi* ratifying the Schengen Treaty[34] the *Conseil Constitutionnel* considered separately the question of an undermining of the essential conditions for exercise of national sovereignty and the question of a transfer of sovereignty, both offered as grounds for the unconstitutionality of the treaty by those making the reference. The *Conseil Constitutionnel* considered under the essential conditions for exercise of national sovereignty the same three headings as it considered in its decision of 22 May 1985[35]: the duty of the State to guarantee the respect for its institutions; the continuity of the life of the nation; and the guarantee of the rights and liberties of citizens. But the *Conseil Constitutionnel* went on to consider as a separate constitutional complaint the question of whether there had been a transfer of sovereignty. It restricted the notion of transfer of sovereignty to the alleged transfer of the competences of the police by the provisions of the treaty which allowed in certain restricted circumstances the police of another signatory state to pursue in a restricted manner a trans-border fugitive. The *Conseil Constitutionnel* found no transfer of sovereignty because the Treaty provided for possibilities of derogation for reasons of public order or of national security and reserved expressly that the competences of police of each contracting party on its territory would not be restricted. The *Conseil Constitutionnel's* acceptance, in answering the complaints of unconstitutionality, of the distinction made here between the essential conditions for the exercise of national sovereignty and the transfer of sovereignty is important for affirming that the two are not identical.

In this decision,[36] further norms of constitutional control of the treaty other than a transfer of sovereignty or an undermining of the essential conditions for exercise of national sovereignty were considered. These were the indivisibility of the Republic – (which is distinct from respect for the institutions of the Republic (an essential condition for the exercise of national sovereignty)), the republican form of government (which cannot be amended under the Constitution of 1958, (Article 89)) and the disregard of the rights and liberties of constitutional value which attach to non-citizens in their right to asylum[37]

---

34 91–294 DC, 25 July 1991, Rec. p. 91; (1991) *Revue de Droit Public* 1517, *Schengen Treaty*.
35 85–155 DC, 22 May 1985, Rec. p. 15, *Protocol on the abolition of the death penalty*.
36 91–294 DC, 25 July 1991, Rec. p. 91; (1991) *Revue de Droit Public* 1517, *Schengen Treaty*.
37 Paragraph 4 of the Preamble to the Constitution of 1946 provides: "Every man persecuted because of his actions for liberty has the right of asylum in the territories of the Republic."

(which is distinct from the rights and liberties of citizens – an essential condition of the exercise of national sovereignty).

The insistence in the decisions of the *Conseil Constitutionnel*, the parliamentary debates, and the revision of the constitution, on the transfer of competences rather than transfers of sovereignty has the following important consequences:

1. It grounds French constitutional law's restrictive interpretation of European Community law because the nature of the European Community itself is defined in terms other than sovereign. The importance of the reformulation is made clear fully only in the *Conseil Constitutionnel's* decision *TEU No. 1*[38] where it uses the notion of competences, not of sovereignty, on which to build its view of the European Community. This is set out at length in the section on French constitutional law's interpretation of European Community law.[39] Article 88–1 builds on this basis.

2. The French constitutional law concept of sovereignty is conserved intact. This means that areas which are linked into national sovereignty, such as the protection of the rights and liberties of citizens, can maintain their coherence in the legal order.

3. National sovereignty remains inalienable.

4. Participation in the European Community remains, according to French constitutional law, reversible.[40]

During the debate on constitutional revision following *TEU No. 1*,[41] most participants insisted that it was solely a transfer of competences, as opposed to that of sovereignty, which was involved. For example, the "Outline of Reasons" accompanying the Bill submitted by the President of the Republic and the government to the National Assembly stated that the Treaty transfers competences; sovereignty is not mentioned.[42] The Minister for Justice insisted that only transfers of competences were involved, not transfers of sovereignty.[43] The Senate Report maintained that the constitutional amendments did not put the State's sovereignty in doubt in the internal legal order (or the public international legal order).[44] The Minister for Foreign Affairs made clear that the Parliament could not be constrained to transpose the directives on voting and eligibility into French law, but could be subject only to an action for breach of European Community law,[45] thus interpreting the claims of European

---

38 92–308 DC, 9 April 1992, Rec. p. 55; (1992) 28 *Revue Trimestrielle du Droit Européen* 418.
39 See below, Chap. 18, "French Constitutional Law Interpretation of European Community Law in the Ratification of the Treaty on European Union".
40 See below, Chap. 17, "Denunciation and Reversibility".
41 92–308 DC, 9 April 1992, Rec. p. 55; (1992) *Revue Trimestrielle du Droit Européen* 418.
42 Assemblée Nationale Document No. 2623, 22 April 1992.
43 Larché's Report, above, n.14; Gouzes' Report above, n.4.
44 Larché's Report, above, n.14, p. 37.
45 Larché's Report, above, n.14.

Community law as if European Community law was public international law and denying one of the central concepts of European Community law: the duty of the organs of government to uphold European Community law.[46] This area of voting and eligibility is one of three where competences concerning the essential conditions for exercise of national sovereignty were expressly transferred (Article 88–3). The European Community would not be unable to constrain Parliament if sovereignty had been transferred.

The Inalienability of Sovereignty

16–6 This insistence that competences, and not sovereignty, were being transferred was backed up by the insistence on the inalienability of national sovereignty (itself backed up by unamendability). As regards the present incompatibility of French constitutional law with European Community law, it is not necessary to establish that sovereignty could not be transferred to establish that sovereignty was not in fact transferred by the ratification of the Treaty on European Union. A consideration of the issue of future alienability need make no concession on the finding that only certain competences, and not sovereignty, have been transferred and that French constitutional law and European Community law are in a state of constitutionally incompatible stand-off. The question of future alienability goes to the assessment of risk of revolution in French constitutional law, and of revolt needed to avoid a revolution. If sovereignty cannot be alienated, then French constitutional law can in the future only ever permit the transfer of competences, and therefore will revolt against a demand to transfer sovereignty, unless there is a revolutionary break from the French constitutional law concept of sovereignty. The concept of alienability of sovereignty forms part of what is at issue in the concepts of essential conditions for the exercise of national sovereignty and limits to amendment.

The Controlling Norm of the Essential Conditions for the Exercise of National Sovereignty

16–7 The distinction between essential and non-essential (the restriction of which does not per se require constitutional amendment if no other constitutional rule – such as a provision – is affected) conditions of the exercise of national sovereignty is not simply a rewording of the distinction between limitations and transfers of sovereignty. It is a reformulation of the problem of accommodating the French constitutional law notion of sovereignty with the claims of European Community Law.

The understanding of the test of compatibility with the essential conditions for the exercise of national sovereignty advanced here differs from Favoreau's

---

[46] The highest judicial sanction provided by the Treaty on European Union is to fine the Member State, and the ultimate political sanction is withdrawal of membership.

understanding. Favoreau stated in his audience before the Senate Committee[47] during the debate on the revision of the constitution that the new distinction between transfers of ordinary competences and transfers of competences concerning essential conditions for exercise of national sovereignty was almost the same as what he termed the abandoned distinction between limitations and transfers of sovereignty. Because the essential conditions for the exercise of national sovereignty have been affected by that revision which allowed for transfers of competences to the European Community, Favoreau's identification of the transfer of competences concerning essential conditions for the exercise of national sovereignty with the transfer of sovereignty suggests that a transfer of the latter sort has occurred. But a transfer of sovereignty clearly has not occurred as far as French constitutional law is concerned. The old distinction between limitations and transfers of sovereignty appears to remain as regards police powers[48] but not otherwise. Favoreau's interpretation is based not only on a different understanding of the French constitutional law interpretation of European Community law which appears contrary to *TEU No. 1* and *TEU No. 2* as well as Articles 88–1 to 88–3 but also on a different understanding of the controlling norm of essential conditions for the exercise of national sovereignty.

The controlling norms referred to by the *Conseil Constitutionnel* in its decisions on the constitutional conformity of treaties are:

1. All written provisions of the Constitution (including, for example, the republican form of government, which "may not be the subject of revision" according to Article 89 of the Constitution of 1958).

2. Rules and principles of constitutional value (that is, rules and principles other than those in categories of 1 and 3 which are also of constitutional value). For example, in the *Schengen Treaty* decision[49] the *Conseil Constitutionnel* considered separately from category 3 the unwritten rights and liberties of the non-French asylum seeker which have constitutional value and the principle of the indivisibility of the Republic.

3. Essential conditions of/for exercise of national sovereignty (*conditions essentielles d'exercise de la souveraineté nationale*), which are respect for the institutions of the Republic, the continuation of the life of the nation, and the guarantee of the rights and liberties of citizens. The *Conseil Constitutionnel* evolved this controlling norm, to which it first referred its decision *Budgetary and Merger Treaties.*[50] The substantive conditions are considered separately from this consideration of the controlling norm as a whole.[51]

---

47 Larché's Report, above, n.14.

48 91–294 DC, 25 July 1991, Rec. p. 91; (1991) *Revue de Droit Public* 1517, *Schengen Treaty.*

49 *ibid.*

50 70–39 DC, 19 June 1970, Rec. p. 15.

51 See below, Chap. 21, "The Substance of the Essential Conditions for Exercise of National Sovereignty".

There is a basic inconsistency in the notion as it stands of essential conditions for exercise of national sovereignty. The word "condition" itself is ambiguous. It could simply mean "matter", and thus the phrase would read "essential matters concerning the exercise of national sovereignty". However in the alternative it could mean the *sine qua non* of sovereignty. The word must be read with its qualification "essential", which is the more important word because it explains how these matters/conditions/*sine qua non* stand in relation to national sovereignty. On the one hand, these conditions are essential, yet on the other hand, an act of sovereignty in the revision of the Constitution can change them (for example, Articles 88–2 and 88–3 were inserted in order to make ratification of the Treaty on European Union constitutionally permissible after the *Conseil Constitutionnel's* decision that it infringed the essential conditions for the exercise of national sovereignty). The notion of essential conditions implies a framework within which national sovereignty, as it stands at the moment of the application of the norm, must be exercised – "essential" means indispensable, in this context perhaps also enabling, legitimating, and controlling. The essential conditions for exercise of national sovereignty are conditions without which national sovereignty, as understood under the Constitution of 1958 at the moment of application of the norm, cannot be exercised. Thus the concept, and not just the exercise, of national sovereignty is limited by other fundamental commitments in the law, and the essential nature of the limits suggests that sovereignty cannot destroy them completely, unless it could and did destroy itself as well.[52] In any case this has not yet happened. Whether it can happen raises the question of the limitations to amendment.

The Limits on Amendment under the Constitution of 1958

Limits to Amendment on the face of the Constitution and Decisions of the Conseil Constitutionnel

16–8 What are the limits on national sovereignty acting as the constituent power to change the Constitution under the Constitution of 1958? The *Conseil Constitutionnel*, acting under that Constitution, provided the answer in its decision *TEU No. 2*[53] where it held, in considering the argument that the Treaty provisions on the right to vote and eligibility in municipal elections were contrary to the Constitution by virtue of Article 3 of the Constitution notwithstanding the revision made by the insertion of Article 88–3, that:

---

[52] The notion of national sovereignty under the Constitution of 1958 existing without any of the conditions essential for its exercise is obscure. National sovereignty as a fact or political concept recognised by the Constitution of 1958 and waiting in the wings, however, is a comprehensible, but different, notion.

[53] 92–312 DC, 2 September 1992, Rec. p. 76; (1992) *Recueil de Droit Public* 1610.

> "Considering that, subject, on the one hand, to the limitations concerning the periods during which a revision of the Constitution cannot be engaged or pursued, which result from Articles 7 [vacancy of presidency], 16 [declared emergency] and 89, paragraph 4 [integrity of territory], of the constitutional text and, on the other hand, [which result] from the respect of the prescriptions in the fifth paragraph of Article 89 by virtue of which 'the republican form of government cannot be the object of a revision', the constituent power is sovereign, that it is permissible for it to abrogate, to modify or to complete provisions of constitutional import [*valeur*] in the form which it considers to be appropriate; that, thus, nothing opposes the introduction by the constituent power of new provisions into the text of the Constitution which, in the case where they so aim, derogate from a rule or a principle of constitutional import; that this derogation can be just as well express as implied;"

The *Conseil Constitutionnel* went on to consider the argument that the Treaty provisions on Economic and Monetary Union deprived Parliament of competences in violation of Articles 3 and 34 of the Constitution, holding that:

> "within the limits indicated above, the constituent power is sovereign; it is permissible for it to abrogate, to modify or to complete provisions of constitutional import in the form which it considers appropriate;"

The *Conseil Constitutionnel* refused to answer the further question put by those who referred the Treaty: so far as the French juridical order is constructed around the central idea of national sovereignty, how far can revisions of the Constitution go which involve successive undermining of essential conditions for exercise of national sovereignty before the limits of the adequacy of the Constitution for European construction are reached? The *Conseil Constitutionnel* held that it did not have competence under Article 54 to answer this question because it did not relate to the Treaty on European Union.

Whatever answer the *Conseil Constitutionnel* might give to this big question, the decision given means that the stage where this question needs to be considered in determining the constitutionality of a Treaty establishing a European Union was not reached by the ratification of the Treaty on European Union. However, in considering future Rubicon-like limits to European integration, which can be surpassed only by revolution, the first passage cited indicates several limits, leaving aside the limits on the timing of a revision and the limits implicit in the essential conditions for exercise of national sovereignty.

The first limit is implicit in the clause "in the case where [the people] so aim". This suggests that the specific constitutional change made by the people may be limited by other constitutional provisions and principles which would necessitate a harmonious interpretation of the Constitution by the *Conseil Constitutionnel*. However this is not a limit if the people made expressly clear that they wished to override another constitutional provision or principle. But for the people to be so clear, the framers of the proposal would have to be clear to the people, and consequently might not succeed politically with the revision. The second limit is based on Article 89 paragraph 5: "The republican form of government cannot be made the object of a revision."[54]

It is clear from Article 89 and the first passage cited that the constituent power (the President and Parliament in Congress, or the President, both houses of Parliament, and the people pursuant to Articles 89 and 11) has the authority to abrogate provisions of the Constitution, and that it does not have authority under the Constitution to revise contrary to this paragraph.[55] It is not clear from the passage whether the authority to abrogate provisions would extend to the abrogation of so many provisions as to effectively abrogate the Constitution itself, or whether this would be a third limit.

It is clear that there is some limitation as to when the Constitution can be revised. It also appears that the procedure under the Constitution of 1958 must be observed.[56] It is not clear what content the *Conseil Constitutionnel* would give the second limit. But, it appears meaningless to preserve a republican form of government without preserving a republic. And a lot of constitutional requirements can be read into the word "republic". The *ordonnance* of the Provisional Government of the French Republic of 9 August 1944 is an example where a lot was read into the notion of a republican form of government.[57] The provisions of Article 89 could be given a content very similar to the essential conditions for exercise of national sovereignty. Taken together, they support the view that there are other fundamental criteria in French constitutional law which condition national sovereignty under the Constitution of 1958, acting as government according to the Constitution or, according to the Constitution, as constituent power changing it.

The Constitution of 1958 apparently permits important modification. This means that important constitutional law changes can take place constitutionally. There are historical examples under earlier Constitutions – the amending *senatus-consultes* under the Constitution of Year VIII converted the First Republic into an Empire. But this does not mean that all constitutional changes can take place constitutionally, that is, without a revolution in the continuity of French constitutional law. One of the functions of Article 89 paragraph 5, which forbids amendment under the Constitution of 1958 of the Republican form of government, appears to be to distinguish a revolution (break in the legitimation of law) from permissible change.

---

[54] This statement is not an innovation in the Constitution of 1958. Article 89 para. 5 reproduces Article 2 of the Constitutional *loi* of 14 August 1884 revising the Constitution of the Third Republic.

[55] An almost identical provision is to be found in the Constitution of the Fourth Republic: "Article 95. The republican form of Government cannot be made the object of an amending bill". By contrast, the Supreme Court of the United States has held that what constitutes a "republican form of government" guaranteed to the states by Article IV Section 4 of the Constitution is a political question and therefore non-justiciable – *Pacific States Telephone & Telegraph Co. v. Oregon* 223 U.S. 118 (1912).

[56] *cf.* 62–20 DC, 6 November 1962, Rec. p. 27; B. Rudden and L. Kahn-Freund, p. 55, *op. cit.* above, n.27, "Direct amendment on popular election of the President".

[57] See below, para. 16–10, "The Limits to Recognition of the Legal Effects of National Sovereignty as Political Concept or Fact".

Limits to Amendment Implicit in the Controlling Norm of the Essential Conditions for the Exercise of National Sovereignty

16–9 The fact that national sovereignty, as it exists as a political concept or in fact in the people, imposed limits on national sovereignty as it is understood under the Constitution of 1958 does not establish that national sovereignty under the Constitution of 1958 can destroy the essential limits on its exercise. Furthermore, (i) that imposition may be considered to be a declaration of limits otherwise existing according to the legitimation of French constitutional law; (ii) "essential" implies an element of irremovability. The word "exercise" between "essential conditions" and "national sovereignty" does not save the inconsistency in upholding as constitutional a revision of the essential conditions, because this revision is an exercise also, which must also be limited. Yet the *Conseil Constitutionnel* has allowed the competences whose exercise falls within these essential conditions to be amended,[58] although not abrogated, without breaking the continuity of the existing order.

The controlling norm referring to the essential conditions for exercise of national sovereignty make some sense only if the two different meanings of national sovereignty are separated, which is not done clearly in the debates, or in the *Conseil Constitutionnel* decisions. One meaning is national sovereignty as it exists under the Constitution of 1958, and the other is national sovereignty as it exists outside the framework of the Constitution of 1958, in the people as fact or as a political concept. The condition for the exercise of national sovereignty under the Constitution of 1958 could be (and was) changed so that the Constitution is no longer the set of conditions under which as full a national sovereignty, as formerly, which fuller sovereignty remains unaffected outside the Constitution of 1958, can be exercised. This does not surmount the problem of the limitations on the exercise of national sovereignty by the constituent power changing the essential conditions for the exercise of national sovereignty and identifies some slippage between which meaning of sovereignty is applied to the constituent power (which is now, although not in historical origin, a creature of the Constitution of 1958, being comprised of institutions established thereunder acting according to limitations of procedure and substance). It allows for the reestablishment of formerly essential conditions – "formerly" essential because, once changed, national sovereignty under the Constitution of 1958 still continues, albeit in more limited form.

This distinction of meanings is similar to the distinction between sovereignty as it exists in delegated and undelegated form. However the term "delegated sovereignty" does not fully express the meaning of national sovereignty as it exists under the Constitution of 1958 because there is no single delegate of national sovereignty under the Constitution of 1958: Parliament, the executive, the *Conseil Constitutionnel*, the President, and all the constitutional organs

---

[58] 92–312 DC, 2 September 1992, Rec. p. 76; (1992) *Recueil de Droit Public* 1610, *TEU No. 2.*

under the Constitution of 1958, exercise national sovereignty as it exists under the Constitution of 1958 subject to the essential conditions of that exercise (the guarantee of the rights and liberties of citizens, etc.). The delegation of sovereignty was the creation of the Constitution. The term "delegated sovereignty" suggests that there can be some level of sovereignty operating in government below sovereignty with either of the two indicated meanings. The term "delegated sovereignty" *simpliciter* better describes the situation that existed under a National Assembly immediately after the revolution of 1789: that assembly which was the organ of arbitration of constitutionality and the source of the executive's power.

With these two meanings of national sovereignty distinguished in this explanation of the third controlling norm, the problem opposing ratification becomes clearer: the Treaty infringes the three essential conditions[59] for exercise of national sovereignty as it exists under the Constitution of 1958, and therefore an exercise of national sovereignty as it exists under the Constitution of 1958 through the organs of the constituent power (in this case, not the people but the President and the Parliament in Congress) is necessary to remove those infringements by restricting the conditions under which national sovereignty as it was envisaged under the unamended Constitution can henceforth be exercised, and by such restriction the *loi* authorising the ratification of the Treaty on European Union will not be unconstitutional and the Treaty itself not incompatible with the Constitution, and France can comply with that Treaty so far as French constitutional law is concerned (although not necessarily to the extent required by European Community law).

In French constitutional law, the written provisions of the Constitution (the first controlling norm in respect of treaties) and the rules and principles of constitutional value (the second controlling norm in respect of treaties), which together may be referred to as the *bloc de constitutionalité* which is applicable in any constitutional assessment such as an Article 61.2 control of a *loi* on a purely domestic matter, both define (they set out the composition, functioning, competences, and relations of government), and condition the exercise of national sovereignty (conflicts with either of these norms are justiciable and the *Conseil Constitutionnel* decisions are binding). The first two controlling norms therefore comprise part of the meaning of national sovereignty as it exists under the Constitution of 1958. They encompass the substance of the third controlling norm. What is the need for a further controlling norm to determine the existence of a conflict with treaties?

The first explanation is that the substantive criteria of the third controlling norm are in some way more essential than the other rules and principles of constitutional value and constitutional provisions, in the sense that they are

---

59 The guarantee of the rights and liberties of citizens, the institutions of the Republic, and the life of the Nation.

less susceptible to constitutional revision. However, national sovereignty as it exists under the Constitution of 1958 as the constituent power did restrict by amendment these more essential conditions for exercise of national sovereignty under the Constitution of 1958 in the Constitutional *loi* of 25 June 1992. This suggests that the three criteria are picked out as more essential because there is an essential core to these three more essential conditions which cannot be amended within the framework of the Constitution or without the termination of national sovereignty as it exists under the Constitution.

The "most essential" is reached most quickly in the condition of the protection of the rights and liberties of citizens which would involve the transfer of the competence of testing the validity of rules against human rights, a transfer of competence different to the transfer of competences contrary to the other two conditions, where the problem is simply the transfer itself. How the competences contrary to these other two conditions are exercised once transferred is not important, any more than it is important how untransferred competences are exercised within the framework of the Constitution of 1958, providing the limits of the specified transfer are not exceeded. In the condition of the guarantee of the rights and liberties of citizens, on the other hand, *how* the transferred competence would be exercised is all important, because this condition is by its own self-definition more a set of substantive controlling requirements than a competence. To change the requirement is to exceed the competence transferred. In short, how the competence is exercised is determined by the substance of human rights. By contrast, how the competence in, for example Economic and Monetary Union affairs is exercised is not substantively determined by constitutional principles.[60] So even if it is possible to transfer competences of control of rules by human rights (and this has not yet and perhaps cannot be done) it could only be competence in a *Solange II*[61] sense. In that case the German Federal Constitutional Court (*Bundesverfassungsgericht*) withdrew from testing European Community law according to human rights so long as the Court of Justice exercised an equivalent control. In Part II and Part V, below, it is demonstrated that the control is not equivalent because the European Community has a different view of the substance of the rights and the circumstances of their exercise, and of other related concepts such as the common good.

In summary, this explanation points to limits to how far the Constitution of 1958 can be amended without a legal revolution, and points to the protection of human rights as an area where the dilemma of revolt or revolution may be envisaged.

---

60 At least in general. There might be problems if, for example, nationalisation was to be prohibited altogether. *Q.v.* 81–132 DC, 16 January 1982, Rec. p. 18; B. Rudden and L. Kahn-Freund, *op. cit.* above, n.27, pp. 67–71, *On nationalisation*; 86–207 DC, 25–26 June 1986, Rec. p. 61, *De-nationalisation loi.*

61 *Wunsche Handelsgesellschaft* ("*Solange II*" judgment of the *Bundesverfassungsgericht*), [1987] 3 C.M.L.R. 225.

A second possible explanation is that when the Treaty bears on one of the essential conditions, there is a constitutional conflict even though no specific norm or principle is affected. The controlling norm therefore provides a flexible tool for dealing with the structural issues to which federation gives rise. Other rules and principles have been spelled out in the course of French constitutional history but these are fashioned to control internal conflicts. It makes sense to have some newly placed principles, albeit drawn from the same doctrinal sources, to deal with the novel conflicts posed by the European Community. Thus, for example, a competence (such as employment) could logically effect an inner sanctum in the constitution of a state (for example the employment of the head of state) and so there is a need for principles concerning the nature of the federal–state relationship to restrain such effects. But against this explanation is the fact that one of the two other controlling norms, and in particular specific provisions of the Constitution, could always be pointed to where an essential condition for the exercise of national sovereignty was at stake, as was done in *TEU No. 1.*[62] In the light of this it appears from both explanations that the creation of this controlling norm suggests stronger potential resistance to change than in other rules and principles of constitutional value.

The Limits to Recognition of the Legal Effects of National Sovereignty as Political Concept or Fact

16–10 If the constituent power attempts to destroy the limits on amendment above, then there will be a legal revolution at the level of the Constitution of 1958, (that is not merely the destruction of the Constitution but destruction in a way not provided for by that Constitution). This possibility is sufficient for this thesis. This section considers whether the limits extend beyond the present constitutional shape of the French legal order established in the Constitution of 1958. National sovereignty as organs of government and as the constituent power recognised under the Constitution of 1958 (which is comprised either of organs of government or of organs of government and the people) differ in function, not in nature. Neither encompasses the political concept or factual reality.

Historically in French constitutional law, several exercises of national sovereignty in various forms have made and unmade constitutions since the Revolution. These exercises may have caused legal revolutions in the constitutional orders which they replaced. There is a further question of whether there are limits recognised in French constitutional law to the legal effects of what this sovereign can do. The initial problem posed by looking outside the order is one of identification: can a sovereign exist in fact without some

---

62 92–308 DC, 9 April 1992, Rec. p. 55; (1992) 28 *Revue Trimestrielle du Droit Européen* 418; see below, para. 18–10, "Article 88–3: Elections".

order from which this existence must be assessed, and which of the competing ideas of political theory is to be called the political concept of sovereignty? This question is well beyond this work, which identifies the sovereign as the enactor of the Constitution of 1958, the people capable of enacting law. This historic constituent power appears to have several of the same limitations as are recognised as binding the constituent power as now understood under the Constitution of 1958: inalienability of sovereignty, respect for fundamental rights and liberties, and the preservation of the Republic.[63]

The *Conseil Constitutionnel* almost recognised, inconsistently with the restrictions in its later decisions, this third type of national sovereignty, the sovereign people, as the constituent power outside of the Constitution of 1958. In its decision *Direct amendment on the popular election of the President*[64] the *Conseil Constitutionnel* held that the direct expression of the national sovereignty by the people was not subject to review for constitutionality, even though the constitutional methods to which it referred in its judgment in *TEU No. 2*[65] were not observed. The inconsistency is removed by the technical insistence on the jurisdictional grounds of the decision – the *Conseil Constitutionnel* held that the Constitutional *loi* directly enacted by the people was not a *loi* of Parliament and therefore could not be controlled under Article 61.2. The same reason was given for holding the third Treaty on European Union reference to be inadmissible in *TEU No. 3*.[66] This jurisdictional point, however, weakens French constitutional law because such jurisdictional rules give the Constitution its substantive legal, as distinct from political, shape.[67]

In the debates on the Treaty on European Union, the question of what are the limits of the historical constituent power, the popular sovereign, to change or create any constitution was evenly contested. One Committee

---

63 Such limits to what French constitutional doctrine will recognise as lawful do not answer the question whether acts contrary to these limitations can happen in fact.

64 62–20 DC, 6 November 1962, Rec. p. 27; in B. Rudden and L. Kahn-Freund *op. cit.* above n.27, p. 55.

65 92–312 DC, 2 September 1992, Rec. p. 76; (1992) *Recueil de Droit Public* 1610.

66 92–313 DC, 23 September 1992, Rec. p. 94; (1992) *Revue de Droit Public* 1618.

67 An extra-order comment: paradoxically, the decision may have had as background the fear of politicisation of the judicial function in the sense of "*gouvernement des juges*". The book which popularised this phrase considered that judicial review would extend not only to the procedure of adoption of a constitutional amendment but to the substance of that amendment itself: E. Lambert, *Le Gouvernement des juges et la lutte contre la legislation sociale aux États-Unis* (Paris: Giard, 1921). See also M.H. Davis, "A Government of Judges: An Historical Re-View" (1987) 35 *American Journal of Comparative Law* 559 at pp. 561–562. The reason such review was not exercised in 1870 by the Supreme Court of the United States, according to Lambert, was that such exercise would have had no chance of acceptance. Indeed, it would have been met by a (rather Gallic) "*haussement d'épaules*" (p. 110). Lambert compares the situation in the United States to that of the pre-revolutionary *parlementaires* who refused to register royal *ordonnances* contrary to the fundamental *lois* of the kingdom (p. 128). Lambert concludes that even if the Supreme Court has not exercised such control, neither have they taken one of several opportunities to renounce it (pp. 119–120).

member summarised the opinion of many of the Committee when he declared that "the French people cannot, in any case, abandon its sovereignty",[68] the limitation therefore being on alienation. Indeed the reason why an amendment to make specific the inalienable character of sovereignty in Article 3 of the Constitution was rejected was because the inalienable character of sovereignty was incontestable, therefore its introduction into Article 3 could only have a reducing effect.[69] In other words, reduction of inalienability to positive constitutional law would cast doubt on its self-evidence and open the way to attempts to get at inalienability by restrictive revision of the amended Article 3.

On the other hand, there were those who argued for no limitation on what the sovereign could do in substance. Dean Vedel was of the opinion that the constituent power is "totally sovereign"[70] – it is tied by rules of procedure and form but there is nothing it cannot modify, including the Declaration of the Rights of Man, the fundamental principles recognised by the laws of the Republic, etc. Yet Dean Vedel had difficulty with the alienability of sovereignty.[71] Professor Luchaire stated:

> "if one could raise questions on the supraconstitutional value of the notion of sovereignty, the revolutionaries of 1789 knew that no generation is able to claim to subject a future generation to its laws."[72]

Yet Professor Luchaire claims at the same time that the transfers to the European Community, which he claims are effectively transfers of sovereignty, cannot be reclaimed. This raises a distinction between the incapacity of any act of a holder of sovereignty to bind its successors and the termination of sovereignty itself. Although such a termination must result from an act of a holder of sovereignty, presumably the termination is not to be understood as an act binding the successive holders of sovereignty but rather as giving rise to a new sovereign Community which prevents the resurrection of the old national sovereignty.

Part of the *sine qua non* of the legitimation of French law is the promotion and protection of human rights, one of the essential conditions for exercise of national sovereignty recognised by the *Conseil Constitutionnel*, one of the recurring themes in French constitutional law, but also one of the legitimating bases for the act of making constitutional law out of constitutional theory – the French Revolution. Sovereignty is one of the foundations of France's

---

68 Gouzes' Report, above, n.4.

69 National Assembly, *Rapport supplémentaire au nom de la commission des lois constitutionelles, de la législation et de l'administration générale de la République sur le projet de loi constitutionelle* (No. 2623) ajoutant à la Constitution un titre: "De l'Union européenne", No. 2684 by G. Gouzes, 11 May 1992. (Gouzes' Supplemental Report) p. 6.

70 National Assembly, *Observations et amendements présentés au nom de la commission des affaires étrangéres, saisie pour avis*, No. 2676 (Annexe), by J.-M. Caro, 4 May 1992. (Caro's Report) p. 15.

71 See below, para. 17–3.

72 Gouzes' Report above, n.4.

independence in the derivation of the validity of norms, but is not the only one. The protection of fundamental rights is considered further below.[73]

French constitutional law doctrine legitimating French constitutional law has resisted its own termination before. On 3 June 1944 the French Committee of National Liberation (C.F.N.L.) constituted itself by *ordonnance* into the Provisional Government of the French Republic (G.P.R.F.). On 9 August 1944 it passed an *ordonnance* on the reestablishment of republican legality on the continental territory. The *exposé* of reasons heading the *ordonnance* explained that the first act of the reestablishment of Republican legality is the statement contained in Article 1:

> "Article 1. The form of Government of France is and remains the Republic. In law [*droit*] this [Republic] has never ceased to exist."

It then becomes necessary to provide a framework to deal with the Constitutional Acts and other measures of the Vichy Government (1940–1944). As the *exposé* of reasons made clear, everything which was posterior to the downfall on 16 June 1940 "of the last legitimate government of the Republic is obviously struck with nullity". The *ordonnance* provided:

> "Article 2. In consequence, all constitutional legislative or reglementary acts, as well as measures taken for their execution, under whatever denomination, are null and of no effect . . . ".

However "considerations of practical interest" lead to the provision that the nullity of those legal measures had to be expressly stated. Thus the ordonnance proceeds to declare null all "acts of a constitutional nature" and any other acts. Those acts of the "authority in fact" which were not declared invalid were declared to continue as provisionally valid pending subsequent *ordonnances.* Certain court decisions (Article 8) were declared retroactively valid and certain administrative acts were declared provisionally and retroactively valid (Article 9). The statement of invalidity of the Vichy regime left a gap to be filled; and so a referendum was put to the people on whether they wanted a return to the Constitution of the Third Republic or to enact a new one.

The Provisional Government of the French Republic did not have to proceed this way. Other legal options were available, such as the declaration that measures of the Vichy scheme were retroactively invalid. Instead the Provisional Government of the French Republic took a stand on grounds of the legitimation of French constitutional law and enacted as a measure of positive law the recognition of the illegitimacy of the Vichy Government and the legal invalidity of its acts. This necessarily follows, according to the "Outline of Reasons" which headed the *ordonnance,* from the fact that the republican form of government never ceased to exist in law, despite its cessation in positive law. The restriction on amendment posed by the essential condition for the

---

[73] See below, paras. 21–2 *et seq.*, "Assuring the Guarantee of the Rights and Liberties of Citizens".

exercise of national sovereignty of assuring respect for the institutions of the Republic is considered further below.[74]

Conclusion

16–11 The analysis of the French constitutional law concept of sovereignty shows the conflicts this poses for European Community law demands, particularly in the light of the analysis of French constitutional law's interpretation of European Community law,[75] and of the substance of the essential conditions for exercise of national sovereignty.[76] These conflicts are posed first with French constitutional law as it stands; secondly, with what French constitutional law under the Constitution of 1958 can accomplish without revolution or revolt in response to these and further demands; and thirdly, at a more abstract level if the Constitution of 1958 was abandoned in fact. These conflicts involve the fundamental commitment in French constitutional law to national sovereignty, part of the legitimation of French constitutional law, and the fundamental commitments in French constitutional law which limit national sovereignty and the acts of sovereignty which will be regarded as law.

---

[74] See para. 21–16, "Assuring Respect for the Institutions of the Republic".

[75] See Chap. 18, "French Constitutional Law Interpretation of European Community Law in the Ratification of the Treaty on European Union".

[76] See Chap. 21, "The Substance of the Essential Conditions for Exercise of National Sovereignty".

17. DENUNCIATION AND REVERSIBILITY

17–1 Before the detailed consideration of French constitutional law's interpretation of European Community law there is a question which can be analysed separately which combines the related issues of transfer of sovereignty v. transfer of competences, alienability versus inalienability, and the possible consequences of a conflict between French constitutional law's interpretation of European Community law and European Community law's self-interpretation. The question is whether France can denounce the Treaty on European Union and whether the constitutional revisions may be reversed.

Constitutional Law

The Treaty on European Union

17–2 The Articles in Title XIV state that the Republic participates in the European Union and that France consents to certain transfers of competences which would be otherwise contrary to the essential conditions for exercise of national sovereignty. If these provisions were simply enabling, then the process for denunciation of the Treaty could proceed as normal. However if these provisions mandate participation, then constitutional revision would have to precede denunciation of the treaty.

There appears to be no bar to deletion by amendment of any mandatory effect, if such exists, in these new provisions because of the distinction made between transfers of competences and sovereignty. Thus the Minister for Justice, in trying to guide the Constitutional *loi* Bill through the National Assembly, declared that sovereignty cannot be irreversibly alienated; that all that was happening in the Treaty on European Union was a transfer of competences, which it would always be possible to get back: "France conserves that which the German jurists call the 'competence of its competence'"[1] – that is, the legal capacity to determine what its legal capacities should be.[2]

---

[1] National Assembly, *Rapport au nom de la commission des lois constitutionelles, de la législation et de l'administration générale de la République sur le projet de loi constitutionelle (No. 2623) ajoutant à la Constitution un titre:* "De l'Union européenne", No. 2676, registered 4 May 1992 (Gouzes' Report) p. 42.

[2] *cf.* Luchaire's assertion that France no longer has the competence to decide its own competences and can no longer recover competences transferred, an assertion which can only be supported from the internal standpoint of European Community law but which he offers from the standpoint of French Constitutional Law – F. Luchaire "L'Union Européenne et la Constitution" (1992) *Revue de Droit Public* 955 at p. 959.

Once the Constitution is revised, or alternatively if the Constitution is interpreted as simply authorising but not requiring adhesion to the Treaty on European Union, the question is how any treaty can be denounced. Surprisingly, the Constitution of 1958 is silent. Article 28 of the Constitution of 1946, on the other hand, provided that treaties could be abrogated by a "regular denunciation, diplomatically notified". If the treaty was ratified by a *loi*, with the exception of trade treaties, then the denunciation had to be authorised by the National Assembly. As regards the Constitution of 1958, Professor Luchaire suggests that its silence implies that no *loi* is necessary.[3] Denunciation appears to be up to the President without restriction because if there had been a *loi* in connection with the treaty, its purpose could not have been to ratify but solely to authorise the President to ratify in his discretion. The *loi* authorising ratification or approving a treaty is an ordinary *loi* in the formal sense but without normative content other than a simple authorisation. A *décret* specifies that "the act comprising denunciation by France of a convention, treaty, protocol or international regulation" must be published.[4] An act suspending, as distinct from denouncing, a treaty must be published to a degree or the State will not be able to rely on its suspension.[5] Whether or not the act requires the backing of a *loi* as a matter of French constitutional law has not been considered by the *Conseil Constitutionnel.* It does not appear to be required. As far as the administrative judge is concerned, he would hold that act of denunciation by the President was connected with foreign affairs and probably therefore unreviewable.[6] Whatever the method, it is possible in French law to denounce any treaty.

Future Treaties

17–3 Is it possible for France to ratify a future Treaty establishing a European Community which declared itself irreversible? There are no *Conseil Constitutionnel* decisions on this point. There are, however, two decisions of the *Conseil Constitutionnel* on the absence of a denunciation clause. In its decision of 22 May 1985 on the *Protocol on the abolition of the Death Penalty,*[7] the *Conseil Constitutionnel* upheld the constitutionality of the international engagement, stating that "this agreement can be denounced in the conditions fixed by Article 65 of the European Convention of the Rights of Man". It thus opened the question whether the absence of a denunciation clause in a treaty would be unconstitutional. This was made one of the grounds of attack on the con-

---

3 F. Luchaire, "Le Conseil Constitutionnel et la Souveraineté Nationale" (1991) *Revue de Droit Public* 1499.

4 *Décret* No. 86–707 of 11 April 1986, amending *décret* No. 53–192 of 14 March 1953.

5 Decision of the *Conseil d'État, Préfet de la Gironde c. Mahmedi,* 18 December 1992, Rec. Lebon, p. 446. Conclusions of Government Commissioner Lancy, p. 447.

6 Decisions on foreign affairs matters are unreviewable – Decision of the *Conseil d'État, Association Greenpeace France,* 29 September 1995.

7 85–188 DC, 22 May 1985, Rec. p. 15, *Protocol on the abolition of the death penalty.*

stitutionality of the Schengen Treaty, but the *Conseil Constitutionnel* decided that, considering that the procedures for modification which involved France were subject to reciprocity and to control under Article 54, "the absence of reference to a withdrawal clause does not constitute in itself an abandonment of sovereignty" and thus was not unconstitutional.[8] The absence of a denunciation clause was not raised in the Treaty on European Union decisions.

The further question, not of the constitutional importance of the absence of a denunciation clause, but of an irreversible hypothetical treaty was considered in the Treaty on European Union debates (not of course in the *Conseil Constitutionnel* decisions because the Treaty did not claim irreversibility although Article 240 (EEC) and Article Q (EU) both provide identically that "[t]his Treaty is concluded for an unlimited period"). Goquel, honorary Secretary General of the *Sénat* and a former member of the *Conseil Constitutionnel*, replied to this question posed by the *rapporteur* for the *Sénat*, Larché:

> "France cannot be constitutionally bound in an irreversible manner by an international engagement, because the Declaration of the Rights of Man and of the Citizen recognised inalienable and sacred rights in the citizen. This principle signifies that, even if the present generation infringed national sovereignty, a future generation could reclaim it. *A fortiori* it was inconceivable that a rule resulting from an international treaty could be considered as irreversible, whereas any constitutional provision could be the subject of a revision, with the exception of the republican form of Government."[9]

Dean Vedel expressed a similar view, holding that no Treaty, nor any provision of the constitution, is irreversible.[10] The principal National Assembly report concluded:

> "in the same way as a human constitution is not eternal, no treaty is irrevocable; that which an international agreement has done, another can undo . . . by the same manifestation of the sovereignty which continues to reside where it is found, that is in the people."[11]

The Relevance of the Public International Law of Treaties

17–4 The *Conseil Constitutionnel* has carefully treated the European Community treaties on the same basis as other public international law treaties in its review under Article 54. The *Conseil Constitutionnel*, having referred to paragraph 14

---

8 91–294 DC, 25 July 1991, Rec. p. 91; (1991) *Revue de Droit Public* 1517, *Schengen Treaty*.

9 Senate, *Rapport fait au nom de la commission des lois constitutionelles, de législation, du suffrage universel, du règlement et d'administration générale sur le projet de loi constitutionelle adoptée par l'Assemblée Nationale ajoutant à la constitution un titre*: "Des Communautés européennes et de l'Union européenne", No. 2676 (Annexe), by J. Larché', 27 May 1992. (Larché's Report). p. 93.

10 National Assembly, *Observations et amendements présentés au nom de la commission des affaires étrangères, saisie pour avis*, No. 2676 (Annexe) by J.-M. Caro, 4 May 1992. (Caro's Report).

11 Gouzes' Report, above, n.1, p. 32.

of the Preamble of the Constitution of 1946 and the reference to it by the Preamble of the Constitution of 1958, pointed out that among the rules of public international law was the rule *pacta sunt servanda* which it describes as meaning that any treaty in force binds the parties and must be executed by them in good faith.[12] However the roundabout way the *Conseil Constitutionnel* put this indicates its care not to state that the rule of *pacta sunt servanda* had superior authority to any possibly conflicting rule of constitutional value, thus preserving consideration of a possible situation where withdrawal from a treaty could be constitutionally required but would be in breach of *pacta sunt servanda.*

It appears that French constitutional law recognises all the public international law grounds for withdrawing from a Treaty establishing a European Community which apply to any international treaty. These were considered particularly in the Senate Report[13]; Dean Vedel referred to them as demonstrating that no Treaty could be irreversible. Two of these mechanisms of public international law appear to safeguard the fundamental interests of France:

1. The principle *omnis conventio intelligitur rebus sic stantibus.* This principle is to be understood in the light of Article 62 of the Vienna Convention on the Law of Treaties under which a treaty ceases to be obligatory as soon as (a) there is a fundamental change of circumstances, (b) the circumstances which form the basis of the agreement have changed, or (c) the change in circumstances radically transforms the importance of the obligations left to be carried out. *Rebus sic stantibus* is a tacit condition said to attach to all treaties and to be incapable of exclusion by express treaty provision.

   In the context under consideration, if the Treaty on European Union no longer conformed to its French constitutional description, then as far as French constitutional law is concerned the principle allows denunciation of the international obligation. The only possibility where this would not be so is if the *Conseil Constitutionnel* recognised a higher external authority's contrary interpretation of the principle as superior to its own. But this external authority could not be the Court of Justice despite Article 219 (EC)[14] because this would defeat the logic of the principle. And there are big problems in involving the International Court of Justice: France would have to consent to this separately; the European Community has no *locus standi* under the Statute of the International Court of Justice (Article 42);

---

12 92–308 DC, 9 April 1992, Rec. p. 55; (1992) 28 *Revue Trimestrielle du Droit Européen* 418, *TEU No. 1.*

13 Larché's Report, above, n.9.

14 "Member States undertake not to submit a dispute concerning the interpretation or application of this Treaty to any method of settlement other than those provided for therein."

and if another Member State was to be the other party, it would be putting itself in breach of Article 219 (EC) as well.

2. This principle is supported by the public international law principle that States cannot contract perpetual obligations. It is also supported in French constitutional law by the holding in the *Schengen Treaty*[15] decision that the absence of a termination clause does not constitute an abandonment of sovereignty, which suggests that the power to terminate is retained.

[15] 91–294 DC, 25 July 1991, Rec. p. 91; (1991) *Revue de Droit Public* 1517.

18. FRENCH CONSTITUTIONAL LAW INTERPRETATION OF EUROPEAN COMMUNITY LAW IN THE RATIFICATION OF THE TREATY ON EUROPEAN UNION

18–1 This chapter seeks to demonstrate how the conceptual issues involved in the French constitutional law interpretation of European Community law considered above have resulted in the restrictive interpretation given to European Community law by French constitutional law in the process of the ratification of the Treaty on European Union. Professor Favoreau turned attention to the importance of the destination of the transfer stating that this was more important than the question of the content – sovereignty or competences – of the transfer.[1] The destination is important but not critical to the transferor: the *Conseil Constitutionnel's* view of the European Community is directly informed by its insistence that it is competences that are being transferred. Both destination and content of transfer are important because, according to French constitutional law, it is these transfers which create the powers of decision of the institutions of the European Union and European Communities.[2]

Favoreau continued:

> "[T]hus, the *Conseil Constitutionnel* has underlined heavily that the European Community was an international organisation and not a future federal State, a point of view not always shared by the other, notably the small, States of the Community. However, if it [the *Conseil Constitutionnel*] has taken the precautions which it could, the *Conseil Constitutionnel* is not the judge of the evolution of the Community."

Clearly the *Conseil Constitutionnel* cannot be the controlling judge of the Community's evolution, but it is the judge of how French constitutional law interprets the European Community and what it has transferred to it.[3]

---

1 National Assembly, *Rapport au nom de la commission des lois constitutionelles, de la législation et de l'administration générale de la République sur le projet de loi constitutionelle (No. 2623) ajoutant à la Constitution un titre:* "De l'Union européenne", No. 2676, registered 4 May 1992 (Gouzes' Report) p. 51.

2 See paragraph 5 of the extract quoted below in para. 18–2.

3 It can be argued also that the domestic interpretation of the relation between national constitutional and European Community law could act as a limitation of European Community law's self-interpretation, because European Community law is either dependent on transfers for the characteristics which distinguish it from public international law (see Advocate-General Warner's approach in Case 7/76 *IRCA* [1976] E.C.R. 1213 and Opinion 2/94 *Accession of the European Community to the European Convention for the Protection of Human Rights and Fundamental Freedoms,* 28 March 1996, on Article 3b (EC)

The *Conseil Constitutionnel's* Interpretation of the European Community

18–2 It was not until *TEU No. 1*[4] that the importance of the *Conseil Constitutionnel's* insistence on competences and essential conditions for exercise of national sovereignty was made clear. This is worth setting out at length:

> "1. Considering that the French people have, by the preamble to the Constitution of 1958, proclaimed solemnly 'their commitment to the rights of man and to the principles of national sovereignty such as they are defined by the Declaration of 1789, confirmed and completed by the preamble to the Constitution of 1946';
>
> 2. Considering that, in its Article 3, the Declaration of the rights of man and of the citizen announces that 'the principle of all sovereignty resides essentially in the nation'; that Article 3 of the Constitution of 1958 provides, in its first paragraph, that 'the national sovereignty belongs to the people who exercise it by its representatives or by means of a referendum';
>
> 3. Considering that the preamble of the Constitution of 1946 proclaims, in its fourteenth paragraph, that the French Republic 'complies with the rules of public international law' and, in its fifteenth paragraph, that 'under reserve of reciprocity, France consent to the limitations of sovereignty necessary to the organisation and the defense of the peace';
>
> 4. Considering that, in its Article 53, the Constitution of 1958 sanctions, as does Article 27 of the Constitution of 1946, the existence of 'treaties or accords concerning international organisations'; that these treaties or agreements cannot be ratified or approved by the President of the Republic except by virtue of a *loi*;
>
> 5. Considering that it results from these texts of constitutional value that respect for national sovereignty does not form an obstacle to whatever, on the basis of the above cited provisions of the preambles of the Constitution of 1946, France may conclude, subject to reciprocity, as international engagements with a view to participating in the creation or the development of a permanent international organisation, endowed with legal personality and invested with powers of decision by the effect of transfers of competences consented to by the Member States;
>
> 6. Considering nevertheless that in the case where international engagements subscribed to this end contain a clause contrary to the Constitution or infringe the essential conditions for exercise of national sovereignty, the authorisation to ratify them requires a constitutional revision;
>
> 7. Considering that it is with regard to these principles that it falls by right to the *Conseil Constitutionnel* to proceed to the examination of the Treaty on European Union" (numbering added).

---

and the principle of transferred powers) or is legitimated by reference to the attainment of dynamic, vague political objectives, which legitimation relies in part on what has been and can be achieved in fact, and thus relies on the application of European Community law in France. See Part VI, para. 36–3, "Further Support from within European Community Law".

4 92–308 DC, 9 April 1992 Rec. p. 55; (1992) 28 *Revue Trimestrielle du Droit Européen* 418.

Paragraph 5 amounts to the sketch of a French constitutional law definition of the European Community by the *Conseil Constitutionnel* and formed the basis of the amending Article 88–1 considered below. It is an express denial of the nature of European Community law as it sees itself: "it contradicts completely long-standing case law of the European Court. It also gives an image of the European Communities which contradicts the whole process of European Union."[5]

The *Conseil Constitutionnel's* treatment of four aspects of the European Community will illustrate this interpretation of the European Community as a whole. These are the European Parliament, citizenship, the right to vote in elections to the European Parliament, and majority voting in the Council. The *Conseil Constitutionnel's* treatment of these aspects demonstrates also how the *Conseil Constitutionnel* embedded the assurances of the supporters of the ratification of the Treaty on European Union, who played down its federal aspect, in its interpretation of European Community law.

The European Parliament

18–3 In its decision of 30 December 1976 *European Community Council Decision for direct elections to European Parliament*[6] the *Conseil Constitutionnel* upheld the constitutionality of the decision because it found that universal direct election to the European Parliament created neither a sovereignty nor an institution incompatible with respect for national sovereignty nor did it undermine the Republic's institutions, notably the parliament. The powers of the European Parliament were a matter for the internal distribution amongst the European Community institutions of competences conferred by the treaties. The Conseil Constitutionnel considered the European Parliament in the same terms in *TEU No. 1*[7] where it held that the Treaty on European Union did not modify the legal nature of the European Parliament, and that the European Parliament did not constitute a sovereign assembly, was not called upon to exercise concurrently national sovereignty, and was a creature of a legal order separate to the institutional order of the French Republic.

Union Citizenship

18–4 As regards citizenship, the *Conseil Constitutionnel* considered the concept added by the Treaty on European Union as Part Two of the Treaty establishing the European Community solely in terms of its constituent rights. This

---

5 S. Boyron, "The *Conseil Constitutionnel* and the European Union" [1993] *Public Law* 30 at p. 34.

6 76–71 DC, 30 December 1976, Rec. p. 15; in B. Rudden and L. Kahn-Freund, *A Source-Book on French Law* (Oxford: Clarendon Press, 1991) pp. 58–60, "European Community Council Decision for direct elections to European Parliament".

7 92–308 DC, above, 9 April 1922, Rec. p. 55; (1992) 28 Revue Trimestrielle du Droit Européen 418, *TEU No. 1.*

in itself is a denial, as indeed it was denied by the governments of the Member States during the debate in Denmark, of the constitutional importance of the concept in European Community law. This limited interpretation was affirmed in the Edinburgh Summit. Section A of the Edinburgh Declaration[8] provides as follows:

> "The provisions of Part Two of the Treaty establishing the European Community relating to citizenship of the Union give nationals of the Member States additional rights and protection as specified in that Part. They do not in any way take the place of national citizenship."

The Treaty on European Union could have provided for such rights to adhere to nationals of the Member States by virtue of their nationality, rather than by virtue of their citizenship of the Union which adheres to them by virtue of their nationality. Even if the Court of Justice follows the interpretation of the Edinburgh Declaration, the concept of citizenship will have a constitutional importance for European Community law which will go beyond the rights incidental to it. Therefore the *Conseil Constitutionnel's* interpretation and the Court of Justice's interpretation both of citizenship and of matters which rely on the idea of a political community of citizens will probably diverge.

The *Conseil Constitutionnel* found that only three of the rights attaching to Union citizenship needed to be examined: the right to vote and the right to stand in municipal elections (considered below under Article 88–3); and the right to vote in European Parliament elections. The *Conseil Constitutionnel* found that the right to vote in European Parliament elections was not unconstitutional. The fact that the *Conseil Constitutionnel* specifically and at relative length considered a provision in order to uphold its constitutionality is very significant. There are hundreds of provisions which the *Conseil Constitutionnel* could have analysed but did not. Those in favour of ratification correctly pointed out in the debate that this meant the unconsidered provisions were not unconstitutional. The *Conseil Constitutionnel* picked out only the right to vote in European Parliament elections and Article F(2) (EU) on the guarantee of the rights and liberties of citizens in order to set out the interpretation in which these rights are constitutional – in other words, to make reservations of interpretation.[9]

The Right to Vote in European Parliament Elections

18–5 In considering the combination of the European Community law concepts of citizenship and the European Parliament in the rights to vote, the *Conseil Constitutionnel* took the opportunity to point out again that the

---

8 Decision of the Heads of State and Government, Meeting within the European Council, Concerning Certain Problems Raised by Denmark on the Treaty on European Union [1992] O.J. C348/2.

9 For the French constitutional law interpretation of Article F(2) (EU) see below, para. 21–3, "As a Competence".

European Parliament has its legal foundation not in the Constitution of 1958 but in international engagements subscribed "in the framework of the dispositions of constitutional value previously mentioned", which presumably means within the framework of the provisions cited in paragraphs one to three of the extract above, as well as the norms of constitutional control. The *Conseil Constitutionnel* states that "the European Parliament, like other Community institutions, acts 'within the limits of the competences which are conferred on' by each of the [Community] treaties".

Voting in Council

18–6 As regards majority voting, the *Conseil Constitutionnel* held unconstitutional only the existence of majority voting after 1 January 1996 in considering Article 100c (EC) on common rules for visas and control of movement of third party nationals. This view of unanimity in Council giving a Member State a veto is an intergovernmental view of the Council which does not correspond to the European Community law view, according to which the Council will not be meeting or discussing in the same way as States negotiate an international engagement in the usual sense of that term: the Council is an institution, created by European Community law, acting within the Community legislative process and in the framework of and bound by the Court of Justice's interpretation of European Community law.

The Interpretation in the Debates

18–7 The importance of the *Conseil Constitutionnel's* definition of the European Community was well understood in the debates on ratifications. Favoreau underlined that the *Conseil Constitutionnel* refused to consider the European Community legal order as qualitatively different, *vis-à-vis* the internal order, from public international law.[10] The Minister for Justice repeated that only a transfer of competences was involved.[11]

The importance of the *Conseil Constitutionnel's* interpretation was highlighted in the debates by an awareness that more integrationist interpretations are possible even by lawyers who respect the semantic limits of interpreting law more highly than those focussed on the attainment of objectives. For example, Caro's Report (see above, chapter 16, n.70) drew attention to the difference between the goal of the Council of Europe (the Charter

---

[10] Gouzes' Report, above, n.1.

[11] Senate, *Rapport fait au nom de la commission des lois constitutionelles, de législation, du suffrage universel, du règlement et d'administration générale sur le projet de loi constitutionelle adoptée par l'Assemblée Nationale ajoutant à la Constitution un titre:* "Des Communautés européennes et de l'Union européenne", No. 2676 (Annexe), by J. Larché, 27 May 1992 (Larché's Report).

of the Council of Europe provides in Article 1 that its goal is a "closer union amongst its members"), and the statement in the preamble of the Treaty on European Union on the resolve "to continue the process of creating an ever closer union among the peoples of Europe, in which decisions are taken as closely as possible to the citizen in accordance with the principle of subsidiarity". The awareness of the divergence between European Community law and French constitutional law was perhaps brought out most clearly in the Senate Report which considered the control exercised by the Court of Justice.[12] The Report compared the decision of the *Conseil Constitutionnel TEU No. 1*[13] with the decision of the Court of Justice in *Internationale Handelsgesellschaft*[14] of 17 December 1970, one of the most important constitutional decisions in European Community law, which held that the incompatibility between fundamental national constitutional rights or national constitutional structures and European Community law could not affect the uniformity of application of European Community law. The Report stated that this Court of Justice decision could not be followed in France because it would be contrary to national sovereignty and the objectives of Article 54, and went on to state:

> "Thus confronted with an eventual divergence of jurisprudence between the Court of Justice of the European Communities and the *Conseil Constitutionnel*, the French public powers cannot but follow the French constitutional jurisdiction whose decisions, in France, bind all, in conformity with Article 62 of the Constitution."

This is directly contrary to the fundamental European Community law notion of the duty to observe European Community law of all the organs of national government.

As regards one particular aspect of the Treaty on European Union, the right of citizens of the Union to vote in European Parliament elections, the debates again indicate that the *Conseil Constitutionnel's* constitutional interpretation is particular. The significance of the *Conseil Constitutionnel's* deviation from its method in that decision of considering only unconstitutional provisions was remarked upon.[15] The deviation indicates that the Conseil Constitutionnel had a reservation of interpretation to make. Gougel and Favoreau were concerned that this aspect of the Treaty on European Union would result in a new concept of "European people" in place of the peoples of the Member States together with a European sovereignty superior to national sovereignties.[16] This concern is particularly understandable in the light of the importance of the French constitutional law concept of people[17] and the

---

12 Larché's Report, above, n.11, pp. 51–52.

13 92–308 DC, 9 April 1992, Rec. p. 55; (1992) 28 *Revue Trimestrielle du Droit Européen* 418.

14 Case 11/70 *Internationale Handelsgesellschaft* [1970] E.C.R. 1125.

15 Gouzes' Report, above, n.1, p. 21.

16 Larché's Report, above, n.11.

17 91–290 DC, 9 May 1991, Rec. p. 50; West *et al., The French Legal System* (London: Fourmat Publishing, 1992) pp. 194–195, "Loi on the status of Corsica".

link between this concept and the constituent power. Given the expansionist history of the development of European Community law out of an international economic treaty which made little mention of persons at all, it hardly seems far-fetched to suggest that integrationist lawyers and political scientists will use this as a concept on which to hang federalist visions. Luchaire has already asserted that it is not only the French State which participates in the Union but each Frenchman.[18] But the *Conseil Constitutionnel* has in French constitutional law denied the basis of such an assertion by its interpretation which reduces the concept into its constituent rights. This reduction is supported by the "Outline of Reasons" to the Constitutional *loi* Bill of 25 June 1992 which states that Union citizenship adds to French citizenship and translates notably into the right to vote in municipal elections.[19]

Article 88–1: The European Communities and the European Union

18–8 "The Republic participates in the European Communities and in the European Union, composed of States which have freely chosen, in virtue of the treaties which they have instituted, to exercise in common certain of their competences."

This Article is a result of an amendment adopted by the National Assembly on the first hearing of the Constitutional *loi* Bill to amend the Constitution in the wake of the *Conseil Constitutionnel's* decision. The amendment is self-evidently based on the insistence that competences were being transferred and sovereignty retained, and is the sole success of a whole cluster of proposed and rejected amendments which sought to define the European Community in French constitutional law terms. It comes close to the view of the European Community as an international organisation given by the *Conseil Constitutionnel* in paragraph five of the extract quoted above. The originator of the amendment, Juppé, also proposed an amendment giving the Luxembourg Compromise constitutional value,[20] which failed. An even more striking example of this line of proposals was that of Catala, which stated that: "This Union is in conformity with the principles of Democracy. It respects the fundamental principles of Law and the French legal constitutional order."[21] The intent of these proposals was to limit the internal effect of the European Community also but, in spite of this intent, Article 88–1 might be construed as creating also a risk of increasing the European Community's constitutional status by

---

[18] F. Luchaire, "L'Union Européenne et la Constitution" (1992) *Revue de Droit Public* 955 at p. 958.

[19] Assemblée Nationale Doc. No. 2623, 22 April 1992; the enacted *loi* is No. 92–554 of 25 June 1992, J.O. p. 8406, 26 June 1992.

[20] National Assembly, *Observations et amendements présentés au nom de la commission des affaires étrangères, saisis pour avis*, No. 2676 (Annexe), by J.-M. Caro, 4 May 1991 (Caro's Report).

[21] Gouzes' Report, above, n.1, p. 90.

stating in the Constitution France's participation in the European Community. The proposals contrasted with Article 88–2 and Article 88–3 which were carefully drafted by the government to avoid transfer of competence beyond the minimum necessary to comply with the *Conseil Constitutionnel's* decision in order to allow for ratification. However Article 88–1 is closely based on the *Conseil Constitutionnel's* interpretation of the Treaty on European Union and consequently its likely effect is to enhance the status of that interpretation by writing it into the Constitution. When the Treaty on European Union was referred to the *Conseil Constitutionnel* after the constitutional revision, the *Conseil Constitutionnel* dealt with the issue of conflicts between European Community law and French constitutional law in its decision in *TEU No. 2*[22] in the same fashion as in *TEU No. 1*[23] – that is, treating European Community law as qualitatively the same as public international law. This decision therefore indicates that the importance of Article 88–1 will be in its restrictive view of the European Community rather than in the internalization into the Community of France's participation in the European Community and the European Union.

Luchaire has stated that "In reality, this provision has no legal effect because it neither adds nor subtracts anything from the Community agreements."[24] This assertion that national constitutional interpretation of European Community law has no effect on European Community law's own self-interpretation is arguable, at least so far as European Community law claims to have a nature different to public international law by virtue of constitutional transfers. But this point aside, the assertion misses the importance of the Article in cementing French constitutional law's interpretation of the European Community in the French legal order. The Senate Committee commenting on the amendment stated that it "permits the better measuring of the fundamental difference between the exercise in common of certain state competences and a pure and simple transfer of national sovereignty."[25] The Article makes clear that in French constitutional law the European Community is composed of States freely choosing to participate by virtue of international agreements and thus denies in French constitutional law any European Community claim to federalism.

Article 88–2: Economic and Monetary Union and Control of External Frontiers

18–9 "Subject to reciprocity, and according to the terms provided by the Treaty on European Union signed on the 7 February 1992, France consents to transfers

---

22 92–312 DC, 2 September 1992, Rec. p. 76; (1992) *Revue de Droit Public* 1610.

23 above, n.13.

24 F. Luchaire, above, n.18, at 957, 9 April 1992, rec. p. 55; (1992) *Revue Trimestrielle du Droit Européen* 418.

25 Larché's Report, above, n.11, p. 27.

> of competences necessary to the establishment of the European economic and monetary union as well for the determination of the rules relating to the crossing of the external frontiers of the Member States of the European Community."

Unlike Article 88–1, Articles 88–2 and 88–3 were a direct response to the constitutional blocks to ratification of the Treaty on European Union set out in *TEU No. 1.*[26] Article 88–2 revises the Constitution to allow the transfer of competences in the areas of Economic and Monetary Union and the entry and stay of persons into the internal market which the *Conseil Constitutionnel* had found contrary to the essential conditions for the exercise of national sovereignty and consequently to be contrary to the Constitution. The *Conseil Constitutionnel* did not specify which conditions were involved. Because the subject matter of the competences involved fell into the domain of *loi* under Article 34, one might assume that the condition involved was respect for the institutions of the Republic. It clearly was not the condition of the guarantee of the rights and liberties of the citizens: even so far as this condition includes the right to sovereignty, the *Conseil Constitutionnel* held that sovereignty, as distinct from the conditions for its exercise, was not affected.[27] The *Conseil Constitutionnel's* concern was that the competence was being transferred, not how the competence would be exercised once transferred.

The 60 senators who seised the *Conseil Constitutionnel* of the Treaty on European Union under Article 54 after the revision of the Constitution claimed that the transfer of competences involved in Article 88–2 were in violation of Article 3 (on sovereignty) and Article 34 (on the domain of *loi*) of the Constitution and that as a consequence these Articles had to be modified. The *Conseil Constitutionnel* in *TEU No. 2* held that it was within the power of appreciation of the constituent to choose to add new provisions to the Constitution in lieu of amending the old: "it is permissible to [the constituent power] to abrogate, modify or complete provisions of constitutional value in the form it considers appropriate."

The *Conseil Constitutionnel* found the whole notion of Economic and Monetary Union contrary to the Constitution because it would result in the third phase in a monetary policy and a single currency according to terms and conditions such that a Member State would find itself deprived of its own competences in a domain where the essential conditions for the exercise of national sovereignty were involved.[28] As regards Economic and Monetary

---

26 92–308 DC, above, n.23.

27 *q.v.* Larché's Report, above, n.11, p. 93, quoted above, in para. 17–3, "Future Treaties".

28 This decision is consistent with the *Conseil Constitutionnel's* earlier decision when it held that this treaty did not affect relations between states and the European Community but only relations between European Community institutions (70–39 DC, 19 June 1970, Rec. p. 15, *Budgetary and Merger Treaties*) because of the *Conseil Constitutionnel's* view of the nature of the European Community as an international organisation and the very different nature of the Budgetary and Merger Treaty from the Treaty on European Union, as a treaty not affecting directly competences formerly exercised by States alone.

Union, in *TEU No. 2*[29] the *Conseil Constitutionnel* held that Article 88–2 removed the constitutional objection.

In 1993 a *loi* Bill was passed to organise the autonomy of the Bank of France from the government, as required by the Treaty on European Union and thought to be covered by this Article. However the bill was referred to the *Conseil Constitutionnel* which found it unconstitutional and not saved by Article 88–2 as the Treaty on European Union was not yet in force because the ratification process by all the Member States was not yet over.[30]

As regards the provisions for the entry and movement of persons into the internal market, the *Conseil Constitutionnel* had found in *TEU No. 1* a more specific constitutional objection – the introduction of majority voting on these matters in Article 100c(3) (EC) after 1 January 1996 – which, as the *Conseil Constitutionnel* summarised in *TEU No.2*, affected "the exercise by the State of competences which arise from (*relèvent de*) essential conditions of its sovereignty". Article 100c(5) (EC), to which the *Conseil Constitutionnel* referred, specifies that the Article cannot undermine the exercise of responsibilities which fall to the Member States for the maintenance of public order or the safeguard of internal security. Either the *Conseil Constitutionnel* found these grounds unduly restrictive *per se*, which is hard to believe given the breadth of the concept of "*ordre public*", or it recognised that the concept of public order had different meanings in French and European Community law, or it did not trust the European Community law interpretation of derogations. In Luchaire's opinion,[31] the finding of unconstitutionality "gave witness to a certain severity" in the *Conseil Constitutionnel's* treatment. In *TEU No. 2* the *Conseil Constitutionnel* found that Article 88–2 "has the effect of lifting the obstacles of a constitutional order". The Senate report asserted that even after the constitutional revision, the operation of Article 100c (EC) could not exceed the framework of the maximum transfers to which a sovereign state can consent without putting its "global sovereignty" into doubt, either in the internal or in the international legal order.[32]

Article 88–3: Elections

18–10 "Subject to reciprocity, and according to the terms provided by the Treaty on European Union signed on the 7 February 1992, the right to vote and eligibility to the municipal elections may be accorded only to citizens of the Union

---

[29] 92–312 DC, 2 September 1992, Rec. p. 76; (1992) *Revue de Droit Public* 1610.

[30] 93–324 DC, 3 August 1993, Rec. p. 208, *Statute of the Bank of France.* This decision is in keeping with the rationale of 70–39 DC, 19 June 1970, Rec. p. 15, *Budgetary and Merger Treaties*, that the condition of reciprocity is satisfied by a treaty provision specifying that the treaty does not take effect until the deposit of the last instrument of ratification.

[31] F. Luchaire, *op. cit.* above, n.18.

[32] Larché's Report, above, n.11, p. 37.

resident in France. These citizens may not hold the office of mayor or deputy mayor, nor participate in the election of senators. An Organic *loi* voted in the same terms by the two assemblies shall determine the conditions of application of the present article."

In *TEU No. 1*[33] the *Conseil Constitutionnel* held that Article 8b(1) (EC), which contained the rights referred to in Article 88–3,[34] was contrary to specific provisions of the Constitution. These provisions were Articles 3, 24, and 72 which implied that only French nationals were eligible and had the right to vote in elections which had as their goal the designation of the deliberating organ of a territorial collectivity of the Republic, and notably the designation of municipal councillors or members of the Council of Paris. Interestingly, the *Conseil Constitutionnel* held that the future possibility of derogating measures under the Treaty did not affect the *Conseil Constitutionnel's* duty to consider the constitutionality of the provisions as they stood.

Article 88–3 was the most debated of all the individual articles. After revision, the constitutionality of Article 8b(1) (EC) was questioned in the *Conseil Constitutionnel* on four grounds.[35] First, the senators alleged disregard of Article 3 of the Declaration of 1789 on the principle of all sovereignty resting in the nation. The *Conseil Constitutionnel* stated that it had held that there was no contrariness between Article 3 of the Declaration of 1789 and Article 8b(1) (EC) in *TEU No. 1*[36] and so the senators' argument conflicted with that ruling.

Secondly, the senators claimed that the contested rights were contrary to Article 3 of the Constitution. The *Conseil Constitutionnel* replied with the passage on the sovereign power of the constituent to revise the Constitution,[37] and that Article 88–3 had sufficiently revised the Constitution.

Thirdly, the senators asserted that Article 24 of the Constitution (on the Parliament) remained an obstacle to ratification. The problem is that Union citizens can elect (and be elected) as municipal councillors, and these councillors elect the Senate. One of the functions of municipal elections is therefore to serve as a stage in the election of the Senate. As Goguel pointed out, the only way to preserve the Senate as the representative of the French people and of the territorial collectivities of the Republic is to refuse participation to Union citizens at each stage of the election.[38] The *Conseil Constitutionnel* held that the revision of the Constitution by Article 88–3 was sufficient to remove the constitutional obstacle.

---

33 92–308 DC, 9 April 1992, Rec. p. 55; (1992) 28 *Revue Trimestrielle du Droit Européen* 418.

34 The Council of the European Union has since passed a directive on the right to vote and stand in municipal elections – Council Directive 94/80 of 19 December 1994 which is to be implemented in national law by 1 January 1996.

35 92–312 DC, 2 September 1992, Rec. p. 76; (1992) *Revue de Droit Public* 1610, *TEU No. 2.*

36 In fact the *Conseil Constitutionnel* had not referred to Article 3 of the Declaration in *TEU No. 1.*

37 See above para. 16–8, "Limits to Amendment on the Face of the Constitution and Decisions of the *Conseil Constitutionnel*".

38 Larché's Report, above, n.11.

Fourthly, the senators argued that whereas the Treaty on European Union asserted a right, Article 88–3 only provided that the right "may be" accorded, and was thus insufficient to remove the constitutional objection. However the *Conseil Constitutionnel* met this objection by an interpretation of the third sentence of Article 88–3. It held that the reference to an Organic *loi* postulated that this text would itself be in conformity with the prescriptions ordered at the Community level for the implementation of Article 8b(1) (EC), and so the revision was sufficient. It is interesting to note here that this is the only context in which the *Conseil Constitutionnel* has held that organs of the Republic must conform to the prescriptions enacted at Community level for the implementation of an Article. This need not be taken as a denial of the effect of the *Conseil Constitutionnel's* reservations of interpretation on other questions of European Community law in the event of a different interpretation of European Community law,[39] because in this context the *Conseil Constitutionnel* was construing Article 88–3 in order to make it conform with the revisions required in virtue of its own judgment in *TEU No. 1.*[40]

Article 88–4: Resolutions

18–11 "The Government shall submit to the National Assembly and to the Senate, as soon as their transmission to the Council of the Communities, propositions of Community acts containing provisions of a legislative nature. During the sessions [of Parliament] or outside of them, resolutions may be voted in the framework of the present article, according to the terms fixed by the standing orders of each assembly."

The first thing to note about this amendment, added by the National Assembly on the first reading of the Constitutional *loi* and modified by the Senate, is that it does not directly affect French constitutional law's relationship with European Community law, but rather the division of powers between the Government and the Parliament. It is however indirectly relevant to French constitutional law's relation to European Community law because the increase in consciousness might lead to an increase in references to the *Conseil Constitutionnel*, particularly if the deputies and senators see their resolutions ignored.[41] The Article resulted from Parliament's concern over their lack of involvement at the decision-making stage of measures which later affected the domain of *loi.* In the parliamentary debates Declaration (No. 13) (EU) on the role of national parliaments in the European Union was interpreted as an encouragement to the amendment; it provides "[t]he Conference con-

39 This technique is considered below, para. 20–3, "Effect of Reservations of Interpretation".
40 92–308 DC, 9 April 1992, Rec. p. 55; (1992) 28 *Revue Trimestrielle du Droit Européen* 418.
41 In the first semester of 1994 there were 14 resolutions passed by the National Assembly and eight by the Senate. In 1993 there was a grand total of eight resolutions: B. Rullier, "L'application de l'article 88–4 de la Constitution au premier semestre, 1994" (1994) 19 *Revue Française de Droit Constitutionnel* 553.

siders that it is important to encourage a greater participation of national Parliaments in the activities of the European Union . . . ". The Senate report remarked "[c]uriously, this essential provision adjoins the declaration on the well-being of animals . . .". The Article is considered here in order to indicate the relationship between the political institutions of France and to consider in general terms whether it gives rise to any changes in the jurisdiction of French courts to entertain conflicts between French constitutional law and European Community law.

The power to adopt resolutions had to be conferred by constitutional revision. In an early decision *Standing Orders of the National Assembly*[42] the *Conseil Constitutionnel* held the passing of resolutions to be unconstitutional on the ground that the mechanisms for controlling government action were limited to Articles 49 and 50 on the resignation of the government after the passing of a motion of censure or disapproval of the government's general policy; so far as resolutions could fall within the right of initiative of members of Parliament, this right was covered by Article 34; the standing order containing the right to vote resolutions was not valid because standing orders can only relate to the internal measures concerning the functioning of the Assemblies. Under the Third Republic, resolutions were in effect injunctions addressed to the government. The *Conseil Constitutionnel* has censured injunctions on numerous occasions.[43] As Favoreau pointed out,[44] the opinion of Parliament cannot engage the government because the conduct of national politics is their responsibility under Article 20 and the power to negotiate and ratify treaties belongs to the President under Article 52.

During the Constitutional revision, the Senate changed the text of the amendment by substituting "résolution" for "avis", which measure belonged more to a consultative organ such as the *Conseil d'État*, and stated that the Parliament had been deprived of this competence by a decision of the *Conseil Constitutionnel*.[45] The Senate report stated that resolutions under this Article "without having an imperative effect, have more than indicative value" and that the purpose is to permit Parliament to make its views clear on Community acts which fall within "the natural competence of Parliament".[46] Vedel draws a dubious parallel with the consultation of overseas territories under Article 74, whilst Gicquel considered that it would be better to have downstream control under Article 37 which leaves it up to the government to try to declare *lois* outside Parliamentary competence. However this mode of control remains open and the Parliament could still try to pass *lois* on matters on which they disagreed with the government's decision in the Council.

---

42 59–2 DC, 17, 18, 24 June 1959, Rec. p. 58, *Standing Orders of the National Assembly.*

43 66–7 FNR, 21 December 1966, Rec. p. 37, *Indemnification of French Repatriates.* 76–73 DC, 28 December 1976, Rec. p. 41, *Examination of the* Loi *on Finances for 1977.* 78–102 DC, 17 January 1979, Rec. p. 26, *The Seventh Plan.*

44 Larché's Report, above, n.11.

45 Larché's Report, above, n.11.

46 *ibid.* at p. 53.

The status and importance of resolutions under Article 88–4 were uncertain. Their historical pedigree suggested their importance, but on the other hand they could have been viewed merely as a variation on the functioning of the parliamentary delegations to the European Community already provided for.[47] Their position has been clarified since the constitutional amendment. The National Assembly and the Senate added to the *règlement* by resolution to give effect to this provision.[48] The *Conseil Constitutionnel* was asked to rule on the constitutionality of those resolutions and decided that the resolutions could only be opinions and could not undermine the Government's constitutional responsibility.[49] In its decision on the resolution of the National Assembly the *Conseil Constitutionnel* was careful to make reservations of interpretation in order to protect the prerogatives of the government whilst upholding the constitutionality of the measure.[50] In its decision on the Senate's resolution the *Conseil Constitutionnel* deprived of effect a provision specifying that the President of the Senate could ask the government to refer to the High Assembly a proposed European Community act involving provisions of a legislative nature.[51] The Prime Minister, by circular of 21 April 1993,[52] set out the procedures to be followed for resolutions under Article 88–4 and by circular of 19 July 1994 completed his instructions to ministers on the subject, inviting them to take into account in European Community negotiation the position expressed by the French Parliament.[53]

Conclusion

18–12 The *Conseil Constitutionnel* considers French constitutional law to be compatible currently with the French constitutional law view of European Community law, but the French constitutional law view of European Community law is radically different to the European Community law view, so the two orders are in a conflictual stand-off.

---

47 By *loi* No. 90–385 inserting an Article VI *bis* para. IV into the *ordonnance* No. 58/1100 of 17 November 1958 on the functioning of the parliamentary assemblies.

48 On 19 November 1992, Article 151–1 (Assembly), and on 15 December 1992 (Article 73*bis* (Senate)).

49 D. Rousseau, "Chronique de jurisprudence constitutionnelle 1992–1993" (1994) *Revue de Droit Public* 101 at pp. 122–123; C. Tchakaloff, "*Les mésures françaises d'application des normes communautaires*" (1994) 10 *Revue française de Droit Administratif* 115 at pp. 115–116; M.-F. Verdier, "La révision constitutionnelle du 25 juin 1992 nécessaire à la ratification du traite de Maastricht et à l'extension des provisions des assemblées parlementaires françaises" (1994) 4 *Revue de Droit Public* 1137 at pp. 1162–1163 where Verdier is of the opinion that although the resolutions are non-binding, Article 88–4 has increased the powers of the two assemblies and, by reinforcing the role of the Senate, reinforced bicameralism.

50 92–314 DC, 17 December 1992, Rec. p. 126, *Standing Orders of the National Assembly.*

51 92–315 DC, 12 January 1993, Rec. p. 9, *Standing Orders of the Senate Assembly.*

52 J.O. p. 6495, 22 April 1993.

53 *La Semaine Juridique (Actualités)*, 3 August 1994, J.O. of 21 July 1994 p. 10510.

19. THE CONDITION OF RECIPROCITY

19–1 There is a limit to the acceptance of European Community law by French constitutional law which has not yet been dealt with – the condition of reciprocity. It is relatively straightforward. Article 55 of the Constitution provides that a ratified treaty will have an authority superior to *loi* under the condition that it is applied by the other party. This is a condition new to the Constitution of 1958 which was not present in Article 26 of the Constitution of 1946. It is difficult to control compliance with it.[1] However the interpretation of the condition as it applies to multilateral, as distinct from bilateral, treaties is that the condition is satisfied by a clause which states that the treaty does not take effect until the deposit of the last instrument of ratification.[2] All European Community treaties contained such a provision and are now unified in Article R (EU) so the French constitutional law condition of reciprocity appears to be a non-issue as regards European Community law. Furthermore, the *Cour de Cassation* for its part has held that the condition of reciprocity cannot be argued before national jurisdictions because Article 170 (EC) provides for an action against a failure of a Member State to fulfill its obligations under the treaty.

Nonetheless there appear to be two situations where the condition of reciprocity may remain relevant for European Community law in France. The first is that in the event of failure to ratify a Community treaty by one of the signatories, that treaty may not be applied in France. The application of the requirement of reciprocity in this case appears to have been passed out by the later decision *Statute of the Bank of France* according to which the failure of any Member State to ratify part or all of the Treaty on European Union makes its application in France unconstitutional because it would not be in force.[3]

The second situation arises by virtue of the repetition of the condition of reciprocity in Articles 88–2 and 88–3. However this repetition does not require reciprocal application of the same European Community rules in the areas of these competences but a reciprocal transfer of competences. This suggests that derogations granted by Community law to certain Member States, such as to Luxembourg as regards voting and eligibility, would not activate this condition.

---

1 C. Debasch and J.-M. Pontier, *Les Constitutions de la France*, (2nd ed., Paris: Dalloz, 1989).
2 70–39 DC, 19 June 1970, Rec. p. 15, *Treaty amending the budgetary provisions of European Community Treaties.*
3 93–324 DC, 3 August 1993, Rec. p. 208.

20. INTERNAL CONFLICT AND RESERVATIONS OF INTERPRETATION

20–1 This chapter considers the controlling technique of reservations of interpretation and how the *Conseil Constitutionnel* approaches internal constitutional conflicts by requiring changes in the status quo to be clear and by harmonising with the status quo where possible. Both these points affect conflicts, actual and potential, between European Community law's self-interpretation and French constitutional law's interpretation of European Community Law, because the *Conseil Constitutionnel* has made several reservations of interpretation on European Community law, and because there is now a new Title XV in the Constitution which must be harmonised with the rest of French constitutional law.

Internal Conflicts in the Constitution

20–2 The internal conflict between Articles 88–2 and 88–3 and other provisions of the Constitution, notably Article 3, has been considered under those Articles. The *Conseil Constitutionnel* held that the amendments could take the form of specific Articles and that other provisions of the Constitution could not then be called on to contest the amendments.[1] The more important question of the possible internal conflict between Article 88–1 and another Article was not raised, which is logical because it was not designed as a derogating Article and could not be because it conformed to the *Conseil Constitutionnel's* interpretation of the European Community. However the *Conseil Constitutionnel's* role in the resolution of internal conflicts in the Constitution will be relevant in fleshing out the French constitutional law conception of European Community law in the event of a constitutionally suspect claim by European Community law. In this context two of the *Conseil Constitutionnel's* decisions are on point.

First, in *TEU No. 2* the *Conseil Constitutionnel* suggested that the intent of an amending Article to derogate has to be clear.[2] Secondly, in its decision *On nationalisation*[3] the *Conseil Constitutionnel* confronted the potential conflict between the right to property contained in Article 17 of the Declaration of 1789 on the one hand and, on the other hand, the combination of paragraph 9

---

1 92–312 DC, 2 September 1992, Rec. p. 76; (1992) *Revue de Droit Public* 1610, *TEU No. 2.*

2 See above, paras. 16–8 *et seq.*, "Limits on Amendment".

3 81–132 DC, 16 January 1982, Rec. p. 18; B. Rudden and L. Kahn-Freund, *A Source-book on French Law* (Oxford: Clarendon Press, 1991) pp. 67–71, *On nationalisation.*

of the socialist-inspired Preamble of the Constitution of 1946 which encourages nationalisation with Article 34 of the Constitution of 1958 which provides that nationalisation falls within the domain of *loi*. The *Conseil Constitutionnel* held that the purpose of the Preamble of the Constitution of 1946 was to complete the Declaration of 1789, not to conflict with it. The *Conseil Constitutionnel* thus imposed strict reservations of interpretation on the nationalising *loi*, declaring "the fundamental character of the right to property whose conservation characterizes one of the goals of political society". A similar argument could be made if a European Community rule conflicted with a rule of French constitutional law if not otherwise saved by the new Title. The new Title might receive a limited interpretation (particularly in the light of the *TEU* decisions) which would not cure the conflict.

Effect of Reservations of Interpretation

20–3 The *Conseil Constitutionnel* uses the technique of reservation of interpretation[4] to compensate for the abstract and preventative nature of its constitutional control. The technique enables the *Conseil Constitutionnel* almost to legislate: while it cannot enact rules it can control the meaning of enacted rules, rather than simply uphold their constitutionality or declare their unconstitutionality. This is a familiar technique in French constitutional law which conditions the constitutionality of the upheld provisions: "Interpretation may well be a kindness in preference to a nullity."[5] The technique dates from a very early decision of the *Conseil Constitutionnel* mentioned above in connection with parliamentary resolutions[6] and is an umbrella category for the three effects a *Conseil Constitutionnel* interpretation can have: the effect of restriction where the *Conseil Constitutionnel* states the interpretation which is constitutional; the effect of addition where a provision is fleshed out to make it constitutional; and the effect of injunction where the administration is informed on how to enforce the law.

For example, in *Foreigners in Transit Zones*[7] the *Conseil Constitutionnel* held that an Article of the referred *loi* which conferred on the administration the power to hold a foreigner in a zone of transit without the possibility of judicial review was not contrary to paragraph 4 of the Preamble to the Constitution of 1946 under the reserve of interpretation that the detainee's claim for asylum was manifestly unfounded. Another example is the decision of 25–26 June 1986 where the *Conseil Constitutionnel* upheld the constitutionality of an Empowering *loi* stating, in article one of its ruling: "Under the strict reservations of interpretation expressed above, the *loi* authorising the Government

---

4 On this see J. Bell, *French Constitutional Law* (Oxford: Clarendon Press, 1992) pp. 53–55.
5 *ibid.* p. 55.
6 59–2 DC, 17, 18, 24 June 1959, Rec. p. 58, *Standing Orders of the National Assembly.* See above, para. 18–11, "Article 88–4: Elections".
7 92–307 DC, 25 February 1992, Rec. p. 48.

to take diverse measures of an economic and social character are not contrary to the Constitution". A most striking example of the *Conseil Constitutionnel* making multiple directives on interpretation was its decision *On the Control of Immigration.*[8]

The *Conseil Constitutionnel* is not as explicit in its resolution in *TEU No. 1*[9] as in the case just cited, but it gives the whole order of European Community law as well as certain features considered above a very particular interpretation. The *Conseil Constitutionnel* considered the European Parliament in its decision in order to lay down the French constitutional limits of that institution – the *Conseil Constitutionnel* did not consider many other not unconstitutional features of the Treaty on European Union[10], and all features not specifically focussed on were impliedly held to be constitutional.[11] The question of the rights and liberties of citizens is dealt with below.[12] Luchaire is decidedly against the possibility that reservations of interpretation could attach to the Treaty on European Union.[13] He bases his opinion on two points: first, that it is not the *Conseil Constitutionnel* but "the Court of Justice of the European Communities which has sole jurisdiction to interpret Community law"; secondly, because the *Conseil Constitutionnel* could not risk basing a finding of constitutionality on an interpretation which might not be retained by the Court of Justice. In response to the first point, the French constitutional law interpretation of European Community law is important so far as European Community law falls within the jurisdictions of France. The *Conseil Constitutionnel* and Article 88–1 deny sovereignty to the European Community, and consequently to its institutions. In response to the second point, it may be because the interpretation by the Court of Justice is not controllable that the *Conseil Constitutionnel* considered reservations of interpretation to be necessary. Luchaire considered that reservations of interpretation could have no part in the constitutional control of the Treaty on European Union because "in effect, whereas the decisions of the *Conseil Constitutionnel* bind all the authorities (Article 62 of the Constitution) as well in its holding as in those of the reasons which are the necessary support, it is only thus in the French legal order." This makes precisely the opposite point intended: the reasons given by the *Conseil Constitutionnel* for the constitutionality of the Treaty on European Union bind all authorities in France and that is presumably why they were given.[14]

---

[8] 93–325 DC, 13 August 1993, Rec. p. 224; (1993) *La Semaine Juridique (Textes)* 373.
[9] 92–308 DC, 9 April 1992, Rec. p. 55; (1992) 28 *Revue Trimestrielle du Droit Européen* 418.
[10] *ibid.*
[11] 92–312 DC, 2 September 1992, Rec. p. 76; (1992) *Revue de Droit Public 1610, TEU No. 2.*
[12] See below, para. 21–2. For a consideration of Article F(2) (60), see below, para. 21–3.
[13] F. Luchaire, "L'Union Européenne et la Constitution" (1992) *Revue de Droit Public* 589 at p. 593.
[14] This has been doubted by N. Guimezanes, "L'arrêt de l'immigration en France? Commentaire de la loi No. 93–1027 du 24 août 1993 sur la mâitrise de l'immigration" (1994) *La Semaine Juridique (Doctrine)* 1.

21. THE SUBSTANCE OF THE ESSENTIAL CONDITIONS FOR EXERCISE OF NATIONAL SOVEREIGNTY

21–1 This controlling norm is the foundation for the *Conseil Constitutionnel's* treatment of European Community law.[1] It has been considered above.[2] The analysis has sought to show that not only is French constitutional law's interpretation of European Community law limited,[3] but that a closer future relationship will run into difficulties and run up against restrictions on amendment.[4] In this chapter the bases of the essential conditions for exercise of national sovereignty, which bases condition the concept of sovereignty and legitimate French constitutional law, are considered.

Assuring the Guarantee of the Rights and Liberties of Citizens

21–2 This section focusses on the nature and role of fundamental rights in French constitutional law but does not attempt to draw up a list of these rights. Such a list would not be identical to the list in European Community law.[5]

As a Competence

21–3 There are only a few cases which have discussed the potential conflict between an international obligation and the duty of the State to guarantee the rights and liberties of citizens.[6] That duty was stated in one case to be one of the three essential conditions for the exercise of national sovereignty.[7] In

---

1 The first time the *Conseil Constitutionnel* used the rights and liberties of the citizens as a norm of control for the constitutionality of *lois* was in 71–44 DC, 16 July 1971, Rec. p. 29, *Freedom of Association.*

2 See above, para. 16–7, "The Controlling Norm of the Essential Conditions for the Exercise of Natural Sovereignty".

3 See above, Chap. 18, "French Constitutional Law Interpretation of European Community Law in the Ratification of the Treaty of the European Union".

4 See above, para. 16–8, "The Limits on Amendment".

5 French Delegation to the IX Conference of European Constitutional Courts, "Protection constitutionnelle et protection internationale des droits de l'homme: concurrence ou complémentarité" (1993) *Revue française de Droit Administratif* 850 at pp. 858 and 869.

6 While the Decision of the *Conseil Constitutionnel* 74–54 DC, 15 January 1975, Rec. p. 19; [1975] Rec. Dalloz Sirey 529, *Abortion loi* concerned a potential conflict between, on the one hand, the duty of the State to guarantee the rights and liberties of citizens and, on the other, international obligations, the *Conseil Constitutionnel* held that it lacked jurisdiction under Article 61 to consider the conflict.

7 85–188 DC, 22 May 1985, Rec. p. 15, *Protocol on the abolition of the death penalty.*

TEU No. 1[8] the only essential condition for the exercise of national sovereignty which the *Conseil Constitutionnel* considered separately by name was the guarantee of the rights and liberties of citizens. In two paragraphs whose importance is matched by brevity, the *Conseil Constitutionnel* referred to Article F(2) (EU) (which provides that the Union will protect those fundamental rights which are guaranteed by the European Convention on Human Rights and Fundamental Freedoms, and those which result from the common constitutional conditions of the Member States, as general principles of European Community law). Then the *Conseil Constitutionnel* stated cryptically:

> "Considering that the requirements of paragraph 2 of Article F, paired with the intervention of the national jurisdictions ruling in the framework of their respective competences, are in a position to guarantee the rights and liberties of citizens; that in this respect the international engagement submitted to the *Conseil constitutionnel* does not attack rules and principles of constitutional value."

The *Conseil Constitutionnel* raises, indeed raises first of all other considerations falling within the controlling norms, the provision of Article F(2) (EU) from the many provisions in the Treaty on European Union, not for the purpose of holding it unconstitutional, but to make the reservations of interpretation which make it constitutional. The *Conseil Constitutionnel* appears to focus the whole human rights protection issue in the European Communities as well as in the European Union around this article, although this is incorrect as a matter of European Community law.[9] The reason why Article F(2) (EU) is constitutional is given in the second clause: national jurisdictions continue to intervene in the framework of their respective competences. This clause makes clear that no competence is transferred. With this statement the *Conseil Constitutionnel* appeared to adopt the view that the European Community law protection of human rights does not affect the continuing protection which can be asserted at national level if the European Community law protection falls short of the national standard. Where there is no conflict, the question of national control does not arise. In this paragraph the *Conseil Constitutionnel* also refers to "the rules and principles of constitutional value": which covers the content of the essential conditions for exercise of national sovereignty of the protection of the rights and liberties of citizens. The continuing competence of French jurisdictions to protect human rights implies that neither the Treaty on European Union nor the other European Community treaties jeopardise that protection in French constitutional law. Conflicts may result. An alternative interpretation of that cryptic passage is that the *Conseil Constitutionnel* was not concerned with the protection of fundamental rights in European Community law but only with this provision which, being non–justiciable by the Court of Justice, could not give rise to conflicts of competence

---

8 92–308 DC, 9 April 1992, Rec. p. 55; (1992) 28 *Revue Trimestrielle du Droit Européen* 418.

9 The Court of Justice of the European Communities, according to Article L (EU), does not have competence over Article F (EU).

with national courts, who would remain, just as they would in respect of other international treaties without a special court, in a position to consider the interpretation of that Article. However this interpretation goes against the thrust of the decision of the *Conseil Constitutionnel* and does not fit adequately the meaning of "in the framework of their respective competences".

The *Conseil Constitutionnel* considered in the Schengen Treaty[10] the potential threat of an international obligation to the duty of the State to guarantee the rights and liberties of citizens. Article 2 of the Schengen Treaty provided that the frontiers of States which were internal to the area covered by that treaty could be crossed in any place without control of persons. Those who seised the *Conseil Constitutionnel* argued that this undermined the security of persons proclaimed by the Declaration of 1789 as well as paragraph 11 of the Preamble of the Constitution of 1946 which guaranteed the protection of health, material security, rest and leisure. The *Conseil Constitutionnel* dismissed as irrelevant the complaint based on paragraph 11 but it considered the other complaint in an interesting way, holding that the principle contained in Article 2 of the Schengen Treaty "could not be regarded as disregarding the objective of constitutional value of the safeguard of the public order, which implies notably that the protection of the person will be assured." This was for three reasons: first, there were controls on the external borders; secondly, the re-establishment for a limited period of controls on the national borders was authorised when required by public order or national security; and thirdly, there was no fetter on police competences within the national territory. It is important that the *Conseil Constitutionnel* considered the maintenance of public order under the essential condition for the exercise of national sovereignty of the guarantee of the rights and liberties of citizens, because it points to the intrinsic connection between such concepts of public order and fundamental rights and liberties. This connection, which will be considered below, makes clear that a right is given meaning by other legal concepts which are inherent in a legal order of a political community, and that consequently the right cannot be severed from this order and protected, for example, at the European Community level where there are different ideas of what constitutes public order, without changing the substance of the right itself.[11]

The preceding three decisions all concerned the *Conseil Constitutionnel's* Article 54 control of the ratification of a treaty. A further decision, *Juge unique, juge inique*[12] ("One judge is an unjust judge"), which arose out of the *Conseil Constitutionnel's* Article 61.2 control of the constitutionality of a *loi* on a domestic matter, is nonetheless relevant here because it reinforces the point that

---

[10] 91–294 DC, 25 July 1991, Rec. p. 91; (1991) *Revue de Droit Public* 1517.

[11] See para. 21–14 below, "Rights and Freedoms Understood in a Framework of Interdependent Concepts".

[12] 77–58 DC, 23 July 1975, Rec. p. 16; (1976) Actualités Juridiques 44, *Juge unique, juge inique*. See B. Nicholas, "Fundamental Rights and Judicial Review in France" [1978] *Public Law* 162.

the transfer of competence in the matter of the rights and liberties of the citizen is unconstitutional. The referred *loi* delegated to the President of an ordinary court a discretion to allow any *délit* to be tried by a single judge. The *Conseil Constitutionnel* held that to vest such a discretion in the President of an ordinary court was unconstitutional, because the Parliament cannot delegate its responsibility under Article 34 to another authority where the rights and liberties of the citizen are in question. This constitutional point on permissible delegation could arise in the control of the ratification of international treaties under Article 54.

The amendment of Article 53 of the Constitution has affirmed the importance of France retaining its competence in matters of fundamental rights. Every other contracting state must be bound by identical obligations to France concerning the protection of human rights and fundamental freedoms, and even then France retains the competence to grant asylum.[13]

In summary, a delegation of control of the guarantee of the fundamental rights and liberties of citizens is unconstitutional. No amendment to allow for such a delegation was attempted in the ratification process for the Treaty on European Union because, according to the *Conseil Constitutionnel*, the Treaty on European Union and impliedly the other European Community treaties as well did not affect the French constitutional law control or the duty on all courts to observe the State's obligation in this regard. The reason for continuing the analysis of the protection of the rights and freedoms of citizens is to show on the one hand that they have a specific nature and function in French constitutional law such that they constitutes a fundamental commitment in French constitutional law and on the other hand that this fundamental commitment differs from the protection by European Community law of fundamental rights and there is a possible conflict with European Community law over such protection.[14] Not only is the importance of the commitment such that French jurisdictions should be particularly careful in this area to police the applicability of a European Community law interpretation which differs from that of French constitutional law, but further it is at least doubtful whether in the future French constitutional law could countenance a transfer of competence in this area without risking the legitimation of the French legal order.

Sources of the Rights and Liberties of Citizens

21–4 To determine what constitutes the rights and liberties of citizens is not an easy task. This section considers three types of sources: first, the authoritative standards by reference to which constitutional norms are identified

---

[13] See above, para. 16–3, "Constitutional Basis of Public International Law".

[14] See above, Part II, paras. 8–59 *et seq.* "European Community Law Fundamental Rights", and Part V, Chap. 30, "Conflicts – National Constitutional Law Right v. European Community Law Right".

("formal sources"); secondly, the material sources from which the statements of rights may be taken; thirdly, the legitimation and nature of the rights thus identified.

Formal Sources

21–5 The *Conseil Constitutionnel* often makes reference to "principles having constitutional value" or "principles and rules of constitutional value".[15] This rubric covers rules and principles stated in written texts, fundamental principles of the laws of the Republic which are sometimes stated, sometimes extrapolated, general principles of law, and some objectives of constitutional value.[16] Such a standard leaves the *Conseil Constitutionnel* with considerable scope to define unwritten French constitutional law both in declaring what these rules and principles are, and in giving them specificity. The *Conseil Constitutionnel* has also made reference to "essential principles on which the protection of individual liberty rests"[17] and to "the spirit of the Constitution".[18]

Material Sources

21–6 The material sources provide statements of the rights and liberties of citizens. The Constitution of 1958, which is quite technical partly as a result of the circumstances of crisis and urgency in which it was born, does not itself have any declaration of rights. Rather the Constitution "orders out" in the important first paragraph of its short Preamble, which Preamble runs the ideas of rights and sovereignty together:

> "The French people solemnly proclaims its attachment to the Rights of man and to the principles of national sovereignty such as they are defined by the Declaration of 1789, confirmed and completed by the Preamble of the Constitution of 1946."

The first paragraph of the Preamble of the Constitution of 1946 refers not only to the Declaration of 1789 but also to "the fundamental principles recognised by the *lois* of the Republic".

The *Conseil Constitutionnel* has in its decisions referred to all of these material sources. For example, in *Freedom of Association* the *Conseil Constitutionnel* made clear that it would judge the constitutionality of *lois* according to a wide body of constitutional norms.[19] In that case the *Conseil Constitutionnel* had to consider the constitutionality of a *loi* completing the *loi* of 1 July 1901 concern-

---

15 "*Régles et principes de valeur constitutionnelle*".
16 J. Bell, *French Constitutional Law* (Oxford: Clarendon Press, 1992) at p. 65.
17 76–75 DC, 12 January 1977, Rec. p. 33; B. Rudden and L. Kahn-Freund, *A Source-Book on French Law* (1991), pp. 65–66, On Police Search Powers.
18 62–20 DC, 6 November 1962, Rec. p. 27; B. Rudden and L. Kahn-Freund (1991) *op. cit.*, p. 55 Direct amendment on popular election of the President.
19 71–44 DC, 16 July 1971, Rec. p. 29.

ing articles of association.[20] The *Conseil Constitutionnel* held unconstitutional Article 3 of the referred *loi* which instituted a procedure for subordinating the acquisition of legal capacity of a declared association to the control of their conformity with the law by the judicial branch. Previously the sole condition to the self-constitution of an association was the deposit of a declaration. As the ground for its holding, the *Conseil Constitutionnel* relied on the fact that:

> "in the number of fundamental principles recognised by the *lois* of the Republic and solemnly reaffirmed by the preamble of the Constitution, is to be traced the principle of the freedom of association".

In its important decision upholding the constitutionality (and conformity to treaties) of a *loi* providing for a limited freedom to abort,[21] the *Conseil Constitutionnel* referred to the principle in the preamble of the Constitution of 1946 according to which the state guarantees "to the child the protection of health". However, given the conditions attached to the availability of abortion, the *Conseil Constitutionnel* upheld the *loi.*

Nature and Legitimation of French Constitutional Law Fundamental Rights

21–7 The nature or legitimation of the rights and freedoms of citizens considered here does not directly concern political theories but rather the intra-order explanation given by the self-description of the rights and freedoms themselves as they come from the material sources. The legitimation therein propounded has authority in the legal order and consequently is not "abstract" in the sense of abstracted from the practical importance of the rights and freedoms in French constitutional law.

Before embarking on the consideration below, it is important to reiterate that the Parliament is still left considerable scope by the *Conseil Constitutionnel* to define and balance rights in the exercise of its *loi*-making functions under Article 34.[22] The Parliament has traditionally been regarded as the institution set up by the Constitution as the ultimate interpreter of the constitutional rights of citizens (the *Conseil Constitutionnel* now has this function).[23] The discretion accorded to Parliament by the *Conseil Constitutionnel* has not transferred to rule-makers at the European Community level.

Foundation of Constitution and End of Polity

21–8 The protection of rights is a *sine qua non* of the Constitution:

> "Article 16. Any society in which the guarantee of rights is not assured, nor the separation of powers determined, has no constitution." (Declaration of 1789)

---

20 "*Contrat d'association*".

21 74–54 DC, 17 January 1975, Rec. p. 19, *Abortion loi.*

22 See above, para. 14–2, "The *Conseil Constitutionnel* – Background".

23 There is a particular exception to this on the face of Article 66 of the Constitution which provides that the judiciary as the guardian of individual liberty is to ensure respect for the principle that no one is to be detained arbitrarily, but this respect is to be ensured "in circumstances provided by *loi*".

In stark contrast to the dynamic federal goal of the European Community, the Declaration states:

> "Article 2. The goal of every political association is the conservation of the natural and imprescriptible rights of man. These rights are liberty, property, and freedom from oppression."

The protection of rights is then the goal of France as legal order and as polity. This is reinforced by the preamble to the Constitution of 1791 which states:

> "The National Assembly, wishing to establish the French Constitution on the principles which it has just declared, abolishes irrevocably the institutions which injure the freedom and equality of rights."

With the very establishment of the State dependent on this natural law notion of rights,[24] it is not surprising that the goal of government should be their protection. The Preamble to the Declaration of 1789 provides:

> "The representatives of the French people, constituted in the National Assembly, considering that the ignorance, the forgetting or the contempt for the rights of man are the sole causes of the public troubles and of the corruption of governments, [declare these natural rights] . . . so that this declaration, constantly present to all the members of the social body, will remind them without let-up of their rights and their duties; so that the acts of the legislative power and those of the executive power, being able to be at each instant compared with the goal of every political institution, may be more respected."

The Declaration to the Constitution of 1793 states in the preamble that the purpose of declaring the natural human rights is so that:

> "the people has always before its eyes the basis of its freedom and its happiness [*bonheur*]; the magistrate the rule of his duties; the legislator the object of his mission . . .
>
> First Article . . . Government is instituted to guarantee to man the enjoyment of his natural and imprescriptible rights."

Non-Positivist Nature of Rights and Freedoms

21–9 There are several interrelated characteristics which determine the nature of the fundamental commitment to rights.

21–10 *God* Although the Constitution of 1958 declares itself to be a secular republic, God was mentioned in the preambles to earlier constitutional documents. Thus in the Declaration of 1789 the Assembly recognised and declared the rights of man "in the presence and under the auspices of the Supreme Being" and refers to these rights as sacred. In the Declaration of the Rights of Man and of the Citizen in the Constitution of 24 June 1793, based largely on the Girondin Constitution, the rights were proclaimed "in the presence of the Supreme Being". In the Constitution of the 5 Fructidor Year III[25] the French people proclaimed the rights and duties in the same

---

[24] Article 2: "natural and imprescriptible rights of man"; see further this paragraph and below, para. 21–12, on Natural Rights.

[25] 22 August 1795.

presence. The right to property is referred to in Article 17 of the Declaration as "sacred".

21–11 *Recognition, not Creation* There is a continual insistence that constitutional rights are merely declared by the constitutions, and therefore pre-exist them. This pre-existence implies a force independent from positive law enactment. There is also a recurrent theme of self-evidence and incontestability. The Declarations of rights are just that: declarations, not bills or enactments. In the Declaration of 1789 the representatives of the French people, as the constituent assembly, expounded (*exposer*), acknowledged (*reconnaître*), and declared the rights therein. The claims of the citizens to have these rights recognised rested on "simple and incontestible principles". The Constitution of 3–4 September 1791, which was headed by the Declaration of 1789, in its preamble acknowledges and declares rights and states that the Law ("*la Loi*") will not recognise any engagement contrary to them. In its first title, "Fundamental Provisions Guaranteed by the Constitution" it states that a list of rights are put on the record (*consigner*) by the Constitution. The Constitution of 1793 begins with another declaration which expounds the rights. In the Declaration of the Rights and Duties of Man and Citizen of the Constitution of 1795, "the French people proclaim . . . the following declaration of rights . . .".

21–12 *Natural Rights* The rights so declared are termed natural rights and adhere to man, not to legal persons. Furthermore, tying in to the two characteristics outlined above of the fundamental commitment to rights of God and Declaration, these rights are inalienable and sacred. Thus it is "the natural, inalienable, and sacred rights of man" which are referred to in the introductory paragraph of the Declaration of 1789; the phrase "natural and imprescriptible rights" is used in Article 2; and Article 4 refers to "the natural rights of every man". In the Constitution of 1791 itself the preamble refers to natural rights, as does the preamble of the Constitution of 1793; it also repeats, in Article 1, the phrase "natural and imprescriptible rights". Article 6 asserts: "Freedom . . . has nature for principle". The preamble of the Constitution of 1946 declares that "every human being . . . possesses inalienable and sacred rights". The preamble of the Constitution of 1958 refers to the "Rights of man".

21–13 *Rights of Foreigners* The fundamental constitutional rights recognised or acknowledged in man are not confined to citizens, which displaces the notion of the protection of fundamental rights being legitimated in French constitutional law by social contract between citizens (this is not to say that certain rights will not be confined to citizens, particularly certain civic rights in the political process):

> "Considering nevertheless that if the legislator can take in regard to foreigners specific provisions, it must respect the fundamental rights and liberties of

> constitutional value recognised in all who reside on the territory of the Republic; that if they must be reconciled with the safeguard of public order which constitutes an objective of constitutional value, figuring among these rights and liberties individual liberty and security, notably the liberty to go and to come, the liberty of marriage, the right to lead a normal family life; that furthermore foreigners enjoy rights to social protection, from as soon as they reside in a stable and regular manner on French territory; that they must benefit from the availability of judicial protection for the guarantee of these rights and liberties."[26]

The *Conseil Constitutionnel* had acknowledged before this decision that the asylum-seeker had unwritten rights and liberties of constitutional value.[27]

Rights and Freedoms Understood in a Framework of Interdependent Concepts

21–14 The Declaration in the Constitution of 1793 puts it succinctly: "The end [*but*] of Society is the common good." The fundamental commitment to rights is not dependent on atomistic individualism. The second half of the Declaration of 1789 states that natural, inalienable, and sacred rights are laid out:

> "so that the claims of citizens, founded nevertheless on simple and incontestable principles, tend always towards the maintenance of the Constitution and to the happiness of all. – In consequence the National Assembly recognises and declares, in the presence and under the auspices of the Supreme being, the following rights of Man and the Citizen."

Given this connection between rights on the one hand and the concepts of society and the common happiness, it is logical that these concepts should be involved in the ordering of rights. Ordering does not mean solely ranking or limiting rights, but rather organising a framework of balances in accordance with the conception of a society based on natural rights, which organisation will function to resolve the inevitable competition between claims in a given case. Thus the Declaration of 1789 provides:

> "Article 4. Freedom consists in being able to do everything which does not harm another; thus, the exercise of the natural rights of each man has only the limits which assure to other members of society the enjoyment of their own rights.
>
> Article 5. Legislation [*la Loi*] has the right to prohibit only actions harmful to society."

Article 10 (Declaration of 1789) limits the manifestation of opinions by "public order" (*l'ordre public*); Article 17 limits the right to property by "public necessity". The latter limitation was confirmed by the *Conseil Constitutionnel* in the decision *On nationalisation*[28] which referred to Article 17 and also to

---

26 93–325 DC, 13 August 1993, Rec. p. 224; (1993) *La Semaine Juridique (Textes)* 373, *On the Control of Immigration.*

27 91–294 DC, 25 July 1991, Rec. p. 91; (1991) *Revue de Droit Public* 1517, *Schengen Treaty.*

28 81–132 DC, 16 January 1982, Rec. p. 18; B. Rudden and L. Kahn-Freund (1991), *op. cit.* above, n.17, pp. 67–71, *On nationalisation.*

limitations in the "public interest". Article 1 (Constitution of 1791) states that liberty consists only in the liberty to do all which does not harm the rights of others or public security; therefore the law can penalise those acts which are harmful to society because they attack either the public safety or the rights of others. In general, then, "Legislation can ordain only that which is just and useful to society; it can prohibit only that which is harmful".[29]

There is a relation between rules and principles of constitutional value, including fundamental rights, and objectives of constitutional value. Genevois states: "the objective of a constitutional value appears as the necessary corollary of the implementation of a constitutionally recognised value"; interestingly he draws a parallel with Case 4/73 *Nold v. Commission.*[30] One example is the *Schengen Treaty*[31] case considered above where the constitutional objective of *ordre public* was considered under the heading of the rights and liberties of citizens as an objective which was itself a means to guaranteeing the right to personal protection. Another example is *Press Pluralism*[32] where the *Conseil Constitutionnel* stated that the pluralism of daily newspapers was "in itself an objective of constitutional value" because it was a way of ensuring that Article 11 of the Declaration of 1789 on the freedom of thought and opinion could be secured. In a later case arising from the wish of the Chirac government to relax the Socialist-imposed restrictions on ownership of newspapers, the *Conseil Constitutionnel* stated that:

> "it is not less permissible for it [the legislature] to adopt, for the realisation or conciliation of objectives of constitutional nature, new methods, the appropriateness of which it is up to it to appreciate, and which can comprise the amendment or repeal of provisions which it considers excessive or useless; that, nevertheless, the exercise of this power cannot result in depriving requirements of constitutional character from legal guarantees."[33]

Objectives of constitutional value can operate, as in this case, as a restriction on the power of the legislature; they can also operate as a restriction on rights and freedoms against which these objectives may be balanced. Thus in the Schengen Treaty decision *ordre public* was a restriction on the freedom of non-citizens to uncontrolled movement, and it has been held as a justification to restrict the freedom of citizens too, such as in the imposition of identity checks because:

> "the prevention of threats to public order, especially of threats to the security of persons and property, are necessary for the implementation of principles and rights of constitutional value; that the inconvenience that the application of [the relevant provisions] might represent to the freedom of movement is not excessive".[34]

---

29 Article 4, Declaration of 1793.

30 [1974] E.C.R. 491.

31 91–294 DC, 25 July 1991, Rec. p. 91; (1991) *Revue de Droit Public* 1517.

32 84–181 DC, 10 and 11 October 1984, Rec. p. 73.

33 86–210 DC, 29 July 1986, Rec. p. 110, *loi reforming the legal regime for the press.*

34 80–127 DC, 19 and 20 January 1981, Rec. p. 15, *loi reinforcing security and protecting the freedom of persons.*

Objectives of constitutional value, then, are part and parcel of the French constitutional law notion of rights and freedoms and go hand in hand in their specification and in the identification of the common good.[35]

Summary

21–15 In summary, the goal of Government in France is to promote rights. The promotion of rights is also an essential condition for the exercise of national sovereignty. These are not just any type of rights, but natural, inalienable, human, interdependent rights, declared in the presence of God, and critically important to the notion of a constitution. Such rights, and a legal order based on them, cannot admit of suspension or invalidity when faced with the competing claims of another legal order. Within French constitutional law, not all these rights can be individually absolute. So they are limited according to juridically developed concepts of public order, general interest, public necessity, etc. Rights must be balanced constitutionally also against the rights of others, and in some cases via techniques such as proportionality against the general interest.[36] These are not just any notions of public order, general interest, etc., but are dependent on a society founded on natural rights, a society whose institutions are "founded on the common ideal of freedom, equality, and fraternity".[37] These limiting notions are an integral, inseparable part of the constitutional conception of the polity as a whole, France.

Bell devotes a whole chapter[38] to establish the proposition that judicial review of *lois* in France is concerned with the purpose and rationality of *lois*. This purpose and rationality of *lois*, how they restrict and promote rights, can only be understood within a complete political community.

Moreover, whatever discretion Parliament enjoys in this regard it enjoys by virtue of its nature as an organ of sovereignty within the polity. The restriction of the essential conditions for the exercise of national sovereignty under the Constitution of 1958 has not yet affected the community so far as the protection of these rights are concerned. Such restriction would pose the dilemma of revolt or revolution.

Assuring Respect for the Institutions of the Republic

21–16 Like the protection of the rights and liberties of citizens, the institutions of the Republic are part of the very essence of the State as it is conceived

---

[35] These objectives are very different to those of European Community law. See above Part III.

[36] 88–244 DC, 20 July 1988, Rec. p. 119; B. Rudden (1991) *op. cit.* above, n.17, pp. 67–71, "The Renault Ten I".

[37] Preamble of Constitution of 1958. *cf.* the use of "Prudence, Justice and Charity" in the preamble to the Constitution of Ireland of 1937.

[38] J. Bell (1992) *op. cit.* above, n.16 Chap. 6.

under the Constitution of 1958 and so far as French constitutional law recognises independently the institutions as political concepts or facts. Presumably the phrase 'the institutions of the Republic' refers to the Republican institutions of government (not, for example, to the family) – the Parliament, the Executive, the Judiciary, and the President. The range of meaning which could be given to the norm of assuring their respect is immense. On the one hand, the institutions could mean little more than the buildings, the people who function in them, and their procedures, irrespective of substance, power, or competences.

On the other hand, the institutions of the Republic could mean a lot: the means through which national sovereignty is exercised and the right and liberties of citizens guaranteed, with the implication of the necessary power to act as such a means. The notion of "Republic" itself has many possible meanings. As West puts it:

> "In a negative sense, the Republic is to be contrasted with the monarchy and the inheritability of public functions. In a positive sense, it refers to a particular form of political organisation which is the product of history and is bound up with the related notions of nation, democracy, and *l'État de droit.*"[39]

The *Conseil Constitutionnel* has not elucidated what meaning it has in mind. When it held in *TEU No. 1*[40] that the eligibility and right to vote in municipal elections were contrary to the Constitution because of the knock-on effect on the Senate, it referred specifically to Articles 3, 24, and 72 of the Constitution and not to the essential condition of exercise of national sovereignty of the assurance of respect for the institutions of the Republic.

The institutions of the Republic must be linked on any interpretation to the Republican form of government which, as was affirmed in *TEU No. 2*,[41] cannot be amended according to Article 89.5 of the Constitution of 1958.[42] The assuring of respect for the institutions of the Republic is therefore a norm of control which expresses fundamental commitments in French constitutional law which may not be amendable.[43]

Assuring the Continuation of the Life of the Nation

21–17 The *Conseil Constitutionnel* has not elucidated what it means by this controlling norm. It is very vague. It appears that the Treaty on European Union did not affect this norm because the *Conseil Constitutionnel* did not specify it in *TEU No. 1.*

---

39 A. West *et al.*, *The French Legal System: An Introduction* (London: Fourmat Publishing: 1992) p. 138.

40 92–308 DC, 9 April 1992, Rec. p. 55; (1992) 28 *Revue Trimestrielle du Droit Européen* 418.

41 92–312 DC, 2 September 1992, Rec. p. 76; (1992) *Revue de Droit Public* 1610.

42 The use of this concept in the *ordonnance* of 9 August 1944 of the Government of the Republic has been referred to above in para. 16–10, "The Limits to Recognition of the Legal Effects of National Sovereignty as Political Concept or Fact".

43 See above, para. 16–10.

It is difficult to discuss the juridical concept of nation apart from national sovereignty.[44] In the classical theory of sovereignty behind the Revolution, the nation is the legal person which holds sovereignty. This understanding of sovereignty denied the legitimacy of the divine right of the monarch to rule. The Nation guards the essence of sovereignty and can, according to opinion, delegate it to the people or the country (so far as the country is distinct from the actual inhabitants).[45] It would seem a logical result of this definition that the people as delegates could not destroy the Nation which delegates. According to Hariou, only in the Nation is sovereignty uncontrollable.[46] The revolutionary concept of national sovereignty was not popular sovereignty because the people were seen as not always capable of acting in the general interest. There was thus a non-positivist element to the concept of national sovereignty from the beginning. By the time Article 3 of the Constitution of 1958 expressly stated that sovereignty belongs to the people, the concept of national sovereignty was restricted by other fundamental commitments in French constitutional law enforced by the courts such as the rights and liberties of citizens. Furthermore, the concept of people now has a value beyond that of the aggregation of eligible voters (and thus perhaps beyond their constituent power) – the French people is not merely a collective noun expressing all the French together, but rather is itself a concept of constitutional value.[47]

The notion of Nation separate from sovereignty appears to express the idea of the "political community as a whole".[48] Therefore the controlling norm of assuring the continuation of the life of the nation, which points to that which cannot be infringed without the revision of the Constitution, is dependent on the political concepts and facts. Thus if the European Community was, through economics, the fundamental freedoms, the marketing of its image, and the exercise of all its attributed competences, to remove the political factual presuppositions of the existence of a nation, the *Conseil Constitutionnel* may find that this constitutional bar to the claims of European Community law dissolves. On the other hand, despite whatever legal changes may occur, if the Nation exists as a political fact then under French constitutional law doctrine it alone would be the origin of sovereignty, and consequently have the competence to decide the scope of its competences. The continuation in fact of what is recognised in French constitutional law as the French nation means that the people of that Nation can reclaim sovereignty so long as the Nation continues. Therefore popular sovereignty is, in addition to the points above[49],

---

44 The history of the concept of national sovereignty has been discussed above in Chap. 16, "Sovereignty".

45 G. Cornu, *Vocabulaire Juridique* (Paris 1987; Presses Universitaires de France).

46 J. Bell, (1992) *op. cit.* above n.16, p. 23.

47 91–290 DC, 9 May 1991, Rec. p. 50; West *et al.* (1992) *op. cit.* above, n.39, pp. 194–195, "*Loi* on the status of Corsica".

48 A. West *et al.* (1992) *op. cit.* above, n.39, p. 155.

49 See paras. 16–6 *et seq.*

also inalienable in the sense that there remains an appeal to the concept of the Nation.

Summary

21–18 The substance of essential conditions for the exercise of national sovereignty is the substance of the interdependent foundations of French constitutional law. The interpretation of European Community law to restrict its direct confrontation in decided cases with these conditions places French constitutional law in stand-off conflict with European Community law's self-interpretation. Like the concept of national sovereignty to which they are related, they form a barrier to the deeper penetration of European Community law which cannot be removed without legal revolution under the Constitution of 1958 and with serious problems in the creation of another French constitution.

CONCLUSION

The necessity to come to grips with European Community law, particularly in the process of ratification of the Treaty on European Union, has given the *Conseil Constitutionnel* and the Parliament a chance to define the position of French constitutional law without the immediate threat of violent revolution or *coup d'état* and to affirm the status and practical importance of French constitutional law in the French legal order whose final end is the conservation of the natural and imprescriptible rights of man.[50] The authority of European Community law before French jurisdictions depends on French constitutional law, and French constitutional law's view of European Community law is restrictive. Although the separation of jurisdictions in France makes the reconstruction of French constitutional law and the identification of the risk of conflicts difficult, nonetheless such risks are present. The conflicts are certainly present. Given the institutional setup in France and the political respect due to the National Assembly, the way conflicts were identified, debated and preserved in the ratification of the Treaty on European Union may be the way in which conflicts between French constitutional law and European Community law come to a head, for example sparked by a future treaty or measure, and result in revolt or revolution if there is the political will to force the issue. The integration of European Community law into French constitutional law attacks the way in which the division of powers between the institutions of Government, and the rights and obligations of the individual in respect of the State, are balanced. French constitutional law differs from European Community law also in its legitimation. Further European Community law inroads into French constitutional law will call into question the legitimation of French constitutional law, and risk legal revolution if amendment to make way for these inroads is attempted, or if jurisdictions attempt such amendments by judicial *fiat*.

[50] Article 2, Declaration of 1789.

ANNEX TO PART III

22. THE *CONSEIL D'ÉTAT* AND THE *COUR DE CASSATION*

22–1 There is no procedural bridge between the *Conseil Constitutionnel* and the other administrative and judicial French jurisdictions: the *Conseil d'État*, the supreme court of the administrative law jurisdiction, and the *Cour de Cassation*, the supreme court of the civil and criminal law jurisdiction. Proposed constitutional amendments to that effect in 1990 and 1991[1] and in 1993[2] have not succeeded.[3] The policing of the supra-legislative but infra-constitutional status of international treaties is largely the business of these other jurisdictions. Unlike the *Conseil Constitutionnel*, these jurisdictions have the possibility of making an Article 177 (EC) reference to the Court of Justice which would make clear within a case European Community law's self-interpretation. There are three main points to be considered by this short exploration[4] of the jurisdiction of the *Conseil d'État* and *Cour de Cassation*:

1. the extent of their jurisdiction to decide on possible conflicts between European Community law and French constitutional law (including French constitutional law's interpretation of European Community law);
2. the likely result of such conflicts where they have such jurisdiction; and
3. the difference between their interpretation of the constitutional structures of European Community law and European Community law's own interpretation, which is also a further source of conflict (which might necessitate constitutional or legislative change and thereby the opportunity for conflicts between French constitutional law and European Community law and to come to the fore). In French constitutional law, Article 62 on the binding authority of the *Conseil Constitutionnel* binds these jurisdictions.[5]

An effort is made to limit the complexities of what follows to those necessary to establish the proposition that the extent of the enforcement of

---

1 J. Bell, *French Constitutional Law* (Oxford: Clarendon Press 1992) p. 56.

2 *La Semaine Juridique*, 31 March 1993, pp. 1–3.

3 See above, para. 14–6, "Control of *Lois*".

4 For an overview in English of the application of European Community law in French Courts see Roseren, "The Application of Community Law by French Courts from 1982 to 1993" (1994) Common Market Law Review 315.

5 This was also the view of the Senate quoted above in para. 18–2, "The *Conseil Constitutionnel* Interpretation of the European Community".

European Community law against all other rules depends on the compatibility of European Community law with French constitutional law. In considering the *Conseil d'État* and the *Cour de Cassation* it may be helpful to keep in mind the principal three cases in which a conflict may occur between French constitutional law and European Community law within the current constitutional and treaty framework.[6]

The *Conseil d'État*

22–2 The method adopted here is to analyse the *Conseil d'État's* jurisdiction in respect of three formal sources of French law: *lois, règlements,* and individual decisions. The types of conflict which might occur are case one and case two.[7] The authority of the *Conseil Constitutionnel* over the *Conseil d'État* has already been mentioned.[8]

Application of public international law treaties

22–3 Formerly, the *Conseil d'État* would not interpret a treaty at all, referring the question to the Minister for Foreign Affairs.[9] Now, where the interpretation is not clear, the *Conseil d'État* will still consult the Minister for Foreign Affairs but his interpretation will be only one element in its decision.[10] As

---

6 These are the same three cases which are highlighted in connection with the *Conseil Constitutionnel* in Chap. 14, namely:

(i) where a directly effective European Community measure or treaty is outside of the French constitutional law interpretation of European Community law and contrary to French constitutional law;

(ii) where a domestic measure (*loi, règlement,* or *décision*) would be unconstitutional if not based on a European Community law measure but that European Community law measure is unconstitutional in the sense of case (i);

(iii) where a domestic measure is taken not on the basis of European Community law but to promote a constitutional principle (for example, the right to property) which conflicts with an European Community law rule which is outside the French constitutional law interpretation of European Community law.

7 *ibid.*

8 See above, para. 14–3, "The *Conseil Constitutionnel* – Authority".

9 Decision of the *Conseil d'État, Jabin-Dudognon,* 1 July 1938, Rec. Lebon p. 607.

10 Decision of the *Conseil d'État, Groupe d'information et de soutien des travailleurs immigrés,* 29 June 1990, Rec. Lebon p. 171. Opinion of the Government Commissioner Abraham p. 173. This decision was a major reversal of long-standing jurisprudence. One of the reasons suggested by the Government Commissioner to ground a reversal was based on a decision of the *Conseil d'État* of the previous year, *Nicolo,* 20 October 1989, Rec. Lebon p. 190; (1989) *Revue française de droit administratif* 823, from which it resulted that the *Conseil d'État* could test the validity of a posterior *loi* against a treaty because Article 55 of the Constitution. Abraham considered that the applicability of a *loi* could not be dependent on the interpretation of a minister: *ibid.* p. 179.

Subsequently, an earlier decision of the *Conseil d'État* which declared itself bound by the interpretation given by the Minister for Foreign Affairs formed the basis for a

regards European Community law, the *Conseil d'État* can make Article 177 (EC) references but it often applies the *acte claire* doctrine. The *Conseil d'État* will also raise an issue of the interpretation of a treaty *ex officio*, considering it to be a point of public order.[11] In general, leaving aside the question of conflict, the *Conseil d'État* will interpret a treaty to determine if the contracting parties intended to confer directly rights to individuals.[12] While the *Conseil d'État* normally accords a decision of an international tribunal the authority of the judged action (*l'autorité de la chose jugée*), that is, binding force in respect of the dispute between the parties, the *Conseil d'État* has interpreted provisions of an international agreement contrary to the international tribunal charged with its interpretation, which is indicative of its retention of ultimate competence in interpretation.[13] The *Conseil d'État* does not distinguish its approach to European Community law from its approach to public international law treaties in general.[14]

Control of *Lois*

22–4 The *Conseil d'État* has no jurisdiction to test the constitutionality of *lois*[15] – that jurisdiction is the preserve of the *Conseil Constitutionnel*. This statement must be nuanced. First, the *Conseil d'État* subjects *ordonnances* made under

---

ruling by the European Court of Human Rights that France was in breach of the European Convention for the Protection of Human Rights and Fundamental Freedoms because the *Conseil d'État* had not behaved as a tribunal in the sense of Article 6(1) of the Convention. *Beaumartin v. France*, 24 November 1994, Series A, No. 296–B.

11 Decision of the *Conseil d'État, Donyon*, 23 February 1990, Rec. Lebon p. 773. This approach predated the judicial obligation and power conferred by European Community law established in Case C–312/93 *Peterbroeck v. Belgium* [1995] E.C.R. I–4599 and Joined Cases C 430 & 431/93 *Van Schijndel e.a. v. Stichting Pensioenfond voor Fysiotherapeuten*, [1995] E.C.R. I–4705. See above, Part II, "European Community Law".

12 Decision of the *Conseil d'État, Ministre du budget c. Valton e.a.*, 20 April 1984, Rec. Lebon p. 148, considering the European Social Charter, Article 4(4), and the right to reasonable warning before the termination of employment.

13 Decision of the *Conseil d'État, Subrini*, 11 July 1984, Rec. Lebon p. 259, interpreting Article 6(1) of the European Convention on Human Rights and Fundamental Freedoms – the right to a fair hearing.

14 Arguably, the evolution of its approach to public international law treaties has been prompted in part by coming to grips with European Community law.

15 The traditional doctrine in the *Conseil d'État* is that of the *loi écran* which prevents the *Conseil d'État* considering the constitutionality of an executive act providing that it is *intra vires* a *loi*, whose constitutionality will not be questioned. The extent to which the *Conseil d'État* applies this doctrine can be seen from its judgment in a proceeding for judicial review of the legality of the punishment of imprisonment provided by government decree for minor offences. Decision of the *Conseil d'État Confédération française democratique du travail et confédération générale du travail*, 3 February 1978, Rec. p. 47. A prior judgment of the *Conseil Constitutionnel* cast doubt on the constitutionality of providing for such a penalty by executive act (73–80 L, 28 November 1973, Rec. p. 45, (*Contraventions*)). Despite this, the *Conseil d'État* upheld the decree because it resulted from the legislative provisions of the Penal Code "whose constitutionality it did not fall to the *Conseil d'État* to judge in deciding a dispute".

Article 38 of the Constitution of 1958 to control for validity.[16] This is significant because *ordonnances* are measures which Parliament authorises the government to take, which measures normally belong in the domain of *loi* and after ratification by Parliament have the status of *lois* and thus can amend earlier *lois*. Thus before this decision *ordonnances* might have been thought to be protected from the *Conseil d'État's* scrutiny by the principle of the separation of powers. Secondly, and more importantly in this context, the *Conseil d'État* will apply European Community law over an incompatible *loi*. The question is whether the *Conseil d'État* can apply European Community law over an incompatible *loi* on the basis and to the extent required by European Community law, in particular, whether the *Conseil d'État* will apply the reservations of the *Conseil Constitutionnel* over an inconsistent European Community law in the event of a conflict between the French constitutional law perception of European Community law and European Community law's self-perception.

Initially the *Conseil d'État* refused to disapply a national *loi* which conflicted with European Community law on the grounds that it had no jurisdiction to consider the validity of a *loi* because of the principle of the separation of powers. Thus in its *Semoules* decision[17] the *Conseil d'État* held that a decision by the Minister for Agriculture authorising the importation of semolina from Algeria free from the levy required by a Regulation (EEC) was not in excess of his power, because the decision was pursuant to provisions of legislative status[18] which maintained a special customs regime for such imports.

The *Conseil d'État* had no difficulty in considering the compatibility of an anterior *loi* with a treaty.[19] It was not until *Nicolo*[20] that the *Conseil d'État* decided that Article 55 of the Constitution was intended to have the effect of binding it to test the compatibility of a posterior *loi* with a conflicting European Community rule. The *Conseil d'État's* judgment has the effect of ranking the effective application of Article 55 above the constitutional principle of the separation of powers as it had formerly interpreted it. More importantly in this context, it means that the *Conseil d'État* bases its application of European Community law on French constitutional law. This puts the *Conseil d'État* in

---

16 Decision of the *Conseil d'État, Fédération nationale des syndicats de police*, 24 November 1961, Rec. p. 658.

17 Decision of the *Conseil d'État, Syndicat Général des Fabricants des Semoules de France*, 1 March 1968, Rec. p. 149; (1968) 24 *Actualité Juridique, Droit Administratif* 238.

18 This decision was an application, in a case where European Community law was in issue, of the doctrine of *loi écran*, to the effect that once the *Conseil d'État* is satisfied that an executive measure is *intra vires* a *loi*, the measure will not be held invalid on the grounds of unconstitutionality.

19 Decision of the *Conseil d'État, Klaus Croissant*, 7 July 1978, Rec. p. 292, where the *Conseil d'État* applied the Franco-German Extradition Treaty of 29 November 1951 over a 1927 *loi*, on the grounds that the Treaty took precedence because it was later in time and Article 55 of the Constitution gave the Treaty an authority superior to *loi*.

20 Decision of the *Conseil d'État, Nicolo*, 20 October 1989, Rec. p. 190; (1989) *Revue française de droit administratif* 823.

conflict with European Community constitutional doctrine. The judgment suggests that the *Conseil d'État* will apply the French constitutional law interpretation of European Community law (including the *Conseil Constitutionnel's* reservations of interpretation) because if the *Conseil d'État* looks to its constitutional provisions in order to have the jurisdiction to apply European Community law even though European Community law gives that jurisdiction directly (according to European Community law), it will also look to French constitutional law for guidance on what has been and might be properly admitted via Article 54. (This is considered further below.)

Mr Nicolo sought to annul the electoral operations (administrative acts) which took place in France for the election of representatives to the European Parliament. The applicable *loi*, interpreted in the light of the relevant Articles in the Constitution, meant that the overseas territories and departments were necessarily included in the elections. The *Conseil d'État* considered the compatibility of these legislative provisions with Article 227(1) (EEC) which specified that the treaty applied to the "French Republic". Although no incompatibility was disclosed, this decision appears to mean that the *Conseil d'État* will suspend the application of a *loi* which is incompatible with a European Community rule. This *volte-face* occurred against the background of the *Cour de Cassation's* long-standing decision in *Sociétés des cafés Jacques Vabre* and a decision of the *Conseil Constitutionnel A.N., Val-d'Oise (fifth electoral ward)*.[21] In that decision the *Conseil Constitutionnel*, acting as electoral judge under Article 59, refused to consider the constitutionality of a provision of the Electoral Code, which would have been outside its Article 59 competence to review for regularity, but did consider the conformity of the provision with the European Convention on Human Rights and Fundamental Freedoms. When exercising its Article 59 jurisdiction the *Conseil Constitutionnel* is in the same position as an administrative court.[22] Also important was *Abortion loi*[23] where the *Conseil Constitutionnel* held that considering the compatibility of a *loi* with a treaty was not a control of the constitutionality of a *loi*.

The *Nicolo*[24] rationale appears to apply to any provision of European Community law. As Abraham pointed out, once the obstacle to the competence to suspend the application of a *loi* has been removed, as in *Nicolo*, then the origin of the European Community rule, treaty or secondary legislation, should not make any difference.[25] In *Boisdet* the *Conseil d'État* extended its

---

21 88–1082/1117, 21 October 1988, Rec. p. 183.

22 This proposition was asserted by Government Commissioner Frydman, in Decision of the *Conseil d'État, Nicolo*, 20 October 1989, Rec. p. 190, 196; (1989) *Revue française de droit administratif* 823.

23 74–54 DC, 15 January 1975, Rec. p. 19. See above, para. 14–7, "Article 61.2 – Constitutional Control of *Lois*".

24 Decision of the *Conseil d'État*, 20 October 1989, Rec. p. 190; (1989) *Revue française de droit administratif* 823.

25 R. Abraham, *Droit international, droit communautaire et droit français*, p. E.S. (1st ed., Paris: Hachette, 1989), with Update, 1990: see Update at p. 7.

acceptance of the primacy of European Community law to Regulations,[26] and in its two decisions *Rothmans* and *Philip Morris* (hereafter *the Cigarette Cases*) to Directives.[27] In these latter decisions the *Conseil d'État* relied on the Court of Justice's interpretation of the Directive at issue in its decisions declaring that France was in breach of its European Community law obligations in failing to implement the Directive. The Government Commissioner in *the Cigarette Cases*[28] referred to the decisions[29] of the *Conseil Constitutionnel* for authority that secondary European Community law has the same effect as treaties as far as Article 55 is concerned.

The structure of the *Conseil d'État's* jurisdiction, as it emerges from *Nicolo* and the doctrine of the *loi écran*, suggests that there may be an argument to the effect that, since the *Conseil d'État* will not judge the constitutionality of a *loi*, then *a fortiori* it will not judge the constitutionality of European Community law which has a superior authority under Article 55. But there are counter-arguments. First, the separation of powers does not apply to the testing of European Community law, because this is not an emanation of Parliament. Secondly, the thesis behind *Nicolo*, that Article 55 establishes a hierarchy of norms and cannot be rendered a dead letter,[30] logically extends to the application of the implicit hierarchy in Article 55 of Constitution over treaty. More generally, the *Nicolo* thesis extends to not leaving the Constitution as a whole as a dead letter, at least so far as the jurisdiction of the *Conseil Constitutionnel* has not been invoked. The *Conseil d'État* has to look to the Constitution (Article 55) to apply European Community law, which implies that it is bound by the constitutional limits thereon. This interpretation is supported by the rejection by the *Conseil d'État* of the European Community law on the direct effect of Directives.[31] Further, in the light of the *Conseil d'État's* protracted refusal until *Nicolo* to apply European Community law over a conflicting *loi*, it does not seem likely that it will readily apply European

---

26 Decision of the *Conseil d'État*, 24 September 1990, Rec. Lebon p. 251.

27 Laroque, in decisions of the *Conseil d'État*, *Société Arizona Tobacco Products and Philip Morris France*, 28 February 1992, Rec. Lebon p. 78, and *SA Rothmans International France* and *SA Philip Morris France*, 28 February 1992, Rec. Lebon p. 80.

28 *ibid.*, and in (1992) *Actualités Juridique, Droit Administratif* 210 at pp. 213–214.

29 77–90 DC, 30 December 1977, Rec. p. 44, *On the Finance Rectification* loi *of 1977* concerning a *loi* fixing the specifics for a regulation consequent upon a regularly ratified Council Decision (70–39 DC, 19 June 1970, Rec. p. 15, *Budgetary and Merger Treaties*) and upon the Treaty establishing the European Economic Community. As regards treaties in general, the *Conseil Constitutionnel* held in 86–207 DC, 25–6 June 1986, Rec. p. 61, *De-nationalisation loi*, that "there is no place to differentiate between the treaty itself and the international norm which is derived from it".

30 Conclusions of the Government Commissioner Frydman in decision of the *Conseil d'État*, *Nicolo*, 20 October 1989, Rec. p. 190, at p. 194.

31 See below, para. 22–6, "Conflict between the *Conseil d'État's* Interpretation of Direct Effect and Supremacy of European Community Law and European Community Law's Self-Interpretation".

Community law over the Constitution as well, which step would itself raise difficulties on the foundation of *Nicolo*.[32]

Control of *Règlements*

22–5 Because the *Conseil d'État* considers both the constitutionality and the European Community legality of a *règlement*, it will have plenty of scope to consider potential conflicts between French constitutional law and European Community law, for example if a *réglement* is made under the authority of European Community law but is contrary to the Constitution.

The review by the *Conseil d'État* of *règlements* was not blocked by the constitutional principle of separation of powers.[33] Both previous to and since the Constitution of 1958 rules made by the executive can be challenged against the delegating *loi*.[34] But the Constitution of 1958 granted the government residuary, sovereign rule-making power outside the domain of *loi* (or inside with parliamentary approval). The Constitution is thus the delegating statute and the *vires* of government rules fall to be tested against it, or not at all. In *Syndicat général des ingénieurs-conseil* the *Conseil d'État* held:

> "[T]he general principles of law (*droit*) which, resulting notably from the Preamble of the Constitution, bind all regulatory authority even in the absence of legislative provisions."[35]

The *Conseil d'État* has recognised also:

> "principles resulting from the Declaration of the Rights of Man and the Citizen and from the Preamble of the Constitution, in the absence of reservations formulated with respect to the said principles by the *loi*".[36]

The *Conseil d'État* will test the validity of a *règlement* also against a conflicting provision of European Community law. In a decision of 7 October 1988 the *Conseil d'État* awarded the Group of Opponents to Hunting a decree annulling the Minister of the Environment's *arrêté* allowing hunting of wildfowl in a period prohibited by a European Community directive.[37] The *Conseil d'État* stated:

---

[32] Abraham, albeit considering only the case of a posterior Constitutional *loi*, has stated "There is little likelihood that the administrative judge would apply in this case an identical reasoning to that in the *Nicolo* judgment, by setting aside the posterior constitutional provision." – *Droit international, droit communautaire et droit français* P.E.S., (1st ed., Paris: Hachette, 1989 with Update, 1990): Update p. 4.

[33] Decision of the *Conseil d'État, Syndicat général des ingénieurs-conseils*, 26 June 1959, Rec. p. 394; [1959] *Recueil Dalloz Sirey* 202.

[34] Opinion of the *Conseil d'État* of 6 February 1953, in West *et al.*, *The French Legal System: An Introduction* (London: Fourmat Publishing, 1992) p. 189.

[35] Decision of the *Conseil d'État*, 26 June 1959, Rec. p. 394; [1959] *Recueil Dalloz Sirey* 202.

[36] Decision of the *Conseil d'État, Syndicat des propriétaires de forêts de chênes – lièges d'Algérie*, 7 February 1958, Rec. Lebon p. 74. The decision predated the Constitution of 1958. The *Conseil d'État* allowed an expropriation *loi* to derogate from the principles contained in the Declaration of the Rights of Man and the Citizen and from the Preamble of the Constitution.

[37] Decision of the *Conseil d'État, Rassemblement des opposants à la chasse*, 7 October 1988, Rec. p. 335. See also the decision of the *Conseil d'État, Confédération nationale des Sociétés de*

"Considering that it clearly falls within the competence of the conditions of Article 189 of the Treaty of 25 March 1957 that the directives of the Council of the European Economic Community bind Member States 'as to the result to be achieved'; that if, to achieve the result which they [the Member States] define, the national authorities, who are bound to adapt the legislation and the regulations of the Member States to the directives, remain those solely competent to decide the form to be given to the execution of these directives and to fix themselves, under the control of national jurisdictions, the proper means to make them produce their effects in domestic law, these authorities cannot legally enact regulatory [*réglementaires*] provisions which would be contrary to the objectives defined by the directives which they concern."

Consequently the *Conseil d'État* will not apply a *règlement* which is contrary to the objectives of a directive. However this judgment raises a second point, based on the *Conseil d'État's* interpretation that Member States remain solely competent to decide the means of implementation. Although this interpretation is consistent with Article 189 (EC) it is in conflict with the interpretation of that Article in the case law of the Court of Justice which is trying to compensate for the lack of uniformity and efficacy caused by Member States' divergent implementation of European Community law.[38] This conflict is a subset of the conflict considered in the next paragraph.

Conflict between the Conseil d'État's Interpretation of Direct Effect and Supremacy of European Community Law and European Community Law's Self-Interpretation

22–6 The basis of the *Conseil d'État's* approach to European Community law cannot be fully discerned from its cryptic judgments. Government Commissioner Freydman, whose opinion the *Conseil d'État* followed in *Nicolo* when it reversed its former approach to European Community law, sets it out explicitly[39]. European Community law is public international law and is to be treated thus; its status in French law is a result of Article 55; conflict between the European Community treaty and another treaty is to be resolved by the application of the Vienna Convention; observance of all public international law is conditional upon satisfaction of the condition of reciprocity which may necessitate the seeking of the opinion of the Minister for Foreign Affairs; to base the control by the *Conseil d'État* of the compatibility of *lois* with European Community law on the specificity of the latter would be "the worst of solu-

---

protection des animaux, 28 September 1984, Rec. p. 481, and decision of the *Conseil d'État*, *Fédération française des sociétés de protection de la nature*, 7 December 1984, Rec. p. 410, where the *Conseil d'État* held that an administrative decree transposing an European Community directive could be quashed on the ground that it conflicted with the objectives of the Directive.

[38] See above, Part II, "European Community Law".

[39] Decision of the *Conseil d'État*, 20 October 1989, Rec. Lebon p. 190, 197–198; (1989) *Revue française de Droit Administratif* 823.

tions . . . without *any* legal basis."[40] The Government Commissioner referred expressly to the *Costa v. ENEL* and *Simmenthal* line of Court of Justice jurisprudence in order to state:

> "We do not believe that you can follow the Court in this praetorian jurisprudence which, in truth, appears to us at least criticisable. To do this, you would engage in effect in a logic, difficult to justify, of *supranationality*, to which moreover the Treaty of Rome does not expressly subscribe and which would lead – whatever may be thought about it on the political level – to the holding of this treaty definitively unconstitutional."[41]

To this grounding of the *Nicolo* decision is to be added the opinion of Government Commissioner Laroque in the *Cigarette* Cases which makes clear that Directives bind France because they are public international law, "without going so far as to confirm the conception of absolute primacy of Community law, *au besoin même supra-constitutionnelle*, as the Court of Justice of the European Communities understands it."[42]

As regards Directives in particular, the *Conseil d'État* has a view of European Community law and its effect in French law which conflicts with European Community law: only the national authorities who are competent to adopt French legislation and regulations are competent to decide the correct form and means whereby Directives are given effect in the internal legal order. Directives are not capable of giving rise to directly effective individual European Community law rights. This position, which was established in *Cohn Bendit*, has not been reversed. This important *Conseil d'État* judgment of 22 December 1978[43] arose out of an action by Cohn-Bendit, based on Directive 221/64 on the coordination of measures providing for a special regime for foreign nationals and justified by public order, health, or security, to annul the Minister of the Interior's decision not to withdraw an expulsion order. The *Conseil d'État* pointed out that no provision of Article 56 (EEC) allowed directly applicable measures to be taken in this domain. Whereas Directives bound the Member States to adapt legislative and reglementary measures to secure the European Community law objectives, the Member States alone were competent to decide how to do this. It followed that Cohn-Bendit could not attack the Minister's decision (an individual administrative act) on the basis of a European Community law right. He had to contest the legality of the reglementary measures taken pursuant to the Directive. In no circumstances could an individual administrative act be directly subordinated to a Directive. Because of this interpretation of Community law competence, the

---

40 *ibid.* p. 198 (original emphasis).

41 *ibid.* p. 198.

42 Decisions of the *Conseil d'État, Société Arizona Tobacco Products and Philip Morris France*, 28 February 1992, Rec. Lebon p. 80 and *SA Rothmans International France* and *SA Philip Morris France*, 28 February 1992, Rec. Lebon p. 78, (1992) *Actualités Juridique, Droit Administratif* 210 at p. 213.

43 Decision of the *Conseil d'État, Cohn-Bendit*, 22 December 1978, Rec. Lebon p. 524.

Conseil d'État annulled the decision of the Administrative Tribunal of Paris which had made Article 177 (EEC) references to the Court of Justice. The *Conseil d'État* has affirmed its reasoning in *Cohn-Bendit* in the later case of *Zakine*,[44] where it held that the provisions of a Directive could not be invoked to support an appeal against a decision of the Veterinary Council refusing enrollment.

The remedies of a plaintiff who wishes to assert rights under a Directive have improved. In *Alitalia*[45] the *Conseil d'État* held that not only could a national measure contrary to the objectives of a Directive be held invalid, but also individuals have a right to ask the administration to take measures necessary for the implementation of a directive such as the abrogation of conflicting rules. In the *Cigarette Cases* the *Conseil d'État* held both that individual ministerial decisions concerning the price of tobacco were illegal because the *décret* on which they were based was without legal basis because it was taken on the basis of a *loi* which was incompatible with a European Community Directive implementing Articles 30 and 37 (EEC), as interpreted by the Court of Justice, and also that the plaintiff has a right to damages against the state for non-implementation of its obligations.[46]

But an individual still has no right that is directly effective against the State under a Directive,[47] in flat contradiction to the jurisprudence of the Court of Justice on the effect of directives and indeed on the nature of Community law. In particular, the insistence that a plaintiff challenging an administrative decision in an individual case also challenges the validity of the *réglement*, *décret*, or *lois* grounding that decision also appears to be contrary to the decision of the Court of Justice in Case 36/75 *Rutili*, which established that the conformity of individual decisions with provisions of a directive should be examined.[48] For many actions, this division of interpretation between the *Conseil d'État* and the Court of Justice is an inconvenience which gives rise to an additional procedural step in French administrative law – a challenge to the provision authorising the decision must precede and challenge the decision itself. However this divergence is the result of profound disagreement over the depth of penetration of European Community law. Furthermore, it is not clear that this negative approach will always reach the same result on

---

44 Decision of the *Conseil d'État*, *Zakine*, 13 December 1985, Rec. Lebon p. 515. See also decision of the *Conseil d'État*, *Ministère de l'Agriculture c. Société coopérative agricole* "Coop 2000", 27 July 1990, Rec. Lebon p. 226.

45 Decision of the *Conseil d'État*, 3 February 1989, Rec. Lebon p. 44.

46 This right to damages rests on established principles of French administrative law and predates the development of the *Francovich* remedy by the Court of Justice – see above, Part II, para. 8–31, "Case 26/62 *Van Gend en Loos* – Directives".

47 The *Conseil d'État* reaffirmed its previous decision on this point in its decision *Compagnie Générale des Eaux*, 23 July 1993, Rec. p. 225; [1994] 2 C.M.L.R. 373 at 375–376.

48 [1975] E.C.R. 1219; F. Hervouet, "Politique Jurisprudentielle de la Cour de Justice et des Juridictions Nationales: Réception du Droit Communautaire par le Droit Interne" (1992) *Revue de Droit Public* 1257 at pp. 1287–1288.

the upholding of a directly applicable European Community law right: the right to ask the administration to implement a Directive is a different matter to the assertion and upholding by a national court of a directly effective right in that Directive.

The *Cour de Cassation*

22–7 The *lois* of 16 and 24 August 1790 on the organisation of the judiciary entrench the principle of the separation of powers: "Article 10: The tribunals cannot take directly or indirectly any part in the exercise of the legislative power, nor impede or suspend the execution of the enactments of the legislative body . . . ". This legislation was a reaction to what was widely perceived as the interference of the *parliaments* (courts) with reform legislation. These provisions are still in force; the *Cour de Cassation* will not consider a challenge to the validity of a *loi.*[49] In considering whether the decision of an inferior judge is tainted with a violation of law, the *Cour de Cassation* takes "*loi*" in its widest sense to include customs and general principles of law.[50]

However, reversing long-standing jurisprudence[51] and relying in part on French constitutional law expounded by the *Conseil Constitutionnel*, the *Cour de Cassation* has held that it will apply a European Community rule over a subsequent law in the case of *Administration des Douanes c. Sociétés "Cafés Jacques Vabre"*.[52] The importations of coffee from the Netherlands had been subject to a discriminatory higher consumption tax. In the main action the importer's customs broker sought restitution of the excess paid and the importer sought damages for losses arising from deprivation of funds. The *Cour de Cassation* held that Article 95 (EEC) had an authority superior to even posterior laws according to Article 55 (Constitution of 1958). A judge cannot declare the unconstitutionality of a *loi* but,

---

[49] 1 October 1985, *Bulletin de la Cour de Cassation* I.232.

[50] B. Rudden and L. Kahn-Freund, *op. cit.* above, n.17, p. 275.

[51] The *Cour de Cassation* had long given treaties a status equal to *loi*, and consequently given precedence to *loi* which postdated a treaty. This was known as the Matter doctrine, taking its name from an opinion of Advocate-General Matter which predated the Constitution of 1958 in *Cour de Cassation, Sanchez c. Consorts Gozland*, 22 December 1931, [1931] Rec. Sirey 257.

[52] *Cour de Cassation mixte*, 24 May 1975, [1975] Rec. Dalloz Sirey 505. The *Cour de Cassation* has long held itself competent to interpret treaties, as distinct from applying them over a subsequent *loi*, where the dispute has as its object private interests which *loi* has given the judicial power the duty of settling in case of dispute (*Cour de Cassation, Fox, Bumbury et consorts c. Duc de Richmond* [1839] Rec. Dalloz Sirey I.257) although there are differences between the chambers of the *Cour de Cassation* as to its precise role in this regard. The *Cour de Cassation* will still not apply international treaties which it interprets as creating obligations between States only. *Cour de Cassation, CPAM de Seine et Marne c. Ponnau*, 13 April 1994, (1994) *La Semaine Juridique* (Jurisprudence) S.2286 (concerning the United Nations Convention on the Rights of the Child).

"considering that the Treaty of 25 March 1957, which, in virtue of [Article 55] of the Constitution, has an authority superior to *lois*, institutes its own juridical order integrated into those of the Member States; that in reason of this specificity, the juridical order which it has created is directly applicable to nationals of these States and binds their jurisdictions".

The *Cour de Cassation* held that the Court of Appeal had properly decided to apply Article 95 (EEC) in the instant case to the exclusion of the Customs Code.

Although the reasoning of the *Cour de Cassation* is enigmatic, the background to the holding can be seen in the lengthy opinion of *Procureur générale* Touffait, which is based on two distinct grounds. First, on national law, the *Procureur générale* drew attention to the thesis of the Government Commissioner (Mme Questiaux) in the *Conseil d'État* case *Syndicat général des Fabricants des Semoules de France*[53] that to consider the conformity of a *loi* with a Treaty involved a consideration of its constitutionality (which would be anathema to the *Cour de Cassation*). But the *Procureur générale* drew support from the later decision of the *Conseil Constitutionnel Abortion loi*[54] where the *Conseil Constitutionnel* held that, because Article 61 gave it only power to consider the constitutionality of *lois*, it could not control the compatibility of *lois* with treaties; the provisions of Article 55 establishing the principle of superior authority of treaties to *lois* did not imply that the *Conseil Constitutionnel* was the jurisdiction to ensure respect for that principle.[55] The *Procureur générale* concluded from this that the principle must be observed by other jurisdictions to whom the problem is posed under penalty of "*déni de justice*". If the *Conseil Constitutionnel* does not consider the application of Article 55 to be judicial review of constitutionality, then the *Cour de Cassation* will not be reproached for applying it.

Secondly, the *Procureur générale* based his conclusions on European Community law, which he urged the *Cour de Cassation* to adopt as the sole basis for its judgment.[56] He adopted the reasoning of the Court of Justice in *Costa v. ENEL* that the direct effect and supremacy of European Community law resulted from the nature of the legal order instituted by the Treaty. The *Procureur générale* considered that to base the status of European Community law on national law, although it might work in French law, would invite discrepancies between Member States.[57] The *Procureur générale* concluded that the transfer by the Member States from their own internal legal order to the

---

53 Decision of the *Conseil d'État*, 1 March 1968, Rec. Lebon p. 149; (1968) 24 *Actualité Juridique, Droit Administratif* 238.

54 74–54 DC, 15 January 1975, Rec. p. 19.

55 See above, paras. 14–6 to14–9, "Control of *Lois*".

56 [1975] Rec. Dalloz Sirey 497 at 504.

57 It is illustrative of how far the *Procureur générale* was willing to base his reasoning and authority on European Community law that he considered, as a ground for a result in the French legal order, what the result might be in the legal orders of other Member States.

Community legal order meant a definitive limitation of sovereign rights against which a unilateral ulterior act, incompatible with the notion of Community could not be asserted. The *Cour de Cassation* did not go as far as the *Procureur générale* urged, and instead based its conclusion on both French constitutional law and European Community law grounds. Indeed the decision is a fudge, not just because of its dual basis but because of an important distinction made in the language of the decision: the wording indicates that it is the Treaty itself which creates a juridical order of such a nature that it is integrated into domestic orders. The reference to Article 55 applies only to superiority. The legal basis for direct effect differs from the legal basis for supremacy, a conclusion which is at variance both with European Community law and French constitutional law as expounded by the *Conseil Constitutionnel.* It is also at variance with the approach of the *Conseil d'État* in *Nicolo* where the specificity of European Community law was not relied on.[58]

In a later case the *Cour de Cassation* appears to rely on the European Community law basis alone.[59] This approach was reinforced in the case of *The Republic v. Weckerle.*[60] The appellant managing director challenged his convictions for breach of the Driving Hours Regulation on the ground, *inter alia,* that the accumulation of 112 summary offences was contrary to the principle of proportionality protected in European Community law. The *Cour de Cassation* was willing to consider the application of this principle, which is not unusual given that they were applying European Community law, but held that the principle was satisfied because the sanctions were a deterrent (rather confusingly, the *Cour de Cassation* also relied on the fact that the sanctions were in line with those applicable to breaches of national rules). The *Cour de Cassation* refused to make an Article 177 (EEC) reference on the questions, presumably in application of the Case 283/81 *CILFIT*[61] doctrine. As to how its consideration of the principle of proportionality was grounded, the *Cour de Cassation* appeared to rely directly on the Treaty establishing the European Economic Community:

> "the system of national sanctions applicable to breaches of Community rules concerning the working conditions in road transport is not incompatible with the principle of proportionality introduced by the EEC Treaty."[62]

---

58 See above, para. 22–6. The Government Commissioner stated that such an approach would be "the worst of solutions . . . without any legal basis". Decision of the *Conseil d'État,* 20 October 1989, Rec. Lebon p. 190, pp. 197–198.

59 *Cour de Cassation* (Third Civil Chamber), *Von Kempis v. Epoux Geldof,* 15 December 1975, [1976] Rec. Dalloz Sirey 33. Without referring to the Constitution, the *Cour de Cassation* relied on Article 52 (EEC),

> "which is directly applicable to nationals of the Member States of the EEC and which binds their jurisdictions, prohibits all restrictions on the Freedom of Establishment of these nationals in France and that, as a result, the provisions of French internal law which obliges those who wish to engage in agricultural business in France to get administrative authorisation have ceased to be applicable."

60 *Cour de Cassation* (Criminal Chamber), 15 February 1994, [1995] 1 C.M.L.R. 49.

61 [1982] E.C.R. 3415.

62 Above, n.60 at 52.

Given the refusal of the *Cour de Cassation* to consider constitutional questions and its reasoning which is friendlier to the Court of Justice than other French jurisdictions,[63] there seems to be some doubt as to whether the ordinary courts, which make Article 177 (EC) references to the Court of Justice, will try to keep European Community law within the *Conseil Constitutionnel's* interpretation.[64] However it appears illogical for the *Cour de Cassation* to apply Article 55 as a result of decisions of the *Conseil Constitutionnel*, and at the same time refuse to apply the *Conseil Constitutionnel's* interpretation of the treaties which have authority superior to *loi* by virtue of this Article, which interpretation binds all jurisdictions by virtue of Article 62.

To this reasoning must be added Article 66 of the Constitution which provides:

> "No one may be arbitrarily detained. The judicial authority, guardian of individual liberty, assures the respect of this principle in the conditions provided by *loi.*"

Further, the Constitutional *loi* of 3 June 1958 provides:

> "Sole article . . . 4. The judicial authority must remain independent in order to be in a position to assure the respect of essential liberties such as are defined by the Preamble of the Constitution of 1946 and by the Declaration of the Rights of Man and Citizen to which it refers."

These direct constitutional obligations can be considered in the light of the *Conseil Constitutionnel's* reference in *TEU No. 1*[65] to national jurisdictions ruling on the rights and liberties of citizens in the framework of their respective competences. The combination of these Articles and this decision results in the imposition of a constitutional obligation on the *Cour de Cassation* to be faithful to French constitutional law's interpretation of the limits of European Community law, *a fortiori* in respect of the guarantee of the fundamental rights and freedoms of citizens. Finally, the lower courts may encourage, almost force, the *Cour de Cassation* to change its mind: "There is no hierarchy in the

---

63 This is in some way remarkable because the forerunner of the present *Cour de Cassation* was set up by decree in 1790 after the Revolution to keep the ordinary courts within the *loi.* Indeed it was proposed to call it the *Conseil national pour la conservation des lois* – M. Cappelletti and W. Cohen, *Comparative Constitutional Law: cases and materials* (Indianopolis Bobbs-Merril Company, 1979).

64 The *Cour d'Appel de Paris*, in *Johansson v. Institut National de la Propriété Industrielle*, 16 December 1992, [1994] 1 C.M.L.R. 269 at 271, held:

> "It is not for the national court to assess the legality or the appropriateness of a Community measure, but only to apply it if it is clear, interpret it if it is not, or seek an interpretation from the European Court of Justice if the question is one of last instance or if it considers it necessary to request an interpretation. Therefore, as matters stand, whether the measure affects acquired rights is irrelevant."

On the point of acquired rights, the Court of Appeal held that the Regulation should be interpreted as protecting them.

65 92–308 DC, 9 April 1992, Rec. p. 55; (1992) 28 *Recueil Trimestrielle du Droit Européen* 418, *TEU No. 1.*

interpretation of texts since, finally, the resistance of the Courts of Appeal succeeds in making the supreme jurisdiction give way".[66]

Conclusion

22–8 Both the administrative and judicial jurisdictions have scope to decide on conflicts between European Community law and French constitutional law. There have been instances of conflicts in the past and the possibilities for conflicts continue. The interpretation of European Community law by these jurisdictions does not correspond to European Community law's interpretation and is controlled by French constitutional law. In short, although the *Cour de Cassation,* relative to the *Conseil d'État* and the *Conseil Constitutionnel,* has gone further down the road to the European Community law view, it is bound both by Article 62 of the Constitution and by its duty to protect the French constitutional law conception of fundamental rights.

[66] Perrot, *Institutions Judiciares* quoted in B. Rudden and L. Kahn-Freund, *op. cit.* above, n.17, at p. 277.

PART IV

IRISH CONSTITUTIONAL LAW

INTRODUCTION

Irish law is an important national legal order to study in its constitutional relationship to European Community law for several reasons. First, the importance of natural law in the legitimation of Irish constitutional law is more pronounced than in French constitutional law[1] and is in stark contrast to European Community law. Secondly, Irish law has been constitutionalised, in the sense that constitutional law is not merely a special interest in the general field of public law but permeates the legal order to a very high degree. A destabilisation of Irish constitutional law therefore would have very far-reaching effects in the legal order. Thirdly, and standing in a relation of both part cause and part effect with the second reason, the jurisdictional rules for the application of Irish constitutional law are very generous, so conflicts can come before courts easily. Fourthly, there has not been much systematic work in this area,[2] and none with the same focus.

This part establishes, on the basis of a critical enquiry into the legitimation of Irish constitutional law and Irish constitutional law's perspective of the place of European Community law in the national legal order, the following propositions:

1. Irish constitutional law has a restricted view of the present and future claims of European Community law. The Irish constitutional law description of

---

1 Irish constitutional law in this work means Irish constitutional law which started with the Constitution of 1937. There may be all sorts of past and future legal orders based on what one was or will be able to call Irish constitutional law. This description is important to bear in mind, particularly when one considers the question of amendability. See below, Chap. 29.

2 There are some notable exceptions: the European University Institute LL.M. dissertation of M. Reid, published as *The Impact of European Community Law on Irish Constitutional Law* (Dublin: Irish Centre for European Law, 1991); B. McMahon and F. Murphy, *European Community Law in Ireland* (Dublin: Butterworths, 1989) p. 282. Of particular note is the recent book by G. Hogan and A. Whelan, *Ireland and the European Union: Constitutional and Legislative Texts and Commentary* (London: Sweet & Maxwell, 1995). The authors take issue with statements in this Ph.D. on several occasions (particularly in their Chapters 1 and 8). Their subtle commentary ranges across a host of issues and rejoinder is made here only where important to this work.

European Community law conflicts with European Community law's self-description.

2. The fundamental commitments of Irish constitutional law are likely to come into conflict with European Community law.

3. Further European Community law inroads into Irish constitutional law may call into question both the coherence of Irish constitutional law and the legitimation of Irish law.

4. The possibility of revision of Irish constitutional law to resolve these conflicts is limited.

The starting point of this Part is a reconstruction of Irish constitutional law doctrine by drawing mainly on the primary sources of the text of the Constitution and on decisions of the courts interpreting the Constitution since their authority is guaranteed by the Constitution (Article 26.3.1).

The reconstruction and exposition which occupies Chapters 23 to 25 is to some degree abstract. But it is important to stress that this is a lawyer's exercise, by which is meant an attempt to organise the law as is, that is, from a point of view internal to Irish constitutional law. The legal foundations considered, being at the root of the national legal structure, are in that sense more concrete than minutiae.[3]

---

3 *e.g.* the District Court application of Council Regulation 1436/70 of 20 July 1970, as interpreted in Case 133/83 *R. v. Thomas Scott & Sons Bakers Ltd* [1984] E.C.R. 2863 in the context of the District Court's interpretation and application of the European Communities (Road Transport) (Recording Equipment) Regulations made thereunder, to a Green-Isle frozen foods speculative sales and delivery man driving in a specialised refrigerated van in North County Dublin (within the Dublin Metropolitan District) which fell within the context of a "National Transport Operation" – *Garda Devine v. Fitzgerald*, District Justice Delap, 3 December 1985, [1986] I.L.T.R. 228.

23. LEGITIMATION OF IRISH CONSTITUTIONAL LAW

23–1 Irish Constitutional law is legitimated not only or even ultimately by reference to popular sovereignty but also by reference to Irish constitutional law's version of secular natural law, which is influenced by scholastic philosophy. Whereas the people are ultimately sovereign as the constituent authority wherein power and the right to decide ultimately resides, Irish constitutional natural law is a control on the lawful effects of every act purporting to be law. The legitimation of Irish constitutional natural law has not been systematically expounded.

Natural Law based on Reason: Reconstructing the Doctrine

A Fundamental Conflict

23–2 A former Chief Justice and later judge of the Court of Justice, O'Higgins has stated:

> "it is certain that in relation to a developing jurisprudence on human rights fears will be raised as to a possible conflict between a philosophy of legal positivism and the concept of natural rights founded on natural law."[1]

O'Higgins refers later to "the legal positivism of the Convention on Human Rights and the problems which its acceptance by the Court of Justice as a code would create in relation to the Constitution of some Member States including Ireland"[2]:

> "Irish constitutional jurisprudence owes much to the frank recognition that many of these rights do not derive from the fact that they are written down in the basic law of the State but rather from the very nature of man and from the natural law. What is important in relation to such rights, truly described as fundamental, is that they are confirmed and protected, but not created, by the Constitution . . . [O'Higgins goes over Articles 40–43] There are therefore rights recognised by the Constitution of Ireland which are acknowledged

---

1 Preface to M. Reid, *The Impact of European Community Law on Irish Constitutional Law*, (Dublin: Irish Centre for European Law, 1991) p. 1. See also D. Costello, "Natural Law, the Constitution, and the Courts" *Essays in Memory of Alexis Fitzgerald* in P. Lynch and J. Meenan, (Dublin: Incorporated Law Society of Ireland, 1987) p. 109: "it has more than once been judicially observed that the Constitution rejects legal positivism as a basis for the protection of fundamental rights and suggests instead a theory of natural law from which those rights can be derived. There are strong arguments to support that conclusion."

2 M. Reid (1991) *op. cit.*, p. 2.

> as being antecedent both to it and to all positive law and, as part of a higher law, immune from change and inviolable".[3]

The conflict between European Community law and Irish constitutional law may present therefore an even greater problem than a "constitutional gap" which Ireland can close by constitutional referendum, since for example certain rights are "immune from change and inviolable"[4]: Murphy and McMahon, who consider in contrast to this author that Ireland has unambiguously accepted the legal obligations of membership,[5] acknowledge the particular difficulty posed by the protection of fundamental rights:

> "Ireland also, it seems, fully embraces the doctrine of the 'supremacy of Community law' [as well as direct applicability]. This last statement, however, may pose some theoretical difficulties, especially in relation to fundamental rights provisions of the Constitution, which, according to the Constitution, are in some cases 'antecedent to positive law'. It is suggested that a fundamental right 'antecedent to positive law' in Irish constitutional theory cannot implicitly be overridden by a constitutional amendment (for example the Third Amendment [considered below]). . . ".[6]

The importance of natural law legitimation to Irish constitutional law and to Irish law as a whole runs further than this acknowledgement and is not limited to those rights which positive constitutional law states to be anterior to positive law.

So far in practice this does not often affect the application of the doctrine of supremacy of European Community law in the courts. Nor in purely domestic situations does this legitimation affect in the usual course of business the application of the acts of the *Oireachtas* as the people's representatives and law-making authority and the delegated rules and regulations made thereunder. No judge sets off on a complete legitimation of a rule prohibiting double-parking every time a person is tried for a parking offence. A judge will need to decide very few cases on the basis of Irish constitutional law natural law. However, this legitimation has importance in this study for the reconstruction of Irish constitutional law and the exposition of what is at stake, for the likelihood of conflicts with European Community law and the restrictions on amendment.

Irish constitutional natural law is a test of the validity in the jurisdiction of any positive law applying in the jurisdiction. European Community law is not immune from this test, nor does Article 29.4.5 immunise it.

---

3 T.F. O'Higgins, "The Constitution and the Communities – Scope for Stress?" in O'Reilly (ed.), *Human Rights and Constitutional Law: Essays in Honour of Brian Walsh* (1992) pp. 234–235.

4 See below, para. 29–5, "Limits to Amendment – Self Amendment".

5 See below, Chap. 27, "European Community Law in Irish Constitutional Law".

6 B. McMahon, and F. Murphy, *European Community Law in Ireland* (1989) p. 276.

The Text of the Constitution

23–3 Irish constitutional natural law is a source of law recognised in the text of the Constitution. A textual interpretation, or at most a harmonious interpretation, of the Constitution discloses this. Irish constitutional natural law itself is not an interpretive approach but rather a source which contains its own principles of determination of specific rules, such as the protection of a particular right. In the text of the Constitution itself the natural law basis of Irish constitutional law is most clearly seen from the provisions on fundamental rights, from the provision on sovereignty, and from the Preamble. These establish three propositions: first, that man has rights by virtue of his rational nature and human personality[7]; secondly, that the family has rights as the fundamental unit group of society but also as a moral institution; thirdly, that these rights are antecedent to positive law and inalienable – the Constitution does not create these rights but acknowledges them. For example, Article 40.1. – "All citizens shall, as human persons, be held equal before the law"; Article 41.1.1 – "The State recognises the Family as the natural primary and fundamental unit group of Society, and as a moral institution possessing inalienable and imprescriptible rights, antecedent and superior to all positive law"; Article 42.1 – "The State acknowledges that the primary and natural educator of the child is the Family and guarantees to respect the inalienable right and duty of parents to provide . . . for the . . . education of their children"; Article 43.1.1 – "The State acknowledges that man, in virtue of his rational being, has the natural right, antecedent to positive law, to the private ownership of external goods." In the exceptional cases where parents fail for physical or moral reasons in their duty towards their children, Article 41.5 provides that the State as guardian of the common good shall take their place, "but always with due regard for the natural and imprescriptible rights of the child."

Some Articles protecting fundamental rights do not refer to any higher law basis. It has been pointed out by Costello J. that this absence of reference (for example in Article 40.3.1 or 40.4.1) does not alter the basis of fundamental rights protection:

> "the Constitution does not *confer* on citizens of the State fundamental rights but recognises their existence as being antecedent and superior to positive law and protects them accordingly. . . .
>
> It does not follow, therefore, that because the Constitution ascribes to only some human rights, characteristics of inalienability and imprescriptibility, the Constitution should be construed as implying that other fundamental human rights lack these qualities, or that only those rights are superior to positive law which are so expressly described in the Constitution."[8]

---

7 *per* Henchy J. in *McGee v. Attorney General* [1974] I.R. 284 at 325.
8 *Murray v. Ireland* [1985] I.R. 532 at 538–539.

Jurisprudence

23–4 Two post-1937 decisions,[9] one in 1939 and one in 1965, pointed to "a 'higher law' approach" behind the text of the Constitution.[10] Later, in *State (Nicolaou) v. An Bord Uchtála,*[11] the Supreme Court held against the claim that the father of a child born out of wedlock had an unenumerated "natural right" to have a say in the child's upbringing stating that it "had not been satisfied that any such right has ever been recognised as part of the natural law". The first really trenchant statement of natural law doctrine under the Constitution of 1937 was made in the context of a constitutional attack on a statute which penalised the importation of contraceptives. The provisions of the statute were struck down as unconstitutional by a majority of 4:1 in the Supreme Court, with Walsh J. (in the majority) stating:

> "Articles 41, 42 and 43 emphatically reject the theory that there are no rights without laws, no rights contrary to the law and no rights anterior to the law. They indicate that justice is placed above the law and acknowledge that natural rights, or human rights, are not created by law but that the Constitution confirms their existence and gives them protection . . . [later in the judgment] In this country it falls finally upon the judges to interpret the Constitution and in doing so to determine, where necessary the rights which are superior or antecedent to positive law, or which are imprescriptible or inalienable . . . The very structure and content of the Articles dealing with fundamental rights clearly indicate that justice is not subordinate to the law. In particular, the terms of Article 40.3 expressly subordinate the law to justice."[12]

Other judicial pronouncements are considered in the context of the chapters below.[13] A few other general examples may be given here. The impor-

---

9 Natural law was referred to most notably before the enactment of the Constitution in the minority judgment of Kennedy C.J. in *State (Ryan) v. Lennon* [1935] I.R. 170.

10 *State (Burke) v. Lennon* [1940] I.R. 136 (Gavan Duffy J., High Court); *Ryan v. Attorney General* [1965] I.R. 294 (Kenny J., High Court). See also J.M. Kelly , *The Irish Constitution* (2nd ed., University College Dublin Press, 1984) at pp. 430–432. *Cf.* J.M. Kelly, *Fundamental Rights in Irish Law and the Constitution* (Dublin: Allen Figgis, 1961) p. 44: "as a guide for judges no less than for legislation (and private citizens) natural law affords hardly anything more than the precept of loving justice and hating iniquity, of avoiding evil and doing good"; and pp. 69–73 of *ibid.* (2nd ed., Dublin: Allen Figgis, 1967) where Kelly replies to critics of his exposition in the first edition. However Kelly later changed his mind on the uncertainty caused by the judicial development of fundamental rights, which uncertainty was a major plank in his argument against the value of a natural law based fundamental rights jurisprudence: "It seemed to me that [*Ryan v. A.G.'s*] result was uncertainty together with a concealed encroachment by the Courts on the well-intentioned discretion of the *Oireachtas.* In retrospect I think I took the wrong side." – Book Review of *Privacy and the Law.* The reasoning in *Ryan* has been criticised by G. Quinn, "Reflections on the Legitimacy of Judicial Activism in the Field of Constitutional Law" (1991) Winter *Dlí* 29 at pp. 34–36 on the grounds that the criteria chosen by Kenny J. conflict.

11 [1966] I.R. 567.

12 *McGee v. Attorney General* [1974] I.R. 284..

13 Of recent interest is the decision *Re Article 26 and the Regulation of Information (Services Outside the State for Termination of Pregnancies) Bill, 1995* [1995] 1 I.R. 1 considered below

tant case of *McGee* was followed by a series of cases which have entrenched this judicial acceptance of natural law legitimation as the basis of Irish constitutional law. In *Healy*[14] Gannon J., having cited what Walsh J. said in *McGee*, referred to "rights which are anterior to and do not merely derive from the Constitution . . . ". In *Murphy v. P.M.P.A. Insurance Co*[15] Doyle J. held that a statutory obligation to furnish information pursuant to a contract *uberrimae fidei* (in this case an insurance contract) to a third party was "an encroachment to a greater or lesser degree on natural liberty or natural rights". The Judge stated:

> "The encroachment on what are claimed to be natural rights in this case . . . is not such as stems from the Articles of the Constitution dealing with the rights of the individual. At one time it was thought that the Constitution had provided a comprehensive code of personal rights and that all pre-existing common law personal or natural rights had been subsumed in it. It is now, however, well established that certain natural and personal rights may exist side by side with the Constitution although not specifically referred to or comprehended in the Articles of the Constitution which give personal guarantees."[16]

The phrase "side by side" notably detaches Irish constitutional law natural law rights from the text of the Constitution, at least from the specifics of provisions. In *G. v. An Bord Uchtála*[17] Walsh J. declared that "[t]he child's natural rights spring primarily from the natural right of every individual to life, to be reared and educated, to liberty, to work, to rest and recreation, to the practice of religion, and to follow his or her conscience". In *Northants County Council v. A.B.F.*[18] Hamilton J. (now Chief Justice) referred to "rights recognised by [the Constitution] and the courts created under it as antecedent and superior to all positive law: they are not so recognised by the law or the courts of the jurisdiction [England] to which it is sought to have the infant returned."

The Role of Reason

23–5 It is very important to clarify what is meant by "natural law". The use by judges of phrases such as "natural law" or "nature" does not mean that

---

in para. 23–9 "Fundamental Rights Based on the Judge's Ideas of the Changing Concepts of Prudence, Justice and Charity".

14 *The State (Healy) v. Donoghue* [1976] I.R. 325.

15 [1978] I.L.R.M. 725, noted in Hogan and Whyte, *Kelly: The Irish Constitution, Supplement to Second Edition* (2nd ed., 1988) and in Hogan and Whyte, *Kelly, The Irish Constitution*, (3rd ed., 1994).

16 See also N. McCarthy: "There is now a penumbra of unenumerated rights derived from man's rational being and from time to time discerned by the courts . . . The catalogue remains open." – "Observations on the Protection of Fundamental Rights in the Irish Constitution" in *Constitutional Adjudication in European Community and National Law: Essays for the Hon. Mr. Justice T.F. O'Higgins* (Curtin and O'Keeffe ed., 1992) p. 182.

17 [1980] I.R. 32.

18 [1982] I.L.R.M. 164.

they are accepting the same legitimation of their decisions.[19] The clarification sought here is that of the meaning of natural law in Irish constitutional law, with a view to its importance in the integration of European Community law into Irish constitutional law. The broader questions on natural law, even those raised in the Irish constitutional law context,[20] are only incidentally engaged, if at all.

Walsh J., former senior ordinary member of the Supreme Court and now judge at the European Court of Human Rights, has set out in simple terms the historical and philosophical basis of this legitimation in Irish constitutional law in the foreword to the first edition of *Casey's Constitutional Law in Ireland*[21]:

> "The Constitution of Ireland was born 50 years ago on the edge of a Europe which was busily preparing for the most destructive war in history – one in which Ireland did not become a participant. It was a Europe where the concept of human or natural rights counted for little. Large parts of Europe were governed in accordance with Fascist ideology or Marxist ideology, in which human rights counted for little, if anything. In most of the rest of Europe the doctrine or philosophy of legal positivism reigned supreme. That doctrine did not even admit the existence of natural rights . . . This is the doctrine that man possesses certain rights because he is man and that these rights are not the gift of any positive law or of any state and that they are inalienable rights . . . The sources were to be found in Greek philosophy and later in Roman philosophy. It was adopted and developed by Christian philosophy which came to dominate the thinking on this subject in most of Europe through what became known as Scholastic philosophy . . . The Irish Constitution's espousal of the doctrine of natural rights is traceable to the influence of Scholastic philosophy and, in effect, acknowledges natural law as the basis of this philosophy. In the Europe of 50 years ago it was quite startling not only to propound such ideas in a basic law but also to give these moral concepts the force of law by imposing upon the State the obligation to guarantee and to defend these rights. Yet in the decades after the war the notion of natural rights or human rights was to dominate European legal thinking."[22]

---

19 This appears to be assumed by Hogan, "Unenumerated Personal Rights: *Ryan's* Case Re-evaluated" (1990–1992) XXV–XXVII *Irish Jurist* 95 at p. 109 where a nineteenth-century decision, certain to cause outrage if handed down now, is juxtaposed for rhetorical effect with Walsh J.'s decision in *McGee.*

20 D.M. Clarke "The Role of Natural Law in Irish Constitutional Law" (1982) XVII *Irish Jurist* 187 at p. 188.

21 Reproduced in the 2nd ed., (London: Sweet & Maxwell, 1992).

22 See also B. Walsh, "Reflections on the Effects of Membership of the European Communities in Irish Law" (1987) in C.-D. Ehlerman *et. al., Du droit international au droit de l'intégration, Liber Amicorum Pierre Pescatore*; (Baden-Baden: Nomos, 1987) p. 817. If the European Convention on Human Rights and Fundamental Freedoms became part of national law there would be "serious conflicts with the philosophy underlying the moral concepts which are given force of law in the human rights provisions of the Constitution. Irish constitutional jurisprudence on these provisions is firmly rooted in the natural law or natural rights character of these constitutionally guaranteed rights and totally rejects the philosophy of legal positivism."

It is suggested by the authorities examined in this thesis so far that the natural law theory on which Irish constitutional law rests is not a slave to any particular set of mores, cultural outlook, religious belief, popular demonstration, demagoguery, or mass media-expressed values of the moment. It is concerned with the application of the permanently relevant principles of practical reason to the fundamental commitments of Irish constitutional law which appear to the rational human mind upon reflection to be self-evidently good – such as the commitments Walsh J. stated in the form of rights in *G. v. An Bord Uchtála*[23]: life, knowledge, liberty, work, play, religion and individual moral autonomy. As O'Hanlon J. of the High Court, former Professor of Criminal and Constitutional Law in University College Dublin and former President of the Law Reform Commission, put it:

> "[Natural law] is not contingent on contemporary *mores* or any particular culture, because it resides in the innermost common denominator of all humankind through all generations, that is, human reason. It is the capacity of human reason to identify basic human goods in an essentially consistent manner which makes possible a meaningful discourse on ethics, law and philosophy. It is this which links, for example, a contemporary Irish jurist with the philosophers of ancient Greece and Rome."[24]

Costello P. has stated the basis of Irish constitutional natural law very clearly[25]:

> "The classical exposition of natural law in the Christian tradition is that contained in the writings of Thomas Aquinas and his theory of law is obviously the most relevant for the purpose of considering the role of natural law in the Irish Constitution.
>
> . . .
>
> The key element in his theory is the role of reason
>
> . . .
>
> [Natural law] is in fact nothing more than a body of precepts established by reason
>
> . . .
>
> . . . Aquinas did not explicitly develop a theory of 'natural' rights which can be derived from the precepts which are established by the practical reason. But this can easily be done. If, for example, it is a precept of natural law that human life is to be preserved then the right to life can be shown to be derived from natural law . . . Human positive law must not go contrary to the natural law. If it does it is a 'perversion' of the law. It would follow then that the basic rights which are derived from the precepts of the natural law obtain their validity from that law and not from human positive law, and that they are superior to it.
>
> . . .

---

23 [1980] I.R. 32 at 69.

24 R. O'Hanlon, "Natural Rights and the Irish Constitution" (1993) 11 *Irish Law Times* 8.

25 D. Costello (1987) *op cit.* above, n.2, pp. 110–113.

> If it can be correctly inferred that the Constitution has adopted a theory of law which derives fundamental rights from natural law, it is not the function of judges to debate the merits of the theory."

One of the consequences of Irish constitutional law's reliance on the role of reason rather than authority in the development and application of Irish constitutional law is that the Courts cannot be bound by the doctrine of precedent if they decide that an earlier decision based on natural law was erroneous.[26] The courts' view of what constitutes the applicable Irish constitutional natural law in a given case may change.[27]

The application of reason, or more exactly practical reason, to the values, in the sense of general basic goods, to which the Constitution is fundamentally committed, is how the content of Irish constitutional natural law is determined (what may be referred to loosely as "interpreted"). Irish constitutional natural law carries within itself this method of determination ("interpretation") as a fundamental commitment.

Natural Law based on Theology/Religion: Debunking the Myth

23–6 "These rights [natural rights protected in Irish constitutional law] are sometimes criticised because it is alleged that they smack of a uniquely Catholic concept of fundamental rights being based upon natural law or natural rights. This stems from the mistaken assumption that natural law or natural rights are uniquely Catholic, which of course they are not. As Doctor Forde pertinently observes, the authors of the Declaration of the Rights of Man and of the Citizen in France in 1789 could scarcely have been regarded as pious Catholics."[28]

More importantly in this context, natural law based on religious authority is not that which is pointed to by the Constitution and applied by the Courts.

---

[26] W. Duncan, "Can Natural Law Be Used in Constitutional Interpretation?" (1995) 45 *Doctrine & Life* 125 at p. 126.

[27] Aquinas has succinctly distinguished between theocratic and practical reason as follows:

> "The business of the theocratic reason is with natural truths that cannot be otherwise, and so without mistake it finds truth in the particular conclusions it draws as in the premises it starts from. Whereas the business of the practical reason is with contingent matters which are the domain of human acts, and although there is some necessity in general principles, the more we get down to particular cases the more we can be mistaken." – *Summa Theologiae* Ia 2ae 94, 4 (Blackfriars 1966) Vol. 28, p. 87.

See further C.P. Nemeth, "A Commentary on the Natural Law, Moral Knowledge and Moral Application" (1992) 34 *Catholic Lawyer* 227.

[28] B. Walsh, Foreword to M. Forde, *Constitutional Law of Ireland* (1987). *Cf.*, as an extra-legal statement, Wolfe Tone: "The Rights of Man are the Rights of God, and to vindicate the one is to maintain the other" quoted by P.H. Pearse, "The Separatist Idea" (1976) *The Murder Machine and other Essays*, p. 52.

Consequently criticism of Irish constitutional law natural law as theocratic[29] relies on a mistaken reconstruction of Irish constitutional law, which has been shown above, both in the text of the Constitution and in the jurisprudence of the courts, not to be theocratic. The distinction, as Sheehy has pointed out, is between, on the one hand, the recognition that the Irish constitutional version of natural law based on reason, so far as it can be identified with a philosophical school, draws on Christian, specifically Thomist, philosophy, and on the other hand a claim that it constituted "the covert importation of Catholicism into the fundamental law of our country which itself professes to eschew any form of religious discrimination."[30]

Reid, in her ground-breaking work,[31] links the strong religious tone of the Constitution to Irish constitutional jurisprudence's "firm and continuing reliance on concepts of natural, as distinct from positive, law". But the articles of the Constitution cited above, referring to inalienability of rights inherent in humans because of their rational nature, do not refer to religion. Reid links the Irish constitutional law position on what some see as issues of sexual morality to religious influence via natural law. This is a fallacy, albeit a popular one. In *McGee v. Attorney General*[32] natural law was invoked as part of Irish constitutional law to invalidate provisions of a statute restricting contraception. Contraception is contrary to the Roman Catholic Church's view of natural law,[33] but that does not mean it should, on the Church's view, be prohibited.[34] This is the major instance where natural law was invoked in matters of sexual morality.

---

29 This criticism may also mistake (although the mistake is not logically implied by it) Roman Catholic Church teaching on this subject. The Church claims no special privileges for its doctrines in law on the ground that the vast majority of the population adhere to Roman Catholicism (91 per cent according to the census reported by R. O'Hanlon, "The Judiciary and the Moral Law" (1993) 11 *Irish Law Times* 129 at p. 131). Rather, the Church affirms a duty to speak out on the social consequences of legal change – W. Duncan, "The Divorce Referendum in the Republic of Ireland: Resisting the Tide" (1988) *International Journal of Law and the Family* 62.

30 Monsignor Sheehy (a judge in the Dublin Marriage Appeals Court) develops the view that this philosophy of natural law underlies the common law in England up to the Reformation and still underlies the Irish common law – "The Right to Marry" in O'Reilly (ed.) *op. cit.* above, n.3. Sheehy's view has been expressly adopted by Murphy, J. in *F. v. F.* [1994] I.L.R.M. 401.

31 M. Reid (1991) *op. cit.* above, n.1, LL.M. dissertation for the European University Institute.

32 [1974] I.R. 284.

33 It is also contrary to Finnis' view of natural law – J. Finnis, *Moral Absolutes: Tradition, Revision, and Truth*, (Washington D.C.: The Catholic University of America Press, 1991) pp. 84 *et seq.*.

34 The approach of the hierarchy to the interaction of law and morality has been explained by Rev. Hannon. Debates about the interaction of law and morality in Ireland take on the colour of a debate about church–state relations because the state is identified with law-making and the Church of the majority (Roman Catholic) with leadership in morality. The hierarchy focusses on the morality of the issue in question, not the law. They uphold the autonomy of the secular, meaning that lawmakers should act according to their conscience. This is limited, however, if there is detrimental effect to the common

The prohibition of abortion within the jurisdiction, an issue often linked in political debate with church–state relations,[35] whilst established on the basis of Irish constitutional natural law, has been dealt with by positive law: constitutional amendment by direct referendums.[36] The positive constitutional law may be supported by Irish constitutional natural law, certainly as regards the prohibition in this jurisdiction,[37] but natural law is not the only basis for the constitutional position.[38] It is prejudice to suppose (Reid does not) that the Irish constitutional law position on these issues is supported as a matter of faith only(or faith as the only reason since faith can be a reason) and not reason (and thus open to further rational argument and development, as distinct from mere political pressure).

Secondly, Murphy, in a critique of O'Hanlon J., states "our Constitution does not endorse a uniform objective standard of morality based on the theological doctrine of any one religion's interpretation of natural law" and claims that the case law does not support such a standard.[39] This is a correct statement standing on its own but, first, it is far from clear that O'Hanlon J. was asserting the legal force of theological doctrine, and secondly, the statement does not lead to the conclusion that Irish constitutional law is not legitimated by Irish constitutional natural law.[40]

---

good, which includes public morality. The test to differentiate between public and private morality is the social impact of the behaviour at issue. Fornication and adultery, for example, are not apt for legislative prohibition. If the law making act detrimentally affects the common good then this activates the duty of the hierarchy to expound the doctrine of the Church. P. Hannon, "Law and Morality in Ireland" (1992) Winter *Dlí* 26.

35 M. Smyth, "The Relationship between Law and Morality in Irish Constitutional Law" (1992) Winter *Dlí* 28, states:

> "If one's beliefs concerning abortion, for example, derive from religious conviction, is it sectarian to argue strongly against abortion? It would seem an abuse of language to qualify it as such. The very principle of pluralism can be used to justify such a person arguing against abortion, because he is simply trying to protect a weak and defenceless group of people from those stronger than them . . . During the two referenda there were times when it seemed that the only qualification required to be sectarian was to be a Catholic. The word did not seem to be used to qualify the views of Protestants or Humanists or Athiests, even though their views derived from the ethos of their group."

36 The Eighth, Thirteenth and Fourteenth amendments of the Constitution.

37 Save for circumstances where the life of the mother is at risk: Article 40.3.3 and *Attorney General v. X* [1992] 1 I.R. 1.

38 On the basis of previous jurisprudence, it appears even to be contrary to it – *Re Article 26 and the Regulation of Information (Services Outside the State for Termination of Pregnancies) Bill, 1995* [1995] 2 I.L.R.M. 81. However, according to Whyte, the previous position in Irish constitutional law may have been incorrect: G. Whyte, "Natural Law and the Constitution" (1995) 45 *Doctrine & Life* 481.

39 T. Murphy, "*Democracy, Natural Law, and the Irish Constitution*", (1993) 11 *Irish Law Times* 81.

40 O'Hanlon has responded to this critique in R. O'Hanlon, "The Judiciary and the Moral Law" (1993) 11 *Irish Law Times* 129. O'Hanlon does not assert the legal force of theological doctrine because it is theological doctrine. In pp. 131–132 O'Hanlon sets out an original argument in three steps. First, he refers to the declaration to which judges must subscribe which is made "[i]n the presence of Almighty God" and which con-

What is the evidence for holding Irish constitutional natural law theory to be based on religious belief? The Preamble to the Constitution proclaims that it is adopted by the people of Éire:

> "In the Name of the Most Holy Trinity, from Whom is all authority and to Whom, as our final end, all actions both of men and States must be referred . . . Humbly acknowledging all our obligations to our Divine Lord, Jesus Christ, Who sustained our fathers through centuries of trial".

It is to be noted that the Irish version, which pursuant to Article 25.5.4 and Article 8.1 is authoritative in case of conflict, uses the word *dírithe* where the English text uses "referred". *Dírithe* suggests "directed to", that is, action oriented to God as goal, whereas "referred" carries a connotation of comparison or referral to judgment. Article 6 states that "All powers of government . . . derive, under God, from the people . . .". As O'Higgins C.J. stated in *Norris v. Attorney General*: "It cannot be doubted that the people . . . [in the Preamble] were proclaiming a deep religious conviction and faith and an intention to adopt a Constitution consistent with that conviction and faith and Christian beliefs."[41] Denham J. stated in *Re a Ward of Court*,[42] quoting Walsh J. in *Quinn's Supermarket v. Attorney General*,[43] that the reflection in the Constitution that the Irish were a religious people aids in interpreting the law and the Constitution, and continues: "In regard specifically to the right to life it enables the interpretation to be inclusive of a spiritual or religious component."

On the basis of such evidence there are those eager to say that the decisions of the courts are tied not just to Christian philosophy but to a Roman

---

cludes with "May God direct and sustain me". Secondly, he refers to Article 6 according to which all powers of government are derived under God. It is an uncontentious point that the powers of government include the judicial power. Thirdly, he points to the problem posed to a judge who believes in the Catholic God: the interpretation of such a judge of the meaning of God will point to certain conclusions on what powers government could have derived from the people and what he has sworn to do. A counter-argument of interpretation is that the meaning of "God" in the declaration and the Constitution is not a Catholic meaning (this appears to be a reasonable argument), and further, the "God" is one who countenances, or does not avert to, abortion (which is a more suspect argument in the light of the Constitution as a whole, the people it governs, and the history of its enactment). But whatever one's views on the merits of O'Hanlon's argument (as it is understood here) and the counter-arguments proposed, O'Hanlon's rejection of the unconstitutionality of the intentional termination of unborn life does not turn on this original argument but rather on the view that it is contrary not only to positive constitutional law but also to Irish constitutional law natural law, which is not dependent on this original argument. Criticisms of O'Hanlon's pieces in the *Irish Law Times* appear to underestimate the combination of subtlety and solidity in addressing highly charged issues in the short space allowed. There is a risk that critics set out a caricature of an argument and affix a name to it and thereby avoid addressing the reasoned and reasonable arguments which may ground a politically incorrect, or in the Pope's words "uncomfortable" (John Paul II, *Crossing the Threshold of Hope* (London: Jonathan Cape, 1994, trans. Alfred A. Knopf Inc.) p. 204) point of view.

41 [1984] I.R. 36 at 64.

42 [1995] 2 I.L.R.M. 401 at 458.

43 [1972] I.R. 1.

Catholic exposition of natural law because the Roman Catholic Church claims to be the authoritative expounder amongst its faithful of natural law doctrine. Given such commentary, it is necessary to consider what the legal recognition of the importance of Christianity in Ireland means: it supports the Christian philosophical basis to Irish constitutional natural law and it restricts an absolutist view of the sovereignty of the people.

It does not mean that Christian belief is the touchstone of the validity of law. Suppose one were to accept the hypothesis of O'Higgins C.J. in *Norris* that the intention of the historical enactors of the Constitution, the people in 1937, is determinative of its basis (which is disputable). Suppose one were to reject other hypotheses, for example that the people intended primarily to react against the centuries of religious intolerance imposed on them under the constitutional structures of Great Britain by declaring an identity. The O'Higgins hypothesis still does not establish that this enactor's intention was to bind future generations to a law uniformly consistent with Christian, let alone Roman Catholic, beliefs. Whatever the supposed intention which may be attributed to be in the minds of the historical positive law enactor of the Constitution, what they in fact enacted is on its own terms declaratory and not constitutive of certain natural law principles, rights, and basic goods.[44] A written constitution, although primarily a legal document, has important political and social symbolical value. It would be odd if there was no symbolic recognition of Christianity in a country where over 95 per cent of the population still profess themselves to be Christians, and in the Republic, almost all of those Roman Catholics.[45]

The invocation of Christianity has other importance. Where the democratically elected legislature decides to regulate matters of public or private morality, for example the commercial retail of pornographic material, certain matters in family law, or the practice of homosexual sexual relations, the Christian values ascribed to the population are susceptible to being invoked as a source for the values grounding the position taken in the restrictive law.

---

44 This is far from saying that Irish constitutional natural law is a cover for a judicial free-for-all. Finnis' *Natural Law and Natural Rights* (1980) restatement and advance of natural law theory as it derives from the Thomist line of philosophy is indicative of the intellectual rigour which such an approach imports. As an approach based on reason and the recognition of certain fundamental commitments to be anterior and superior to positive law, natural rights are derived by the application of the permanently relevant principles of practical reasonableness (such as no arbitrary preference amongst persons or values) to commitments such as knowledge and life, in order to accord to an individual the benefit of another's obligation in respect of the enjoyment of a good.

45 Many legal orders make reference to religion. Some still claim to control religious doctrine: in England, ecclesiastical law even in purely spiritual matters remains part of the law of the State, albeit an area where Parliament has delegated its competence to the General Synod of the Church of England – D.M. Walker, "Law and Religion", in *The Oxford Companion to Law* (Oxford: Oxford University Press, 1980), pp. 723–724.

This is exactly what was done in *Norris v. Attorney General*[46] in the majority judgment. Norris sought a declaration of the unconstitutionality of sections of two Victorian statutes, which criminalised homosexual sexual acts between consenting adult males in private, on the grounds that it infringed his unenumerated constitutional right to privacy (his "right to be let alone" as it was put in the case). No issue was argued or decided on the basis of natural law: neither was the right asserted nor the legislation upheld on this ground. Because of the contentiousness of the issues here, it is useful to examine the basis of this judgment irrespective of one's opinion of desirability of the outcome. There are three key points.

First, O'Higgins C.J., supported by Finlay P. and Griffin J., rejected the proposition that there was a "'no go area' in the field of private morality":

> "I do not accept this view either as a general philosophical proposition concerning the purpose of law or as having particular reference to a right of privacy under our Constitution. I regard the State as having an interest in the general moral well-being of the community and as being entitled, where it is practicable to do so, to discourage conduct which is morally wrong and harmful to a way of life and to values which the State wishes to protect.
>
> A right of privacy or, as it has been put, a right 'to be let alone' can never be absolute. There are many acts done in private which the State is entitled to condemn, whether such be done by an individual on his own or with another. The law has always condemned abortion, incest, suicide attempts, suicide pacts, euthanasia or mercy killing. These are prohibited simply because they are morally wrong and regardless of the fact, which may exist in some instances, that no harm or injury to others is involved."[47]

Henchy J. dissented because the legislation was overbroad but maintained that the State could have a constitutional duty to intervene in sexual morality on the grounds of public order and morality, the protection of those in need of protection, of support for marriage, for the family, the requirements of public health, and other requirements of the common good.[48] This rejection of an absolute right to non-interference in private morality and the recognition of the competence of the State is not based by the Court on natural law. That is a completely different issue, whatever one might feel about the outcome in the case.[49] The question of restricting State activity in this area

---

46 [1984] I.R. 36.

47 *ibid.* at 64.

48 G. Quinn (1991) *op. cit.* above, n.10 at p. 34.

49 As an aside, it can be usefully questioned whether the State should regulate private morality at all, despite the fact that it is regulated by every State and, as the Chief Justice pointed out, in numerous fields (many of which he did not list). However there is a problem with distinguishing between private and public morality, and further all morality arguably has social effects – C. Daly, *Law and Morals* (Dublin: Four Courts Press, 1993). See also *Re a Ward of Court* [1995] 2 I.L.R.M. 401 at 459, *per* Denham J.: "The State has an interest in the moral aspect of society – for the common good." Notwithstanding these effects, however, it is not contentious that if morality is to be regulated at all, there are questions of degree. It seems to this author (although probably too far into an external perspective

as a constitutional principle appears to be one of degree. This of course does not stop the legislature from restricting its own intrusions.

Secondly, Christian morality may be one of the sources for the State's choice of the values which it wishes to protect. The Chief Justice also had regard to other sources, from history and comparative law (the United Kingdom) to the reports of doctors.

Thirdly, according to the Chief Justice the impugned prohibition was not concerned solely to avoid a moral wrong: (a) the prohibition could also be a paternalistic attempt to protect individuals from a life of loneliness and possible suicide; (b) the prohibition protected others from harm from disease, from an attack on the institution of the family, and from risk that a "mildly homosexually oriented person" may be lead into "a way of life from which he may never recover".

Therefore, *Norris* was not decided on the basis of Irish constitutional natural law.

To illustrate the rejection of a religious determination of legal doctrine two sets of cases can be examined. The first is in the law of marriage. As far back as 1912 the distinction between a "valid marriage under the law for the time being in force in the State" and marriage according to Roman Catholic doctrine was made in *Ussher v. Ussher*,[50] a case which Kelly called "a clear authority for the mutual independence of the State and canon law" although decided before the enactment of the Constitution. The President of the Circuit Court (O'Briain P.) made reference to *Ussher* in *The People (Attorney General) v. Ballins*,[51] a case which postdates the Constitution. In *Ballins* a woman, who was first married in a registry office and then by a priest to another man, was convicted of bigamy even though she was only married once in the eyes of the Church. The President averted to a direct conflict between canon law and civil law because in civil law the accused was validly married in the Registry Office and in Canon law she was not. The President stated:

> "The position of a Judge who is called upon to administer the Civil Law that for historical reasons conflicts with the Canon Law which is binding upon the majority of the people of this State is equally unenviable. I do not intend to let that affect my interpretation of the Criminal Law or in any way to derogate from its effect."[52]

Finally, an argument that the New Testament and Mosaic law provided for divorce meant that the State had to provide for it was struck out by O'Hanlon J. for failure to disclose a reasonable cause of action.[53]

---

to be qualified to comment) that the degree of regulation of morality, if morality is to be regulated at all, is one which ought to change with changing social attitudes, although it must always be limited by natural rights. (This is distinct from asserting that the protection of fundamental Irish constitutional natural law rights should change with changing social attitudes.)

50 [1912] 2 I.R. 445.

51 [1964] Ir. Jur. Rep. 14.

52 *ibid.* at 15.

53 *Robert Draper v. Attorney General*, unreported judgment of the High Court, *Irish Times*, 25 November 1986, discussed by J. Casey, (1992) *op. cit.* above, n.21, p. 501.

Secondly, in the law on contraception, *McGee*[54] has already been noted. In *Irish Family Planning Association v. Ryan*[55] the High Court, upheld on appeal by the Supreme Court, quashed a decision of the Censorship Board prohibiting a family planning booklet which gave information on contraception.[56] Kenny J. *per curiam* raised a doubt on the constitutional validity of the prohibition by the Censorship Board of the sale of a book which advocates "the unnatural prevention of conception" in the light of the rights declared, on the basis of natural law, in *McGee.*[57]

On the evidence of the constitutional text and case law, religion-based morality has a limited role in Irish law but does not constitute its constitutional legitimation. Irish constitutional law and Christian doctrines may coincide in decisions based on natural law because of their identification of the same precepts of natural law, such as the right to life,[58] or they may diverge, such as in the regulation of contraception. Convergence is caused by the identification in Irish constitutional law by the application of the permanently relevant principles of practical reason to basic human goods, of the same natural law precepts which a Christian church may identify by its own method (for example on the authoritative interpretation of the divine word of God as revealed in sacred texts by the Church designated by God in the person of his only Son). This convergence is not by the identification by Irish constitutional law of Christian doctrine.

It is in support of natural law based on reason that the regularly cited article of Henchy J. is to be understood.[59] The then Professor of Roman Law, Jurisprudence, and Legal History in University College, Dublin wrote, in the context of establishing the legal basis for the Supreme Court to overrule precedents, that the Constitution rejects the juridical positivism the corollary of which was that the House of Lords refused to overrule a previous decision "be it ever so erroneous or unjust".[60] He stated: "If a judicial decision rejects the

---

54 [1974] I.R. 284.

55 [1979] I.R. 295.

56 *ibid.* The Supreme Court, *per* O'Higgins C.J., Henchy, Griffin, and Parke JJ. concurring, held that the Board exercised unjustly its discretion by failing to communicate to the publisher that the Board was considering a ban on the booklet, and further held that it was not possible to ban the booklet as indecent or obscene.

57 *McGee v. Attorney General* [1974] I.R. 284, at 311.

58 Whether these doctrinal positions still coincide following the amendment of Article 40.3.3 to qualify the right to life by the right to travel and the right to information (see also *Re Article 26 and the Regulation of Information (Services outside the State for Termination of Pregnancies) Bill, 1995* [1995] 2 I.L.R.M. 81) is unclear. There appears to be a divergence with the view of the Church – see for example Pope John Paul II, *Crossing the Threshold of Hope*, above, n.40 and, the Irish Bishop's Conference, "The Value of Human Life" (1995) 262 *Position Paper* 281, published after *Attorney General v. X* [1992] 1 I.R. 1, criticises that decision as departing from natural law on the mistaken basis that natural law is exterior to the Constitution, rather than one of the purposes for its enactment and part of it.

59 S. Henchy, "Precedent in the Irish Supreme Court" (1962) 25 *Modern Law Review* 554.

60 *ibid.* at p. 550. The House of Lords changed its mind a few years later with its Practice Statement. Such a position is not required by positivist theory.

divine law or has not as its object the common good, it has not the character of law." His concern was with "the extent to which the Irish legal system succeeds in meeting the needs of contemporary society"[61] and declared that it would be "at variance with *reason* for the Supreme Court to consider itself bound to accept automatically as law decisions of the House of Lords which rest on a *conception of law different* from that enshrined in our Constitution."[62] This is not an effort to give legal force to religious dogma.

The legitimation of Irish constitutional law is not based on the discovery of the will of a God posited by any set of beliefs whose human interpreter is outside the courts.[63] The content of natural law in Irish constitutional law is not to be determined by belief.

That does not mean that lay or religious moral philosophers cannot give evidence. Kenny J. in *Conroy v. Attorney General*[64] heard the evidence of a Professor of Moral Theology in Maynooth in order to determine the moral quality of the act involved in the offence of drunken driving because this was one of the legal tests (not the only one) for deciding whether an offence should be regarded as major or minor under the Constitution (Article 38.2 – "Minor offenses may be tried by courts of summary jurisdiction"). However his evidence was not accepted on the basis of religious belief:

> "His evidence about the moral gravity of a section 49 offence was not based on the theological or moral doctrines of the Roman Catholic Church but on that moral gravity which may be derived from and measured by the natural law or natural ethics . . . '.

The view that such evidence can be given was disfavoured by Walsh J. in *McGee*[65]:

> "In a pluralist society such as ours, the Courts cannot as a matter of constitutional law be asked to choose between the differing views, where they exist, of experts on the interpretation by the different religious denominations of either the nature or extent of . . . natural rights as they are to be found in the natural law."

Walsh J.'s judgment has been quoted at length by Murphy J. in *F. v. F.* who refused to hear the evidence of a moral theologian on natural law. Murphy J. laid particular emphasis on the following sentence in Walsh J.'s judgment:

> "In this country it falls finally upon the Judges to interpret the Constitution and in doing so to determine, where necessary, the rights which are superior or antecedent to positive law or which are imprescriptible or inalienable."[66]

---

61 *ibid.* at p. 558.
62 *ibid.* at pp. 550–551 (emphasis added).
63 The latter was liberally quoted by T. Murphy, "Democracy, Natural Law, and the Irish Constitution" (1993) 11 *Irish Law Times* 81.
64 [1965] I.R. 411.
65 [1974] I.R. 284 at 318.
66 [1994] 2 I.L.R.M. 401 at 408.

Murphy J. identified the basis for refusing to hear evidence as the obligation of the judge to interpret the law: "it is not permissible for me to abdicate that function to any expert, however distinguished." However this view has been disfavoured in turn by Lynch J. in *Re a Ward of Court*[67] who admitted the oral evidence of two Roman Catholic moral theologians to the effect that the discontinuance of feeding of the ward to lead to her death was acceptable, and also admitted documents prepared by the Church of Ireland and the Church of England. Lynch J. stated that in determining lawfulness under the Constitution "the views of theologians of various faiths are of assistance in that they endeavour to apply right reason to the problems for decision by the Court."[68] The fact that many natural lawyers might disagree with the outcome of the case does not mean that it was not an Irish constitutional natural law determination, but rather is indicative of Irish constitutional natural law developing in a process of arguments based on right reason to find the permanently right answer, although the courts may err.

The position adopted in Irish constitutional law on religion is concisely summed up in the first three provisions of the only article dealing with it, Article 44:

> "1. The State acknowledges that the homage of public worship is due to Almighty God. It shall hold His Name in reverence, and shall respect and honour religion.
> 2. The State guarantees not to endow any religion.
> 3. The State shall not impose any disabilities or make any discrimination on the ground of religious profession, belief or status."

Article 44.1 must be read in the light of Walsh J.'s, statement in *Quinn*[69]: "homage to God is not limited to Christianity". Also worth mentioning here is *E.R. v. J.R.*,[70] where Carroll J. after going out of her way and away from the facts of the case to make clear that her use of the term "minister of religion" was non-denominational, held that "[a]dvice given by a minister of religion has an added dimension which is not present between lay people."

In the light of the above evidence, to deny Irish constitutional natural law as the legitimation of Irish constitutional law on the ground that it is dependent on religious authority or beliefs and that such dependence cannot be the correct construction of Irish constitutional law, is an impoverished denial.[71]

---

67 Decision of 15 May 1995 (High Court). The admissibility of such evidence was implicitly upheld by the Supreme Court – [1995] 2 I.L.R.M. 401.

68 Lynch J., in an interesting dictum, considered that such evidence was useful to "discuss the moral and ethical issues raised by this sort of case with a view to ascertaining what the law ought to be and thus to assist in declaring what is indeed the law of the land."

69 *The State (Quinn) v. Ryan* [1965] I.R. 70.

70 [1981] I.L.R.M. 125.

71 This work does not engage arguments on whether there are coherent critiques of abstract natural law theory or whether there are good arguments criticising Irish constitutional natural law legitimation as not being the basis of Irish constitutional law which is "best" for "Ireland" or "the Irish people", however these might be defined out-

Unenumerated Personal Rights Resulting from the Nature of the State

23–7 In one maverick decision the basis of the protection of unenumerated personal rights in Irish constitutional law was located in the nature of the State.[72] Kenny J. stated in the case of *Ryan v. Attorney General*:

> "I think that the personal rights which may be invoked to invalidate legislation are not confined to those specified in Article 40 but include all those rights which result from the Christian and democratic nature of the State."[73]

This was a landmark decision which established that unenumerated fundamental rights were constitutionally protected (and recognised the right to bodily integrity as one of these). However the learned judge gave a false impression of whence these rights stemmed. As Kelly pointed out: "The State is, indeed, described expressly as 'democratic' in Article 5 . . . [but] the State is nowhere in the Constitution described as Christian".[74] As Hogan remarks, "there is much to suggest the contrary view", making specific reference to Article 44.2 prohibiting the State endowing any religion.[75] The Supreme Court endorsed Kenny J.'s view that fundamental rights unspecified by the Constitution were protected under it, but importantly did not confirm Kenny J.'s interpretation of their source. At this stage in this Part, it should be clear that it is not human rights which result from the nature of the State, but the nature of the State which results from the promotion and protection of the rights, specified and unspecified by the text of the Constitution, and other concepts such as the common good (considered below) which form part of the natural law legitimation of Irish constitutional law.

Fundamental Rights based on a Contract between State and Citizens

23–8 The legitimation of fundamental rights by Irish constitutional law natural law is supported not only by the authority in support of it and the paucity of authority for another coherent legitimation, but also by the particular difficulty of relying on a contractarian doctrine in a legal order which pro-

---

side of Irish constitutional law. The words of Costello P., that "it is not the function of judges to debate the merits of the theory" ((1987) *op. cit.* above, n.1, p. 113), apply *mutatis mutandis* to the reconstruction of the internal point of view.

72 This basis is to be distinguished from the view that unenumerated rights can be identified because their denial would violate "those fundamental principles of liberty and justice which lie at the base of all our civil and political institutions" – W.J. Brennan, Jr., "The Ninth Amendment and Fundamental Rights" in O'Reilly (ed.) (1992) *op. cit.* above, n.3.

73 [1965] I.R. 294 at 312.

74 J.M. Kelly, *The Irish Constitution,* (2nd ed., University College Dublin, 1984) p. 432.

75 G.W. Hogan, (1990–1992) *op. cit.* above, n.19, p.105. *Cf. Re a Ward of Court* [1995] 2 I.L.R.M. 401, at 459, *per* Denham J.

tects the fundamental rights of foreigners.[76] The constitutional provisions are inconsistent.[77] On the one hand, many of the rights are guaranteed expressly to citizens only, including the right to be held equal before the law (Article 40.1), the right to a good name (Article 40.3.2), the right to free expression (Article 40.6.1.i), the right to freedom of assembly (Article 40.6.1.ii) and the right to associate and form unions (Article 40.6.1.iii), the right to liberty (Article 40.4.1), and the right to inviolability of the dwelling (article 40.5); this is also the case for the general statement of protection of rights in articles 40.3.1–3 upon which the development of unenumerated rights is partly based. On the other hand, some rights, such as those concerning education, religion, the family, and private property do not have this qualification.

One judicial view was that Article 40.3 stated rights which attached to citizenship, as defined in Article 9, and fell as a duty on the State.[78]

Confining fundamental rights to citizens does not square with their natural law basis: "The natural law is of universal application and applies to all human persons, be they citizens of this State or not."[79] In *Northampton County Council v. A.B.F. and M.B.F.* Hamilton J. held that an English father could invoke the family guarantees: "[i]n my opinion it would be inconceivable that the father of an infant child would not be entitled to rely on the recognition of the family contained in Article 41 for the purpose of enforcing his rights as the lawful father of the infant." Barrington J. has held that the constitutional rights guaranteed under Articles 40 to 44:

> "derive not from a man's citizenship but from his nature as a human being... the Constitution accepts that those rights derive not from the law but from the nature of man . . . The fact that the wording of Article 40., s.3, commits the State to protect and vindicate the life of 'every citizen' does not justify the inference that it relieves the State of the obligation to defend and vindicate the lives of persons who are not citizens. This is because the whole scheme of moral and political values which are clearly accepted by the Constitution indicates otherwise."[80]

---

[76] For a summary of the substantive law on the protection of the rights of foreigners, see J. Casey, *Constitutional Law in Ireland* (1992) *op.cit.* above, n.21, 2nd ed., 1992, pp. 354–358 and Hogan and Whyte, *Kelly, The Irish Constitution*, (3rd ed., 1994), pp. 679–682. There may well be a contractarian theory to cope with this problem. But the proposed of such a theory in this context would have to show it is adopted as a matter of Irish constitutional law.

[77] If there was a clear provision extending the benefit of all fundamental rights to foreigners then this might support an argument that citizens had contracted with the State for the benefit of foreigners and citizens alike.

[78] *The State (Nicolaou) v. An Bord Uchtála* [1966] I.R. 567 at 617, *per* Henchy, J. *Cf.* at 599–600, *per* Teevan J. When Costello J. refers to social rights in *O'Reilly v. Limerick Corporation* [1989] I.L.R.M. 181 at 192, he describes them as inhering in the citizen. But this is not significant because all the plaintiffs in the case were citizens and because he also referred in the same sentence to basic human rights resulting from the "concept of *man*" (emphasis added) enshrined in the Constitution as inhering in citizens.

[79] *Northampton County Council v. A.B.F. and M.B.F.* [1982] I.L.R.M. 164 at 166, *per* Hamilton J.; see also *Kennedy v. Ireland* [1987] I.R. 587 at 593, *per* Hamilton P.

[80] *Finn v. Attorney General* [1983] I.R. 154 at 159–60, establishing that the reference to citizens as the holders of constitutional rights was not a bar to the recognition of the right

In *T.M. and A.M. v. An Bord Uchtála*, where the Supreme Court construed the Adoption Acts 1952–1988 as applying to children born outside the jurisdiction to foreign parents, O'Flaherty J. stated that rights under Article 42.5 were not confined to citizens and that the requirements imposed on the State were "of universal application".[81]

Another ground for rejecting a contractarian legitimation of fundamental rights is the status of the family as a moral institution (Articles 41 to 42). Irish constitutional law allows the family to be the holder of constitutional rights but requiring the party asserting that right to be a legal person in its own right. Thus, for example, a single member or members joined together as plaintiffs can assert the rights of the family,[82] and if such rights are breached there may be a remedy in damages assessed on the basis of individual loss.[83] However when the Matrimonial Home Bill 1993 was referred to the Supreme Court to decide upon its constitutionality, the rights of the Family were asserted in the abstract as belonging to the Family as such. It appears from *F. v. F.* that a party may rely on the constitutional protection of the family as the fundamental unit group in society in a case arising from an intra-familial dispute.[84]

Unenumerated Personal Rights resulting from Judges' Ideas of Changing Concepts of Prudence, Justice and Charity

23–9 There have been cases for the proposition that Irish constitutional natural law rights are to be interpreted in the light of the Preamble, in particular the purpose of the Constitution to promote the common good with due observance of prudence, justice and charity so that the dignity and freedom of the individual may be assured. This proposition has been changed by case law which considers that these concepts change. The origin of this line of cases is statements by Walsh J. in *McGee*[85] who continued:

> "the judges must, therefore, as best they can from their training and their experience interpret these rights in accordance with their ideas of prudence, jus-

---

to life of the unborn: "I would have no hesitation in holding that the unborn child has a right to life and that it is protected by the Constitution."

81 [1993] I.L.R.M. 577 at 589.

82 *Fajujonu v. Minister for Justice* [1990] 2 I.R. 151.

83 *O'Reilly v. Limerick Corporation* [1989] I.L.R.M. 181 at 192. However in *Greene v. Minister for Agriculture* [1990] 2 I.R. 17, Murphy J. dismissed a married couple's claim for damages resulting from a scheme which was found to violate Article 41 on the ground that the duty cast on the State did not give rise to a corresponding individual right to damages for its breach. *Cf. P.H. v. John Murphy & Sons Ltd.* [1987] I.R. 621 at 626, where Costello J. held that "[t]he *rights* which the Family enjoys *vis-à-vis* the State are those which are correlative to the duties imposed by [Article 41.1.2] and can be ascertained by reference to those duties." Costello J. held that an action in damages would lie for an intentional, but not a negligent breach by a state official of article 41.1.

84 Above, n.33, (Murphy J.). However, the individual rights asserted in that case were held to be protected under Article 40.3 and not under the provisions on the family.

85 *McGee v. Attorney General* [1974] I.R. 284 at 318.

> tice and charity. It is but natural that from time to time the prevailing ideas of these virtues may be conditioned by the passage of time: no interpretation of the Constitution is intended to be final for all time. It is given in the light of prevailing ideas and concepts."

There are many propositions in that statement. First, Walsh J. was concerned to exclude the evidence of experts as facilitating the judge's task. This proposition is now disfavoured.[86] Secondly, no interpretation of the Constitution can be final for all time. This is uncontentious.[87] Thirdly, the prevailing ideas of prudence, justice and charity may be conditioned by the passage of time. This is also uncontentious, as what prevails changes over time as a matter of fact (and such change is in this sense "natural").

It is unclear from Walsh J.'s statement whether there is a fourth proposition which can be extrapolated. The statement has been relied on, however, with refinements on numerous occasions,[88] to evolve the fourth proposition that unenumerated Irish constitutional natural law rights are to be derived via judges' changing ideas of the changing ideas of prudence, justice and charity. If this is what Walsh J. meant, it is radically inconsistent with his clear statements on the Thomist philosophic influence, and on the role of reason, in Irish constitutional natural law. Whilst the prevailing ideas of these concepts change, the concepts themselves do not. The process remains one of trying to identify the correct definition of the right in the light of rational argument which right may remain the same as circumstances change and which is derived from the application of reason to the fundamental commitments in Irish constitutional law and not from acceptance. The fourth proposition, if accepted, would bring in by the back door the risk that the anti-majoritarian protection afforded by human rights would be lost in the test of the socially prevailing view of these concepts (and *a fortiori* the socially prevailing view of what these concepts mean in a specific situation or in respect of a specific right). This reduces the protection of Irish constitutional natural rights to a dependency on consensus (either on the right at issue or on the concepts of prudence, justice and charity), which is ultimately a question of fact.[89]

---

86 *Re A Ward of Court*, decision of Lynch J. of 15 May 1995.

87 A fixed interpretation would be contrary also to Irish constitutional natural law since, being based on reason, it must always be open to new rational arguments. This is distinct from the (false) proposition that there are not permanently correct answers to certain problems.

88 *The State (Healy) v. Donoghue* [1976] I.R. 325 at 347 (O'Higgins C.J.); *F. v. F* [1994] I.L.R.M. 401 at 411 *per* Murphy J.; *Attorney General v. X* [1992] 1 I.R. 1 at 53, *per* Finlay C.J.; *In Re Article 26 and the Regulation of Information (Services for the Termination of Pregnancies) Bill, 1995* [1995] 1 I.R. 1.

89 If the test was the socially prevailing view (or, alternatively, the view of the people) of the concepts of prudence, justice and charity instead of the socially prevailing view of the rights themselves, then judges would be implicitly asserting that they were better able to derive rights on the basis of these consensus concepts than the contributors to the socially prevailing view (or the people) on whose consensus they were relying.

Consequent upon this mode of derivation of right is the risk that judges close themselves off from rational arguments from counsel (perhaps supported by expert evidence) as to what the rights are.

While the decisions post *McGee* accepted and developed Irish constitutional natural law, this incoherent (so far as coherent in itself, inconsistent with that doctrine) and radically dangerous fourth proposition appeared to assume independent force in *Re Article 26 and the Regulation of Information (Services for the Termination of Pregnancies) Bill, 1995*. The Supreme Court in that case, immediately after quoting Walsh J.'s now disfavoured rejection of expert evidence, stated:

> "From a consideration of all the cases which recognised the existence of a personal rights which was not specifically enumerated in the Constitution, it is manifest that the Court in each such case had satisfied itself that such personal right was one which could be reasonably implied from and was guaranteed by the provisions of the Constitution, interpreted in accordance with its ideas of prudence, justice and charity."

This is by no means manifest, as the chapters above demonstrate, nor did the Court make any effort to show why it was manifest, confining itself to setting out quotations from case law some of which might support this extrapolated proposition and some of which contradict it. The difficulty is not with the very open-ended proposition that constitutional natural rights are reasonably implied from and guaranteed by the provisions of the Constitution, since Irish constitutional natural law has an anchor in the text. The difficulty is with their derivation via the Court's ideas of prudence, justice and charity.

The unreasoned reliance on the fourth proposition appears to have been a response to "counsel's general argument that natural law was superior to the Constitution."[90] This appears to misunderstand the distinction between natural law (a phrase which covers a wide body of disparate theories of law and morality) and Irish constitutional natural law, which is interiorised.[91] This misunderstanding, coupled with the rabbit in the hat treatment of the question of the validity, as distinct from the meaning, of the provision, appears to have led the Court to state the obvious as conclusive of the controversy over Irish constitutional natural law and the validity of the amendment: "The Courts, as they were and are bound to, recognised the Constitution as the fundamental law of the State to which the organs of the State were subject and at no stage recognised the provisions of the natural law as superior to the Constitution." The effect of these statements on Irish constitutional natural

---

90 *Re Article 26 and the Regulation of Information (Services for the Termination of Pregnancies) Bill, 1995* [1995] 1 I.R. 1 at 43.

91 See above, para. 23–2, "Natural Law Based on Reason: Reconstructing the Doctrine". See also Irish Bishops' Conference (1995) *op. cit.* above, n.58, at p. 282, commenting on *Attorney General v. X* [1992] 1 I.R. 1: "Its arguments appear to be made on the basis that the natural law is exterior to the Constitution."

law appears to be limited to the restricted effect the result in the opinion has on the vexed question of amendability,[92] although even in that regard one commentator considers that the result might be regarded as in accordance with even obliged by natural law.[93]

The Court expressly accepted its role in determining "the rights which are superior or antecedent to positive law or which are imprescriptible or inalienable."[94] Although the Court relied in this regard on the "fourth proposition", that proposition is too contra-indicated by authority, the coherent recognition of the legitimation of Irish constitutional natural law, reason, and risk, to be a permanent stumbling block for the development of Irish constitutional natural law.

Hogan, like the Supreme Court in *Re Article 26 and the Regulation of Information (Services for the Termination of Pregnancies) Bill, 1995*,[95] interprets the original statement of Walsh J. in *McGee* as the fourth proposition and states:

> "This is practically tantamount to an open invitation to the judiciary to become latter-day philosopher-kings via the guise of constitutional adjudication. One does not want to be too dismissive – since natural law theory is valuable in stressing the link between positive law and morality – but not even its most valiant supporters appear to have suggested that natural law theory provides an objective method whereby the existence of a particular personal right can be ascertained."[96]

---

92 See below, para. 29–6, "Popular Sovereignty and its Natural Law Limits in Irish Constitutional Law". The statement, "it is manifest that the Court in each such case had satisfied itself that such personal right was one which could be reasonably implied from and was guaranteed by the provisions of the Constitution, interpreted in accordance with its ideas of prudence, justice and charity", does not ground the Court's conclusion, since the issue was whether the purported adopted provision was a valid provision (that is, a provision which the people could validly enact into law without other wholesale changes to the Constitution), not what the provision meant. Whilst the people could have enacted a Constitution with no reference to natural law, or indeed with no fundamental rights protection at all, what they in fact enacted was a Constitution which recognised the binding force of natural law, which recognition limits what the people can now enact without causing a legal revolution.

93 According to G. Whyte, "Natural Law and the Constitution" (1995) 45 *Doctrine & Life* 481.

94 *Re Article 26* [1995] 1 I.R. 1 at 42.

95 [1995] 1 I.R. 1.

96 G.W. Hogan (1990–1992) *op. cit.* above, n.19, at p. 110. *Cf.* Humphreys, "Interpreting Natural Rights" (1993–1995) XXVIII–XXX *Irish Jurist* 221. Humphreys advocates in this article, consistently with his earlier article "Constitutional Interpretation" (1993) 15 D.U.L.J. 59, a reflective, interesting and, in the Irish context, new and alternative approach to Irish constitutional natural law. (Because of lack of judicial support to date it is not treated in the text above as a separate approach to Irish constitutional natural law.) Humphreys advocates in part something akin to an application of Cappelletti's comparative phenomenological approach (*The Judicial Process in Comparative Perspective* (Oxford: Clarendon Press, 1989)), where comparative study of certain other legal systems yields a common result in human rights protection, in the context of the discernment of the content of Irish constitutional natural rights. However, it is important to distinguish between the usefulness of the fact of acceptance of human rights in other

But the fourth proposition is not the correct statement of the Irish constitutional natural law position, which provides as objective a method as possible. Whilst Irish constitutional natural law cannot (and does not seek to) claim neutrality as regards the good, since certain fundamental commitments such as life are taken as the point of departure, neither can the text of the Constitution which itself grounds those commitments. Hogan, as a rigorous lawyer, is naturally concerned with judicial discretion. As an objective commentator he acknowledges that "[t]here is no mechanism whereby the existence of [unenumerated] rights can be objectively ascertained"[97] and proposes, following Kelly, the constitutional adoption of a list of rights. There are two immediate problems with this approach. The first, recognised by Hogan,[98] is that such enumeration does not remove judicial discretion,[99] but merely lessens it. The second is that apart from the adoption of express constitutional rights the author appears to ground the protection of fundamental rights on the will of the majority.[100] From the perspective of Irish constitutional law, the adoption of such a principle would cause a legal revolution.

Any proposal for the adoption (an opportunity which may be seized in the present climate, perhaps focussing on the tension between natural law and democratic theory[101]) by the judiciary or by amendment, of a mechanism or doctrine of interpretation professed in the language of liberalism, democracy, inclusiveness, or neutrality is likely to be welcomed, not primarily because of its inherent persuasive force or because of the evidence in Irish constitutional law which can be marshalled to ground its adoption, but because its results and language may be more politically correct.[102] But a popular legal

legal systems to alert domestic judiciary to complementary or alternative interpretations, on the one hand, and the derivation of Irish constitutional natural rights, which are based on reason, on the other. Irish constitutional natural law operates as a break on majority determination of the rights of man, be it by representatives, the people, or the cumulations of other legal systems.

97 G.W. Hogan (1990–1992) *op. cit.* above, n.19, at p. 114.

98 *ibid.* at p. 116.

99 This is put clearly by Humphreys (1993–1995) *op. cit.* above, n.96, pp. 226–227, where he undermines the contrast between objectivity represented by literalism and subjectivity represented by unenumerated rights.

100 However this may not be what the author intends.

101 This tension has been highlighted by A. Whelan, "Constitutional Amendments in Ireland: The Competing Claims of Democracy", in G. Quinn *et al., Justice and Legal Theory in Ireland* (Dublin: Oak Tree Press, 1995), and G. Quinn, "Book Review of J.M. Kelly, *A Short History of Western Legal Theory*" (1993–1995) XXVIII–XXX *Irish Jurist* 408 at p. 412, and G. Quinn, (1991) *op. cit.* above, n.10, p. 36.

102 This is similar to a point first made by Humphreys (1993–1995) *op. cit.* above, n.96, at p. 227: "'Objectivity', in the context of the debate on how to read a text, is a politically charged synonym for nothing other than whatever method enjoys success and acceptance in the interpretative community."

revolution is no less a revolution; and Irish constitutional natural law is a source of law, not an interpretive method.[103]

Hogan and Whelan state that Irish constitutional natural law as expounded in this work can be accepted "solely because it is expressed in terms too general to invite dissent."[104] But the fact that dissent occurs at the point of the specification of the meaning of rights in particular cases should encourage reasoned argument as to the correct application of the principles of practical reason to the fundamental commitments of Irish constitutional natural law, not to the dismissal of it. Irish constitutional natural law is based on a Thomistic conception which involves the application of the principles of practical reason to the fundamental commitments of Irish constitutional law which appear to the rational mind upon reflection to be self-evidently good, such as life, liberty and the pursuit of truth. Certain Irish constitutional fundamental rights are possessed by individuals by virtue of their rational nature and human personality[105]; they are antecedent to positive law and superior to it. As regards the common good, this is the set of conditions in society which enables individuals and families to best pursue in their lives the fundamental commitments and values espoused by the Constitution.[106] A subset of these conditions are the necessary arrangements for a functioning democracy.[107]

---

103 From an external perspective, the causing of a legal revolution is not of itself a conclusive reason for not advocating (popular or unpopular) revolutionary change, but supplies reasons, additional to the loss of the good in the present order of Irish constitutional natural law, for avoiding such a course, not least the weakening of the rule of law (a concern related to Hogan's concern about judicial discretion *op.cit.*, above, n.19) and the danger posed by political correctness to the protection of human rights based on fundamental permanent goods which themselves fall in and out of popularity.

104 G. Hogan and A. Whelan, *Ireland and the European Union: Constitutional and Statutory Texts and Commentary* (1995) p. 128.

105 *McGee v. Attorney General* above, [1974] I.R. 284 at 325, *per* Henchy J.

106 D.R. Phelan, "The Concept of Social Rights" (1994) 16 D.U.L.J. 105 at 114 (N.S.).

107 However Irish constitutional natural law has restrictive implications for the legal scope of majoritarianism and the status of an amendment of the Constitution which is contrary to Irish constitutional natural law. See below, para. 29–6, "Popular Sovereignty in its Natural Law Limitations in Irish Constitutional Law".

Waiver of Constitutional Rights may not be Possible

23–10 The rights inhere in the holder irrespective of the momentary exercise of his will, and duties imposed by Irish constitutional natural law cannot be avoided. (The question of whether or not natural rights can be waived has similarities to the question of whether or not sovereignty can be irreversibly alienated.)

No general rule on waiver can be determined from the content of the Articles themselves. The wording of Article 42 (on the "inalienable right and duty" of parents to educate their children) and Article 41 (asserting the "inalienable and imprescriptible rights" of the family) embeds in positive law these natural rights. Kenny J. considered Article 41 in *Ryan v. Attorney General*[108]: "'Inalienable' means that which cannot be transferred or given away . . . ". On the other hand Article 40, as Walsh J. pointed out, speaking for the Court in *State (Nicolaou) v. An Bórd Uchtála,*[109] contains no express provision which "restricts the surrender, abdication, or transfer of any of the rights guaranteed in that article by the person entitled to them". But these differences in the articles do not mean that each right has a separate rule on waiver depending on the wording of the article which refers to it.

There is a general rule which was stated by Walsh J. in *G v. An Bórd Uchtála*[110] (having cited *Nicolaou*): "Natural rights may be waived or surrendered by the persons who enjoy them provided such waiver is not prohibited either by natural law or positive law." To understand this important rule one must recall that rights which are expressly mentioned in the Constitution may also be natural rights (it would be bizarre if only non-natural rights were listed). Therefore this statement means that natural rights, whether or not listed, may be waived only where Irish constitutional natural law allows, and that listed rights, whether or not natural, may be waived also where positive law allows (provided such waiver is not contrary to Irish constitutional natural law).

Waiver is distinct from the question of the interplay between rights which may result in conflict or harmonisation in certain circumstances. In *Re a Ward of Court*[111] Hamilton C.J. held that the right to bodily integrity extends to the right to forego life-saving treatment, and the right to life extends to the right to a natural death but that the right to life does not include the right to have

---

108 [1965] I.R. 294.
109 [1966] I.R. 567.
110 [1980] IR 32.
111 [1995] 2 I.L.R.M. 401.

life terminated or accelerated: no person has a right to this.[112] An extraordinary facet to this case was that the Court assumed that the exercise of such rights by the Court for the ward, as distinct from by the ward, did not affect the analysis.

Resolution of Internal Constitutional Conflicts

23–11 This is a very important question because due to the dualism of the Irish legal system the status of European Community law before national courts, which depends in the first instance on statute, depends ultimately on special constitutional provisions (Article 29.4.3 to 29.4.5). These will be considered later, and only conflicts not concerning European Community law will be considered here. In order to solve a conflict of rules of the same status (for example legislative, or administrative) one must decide which takes precedence, and thereby establish a hierarchy – the ranking of one over the other in case of conflict. This process necessitates the identification of a principle or rule of recognition by which the hierarchy can be established. Conflicts of constitutional norms are no exception. Studying the outcome of these conflicts can teach not only about the norms in issue but also the hierarchy of norms and the doctrine which holds it together.

It is a principle of interpretation that such conflicts are to be to avoided if possible by seeking to "achieve the smooth and harmonious operation of the Constitution".[113] Partly as a consequence of this, cases of conflict between constitutional rights have been few, and the issue has been resolved by acknowledging a hierarchy of constitutional rights.

The two most important early cases concern really only a single fundamental commitment, and therefore the problem was more one of definition than of balancing. *Quinn's Supermarket v. Attorney General*[114] involved a conflict between the right to practice religion (Article 44.2.2) and the guarantee against discrimination on the grounds of religion (Article 44.3.3). The case arose by way of challenge to the validity of a Ministerial Order[115] which exempted Jewish shops from hours of trading regulations to enable Jews to buy meat ahead of the Sabbath, on which they were prohibited from trading by their religion. This was a conflict within Article 44, which has religion as its fundamental commitment. It was resolved by Walsh J. (Ó Dálaigh C.J. concurring) in the following way:

---

112 This case is discussed further below, in para. 23–12.

113 *Tormey v. Ireland* [1985] I.R. 289, *per* Henchy J.; *Attorney General v. X* [1992] 1 I.R. 1 at 57, *per* Finlay C.J.

114 [1972] I.R. 1.

115 Made in 1948 pursuant to s.25 of the Shops (Hours of Trading) Act 1938.

> "the primary object or aim of Article 44, and in particular the provisions of section 2 of that Article, was to secure and guarantee freedom of conscience and the free profession and practice of religion . . . It would be completely contrary to the spirit and intendment of [Article 44.2] to permit the guarantee against discrimination on the ground of religious profession or belief to be made the very means of restricting or preventing the free profession or practice of religion."[116]

The subsequent case of *McMahon v. Attorney General*[117] concerned a similar problem, a conflict within a single fundamental commitment to voting between the right to vote and the voter's right to secrecy of the ballot (Article 16.1). Perfect secrecy of the ballot was unobtainable if a blind person was to be allowed to vote. Ó Dálaigh C.J. referred to *Quinn's Supermarket* and held:

> "The right to vote of the incapacitated person has to be reconciled with the general right to vote by secret ballot. The latter right, which by its very nature is a guarantee of the free exercise of the right to vote, cannot be made the means of preventing the exercise of the right to vote simply because the incapacity of some electors renders absolute secrecy impossible."

The real problem occurs when the fundamental commitments to which the constitutional rights relate differ. The first mention of a hierarchy of constitutional rights occurred in *The People (Director of Public Prosecutions) v. Shaw*[118] where the continuing police custody of a suspected murderer of a young woman, which may have been in breach of his constitutional rights, had to be offset against the right to life of his victim, who, the police thought, could have still been found alive. Four of the Supreme Court justices upheld the detention on the grounds that it fell within the "extraordinary excusing circumstances" of the doctrine involved in the prisoner's rights in question, and thus the primary concern for the woman's right to life was justified.

Kenny J. however, referred to a hierarchy of constitutional rights, wherein the higher ranked right prevails. This judgment must be treated with caution. He stated: "When a conflict of constitutional rights arises, it must be resolved by having regard to (a) the terms of the Constitution, (b) the ethical values which all Christians living in this State acknowledge and accept and (c) the main tenets of our system of constitutional parliamentary democracy . . . ". This judgment, with which none of the other justices concurred, does not represent the Irish constitutional law on this problem, which has been expounded in *Attorney General v. X.*[119] Before considering this exposition, two comments on Kenny J.'s approach may be made:

---

116 Walsh J. held that an Order which allowed Jewish shops to open at hours which would not place any stress on the observance of the binding dietary laws of the Jewish religion "would be not merely valid, but would be necessary" (*Quinn's Supermarket v. Attorney General* [1972] I.R. 1 at 25). However the challenged Order exempted Jewish meat shops from all regulation of opening hours, including on weekdays, was found constitutionally invalid as being more discriminatory than necessary to attain that objective (at 27).

117 [1972] I.R. 69.

118 [1982] I.R. 1.

119 [1992] 1 I.R. 1.

1. the acceptance of values (Kenny J.'s factor (b)) is not the calibration by which constitutional rights should be ranked, because one of the primary purposes of such rights is to avoid the imposition of values by the majority, even the vast majority, on the minority;

2. Kenny J.'s factors (a) and (c) are not helpful in practice, since as regards (a) the Constitution does not specify any priority of rank, and as regards (c) there is no explanation of how the tenets of a system of parliamentary democracy are relevant to ranking constitutional rights. Kenny J. is the judge who tried to base unenumerated constitutional rights on the Christian and democratic nature of the State.[120]

The first consideration of the role of natural law in solving constitutional conflicts was by Costello J. in *Murray v. Ireland*,[121] in the context of a claim by two married prisoners that their incarceration should not be allowed to frustrate their right to beget children. Costello J. referred to the "scale of values protected by the Constitution",[122] and considered two rights: the expressly guaranteed right to life referred to in Article 40.3.2, and the unenumerated right not to be tortured. Costello J. considered that the fact that neither of these rights "is expressly described as being inalienable and imprescriptible or as being superior to positive law" did not affect their importance as basic human rights. He continued:

> "So, if the court is required to make a valuation between two constitutionally protected human rights, (as it was required to do in *People v. Shaw*[123]), it should have particular regard to the *intrinsic nature of the rights* concerned, a view consistent with the views of Mr. Justice Griffin at p. 56 and Mr. Justice Kenny at p. 63 of that report." (Emphasis added.)

The focus in case of conflict is therefore on Irish constitutional natural law legitimation, not on the question of whether the rights are written or unenumerated, or described as inalienable, imprescriptible, and superior to positive law or not.

In *Attorney General v. X* Finlay C.J., Hederman and Egan JJ. held that if there was a conflict with the right to travel *simpliciter* and the right to life (of the unborn) than the right to life would take precedence.[124] This ranking, although not the idea of a hierarchy, appears to have been overturned by the Thirteenth Amendment to the Constitution Act, 1992. The members of the Supreme Court were of the unanimous opinion that if a harmonious interpretation of the Constitution did not resolve the conflict between rights, then

---

[120] See above, para. 23–7, "Unenumerated Personal Rights Resulting from the Nature of the State".

[121] [1985] IR 532.

[122] *ibid.* at 538.

[123] [1982] I.R. 1.

[124] [1991] 1 I.R. 1 at 57, *per* Finlay, C.J. This ranking was not placed expressly on a natural law basis.

a hierarchy must be applied, and the right to life heads the hierarchy. This has been reaffirmed in *Re A Ward of Court*[125] where Hamilton C.J. held that if there had been an interaction of rights not capable of harmonisation in the case, the right to life would take precedence[126]: "I deem the right to life to be the highest in the hierarchy of rights."[127]

---

125 [1995] 2 I.L.R.M. 401.

126 *ibid.* at 425.

127 *ibid.* at 437. See also Denham J., whose statements appear somewhat inconsistent: "The right to life is the pre-eminent right" (at 457) but goes on to state on the one hand that the requirement to defend the right is not absolute (at 457), and more importantly that "the ward's life is respected, this is an absolute" (at 465).

24. CONCEPTS OF IRISH CONSTITUTIONAL LAW

24–1 Although the legitimation of Irish constitutional law depends ultimately on Irish constitutional natural law, there are other important grounding concepts of Irish constitutional law: the sovereignty of the State; the sovereignty of the people; the common good; and society. These concepts are particularly important to explain the legitimation of Irish constitutional law and the meaning, scope and permissible limitation of Irish constitutional rights: they have specific meanings in Irish constitutional law which differ from European Community law (for example the common good); they give rise to the possibility of conflict; and they are a basis for the argument that there are limits on amendability without legal revolution.

Sovereignty of the State

24–2 According to the Supreme Court, an independent sovereign state was created by the Constitution of 1922 – *Saorstát Éireann*:

> "by virtue of the provisions of the Constitution of 1922 what was being created was a brand new sovereign State and that the function, power or position of the King in that sovereign State was such only as was vested in him by that Constitution and by the State created by it".[1]

This date has been disputed by Kelly[1a] but in either opinion it is clear that Ireland was a sovereign and independent State with the enactment of the Constitution in 1937 – "Article 5. Ireland is a sovereign, independent, democratic state."

Sovereignty is a difficult concept with disputed meanings in legal and political theory and different meanings in different legal orders. Instead of examining its possible meanings in legal theory, the sole concern of this chapter is to consider the meaning sovereignty has in Irish constitutional law. In Irish constitutional law sovereignty has three different meanings, according to the following three contexts:

1. Domestic state action controlled by Irish constitutional law;
2. External state action controlled by Irish constitutional law;
3. Internal or external state action controlled by another legal system.

---

[1] *Webb v. Ireland* [1988] I.R. 353 at 382 *per* Finlay C.J.

[1a] J.M. Kelly, "Hidden Treasure and the Irish Constitution" (1988) 10 D.U.L.J. (N.S.) 5.

These meanings have been clarified by case law. The first two meanings of sovereignty place the exercise of sovereignty by the State under the control of the Constitution. The last meaning is an assertion by Irish constitutional law of the State's place in international law.

1. Walsh J. in a judgment in *Byrne v. Ireland*[2] in which Ó'Dálaigh C.J. and the Supreme Court majority concurred (and which was later expressly affirmed by Finlay C.J. in *Webb*[3]), held:

   > "Article 5 means that the State is not subject to any power of government save those designated by the People in the Constitution itself, and that the State is not amenable to any external authority for its conduct . . . the learned trial judge misconstrued the intent of Article 5 if he construed it as a constitutional declaration that the State is above the law."[4]

   Budd J. in *Byrne* held: "The State is not internally sovereign but, in internal affairs, subject to the Constitution which limits, confines and restricts its power."[5] Budd J. was of the opinion that sovereignty in Article 5 referred to independence in international relations. Kelly commented on *Byrne*: "the 'sovereign' nature of the State, while unimpeachable *vis-à-vis* other States, did not operate *internally* so as to put the State, as a juristic person, above the law."[6]

2. Ireland's external actions as a member of the international community will be controlled by the courts where the Constitution so requires. Article 29.4 provides that the Government shall in connection with external relations exercise its power in accordance with Article 28 of the Constitution. Article 28.2 makes the Executive power subject to the provisions of the Constitution.

   In *Crotty v. An Taoiseach*[7] the Supreme Court granted an injunction restraining the government from depositing the instrument of ratification of the Single European Act. All the judges held that the courts had a duty to intervene in the conduct of foreign affairs where any organ of government was acting in breach of the Constitution. Finlay C.J. and Griffin J. dissented from the award of an injunction because of their construction of Title III of the Single European Act on "European Cooperation in the Sphere of

---

2 [1972] I.R. 241. In this case the Supreme Court established that the State was not immune from suit and could be sued for the negligence of its servants and agents. The declaration in Article 5 that Ireland is a sovereign State did not (as Murnaghan, J. in the High Court had thought) exclude an action against the State. The prerogative of immunity from suit did not survive the Constitution of the Irish Free State 1922.

3 *Webb v. Ireland* [1988] I.R. 353.

4 *Byrne v. Ireland* [1972] I.R. 241 at 264.

5 *ibid.* at 299.

6 J.M. Kelly, *op. cit.* above, n.1a, at p. 24.

7 [1987] I.L.R.M. 400.

Foreign Policy" which they held did not bind the State's "unfettered right to decide"[8] which was the meaning of sovereignty in this context. However, both judges held in principle that the courts could intervene in the conduct of foreign relations: Finlay C.J. stated that the courts must intervene where an individual pleads breach of his constitutional rights.[9]

The other three judges (Walsh, Henchy, and Hederman, JJ.) agreed to issue an injunction, which suspended the coming into force of the Single European Act in European Community law and precipitated a referendum. This case was concerned primarily with whether the proposed method of ratification for such a treaty by approval of *Dáil Éireann* pursuant to Article 29.5.2 was in accordance with the Constitution. The majority held that the Constitution prevented review of the State's conduct of foreign relations as far as statements of policy were concerned, but not as regards binding treaties. Hederman J. held that the essential point was whether the State can bind itself by any act of its organs of government to submit powers bestowed by the Constitution to the advice of other States. He held that the organs of State could not contract to fetter powers bestowed unfettered by the Constitution: "They are the guardians of these powers – not the disposers of them."[10] As Walsh J. put it: "It is not within the competence of the Government, or indeed the Oireachtas, to free themselves from the restraints of the Constitution or to transfer their powers to other bodies unless expressly empowered so to do by the Constitution."[11] This is a very important statement because the Irish constitutional provisions on the European Union and European Communities introduce a bar to constitutional challenges in Irish courts to the application of Community law. They do not empower the organs of government to transfer competences.[12] Walsh J. rejected the claim that the courts have no competence until treaties are translated into domestic law: on his analysis of the Single European Act[13] the treaty materially qualified the right to say yes or no. The judgment of Henchy J. was framed in wider terms and is considered below, in paragraph 24–4.

3. As regards the control of State action by another legal order, Article 5 is a statement in Irish constitutional law of Ireland's position in public international law and marks a definitive constitutional break with any special constitutional tie to the United Kingdom. Walsh J. stated in *Crotty v. An Taoiseach*:

---

8 *ibid.* at 446.

9 *ibid.* at 452. This was also Griffin J.'s opinion, based on an interpretation of *Boland v. An Taoiseach* [1974] I.R. 338.

10 *Crotty v. An Taoiseach* [1987] I.L.R.M. 400 at 469.

11 *ibid.* at 454.

12 This is considered further below in Chap. 27, "European Law in Irish Constitutional Law".

13 *Crotty v. An Taoiseach* [1987] I.L.R.M. 400 at 458–459.

> "The State would not be completely sovereign if it did not have in common with other members of the family of nations the right and power in the field of international relations equal to the right and power of other States."[14]

To this may be added Walsh J.'s remarks in *Byrne v. Ireland*[15] (quoted above) that "the State is not amenable to any external authority for its conduct".

In sum, the State is not sovereign in the sense of an unlimited "power of government" (the phrase used in *Webb*[16]) except as an assertion of Irish constitutional law of its place in public international law. This assertion in *Crotty* of the State's sovereignty in public international law indicates that Irish constitutional law does not regard the State's status as a sovereign state in public international law to be reduced by its membership of the European Union.

Sovereignty of the People

24–3 In Irish constitutional law it is the people who are ultimately internal sovereign[17]; as regards external sovereignty the people control the State's exercise of foreign affairs through the Constitution. The State is externally sovereign in the sense that it is not bound to other states except so far as is provided by the Constitution. The State is not internally sovereign. The sovereignty of the people has been judicially stated in the first major case on the concept of sovereignty in Irish constitutional law:

> "[T]he State is the creation of the People and it is to be governed in accordance with the provisions of the Constitution which was enacted by the People only, and that in the last analysis the sovereign authority is the People."[18]

In *Webb v. Ireland*[19] Walsh J referred to "the People as the sovereign authority having by the Constitution created the State, and by Article 5 declared it to be a sovereign State . . . ".[20] In *McKenna v. An Taoiseach*[21] the Supreme Court reaffirmed the importance of the role of the people in the functioning of democracy, "which is not exclusively a parliamentary democracy; it has elements of a plebiciary democracy".[22] "Power derives from the people".[23]

---

14 *ibid.* at 454.

15 [1972] I.R. 241.

16 *Webb v. Ireland,* [1988] I.R. 353.

17 "It is the people who are paramount . . . The State is not internally Sovereign but, in internal affairs, subject to the constitution, which limits, confines and restricts its powers." – Budd J. in *Byrne v. Ireland* above, n.2, adopted with approval in *Re Article 26 and the Regulation of Information (Services for the Termination of Pregnancies) Bill, 1995* [1995] 1 I.R. 1.

18 *Byrne v. Ireland* [1972] I.R. 241 at 262 *per* Walsh J., majority concurring, affirmed in *Webb v. Ireland* [1988] I.R. 353.

19 [1988] I.R. 353.

20 *ibid.* at 393.

21 [1995] 2 I.R. 10.

22 *ibid. per* O'Flaherty J. at 43.

23 *ibid. per* Denham J. at 54.

Although the people are the ultimate internal sovereign, the notion of sovereignty is itself limited by Irish constitutional natural law and the Irish constitutional law concept of the common good.[24] The legitimation of Irish constitutional law does not ultimately depend on the will of the people. Whether the people as a constitutional concept means, in connection with sovereignty something more then those persons on the register of presidential electors cannot be stated with certainty. However the Irish language text uses the word *pobal* which also has the meaning of community, and indeed has this meaning in the Constitution itself, since "*leas an phobail*" translates as the good/well-being of the community – the common good.

The Common Good

24–4 The meaning of the concept of the common good has not been systematically expounded.[25] The notable exception to this is Judge Costello:

---

24 The common good is considered below in, para. 24–4. There is a tension between natural law theory and most democratic political theories (see A. Whelan, "Constitutional Amendments in Ireland: The Competing Claims of Democracy", in G. Quinn *et al.*, *Justice and Legal Theory in Ireland* (Dublin 1995), and G. Quinn, "Book Review of J.M. Kelly, *A Short History of Western Legal Theory*" (1993–1995) XXVIII–XXX *Irish Jurist* 408 at p. 412). This general tension is translated in the Irish context into a tension between Irish constitutional natural law and the sovereignty of the people. However this tension need not lead to incoherence, nor to an "undemocratic" legal order, although not a legal order in which democracy is taken to mean majority rule. Sovereignty is a limited concept in Irish constitutional law, which is not to say that as a political fact the people could not do things in breach of Irish constitutional natural law. The question is whether or not such acts can have legal effects. The people could have enacted a Constitution which did not import natural law, but they recognised it as binding, and so remain bound unless they succeed, as a political matter, in radically altering the legitimation of Irish constitutional law. If they do so succeed, then such acts will have legal effects in the new order, although will be illegal according to the old. It is important, however, to indicate that there is a further possible level of analysis here, perceived only in peripheral vision in this thesis which would apply to the purported adoption of any Constitution. That is that the people, when they act politically in order to achieve something in law, are bound by the subject matter (law) in which they wish to act, and so cannot act unrestrainedly with legal effects, although they may be able to act unrestrainedly (a question of political fact) without legal effects. This boils down to an external conception of what law is. The conception which the people recognised when they did act in 1933 was a conception of natural law limits to the exercise of power, irrespective of the democratic mechanics and institutionalisation of its exercise. By way of analogy, one can think of a free individual who wishes to make music. He raps his elbow against a blackboard, unwraps a sandwich, and squeaks close to middle C. Is that music? That depends on the meaning of music. The individual could have sung a *Te Deum* or chanted *Olè, olè, olè.*

25 This paragraph does not claim to be a systematic exposition; it focuses on those aspects of the concept necessary to establish the propositions set out in the Introduction to this Part. The concept has been systematically expounded in Ireland outside of Irish law – *see* J. Newman, *Foundations of Justice: A Historico-Critical Study in Thomism* (Cork:

> "It is not usual for contemporary draftsmen of Bills of Rights, or of statutes and international conventions dealing with fundamental rights, to employ the phrase 'the common good' – the 'general welfare' being preferred to convey more or less the same notion. . . . It is a phrase which the Constitution has derived from the classical Christian writings on natural law. It features prominently in Aquinas' works and is linked to his thinking on the nature of the political community."[26]

The common good is related to the moral aspect of society.[27]

The common good could mean only the good of the people, since this would be the flipside to the dual meaning of the word "*pobal*". But this has overtones of majoritarianism which the rest of Irish constitutional law firmly rejects: the protection of Irish constitutional natural law rights is not merely about keeping the delegated organs of government within the *vires* allowed them by an omnipotent sovereign majority; rather, it is a *sine qua non* in the legitimation of Irish constitutional law. Interpreting the Constitution as a whole, then, this restriction of meaning must be rejected.

The common good is very much embedded as a creature of Irish constitutional law and as the common good of the Irish people. In *Webb v. Ireland*[28] Finlay C.J., supported by Walsh J.,[29] emphasised the Constitution's "constant concern for the common good" in deciding that there should be ownership by the State of objects which constitute antiquities of importance.

The common good appears to be a restriction of the idea of people as unlimited sovereign. The common good is mentioned directly in the Constitution several times. It is set as one of the goals of the Constitution and reasons why the people adopted the Constitution, tempered by the concept of Justice: "seeking to promote the common good, with due observance of Prudence, Justice and Charity . . . Do hereby adopt and give themselves this Constitution."[30] Article 6 provides that the people have the right "in final appeal, to decide all questions of national policy, according to the requirements of the common good". This Article does not assert an untrammelled

---

Cork University Press, 1954) pp. 34–42, where the author relates it directly to the concept of legal justice, as the object thereof. The author argues that the common good of the State is the principal common good of human societies, the common goods of lesser communities such as families being integrated into it. The common good of the State comprises both the material and moral conditions for the living of the good life and also the attainment of the good life itself ("In this sense the common good depends for its attainment on the personal action of the individual citizens": p. 38). The common good of the State is subordinate to the ultimate common good of man as a citizen in the City of God and comprises both God and the possession of God (or beatitude).

26 D. Costello, "Natural Law, the Constitution, and the Courts" (1987) in P. Lynch and J. Meenan, *Essays in Memory of Alexis Fitzgerald* (Dublin: Incorporated Law Society of Ireland, 1987) pp. 110–113.

27 *Re a Ward of Court* [1995] 2 I.L.R.M. 401 at 459, *per* Denham J.: "The State has an interest in the moral aspect of society – for the common good".

28 [1988] I.R. 353 at 383.

29 *ibid.* at 390.

30 See also *McGee v. Attorney General* [1974] I.R. 284 at 318–319, *per* Walsh J.

sovereign power to decide; it states a right, which as a power of government is expressly stated in the Article to be under God, to be exercised subject to the requirements of the common good.

The common good is mentioned several times in the Constitution as a grounds for restricting the exercise of individual rights. For example, Article 40.6.1.i provides that the State guarantees liberty for the exercise of the right of citizens to express freely their convictions and opinions but also provides for the constitutionality of restrictions to this right because the education of public opinion is "a matter of such grave import to the common good". As regards the right to property the State may reconcile its exercise "with the exigencies of the common good" (Article 43.2.2). The courts have held that they may have recourse to the directive principles of social policy in deciding on the meaning of the common good in the restriction of unenumerated constitutional rights.[31]

In Article 41.5 the State is referred to as the "guardian of the common good". In Article 43.2.2 the State is declared to be able to limit by law the exercise of the natural right to the private ownership of external goods with a view to reconciling its exercise "with the exigencies of the common good". This is backed up by Article 45.2:

> "The State shall, in particular, direct its policy towards securing . . .
> ii. That the ownership and control of the material resources of the community may be so distributed amongst private individuals and the various classes as best to subserve the common good.
> iii. That, especially, the operation of free competition shall not be allowed so to develop as to result in the concentration of the ownership or control of essential commodities in a few individuals to the common detriment."

A general definition of "common good" may be attempted on the basis of the above legal evidence. The common good appears as an abstract term for the set of conditions in society which enables persons to pursue best in their lives the fundamental commitments espoused by the Constitution.[32] The conditions of the common good act as a counterweight to the uncontrolled pursuit of the good of an individual but at the same time facilitate an individual in the securing of his or her good in life within society. The common good in Irish constitutional law is clearly not equivalent to the greatest good for the greatest number. Nor is it solely concerned with providing a calibration for settling conflicts between two competing constitutional rights. Rather it appears to mean, as a concept which is used to limit the exercise of natural constitutional rights, a set of conditions which enables the members of Irish

---

31 *Landers v. Attorney General* (1975) 109 I.L.T.R. 1; *Attorney General v. Paperlink Ltd.* [1984] I.L.R.M. 373.

32 See also D.R. Phelan, "The Concept of Social Rights" [1994] 16 D.U.L.J. 105 at p. 114. This conception of the common good is closely related to that of J. Finnis, *Natural Law and Natural Rights* (Oxford: Oxford University Press, 1980).

society, both persons[33] and families, to pursue as far as possible the fundamental commitments of Irish constitutional law reflected in their natural rights.

The Irish constitutional law concept of the common good is specific to the Irish legal system and contributes to the potential for conflict with European Community law. The common good was at the root of the *ratio decidendi* in Henchy J.'s judgment in *Crotty v. An Taoiseach*[34] where, having stated that the ultimate source and limit of the Government's powers in the conduct of foreign relations were to be found in Article 6, he declared:

> "It follows that the common good of the Irish People is the ultimate standard by which the constitutional validity of the conduct of foreign affairs by the Government is to be judged. In this and in a number of other respects throughout the Constitution the central position of the common good of the Irish people is stressed as one of the most fundamental characteristics of Ireland as a sovereign, independent, democratic state."[35]

Title III of the Single European Act caused constitutional problems because it required the curtailment of the freedom of action of each Member State "in the interests of the common good of the Member States as a whole."[36] The Irish constitutional law common good was thus in conflict with the common good identified by Title III (which was, in this case, the common good of the Member States as a whole).

Society

24–5 Society is a creation of the Constitution, not the Constitution a creation of society. The Constitution is the foundation which will help society evolve and not an instrument which will follow wherever current pressures of society might lead.[37] This is not surprising given that one of the main purposes of the Constitution which, unlike the Constitution of *Saorstát Éireann,* made a final break with Great Britain,[38] was to give national definition to society. Article 1 of the Constitution asserts the right of the nation "to develop its life, political, economic and cultural, in accordance with its own genius and tra-

---

33 These do not have to be citizens. See above, para. 23–8, "Fundamental Rights based on a Contract between State and Citizens".

34 [1987] I.L.R.M. 400.

35 *ibid.* at 463.

36 *ibid.*

37 This is not to deny that society also exists as a state of facts, although people would disagree, depending on their conception of society, as to which state of facts.

38 Article 29.4.2 in fact provided cover for the functions the Crown exercised pursuant to the Executive Authority (External Relations) Act 1936: the accreditation of diplomatic representatives and the signing of treaties. However Article 29.4.2 made no reference to the Crown, and its functions were transferred to the President by the Republic of Ireland Act 1948.

ditions." Furthermore, it is indicative of a cultural as well as a conceptual attitude towards law which emphasises its symbolic value.[39]

The idea of society created by the Constitution was stated in the case on whether the British royal prerogative of treasure trove had been carried over into law.[40] The Supreme Court began by affirming that the State was the creation of the people, that it was to be governed according to the Constitution, and consequently that the State and its agents had no immunity from suit.[41] The Court then held that there was no royal prerogative of treasure trove, but this did not mean finders keepers. Finlay C.J. held: "It would appear to me to be inconsistent with the framework of the society sought to be created and sought to be protected by the Constitution that such objects should become the exclusive property of those who by chance may find them."[42] Walsh J. supported the Chief Justice in almost identical terms, holding that such a result "would be inconsistent with the framework of the society which is created by the Constitution and which is sought to be protected by that Constitution . . . ".[43]

There are several provisions of the Constitution which touch directly on the concept of Irish society. For example, Article 1 asserts the right of the Irish nation "to develop its life, political, economic and cultural, in accordance with its own genius and traditions." Article 41.1.1 is an example that society is viewed in part as a projection of constitutional principles (which have their basis in natural law[44]); Article 41.1.1 also marks the distinctiveness

---

[39] Duncan has pointed out, in the context of the ideal of permanency of marriage, that there is a:

> " . . . special Irish attitude towards law – an emphasis on its symbolic value . . . By holding fast to that ideal, even when it is recognized to be one which many cannot attain in practice, the law is setting a standard, reflecting a broadly accepted national aspiration and possibly even offering an example and inspiration to other countries. Such a theory assumes that law has an educative function and that radical changes in the standards which it sets can influence conduct over time."

W. Duncan, "The Divorce Referendum in the Republic of Ireland: Resisting the Tide" (1988) *International Journal of Law and the Family* 62 at pp. 71–72. This is an important point. It might be added that the emphasis on the standard-setting function of law is not specially Irish or special to the area of constitutional rights (for example, it is one of the main emphases of criminal law).

[40] *Webb v. Ireland* [1988] I.R. 353.

[41] *Byrne v. Ireland* [1972] I.R. 241.

[42] *Webb v. Ireland* [1988] I.R. 353 at 383.

[43] *ibid.* at 390–391. This case introduced the concept of "national heritage" into constitutional law. See J.M. Kelly, *op. cit.* above, n.1a.

[44] Article 41.1.1 provides:

> "The State recognises the Family as the natural primary and fundamental unit group of Society, and as a moral institution possessing inalienable and imprescriptible rights, antecedent and superior to all positive law."

It is significant that the word "Society" takes a capital "S". This supports the argument that there is a constitutional concept of society which differs from society in fact (whatever that might be). Similarly with "the Family". Interestingly, there is never a capital "P" for "the people" in the Constitution.

of a society where the family is recognised as the fundamental unit group.[45] Article 45 contains the "Directive Principles of Social Policy" which are stated to be "for the general guidance of the *Oireachtas*". These contain a host of social objectives and policies concerned with the protection of weaker members of society and the promotion of the common good. The *Oireachtas* has expressly referred to these principles.[46] Furthermore, the courts have in fact had regard to this article to inform the content of unenumerated personal rights,[47] in considering the validity of pre-Constitution statutes,[48] and in the construction of the common law.[49] In *Attorney General v. Paperlink Ltd.* Costello J. held:

> "I am not precluded by the introductory words of the Article from considering the principles of social policy set out in it for a limited purpose, namely, for assisting the court in ascertaining what personal rights are included in the guarantees contained in Article 40.3.1 and what legitimate limitations in the interests of the common good the State may impose on such rights."[50]

The importance of the constitutional vision of society for fundamental constitutional rights is illustrated by Hamilton P.'s judgment in *Kennedy v. Ireland* where he found an unenumerated right of privacy, and continued:

> "Its exercise may be restricted by the constitutional rights of other, or by the requirements of the common good, and it is subject to the requirements of public order and morality . . .
>
> . . .
>
> The nature of the right to privacy must be such as to ensure the dignity and freedom of the individual in the type of society envisaged by the Constitution, namely, a sovereign, independent and democratic society."[51]

---

[45] Ireland is not alone here. Article 21 of the Constitution of Greece provides that the family "as the foundation of the preservation and the advancement of the nation, as well as marriage, motherhood and childhood, shall be under the protection of the State." Article 6(1) of the German Constitution provides that "Marriage and the family shall enjoy the special protection of the State." Article 3.9.1 of the Spanish Constitution provides "The public authorities shall ensure the social, economic and legal protection of the family".

[46] An early example being the Central Bank Act 1942 which repeats in s.6(1) the intent expressed in Article 45.2.iv, "that in what pertains to the control of credit the constant and predominant aim shall be the welfare of the people as a whole."

[47] *Murtagh Properties v. Cleary* [1972] I.R. 330 at 335–336, *per* Kenny J.; *Landers v. Attorney General* (1975) 109 I.L.T.R. 1, *per* Finlay P.; *Rogers v. I.T. & G.W.U.* [1987] I.L.R.M. 51, *per* Finlay P.; *Attorney General v. Paperlink Ltd.* [1984] I.L.R.M. 373, *per* Costello J.

[48] *McGee v. Attorney General* [1974] I.R. 284 at 291, *per* O'Keeffe P.; *Murtagh Properties v. Cleary* [1972] I.R. 330.

[49] *Kerry Co-Operative Creameries v. An Bord Bainne* [1991] I.L.R.M. 851 at 870–871, *per* McCarthy J., limiting the restriction on application of Article 45 to the making of laws by the Oireachtas.

[50] [1984] I.L.R.M. 373 at 386.

[51] [1987] I.R. 587 at 592–593.

25. THE CONSTITUTIONALISATION OF IRISH LAW

25–1 The next step in this Part is to show how important Irish constitutional law and Irish constitutional natural law legitimation is for the whole of Irish law. The Constitution is no mere political statement; the fundamental rights acknowledged thereunder are no mere aspirations. Nor is Irish constitutional law important solely, for example, for the control of the validity of a statute or the assertion of a constitutional right against State action. A conflict between Irish constitutional law and European Community law has direct implications for the whole legal order. The constitutionalisation of law is easier to demonstrate in this Part than in Part III: there is no French-style rigid division between public and private law (the latter based on the *codes* such as the famous *code civil*) and there is only one set of ordinary courts, which are established and regulated primarily by the Constitution itself (Articles 33–37). There are several distinctive features of Irish constitutional law which characterise its importance in the legal system as a whole.

Here it is considered how far Irish constitutional law branches into administrative and private law, and the overriding duty of the courts to vindicate constitutional rights, which duty enables judges to override legal restrictions on how, when, against whom, and by whom these rights may be asserted.

How Conflicts can Occur Jurisdictionally

25–2 This a short paragraph because there is only one system of courts, the constitutional control of enactments is well-developed, a rigid separation of powers was never entrenched, and there are no restrictions on jurisdiction in constitutional matters, save:

(i) Article 34.3.2 which provides that no question on the constitutionality of a post-Constitution law can be argued except in the High and Supreme Courts;

(ii) Article 28.3.3 on the invalidation of laws of the *Oireachtas* expressed to be for the purpose of securing the public safety and the preservation of the State in time of war or armed rebellion;

(iii) Article 34.3.3 on statutes the constitutionality of which was already upheld by the Supreme Court when referred as a Bill pursuant to Article 26.[1]

---

[1] An analysis of the restrictions on the restrictions provided by these last two exceptional cases is outside the scope of this work.

Access to the High and Supreme Courts on constitutional issues from all other courts or tribunals is easy. It is possible in the event of a conflict with Irish constitutional law to get a court decision binding on all tribunals, organs of government, and private and corporate individuals within the jurisdiction. Judicial review of almost any act of power is well-established, from executive action in external affairs in *Crotty v. An Taoiseach*,[2] to a measure implementing a European Community law obligation in *Condon v. Minister for Agriculture*[3] or the European Communities Act in *Meagher v. Minister for Agriculture*,[4] from a contractual dispute between private parties in *Ryan v. V.I.P. Taxi Co-operative*[5] to the deprivation of a human right in *Attorney General v. X.*[6]

The Extension of Constitutional Justice into Administrative Law and Contract Law

25–3 Although administrative law is a branch of public law it is distinct from what can be properly called constitutional law in some legal orders. For example, in France the administrative courts apply general principles ("*principes généraux*") and not principles of constitutional value ("*principes de valeur constitutionnelles*"). In Ireland the common law principles of natural justice (*nemo iudex in causa sua; audi alteram partem*) have been subsumed into the broader category of principles of constitutional justice.[7] If European Community law requirements conflict with natural justice (such as in the procedures for the administration of a European Community law program) then there is a risk of conflict with Irish constitutional law. Furthermore, if integration of European Community law into Irish constitutional law renders the latter incoherent because it upsets the hierarchy of fundamental rights, there would be a knock-on effect in administrative law.

Constitutional justice appears to be based in large part on the protection of constitutional rights, and in lesser parts both on the unenumerated right to fair procedures, and on an Aristotelian-influenced interpretation of equality before the law. Walsh J.'s interpretation of equality before the law in Article 40.1 is that it "imports the Aristotelian concept that justice demands that we treat equals equally and unequals unequally."[8] It has been seen above how positive law is regarded to be ranked beneath the requirements of justice:

---

2 [1987] I.L.R.M. 400.

3 *Condon v. Minister for Agriculture* (1993) 2 *Irish Journal of European Law* 151.

4 [1994] 1 I.R. 329.

5 Unreported, High Court, Lardner J., January 10, 1989; *Irish Times*, 10 April 1989.

6 [1992] 1 I.R. 1.

7 For a detailed exposition of this phenomenon see G.W. Hogan and D.G. Morgan, *Administrative Law in Ireland* (2nd ed., London: Sweet & Maxwell, 1992).

8 *De Burca v. Attorney General* [1976] I.R. 38 at 68; see Aristotle, *Politics*, iii, 9.

"the concept of justice, which is specifically referred to in the preamble in relation to the freedom and dignity of the individual, appears again in the provisions of Article 34 which deal with the Courts. It is justice which is to be administered in the Courts and this concept of justice must import not only fairness and fair procedures, but also regard to the dignity of the individual. No court under the Constitution has jurisdiction to act contrary to justice."[9]

The distinctive mark of constitutional justice which will be considered in the following examples of judicial review on constitutional grounds of the acts of various bodies is the way in which its requirements are applied by way of judicial review of non-state action.

The seminal case of *In Re Pádraig Haughey*[10] established the right to fair procedures, and the right to have other constitutional rights protected at the procedural stage. Ó'Dálaigh C.J., (Walsh and Budd, JJ., concurring) held:

"Article 40, s.3, of the Constitution is a guarantee to the citizen of basic fairness of procedures. The Constitution guarantees such fairness, and it is the duty of the Court to underline that the words of Article 40, s.3, are not political shibboleths but provide a positive protection for the citizen and his good name . . . in proceedings before *any tribunal* where a party to the proceedings is on risk of having his good name, or his person or property, or *any of his personal rights* jeopardised, the proceedings may be correctly classed as proceedings which may affect his rights, and in compliance with the Constitution the State, either by its enactments or through the Courts, must outlaw any *procedures* which will restrict or prevent the party concerned from vindicating those rights." (Emphasis added.)

This passage also suggests that the tribunal involved need not be created by or exercise a public power.

Provided that there is a procedure available to a claimant to protect constitutional rights in private relations, the type of procedure available is not of central concern to the argument here. However, the courts' former willingness to allow the procedure of judicial review to be used to review a tribunal's procedures where the relationship between the applicant and the decision-maker is based exclusively on the private law of contract[11] is noteworthy for the flexibility of the judiciary in protecting constitutional rights, although it is quite possible that the courts will insist on a more appropriate procedure such as raising constitutional rights as a claim in plenary proceedings. The case of *O'Neill v. Beaumont Hospital Board*[12] concerned the dismissal of a consultant neurosurgeon pursuant to the terms of a common consultant's contract which had been adopted by more than one hospital. The contract provided for a procedure for review by the hospital board but

---

9 *The State (Healy) v. Donoghue* [1976] I.R. 325 at 348.

10 [1971] I.R. 217 at 264.

11 For a succinct exposition of the expansion of the scope of judicial review, see H. Delaney, "The Scope of Judicial Review – a Question of the Source or Nature of Powers" (1993) 11 *Irish Law Times* 12.

12 [1990] I.L.R.M. 419.

the High Court (Murphy J.), upheld by the Supreme Court, found that the decision was void on the ground of bias. In *O'Neill v. Iarnród Éireann*[13] the Supreme Court granted leave to issue proceedings for judicial review by way of *certiorari* to quash a decision to dismiss an employee.

In both these cases, the relationship between the parties was governed by the private law of contract, but the respondent authority had been set up by statute. However, in the case of *Ryan v. V.I.P. Taxi Co-Operative Ltd.*[14] not only was the relationship between the parties exclusively one of contract with the disciplinary jurisdiction derived purely from a contractual source, but also the respondent was a private company. Lardner J. in the High Court granted an applicant an order of *certiorari* quashing the decision of a disciplinary committee of the respondent society. This marks a further extension of the use of judicial review by the ordinary courts on the grounds of constitutional justice to that of a purely private relationship between purely private parties.

In *O'Neill v. Beaumont Hospital* the judges voiced their grave doubts about whether judicial review was the appropriate procedure where there was no state exercise of a public power but did not wish to decide the issue without full argument thereon. From the tone of the *dicta* it appears likely that the law will be changed by a suitable case. There is contrary High Court authority. In *Murphy v. The Turf Club,*[15] Barr J. refused an application for judicial review on the ground that judicial review may be against the decision of a body which does not derive its powers from statute or common law where those powers are of a public law nature, but not where they are of the nature of voluntary contract.[16] Hederman J. stated in *O'Neill v. Iarnród Éireann* that "relief sought under [the procedural rules for judicial review] lies only against public authorities in respect of the duties conferred upon them by law."

However, were such a change in the law to take place it might only affect the procedure by which such issues could be raised and would not necessarily affect the courts' willingness to settle disputes between private parties by application of the same substantive Irish constitutional law or constitutional justice. Thus Hederman J. in *O'Neill v. Iarnród Éireann* went on to consider *In Re Pádraig Haughey*[17] and say that "a constitutional issue of justice and fairness which may arise between private parties, can only be determined by ordinary court procedure." The judge expressed willingness to follow *Glover v. BLN*[18] as authority for the proposition that if a contract provides special procedures for dismissal constitutional issues may arise to be dealt with in private law proceedings. In *O'Neill v. Beaumont Hospital* Murphy J. held that the

---

13 [1991] I.L.R.M. 129.

14 Unreported, High Court, Lardner J., 10 January 1989; *Irish Times*, 10 April 1989.

15 [1989] I.R. 171.

16 The applicant was challenging the respondent's revocation of his licence to train horses, Barr J. held that the relationship between the applicant and respondent was exclusively one of contract, and that the respondent's purported revocation of the applicant's licence was not an exercise of public law powers.

17 [1971] I.R. 217.

18 [1973] I.R. 388.

contract had to be interpreted in the light of the duties required by the rules of constitutional justice. The divisional Supreme Court (*per* Finlay C.J. with Walsh and Budd JJ., concurring) proceeded as if the proceedings had been instituted by way of plenary summons and statement of claim and the plaintiff was claiming an interlocutory injunction based on "contractual rights and the implied constituents of those rights". Constitutional justice operates both positively and negatively: negatively, for example, to hold a decision produced by biased procedures as void; positively, for example, to require the right to state a case to be implied into contractual procedures. Thus Irish constitutional law may be used in the future to require procedures to be read into contracts as implied terms, which contracts would otherwise fall short of the standards constitutional justice expects in the circumstances. In conclusion, whether or not the procedure of judicial review of private law contracts continues to be allowed as in *Ryan v. V.I.P. Taxi Co-Operative Ltd.*,[19] constitutional justice will continue to entrench its position in private law.

The Extension of Constitutional Rights into Private Relations

25–4 Apart from constitutional justice and its progeny, the right to constitutionally just procedures, Irish constitutional law also requires in private legal relations the observance of constitutional personal rights.[20] Irish constitutional law acknowleged early the horizontal direct effect of constitutional norms, specifically, the effect of constitutional rights on relations between private parties. In *Educational Company of Ireland v. Fitzpatrick*[21] O'Dálaigh J. said: "Liberty to exercise a right, it seems to me, *prima facie* implies a correlative duty on others to abstain from interfering with the exercise of such right." In the second phase of that case Budd J. stated in clearer terms:

> "Obedience to the law is required of every citizen, and it follows that if one citizen has a right under the Constitution there exists a correlative duty on the part of other citizens to respect that right and not to interfere with it."[22]

---

19 Unreported, High Court Lardner J., 10 January 1989; *Irish Times*, 10 April 1989.

20 There is a continuing debate in this general area in the United States: H.J. Friendly, "Conference on the Public–Private Distinction" (1982) 130 *University of Pennsylvania Law Review* 1289; M.J. Horwitz, "The History of the Public/Private Distinction" (1982) 130 *University of Pennsylvania Law Review* 1423: "Private power began to be increasingly indistinguishable from public power precisely at the moment, late in the nineteenth century, when large-scale corporate concentration became the norm" (at p. 1428), (the Irish authorities cited in the text all concern actions by humans against corporations); D. Kennedy, "The Stages of the Decline of the Public/Private Distinction" (1982) *University of Pennsylvania Law Review* 1349.

21 [1961] I.R. 323.

22 *ibid.* at 345.

Walsh J. referred to this in *Meskell v. Córas Iompar Éireann*[23] where it was established that trade unions had a duty to respect the constitutional rights of others, including the unenumerated constitutional right to dissociate. In that case he held that the agreement between the trade unions (private associations) to cause the plaintiff's dismissal "was an actionable conspiracy because the means employed constituted a breach or infringement of the plaintiff's constitutional rights." A right to recover damages from the trade unions resulted. The right to life cases confirm this duty on other citizens.

The right to life cases also clarified a second basis for the extension of constitutional rights into private relations. This basis is the duty of the courts to give effect to the Constitution.[23] This is not simply the legal duty of judges to give effect to the law. It is a constitutional duty on judges to give effect to constitutional norms. Where the norm is founded in natural law, so will be the duty. This is important because Irish constitutional law thereby imposes an overriding personal moral obligation on judges not to disregard the efficacy of the norm, which makes it impossible for a judge to "wear two hats" in the event of a conflict between such a norm and a European Community law rule.[25] In one of the first right to life cases it was held:

> "The Court is under a duty to act so as not to permit any body of citizens to deprive another of his constitutional right, to see that such rights are protected and to regard as unlawful any infringement or attempted infringement of such constitutional right as constituting a violation of the fundamental law of the State."[26]

The state of the law has been summed up by Walsh J. writing extra-curially:

> "[T]he Constitution does not speak to the State alone. It is capable of encompassing relationships between individuals or between groups as well as between them and the State. Constitutionally guaranteed rights are protected from infringement by individuals or groups of individuals . . . [refers to the case-law, *Drittwirkung* and Austrian and Swiss Jurisprudence] This is due in a large measure to the fact that structural innovations in contemporary society have in many instances obliged States to share their power with influential groups of individuals or large-scale private organisations who wield considerable economic or even political power, such as corporations, trade unions, political parties or other institutions . . . The protection of individual rights against

---

23 [1973] I.R. 121.

24 It would be interesting to study whether the acceptance of these ideas of horizontal direct effect and duty to ensure efficacy has been encouraged by the same doctrines in European Community law. It would be ironic because the greater the importance of Irish constitutional law in the legal order the more difficult it is to prevent a conflict between European Community law and Irish constitutional law threatening the whole national legal order, a structure on which European Community law is dependent for its implementation.

25 D.R. Phelan, "Two Hats, One Wig, No Halo" (1995) 45 *Doctrine & Life* 130; see also the judgment of Maguire C.J. in *Re O'Laighleis* [1960] I.R. 93, quoted below in para. 26–2.

26 *Attorney General (S.P.U.C.) v. OpenDoor Counselling* [1987] I.L.R.M. 477.

other social groups or powerful groups is not in itself a new development. What is significant is the introduction into the jurisprudence of [Austria, Germany, Belgium and Italy] of the right of recourse to constitutional norms. If liberty is to be valued both as an end and as a means the Constitution must offer protection against the encroachment of powerful groups upon man's right to develop his faculties in accordance with the ideals of human dignity. Therefore it must ensure liberty and justice for all individuals. This covers liberty and justice in the economic field and in fields such as professional discipline, statutory monopolies and trade unions."[27]

Locus Standi in Proceedings against Public and Private Parties

25–5 A party may uphold a constitutional right where there is no injury marking it out as having a special interest. This party need not even be human – it may be a public interest group. The standard rules on *locus standi*[28] have given way where they would restrict the protection of the Constitution and constitutional rights, or at least in those exceptional actions where no one would be in a better position to assert the constitutional rights. This reinforces both the legal importance of constitutional rights in the courts, and the chances of justiciable conflicts between European Community law and Irish constitutional law.

Against Private Parties

25–6 Not only may private parties assert their own constitutional right against private party infringers of that right, but also a private party may bring an action to defend the constitutional right of another where that person is unable to defend itself. In *S.P.U.C. v. Coogan*[29] Finlay C.J. held that any person who has a bona fide concern and interest, in the sense of an objective or proximate interest, in the protection of the right to life of the unborn has *locus standi* to bring an action (in this case against a student union), at least where the constitutionality of a statute is not in issue. The action was brought by the Society for the Protection of Unborn Children to enforce Article 40.3.3 against the defendant, who was carrying out activities declared to be prohibited in *Attorney General (S.P.U.C.) v. Open Door Counselling.*[30]

There were two sets of reasons given for the extension of Irish constitutional law to allow a private party to assert against another private party the constitutional right of a third party. First, there is the duty on the courts to

---

[27] B. Walsh in *Foreword* to, M. Forde, *Constitutional Law in Ireland* (Cork and Dublin: Mercier, 1987).

[28] *Cahill v. Sutton* [1980] I.R. 269 at 285.

[29] [1990] I.L.R.M. 70.

[30] [1987] I.R. 593.

uphold the Constitution. The Chief Justice based his judgment on, *inter alia,* the following two reasons:

1. once a party with a bona fide concern and interest had invoked the jurisdiction of the courts, the courts would be failing in their duty as an organ of the State bound under Article 40.3.1 to defend and vindicate personal rights;
2. if the right to sue was restricted to the Attorney General, it would be a major curtailment of the duty and power of the courts to defend the Constitution.

Secondly, there is the horizontal direct effect of constitutional norms coupled with the public interest in their preservation. Walsh J. in *S.P.U.C. v. Coogan* denied that constitutional rights are merely public rights "in the classic sense". He held:

> "The right to life of each of the unborn is the private human right of that life . . . what is in issue in this case is the defence of the public interest in the preservation of that private right which has been guaranteed by the constitution . . . . every member of the public has an interest in seeing that the fundamental law of the State is not defeated."[31]

Against the State

25–7 In *Crotty v. An Taoiseach*[32] Barrington J. held in an *ex tempore* judgment of an interlocutory application that a citizen had standing to challenge the legislative authorisation of the Single European Act (without which the State would not be bound – Article 29.5.2) despite his lack of special interest in that state action. Barrington J. held that the applicant had *locus standi* because as a citizen the applicant had a constitutional right to be consulted if a referendum on the amendment to the Constitution was necessary, which the applicant claimed. (Barrington J. also held that the citizen's challenge to the ratification of the Single European Act raised issues in common with him and other citizens where "weighty countervailing circumstances", provided for by Henchy J. in *Cahill v. Sutton*[33] as an exception to the more restrictive *locus standi* rules which normally apply, could be properly invoked.) Barrington J. was later unanimously upheld on his interpretation of the law of *locus standi* by the Supreme Court in reserved judgments.

The Provision of Remedies

25–8 Walsh J. held in a seminal decision in *Byrne v. Ireland*[34]:

---

31 Above, n.29, at 75.
32 [1987] I.L.R.M. 400.
33 [1980] I.R. 269.
34 [1972] I.R. 241.

> "Where the people by the Constitution create rights against the State or impose duties upon the State, a remedy to enforce these must be deemed to be also available."

It has been seen that in the later case of *Meskell v. CIE*[35] this meant a remedy in damages had to be provided as of right against a private defendant. In *Crotty v. An Taoiseach*[36] this meant the remedy which had to be provided was an injunction restraining the government, backed by the Oireachtas, from acting unconstitutionally in the sphere of external relations. The case of *McKinley v. Minister for Defence and Others*[37] concerned a claim for loss of consortium brought by the wife of a former member of the Defence Forces for loss of her husband's services because of scrotal injury. The Supreme Court remitted the action, dismissing the appeal from Johnson J. who had refused to strike out the claim as stating no cause of action. The Supreme Court held (*per* Hederman, McCarthy, and O'Flaherty JJ.) that the English common law limitation of the action for loss of consortium to a claim brought by a husband for loss of services to his wife was inconsistent with the wife's rights under Article 40.1 (equality before the law) and Article 41 (on the family). The judges further held that the courts' jurisdiction was not confined to declaring that an existing common law rule was invalid but extended to declaring that the plaintiff had a constitutional right to compensation.

The Relaxation of Procedural Requirements

25–9 "Notwithstanding any rules of procedure or standing, the courts will jealously guard the right of the individual to be protected from laws, actions or conduct which impinge upon constitutional rights. Where constitutional rights are at stake, the rules of court themselves are at stake."[38]

Procedural rules are relaxed, or at least exceptions made, when the protection of constitutional rights is at issue.[39] It has already been seen above (a) how the Court allowed the procedure of judicial review where issues of constitutional justice arose in contractual relations, despite an expressed preference for plenary procedure and (b) how the rules of *locus standi* facilitate the court protection of constitutional rights. In *The State (Gallagher, Shatter & Co.) v. de Valera (No. 2)*, Barrington J. held that constitutional issues need not always be raised by plenary procedures, stating:

---

35 [1973] I.R. 121.

36 [1987] I.L.R.M. 400.

37 [1992] 2 I.R. 333, noted by G.W. Hogan (1992) 14 D.U.L. J. 115.

38 A.M. Collins and J. O'Reilly, *Civil Proceedings and the State in Ireland* (Dublin: Round Hall Press, 1990) p. 113, citing *Shannon v. Ireland* [1984] I.R. 548 at 555.

39 The habeas corpus line of authorities, not considered here on account of space, supports this contention.

"the great issues decided in the *Sinn Féin Funds* case were first raised in that most humble of all applications – an *ex parte* application for the payment of money out of court."[40]

40 G.W. Hogan and G. Whyte, *Supplement to Second Edition of J.M. Kelly: The Irish Constitution*, (Dublin: University College Dublin, 1988) p. 136.

26. PUBLIC INTERNATIONAL LAW IN IRISH CONSTITUTIONAL LAW

26–1 Article 29 is dedicated to international relations including the relationship of public international law treaties and principles to domestic law. Also included as a subheading of international law is European Community law, although the treatment accorded to it differs from public international law proper. The chapters above reconstructed the bases of Irish constitutional law as natural law based on reason as well as a restricted concept of popular sovereignty. It is of note that in looking outward to the international relations of the State the Constitution takes its two foundational principles to be international justice and morality (Article 29.1):

> "Ireland affirms its devotion to the ideal of peace and friendly cooperation amongst nations founded on international justice and morality."

Coming as the first provisions in Article 29, these principles on the international relations of the State might be interpreted as controlling criteria.[1]

Article 29.2 proclaims the State's adherence to the principle of the pacific settlement of international disputes by arbitration or judicial determination. However the State has not made a declaration under Article 36(2) of the Statute of the International Court of Justice which would make its jurisdiction compulsory in relation to a dispute with any other state accepting the same obligation.

Dualism

26–2 The dualist nature of the legal system as regards international agreements is stated simply and squarely in Article 29.6: "No international agreement shall be part of the domestic law of the State save as may be determined by the *Oireachtas.*" Before a determination by the *Oireachtas,* it is therefore clear that an international agreement has no force before the courts. There is nothing in this Article to suggest that the status of an international agreement can be anything other than that determined by the *Oireachtas,* or that a determination of the *Oireachtas* under Article 29.6 can have any different status to any other determination of the *Oireachtas.* A determination under Article 29.6 could never give an international agreement the same status as

---

1 This Article was impliedly referred to by Finlay C.J. (*nem. diss.*) in *McGimpsey v. Ireland* [1990] 1 I.R. 110 at 121, where the Chief Justice appeared to hold that an international agreement, attacked on constitutional grounds, which the State enters into in accordance with the principles in this Article would be supported (but not immunised) thereby.

constitutional law because Article 29.6 does not purport to grant the *Oireachtas* the power to amend the Constitution through the importation of treaties.

The dualism of the system has been consistently spelled out by the courts in relation to the European Convention on the Protection of Human Rights and Fundamental Freedoms, to which the State is a party. In *Re Ó'Laighléis*[2] the applicant claimed that he could not be lawfully interned under the Offences against the State (Amendment) Act 1940 because it was inconsistent with the Convention and therefore inoperable. Maguire C.J., in holding that the Court could not give effect to the Convention, made reference to Article 29.6, to Article 15.2.1 which provides that "the sole and exclusive power of making laws for the State is vested in the *Oireachtas*: no other legislative authority has power to make laws for the State", and to the fact that the *Oireachtas* has not determined that the Convention was part of the domestic law of the State. The Chief Justice also referred to the duty of judges:

> "No argument can prevail against the express command of section 6 of Article 29 of the Constitution before judges whose declared duty is to uphold the Constitution and the laws."[3]

The authority of judgments of the European Court of Human Rights to bind Irish courts has also been roundly rejected.[4] In *Norris* O'Higgins C.J. held that the Convention could not affect in any way questions arising under domestic law. This rejection extends to judgments against Ireland herself.[5] None of the above prevents the judgments of the European Court from being binding according to the terms of the European Convention on the Protection of Human Rights and Fundamental Freedoms (Article 34.4 of that Convention) in public international law, or their use to Irish courts as aids to the interpretation of national (and possibly European Community) law. This position has been affirmed by O'Hanlon J. in *Desmond v. Glackin*,[6] holding that the judgments of the European Court could have persuasive effect when considering the common law in the light of Irish constitutional law guarantees.[7]

General Principles of Public International Law

26–3 The position of general principles of international law in domestic law is different to that of international treaties. Article 29.3 provides:

> "Ireland accepts the generally recognised principles of international law as its rule of conduct in its relations with other States."

---

2 *Re Ó'Laighléis* [1960] I.R. 93; approved in *Application of Woods* [1970] I.R. 154.

3 *Re Ó'Laighléis*, above, at 125.

4 *Norris v. Attorney General* [1984] I.R. 36; *O'B. v. S.* [1984] I.R. 316.

5 *E. v. E.* [1982] I.L.R.M. 497, *per* O'Hanlon J.

6 [1992] I.L.R.M. 490 at 513.

7 O'Hanlon J. held also that the provisions of the Convention could be considered when determining issues of public policy.

These general principles may be pleaded before the courts, who have recognised that their content is not frozen for the purposes of domestic recognition to that prevailing in 1937.[8]

There are several possibilities for the status of such principles in domestic law. The frontier to the application of Article 29.3 which could be defended on the basis of its wording is that between control of external executive State action and control of any rule of internal law, be it administrative, legislative, or common law. But as *Government of Canada v. Employment Appeals Tribunal* testifies, the general principles of international law on the doctrine of sovereign immunity have already been admitted into consideration in deciding to bar an action based on common law.[9] Article 29.3 is a direct constitutional recognition, unlike the implied permission to incorporate international agreements granted to the *Oireachtas* in Article 29.6. Therefore general principles could possibly have a status higher than statutes. There is no *ratio decidendi* on this issue although there is an *obiter dictum* against, in the case of *State (Sumers Jennings) v. Furlong,* where Henchy J. treated the status of principles as the same as conventions:

> "Having regard to the statement in Article 6 of the Constitution that the legislative powers of the State derive, under God, from the people and the wording of section 3 of Article 29, I would respectfully adopt the *dictum* of Davitt P. in the *Ó Laighléis*[10] case: 'Where there is an irreconcilable conflict between a domestic statute and the principles of international law or the provisions of an international convention, the Courts administering the domestic law must give effect to the statute.'"[11]

But this is not a necessary implication of Article 29.3. The statement has been distinguished by the Law Enforcement Commission in which the Irish delegates[12] (including Henchy J.)[13] voiced a contrary view:

> "The constitutional provision is in terms an express commitment on the part of the State. The Courts can intervene to set aside any executive or legislative act which contravenes this or any other constitutional provision. Whether such contravention is in the form of legislative or executive action it is open to intervention by the courts. . .
>
> . . . a breach by the State or by any organ of the State of a generally recognised principle of international law would not necessarily be justiciable in the domes-

---

8 *Government of Canada v. Employment Appeals Tribunal* [1992] I.L.R.M. 325 (concerning the principle of sovereign immunity).

9 [1992] I.L.R.M. 325. See also *Report of the Law Enforcement Commission to the Secretary of State for Northern Ireland and the Minister for Justice of Ireland* (London: HMSO, 1974), p. 23: "the test should be what they [the general principles of international law] are at the time the court is called upon to intervene."

10 [1960] I.R. 93.

11 *The State (Sumers Jennings) v. Furlong* [1966] I.R. 183 at 190. The statement is *obiter* because Henchy J. found that, even if the rule advocated by the prosecutor was a general principle of international law, was not sufficiently broad to cover the case, contrary to the prosecutors contention (at 191).

12 Walsh J., Henchy J., Declan Quigley and Thomas A. Doyle.

13 Indeed Henchy J.'s rejection of the proposed change in extradition laws was based entirely on an understanding of Article 29.3 which contradicts that statement in *The State (Summers Jennings) v. Furlong* [1966] I.R. 184 – see note to p. 14 of the Report *op.cit.*, above, n.9.

> tic courts in all cases. It would, however, be justiciable if the effect of the breach operated within the municipal sphere and more especially if it threatened fundamental personal rights. . . .
> These members cannot advise that the Government of Ireland could legally enter into any agreement or that the legislature could validly enact any legislation affecting its relations with other states which would be in breach of the generally recognised principles of international law."[14]

If one jumps forward in the analysis here to the consideration of possible conflicts with European Community law, one can see that Article 29.3 creates the possibility that there could be a conflict which Irish courts would have to resolve for the purposes of Irish law between the general principles of international law and a rule of European Community law. The courts would have to decide how to harmonise the recognition given in Article 29.3 with the recognition of European Community law in Article 29.4.3 to 29.4.5.

This conflict could arise whether or not general principles of international law were recognised as having a status superior to statute.[15]

1. In the case where general principles are not recognised as having a status superior to statute, one could argue that this simply means that the constitutionality of the European Communities Act 1972 (as amended) could not be called into question on this ground, but the authority of the rules dependent on it could be (before the national courts).

   A counter-argument could be made against this proposition. Normally, where a rule with an unconstitutional effect (such as the denial of fair procedures) and an authority dependent on a post-Constitution statute is challenged, the statute is given the benefit of the presumption of constitutionality and so is interpreted, if possible, as not authorising that rule (which is struck down). But if it is clear that the authority of the rule is *intra vires* a provision of the statute, then that provision itself must be struck down. However the European Communities Act not only is presumed to be constitutional *vis-à-vis* the general principles of international law (like any other act), it is moreover unchallengeable on this ground by virtue of Article 29.4.5. This leaves the rules (European Community rules or implementing measures) whose root of title is dependent thereon in the same position *vis-à-vis* the general principles as delegated legislation made pursuant to a statute

---

[14] Above. n.9, pp. 22–24. This view determined the conclusion of the *Report* (p. 41, para. 112(b)).

[15] This problem is stated in terms of clearcut hierarchy. That is not to deny that, whatever the outcome on hierarchy, public international law principles might have a role anyway in the interpretation of statutes. (This appears certainly to be the case in respect of international treaties – *The State (DPP) v. Walsh* [1981] I.R. 412 (Henchy J.); *Ó'Domhnaill v. Merrick* [1985] I.L.R.M. 40 (Henchy J.); *Desmond v. Glackin (No. 1)* [1993] 3 I.R. 1 (O'Hanlon J.)). However it is hard to accept an argument that some public international law principles would have status superior to statute, and some not, depending on the public international law principle.

which has survived an Article 26 reference (which means its constitutionality cannot be called into question – Article 34.3.3, *vis-à-vis* the Constitution as a whole.[16]

But it is not clear that such delegated legislation would be treated with this respect, given that the Article 26 system is a completely different system of judicial review to that normally practiced by the courts, and is not favoured by them precisely because it immunises from judicial review for all time a statute which passes this scrutiny.[17] The question has not been decided. Similarly, the authority of rules whose authority derived from the European Communities Act which, like all statutes in this hypothesis, was immune to attack via Article 26.3, might nonetheless be open to attack on this ground.

2. More importantly, concern over the immunity of rules made pursuant to statutes is a reason for not holding the statutes themselves to be immune from Article 29.3 attack. Article 29.3 need not be interpreted as ranking the general principles of international law below those of statutes (whereas Article 34.3.3 leaves the courts with little room to manoeuvre out of the immunity of a statute which has passed Article 26 scrutiny). Far from it. Ranking principles recognised by the Constitution as below the status of statutes would be an unusual interpretation of the Constitution.[18]

3. In the case where general principles are recognised as having a status superior to statute then both the constitutionality of the European Communities Act and the European Community rules which form part of domestic law thereunder could be tested against these principles, and the question becomes one of the interpretation of Article 29.3 and 29.4.

---

16 Although as Anthony Whelan has pointed out, the challenge to the sub-statutory rules on the basis of Article 29.3, if such a challenge cannot impugn a statute, is not analogous to their attack on the basis of the Constitution, because the presumption of constitutionality of the statute, which might facilitate a reading of the statute which makes the sub-statutory rules *ultra vires*, does not apply. However, this difference is minimised because a different presumption which operates very similarly in respect of statutes – that they are to be interpreted in accordance with public international law treaties and arguably public international law principles (see above, n.15) – does apply, at least so far as Article 29.3 and Article 29.4 interact.

17 *Re Article 26 and the Housing (Private Rented Dwellings) Bill, 1981* [1983] I.R. 181 at 186–187. See also J. Casey, *Constitutional Law in Ireland* (London: Sweet & Maxwell, 1992) pp. 267–271, on the question of the constitutionality of a statute where the compatibility of the Bill was upheld in an Article 26 reference but the rationale for declaring the compatibility of the Bill ceases to have support.

18 See the *Report* quoted in the text, above, n.9.

27. EUROPEAN COMMUNITY LAW IN IRISH CONSTITUTIONAL LAW

27–1 "Perhaps this unambiguous acceptance of the legal obligations associated with membership of the European Communities reflects a desire to move out from the shadow cast so long by our dominant neighbour."[1]

Whilst the legal relations of Ireland with the European Communities have been smooth more often than not, this does not mean an unambiguous acceptance of legal obligations so much as a pragmatic avoidance of direct and potentially damaging conflict.[2] Even if Irish constitutional law were legitimated solely by reference to popular sovereignty (it is not), Irish constitutional law and European Community law would be in conflict and prone to these conflicts coming to a head in courts because of the limited recognition which Irish constitutional law gives to European Community law.

History of Membership

27–2 Ireland became a member of the European Communities along with the United Kingdom and Denmark from 1 January 1973. The Treaty of Accession was signed in Brussels on 22 January 1972 whereupon Ireland became a member subject to the deposit of the instrument of ratification with the Government of the Italian Republic. In order to ratify the treaty a referendum was necessary to amend the Constitution. This procedure is set out in Article 46. The Third Amendment of the Constitution Bill 1972 was initiated in *Dáil Éireann* and passed by both houses of the *Oireachtas,* and then submitted to the people. The referendum was held on 10 May 1972 and was approved by 83 per cent of those who voted. After this positive result, the Act was signed forthwith by the President and duly promulgated as law in accordance with Article 46.5 on 8 June 1972. This Act inserted Article 29.4.3 into the Constitution. The European Communities Act 1972 was also passed at the same time. The instrument of ratification was deposited on 16 December 1972.

The accession of three new members, Greece, Spain and Portugal, did not necessitate Irish constitutional change.

---

1 B. McMahon and F. Murphy, *European Community Law in Ireland* (Dublin: Butterworths, 1989) p. 282. One must ask, in considering the acceptance of European Community law in Irish constitutional law, whether it is the country's future, this time self-imposed, to move always between the mists of myth and the shadows of political superiors.

2 Not an attitude which first appeared with membership of the European Communities.

However the Single European Act did. Despite its name, the Single European Act was an international treaty signed by the Member States. The Single European Act amended the constituent European Community treaties in several respects. The constitutionality of an Irish Act, the European Communities (amendment) Act 1986, which purported to introduce into Irish law various parts of the Single European Act, was challenged in *Crotty v. An Taoiseach*.[3] The challenge failed against the Act, but succeeded against the State's ratification of Title III of the Single European Act. Title III concerned cooperation in the field of foreign policy and was a commitment separate to the European Community treaties (that is, the treaties of the three communities) of which it did not form a part. The State, enjoined by the Supreme Court from ratifying the Single European Act, had to hold a referendum on the Tenth Amendment of the Constitution Act 1987, which was passed on 6 May 1987 by 70 per cent of the votes cast in a 45 per cent turnout. The Act inserted a second sentence into Article 29.4.3. The constitutional process delayed the coming into force of the Single European Act until the summer of 1987.

The Treaty on European Union was signed at Maastricht on 7 February 1992. Ireland was the fourth Member State to deposit its instrument of ratification, which it did on 23 November 1992. The treaty came into force, following a delay by the Federal Constitutional Court of Germany, on 1 November 1993. The Treaty on European Union necessitated a constitutional amendment and the Eleventh Amendment of the Constitution Act 1992 was passed in a referendum and promulgated as law on 23 December 1992. This amended Article 29.4.3 and added four new sections. The European Communities Act 1972 was also amended.

Ireland held the presidency of the Council of the European Union in the second half of 1996, when the intergovernmental conference was convened pursuant to Article N (EU) to consider revision of the Treaties. To date, no amending treaty has been signed.

The Amendment of National Law to Pre-empt Conflicts

Constitutional Amendments

27–3 The constitutional provisions dedicated to European Community law are considered in later Sections. This Section is confined to a consideration of why constitutional amendment was necessary for Ireland to join the Community in 1973. At the time of accession (pre-*Crotty*), it was not clear that the courts could pose a bar to the State joining the European Communities, in the sense of a bar to the government's ratification of the treaty. Since the

---

[3] [1987] I.L.R.M. 400.

treaty entailed a charge on public funds it also had to be approved by the Dáil. Although both the executive and the legislature are under a duty to observe the Constitution, it was not established at the time that these ratifying functions were reviewable. This is important because no such constitutional change is mandated by European Community law. The reception of European Community law into the national legal order is, according to European Community law, direct.[4] The dependency of European Community law on Irish law (constitutional, statutory, and regulatory) for its enforcement is in conflict with European Community law's fundamental constitutional claim. Costello J.'s description of the effect of the constitutional provisions as giving effect to European Community law in the manner which European Community law provides is inaccurate.[5]

However, as a matter of Irish constitutional law, the amendment was necessary. Leaving aside for the moment conflicts of individuals' rights and of the substance of law, there were several conflicts concerning who exercised power, both on an abstract and on a practical level:

1. On an abstract level, Article 5 of the Constitution provides that: "Ireland is a sovereign, independent, democratic State." This appears to apply to the external sovereignty of the State. The European Economic Community was at least a sophisticated international organisation which would have implications for the understanding of such sovereignty. Article 6 provides that all powers of government derive from the people who in final appeal decide all questions of national policy. This appears to apply to the internal sovereignty of the people. It was clear since Case 26/62 *Van Gend en Loos*,[6] if not to the original signatories, that membership had implications for sovereignty. Exactly what these implications are, according to Irish constitutional law or public international law, is a very difficult question. The implications for sovereignty will vary from national legal order to national legal order depending both on how a legal order views sovereignty and on how a legal order has adapted to the European Community law challenge. From the perspective of European Community law, however, it was clear that it involved a limitation of sovereign rights (note: not a limitation of the exercise of sovereign rights, but a limitation of the rights themselves).[7]
2. On a practical level, the following provisions are clearly inconsistent with the powers of the various Community institutions:
   (a) Article 6 provides that legislative, executive and judicial powers could be exercised only by the bodies established by the Constitution;

---

4 See above, Part II, "European Community Law" and in particular the discussion at para. 7–13.
5 *Pigs and Bacon Commission v. McCarron*, unreported, Costello J., High Court, June 30, 1978.
6 [1963] E.C.R. 1.
7 See above, Part II, "European Community Law", para. 8–16 "Sovereignty".

(b) Article 15.2 provides that the only body to make laws for the country shall be the *Oireachtas*;
(c) Articles 34 to 38 provide that only the courts established in accordance with the Constitution have power to administer justice, that the High Court has full original jurisdiction (Article 34.3.1) and that the final court of appeal is the Supreme Court (Article 34.4.3);
(d) Article 28.2 provides that the executive power shall be exercised by the government. There were in 1973 already areas where the Community institutions acted in the place of or with the cooperation of the Member States, such as intra-Community competition matters. (Generally, European Community law is executed within the country through agencies of government who derive their legal existence ultimately from the Constitution, although their powers may in some areas be derived from European Community law. A good example of the crossover of the exercise of executive power is *Clover Meats v. Minister for Agriculture*[8] where Barrington J. held that the Minister for Agriculture was allowed to set off debts owed to him by Clover Meats – insolvent at the time – against moneys due Clover Meats from the Minister as Intervention Agent for the European Commission);
(e) Article 29.4.1 provides for the exercise of the executive power of the State in external relations. This could be in conflict with the Community role in the negotiation and conclusion of treaties.

There were two possible drafting choices in order to avoid these and less immediately obvious conflicts. First, attempt to amend every article which might be contrary to European Community law. No Member State has done this, not least because of the obvious difficulties and uncertainties it entails. However, pointing out this option helps to understand the second, chosen option, which is to provide in the Constitution for a block to the application of the Constitution to European Community law or to acts necessitated thereby.

This extraordinary provision makes sense historically, but might not have been the option chosen had the Constitution been enacted at the same time or after Ireland (Ireland in the sense of the State recognised by public international law) joined the European Communities, although France enacted the Constitution of 1958 after it became a founding member. It is very difficult to bring about, by the insertion of one provision in a 36-year old Constitution, the effect of the tail wagging the dog capable, in conjunction with the European Communities Act 1972, of funnelling a whole new system of law past the rest of the Constitution of which it forms a textual part and into the national courts. As a *sine qua non* for such an endeavour to succeed, it would have to be more explicit.

---

8 (1992) 1 *Irish Journal of European Law* 162.

An extremely important implication of the method of introducing a barring provision into the Constitution is that it does not purport to transfer sovereign rights; that is, legally recognised power.[9] The Constitution presumes the European Community to have authority independently of the transfer of sovereign rights, from the international agreements entered into by the State. Thus Irish constitutional law sees European Community law as essentially public international law, but which has different effects by virtue of this bar. It does not grant the European Community sovereign authority, in the sense that this is understood in Irish constitutional law. Irish constitutional law does not see European Community law as deriving the validity of its norms from any source other than public international law.

Statutory Amendments

27–4 For European Community law to have effect it was not sufficient to place a bar to its constitutional invalidity (in the eyes of Irish constitutional law). The *Oireachtas* has to determine how far the treaties and the law made thereunder become the domestic law of the State.[10] This it did in the European Communities Act 1972. As Barrington J. explained in *Crotty v. An Taoiseach*:

> "Had the *Oireachtas* not passed the European Communities Act, 1972, Ireland might still have been a member of the Community in international law but it would have been in breach of its obligations in international law under the Treaty of Rome and under the Treaty of Accession. This would not have been a matter in relation to which the domestic courts of this country would have had any competence because the Treaty would not have been part of domestic law. The immunity from constitutional challenge conferred by the second sentence of the Third Amendment on laws enacted, acts done, or measures adopted by the Community or its institutions would therefore have been meaningless as these laws, acts, or measures would not have been part of the domestic law of this country."[11]

This passage succinctly summarises the consequences in Irish law had the European Communities Act 1972 not been passed. However the learned judge may have been wrong so far as the judgment suggests that failure to pass the Act would place Ireland, as a matter of European Community Law, breach of the Treaty of Rome and the Treaty of Accession. If the full logic of European Community Law holds sway, Ireland is in breach of these Treaties

---

9 If this were to be attempted, the attempt would have to be explicit. As Walsh J. has stated (quoted above in para. 24–2): "It is not within the competence of the Government, or indeed the *Oireachtas*, to free themselves from the restraints of the Constitution or to transfer their powers to other bodies unless expressly empowered to do so by the Constitution." – *Crotty v. An Taoiseach*, [1987] I.L.R.M. 400 at 454. Although this statement supports the point that the attempt needs to be explicit, it ought not obscure the point that the idea of licence for transfer of powers is not in the route followed in Irish constitutional law. Rather, the constitutional amendments have sought to introduce a constitutional bar to constitutional jurisdiction.

10 See above, para. 26–2, "Dualism".

11 [1987] I.R. 713 at 757.

as interpreted by the Court of Justice anyhow, since the courts do not recognise the direct duty to uphold European Community law.[12]

The European Communities Act provides:

> " Section 2 – From the first day of January, 1973, the treaties governing the European Communities and the existing and future acts adopted by the institutions of those Communities and by bodies competent under the said treaties shall be binding on the State and shall be part of the domestic law thereof under the conditions laid down in those treaties."[13]

Section 1 defines "the treaties governing the European Communities" to include, *inter alia,* the Single European Act and parts of the Treaty on European Union.[14] The "conditions laid down in those treaties" arguably (from the point of view of Irish constitutional law) include the doctrines of supremacy and direct effect as interpreted by the Court of Justice. The Act appears to ground, as a matter of Irish law, European Community law as part of the domestic law of the State. But the courts' reference to section 2 is itself a refusal to acknowledge the Court of Justice's Case 26/62 *Van Gend en Loos* doctrine. So far as the European Community law self-description is accepted, this means that the 1972 Act appears to recognise the supremacy of European Community law over any internal source of law. Of course, section 2 cannot thereby affect the relationship between European Community law and Irish constitutional law, and this is one reason why constitutional amendment was necessary to avoid this act being held unconstitutional. But it can form the root for the Irish law version of the supremacy of European Community law over rules whose origin is from a formal source lower in the hierarchy of Irish legal norms than legislation, and of legislation enacted prior to 1973. The section is, however, a shaky basis for European Community law, as the points below show.

There are three possible ways in which this provision does not succeed in avoiding conflicts with legislation:

1. The legislation has the same problems *vis-à-vis* subsequent legislation as the European Community Act 1972 in the United Kingdom. So, for example, if a subsequent statute enacted by the democratically elected *Oireachtas* specifically derogated from a European Community rule, could this 1972 Act be invoked against it? There is no existing doctrine to say it could. There is nothing in Irish law to weaken the effectiveness of a statute saying "European Community law shall not be part of the domestic law of the state" or, "European Community law shall not be part of the domestic law of the state so far as it conflicts with fundamental rights protected under the Constitution." European Community law has a similar status in the

---

12 See above, Part II, "European Community Law".

13 As amended by the European Communities (Amendment) Act 1992.

14 *i.e.* the Protocols, Titles II, III, IV, and Articles L, M, P, and other provisions of Title VII so far as they relate to another treaty governing the European Communities.

Irish hierarchy of norms as a statute, the status being conferred by a statute which benefits from a jurisdictional immunity of debated extent. European Community law does not have a status superior to constitutional law; rather, the interaction of the 1972 Act and Article 29.4 generally preserves its application.

2. Secondly, the national courts are the judge of the meaning of "the conditions laid down in those treaties" contained in section 2.[15] (There is no question that under the conditions laid down in those treaties, from the perspective of European Community law, the Court of Justice is the judge of what are the conditions laid down in those treaties. But that is not the same thing.) The same analysis as that which applies to Article 29.4.5 [a] (see below paras. 27–7 *et seq.*) applies here – it is ultimately a question for the national courts, which are not bound to follow the Court of Justice interpretation of conditions in the treaties as regards this text. This analysis is reinforced here by section 2 itself, because to ascribe the European Community law meaning to the phrase would make a complete nonsense of the provision. Under the European Community law interpretation, the integration of European Community law into domestic law is not dependent on national law at all.[16] So the national courts would be looking to a European Community law interpretation of a phrase in a national statute which interpretation is that the statute is irrelevant to the status of European Community law in national courts.

3. Based on the analysis of 2, it is up to the national courts to make out what it means to be part of the domestic law (save that the national courts cannot give acts adopted by the institutions a status higher than legislation, because no European Communities Act, being a statute, could do so).

Article 29.4.3 and Article 29.4.4: Membership

27–5 Articles 29.4.3 and 29.4.4 provide for membership. They are straightforward:

> "3. The State may become a member of the European Coal and Steel Community (established by Treaty signed at Paris on the eighteenth day of April, 1951), the European Economic Community (established by Treaty signed at Rome on the twenty-fifth day of March, 1957) and the European Atomic Energy Community (established by Treaty signed at Rome on the twenty-fifth day of March, 1957). The State may ratify the Single European Act (signed on

---

[15] There is no counterpart in the Irish statute to the United Kingdom's s.3(1) of the European Communities Act 1972, which provides that any question as to the effect of any of the Treaties or of Community legislation must be decided "in accordance with the principles of any relevant decision" of the Court of Justice.

[16] See above, Part II, "European Community Law".

behalf of the Member States of the Communities at Luxembourg on the seventeenth day of February, 1986, and at the Hague on the twenty-eighth day of February, 1986).

4. The State may ratify the Treaty on European Union signed at Maastricht on the seventh day of February, 1992, and may become a member of that Union."

These articles are drafted in deliberately narrow terms. They permit membership of these Communities – but nothing compels the State to join or to remain a member. The provisions are enabling only. This means that, as far as Irish constitutional law is concerned, Ireland can cease to become a member without a referendum.[17] Such an act, whilst compatible with Irish constitutional law, would be in conflict with European Community law because European Community law allows Member States to leave, if at all, only by amendment of the constituent treaties, which must be unanimous.[18]

These articles are also potentially restrictive and so they may be the focus of conflicts as European Community law develops. In *Crotty*[19] the question arose as to whether the Single European Act so amended the Community as to take it outside the permission in Article 29.4.3 (as it then was). Although the referendum precipitated by this case was passed, the analysis remains pertinent even after the permission to ratify the Treaty on European Union was inserted in Article 29.4.4. Unlike Germany and France, there was no case in Ireland on the Treaty on European Union because the unconstitutionality of the State's membership without a constitutional amendment was presumed in the light of *Crotty*. *Crotty* is therefore the only case solely dedicated to an analysis of the constitutional problems posed by membership. In *Crotty* the constitutionality of the European Communities (Amendment) Act 1986 (allowing for the Minister to make the provisions of the Single European Act referred to part of domestic law) was decided on the basis of the licence to join the Community.

It was not contended that ratification was necessitated by the obligations of membership, and therefore does not affect the analysis of Article 29.4.5 [clause a]. The majority of the Supreme Court (Walsh, Henchy, and Hederman, JJ.), in granting an injunction preventing the government's ratification of the Single European Act by deposit of the instrument of ratification and making it subject to prior authorisation by the people through constitutional amendment, held that Title III of the Single European Act dealt with matters outside

---

17 But it might be argued that by such unilateral withdrawal the Executive would be in breach of Article 29.3. However, even if such an argument was successful, a referendum could cure the problem, whereas the problem would remain in European Community law.

18 If a Member State wished to leave, such agreement would likely be forthcoming as a political matter, certainly as regards a small Member State.

19 *Crotty v. An Taoiseach* [1987] I.L.R.M. 400.

the scope of the existing treaties and therefore were not covered by the licence contained in Article 29.4.3.

This dramatic case, which has been extensively noted,[20] commenced as an application for an interlocutory injunction restraining the State from depositing the instrument of ratification. The resolution of the Dáil had already been passed (necessary because the treaty involved a charge on public funds) and the President had affixed the Seal of Ireland in accordance with the advice of the Government. The analysis of both the High Court and the Supreme Court is considered here, because although the Supreme Court reversed the High Court and granted the injunction sought, the courts differed primarily over the interpretation of whether Title III was within or without the licence to join the Community.

The Divisional High Court considered that the permission to become a member of the European Economic Community was intended to identify the Community which the State could join, not to freeze its boundaries. The terms of the licence granted by the permission were not to be read restrictively: the immunity granted was "a licence to join a living dynamic Community".[21] Therefore not every amendment to the constituent treaties would necessitate a new amendment to the Constitution. The most important factor pointed to was the objectives of the Treaties: the High Court held that the Single European Act represented nothing more than "an evolution of the Community within the terms of its original objectives".[22]

The Supreme Court held that the constitutional permission covered:

> "amendments of the Treaties so long as such amendments do not alter *the essential scope or objectives* of the Communities. To hold that the first sentence of Article 29.4.3 does not authorise any form of amendment to the treaties after 1973 without a further amendment of the Constitution would be too narrow a construction; to construe it as open ended authority to agree, without further amendment of the Constitution, to any amendment of the treaties would be too broad."[23]

Therefore the scope of the permissions granted the State are limited to adhering to Communities whose "essential scope or objectives" do not change. This is an extremely vague test – the essential scope of the Community is far from clear, and what can come under its objectives is potentially limitless. But, most importantly, the assessment of what are the essential scope and objectives of the Communities remains for the purposes of Irish constitutional law an assessment of the Irish courts. For example, according to the

---

20 For example J. Casey, "*Crotty v. An Taoiseach*: A Comparative Perspective" in J. O'Reilly, (ed.), *Essays in Honour of Brian Walsh* (Dublin: Butterworths, 1992) p. 189; G.W. Hogan, "The Supreme Court and the Single European Act" (1987) XXII *Irish Jurist* 68.

21 *Crotty v. An Taoiseach* [1987] I.L.R.M. 400 at 435.

22 *ibid.* at 438.

23 *ibid.* at 444 (emphasis added).

Divisional High Court, the licence was to join a Community "of the kind described by the defendants".[24] The defendants had specified that:

> "[t]he quest for common constitutional values is not designed to deprive nationals of Member States of fundamental rights guaranteed to them by their respective national constitutions. Rather it is designed to protect individuals against the harsh or unfair legislative or administrative acts of the Community".[25]

Although it is correct that the protection of fundamental rights by the Court of Justice is not designed to deny national constitutional rights, what this comment seems to be getting at is that there is no risk to the protection of national constitutional rights in areas falling within European Community competence, which of course there is. The protection of fundamental rights by the Court of Justice originated to avoid threats to the supremacy, direct effect, efficacy and uniformity of European Community law posed by protection of national constitutional rights by national courts.[26] The licence accorded by Irish law to the state is therefore insufficient from the perspective of European Community law. Finlay C.J. also expressly pointed out that it was not shown that the new powers given to the Council "create a threat to fundamental constitutional rights".[27]

In general, the following two important clarifications on European Community law's position in Irish constitutional law can be deduced from the *Crotty* analysis:

1. Should the European Community law interpretation of essential scope and objectives of the Community go beyond that of Irish constitutional law, then the European Communities Act (as amended) would be open to constitutional challenge so far as it purports to import into domestic law a rule which goes beyond the Irish constitutional law version of the essential scope and objectives of the Community.[28] Barrington J. stated:

> "Should such challenge be successful such Acts of the institutions of the Community as depend on [the European Community Act] for their status in domestic law would lose that status and would be of no effect in domestic law. Such a result might be embarrassing for the Government, and might involve the State being in breach of its international obligations, but such considerations could not prevent this Court from fulfilling its constitutional duty should the matter be made out in a case properly before it."[29]

---

24 *ibid.* at 435.

25 *ibid.* at 429.

26 See above, Part II, "European Community Law", and below, Part IV, "Conflicts".

27 [1987] I.L.R.M. 400 at 447, see also Barrington J. at 436.

28 See particularly *ibid.* at 435.

29 *ibid.* at 435 Barrington J. pointed to the possibility of breach of international obligations. This is radically different to the European Community law view of such a breach. It indicates that Irish constitutional law perceives the failure to apply European Community law as engaging public international law responsibility only, and no special direct European Community law duty. For the different perspective of European Community law, see above, Part II, "European Community law".

2. State acts or measures implementing European Community law which go beyond this Irish constitutional law version of the essential scope and objectives of the Community would not be "necessitated" by the obligations of membership within the terms of Article 29.4.5 and therefore open to attack. This is a very real possibility.[30]

These clarifications are just as applicable after the referendum to allow for the ratification of the Treaty on European Union – although there was no case, there is no reason to presume that Irish constitutional law cannot take a position on what is within the essential scope or objectives of the Treaty on European Union when the case arises.[31]

Article 29.4.5

27–6 "5. No provision of this Constitution [clause a] invalidates laws enacted, acts done or measures adopted by the State which are necessitated by the obligations of the European Union or of the Communities, or [clause b] prevents laws enacted, acts done or measures adopted by European Union or by the Communities or by the institutions thereof, or by bodies competent under the Treaties establishing the Communities, from having the force of law in the State." (Lettering added.)

There are two important preliminary points to be made about this Article: first, from the perspective of European Community law it is irrelevant; secondly, it is not the only Article attempting to restrict judicial review.[32]

This provision attempts to do two distinct things in its two clauses, which will be analysed separately. Overall, the provision constitutes a bar to constitutional challenges to European Community law rules and Irish implementing measures. It is not enabling. It does not make European Community law

[30] Walsh J. has stated in *S.P.U.C. v. Grogan* [1990] I.L.R.M. 350 at 357:
"it cannot be one of the objectives of the European Communities that a Member State should be obliged to permit activities which are clearly designed to set at nought the constitutional guarantees for the protection within the State of a fundamental human right."

[31] The Court of Justice has not held a European Community act to be outside the objectives of the European Community. Given the increase in the scope of the objectives in the Treaty on European Union (Article B) and the amendment of Article 2 (EC), this is not likely to happen. However the Court of Justice has held that certain acts of constitutional importance could not be taken on the basis of Article 235 (EC) – Opinion 2/94 *Accession by the Community to the European Convention for the Protection of Human Rights and Fundamental Freedoms*, 28 March 1996. This presents an opportunity for a more restrictive view of the objectives of the European Community to be taken by a national court. Prior to this case, a restrictive view was taken by national courts, for example the *Conseil Constitutionnel*, and the German Federal Constitutional Court in *Brunner v. The European Union Treaty* [1994] 69 C.M.L.R. 57.

[32] Article 28.3 and Article 34.3.3 do also: see above, para. 25–2, "How Conflicts Can Occur Jurisdictionally".

[33] *Crotty* [1987] I.L.R.M. 400 at 434.

rules part of domestic law. As Barrington J. put it, if the constitutional provision "is the canopy over their heads, the European Communities Act 1972 is the perch on which they stand".[33]

Article 29.4.5 [a][33a]

27–7 O'Higgins, former Chief Justice of the Supreme Court and judge of the Court of Justice of the European Communities, has stated that it is up to the High Court under Article 34.3.2 of the Constitution to determine whether a law, act, or measure is necessitated by Community membership.[34] Gallagher, S.C., disagrees, on the ground that a party can demand as of right that a reference be made to the Court of Justice under Article 177 (EC) because a question on the interpretation of Community laws is involved.[35] This paragraph argues that the courts may hold a provision of Irish law to be invalid and not saved by Article 29.4.5 [clause a] where this or a similar provision is required by European Community law, and therefore this Article does not bar conclusively conflicts between Irish constitutional law and European Community law.

The recurring practical importance of the constitutional analysis of this provision is highlighted by the Supreme Court decision in *Meagher v. Minister for Agriculture*.[36] This case concerned section 3(2) of the European Communities Act 1972, as amended, which provides the machinery for the implementation of Community law (ministerial statutory instrument with minimum parliamentary control). Johnson J. in the High Court, had held that this provision was not protected by Article 29.4.5, because this mode of implementation was not necessitated by the obligations of membership of the Communities. Once outside the Article 29.4.5 protection, the provision fell on several grounds. The Supreme Court, reversing Johnson J., upheld the constitutionality of the provision and thereby avoided the serious implications for the body of statutory instruments made under this section.

In considering clause [a], two points need to be kept in mind. First, one must distinguish between the interpretation of the abstract question of what is necessitated as an obligation of membership of the European Communities and the interpretation of texts. Secondly, the order approach must be kept constantly

---

33a This section draws heavily on D.R. Phelan, "'Necessitated' by the obligations of Membership? Article 2.9.4.5° of the Constitution" (1993) 11 *Irish Law Times* 272.

34 T.F. O'Higgins, "The Constitution and the Community – Scope for Stress" in J. O'Reilly, (ed.), (1992) *op. cit.* above, n.20, pp. 227 and 229.

35 P. Gallagher, "The Constitution and the Community" (1993) 2 *Irish Journal of European Law* 129 at pp. 130–132.

36 [1994] 1 I.R. 344 (Sup. Ct.) 329 (High Ct.), analysed by G.W. Hogan, "The Implementation of European Union Law in Ireland: The *Meagher* case and the democratic deficit" (1994) 2 *Irish Journal of European Law* 190.

in mind. European Community law is applied in the Irish courts ultimately only by virtue of the provisions of Article 29.4.5. On the one hand, the question of what is necessitated by membership of the European Community is frequently decided by the Court of Justice as a matter of European Community law binding all Member States. On the other, Article 29.4.5 is a constitutional text which, according to both constitutional and European Community law, can only be authoritatively interpreted by the Irish courts.[37]

Let us suppose that the executive or the *Oireachtas* (hereafter referred to loosely as "the State") adopts measure X pursuant to European Community obligation Y. We need not concern ourselves yet with the origin of the obligation (directive or treaty) or with the type of measure (implementation by legislation or ministerial regulation, ratification of a new treaty, etc.). We suppose further that X is clearly unconstitutional (we do not yet consider the grounds of unconstitutionality) if it is not saved by Article 29.4.5. A party challenges the constitutionality of X in the High Court. Let us presume the challenge is brought in an action against the State. (Depending on X, the challenge may come in a dispute between two private parties where one party claims a right pursuant to X and the other party claims the exercise of that right would subvert a constitutional rule. The analysis remains the same.) The State admits the measure would be unconstitutional save for Article 29.4.5 which it pleads in defence. The High Court is of the opinion that X is not necessitated by the obligations of membership, and is unconstitutional and void.

So far, this is what happened in *Meagher*. But now let us suppose that the State seeks an Article 177 (EC) reference. The meaning of Article 177 (EC), as interpreted by the Court of Justice, falls within [clause b] of Article 29.4.5, according to which no provision of the Constitution may be invoked to prevent it having the force of law before the Irish courts. The force of law is granted by the European Communities Act. The first paragraph of Article 177 (EC) provides:

> "The Court of Justice shall have jurisdiction to give preliminary rulings concerning:
> (a) the interpretation of this Treaty;
> (b) the validity and interpretation of acts of the institutions of the Community;
> (c) the interpretation of the statutes of bodies established by the Council, where those statutes so provide."

Consequently the referred question must be one of European Community law. There is no question of referring a question on the interpretation of Article 29.4.5. The State therefore proposes the question: "Does obligation Y necessitate X?" Article 177 (EC), paragraph two provides:

> "where such a question is raised before any court or tribunal of a Member State, that court or tribunal may, if it considers that a decision on a question

[37] *S.P.U.C. v. Grogan* [1989] I.R. 753 at 770, *per* McCarthy J.: "The sole authority for the construction of the Constitution lies in the Irish courts . . .".

> is necessary to enable it to give judgment, request the Court of Justice to give a ruling thereon."

Let us presume that if the High Court decided in its discretion that it would be helpful to make this reference,[38] the Court of Justice would answer it.[39] We will focus on a scenario in which the High Court disposes of the case and the State appeals to the Supreme Court under Article 34.4.3[40] and looks for a reference.

Article 177 (EC), paragraph 3 provides:

> "where any such question is raised in a case pending before a court or tribunal of a Member State, against whose decisions there is no judicial remedy under national law, that court or tribunal shall bring the matter before the Court of Justice."

Section 2 of the European Communities Act 1972 in conjunction with Article 29.4.5 [clause b] binds the Supreme Court to obey this European Community law provision. So the State must get its reference? Not necessarily. Article 177 does not give the right to a reference to any party before the courts of any Member State who decides to raise a question on European Community law. Both according to Article 177 (EC) paragraph 3 (interpreted in Case 283/81 *CILFIT v. Minister for Health*[41]) and according to constitutional law (*Doyle v. An Taoiseach*[42]), the question must be necessary for the national court to give judgment in the case. If it is, then both under the European Community law "*acte clair*" doctrine and constitutional law, the further question of whether a reference of that question is necessary to give judgment must be determined by the national court. This is the key. Is a ruling on a European Community law question necessary for the High Court to interpret Article 29.4.5 and thereby dispose of the case before it?

---

38 It is unlikely that the decision to make such a reference would be reviewed by the Supreme Court, since this has already held that it is not a decision within the meaning of Article 34.3.3 over which the Supreme Court has appellate jurisdiction. *Campus Oil Ltd v. Minister for Industry and Energy (No. 1)* [1983] I.R. 82 at 87, *per* Walsh J., criticised by Hogan and Whyte, *Kelly, Supplement to The Irish Constitution to the Second Edition* (Dublin, 1988) p. 40 (see also 3rd ed., 1984 at pp. 284–285) as a "questionable example of harmonious interpretation of the Constitution". (This decision is further considered in the Section on Article 29.4.5 [clause b]). Presumably such appellate jurisdiction could be granted by statute, or this ruling in *Campus Oil* might be reversed if some important Irish constitutional law issue was at stake.

39 Case C–159/90 *S.P.U.C. v. Grogan* [1991] E.C.R. I–4685, where the Court of Justice answered a High Court reference held by the Supreme Court in *S.P.U.C. v. Grogan* [1989] I.R. 753 to be unnecessary as a matter of Irish constitutional law.

40 Article 34.4.3 provides:

> "The Supreme Court shall, with such exceptions and subject to such regulations as may be prescribed by law, have appellate jurisdiction from all decisions of the High Court, and shall also have appellate jurisdiction from such decisions of other courts as may be prescribed by law."

41 [1982] E.C.R. 3415.

42 [1986] I.L.R.M. 693 at 714, *per* Henchy J.

This is a question of establishing an element of the constitutional law test for what is necessitated by the obligations of membership within the meaning of Article 29.4.5. There are many possibilities for the general test, some of which have been articulated. For example:

1. Only matters which can be made the subject of Regulation or Directive, and, by implication, not treaties.[43]

2. Acts which are the fair and reasonable implementation of details. In *Condon v. Minister for Agriculture and Food*[44] Lynch J., in considering this test, was satisfied that the implementing measures were within the Article 43 permission to the State to regulate the right to private property in accordance with the principles of social justice and the common good.

3. Any acts which are in general fulfillment of an obligation of membership. In *Lawlor v. Minister for Agriculture*[45] Murphy J. considered *obiter* that even if the halving of the value of a milk quota without warning or compensation constituted an unjustified attack on the plaintiff's constitutional rights (specifically, his right to private ownership of external goods under Article 44.3 and to private property in Article 40.3.2 this would be protected by [clause a] even if the implementing measure was not required in all its parts to be enacted by the obligations of membership of the Community. This remark is also disputable (see below).

4. Murphy J. in *Greene v. Minister for Agriculture*[46] quoted himself in *Lawlor* and went on to make out that a Minister had a measure of "choice, selection or discretion" in implementing a Directive, because that was the function of a Directive. The learned judge made the non-consequential leap in argument that an exercise within this discretion would be necessitated for the purposes of Article 29.4.5 [clause a]. This is based on a misunderstanding of the nature of a Directive, which accords a discretion in European Community law to a Member State, and not to a particular implementing authority.[47] One of the reasons for using a Directive as a legislative instrument is precisely to allow the Member State to implement in a manner and a substance consistent with domestic requirements, including constitutional requirements. Murphy J. in *Greene* went on to find the actual exercise of discretion[48] so far-reaching and detached from the result to

---

43 B. Walsh, "Reflections on the Effects of Membership of the European Communities, in Irish Law"; in F. Capotorti *et al.* (eds.), *Du Droit International au Droit de l'Intégration, Liber Amicorum Pierre Pescatore* (Baden-Baden: Nomos, 1987) pp. 805, 813.

44 (1993) 1 *Irish Journal of European Law* 151 at p. 156, *per* Lynch J.

45 [1990] 1 I.R. 356 at 377.

46 [1990] 2 I.R. 17 at 25.

47 See also A. Whelan, "Constitutional Law – *Meagher v. Minister for Agriculture*" (1993) 15 *Dublin University Law Journal* 152 at p. 156.

48 These were administrative schemes implementing Council Directive 75/268/EEC authorising Member States to introduce aids to encourage hill farming. The implemented

be achieved that it was not necessitated, and therefore fell outside the protection afforded by [clause a]. The plaintiffs were entitled to a declaration that the scheme was *ultra vires* the Minister because he failed to perform his constitutional duty to safeguard the institution of marriage imposed by Article 43.

5. Casey's sounder test of something imperatively required or mandated by membership.[49]

However, we are concerned solely with that element of the test which establishes whether, if a reference was made, and the Court of Justice ruled as a matter of European Community law that obligation Y necessitates X, the High Court would have to follow the Court of Justice's decision. That is, must the interpretation of Article 29.4.5 follow European Community law? If yes, then the reference would be necessary, and therefore as of right. If no, then the State would have no right to a reference, and X would remain void (what may happen thereafter is considered below). The answer is not immediately obvious.

We need to pause here to remark that in some cases, maybe most, the High Court may decide as a matter of practice to make a reference on the State's request and would follow the Court of Justice's ruling. Perhaps it is rarely that the State would have to assert the right to a reference, as distinct from a reasoned request. Furthermore, the Court of Justice may itself hold that the State's action is not necessitated. However that may be, the answer for all cases to the question of whether or not a reference must be made as of right depends on whether the High Court has the power not to follow the Court of Justice, even if this power is seldom exercised.

We pause also to distinguish our question from that considered by the Supreme Court in *Meagher v. Minister for Agriculture*,[50] where no Article 177 (European Community) reference was sought. *Meagher* principally[51] concerned

---

scheme disqualified farmers whose off-farm income "combined with that of their spouses" did not reach a certain figure, which discriminated against married couples and in favour of couples living together.

[49] J.P. Casey, *Constitutional Law in Ireland* (2nd ed., London: Sweet & Maxwell, 1992) p. 170.

[50] *Meagher v. Minister of Agriculture*, above, n.36 extensively analysed in G.W. Hogan and A. Whelan, *Ireland and the European Union: Constitutional and Statutory Texts and Commentary* (London: Sweet & Maxwell, 1995), Chap. 4. See further A. Whelan, "Constitutional Law – *Meagher v. Minister for Agriculture*" (1993) 15 *Dublin University Law Journal* 152, and G.W. Hogan, "The *Meagher* Case and the Executive Implementation of European Directives in Ireland" (1995) 2 *Maastricht Journal of European and Comparative Law* 174.

[51] The case also concerned the validity of ministerial regulations made under s.3(2) of the European Communities Act 1972 and search warrants and summonses issued thereunder. Following the structure of analysis in *East Donegal Co-operative* [1970] I.R. 317 that ministerial powers must be exercised according to the principles of constitutional justice these regulations were unanimously upheld as *intra vires* s.3(2) on the grounds that (i) the substance of those regulations was necessitated by the directive and the method was "appropriate", *per* Blayney J.; and (ii) the regulations merely give effect to

the admitted conflict between section 3(2) of the 1972 Act, which allows the minister to make regulations "repealing, amending or applying, with or without modification, other law exclusive of this Act", with the exclusive law-making power of the *Oireachtas* contained in Article 15.2.1. The Supreme Court held that [clause a] saved section 3(2) from unconstitutionality because:

> "having regard to the number of Community laws, acts done and measures adopted which either have to be facilitated in their application to the law of the State or have to be implemented by appropriate action into the law of the State, the obligation of membership would necessitate facilitating these activities, in some instances at least, and possibly in the great majority of instances, by the making of ministerial regulation rather than legislation of the *Oireachtas*."

This (the sole) reason is interesting because the machinery in section 3(2) is not, as a matter of Community law, necessitated as an obligation of membership. Community law has no rules on what the domestic machinery should be, so long as the result complies with Community law. The result may be reached by any effective means, for example, implementation by all the autonomous regions in a federal state, by legislation, by constitutional referenda, according to the choice of the national system. Therefore the Supreme Court decisions turns on giving a different meaning to "necessitated by the obligations of membership" than that given by Community law. It is an Irish constitutional law meaning, albeit one which in this case is more *communautaire* than Community law itself. But this *communautaire* decision suggests that the question whether the Irish courts must follow the Community law interpretation of what is "necessitated" is to be answered "no".

It can be argued that the constitutional law interpretation must follow the European Community law interpretation because once the Court of Justice has decided that X is necessitated by membership then an interpretation of Article 29.4.5 that X is not necessitated is perverse and unreasonable and therefore not according to the canons of constitutional interpretation. At first glance, this appears to be correct. But there are several reasons why it is not correct.

It is easier to understand why if the constitutional rule ("Z") which X violates is particularly important (for example, a basic principle on the separation of the judicial and other powers of government, on the people's right to be consulted in a referendum, a human right, etc.). It is interesting to note in this regard that Denham J. made the express reservation in *Meagher v. Minister for Agriculture*[52] that there was no argument or issue of a constitutional right or of the validity of the directive or its principles or policies under the treaties. It is perfectly legitimate as a matter of constitutional construction to apply any of the following methods of interpretation:

---

the principles and policies in the directive, applying by way of analogy the test for the validity of delegated legislation in *Cityview Press v. An Chomhairle Oiliúna* [1980] I.R. 381 at 399, *per* Denham J. Finlay C.J. and O'Flaherty and Egan J.J., concurred in all the judgments.

[52] *Meagher v. Minister for Agriculture* [1994] I.R. 344 (Sup. Ct.) 329 (High Ct.).

1. A historical interpretation (*e.g. The People (D.P.P.) v. O'Shea,*[53] *per* Henchy J. dissenting) of Article 29.4.5 along these lines: in amending the Constitution the people did not intend to allow the rendering inapplicable of Z by a measure such as X.

2. An interpretation of Article 29.4.5 and section 2 of the European Communities Act 1972 in the light of the Constitution (*e.g. Tormey v. Ireland*[54]) as a whole, holding that the tail cannot wag the dog.

3. A teleological interpretation according to which Article 29.4.5 must be read in the light of the goals of the Constitution, which precludes the overriding of Z by X (*e.g. Nestor v. Murphy,*[55] *per* Henchy J.). (In other words, in holding that Y does not oblige X, the High Court might apply the same method of interpretation to the Constitution which the Court of Justice may have used on Community law texts to hold that Y obliges X.)

4. An interpretation of Article 29.4.5 in the light of its interaction with a particular article (*S.P.U.C. v. Grogan,*[56] *per* Walsh J. (Hederman J. concurring)). There may be other methods.

5. A textual interpretation according to which the protection afforded by Article 29.4.5 may be limited because it is a shield solely against *provisions* of the Constitution, not against natural law rules recognised under it. This point applies to [clause a] and [clause b] equally and will be pursued in more detail in the analysis of [clause b].

It should be clear that whatever is involved in the constitutional test, it is an Irish constitutional law test, and there is no element which obliges the courts to follow the European Community law interpretation.

There is another reason why the constitutional test does not require the following of a Court of Justice ruling, apart from the above argument. This reason turns on the distinction between what is necessitated by European Community law and what is necessitated by European Community membership. The latter is partly a political question, and one of which the Court of Justice is not necessarily the authoritative interpreter even as a matter of European Community law. This distinction may be in itself determinative of the question of whether the courts must follow a Court of Justice ruling. This is not developed here on account of space and the desire to focus the analysis to demonstrating that, even if the distinction between necessitated by European Community law and European Community membership is evanescent (which is not admitted), the courts still need not follow a Court of Justice ruling.

---

53 [1982] I.R. 384.
54 [1985] I.R. 289 at p. 295–296, *per* Henchy J.
55 [1979] I.R. 326.
56 [1989] I.R. 753.

This analysis, it is hoped, stands on its own as the correct understanding of the Third Amendment. However it is easier to see as the correct interpretation of Article 29.4.5 when one considers the changes brought about by the Eleventh Amendment, *viz.* that the Constitution cannot invalidate State measures "necessitated by the obligations of membership *of the European Union* or of the Communities" (emphasis added). Collins has pointed out that there are obligations under the Treaty on European Union in the fields of common foreign and security police (Title V of that Treaty) and justice and home affairs (Title VI) which the Court of Justice is not competent to consider.[57] Therefore as a matter of the law of the European Union, the authoritative arbiter of what is necessitated by such obligations will not be the Court of Justice. Perhaps it will be the Member States acting together. Perhaps it will be the International Court of Justice if two Member States choose to litigate the issue against each other. Whoever it is, the decision need not be followed by the High Court in the interpretation of Article 29.4.5 for the same reasons as those given above in respect of the European Communities. Indeed, if the High Court were to follow the interpretation of the Member States of the European Union, it is difficult to see what purpose the test of necessity in Article 29.4.5 serves.

Furthermore, as Collins points out, unlike the Court of Justice's control of European Community law under Article 164 (EC) according to, for example, its version of the principles of the rule of law and fundamental rights,[58] there is no such control for certain measures taken under the Treaty on European Union. There is a serious concern that if the Irish courts interpret Article 29.4.5 [clause b] to deprive them of the power to test the application of such measures in Ireland against constitutional law, which on its face it does, then laws may be applied in Ireland with no judicial control whatever, even at the European Community law level.

However the Irish courts interpret [clause b], it is difficult to see why they would interpret [clause a] in such a way as to immunise state action taken on foot of the obligations of membership of the European Union from challenge on the grounds of its incompatibility with the Constitution. This is not to say that, if such an interpretation was the only legal one possible, the Irish courts would not respect the semantic limits of the law. But for the reasons given above this is not even the preferable semantic interpretation, least of all the only possible one.

---

57 A. Collins, "The Eleventh Amendment – Problems and Perspectives" (1992) 10 *Irish Law Times* 209.

58 These of course need not correspond to the Irish constitutional law version of the principles of the rule of law and human rights: "Furthermore, it must be emphasised that legal concepts do not necessarily have the same meaning in Community law and in the law of the various Member States" – Case 283/81 *CILFIT v. Ministry of Health* [1982] ECR 3415 at 3430.

But there is a final, conclusive argument for this interpretation. It is so completely accepted that section 2 of the European Communities Act 1972 is necessitated by the obligations of membership[59] that this is not questioned. Yet, in the perception of European Community law, section 2 is not only not necessitated by the obligations of membership, it is at best irrelevant and arguably contrary to European Community law because of the doctrine of direct effect.[60] Therefore the meaning of necessitated by the obligations of membership in [clause a] is an Irish constitutional law meaning because this acceptance of the necessity of section 2 must be one based outside European Community law. If the interpretation of Hogan and Whelan that [clause a] is a *renvoi* to European Community law requirements[61] was accepted over the arguments advanced here but their arguments on the requirements of European Community law rejected,[62] then section 2 is unconstitutional for over-reaching the power of the Oireachtas. Even if it were not unconstitutional, it would be a ripe target for an Article 177 (EC) reference to determine its compatibility with European Community law. If the test of necessity is not an Irish constitutional law test, then section 2 is probably both unconstitutional and contrary to European Community law.

The results of this analysis are the following:

1. The Irish courts do not have to follow the Court of Justice's European Community law interpretation of what is necessitated by the obligations of membership of the European Communities in deciding whether measures by the executive or the *Oireachtas* are necessitated by the obligations of membership for the purposes of the Article 29.4.5 immunity granted such measures. Likewise, with the necessary changes, for the European Union.
2. Such a measure may be held, and remain, void as unconstitutional.
3. There is no right to an Article 177 (EC) reference from the High Court or the Supreme Court on the interpretation of the European Community obligation on which this national measure is based for the purposes of showing it to be necessitated.

This does not mean that Ireland might not be in breach of its European Community obligations. Ways to test this would be for the Commission under Article 169 (EC), or another Member State, under Article 170 (EC) or even Article 182 (EC), to bring the matter before the Court of Justice, or for a

---

59 See, *e.g. Crotty v. An Taoiseach* [1987] I.L.R.M. 400, judgment of Barrington J., quoted above in para. 27–4.

60 See above, Part II, "European Community Law".

61 (1995) *op. cit.* above, n.50, Chap. 3.

62 See above, para. 7–13.

court to so decide then in its discretion to make a reference on the matter. If a court did not the extreme unlikelihood of the other possibilities means that the practical result is that X remains void and the European Community question is never decided. However it is conceivable that the Commission would initiate an action. Constitutional problems are no defence – Case 77/69 *Commission v. Belgium*[63]: "the liability of a Member State under Article 169 arises whatever the agency of the State whose action or inaction is the cause of the failure to fulfil its obligations, even in the case of a constitutionally independent institution". (The State would have a difficult time deciding what to argue, (for example, it may be constitutionally bound to defend the decision of the Supreme Court).) In any type of case other than a preliminary reference, the Court of Justice may not pronounce on the necessity of X, but rather confine itself to stating that the result required by Y has not been achieved. The Court of Justice may make three possible rulings:

1. It may decide that X is not necessitated by Y. Y can be satisfied by some other State measure ("W"). The Court of Justice may or may not hold Ireland in breach of its obligations for not trying W, depending on how the action was framed. W may or may not cause constitutional problems.

2. The Court of Justice may rule that X is necessitated by Y. (Of course the Court of Justice would not hold that the High Court's decision was in error, as that was a decision on the interpretation of national law.) Providing the time limit for implementation of Y has elapsed, the Court of Justice may find that Ireland has failed to fulfil its obligations under the Treaty. Under Article 171 (EC), Ireland would be required to take the necessary measures to comply with the judgment. The State would then have several options to remedy its breach of Community law. It is also possible, albeit unlikely, that such a decision would be characterised by the courts as an act of an institution for the purposes of [clause b].

3. The Court of Justice may make the same ruling as the second ruling above, but add further that Y is directly effective and lay down what directly effective rights and obligations it gives rise to. Ireland would still be in breach of its obligations,[64] and would have the same options. But there is an important consequence in constitutional law if the directly effective rights and obligations of Y conflict with Z. Suppose a party disputed before the High Court an action based on the directly effective parts of Y. This would now fall to be analysed under Article 29.4.5 [clause b] because Y, unlike X, is a law, act or measure adopted by the Communities and of which the Court of Justice is the authoritative interpreter. Under [clause b] there is no constitutional test of necessity.

63 [1970] E.C.R. 237 at 243, para. 15.

64 Case C–208/90 *Emmott v. Minister for Social Welfare*: [1991] I E.C.R. I–4269 at 4299, paras. 20 to 23 (the direct effect of Social Security Directive established in earlier cases (Case 286/85 *McDermott and Cotter* [1987] E.C.R. 1453 and Case C–377/89 *McDermott and Cotter* [1991] E.C.R. I–1155) did not relieve Ireland from its obligation to implement).

Unless some other argument is made and accepted, such as those proposed below in paragraph 27–8, the end result is that Z is rendered inapplicable in favour of the European Community law rule by virtue of the European Communities Act and Article 29.4.5 [clause b], just as it would have been if Y was contained in a Regulation and was therefore binding and directly applicable [Article 189 paragraph 2 (EC)]. Given that this is a possible effect of the European Communities Act and [clause b], certainly a possible effect in cases where there is no fundamental commitment of Irish constitutional law at issue, it could be argued by application of the principle of harmonious interpretation of the Constitution that this outcome ought to influence a more *communautaire* interpretation of [clause a]. However, harmonious interpretation must take into account the entirety of the Constitution and the necessity of a European Communities Act, and the possible effect of [clause b] will be only one factor.

Therefore the understanding of Article 29.4.5 proposed here does not of itself affect the final result of the issue of the supremacy of European Community law over constitutional law. However it does have practical effects for the testing of State measures purportedly enacted in pursuance of European Community obligations against the Constitution, and thus for the possibility of conflicts, and for the right to an Article 177 (EC) reference on the question of what is necessitated.[65]

Article 29.4.5 [b]

27–8 The first point to make about [clause b] is that there is no test of necessity. Whether or not a law has been enacted, an act done, or a measure adopted appears to be relatively clearcut. No provision of the Constitution, under this provision, can bar them from having the force of law in the State. This appears to be an effective and strongly worded provision which has helped the avoidance of any complete blow-up between Irish courts and the Court of Justice. As an exercise in drafting to avoid Ireland being held in breach of its Community obligations, it has so far succeeded as a practical matter.

The provision appears at first sight, if one accepts in this instance the inversion of the principle of interpretation of *generalia specialibus non derogant* into *lex specialis derogat generalibus*, to be the end of the question of conflicts with directly effective European Community law rules (problems with the statute and implementing measures apart and the problem of the permanent state of constitutional disobedience caused by the presence of these measures left to one side). Not so. There are several possible limitations in the very wording of this provision:

---

[65] This latter point receives some support from the *dicta* of Finlay C.J. in *S.P.U.C. v. Grogan (No. 1)* [1990] I.L.R.M. 350 at 357.

1. Does this recitation of instruments (law, act, or measure) include decisions of the Court of Justice? If not, are Irish courts hereby bound to accept the Court of Justice interpretation of laws, acts and measures as coming within this constitutional provision? Without going into the questions, which have not been answered by the courts, even if the answer is yes to both questions there are further problems,

2. "provision": this does not cover the preamble or Irish constitutional natural law.

3. "prevent": the provision erects a bar – it does not grant European Community law constitutional status, nor make any transfer to the European Community, nor ground an assertion that a statute cannot overrule the European Communities Act. Most importantly, it does not prevent a statute or other instrument overruling directly effective European Community law. That would be a matter for the interaction of such a statute or instrument and the European Communities Act 1972.[66]

4. "force of law": similarly, it is not clear what status of law this is to be. "Force of law" is not "force of constitutional law". In particular, barring the challenge to the force of law of the European Community law rule on the basis of constitutional provisions does not mean that the European Communities Act 1972 can confer on a European Community law rule a status superior to a subsequent statute. On this interpretation therefore, section 2 of the European Communities Act 1972 must either be read very restrictively or is unconstitutional as an unlawful delegation of the sovereignty of the *Oireachtas*, unless it is saved by a [clause a] Irish constitutional law interpretation of what is necessitated by membership.

   What appears to be meant is an enforceable rule. But that is not necessarily so. Even if it is so, and apart from the question of the status of law, the word "law" here introduces the potential restrictions which Irish con-

---

66 It could be argued that [clause b] prevents the legislative power of the *Oireachtas* being invoked to disrupt the effectiveness of European Community law, because [clause b] prevents all provisions, including Article 15 on the legislative power of the *Oireachtas*, being invoked. But this is tenuous because it is not Article 15 which prevents European Community law having the force of law but the statute (which results from the exercise of power in Article 15). If it had been intended to prevent a repealing statute without constitutional revision, [clause b] could have read "No statute or provision of this Constitution . . .". More importantly, this argument goes against the whole idea of Article 29.4 of setting up a jurisdictional bar to constitutional review and grounding European Community law in statute law. Further, if one views the grounding effect of the European Communities Act for directly effective provisions of European Community law to be contrary to European Community law, this argument would mean that the Oireachtas lacked power to enact those parts of the European Communities Act.

stitutional law sees as applying to any rule in order for it to be "law",[67] such as the restriction of the observance of fundamental rights.

Combining points 2 to 4 with the analysis of the European Communities Act,[68] the most favourable construction of [clause b] from the point of view of the enforceability of European Community law in the courts is that it purports to introduce to some degree a bar to the direct adjudication of conflicts between European Community law and Irish constitutional law. But such a bar is irrelevant because European Community law is not directly in force in domestic law: such a state of law would be in contravention of Article 29.6. [Clause b] is not sufficiently strongly worded to be interpreted as derogating from that Article. The status of European Community law rules depends on the European Communities Act 1972. To assert the enforceability of European Community law rules is to claim that the Act is necessitated by the obligations of membership. Therefore [clause b] is irrelevant. It is no help to the enforceability of European Community law rights that their "force of law" cannot be challenged on the basis of constitutional provisions, if they are not given any purported status before the national courts. [Clause b] might, however, be relevant in addition to [clause a] to ground the constitutionality of the European Communities Act 1972.

Even if it is not accepted on the basis of this textual analysis that [clause b] is otiose, or if it is accepted as having the above use in respect of the 1972 Act, the rules of constitutional interpretation recited above in connection with [clause a] operate to restrict its effect, and thus give rise to possibilities of conflict with Irish constitutional law.

A position once put forward by Walsh J. should be rejected here.[69] In deciding that a High Court decision to make an Article 177 (EC) reference was not a decision within the meaning of Article 34 of the Constitution and thus did not give rise to a right of appeal,[70] Walsh J. held:

> "by virtue of the provisions of Article 29.4.3 of the Constitution, the right of appeal to this Court from such a decision must yield to the primacy of article 177 of the Treaty. That article, as a part of Irish law, qualifies Article 34 of the Constitution in the matter in question."[71]

---

67 Interestingly, the Court of Justice has shown the way on how far such a word can be interpreted, as in its application of Article 164 (EEC) in the Opinion 1/91 *On the Draft European Economic Area Treaty* [1991] E.C.R. I–6079.

68 See above, para. 27–4, "Statutory Amendments".

69 *Campus Oil v. Minister for Industry* [1983] I.R. 82 at 87.

70 Similar criticisms to those considered here can probably be levied against the decision in *Doyle v. An Taoiseach* [1986] I.L.R.M. 693 at 714 which states that "Community law has the paramount force and effect of constitutional provisions."

71 The learned judge made an Irish constitutional law interpretation of Article 177 (EEC) which conflicts with European Community law in holding that a right of appeal of a decision to make an Article 177 reference "would be contrary to both the spirit and the letter of Article 177". This is not the case in European Community law, as the learned

The learned judge misstated in that passage the nature of European Community law in Irish law. The decision has been decisively criticised by Kelly as proceeding on the mistaken basis that the European Community Treaty has been incorporated by reference into the constitutional order, which on the analysis above is wrong. As Kelly put it, the decision approaches "the radical proposition that Article 29.4.3 has the effect of scheduling every Article of the Treaty of Rome to the text of the Constitution."[72]

Why Conflicts Can Occur

27–9 There are many potential weak points in the constitutional and statutory provisions to the position of European Community law in Irish law, which weak points reflect the strength of constitutional coherence which remains. There is no unquestionable acceptance of European Community law or measures based on European Community law in the constitutional and statutory provisions dedicated to European Community law, let alone in Irish constitutional law as a whole. The following weak points, *inter alia*, have already been indicated:

- Irish constitutional law has a different perspective as to what constitutes European Community law from European Community law's self-description;
- the possible limitations to the licence to join in Article 29.4.3, to what is necessitated by the obligations of membership in Article 29.4.5 [clause a], and to the bar to constitutional challenges based on other constitutional provisions in [clause b];
- if [clause b] is not otiose, it goes only to support the constitutionality of the European Communities Act 1972 and is very restricted both on a textual analysis and in the light of the principles of constitutional interpretation;
- the status of European Community law depends on statute, which opens it to debasement by other statutes;

judge appears to have accepted, in citing Case 146/73 *Rheinmühlen-Düsseldorf v. Einfuhr- und Vorratsstelle Getreide* [1974] E.C.R. 139. It is in the light of this willingness to make an Irish constitutional law interpretation of European Community law that his statement "the very purpose of that provision of Article 177 of the Treaty is to enable the national judge to have direct and unimpeded access to the only court which has jurisdiction to furnish him with [an interpretation of the Treaty or of acts of the institutions etc.]" is to be understood: the Court of Justice is the only court which can make this interpretation as a matter of European Community law. Otherwise his judgment is self-contradictory.

72 G.W. Hogan and G. Whyte, *Supplement to Second Edition of J.M. Kelly: The Irish Constitution*, (Dublin: University College Dublin, 1988), p. 40; see also Hogan and Whyte, *J.M. Kelly: The Irish Constitution* (3rd ed., 1994) pp. 284–285.

- there may be a conflict over an Irish constitutional law interpretation of the statutory wording "the conditions laid down in those treaties" which conflicts with a European Community law interpretation of such issues;
- the necessity for constitutional and statutory provision to ground the enforceability of European Community law in Irish courts contradicts Case 26/62 *Van Gend en Loos*;
- to these weak points must be added that the State may withdraw from the European Community without difficulties in Irish constitutional law. The provisions on membership are facilitative, not mandatory. The Constitution is silent on how treaties may be denounced. Presumably denunciation could be by act of the Government pursuant to Article 29.4.1. The only possible limitation is that such denunciation might have to be in accordance with public international law pursuant to Article 29.3. If the State wished to withdraw for reasons insufficient in public international law[73] and Article 29.3 posed a problem, there is no apparent difficulty in the people amending the Constitution to resolve that problem.

The textual and interpretative analyses demonstrate the limitations of the reception of European Community law into Irish law. Do the courts, despite all that has been said about texts, judicial decisions, and the legitimation of Irish constitutional law, uphold European Community law by relying directly on the European Community law duty according to the requirements of European Community constitutional law?

The duty on judges to uphold the Constitution has been used as a grounds for the extension of constitutional protection, because a judge in his decisions cannot ignore it.[74] Every person appointed a judge under the Constitution is required pursuant to Article 34.5.1 to take the following oath:

> "In the presence of Almighty God I . . . do solemnly and sincerely promise and declare that I will duly and faithfully and to the best of my knowledge and power execute the office of . . . without fear or favour, affection or ill-will towards any man, and that I will uphold the Constitution and the laws. May God direct and sustain me."

What happens where this duty to uphold the Constitution conflicts with a European Community law duty to disregard it?[75] There are several judicial statements on the duty of judges in the context of Irish constitutional law considerations of European Community matters. Barrington J. in *Crotty v. An Taoiseach,*[76] stated "It would not be open to the Court [of Justice] to question

---

[73] For sufficient reasons in public international law, see above, para. 17–4, "The Relevance of the Public International Law of Treaties".

[74] See above, Chap. 25, "The Constitutionalisation of Irish Law".

[75] For an analysis going beyond the order approach, see D.R. Phelan, "Two Hats, One Wig, No Halo" (1995) *Doctrine & Life* 130.

[76] [1987] I.L.R.M. 400.

the validity of the Treaty [of Rome] to which it owed its existence any more than it would be open to this Court to question the validity of the Irish Constitution." He went on to state[77] that important and embarrassing consequences in European Community law cannot affect the duty of the court to fulfil its constitutional duty and, in this case, hold the European Communities Act unconstitutional, in a case properly before it. Finlay C.J. stated in *Attorney General v. X*,[78] quoting Kenny J. in *The People v. Shaw*,[79] where he refers to the guarantee by the State to protect and vindicate the personal rights of the citizen (Article 40.3) as imposing an obligation to implement the guarantee "on each branch of the State which exercises the powers of legislating, executing and giving judgment on those laws."

Where the High Court judge in *S.P.U.C. v. Grogan*[80] effectively failed to uphold the Constitution by refusing to grant an injunction to protect constitutional rights when making an Article 177 (EEC) reference, distinguishing a prior Supreme Court judgment on grounds that the Supreme Court considered unconvincing, the Supreme Court on appeal pointed out the judge's failure of duty. Walsh J. stated, "[i]t is not open to any judge to do anything which in effect suspends any provisions of the Constitution for any period whatsoever".[81]

McCarthy J. stated in *Grogan* that although he did not think that the injunction granted would be effective, he thought that if the judges did not shoulder their constitutional duty to grant it "the rule of law will be set at naught".[82] This is important because it ties the individual duty on judges to uphold the Constitution with the notion of law under the Constitution: there cannot be law without observance of Irish constitutional law rules.

The provisions of Article 29.4 are limited. If this Article, in combination with the European Communities Act, is regarded to some degree as a Trojan horse in the middle of the Constitution, one cannot expect judges to salute each new European Community law rule which emerges from its belly.

What types of conflict between Irish constitutional law and European Community law can occur? Three: first, between statute law and European Community law; secondly, between public international law and European Community law: third, between Irish constitutional law and European

---

77 *ibid.* at 435, quoted in the text above.
78 [1992] 1 I.R. 1.
79 [1982] I.R. 1.
80 [1989] I.R. 752.
81 *ibid.* at 767–768. *q.v.* R. Dworkin *Taking Rights Seriously* (London: Duckworth, 1977): "If a judge accepts the settled practices of his legal system – if he accepts that is, the autonomy provided by its distinct constitutive and regulative rules – then he must, according to the doctrine of political responsibility, accept some general political theory that justifies these practices."
82 *ibid.* p. 363.

Community law. The first two types of conflict have been flagged and will not be pursued further. The last is considered in substance below in Part V.

What if, in any conflict where Irish law does not accommodate the claim of European Community law for any of the above reasons, the Supreme Court nonetheless upholds European Community law in breach of Irish constitutional law? This would be to cause a constitutional revolution – a discontinuity in the validation of laws – and by implication to seek to establish a new Irish constitutional law legitimation. Thus one can argue within the framework of Irish constitutional law that such a judgment would be illegal. In terms of politics and power, one may lose. Legally, however, it is a revolution. This revolution has not yet taken place. Given the limited textual basis for European Community law, the coherence of Irish constitutional law on the interpretation above has not been broken.[83]

---

83 *c.f.* G.W. Hogan and A. Whelan take a contrary view in (1995) *op. cit.* above, n.50, p. 142:
"If one can speak of a revolution (and the effects, actual and potential, of European legal integration are profound) it took place most likely, in 1972."

28. COPING WITH CONFLICTS

28–1 Chapters 23 to 25 considered the basis of Irish constitutional law. Chapters 26 and 27 considered the limited and dependent position of European Community law in Irish constitutional law, which is contrary to European Community constitutional law demands. Here is considered how Ireland can deal with a conflict between the two.

If the courts do something mandated by the Constitution which results in the denial of a European Community law right, and thereby prevent an Irish constitutional law revolution, there are four possible options for the government:

1. The government could try to ignore the decision and wait for the Commission or another Member State to bring an action against it. Before that time there would be no Court of Justice judgment directly against Ireland. There would not necessarily even be an Article 177 (EC) preliminary ruling by the Court of Justice either because no reference need be made[1] or because the ruling would have been made earlier in the proceedings, would have to leave the interpretation up to a national court, and could not have been a judgment against Ireland (by virtue of the nature of Article 177 references).

   If an action were taken directly against Ireland, which is far from certain as a political matter, and the Court of Justice held against Ireland, then Ireland could ignore this judgment (as, for example, it ignored for a long time the judgment of the European Court of Human Rights in Strasbourg[2]). By hypothesis, there would be no constitutional problem with this course of action. It might lead Ireland into political trouble with other Member States, or if a further action is brought it might lead to the imposition of a fine by the Court of Justice. The latter possibility would depend on a Court of Justice judgment which is within the Court of Justice's discretion, unlike the declaration that Ireland had failed in its obligations. Even if such a penalty were to be declared, Ireland could pay it, or not pay it (which might entail, again, political consequences). There are no consequences in Irish constitutional law. What may be called the "dragging of heels" in *communautaire* terms may be called standing on principle in Irish constitutional law, because of the gap between the two orders.

2. The government could seek a protocol which relieves it of the obligation or allows the obligation to be implemented in some less effective way which

---

1 See above, para. 27–6, "Article 29.4.5 [clause a]".
2 *Norris v. Attorney General* [1984] I.R. 36.

does not entail a measure conflicting with the Irish constitutional law imperative. The willingness of other Member States to agree to such a protocol is a political question which will not be considered here save to say that it would depend on how strongly the government argued and on whether other Member States regarded ensuring the application of the particular conflicting European Community law obligation in Ireland as essential to their interests.

3. The government could seek the amendment of the Treaty or the Directive containing the European Community law requirement to avoid the problem.
4. The government could acquiesce to the European Community law demand and seek a domestic referendum to change the Constitution and remove the Irish constitutional law problem; or further, seek a new Constitution altogether.

This fourth option may not always work. It is the focus of the remainder of the Chapter. As an option it has a limited importance for the overall thesis in this work, because it is by no means clear that this option will be the response to the dilemma of revolt or revolution. Even if it is the response, the dilemma will still be posed with the possible exception of a case where the government successfully[3] puts forward, and the people accept and the courts uphold, the systematic and direct removal of Irish constitutional law fundamental commitments in order to change the legitimation of Irish constitutional law. Such an exceptional scenario would cause a revolution in law.

---

3 R. Humphreys poses a question on a related proposition: "where are the massed ranks of cranial literalists poised to rise up throughout the land in their hundreds of thousands to vote for the passage of [an amendment to negative the existence of unenumerated rights]?" – "Interpreting Natural Rights" (1993–1995) XXVII–XXX *Irish Jurist* 223 at p. 224 (N.S.).

29. LIMITS ON AMENDMENT

The Problematic

29–1 This is a tricky question. It is necessary to separate two propositions. The purpose of this enquiry is not to question the existence of political power, but the legality of its exercise and the potential breach in legitimation by the recognition of the legality of the result. Such an enquiry will not interest those who hold that power is its own justification, save perhaps to illustrate some problems with particular means. As a brute political fact, legal orders can be changed. There is no doubt that in France in 1789 and in Russia in 1917 there were constitutional revolutions. In Ireland, to simplify its legal history, the brehon courts were abolished by the English, and centuries later the right to appeal to the Judicial Committee of the Privy Council in Irish law was abolished by the Irish. The first political act was a legal act only from the point of view of English law, and was a revolution from the point of view of brehon law. The second act was legal according to English law (*Moore v. Attorney General*[1]) but possibly not according to Irish law.[2] The new Constitution creating an autonomous legal order could be established only through legal revolution and a new legitimation.

---

1 [1935] I.R. 472 (Judicial Committee of the Privy Council).

2 The Third Dáil, sitting as a constituent assembly and unfettered by any oath, enacted the Constitution of the Irish Free State 1992 by passing the Constituent Act which contained in the First Schedule the Constitution and in the Second Schedules the Articles of Agreement for a Treaty between Great Britain and Ireland. Section 2 of the Act provided that any provision or amendment thereof contrary to the Treaty would be void. As Fitzgibbon J. pointed out in *The State (Ryan) v. Lennon* [1935] I.R. 170 at 226, this Constituent Assembly "expressly denied to the Oireachtas the power of enacting *any* legislation, by way of amendment of the Constitution or otherwise" which was contrary to the Treaty. Only the Constituent Assembly, and not the Oireachtas it created, had the power to amend the Constituent Act. From this is could be argued that the Constitution of 1937 was outside the scope of the Constituent Act, and caused a legal revolution. As against this argument, however, the authority of the Constituent Assembly which enacted the Constitution of 1922 itself derived from the people (and this proposition is agreed to by Fitzgibbon J. in *The State (Ryan) v. Lennon*, who calls the Constituent Assembly "the mouthpiece of the people" – at 226) and so the enactment by the people of the Constitution of 1937, whilst in breach of the Constituent Act, maintained the same legitimation as that Act. This argument (favoured by this author) coupled with recent Supreme Court jurisprudence, could point the way to a consistent historical legitimation of Irish law since 1922 (or even 1918) at which point there was a legal revolution based on popular sovereignty. That concept is, however, an indeterminate one (looked at from an external perspective) and is in any event insufficient of itself to legitimate Irish constitutional law in general and in particular the controls on the exercise of power and the recognition of legal effect (see above, para. 24–3,"Sovereignty of the People").

The Irish[3] could no doubt as a political act abolish their Constitution and join in a European constitution enacted, for example, by direct suffrage of the citizens of the present European Union. This would presumably be a legal act from the perspective of the new European constitutional law. But it would be illegal from the perspective of the Constitution, and so a discontinuity of constitutional law would occur. The two hypotheses in option 4 in the last chapter both involve the question of how far amendment to the Constitution can go whilst still being legal under Irish constitutional law, which raises the immediate practical question of how far Irish constitutional law has already been amended. By definition, there cannot be an amendment of Irish constitutional law which is illegal according to Irish constitutional law – although there can be an end put to Irish constitutional law and a new notion of Irish constitutional law developed. There would be a legal revolution if a purported amendment, contrary to Irish constitutional law, was upheld.

The Provision on Amendment

29–2 Articles 46 and 47 deal with amendment of the Constitution and referendums. They provide:

"Article 46

1. Any provision of this Constitution may be amended, whether by way of variation, addition, or repeal, in the manner provided by this Article.
2. Every proposal for an amendment of this Constitution shall be initiated in Dáil Éireann as a Bill, and shall upon having been passed or deemed to have been passed by both Houses of the Oireachtas, be submitted by Referendum to the decision of the people in accordance with the law for the time being in force relating to the Referendum.
3. Every such Bill shall be expressed to be 'An Act to amend the Constitution'.
4. A Bill containing a proposal or proposals for the amendment of this Constitution shall not contain any other proposal.
5. A Bill containing a proposal for the amendment of this Constitution shall be signed by the President forthwith upon his being satisfied that the provisions of this Article have been complied with in respect thereof and that such proposal has been duly approved by the people in accordance with the provisions of section 1 of Article 47 of this Constitution and shall be duly promulgated by the President as a law.

Article 47

1. Every proposal for an amendment of this Constitution which is submitted by referendum to the decision of the people shall, for the purpose of Article

---

[3] The meaning of this term outside of the meaning given it in Irish law would have to be determined for the purposes of establishing a putative constituent power. In the circumstances of this hypothesis such a determination would be best (from the point of view of an emerging federal constitution) left to European Community law.

46 of this Constitution, be held to have been approved by the people, if, upon having been so submitted, a majority of the votes cast at such referendum shall have been cast in favour of its enactment into law.

2. 1. Every proposal, other than a proposal to amend the Constitution, which is submitted by referendum to the decision of the people shall be held to have been vetoed by the people if a majority of the votes cast at such referendum shall have been cast against its enactment into law and if the votes so cast against its enactment into law shall have amounted to not less than thirty-three and one-third per cent. of the voters on the register.
2. Every proposal, other than a proposal to amend the Constitution, which is submitted by referendum to the decision of the people shall for the purposes of Article 27 hereof be held to have been approved by the people unless vetoed by them in accordance with the provisions of the foregoing subsection of this section."

The textual limitation to this power to amend will be considered below, in paragraphs 29–3 and 29–4. The limitations derived from the legitimation of Irish constitutional law of natural law and popular sovereignty will be considered in the context of self-amendment.

Manner

29–3 There are clear limits on the manner in which the Constitution can be amended: "if the Constitution is to be amended, it is to be amended in accordance with the machinery established under Articles 46 and 47 of the Constitution and not otherwise".[4] It is important to recall this statement before going into an analysis of the power of amendment of the Constitution because it makes clear that the power cannot be greater than or other than that contained in this Article.[5]

"Provision"

29–4 There are three possible limitations which arise from the use of this word in Article 46.1:

1. The power of amendment does not extend to the Preamble, which sets out several principles and goals of the Constitution: authority comes ultimately from the Holy Trinity which is also the final end; the promotion of

---

4 Divisional High Court, *Crotty v. An Taoiseach* [1987] I.R. 713 at 745.

5 There is, however, an argument to be made that a return to the people of Ireland outside of this Article would maintain the link with the historical legitimation of Irish constitutional law back to the Constituent Assembly of 1922 and the people in 1937 (see the note to para. 29–1, above). This would be similar to the case in France where the president General De Gaulle appealed directly to the people over the heads of the Assembly and this, unprovided for by the Constitution, was not held unconstitutional by the *Conseil Constitutionnel* (who held that they had no jurisdiction to consider the point). The legality of this is questionable. See above, para. 16–10.

the common good; the necessity to observe justice; the goals of the dignity and freedom of the individual and true social order.

2. Neither does it extend to *"Dochum Glóire Dé agus Onóra na hÉireann"*, the sentence which appears at the foot of both the English and Irish texts of the Constitution.
3. Can the wording of Article 29.4.5 ("No provision of this Constitution . . .") apply to the process of amendment to restrict what can be done? A positive answer would mean that by adopting an amendment the people had limited their power of amendment. This is an interesting question but it would only arise in the reverse of the present hypothesis that the amendment of the Constitution is to provide better for European Community law's place in Irish constitutional law. The question gives rise to the general problem of the alienability of sovereignty, discussed below.

Self-Amendment

29–5 Articles 46 and 47 are themselves provisions of the Constitution which presumptively fall within the power of amendment which they contain. If this is the case, then they could be amended to extend to the Preamble. It is not clear how far the amending power can itself be amended – this is a problem which has arisen in other jurisdictions also, notably in India.[6]

The following two considerations apply both to how far Articles 46 and 47 can be amended themselves, and how far amendment may be carried out under the existing Articles. These considerations are the limited nature of popular sovereignty in Irish constitutional law and Irish constitutional natural law.

Popular Sovereignty and its Natural Law Limits in Irish Constitutional Law

29–6 As a concept, like many others in legal theory, the concept of popular sovereignty is very indeterminate. The analysis is limited here to a consideration of what popular sovereignty means in Irish constitutional law, where it is the subject of less constitutional text, and less constitutional jurisprudence, than natural law, in the context of amendability.[7]

The only direct post-1937 authority on this issue is *Re Article 26 and the Regulation of Information (Services Outside the State for the Termination of Pregnancies) Bill, 1995*.[8] This case stands for the proposition that Irish constitutional natural law cannot invalidate an amendment of the Constitution which is adopted

---

6 J. Finnis, "India" in *Annual Survey of Commonwealth Law* (1967), p. 36; (1972), p. 39; (1973), p. 30.

7 See further and more broadly, para. 24–3, "Sovereignty of the People".

8 [1995] 1 I.R. 1.

by the people which alters the pre-existing Irish constitutional natural law interpretation of a fundamental right, which right is acknowledged in a constitutional provision and not specified in that provision to be natural or inalienable or anterior or superior to positive law, and where the purpose of the amendment is clear, and amends the same provision directly. The limited authority of this case has been considered above.[9] However, even as a limited proposition of dubious life span the decision is nonetheless important in giving an option 4 campaign more legal support than heretofore available, and more generally in weakening the development of the full logic of Irish constitutional natural law.

Upon analysis, the power of the people to amend is constrained and amounts to no more than the possibility of vetoing proposed amendments, and even then it is not absolute:

1. The proposal is made in the Dáil as a Bill and must be passed by both Houses of the *Oireachtas* before the people even get to vote on it (Article 46.2). The proposal may not get beyond this stage.

2. The people can approve it (Article 47.1) by a majority of the votes cast. Therefore a minority of eligible voters could amend the Constitution.[10]

3. The people do not enact the proposal into law (unlike the Constitution itself which the People enacted on 14 June 1937). It remains a Bill to be signed by the President (Article 46.5) and promulgated by her. Thus the limited say of the people even at the stage where they vote is itself limited to one stage in the passing of a Bill, but not its enactment: popular approval is a *sine qua non* but not a sufficient cause.

More generally in Irish constitutional law, although the people are above the State in matters of sovereignty (see above, Part I), sovereignty itself is not the most fundamental legal concept in Irish constitutional law, in particular where the scope of the exercise of power is concerned. A Benthamite or an Austinian analysis has no place.[11] Sovereignty is limited in Irish constitutional law, whether it is the people's or the State's. This is a complex theoretical issue which has benefitted once only from direct judicial statements on the

---

[9] See above, para. 23–9, "Unenumerated Personal Right Resulting from Judges' Ideas of Changing Concept of Prudence, Justice and Charity".

[10] This occurred in the Tenth Amendment of the Constitution Act 1987 (providing for the ratification of the Single European Act).

[11] Walsh J. in *McGee v. Attorney General* [1974] I.R. 284 at 310:

> "Articles 41, 42 and 43 emphatically reject the theory that there are no rights without laws, no rights contrary to the law and no rights anterior to the law. They indicate that justice is placed above the law and acknowledge that natural rights, or human rights, are not created by law but that the Constitution confirms their existence and gives them protection."

issue of the limitation of the people's power in Irish constitutional law. Six further points need to be considered.[12]

1. The idea of an unlimited sovereign people in Irish constitutional law is inconsistent with the idea of natural rights being protected because the protection of natural rights is necessary to legitimate Irish constitutional law, whether these rights be declared by the Constitution or identified by the courts. These rights are not protected because, for example, they represent the will of the people through a social contract as the *quid pro quo* for the surrender of liberty.[13]

2. The protection of Irish constitutional law natural rights does not cease when threatened by the will of the "sovereign" people acting in a majority whether this will be declared through elected representatives in the *Oireachtas* or directly through constitutional referendum. This important protection is supported by the very idea of fundamental rights protection. As Walsh J. has put it:

   > "Quite clearly there are fundamental rights which may not be trampled upon even with the active support of the overwhelming majority of the people. . . . the Constitution is concerned with the human tendency to act selfishly and to abuse power."[14]

   It may be argued that this protection against the people in the core areas protected by natural law is of benefit particularly to the weak and socially disfavoured in times of conflict, such as the unborn, the old, or the expendable. Protection against majority action is also important where there are religious minorities and a very large religious majority living under the same system. A cat to be belled here is that a way of making this protection dependent on majority will is the attack on Irish constitutional law doctrine.[15]

---

[12] These are additional to Chap. 24, "Concepts of Irish Constitutional Law".

[13] See above, Chap. 23, para. 8, on "Fundamental Rights Based on a Contract between State and Citizens".

[14] Foreword to J.P. Casey, *Constitutional Law in Ireland* (1st ed., 1987.) p. 9.

[15] Such an attack comes in many guises and may be expressed in terms which make an opposite view sound unreasonable. G.W. Hogan and A. Whelan state:

> "It is nonetheless important to appreciate that the favouring of one (the European Community) external conception [of values] over that indigenous to Ireland (. . .) represents, from Phelan's perspective, a veritable subversion of the Irish constitutional order rather than simply an (extensive) accommodation of a supranational legal order chosen as the vehicle for the advancement of the general interest."

Ireland and the European Union: Constitutional and Statutory Texts and Commentary (London: Sweet & Maxwell, 1995) p. 128. Behind the language of accommodation and pragmatic advancement of the general interest lies a subversion of the protection of human rights to make them susceptible to external overriding because of a narrowly worded provision (Article 29.4) of the Constitution inserted by the voting majority, coupled with a contingent statutory provision.

As a general point without reference to Hogan and Whelan, the threat to fundamental rights in Western Europe is not posed by the unsophisticated thuggery of tin pot dictators,

3. Article 6 places the exercise of sovereignty under God and subject to the requirements of the common good.[16]

4. The rejection of a legal positivist notion of sovereignty as the ultimate legal authority can be implied from *Byrne v. Ireland*.[17] Walsh J. held: "Not only in England but in many other countries in Europe the inviolability of property was acknowledged in law as a right superior even to that of sovereignty itself".[18] That case concerned whether or not the Royal prerogative of sovereign immunity from suit passed over into law after the creation of the State by virtue of its status as a common law doctrine (the common law continued in force so far as it was not inconsistent with the Constitution).

   Walsh J. found that the theoretical basis of the doctrine was either that the king was the fount of all justice and could therefore do no wrong or that the State (which is still in the law of the United Kingdom personified by the monarch) was the originator of all law and rights. This second notion could have no place in Irish constitutional law because, as noted above, the people are the origin of the State, but they do not personify it. "People" does not simply replace "king": "[t]here is no basis, theoretical or otherwise, for a claim that the State can do no wrong . . .".[19] The first notion of the king as fount of all justice is more interesting because it highlights the fact that if one switches sovereigns (people for king) one cannot state in Irish constitutional law that the people are the font of all justice. Such an idea is completely alien to Irish constitutional law, which is firmly attached to the idea of constitutional justice (not a meaning confined to the administrative law principles of *nemo iudex in causa sua* and *audi alteram partem*). This indicates the limitation of the idea of sovereignty in Irish constitutional law to that of ultimate originator of positive law rules and political authority, but not the ultimate check on their validity or application as law. As O'Higgins C.J. put it in *The State (Healy) v. Donoghue*: "No court under the Constitution has jurisdiction to act contrary to justice."[20]

---

but by the calm and perhaps unconscious subversion of the anti-majoritarian and politically unpopular doctrine in legal orders like Irish constitutional law with the rhetoric of reasonableness, pragmatism, openness, and the general interest. The development in the sophistication of the language which denies human rights in discourse parallels the development in the sophistication of the techniques available to deny human rights in practice. The attempt in this Part to evolve, internally and coherently, the position of Irish constitutional natural law, together with the analysis of the limitations of the position of European Community law in Irish law, is doubtless as unpopular as it is imperfect. Its unpopularity is strong evidence for its necessity.

16 See above, para. 24–4, "The Common Good".
17 [1972] I.R. 241.
18 *ibid.* at 263.
19 *ibid.* at 279.
20 [1976] I.R. 325 at 348.

5. The idea of the people having a constitutional right and duty, as opposed to a sovereign power, is another example of the limited nature of the concept of sovereignty in Irish constitutional law. In *Webb v. Ireland,* Walsh J. found there was a constitutional right to objects which belonged to the national heritage:

> "[T]he people as the sovereign authority having by the Constitution created the State, and by Article 5 declared it to be a sovereign State, have the right and the duty, acting by the State which is the juristic person capable of holding property by virtue of the Constitution, to exercise dominion over all objects forming part of the national heritage."[21]

6. Article 1 of the Constitution provides: "The Irish nation hereby affirms its inalienable, indefeasible, and sovereign right . . .". This is the right of the nation, not of the people. The limitations imported by the concept of Nation have yet to be worked out.

Irish Constitutional Natural Law

29–7 The natural law legitimation of Irish constitutional law affects the power of amendment in three ways.[22] First, Articles 46 and 47 must be read in the light of the other provisions of the Constitution, including those which refer to inalienable rights anterior and superior to positive law. Secondly, the power to amend must be considered in the light of limitations on the concept of sovereignty in Irish constitutional law, including natural law limitations to what it can do with effects recognised in law. Thirdly, Article 46.1 refers to the amendment of provisions, and not to that to which the provisions refer. Combined, these three points limit that power, and consequently this Part concludes that it is not possible without a legal revolution to amend Irish constitutional law to comply with the conflicting European Community law claims where such amendment will run into these limits.

The last point, that Article 46.1 refers to provisions only, is insufficient in isolation to limit ultimately the power of amendment, because (if there were no other limitation) all references to natural law in provisions could be deleted, and perhaps Article 46.1 could itself be amended to extend the power of amendment to delete other positive law anchors for Irish constitutional natural law in the Preamble. However the point is clearly extremely important practically, because all those referenda would otherwise have to pass through the procedure provided.

---

21 [1988] I.R. 353.

22 In an important dissenting judgment in *The State (Ryan) v. Lennon* [1935] I.R. 170 at 204, Kennedy C.J. held that there were natural law limits to constitutional amendment, under the Constitution of the Irish Free State. In that case the amendment to that constitution was upheld by a two to one majority.

Let us consider a hypothetical constitution where an article provides that it is "irrevocable". What meaning does "irrevocable" have? It means that the article admits of no revocation. But if the article was put there on the authority of a sovereign (let us say the people), by whose authority is it bound not to change its mind? There is no reason for its former authority when enacting the article to outrank its current or future authority. So the provision is not, in fact, irrevocable, within that legal order.

But such a legal order is not the same as Irish constitutional law. The Constitution does not provide, for example, that the basis of certain rights is natural law, nor provide for some of these rights. Such provision would strengthen the argument that the people could change also that basis and those rights. What the constituent power did in the creation of the Constitution was *to recognise* that the basis of certain rights was in natural law, and recognised certain rights as inherent, around which it has organised its constitutional system. This is not a constitutive act. In the creation of the sovereign State, the popular sovereign recognised that it was itself bound to observe natural rights.

To override Irish constitutional natural rights is to cause a revolution – to establish a new basis for an order.[23] It is a revolution because, *inter alia*, it involves acceptance that an authority can grant itself authority which it never recognised it had. Could the population (note: not "the people" in the Irish constitutional law sense[24]) have provided for a constitutional order which had nothing to do with natural law? The "could" in that question is a matter of political possibility. They were already breaking from the former constitution of *Saorstát Éireann.* One might also ask whether the Blueshirts (an indigenous anti-republican quasi-fascist movement) could have established a Constitution based on the Spanish model of the time. Both questions come from the same discourse. Neither happened.[25]

There is no need to rehash here Chapters 23–26 of this work. Unless the text of the Constitution and judicial pronouncements thereon are to be treated as nothing more than rhetoric, then certain rights under Irish constitutional law are indeed inalienable, anterior and superior to positive law, including

---

[23] G.W. Hogan and A. Whelan (1995) *op. cit.* above, n.15, suggest that this revolution may have occurred in 1972. However it is hard to see how this can be supported given the restrictive nature of the provisions adopted.

The Bishops' Conference has stated:

> "An attempt – even one ratified by a majority of the people – so to amend that Constitution as to violate [the fundamental principles and rights which derive from the dignity of the person] would contradict not only justice and the common good but also the very foundation on which the Constitution itself is built."

"The Value of Human Life" (1995) 262 *Position Paper* 281 at p. 283.

[24] Which is indeterminate – see above para. 24–3, "Sovereignty of the People".

[25] Walsh J. stated in *Crotty v. An Taoiseach* [1987] I.R. 713 at 783–784: "In the last analysis it is the People themselves who are the guardians of the Constitution." But this was in comparison to the State's attempt to bind itself to act contrary to the Constitution in the sphere of foreign policy without consulting the people in a referendum.

positive Irish constitutional law. It is a *sine qua non* of the Irish legal order, from the point of view of its authority, legitimation, and coherence, that these rights are protected. There are Irish constitutional natural law limits to what a rule can be for it to be law in the present Irish legal order, and these limits cannot be changed operating within the Irish constitutional law system, including by the process of referendum. These limits can be changed through the evolution of Irish constitutional natural law in the light of new findings and arguments, but the process remains the same – the application of the basic principles of practical reasoning to certain Irish constitutional fundamental commitments.[26]

[26] See above, para. 23–2, "Natural Law Based on Reason: Reconstructing the Doctrine".

CONCLUSION TO PART IV

The first point is that by the time this stage is reached there must have been enormous political work translated into a concerted attack on the natural law legitimation of Irish constitutional law. And this attack must have been politically successful. This is of very high practical significance. But the legal analysis cannot stop at this political hurdle, because it is a legal analysis, not a political prediction.

Ultimately, arguments for and against the amendability of Irish constitutional law tend to circularity: (i) Irish constitutional law is to some degree unamendable because the validity of law depends also on the Irish constitutional natural law legitimation: (ii) Irish constitutional law is amendable because it is not ultimately based on natural law but on untrammelled sovereignty. But this latter perception poses problems of amendability too: how can sovereignty transfer itself permanently? can the people, sovereign, god create a stone it cannot lift?

These are two different perceptions of Irish constitutional law.[27] The correct intra-order perception is set out in Chapters 23–26.

The popular sovereign is the ultimate legislator, but the validity of law depends on its compatability with Irish constitutional natural law. A third perception might consider popular sovereignty to be limited by a 'higher' law which is not Irish constitutional natural law but is based on a currently popular doctrine, such as one drawn from democratic theory. But there is much less intra-order evidence for such a perception. The protection of fundamental rights is the most likely point of confrontation with European Community law; Irish constitutional natural law is the legitimation of this protection which is most difficult to overcome; so this legitimation is the focus for this thesis. The Irish constitutional natural law legitimation does not exclude the Irish constitutional law doctrine of popular sovereignty, but it does not recognise it as the exclusive test of legal validity. The Irish constitutional law doctrine of popular sovereignty also presents its own doctrinal barriers to European Community law demands, amongst others the extent of the concept itself, the distinction between the existence and exercise of sovereignty, the possibility of alienation and irreversible alienation, and the compatibility with European Community law demands of the concepts of people, independence, and nation.[28]

---

[27] It could be said that a legal revolution is merely a perception. But so then is a political revolution. There is no rock on which to stub a toe. The time for such analyses is not when the rock is needed for self-defence.

[28] The question whether Irish constitutional natural law is the best legitimation for a constitutional order, or whether there should be a constitutional revolution, a completely new constitution which would base a new Irish constitutional law which would grow around it, are separate issues requiring an external perspective for their resolution.

PART V

CONFLICTS

INTRODUCTION

The preceding parts establish that European Community law and national constitutional law are in a standoff of constitutional conflict. The combination of the restrictions in national law grounding the reception of European Community law, the different legitimations of national constitutional law and European Community law, the extent of overlap of substantive areas where both European Community law and national constitutional law make claims, and the ease of seeking constitutional control, means that there are many possibilities for actual conflicts on substantive issues. It is guesswork to predict exactly where such conflicts will arise. Conflicts could arise involving issues which national constitutional law would consider to fall into the areas of private property, family,[1] education, religious freedom, protection of unborn life, judicial remedies and court procedure, freedom of speech, and use of language. This is not to say that different approaches to issues in these areas will necessarily result in conflict.

There are several types of national constitutional law which might give rise to a conflict, for example a policy (such as the promotion of the national language),[2] structure (such as separation of powers issues or judicial process),[3] principle,[4] or right.[5] Without prejudice to the standoff of constitutional conflict, this Part focuses on three types of conflict between national constitu-

---

1 See, *e.g.* in Irish constitutional law, *Greene v. Minister for Agriculture* [1990] 2 I.R. 17.

2 See below, Chap. 32, "National Constitutional Law Policy v. European Community Policy/Right/Principle".

3 In Irish constitutional law, *e.g. Meagher v. Minister for Agriculture* [1994] 1 I.R. 329, considered Part IV. In French constitutional law, for example, the election of local representatives who are themselves involved in electing national representatives impinges on the conditions for the exercise of national sovereignty. See above, para. 18–11, "Article 88–4: Resolutions". Another problem waiting in the wings of French constitutional law is the position of the European Parliament *vis-à-vis* the French Parliament.

4 In French constitutional law, for example, national sovereignty and democracy are referred to as principles: Article 4 of the Constitution of 1958. (See above, Chap. 16, "Sovereignty".) In Irish constitutional law, the *Cotter and McDermott* litigation raised the question of the compatibility of European Community law with the principles against unjust enrichment and double payment. *Cotter and McDermott v. Minister for Social Welfare* (High Ct.) 13 May 1985; Case 286/85 [1987] E.C.R. 1453; High Court, 10 June, 1988;

tional law and European Community law to illustrate in concrete terms the structural concerns of this work, in particular how in practice the demands of European Community law on national law and national courts might create conflicts which are sufficiently fundamental to lead to judicial revolt or legal revolution in national law. These three are, firstly, conflicts between a national constitutional law fundamental right and a European Community law fundamental right; secondly, a conflict in the interpretation of a right with the same name in both national and European Community legal orders, and thirdly, a conflict between constitutional policies. In the examples chosen, the European Community law right or policy is important to European Community law and may give rise to arguments that they are unamendable, which poses the revolt or revolution dilemma in European Community law as well as in national law. However the claims of European Community constitutional law are such that a minor, run-of-the-mill European Community law rule from a secondary source is also supreme and can be directly applicable in national law, and so a major constitutional conflict might arise from what is in European Community law a minor substantive issue.

[1990] 2 C.M.L.R. 141; (Sup. Ct.) 27 July 1989 (order of reference); Case C–377/89 [1991] E.C.R. I–1155. However it is not clear whether constitutional status attached to this principle. In any event, the litigation was inconclusive on the possibility of conflict because after the second Court of Justice decision, holding that these principles were not a defence to the assertion of an European Community law right, the case settled without admission of liability. Order of the Supreme Court, 6 June 1991.

[5] See below, Chaps. 30 and 31.

30. NATIONAL CONSTITUTIONAL LAW NATURAL RIGHT VERSUS EUROPEAN COMMUNITY LAW RIGHT

30–1 The following presentation is unbalanced in terms of space in favour of Irish constitutional law – European Community law conflicts over French constitutional law – European Community law conflicts because the jurisdictional rules and time limits in French constitutional law mean that an Article 177 (EC) reference cannot be made from the *Conseil Constitutionnel* to the Court of Justice. This means that French constitutional law–European Community law conflicts are located primarily within the analysis of French constitutional law's restrictive interpretation of European Community law in the constitutional process of constitutional amendment and ratification of the Treaty on European Union and the analysis of French law's complex jurisdictional rules.

The European Community law structures analysed below in the context of a conflict with Irish constitutional law apply equally in a conflict with French constitutional law. Furthermore, the *Conseil Constitutionnel* held in *TEU No. 1*[1] that the French jurisdictions retain their competence in the protection of fundamental rights.[2] Not only is the list of fundamental rights protected in European Community law and French constitutional law not the same,[3] the nature of French constitutional law rights, and their place in the legal order differs from the place of European Community law rights in the European Community legal order.[4] The right to life of the unborn which is considered in the conflict between an Irish constitutional law natural right and a European Community law right has not been stated expressly to be a French constitutional law right. However there is support in the decisions of the *Conseil Constitutionnel* to consider it as such.[5] The right to life from commencement of life (at conception) is acknowledged by *loi*[6] and is considered by the *Conseil*

---

1 92–308 DC, 9 April 1992, Rec. p.55; (1992) 28 *Revue Trimestrielle du Droit Européen* 418.

2 See above, para. 21–3, "Assuring the Guarantee of the Rights and Liberties of Citizens – As a Competence".

3 See Part III, Chap. 21, "The Substance of the Essential Conditions for Exercise of National Sovereignty".

4 See above, para. 21–7, "Nature and Legitimation of French Constitutional Law Fundamental Rights" and para. 21–14, "Rights and Freedoms Understood in a Framework of Interdependent Concepts".

5 B. Mathieu, "Note sur la décision du Conseil constitutionnel du 27 juillet 1994 relative au respect du corps humain" (1995) *Recueil Dalloz Sirey (Jurisprudence)* 238 at p. 236.

6 *Loi* No. 94–653 and *loi* No. 94–654, both of 29 July 1994.

Constitutionnel to contribute to securing respect of the constitutional principle of the safeguard of the dignity of the human person.[7] It would follow that the right to life from the commencement of life is protected at least as part of that principle. The right, being part of the French constitutional law order, has not an identical meaning with the Irish constitutional law right.[8]

Irish Constitutional Law Natural Right v. European Community Law Right

30–2 The conflict considered here is between the Irish constitutional law right to life of the unborn[9] and the European Community law right to receive services and information concerning services – not a European Community law right as it appeared from the text of the European Community treaties or as feared[10] legislation thereunder, but as developed by the jurisprudence of the Court of Justice.[11] A Protocol, which by virtue of Article 239 (EC) has the same effect as a Treaty article, was inserted into the Treaty on European Union to prevent this conflict:

> "Nothing in the Treaty on the European Union, or in the Treaties establishing the European Communities, or in the Treaties or acts modifying or sup-

---

7 94–343/344 DC, 27 July 1994, Rec. p. 100; (1995) Rec. Dalloz Sirey 237, *lois on respect for the human body and biotechnology*.

8 Apart from the differences expected between meanings of similarly named rights contingent upon the framework of rights, concepts, and jurisdictional rules in which they are protected, topics have been made the subject of French law which have yet to be specifically considered in Irish constitutional law. In particular, the rights of embryos in *in vitro* fertilisation have been protected, but the right to life from the commencement of life does not extend to those embryos which have never been implanted in the womb.

9 The positive law version of this right is set out in Article 40.3.3, a creation of the Eighth, Twelfth, and Thirteenth Amendments to the Constitution:

> "The State acknowledges the right to life of the unborn and, with due regard to the equal right to life of the mother, guarantees in its laws to respect, and, as far as practicable, by its laws to vindicate that right.
>
> This subsection shall not limit freedom to travel between the State and another state.
>
> This subsection shall not limit freedom to obtain or make available, in the State, subject to such conditions as may be laid down by law, information relating to services lawfully available in another state."

10 By some deciding on the merits of voting for or against ratification of the Single European Act, who considered that a right to abort might be imported under a workers' health policy. This was adamantly denied. *Cf.* Council Resolution of 20 December 1995 on the integration of health protection requirements in Community policies, [1995] O.J. C350/2. This Resolution was adopted pursuant to Article 129 (EC) which is in the new Title X, Public Health, inserted by Article G(38) (EU).

11 The rest of this chapter is based on D.R. Phelan, "Right to Life of the Unborn v. Promotion of the Trade in Services: the European Court of Justice and the Normative Shaping of the European Union" (1992) 55 *Modern Law Review* 670.

> plementing those Treaties, shall affect the application in Ireland of Article 40.3.3 of the Constitution of Ireland."[12]

A Solemn Declaration[13] was later made which on its face removes the protection of the Protocol, although its status and effect remain unclear.[14] The present risk of this conflict recurring has been alleviated by a combination of these Treaty amendments, providing for the disuniform application of European Community law, and the adoption of the Twelfth and Thirteenth Amendments to the Irish Constitution in December 1992.[15] However, the Act adopted to implement the Thirteenth Amendment, the Regulation of Information (Services Outside the State for Termination of Pregnancies) Act 1995, provides in section 6 that it is unlawful for a provider of information, advice or counselling, to provide information if such a provider has an interest in a body providing abortion services.[16] This makes contrary to European Community law precisely the connection which would make European Community law apply – an economic link between the provider of information and the provider of abortion. The most important point is that the structures in which the particular controversy analysed here were played out remain

---

12 Protocol (No. 17) Annexed to the Treaty on the European Union and to the Treaties Establishing the European Communities.

13 The text of the declaration is:

> "The High Contracting Parties to the Treaty on European Union signed at Maastricht on the 7th day of February 1992,
>
> Having considered the terms of Protocol No. 17 to the said Treaty on European Union which is annexed to that treaty and to the treaties establishing the European Communities,
>
> Hereby give the following legal interpretation: that it was and is their intention that the protocol shall not limit freedom either to travel between member states or, in accordance with conditions which may be laid down, in conformity with Community law, by Irish legislation, to obtain or make available in Ireland information relating to services lawfully available in member states.
>
> At the same time the High Contracting Parties solemnly declare that, in the event of a future constitutional amendment in Ireland which concerns the subject matter of Article 40.3.3. of the Constitution of Ireland and which does not conflict with the intention of the High Contracting Parties hereinbefore expressed, they will, following the entry into force of the Treaty on European Union, be favourably disposed to amending the said protocol so as to extend its application to such constitutional amendment if Ireland so requests."

14 See G. Hogan and A. Whelan, *Ireland and the European Union: Constitutional and Statutory Texts and Commentary* (London: Sweet & Maxwell, 1995) Chap. 9.

15 These amendments added two new paragraphs to Article 40.3.3 (quoted above, n.9).

16 What may be called the "indirect effect" of European Community law is of note here. The developments in European Community law were possibly a factor encouraging the change in national law to restrict the right to life of the unborn, and were certainly a factor in the ascription of the term "service" to describe abortion. Also possibly a factor was the decision of the European Court of Human Rights in *Open Door Counselling and Dublin Well Woman Centre v. Ireland* (1993) 15 E.H.R.R. 244, where by 15 votes to eight the restriction on the provision of information was found to violate Article 10 of the European Convention on Human Rights and Fundamental Freedoms (the freedom of expression).

the same. Just as few people expected European Community law to cover abortion (and they were considered to be scaremongering), the fact that the substance of the next controversy is unclear does not detract from the certainty of one arising.

The Court has, by reference to its economic and federal teleology of Community objectives, evolved certain legal techniques applicable to human rights which highlight the demands placed on national law, the possibilities of revolt-causing or revolution-causing conflicts between European Community law and national law orders, and the different legitimations of those orders. These techniques, supported by the doctrines of supremacy over, and direct effect in, national law,[17] are brought into play when national constitutional rights which the Court does not adopt as its own[18] are held to have economic implications. The techniques are used to control the conflict which is produced between state and federal competences, between a moral and an economic ideal of what is fundamental based on personhood on the one hand and economics and the achievement of dynamic political goals on the other (and hence different ideas of fundamental rights), and between different legitimations of law. The techniques are as follows. First, the definition of an act as a service solely on account of its economic significance, regardless of the unconstitutional and criminal nature of that act in national law. Secondly, the prohibition as a matter of principle of all impediments to the freedom of services, even if caused by disparities between national constitutional rights. Thirdly, the use of fundamental rights to expand the free movement of services and to incorporate thereby supreme rights, differently legitimated and supported by the doctrines of supremacy and direct effect, for market participants. Fourthly, the testing of national constitutional rights as derogations from economic principle.

The Background

30–3 The focus here is on the structure of argument in Case C–159/90 *Society for the Protection of the Unborn Child v. Grogan* in the light of the Court's supporting decisions and its opinion of constitutional importance on the European Economic Area.[19] Case C–159/90 *Grogan* is the first case where a

---

17 Case 26/62 *Van Gend en Loos v. Nederlandse Administratie der belastingen* [1963] E.C.R. 1; Case 6/64 *Costa v. ENEL* [1964] E.C.R. 585. Both cases are analysed at length in, paras. 8–6 *et seq*, "Case 26/62 *Van Gend en Loos*" and paras. 8–41 *et seq*, "Case 6/64 *Costa v. ENEL*".

18 Case 11/70 *Internationale Handelsgesellschaft v. Einfuhr- und Vorratsstelle für Getreide* [1970] E.C.R. 1125.

19 Opinion 1/91 *Re the Draft Treaty on a European Economic Area* [1991] E.C.R. I–6079, [1992] 1 C.M.L.R. 245; Case C–159/90 *Society for the Protection of Unborn Children (Ireland) Ltd. v. Grogan and others* [1991] E.C.R. I–4685 [1991] 3 C.M.L.R. 849. Where these cases are cited in this part the C.M.L.R. page numbers are given. *Grogan* forms part of a wide-ranging analysis in G. De Burca, "Fundamental Human Rights and the Reach of

private party sought in European Community law the means to avoid restraints on its freedom necessitated by the vindication of the constitutional right of another. S.P.U.C. sought to enjoin, under Article 40.3.3, student unions from publishing addresses of British abortion clinics.[20] Despite the Supreme Court's prohibition on the similar activities of counselling services in *Attorney General (Society for the Protection of Unborn Children (Ireland) Ltd.) v. Open Door Counselling Ltd. and The Dublin Well Woman Centre Ltd.*,[20a] the High Court distinguished this case and made an Article 177 (EEC) reference. The Supreme Court on appeal criticised the distinction and made an interlocutory injunction prohibiting distribution of the information pending the Court of Justice's reply and the High Court's subsequent determination of the case. But the Supreme Court did not interfere with the High Court's jurisdiction to make the reference, citing *Campus Oil v. Minister for Energy (No. 2)*.[21] The Court of Justice held, first, that abortion "constitutes a service within the meaning of Article 60"; secondly, that "the provisions of Article 59 (EC) . . . prohibit any restrictions on the freedom to supply services"; thirdly, that on the facts the link to the provision of services was "too tenuous for the prohibition on the distribution of information to be regarded as a restriction within the meaning of Article 59"; and fourthly, that the Court has no fundamental rights jurisdiction with regard to national rules "lying outside the scope of Community law", as was the instant case because of the insufficiently proximate link between student unions and abortion clinics.[22]

Advocate-General Van Gerven applied the Court's jurisprudence by testing the constitutional right as a derogation because he considered the link sufficient. The Advocate-General's argument brings together several trends in the Court's jurisprudence which could have been decisive had there been follow up litigation based either on an agency relationship between the providers of information and services or directly on the new right of free movement as European citizen (contained in Article 8a (EC)) and recipient of services. The likelihood of confrontation between the Court of Justice and

---

European Community Law" (1993) 13 *Oxford Journal of Legal Studies* 283, and in three parts by J. Kingston and A. Whelan, "The Protection of the Unborn in Three Legal Orders" (1992) 10 *Irish Law Times* 93 at pp. 104 and 166; and is noted by B. Wilkinson, "Abortion, The Irish Constitution and the EEC" [1992] *Public Law* 19; and S. O'Leary, "The Court of Justice as a reluctant constitutional adjudicator: Note on Case 159/90 *S.P.U.C. v. Grogan*" (1992) *European Law Review* 139. Of note should be the forthcoming book, J. Kingston and A. Whelan with I. Bacik, *Abortion and the Law* (1997).

20 The absence of state action is not a problem in Irish constitutional law: "If one citizen has a right under the Constitution there exists a correlative duty on the part of other citizens to respect that right and not interfere with it" – *Educational Company of Ireland v. Fitzpatrick* [1960] I.R. 368 (Budd J., High Ct.).

20a [1988] I.R. 593.

21 [1984] 1 C.M.L.R. 479.

22 Case C–159/90 *Society for the Protection of Unborn Children (Ireland) Ltd. v. Grogan and others* [1991] E.C.R. I–4685, [1991] 3 C.M.L.R. 849 at 891–893.

the Irish courts on this related issue of free movement of persons was affirmed by the widely reported case of a 14-year-old Irish girl. This defendant alleged that she was pregnant by rape (this was subsequently confirmed after the litigation) and offered evidence to demonstrate her suicidal intent. She was initially judicially restrained at the suit of the Attorney General from travelling to the United Kingdom to abort. In *Attorney General v. X*[23] the High Court and three of the five Supreme Court judges held that where the right to life of the unborn is not outweighed by the equal right to life of the mother, an injunction restraining travel to obtain an abortion will issue. This test may be too restrictive according to European Community law. The Twelfth Amendment to the Constitution has reduced the risk of conflict on this issue for the present.[24]

The Scope of the European Community Law on Services

Perspective of Irish Constitutional Law

30–4 The general belief that the abortion issue stood outside European Community law was summarised by Walsh J. of the Supreme Court in the Case C–159/90, *Grogan*[25]:

> "Although the provision of abortions within the law in particular Member States provides profit for those engaged in it that could scarcely qualify it to be described as a service of economic significance of a type which must be available in all Member States."

Both the provision of information on abortion and the act of abortion, which is subject to the *Oireachtas*' extraterritorial law-making power,[26] are criminal

---

[23] [1992] 1 I.R. 1 (judgment of the High Court (Costello J.)) (judgment of the Supreme Court (*per* Finlay C.J., Hederman and Egan JJ.)).

[24] Although there has been no case on point. The wording of the Amendment is itself clear ("This subsection shall not limit freedom to travel between the State and another state"). It does not grant any freedom or right, but limits the application of another right. Its interpretation is therefore unclear, and in particular how it fits into the scheme of the Constitution and the legitimation of Irish constitutional law. The non-restriction of free movement can draw collateral support, however, from *Re Article 26 and the Regulation of Information (Services outside the State for the Termination of Pregnancies) Bill* [1995] 2 I.L.R.M. 81, but this is not directly on point. See above, Part IV, "*Irish Constitutional Law*".

[25] Case 159/90 *Society for the Protection of the Unborn (Ireland) Ltd. v. Grogan* [1990] 1 C.M.L.R. 689 at 704. "The abortion issue does not touch the EEC and its Court" according to J. Weiler, "Protection of Fundamental Rights within the Legal Order of The European Communities" in *International Enforcement of Human Rights: reports submitted to the Colloquium of the International Association of Legal Science* (Heidelberg, Bernhart and Jolowicz (eds.) 28–30 August 1985) pp. 128–129. One of the rejected grounds for the constitutional challenge to the Single European Act in *Crotty v. An Taoiseach* [1987] I.R. 713 at 736 (High Ct.), 763 at 770 (Sup. Ct.) was the threat to fundamental rights if abortion was introduced as worker health care. The Government Information Booklet on the Single European Act (May 1987) stated: "Subjects such as the family, divorce and abortion fall outside the scope of the European Community Treaties" (para. 4.9). Similar assurances were also contained in the Commission's booklet *The Facts*.

[26] This power under Article 3 of the Constitution was expressly referred to by Hederman J. in *Attorney General v. X* [1992] 1 I.R. 1.

offences,[27] and prohibited by the Constitution as an abuse of the right to life unless necessary to save the mother's life.[28] The right was first enunciated by Walsh J in *McGee v. Attorney General* and more explicitly in *G v. An Bord Úchtála* drawing on the Article 40.2 protection of the right to life.[29] It was written into the Constitution expressly in Article 40.3.3 by popular referendum:

> "The State acknowledges the right to life of the unborn and, with due regard to the equal right to life of the mother, guarantees in its laws to respect, and, as far as practicable, by its laws to defend and vindicate that right."

With this legal background S.P.U.C. argued that abortion cannot be regarded as a service because it involves the destruction of life.[30]

Perspective of European Community Law

30–5 The Commission had been answering written questions for over a decade by denying competence; no one had asked the Court of Justice.[31] The text of Article 60 (EC), untouched by amendment, provides only that a service must be normally provided for remuneration; Article 60(d) provides that activities of the professions are covered. Case 286/82 *Luisi and Carbone* established that Article 60(d) covers medical activities, and that Article 59 prohibits restrictions on the receipt as well as on the provision of services. This skeleton framework, half of it judge-made, was sufficient for the Court of Justice in Case C–159/90 *Grogan*:

---

27 The statutory prohibition of abortion is contained in the Health (Family Planning) Act 1979, s.10(b) which reaffirms ss.58 and 59 of the Offences Against the Person Act 1861. The creation or distribution of information advocating abortion is prohibited under s.16 of the Censorship of Publications Acts 1929–1967, as amended by s.12(1) of the Health (Family Planning) Act 1979. Advertisements referring to the procurement of an abortion were prohibited under s.3 of the Indecent Advertisements Act 1889, as amended by s.17 of the Censorship of Publications Act 1929 and s.12(2) of the Health (Family Planning) Act 1979. The most important Act in the area is now the Regulation of Information (Provision of Services Outside the State for the Termination of Pregnancies) Act 1995.

28 Article 40.3.3, the Eighth Amendment to the Constitution passed in a popular referendum in 1983 by 66.45 per cent of the poll, is in the Fundamental Rights section (Articles 40–44) of the Constitution. In A.G. (S.P.U.C.) *Open Door Counselling* [1987] I.L.R.M. 477 at 481 (High Ct.). Hamilton P. stated: "any action on the part of any person endangering human life, must necessarily not only be an offence against the common good, but also against the guaranteed human rights of the human life in person". The text of the amendments to the Article is in the footnotes to para. 30–3, above.

29 [1974] I.R. 284; [1980] I.R. 32.

30 Case C–159/90 *Report for the Hearing*, Reporting Judge Mancini, [1991] E.C.R. I–4685, 4691, 4694–4696.

31 This also emerged from European Parliamentary debates and the Commission's answers to written questions. Question 655/88 [1989] O.J. C111/21 and Question 319/88 [1989] O.J. C111/16, both of 2 May 1989, concerned the RU 486 abortion pill; the Commission answered: "these questions should continue to be resolved on the national level". The Commission replied to a question in European Parliament Debate No. 248, p.223 that it had no specific competence in this area.

> "It must be held that the termination of pregnancy, as lawfully practiced in several member states, is a medical activity which is normally provided for remuneration, and may be carried out as part of a professional activity."[32]

The Court thus proposed a definition of service based on payment and conditional legality in several Member States, perhaps indicating a majority rule. Outside this it did not consider whether the nature of the act could disqualify it, or what the criteria for normality in the provision of remuneration are. Any act or experiment requiring hired expertise is by definition a service,[32a] and if carried out by a medical practitioner, it is by definition a medical service.

European Community Law Characterisation of Irish Constitutional Law Fundamental Right

30–6 Despite the basis of S.P.U.C.'s argument in national criminal legislation and enumerated and unenumerated constitutional rights, and despite the Court's own engagement in moral issues by assuming a human rights jurisdiction, the Court characterised the argument that abortion was not a service under European Community law as simply "moral" and therefore irrelevant. The Court stated that it could not substitute its assessment for those of the Member States where abortion is legal. Yet the characterisation of abortion as legal in other Member States is in itself misleading, as even the Advocate-General conceded: "Abortion is also prohibited in principle in other Member States" where it is illegal unless statutory conditions are met. Sir Basil Hall in his opinion for the European Commission of Human Rights referred to Ireland's views on abortion as "[a] moral view point entrenched in the European tradition despite the absence of any uniform policy in the Member States or the Council of Europe".[33] But the issue is much more than a moral viewpoint entrenched in tradition. Rather it is the protection of a right, a right which is constitutional, natural, human, fundamental, and essential to the legitimation of Irish constitutional law.

More importantly, the Court was not asked to substitute its assessment of the legality of other Member States' abortion laws: it was asked, in question one of the High Court's reference, whether abortion came "within the definition of 'services' provided for in Article 60 of the Treaty".[34] By ruling in the affirmative the Court extended the scope of European Community law by substituting the social legislation of the United Kingdom for the direct

---

[32] [1991] 3 C.M.L.R. 849 at 890, relying on Cases 286/82 and 26/83 *Luisi and Carboni v. Ministero del Tesoro* [1984] E.C.R. 377, [1985] 3 C.M.L.R. 52.

[32a] "[The bourgeoisie] has resolved personal worth into exchange value, and in place of the numberless indefeasible chartered freedoms, has set up that single unconscionable freedom – Free Trade" – K. Marx and F. Engels, "Manifesto of the Communist Party", in *Selected Works* (Moscow, Progress Publisher, 1968-Seventh Printing 1986) p. 38.

[33] See *Open Door Counselling Ltd. and Dublin Well Woman Centre Ltd. and Others v. Ireland*, Report of the Commission, 7 March 1991, (1992) 14 E.H.R.R. 131.

[34] [1991] 3 C.M.L.R. 849.

choice of the people of another Member State to protect the right to life of the unborn and the national constitutional natural law fundamental commitment.

The focus of European Community law on the legality of the act in the country where the abortion takes place also causes practical anomalies in domestic law.[35] The provider of abortion information would have to comply with the rules on qualifications for counselling, age of mother, dates of pregnancy, etc., of the Member States where the relevant clinic is situated.[36] The strange result follows that, if the providers of information do not observe these foreign rules or do not have the necessary foreign law expertise, it is permissible in European Community law for the High Court in Ireland to issue an injunction applying the United Kingdom's Abortion Act,[37] but not to enforce the Constitution.

European Community Law Demands on National Law

30–7 Case C–159/90 *Grogan* represents the low water mark of the Court's regard for national constitutional law. In Case 4/73 *Nold* the Court had stated:

> "In assuring the protection of [fundamental] rights, this Court is required to base itself on the Constitutional traditions common to Member States and therefore could not allow measures which are incompatible with the fundamental rights recognised and guaranteed by the constitutions of such States."[38]

This judgment was thought to protect a constitutional right guaranteed by one Member State: Advocate-General Warner stated in Case 7/76 *IRCA* that Member States did not transfer sovereignty to the Community sufficient to

---

35 In Case C–159/90 *Grogan* [1991] 3 C.M.L.R. 849 at 863, the Advocate-General states that the provision of information must "remain within the limits of what is allowed in the Member State in which the service originates. This detail is important, because the right to provide information may in no case extend beyond the freedom to provide services on the part of the actual provider of the services established in another Member State". The Commission for its part made a distinction in law on the basis of the economic difference between abortion by a private clinic for a fee, which would be a service under Article 60, and abortion by public authority as part of a budget-financed public health program.

36 *e.g.* the Advocate-General referred to the requirements laid down with regard to advice and counselling to prevent routine and commercialised abortions in para. 219(b) of the *German Strafgesetzbuch* [Criminal Code], and the requirements of authorisation for the providers of the information under Articles L162–3, L645 and L647 of the French *Code de la Santé Publique* [Public Health Code].

37 Abortion Act 1967, s.1(1), provides for the lawfulness of abortion only where continuation would involve risk to the life, physical or mental health of the pregnant women greater than termination, or whereunder there is substantial risk that the child will be born seriously handicapped. However it appears to be applied in a manner which suggests that the balance is between a mother's right and a weak public policy against abortion, rather than a balance between competing rights.

38 Case 4/73, *Nold v. EC Commission* [1974] 2 C.M.L.R. 338 at 354; [1974] E.C.R. 491.

overrule a fundamental right,[39] an argument used by S.P.U.C. The passage was affirmed by the Court in Case 44/79 *Hauer* and the German Federal Constitutional Court expressly relied on it in *Wunsche,* which case averted the potential rebellion of German courts against the Court of Justice raised by Case 11/70 *Internationale Handelsgesellshaft.*[40] However, the Court marked a possible new departure in Case 155/79 *AM & S* when it restricted the application of the lawyer-client privilege to "such elements . . . as are common to the laws of the Member States".[41] That formulation implies a reversal of the implication in Case 4/73 *Nold*: after Case 155/79 *AM & S* are fundamental rights to be protected only where that protection is common to the Member States? Mancini (Reporting Judge in Case C–159/90 *S.P.U.C. v. Grogan*) has written:

> "[T]he Court does not have to go looking for maximum, minimum or average standards. The yardstick by which it measures the approaches adopted by the various systems derives from the spirit of the Treaty and from the requirements of a Community which is in the process of being built up."[42]

The Court has used respect for family life in Article 8 of the European Convention for the Protection of Human Rights and Fundamental Freedoms to extend by interpretation the free movement of workers Regulation 1612/68[43] in Case 249/86 *Commission v. Federal Republic of Germany* without even referring to inspiration from the constitutional traditions of the Member States: "That requirement is one of the fundamental rights which, *according to the Court's settled case law,* restated in the Preamble to the Single European Act, are recognised by Community law".[44] Whereas in Case 155/79 *AM & S* the

---

39 Case 7/76 *IRCA v. Amministrazione delle Finanze dello Stato* [1976] E.C.R. 1213. In Case C–159/90 *Grogan,* S.P.U.C. argued that in adopting the Third Amendment to the Constitution, which allowed accession to the Treaty of Rome, or any further amendment, the people themselves lacked power to imperil a constitutional right. See also T.C. Hartley, *The Foundations of European Community Law* (2nd ed., 1988), p. 136: "[I]t is probable that the European Court would accept as a general principle of Community law a principle which is protected in only *one* Member State", (original emphasis); and H.G. Schermers, "The European Community Bound by Fundamental Human Rights" (1990) 27 *Common Market Law Review* 249.

40 Case 44/79 *Hauer v. Land Rheinland-Pfalz* [1980] 3 C.M.L.R. 42 at 64; *Wunsche Handelsgesellschaft ("Solange II"),* judgment of the German Federal Constitutional Court (*Bundesverfassungsgericht*) [1987] 3 C.M.L.R. 225 at 260, para. 38; *Internationale Handelsgesellshaft v. E.V.G.F.* (*"Solange I"*), judgment of the German Federal Constitutional Court (*Bundesverfassungsgericht*) [1974] 2 C.M.L.R. 540 at 549.

41 Case 155/79 *AM & S Europe Ltd v. EC Commission* [1982] E.C.R. 1575 at 1610–1611. See also D. Edward, "Constitutional Rules of Community Law in EEC Competition Cases" in *1992 and EEC/U.S. Competition and Trade Law,* Fordham Corporate Law Institute (New York: Transnational Jun's Publications, Inc. 1990).

42 F. Mancini, *Safeguarding Human Rights: the Role of the Court of Justice of the European Communities* (John Hopkins University, Bologna, Occasional Paper, No.62 March 1990).

43 The Preamble to that Regulation refers to the freedom of movement of workers and their families as constituting a fundamental right. [1968] O.J. Spec. Ed. (II) 475.

44 Case 249/86 [1989] E.C.R. 1263 at 1290 (emphasis added). In Case 159/90, *Grogan* the Court of Justice referred to the Convention but not to the constitutional tradition common to the member states. See generally C.N. Kakouris, "The position of constitutional rules in the hierarchy of rules of law and its importance for the protection of funda-

national legal principle was raised by a corporation as a shield against a Commission competition investigation, Case C–159/90 *Grogan* established the possibility of using Article 59 (EC) as a sword against a constitutional right. It now seems possible within European Community law for the Commission under Article 169 (EC) or a crusading member state under Article 170 (EC) to bring an infringement action against another Member State on the grounds of the incompatible effects the protection of its constitutional rights has on European Community rules. Failure to observe the Court's ruling will leave the Member State liable for a money fine under Article 171(2) (EC). Despite ruling the moral issue to be irrelevant, the Court in Case C–159/90 *Grogan* adopted an approach with enormous moral implications by a recharacterisation of the rights in issue, based on economic principle which denies the validity of the Irish constitutional position in the European Community. By defining abortion as an economic activity in European Community law the Court has placed abortion under the Article 2 (EC) task to promote throughout the Community a harmonious and balanced development of economic activities.[45]

Extension of European Community Law on Services

30–8 Once abortion was established as a service under Article 60, the next impediment to the application of the Article 59 prohibition on restrictions was the absence of overt or covert nationality discrimination in the substance or effects of the constitutional rule. The Court stated shortly that "the provisions of Article 59 of the Treaty . . . prohibit any restriction on the freedom to provide services" thus rejecting the Commission's argument, which was supported by earlier jurisprudence, that Articles 59 and 60 invalidated neutral national regulations with discriminatory effects but did not cover complete prohibitions.[46] It accepted the Advocate-General's invitation to reconcile the "undesirable divergence" between the provision of services and the "Cassis de Dijon"[47] line of authority on the movement of goods.[48] Case C–159/90

---

mental rights in the Community legal order" – *Eighth Conference on European Constitutional Courts* (1990).

45 In *S.P.U.C. v. Grogan and others* [1989] I.R. 753 at 767. Walsh J. stated in relation to abortion: "On the economic plane, there are, no doubt, some distorted minds who would make a case for the elimination of what they would regard as old, useless and unproductive human units." The Court of Justice has unwittingly gone one step further to regard the process of elimination to be an end worth promoting in itself.

46 The Commission relied on Case 15/78 *Société Générale Alsacienne de Banque v. Koestler* [1978] E.C.R. 1971 and Case 52/79 *Procureur du Roi v. DeBauve* [1980] E.C.R. 833. These cases concerned, respectively, a preclusion of recovery of wagering debts and a ban on cable television advertising which, although affecting free movement, were held not to conflict with the treaty provisions because of their non-discriminatory nature.

47 Case 120/78 *Rewe v. Bundesmonopolverwaltung für Branntwein* [1979] E.C.R. 649.

48 The Advocate-General's formulation of the test echoes the Court in Case 8/74 *Procureur du Roi v. Dassonville* [1974] E.C.R. 837.

S.P.U.C. v. Grogan is the culmination of the drive in the cases of Case C–154/89 *Commission v. France*, Case C–180/89 *Commission v. Italy*, Case C–198/89 *Commission v. Greece*, and Case C–76/90 *Säger*, to extrapolate the fundamental principle of the free provision of services free from the qualified Treaty articles which gave it birth, subject only to the judicially evolved qualification of justification in the public interest.[49] The absence of discriminatory intent or effects in the application of national constitutional rights before Case C–159/90 *S.P.U.C. v. Grogan* helped protect them from attack by European Community law. The Court in Case 120/78 "Cassis de Dijon" promoted mutual recognition of national standards by the suppression of obstacles to free movement resulting from disparities in national economic regulation of the alcohol content in fruit liqueurs. The legal technique of mutual recognition formed a bedrock of the Single European Act and the "1992 program". On the eve of Maastricht, the Court showed its willingness to drop the question of discriminatory effects and to suppress obstacles to the provision of services caused by disparities in constitutional rights protection. The Advocate-General argued:

> "To allow measures which are non-discriminatory but detrimental to intra-Community trade in services to fall *a priori* outside the scope of Article 59 of the EEC Treaty would detract substantially from the effectiveness of the principle of the free movement of services, which in an economy in which the tertiary sector is continuing to expand will increase in importance."

The definition of abortion as a service gives individuals rights in national courts. Case 33/74 *Van Binsbergen* established that Article 59 (EEC) is directly effective so far as it prohibits discrimination based on nationality or residence.[50] This case also provides a possible European Community law ground other than public policy for the restriction of the provision of abortion services: rules restricting the activities of a provider of a service who would otherwise avoid the professional rules of conduct which would be applicable to him if he were established in the Member State imposing the restrictions.[51] The question is whether the extended scope of Article 59 to prohibit restrictions on the freedom to provide services caused by disparities in non-discriminatory national laws also creates individual European Community rights which a national

---

[49] Case C–154/89 *Commission v. France* [1981] E.C.R. I–659, para. 12; Case C–180/89 *Commission v. Italy* [1991] E.C.R. 709, para. 15: Case C–198/89 *Commission v. Greece* [1991] E.C.R. 727, para. 16; Case C–76/90 *Säger v. Société Dennemeyer* [1991] E.C.R. I–4221, paras. 8–13, also Opinion of Advocate-General Jacob in that case, para. 22; Case 279/80 *Webb* [1981] E.C.R. 3305, para. 17 (freedom to provide services as a fundamental principle can only be limited by a justified public interest), also Opinion of Advocate-General Slynn in that case at 3330–3333; Case 62/79 *Coditel v. Cine Vog Films* [1980] E.C.R. 881 at 870–873.

[50] Case 33/74 *van Binsbergen v. Bestuur van de Bedrijfsvereniging voor de Metaalnijverheid* [1974] E.C.R. 1299.

[51] *ibid.* at para. 13.

court must protect against state and non-state action.[52] Since these restrictions may be justified by the imperative requirements of the public interest underlying the national rule, the Member States have a degree of discretion which makes direct effect difficult because of the deference of national courts to legislatures on matters of policy. However, Case 41/74 *Van Duyn* established that the safeguard clause of Article 48(3) (EEC) which allows restrictions on the grounds of public policy, security, or health, since these grounds are subject to judicial control (below), did not prevent direct effects.[53] Doubts about justification are to be resolved, as in other cases of doubt as to the scope, application, or interpretation of European Community law, by Article 177 reference (Case 41/74 *Van Duyn*). Consequently an individual may invoke rights under Article 59 in a national court as a defence against the attempt to enforce the constitutional right of another (Irish constitutional rights are enforceable against private parties[54]) by that other or by the State or (depending on a right of action under national constitutional law) by a non-state party with *locus standi.* When the protection of a constitutional right gives rise to economic incidents (as even the right to life does in a market economy) which infringe free market principles and that right is not recognised by the Court of Justice, its existence has become dependent on a plea of derogation to be judged by the Court of Justice according to its restrictive tests.

Contrasting Legitimations

Contrasting Objectives

30–9 This result is a product of legal structures and doctrines. The Court of Justice historically lacks competence in fundamental rights as the Treaties establishing the European Communities contained no reference to human rights, unlike the Charter of the United Nations, or reference to a humanist vision or an ethical philosophy or indeed a political philosophy for a complete political community.[55] In a supranational (now, as was argued above in Part II, a federal) legal structure which involves the transfer of sovereignty and the doctrines of supremacy, and direct applicability this would have meant the harmonisation of the core of national constitutions. The people of Ireland established the Constitution according to the Preamble:

> "In the Name of the Most Holy Trinity, from Whom is all authority and to Whom, as our final end, all actions of both men and States must be referred . . . And

---

[52] Case 26/62 *Van Gend en Loos v. Nederlandse Administratie der belastingen* [1963] E.C.R. 1. Case 43/75 *Defrenne v. SABENA* [1976] E.C.R. 455 which established the doctrine of horizontal direct effects of Treaty Articles.

[53] Case 41/74 *Van Duyn v. Home Office* [1975] 1 C.M.L.R. 1 at 15.

[54] The circumstances for this are set out above, in para. 25–4.

[55] It is worth noting Dworkin's point that liberalism's idea of individual rights is "parasitic on the dominant idea of utilitarianism, which is the idea of a collective goal of the community as a whole." *Taking Rights Seriously* (1977), p. xi.

seeking to promote the common good, with due observance of Prudence, Justice and Charity, so that the dignity and freedom of the individual may be assured, true social order attained . . .".

The dynamic objectives of the European Community stand in complete contrast: completion of the internal market, economic and monetary union, and European Union.[56] The Court of Justice's conception of the general interest is the attainment of these objectives. The Court has developed the Treaties on the one hand as an international agreement "to be interpreted not only on the basis of its wording but also in light of its objectives",[57] and, on the other, as a constitution, to form a quasi-federal normative structure of supremacy and individual rights. In the Court's words: "[T]he EEC Treaty, albeit concluded in the form of an international agreement, none the less constitutes the constitutional charter of a Community based on the rule of law".[58] It is via the objectives of the Treaties, contained for example in the Preambles which as a general rule of interpretation under Article 31 of the Vienna Convention on the Law of Treaties are to be considered an integral part of the text, that the Court has converted the juridical nature of European Community law from international to constitutional law.[59] To attain these objectives the Court of Justice has evolved the federal doctrines of supremacy (Case 26/62 *Van Gend en Loos*), direct effect and individuals as subjects of European Community law (Case 6/64 *Costa v. ENEL*).[60]

Contrasting Views of What Is Fundamental

30–10 General principles of European Community law are likewise "merely means of achieving those objectives" and the provisions from which they are extrapolated "far from being an end in themselves are only means for attaining those objectives".[61] By "general principle" is meant hypothesis, disposition, and sanction: to state that it is a general principle that fundamental rights are observed in Community law means that there will be a sanction for breach of a particular right so recognised, for example the declaration of incompatibility of a national rule or the nullification of a Community rule. A national court upholding a constitutional right in breach of European Community fundamental rights will leave the government open to an action at the suit of the Commission (Article 169 (EC)) or a Member State (Article 170 (EC)) for failure to fulfil European Community law obligations, and ultimately to

---

56 Opinion 1/91 *Re the Draft Treaty on a European Economic Area* [1991] E.C.R. I–6079; [1992] 1 C.M.L.R. 245 at 268 and 272, quoting Articles 2, 8a, 102a (EEC), Article 1 (SEA), and s.2.5 of the Solemn Declaration of Stuttgart of 19 June 1983.

57 *ibid.* [C.M.L.R.] at 268.

58 *ibid.* at 269.

59 See above, Part II.

60 Case 26/62 *Van Gend en Loos v. Nederlandse Administratie der belastingen* [1963] ECR 1; Case 6/64 *Costa v. ENEL* [1964] E.C.R. 585.

61 Opinion 1/91 [1992] 1 C.M.L.R. 245 at 272 and 268.

the Court of Justice's power to "impose a lump sum or penalty payment" under Article 171 (2) (EC).

Case C–159/90 *S.P.U.C. v. Grogan* has clearly established that the meaning of "fundamental" and the catalogue of fundamental rights differ in the Community and Member State contexts.[62] In European Community law a right is fundamental in the sense that it is of basic importance in promoting Treaty objectives; this is the same sense of "fundamental" as in the fundamental freedom of services. Rights which are fundamental in this sense inevitably tend to expand the interpretation of Treaty provisions and fundamental freedoms, and being thus linked to Community law, are in effect incorporated against Member State action (including constitutional rights) through the doctrines of direct effect, individuals as subjects of rights, and supremacy. In national constitutional law a right is "fundamental" in two interrelated ways. First, when the observance of the right is important in achieving the objectives of that society, such as in the Constitution "the dignity and freedom of the individual, true social order". Secondly, when the protection of the right is a necessary part of the legitimation of the State's legal order, where the right may be both a consequence of that legitimation and a goal in and of itself, such as the right to life.

The Extension of European Community Law Demands on National Law by Reference to Fundamentals

30–11 The Advocate-General in Case C–159/90 *Grogan* illustrates the use of fundamental right in the Community sense, by basing himself firmly at the head of the trend in the Court of Justice's jurisprudence. In Case 118/75 *Watson and Belmann* the Court had ruled:

---

62 *cf.* the answer given by the President of the European Commission (J. Santer) to Written Question E–2043/93 on fundamental rights of European Union citizens, where having recited the relevant provisions (Article F(2) (EU), Article K.1 (EU), and various articles in the Treaty establishing the European Community (not including Protocol (No. 17) or the Declaration on Article 40.3.3 of the Irish Constitution)) and the jurisprudence of the Court of Justice, makes the leap in his conclusion: "All these provisions demonstrate that fundamental rights represent basic common values and norms in the Community legal order which the Treaty provisions and legislation adopted under the Treaty have to observe." [1995] O.J. C311/30–31. His use of the phrase "Community legal order" appears to encompass national legal orders, since if the phrase means just European Community law then of course these norms are common to it, being part of it. A conclusion that the presence of these norms in European Community law means that they are common in national legal orders is a non-sequitur and a curious inversion of the approach in Case 4/73 *Nold v. EC Commission* [1974] E.C.R. 491, [1974] 2 C.M.L.R. 338. However the reply may not have intended to have been legally precise and it might be unfair to judge it to a rigorous standard. The President appears to consider the Community legal order embracing the national orders (and even raises the question of compatibility of treaty articles with human rights, considered below in Chap. 37, "Resistance within European Community Law to the Proposed Direction").

> "Articles 48 to 66 . . . implement a fundamental principle of the Treaty and confer on persons whom they protect individual rights which the national courts must protect and take precedence over any national rule which might conflict with them."[63]

In that case Advocate-General Trabucchi warned the Court to remain faithful to the intention of the Member States as expressed in the text, not what the Court perceives to be the ultimate objective:

> "it would be a sound rule to avoid the fiction of using the actual wording of the Treaty to justify the extension to all citizens of the Community of the right to freedom of movement which the Treaty intended only to apply to clearly defined categories of persons [employed persons, persons providing services]."[64]

But the warning was swept away by reference to fundamentals in Case 286/82 *Luisi and Carbon* and in Case 186/87 *Cowan*, where the Court stated that "the freedom to supply services includes the freedom, for the recipients of services, to go to another Member State in order to receive a service there".[65] The Advocate-General in Case C–159/90 *Grogan* sought to extend the right to travel to receive services to the right of the potential traveller to receive unimpeded information about the provider of services, and thereby the right of the provider to provide such information, and thereby (where he failed) the right of the student unions to distribute information.

To do this the Advocate-General drew on Case 362/88 *GB–INNO–BM* and Case C–76/90 *Säger*, and the decision of the European Court of Human Rights in *Markt Intern*. Case 362/88 *GB–INNO–BM* on the free movement of goods was used as authority by way of analogy. In that case the Court of Justice held that an injunction of a Luxembourg court against the Belgian supermarket chain GB–INNO–BM enjoining distribution in Luxembourg of advertisement leaflets, whose contents breached Luxembourg rules for accuracy, was incompatible with Article 30 (EEC). Both the Advocate- General and the Court pointed to the indirect effect the restriction of advertising had on the volume of trade, the Advocate-General stating that "in a market economy the provision of information to market participants on market conditions is an essential precondition of its functioning".[66] The judgment seems to follow the logic that what is essential for the market is necessary in the law: the Court held that the free movement of goods implied the free movement of con-

---

[63] Case 118/75 *The State v. Watson and Belmann* [1976] E.C.R. 1185 at 1200.

[64] *ibid.* 1205. He argued that even the Council could not extend the categories, save by amendment via Article 235 (EEC). A broad interpretation would mean anyone could be classed as a recipient of a service.

[65] Cases 286/82 and 26/83 *Luisi and Carboni v. Ministero del Tesoro* [1985] 3 C.M.L.R. 52, para. 16; Case 186/87 *Cowan v. Tresor Public* [1990] 2 C.M.L.R. 613, para. 15.

[66] Case 362/88 *GB–INNO–BM* [1990] 1 E.C.R. 667, para. 14. On the importance of the indirect effect on the volume of trade see Case 286/81 *Oosthoek's Uitgeversmaatschappi* [1982] E.C.R. 4575. The extension of this line of thinking has been stopped by Joined Cases C–267 & 268/91 *Keck and Mithouard* [1993] E.C.R. I–6079.

sumers to shop under the same conditions as the local population, which freedom is restricted contrary to Articles 30, 31, and 36 (EEC) if they "are deprived of access to advertising available in the country where the purchases are made".[67]

In Case C–159/90 *Grogan* the Advocate-General used the same argument which had overcome a restriction on the consumer's freedom to shop in order to overcome a constitutional right. In Case C–76/90 *Säger*, Advocate-General Jacobs had stated that the freedom to provide services implied the freedom to receive services which in turn required the right to receive unimpeded information.[68]

The facts in *Markt Intern* were that the German Federal Supreme Court (*Bundesgerichtshof*) had ordered the applicants to refrain from publishing certain information on commercial practices, having found that the aim of the information bulletin which contained it "was not intended to influence or mobilise public opinion, but to promote the economic interests of a given group of undertakings". In the view of the German Government the information was an organised attempt to dispose of an awkward competitor by a strategy unlawful under German competition law. The European Court of Human Rights held that Article 10(1) of the Convention is not limited to ideas or forms of expression but protects the right to receive and impart information including information of a commercial nature.[69] Judge Martins, approved by Judge MacDonald, stated: "The socio-economic press is just as important as the political and cultural press for the progress of our modern societies and for the development of every man".

In Case C–159/90 *Grogan* the Advocate-General drew on these cases to conclude that the freedom to supply services, with its necessary corollary – the freedom to shop for abortions – "may be promoted by all, *inter alia*, by means of the provision of information, whether or not for consideration".[70] This view merges the provision of information as part of the service with the

---

67 *ibid.* para. 8. Furthermore, the Court referred to the Council Resolution approving a second program of the European Economic Community for a consumer protection and information policy which sets out basic rights of the consumer, one of which is the right to information and education ([1981] O.J. C133/1). The Treaty on European Union added a new Title XI "Consumer Protection" to Part III of the Treaty establishing the European Economic Community (Policy of the Community). Article 129a(1)(b) provides for specific action by the Community to provide adequate information for consumers.

68 Case C–76/90 *Manfred Säger v. Société Dennemeyer & Co. Ltd.* [1991] E.C.R. 4221 (Opinion of the Advocate-General).

69 *Markt Intern Verlag GmbH and Klaus Beermann*, Reports of the European Court of Human Rights series A volume 165, judgment of 20 November 1989. The restriction on the information was upheld on the narrow ground that the federal court did not go "beyond the margin of appreciation left to national authorities" by the casting vote of the President on a 9:9 split.

70 The Advocate-General also quotes Article 5 of the European Parliament's *Declaration of Fundamental Rights and Freedoms* ([1989] O.J. C120/51) which provides for the right

right of recipients to be informed, into a general promotion of market-relevant information in order to expand the scope of the fundamental freedom to supply services beyond the Treaty articles.[71]

Conflict of Fundamentals

30–12 What happens when the protection of fundamental rights in the national sense is incompatible with Treaty objectives is illustrated by the two leading cases of Case 4/73 *Nold* and Case 44/79 *Hauer.*[72] Although these cases originated in Germany and concerned German constitutional rights, they are important here because they illustrate the European Community law structures in which all national constitutional law rights must make their way. Both concerned commercial aspects of the right to private property, a conception clearly presumed by a Community founded on the free market, conflicting with the Treaty objective of the common market. The family firm Nold claimed that a series of Commission decisions which reorganised the coal industry effectively cutting off small wholesalers from their source of direct supply on account of the size of the minimum purchase requirement was contrary to the quasi-property rights to carry out trade and have the existence of the undertaking protected under Article 14 of the German Basic Law (*Grundgesetz*). The Court of Justice held that "[i]n the Community legal order, it thus appears legitimate, as regards these rights, to maintain certain limits justified by the general objectives [the proper functioning of the community market] pursued by the Community".[73]

In Case 44/79 *Hauer* the fundamental right to property and to freely pursue a trade and profession (Articles 12 and 14 of the Basic Law) conflicted with Council regulations which imposed a three-year ban on the planting of new vines in order to adjust wine growing potential according to the common organisation of the wine market. The Court substituted the permissible limitation of the right in accordance with the general interest (Article 1 of

---

subject to restrictions prescribed by law "to receive and impart information and ideas without interference by public authority and regardless of frontiers". This approach could be seen to be supported by the addition in the Treaty on European Union of a Title XI on "Consumer Protection" which amends Part III of the Treaty establishing the European Economic Community (Policy of the Community).

71 A more extreme view is that once information is covered by Article 59 (EC), its restriction cannot be justified under Article 10 (2) of the European Convention on Human Rights and Fundamental Freedoms – C. Langenfeld, and A. Zimmermann, "The Interrelation between Domestic Constitutional Law, the European Convention on Human Rights and Community Law. Some Remarks on the Recent Decisions in Dublin, Strasbourg and Luxembourg Concerning the Distribution of Information about Abortions in Ireland. English Summary" (1992) 52 *Zeitschrift für auslandisches ofentliches Recht und Volkerrecht* (Heidelberg Journal of International Law) 314.

72 Case 4/73 *Nold v. EC Commission* [1974] E.C.R. 491; [1974] 2 C.M.L.R. 338, Case 44/79 *Hauer v. Land Rheinland-Pfalz* [1980] 3 C.M.L.R. 42.

73 *ibid.* at 355. The objective is stated at 349.

the First Protocol to the Convention, the "common good" in the German Constitution, "social justice" in the Constitution) with the limitation according to the European Community law concept of the general interest in securing Treaty objectives.[74] In both Case 4/73 *Nold* and Case 44/79 *Hauer* the Court recognised the right to property as a fundamental right protected as part of the general principles of European Community law, and claimed that the restriction of the right as understood by the German Constitution did not affect its substance.[75] The Court in Case 44/79 *Hauer* concluded that because restriction was allowed by constitutions, restriction in the Community interest "cannot be challenged in principle".

But different conceptions of the general interest will result in different permissible limitations; the conceptions of the right on the one hand and the general interest on the other interact to define each other. In short, the Community right to property limited by the Community general interests such as the common organisation of the market means a difference in the substance of the national constitutional right which is subject to limitation by concepts such as social justice. This is so unless the meaning of the substance of the right to property is confined to the skeletal idea of private property which is necessarily accepted in all Member States as a precondition of western capitalism. What the Court recognised was the principle of a right to property in accordance with Treaty objectives, and thus the fundamental right of a national constitution has been translated into European Community law as fundamental in the Community sense.[76]

The right to life of the unborn is fundamental in Irish constitutional law in both of the related national senses of that term.[77] First because it aims to

---

74 Case 44/79 *Hauer v. Land Rheinland-Pfalz* [1980] 3 C.M.L.R. 42 at 65.

75 Case 4/73 *Nold v. EC Commission* [1974] ECR 491 at 355; Case 44/79 *Hauer v. Land Rheinland-Pfalz* [1980] 3 C.M.L.R. 42 at 68.

76 Case 5/88 *Wachauf v. Federal Republic of Germany* [1989] E.C.R. 2609 illustrates the Court of Justice's treatment of a constitutional right to private property where it does not conflict with treaty objectives. In that case the Court held that a member state's implementing legislation could not deny the Community fundamental right of a lessee (Wachauf) to the fruit of his labour and investment by refusing compensation for the surrender of his milk quota without the consent of the lessor. This adopted in the context of encouraging surrender of milk quotas the German constitutional right stated by the German Administrative Court (*Verwaltungsgericht*) in its order for Article 177 (EEC) reference. The Court used the following formula:

> "The fundamental rights recognised by the Court are not absolute, however, but must be considered in relation to their social function. Consequently, restrictions may be imposed on the exercise of those rights, in particular in the common organisation of the market, provided that those restrictions in fact correspond to objectives of general interest pursued by the Community . . . "(at 2639).

It has been argued that Case 5/88 *Wachauf* advances integration through the use of fundamental rights by the invalidation of an act of a national legislature implementing Community law – J. Coppel and A. O'Neill, "The European Court of Justice – Taking Rights Seriously" (1992) *Legal Studies* 227.

77 See above, para. 30–10, and Part IV.

achieve the objectives in the Preamble to the Constitution; Finlay C.J. reiterated this in *Attorney General v. X*[78] by adopting Walsh J.'s interpretation of that right: "The judges must interpret these rights in accordance with their ideas of prudence, justice, and charity . . .".[79] Walsh J. in *G v. An Bord Úchtála* stated:

> "The child's natural rights spring primarily from the natural right of every individual to life, to be reared and educated, to liberty, to work, to rest and recreation, to the practice of religion, and to follow his or her conscience. The right to life necessarily implies the right to be born. . . It lies not in the power of the parent to terminate its existence. . . . The child's natural right to life and all that flows from that right are independent of any right of the parent as such."[80]

Secondly, because the protection of the right is necessary to the legitimation of Irish constitutional law[81]:

> "Articles 41, 42 and 43 emphatically reject the theory that there are no rights without laws, no rights contrary to the law and no rights anterior to the law. They indicate that justice is placed above the law and acknowledge that natural rights, or human rights, are not created by law but that the Constitution confirms their existence and gives them protection."[82]

There was never any question in Case C–159/90 *S.P.U.C. v. Grogan,* given Member States' differences, of the Court of Justice adopting the right to life of the unborn as a fundamental right. But the Court's previous jurisprudence on fundamental rights, such as Case 44/79 *Hauer* and Case 4/73 *Nold,* did not indicate how far it would push the logic of its teleology or the extension of its competence, or how much of a chasm exists between the Court's and Member States' conceptions of fundamental rights. "The most basic of all human rights is life itself"[83]; yet the Court not only denied, as a matter of legal principle, any importance to the manifestation of a fundamental constitutional right of a Member State the protection of which is necessary to

---

[78] [1992] 1 I.R. 1.

[79] *McGee v. Attorney General* [1974] I.R. 284 at 318. Finlay C.J. referred also to the adoption of this passage by former Chief Justice O'Higgins in *The State (Healy) v. O'Donoghue* [1976] I.R. 347, where he said: "I find [the passage] particularly and peculiarly appropriate and illuminating in the interpretation of a sub-article of the Constitution which deals with the intimate human problem of the right of the unborn to life . . .".

[80] [1980] I.R. 32 at 69.

[81] See generally Chap. 23, "The Legitimation of Irish Constitutional Law".

[82] *Mc Gee v. Attorney General* [1974] I.R. 284 at 310. Walsh J. continued at 317–318:

> "There are many to argue that natural law may be regarded only as an ethical concept and as such is a reaffirmation of the ethical content of law in its ideal of justice. The natural law as a theological concept is the law of God promulgated by reason and is the ultimate governor of all the laws of men. In view of the acknowledgement of Christianity in the preamble and in view of the reference to God in Article 6 of the Constitution, it must be accepted that the Constitution intended the natural human rights I have mentioned as being in the latter category rather than simply an acknowledgement of the ethical content of law in its ideal of justice."

[83] *S.P.U.C. v. Grogan* [1990] 1 C.M.L.R. 689 at 701, *per* (Sup. Ct.) Walsh J.

the legitimation of that Member State's legal order (and it is up to the Member State to decide that), but it defined the destruction of that right as a service to be promoted to attain the Treaty objectives to which Community fundamental rights aim.[84]

---

[84] C. Joerges, "European Economic Law, the Nation-State and the Maastricht Treaty" in *Europe after Maastricht: An Ever Closer Union?* (Dehousse, ed., Munich: Law Books in Europe, 1994) p. 36:

> "The logic of European integration cannot claim *a priori* superior legitimacy where it dismantles national concerns in the name of market integration. It is one thing to ensure free trade and to thereby overcome the 'state of nature' in international economic relations. It is quite another project to restructure national societies according to the logic of market integration."

S. O'Leary (O'Leary, "The Relationship Between Community Citizenship and the Protection of Fundamental Rights in Community Law" (1995) *Common Market Law Review* 519) has commented on D.R. Phelan, "The Right to Life of the Unborn v. the Promotion of Trade in Services the European Court of Justice and the Normative Shaping of the European Union" (1992) 55 *Modern Law Review* 670, as follows:

> "The author's criticism of the need to recharacterise the rights with which [the Court of Justice] deals, in order to bring them within the mainly economic parameters of Community law, may be well founded. This does not automatically imply, however, that what is fundamental in the Community legal order differs from what is fundamental in the Member States, nor that the Court's technique will necessarily point the Community's protection of fundamental rights in different normative directions."

This author maintains that the recharacterisation does imply a difference in fundamentals because such a recharacterisation would not have been necessary were the fundamentals the same. Even if the rights carried the same names there would be a need to recharacterise because of the difference in functional position of human rights in European Community law applied to restrict derogations, and because of the difference in the shaping concepts such as the common good. Even if this is incorrect, what is fundamental does differ, as this case and subsequent changes in European Community law and Irish constitutional law makes clear. O'Leary objects to the Court not following the Advocate-General in exercising its human rights jurisdiction, and is concerned that the Court of Justice develops the protection of fundamental rights as part of a Community social contract with the Member States and their nationals and the direct involvement of Community citizens in order to legitimise the process of integration. This is a perfectly stateable direction and one which O'Leary has consistently advanced for future Community development, although one which is dependent on change in European Community law and may necessitate revolt or revolution in national constitutional law. (See Chap. 33, para. 4, "Direction Three".)

Ward (I. Ward, "In Search of a European Identity: Review of J. Derrida, The Other Heading: Reflections on Today's Europe" (1994) 57 *Modern Law Review* 315 at p. 326 *et seq.*) agrees that European Community law fundamental rights are derived from economic rather than moral bases. As Ward clarifies, the "fault" in *Grogan* does not lie solely with the Court of Justice, but rather with the notion of right in European Community law. Ward is concerned with the foundation of a European legal order as a morally derived legal order, based on the fundamental Kantian rights of freedom and equality. This also is a stateable future direction for European Community law.

This author is concerned in this work with the constitutional boundaries of the E.C., in what is at stake in the accommodation of the conflicting demands of integrating orders, and the posing of the dilemma of revolt or revolution, which dilemma may arise for decisions in jurisdictional conflicts. Criticism of Court of Justice, as institution, is not the focus, but rather its case law is a focus of attention in having elaborated much of the constitutional law of the European Community – see Part II.

National Constitutional Law Fundamental Rights as Derogations from European Community Law Economic Principle

30–13 Case C–159/90 *Grogan* shows that the protection of fundamental rights which conflict with Treaty objectives will be treated not as modifications of principle but as derogations therefrom.[85] Even if a system of European Community law which in principle aims to destroy a Member State fundamental right where it conflicts with the Court of Justice's construction of Community objectives is acceptable,[86] there is a further question: are Member States' fundamental rights which conflict with Treaty objectives adequately accommodated in European Community law by the technique of derogation?

Article 66 (EC) in conjunction with Article 56 (EC) allows for "special treatment for foreign nationals on grounds of public policy, public security, or public health". These derogations are limited on their face to discriminatory national rules. But Article 59 now prohibits restrictions which result from non-discriminatory national fundamental rights protection, so the Court by the same technique as in "Cassis de Dijon" has begun to develop in the law of free provision of services an umbrella category of justification of non-discriminatory derogations by the general good ("*l'intérêt général*"),[87] under which public policy is treated as a particular instance. Since Case 36/75 *Rutili* it is clear that the Court of Justice decides on the validity of the derogation. In that case the French Government argued that residence in certain areas was contrary to public policy and drew on Case 41/74 *Van Duyn* to support the argument that the question of what was "justified by public policy" (Article 48 (3) (EC)) fell to be decided by national governments.[88] That argument

---

85 For a different and very useful analysis of the structure of derogations, see G. De Burca, "Fundamental Human Rights and the Reach of EC Law" (1993) 13 *Oxford Journal of Legal Studies* 283.

86 The temporary reprieve for the Irish fundamental right because the economic link was too tenuous has been criticised, from a startling perspective, as "cavalier" by Barnard, "An Irish Solution" (1992) *New Law Journal* 526. This reprieve on "the stranglehold of the Catholic church over Irish secular life" together, for good measure, with the failure to overrule the Irish language requirement for teachers in Case 379/87 *Groener v. Minister for Education* [1989] E.C.R. 3967, constitutes in her view:

> "the development of an exception for Ireland and seems to drive a coach and horses through the fundamental principles of Community law. Multiply this manyfold with the future accession of such diverse countries as Hungary, Poland, and Czechoslovakia . . . – each with its own ethnic, cultural and linguistic traditions – and the very foundations of the Community would be fundamentally shaken."

87 Case 279/80 *Webb* [1981] E.C.R. 3305, para. 17; Case C–180/89 *Commission v. Italy* [1991] E.C.R. I–709, para. 18; Case C–198/89 *Commission v. Greece* [1991] E.C.R. I–727, para. 19; Case 159/90 *S.P.U.C. v. Grogan* [1991] 3 C.M.L.R. 849 at 869–870.

88 Case 41/74 *Van Duyn v. Home Office* [1975] 1 C.M.L.R. 1, para. 18: "[T]he particular circumstances justifying recourse to the concept of public policy may vary from one country to another and from one period to another, and it is therefore necessary in this matter to allow the competent national authorities an area of discretion within the limits imposed by the Treaty".

had been supported by Advocate-General Mayras in Case 41/74 *Van Duyn.*[89] However in Case 36/75 *Rutili*, Advocate-General Mayras urged that the Court "must . . . place the concept of public policy in the Community context".[90] The Court held that "the concept of public policy . . . cannot be determined unilaterally by each Member State without being subject to control by the institutions of the Community".[91] The Court saw the restrictions on derogation in Council Regulation 1612/68 and Council Directive 64/221 as "a specific manifestation of the more general principle" in the European Convention on Human Rights and Fundamental Freedoms and recognised in European Community law that there should be no restrictions other than those "necessary for the protection of those interests 'in a democratic society'".

The Court's control of derogations tightened in Case 116/81 *Adoui* and Case 30/77 *R v. Bouchereau*, where it held that the Member State's derogation must be based on "a genuine and sufficiently serious threat to the requirements of public policy affecting one of the fundamental interests of society".[92] If there is such a threat, the question becomes

> "whether the rule pursues an objective which is compatible with Community law, that is to say whether it can rely on imperative requirements of public interest which are consistent with or not incompatible with the aims laid down in the Treaty provisions."[93]

In other words, before the Court's consideration of the validity of the substance of the derogation comes the first question of whether the fundamental interest of a Member State's society is compatible with Treaty objectives. All of the tests according to fundamental rights, the principle of proportionality, and necessity in a democratic society which the Court employs to restrict derogations, are therefore *ipso facto* promoting Treaty objectives because of their functional position[94]:

> "an appraisal as to whether measures designed to safeguard public policy are justified must have regard to all rules of Community law the object of which

---

89 Advocate-General Mayras advised that a "Community public policy" might only exist where the Member States transferred powers via the Treaty to the Community institutions. The Community policy could only be an "*economic* public policy, relating, for example, to the common organisation of the agricultural markets" – *ibid.* at 11.

90 Case 36/75 *Rutili v. Minister for the Interior* [1975] E.C.R. 1219 at 1241.

91 *ibid.* at 1231. The case arose by Article 177 (EEC) reference from the Tribunal Administratif in Paris.

92 Case 30/77 *R v. Bouchereau* [1977] E.C.R. 1999, para. 34; Joined Cases 115 & 116/81 *Rezguia Adoui v. Belgian State and City of Liege*; Case 116/81 *Cornuaille v. Belgian State* [1982] E.C.R. 1665 at 1707–1708, para. 8. However, Case 41/74 *Van Duyn* is still cited regularly in national courts, for example in the High Court in *Attorney General v. X* [1992] 1 I.R. 1.

93 Case C–159/90 *S.P.U.C. v. Grogan* [1992] 3 C.M.L.R. 849 at 872 (opinion of the Advocate-General).

94 This is not the same as saying that the examination of the measure is one of the extent to which the measure promotes Community interests. *Cf.* G. De Burca, "Fundamental Human Rights and the Reach of EC Law" (1993) 13 *Oxford Journal of Legal Studies* 283, at p. 198, n.70.

> is, on the one hand, to limit the discretionary power of the Member States in this respect, and on the other, to ensure that the rights of persons subject thereunder to restrictive measures are protected."[95]

In Case C–260/89, *ERT* the Court held that derogations via Articles 56 and 66 (EEC) must be interpreted "in the light of the general principles of law and in particular of fundamental rights".[96] In areas of substantive competence the Court translates national constitutional rights into Community fundamental rights which tend to attain Community objectives.[97] However in counterbalancing derogations any Community fundamental right irrespective of the meaning of "fundamental" will also be "fundamental" in the Community sense because it functionally helps attain Community objectives by restricting exceptions to uniform application of European Community legal principles. And there can be no danger to the validity of Community law from the adoption and use of untranslated fundamental rights within this technique – quite the opposite, since the purpose is to test national measures which would derogate from the uniform application of European Community law. ERT was a not-for-profit organisation with cultural functions which had a monopoly on domestic broadcasts. The Court in Case C–260/89 *ERT*, like the Advocate-General in Case C–159/90 *S.P.U.C. v. Grogan*, tested the Greek derogation against the freedom of expression contained in Article 10 of the European Convention on Human Rights and Fundamental Freedoms.[98]

In Case C–159/90 *S.P.U.C. v. Grogan* the Advocate-General used the rights to provide and receive commercial information in the jurisprudence of the Court of Justice and European Court of Human Rights in order to expand the scope of the free movement of services and so bring the Supreme Court injunction under Article 59 (EEC). There is no functional contradiction in then having turned to the moral aspects of the right to freedom of expression in order to restrict the public policy derogation:

> "[I]t appears from the case law of the European Court and the European Commission of Human Rights on Article 10 of the European Convention that commercial information qualifies for protection under Article 10 and *a fortiori* information intended to influence public opinion. The information in this case is not distributed by providers of services in Great Britain themselves but by Irish student associations, which distribute the information in Ireland without remuneration, because of their conviction . . .".[99]

The Court held in Case C–260/89 *ERT* that restrictions to freedom of expression by the derogation from the free provision of services, like restrictions to the fundamental rights in Articles 8, 9, 10, and 11 of the Convention,

---

95 Case 36/75 *Rutili v. Minister for the Interior* [1975] E.C.R. 1219 at 1235.

96 Case 260/89 *Elliniki Radiophonia Tileorassi – Anonimi Etairia (ERT-AE) v. Dimotiki Etairia Pliroforissis (DEP)* [1991] E.C.R. I–2925.

97 See above, para. 30–11.

98 Case C–260/89 *ERT* [1991] E.C.R. I–2925, para. 45.

99 Case C–159/90 *S.P.U.C. v. Grogan* [1992] 3 C.M.L.R. 849 at 879.

must be "necessary in a democratic society".[100] This is a considerable advance from the position in Case 36/75 *Rutili* because in that case the Court tested according to necessity in a democratic society the validity of restrictions imposed on rights secured directly by Article 48(3) (EEC), Article 3 of Directive No. 64/221, and Article 8 of Regulation No. 1612/68, and not on rights secured by a free-standing broad value principle such as freedom of expression drawn from an international convention for the purpose not of interpreting or testing the validity of Community acts but for restricting Member States' actions pursuant to a legitimate public interest which affects Community law.[101] The Court's conception of "necessity" and of "democratic society" is in fact another potential restriction in the interest of Treaty objectives on a national constitutional right embedded by popular referendum. The concurring opinion of Commissioner Schermers in the European Commission of Human Rights in *Open Door Counselling and Dublin Well Women Centre v. Ireland*[102] demonstrates that this confusion between market rights and human rights, and European Community law and European Convention for the Protection of Human Rights and Fundamental Freedoms law, a confusion which the Treaty on European Union has increased,[103] will ultimately lead to new values. Schermers, a European Community lawyer, looked to the European Community for what is necessary in a democratic society, calling it "the European (Community) society", and in particular to the freedom of movement of persons which is "not just another economic right" but a fundamental principle of the Community and "part of its cultural richness". He agreed that the injunctions prohibiting the provision of information were not necessary in a democratic society.

---

100 Compare the judgment of Kenny, J. in *Ryan v. Attorney General* [1965] I.R. 294 where he used the concept of democracy as a source of rights apparently antecedent to the Constitution: "There are many rights which flow from the Christian and democratic nature of the State which are not mentioned in Article 40 at all".

101 Case 36/75 *Rutili v. Minister for the Interior* [1975] ECR 1219 at 1232.

102 (1992) 14 E.H.R.R. 131 at 141.

103 Article F(2) (EU) states:

> "The Union shall respect fundamental rights as guaranteed by the European Convention for the Protection of Human Rights and Fundamental Freedoms and as they result from the constitutional traditions common to the Member States as general principles of Community law."

This article does not mean that the European Community is bound by the European Convention for the Protection of Human Rights and Fundamental Freedoms in the international law sense. Decisions of the Court of Justice which purport to apply the European Convention for the Protection of Human Rights and Fundamental Freedoms as European Community law, and thus as part of the domestic law of the Member States, are not appealable to the European Court of Human Rights. A proposal by the Commission to bind the European Community to the European Convention on Human Rights and Fundamental Freedoms has not been followed – Memorandum of the Commission, 4 April 1979, [1979] 2 European Community Bull. Supp. The question of accession is under consideration.

The test of necessity in a democratic society of a public policy derogation is one aspect of the broader test of proportionality. In Case 44/79 *Hauer* the Court had to determine whether the restriction by the implementation of a temporary ban on new vine planting of the right to property in its European Community law version, translated from national constitutions and the Convention in the light of economic objectives, was proportionate to the Community objectives behind it; if not, the Community rule would have had to give way.[104] In Case C–159/90 *Grogan*, the Advocate-General sought to test whether the restriction of the right to freedom of expression by injunction was proportionate to the value of the Member State policy behind it; if not, the Member State policy had to give way.[105] The objection to this is that restrictions by European Community law and by Member State law are not of the same nature. The technique used in European Community law is the same in both Case 44/79 *Hauer* and Case C–159/90 *Grogan*: a method of resolving the inevitable clashes between the general interest and an individual right. However the technique is independent of what is put in the balance: in Case C–159/90 *S.P.U.C. v. Grogan* it is a national fundamental right which may have to give way to a Community fundamental right, that is to a right which will promote the Community interest in securing objectives by virtue of its functional position within derogations, because it is not necessary in a democratic society. In other words the protection of life is never balanced directly against the provision of services; the values involved never clash within a technique. Yet the idea of the principle of proportionality, adopted from German law, is to achieve a balance between the individual and the general which best fits society according to the constitutional scheme. A fundamental right afforded by a Member State will be in the precarious position of derogation at the discretion of the Court of Justice precisely because there is in reality a clash between constitutions differently legitimated pursuing incompatible social goals and ideas of what is fundamental to society and to the legal order.[106]

---

104 The restriction on the translated member state right was held proportionate. Case 44/79 *Hauer v. Land Rheinland-Pfalz* [1979] E.C.R. 3727; [1980] 3 C.M.L.R. 42, para. 23.

105 The Advocate-General believed the particular restriction by the Member State right on the Community freedom to be proportionate on the facts. Case C–159/90 *S.P.U.C. v. Grogan* [1992] 3 C.M.L.R. 849 at 878–885.

106 De Burca (G. de Búrca (1993) *op. cit.* above, n.94 at p. 299) argues that the Treaty freedoms (including, therefore, the freedom to provide abortions for money) have substantial moral and social importance beyond their economic significance because they form part of the creation of "a fairer, more peaceful, and democratic society" (this appears to be an empirical prediction). No doubt the freedoms do have importance beyond economics. Economics has importance beyond economics. But this does not mean that such freedoms are of the same nature as national constitutional fundamental rights, being of the nature set out above in Parts III and IV, and the protection of which is an end in itself. Furthermore, these freedoms and these rights conflict.

De Búrca also argues that the Advocate-General's balancing reflects "a substantive reconciliation within Community law of competing moral choices and human rights." (at p. 300.). But functionally this "substantive reconciliation" is made to restrict a dero-

It is hardly surprising that Irish constitutional law and European Community law should reach different conclusions.[107] When *S.P.U.C. v. Grogan* was in the Supreme Court, Finlay C.J. stated:

> "I am satisfied that where an injunction is sought to protect a constitutional right the only matter which could properly be capable of being weighed in a balance against the granting of such protection would be another competing constitutional right. . . Where the right sought to be protected is that of a life, there can be no question of a possible or putative right which might exist in European law as a corollary to a right to travel so as to avail of services, counter-balancing . . . the necessity for an interlocutory injunction."[108]

In *Open Door Counselling*, Finlay C.J. had already said: "[N]o right could constitutionally arise to obtain information the purpose of the obtaining of which was to defeat the constitutional right to life of the unborn child."[109] By contrast, in Case C–159/90 *Grogan* the Advocate-General in his judgment of the optimal balance of competing values in Community society, was willing

---

gation from the economic freedom to provide and avail of abortions. Such a reconciliation is anathema to national constitutional law. Furthermore, the reconciliation is between the State's interest in public morality on the one hand and individual rights on the other, not the balancing of one right against the other. Finally, the result of the reconciliation differs (in this case, although not necessarily always) with the result of a similar balancing in national constitutional law.

107 The English courts have also experienced difficulty with proportionality in the Shop Acts saga, differing with the Court of Justice as to both the test and the result. In *W.H. Smith Do-It-All Ltd and Payless DIY Ltd. v. Peterborough City Council* [1990] 2 C.M.L.R. 577, Mustill L.J. overturned the Crown Court and applied the decision of the Court of Justice in Case 145/88 *Torfaen Borough Council v. B & Q plc* [1989] E.C.R. 3851, holding that s.47 of the Shop Act 1950 was a measure having equivalent effect to a quantitative restriction on imports and thus prohibited by Article 30 (EEC) unless, *per* "Cassis de Dijon", its socio-cultural purpose is one justified by the Community in principle, and the least restrictive means and proportionality tests are satisfied. However Mustill L.J. wondered: "How could a desire to keep the Sabbath holy be measured against the free-trade economic premises of the Common Market?" (at 596). This was also the view of Hoffman J. in *Stoke-on-Trent City Council v. B & Q plc* [1991] 2 W.L.R. 43 at 57 where the court effectively rejects the Court of Justice's proportionality test. Hoffman J.'s view was adopted by Mummery J. in *Mendip District Council v. B & Q plc* [1991] 1 C.M.L.R. 113. This case was the subject of a preliminary ruling in Case C–169/91, together with Case 306/88 *Rochdale Borough Council v. Anders* [1992] E.C.R. I–6457 and Case C–304/90, *Reading Borough Council v. Payless DIY Ltd* [1992] E.C.R. I 6493 where the Court of Justice itself applied the proportionality test and held that Sunday trading rules were not contrary to Article 30 (EEC). As part of the line of cases starting with Joined Cases C 267 & 268/91 *Keck and Mithouard* [1993] E.C.R. I–6079 (see M. Poiares Maduro, "*Keck*: The end? The beginning of the end? Or just the end of the beginning?" (1994) 1 *Irish Journal of European Law* 30) the Court of Justice has held that such rules are not covered by Art. 30 (EC) – Joined Cases C–69/93 and C–258/93 *Punto Casa and PPV* [1994] E.C.R. I–2355 and Joined Cases C–418/93 *et alia Semeraro Caso Uno v. Sindaco del Commune di Erbuso* [1996] E.C.R. I–2975.

108 *S.P.U.C. v. Grogan* [1990] 1 C.M.L.R. 688 at 699 (Sup. Ct.).

109 *Open Door Counselling* [1988] I.R. 593 (Sup. Ct). Hamilton P. in the High Court ([1987] I.L.R.M. 477 at 500) stated:

> "The qualified right to privacy, the rights of association and freedom of expression and the right to disseminate information cannot be invoked to interfere with such a fundamental right as the right to life of the unborn, which is acknowledged by the Constitution of Ireland."

to let only information by way of assistance pass the proportionality test. But this reprieve for Irish constitutional rights does not cover "other information . . . and does not extend to measures restricting the freedom of movement of pregnant women or subjecting them to unsolicited examination".[110] The High Court in *Attorney General v. X* referred to *S.P.U.C. v. Grogan* and applied the test of proportionality but held the injunction proportional because "in the absence of such a power the protection afforded to the right to life which the Constitution acknowledges would in many cases be worthless".[111] In the Supreme Court the pregnant mother was allowed to travel because of the favourable balance of her right to life against that of the unborn according to the new constitutional test adopted in that case.[112] However Finlay C.J. expressed his future willingness to apply a priority of rights: "[I]f there was a stark contrast between the right of a mother of an unborn child to travel and the right to life of the unborn child, that right would necessarily have to take precedence over the right to travel". Only the right to life of the unborn and the right to life of the mother were on the same normative level and were capable of balancing each other; although there are two rights they are both based on a single supreme value: life. The constitutional natural right to life was an exceptionless legal norm, to which the very rationale of proportional balancing of effects, ends and means, and other rights was anathema.[113] This position has been altered in Irish constitutional law since this conflict (as has the position in European Community law).[114]

The Irish judicial reaction on this issue establishes four important points which fit into the position of European Community law in Irish constitutional law, and any of which would be capable of putting Ireland in breach of its European Community law obligations[115]:

1. When it comes to the enforcement of a constitutional right, the only counterbalance is another constitutional right.[116]

---

110 [1989] 3 C.M.L.R. 849 at 885. In other opinions Advocate-General Van Gerven has held that disproportionality arises "where the rule gives rise to serious screening off of the market" *q.v.* his opinions in Case 145/88 *Torfaen Borough Council v. B & Q Plc.* [1989] E.C.R. 3851, sections 17–25; Case C–312/89 *Conforama* [1991] E.C.R. I–997; Case C–332/89 *Marchandise* [1991] E.C.R. I–1027, para. 12. Van Gerven's approach in Case C–159/90 *S.P.U.C. v. Grogan* and in Case 145/88 *Torfaen*, which was there adopted by the Court, is the same.

111 [1992] 1 I.R. 1.

112 Finlay C.J. gave what appears to be the majority test: "If it is established as a matter of probability that there is a real and substantial risk to the life as distinct from the health of the mother, which can only be avoided by the termination of her pregnancy, that such termination is permissible, having regard to the true interpretation of Article 40.3.3. of the Constitution."

113 *S.P.U.C. v. Grogan* [1990] 1 C.M.L.R. 689 at 701, *per* Walsh J.: "The most basic of all human rights is life itself". See also above, para. 23–12, "Resolution of Internal Constitutional Conflicts".

114 See above, para. 30–2.

115 See more generally Part IV.

116 *S.P.U.C. v. Grogan* [1990] I.L.R.M. 350 at 357, *per* Finlay C.J.

2. An Irish constitutional law interpretation of European Community law was put forward which did not admit of European Community law overriding Irish constitutional law rights, and which did not correspond to the European Community law self-interpretation: Finlay C.J., "where the right sought to be protected is that of life, there can be *no question* of a possible or putative right which might exist in European law as a corollary to a right to travel"[117]; Walsh J., "it *cannot* be one of the objectives of the European Communities that a Member State should be obliged to permit activities which are clearly designed to set at nought the constitutional guarantees for the protection within the State of a fundamental human right."[118]

3. In the event of a clash between European Community law and Irish constitutional law, the conflict must be resolved for Irish constitutional law purposes by an interpretation of the Constitution,[119] which looks at the conflicting Irish constitutional law provision[120] and the limitations of the Article 29.4 provisions (which, *per* McCarthy J., "*may* exclude from constitutional invalidation *some* provisions of the Treaty of Rome the enforcement of which is *necessitated* by the obligations of membership of the European Communities"[121]).

4. There is a direct constitutional duty on judges to observe the above.

There would have been a head-on collision in *Attorney General v. X*[122] between the right to travel to receive a service and the protection of the right to life of the unborn if the Supreme Court had not disposed of the case on Irish constitutional law grounds in favour of the party asserting the European Community law right.[123] The European Community law issue was however considered by the High Court, where Costello J. held that the injunction fell under the public policy exception to European Community law rights, holding:

> "The aim of the Eighth Amendment was to ensure that the right to life of the unborn is adequately protected. I do not think that a measure which empowers a court to stop a woman going abroad (which taken in conjunction with constitutional principles is one of the effects of the Eighth amendment) to terminate the life of the unborn is disproportionate to the aim which the Eighth Amendment seeks to achieve."[124]

---

117 *ibid.* at 357 (emphasis added).
118 *ibid.* at 361, (emphasis added).
119 *ibid., per* Finlay C.J. at 356. See above, Part IV, Chap. 27, "Coping with Conflicts".
120 *ibid.* at 361, *per* Walsh J.
121 *ibid.* at 362 (emphasis added).
122 [1992] 1 I.R. 1.
123 There are interesting but unanswerable questions as to how far European Community law ideas of proportionality might have over time affected Irish constitutional law ideas to reach the result in this case, and also how far the prospect of a clash with the Court of Justice influenced the Supreme Court's willingness to find an Irish constitutional law answer which would not affect the European Community law right in the instant case.
124 [1992] 1 I.R.1 at 17.

This is in contradiction of Advocate-General Van Gerven's analysis. However an increase in policing the right to life of the unborn might have led to the European Court on Human Rights finding in Ireland's favour since the decision that the prohibition was not necessary in a democratic society was based in part on the ineffectiveness of the prohibition on the dissemination of information.[125]

The categorisation of a Member State's conflicting constitutional right as an area of discretion in public policy or interest is itself not always accurate. The term may be an appropriate description of the national public interest in a case which involves the general protection of a civic liberty, such as in Case C–353/89 *Commission v. Netherlands.*[126] In that case the Dutch government claimed that a law requiring a proportion of broadcasts to be made with Dutch technical assistance was justified as a derogation from Article 59 (EEC) by protection of the freedom of expression of different viewpoints in Dutch society. But the existence of a public policy or interest or, in the terms of the Advocate-General, a moral choice is not the crux of what is involved. In a case where, unlike *Attorney-General v. X*, the health of the mother but not her right to life was threatened, European Community law would operate to override not only a policy but also the protection of a particular human life.[127] The result would be the denial of a personal right to life, and the consequent loss of a particular life, by virtue of European Community law rights related to information, travel and services. The general respect for fundamental rights, observed in the actions of the Community executive and the executives of the Member States when acting under colour of Community law gives rise to a dangerous complacency about the structures of the law. The conflicts between rights and between competences is translated in the European Community law structures of derogations into a conflict of interests. The intrusive structures and techniques of European Community law may achieve the same result *vis-à-vis* a Member State's constitutional right through the actions of private parties: the loss of a human life. There is no safe haven for Member States' fundamental rights under derogations.

---

125 *Open Door Counselling and Dublin Well Woman Centre v. Ireland* (1992) Series A, No. 246. See J. Kingston, "Human Rights: The Solution to the Abortion Question", in C. Gearty and A. Tomkins, *Understanding Human Rights* (London and New York: Mansell, 1996) p. 464. *Cf.* the opposite view of G. De Burca (1993) *op. cit.* above, n.94, p. 315.

126 Case 353/89 [1991] E.C.R. I–4069.

127 As Walsh J. has stated, "the Irish constitutional provision against abortion is not based on the question of public morality but is based on the right of the individual life" – "Reflections on the Effects of Membership of the European Communities in Irish Law" (1987) in C.-D. Ehlerman, F. Capotorti, J. Frowein, F. Jacobs, R. Joliet, T. Koopmans, R. Kovar, *Du droit international au droit de l'intégration, Liber Amicorum Pierre Pescatore* (Baden–Baden: Nomos, 1989).

31. DIFFERENT INTERPRETATIONS OF A SIMILARLY NAMED RIGHT

31–1 Unlike the right to life of the unborn, the right to private property is recognised in European Community law,[1] and is even declared to be drawn from the common traditions of the Member States, being first announced at that stage of the Court of Justice's jurisprudence where the Court of Justice, in creating a human rights jurisdiction, made reference to the constitutions of the Member States.[2] Does this mean that no conflict can occur?

No. It has been a recurring theme of this work that the protection of a legal right is given definition and meaning in the legal order in which it is protected.[3] Furthermore, European Community law allows for the limitation of that right by measures necessary to pursue the public interest objectives of the European Community. This is a European Community concept of public interest,[4] in which there is potential for a latent European concept of society.[5]

---

1 See above, para. 30–7, "Conflict of Fundamentals" and Part II, para. 8–6, "Fundamental Rights Currently Included".

2 Case 44/79 *Hauer v. Land Rheinland-Pfalz* [1979] E.C.R. 3727.

3 Monsignor G. Sheehy considers that rights such as the right to marry can only be sensibly considered in the context of a given legal system, "a system which will of necessity itself reflect such factors as its historical roots and development, its cultural milieu past and present, its own concept of the place and purpose of law in society, its religious orientation and beliefs.": "The Right to Marry" in O'Reilly (ed.), *Human Rights and Constitutional Law: Essays in honour of Brian Walsh* (Dublin: Round Hall Press, 1992). Whilst this is correct in the case of many constitutional rights, Sheehy's view that "[t]his is not to say that the right itself varies. It is to say that, from a legal rather than a philosophical point of view, its appreciation and the application of it has to be evaluated in the milieu in which it is exercised" (*ibid.* p. 14), although stateable from a different point of view, differs from the argument in this work, given the focus on intra-order meaning. The change in appreciation and application of a right changes the meaning of the right, and the incidents of the non-vindication of a right by a court vary according to the order from which the right is drawn. This is more than a difference of terminology. As Pearse put it, "[i]f the definition can be varied in its essentials, or added to or subtracted from, it wasn't the true definition in the first place" – "Ghosts" in *The Murder Machine and Other Essays* (Dublin: Mercier, 1976) p. 30.

4 The idea of a common European public interest is at the heart of one conception of the European Community, certainly of the European Community law conception, and is important in diverse contexts: for example, in Article 92(3)(b) (EC) on state aids, where aids may be excepted by the Commission where they promote the execution of a project of "common European interest." The duty on national jurisdictions to respect the decisions of the Court of Justice applies particularly to the Court of Justice's appreciation of "the interest of the Community": Case C–466/93 *Atlanta Fruchthandelsgesellschaft v. Bunesamt für Ernährung und Forstwirtschaft* 9 November 1995, para. 50. In the circumstances of this case (banana dispute between Germany and the Community) the Court of Justice made clear that it is up to it to decide on the proper balance between the Community and the national interest.

5 In Case 5/88 *Wachauf* [1989] E.C.R. 2609 at 2693, para. 18, the Court of Justice

French Constitutional Law versus European Community Law

31–2 In French constitutional law the right to property is specifically declared in Article 2 of the Declaration of the Rights of Man and of the Citizen 1789, as one of the natural and imprescriptible rights of man whose preservation is the ultimate purpose of every political institution. The protection of the right must be understood as one in a framework of fundamental commitments of French constitutional law[6] the limitation of which is itself limited and can occur only in the context of a framework of interdependent French constitutional law concepts,[7] by the constitutionally designated organ, the National Parliament.

Irish Constitutional Law versus European Community Law

31–3 In Irish constitutional law the protection of the right to the private ownership of external goods is acknowledged by Article 43.1.1 to be a natural right antecedent to positive law inhering in man by virtue of his rational being. This is a different right, with a similar name, to that recognised in European Community law. Irish constitutional law allows in Article 43.2.2 for limitation of its right to property by the exigencies of the common good. The notion of the common good has a particular meaning in Irish constitutional law[8] which is tied into the Irish constitutional natural law basis of the right itself. Thus even in a situation where European Community law agreed with Irish constitutional law that "the right to private property" was at issue, the two orders may differ over how it could be limited. For example, in Joined Cases T–466, 469, 473, 474 and 477/93, *O'Dwyer v. Council* the Court of First Instance held that restrictions by the Common Agricultural Policy on the right to private property would not be disproportionate to the objectives pursued by the legislation unless they were "manifestly inappropriate".[9] This is a much laxer test than in Irish constitutional law.

This has yet to arise directly, although it has arisen in the context of a challenge to Ministerial Regulations on milk quotas, where Murphy, J. held the measures justified by the exigencies of the common good.[10] The learned trial judge did not avert to the fact that the common good of the European

considered social function as a possible limit to a fundamental right. It is not possible to have a conception of social function without a conception of society.

6 See above, para. 21–2, "Assuring the Guarantee of the Rights and Liberties of Citizens".
7 See above, para. 21–14, "Rights and Freedoms Understood in a Framework of Interdependent Concepts".
8 See above, para. 24–4, "The Common Good".
9 [1995] E.C.R. II–2071.
10 *Lawlor v. Minister for Agriculture* [1988] I.L.R.M. 400.

Community and that of Irish constitutional law can differ, and that the former cannot justify the restriction of a right in the latter.

Both the concept of common good and that of society have a meaning in Irish constitutional law specific to it, and thus contribute to the different idea of rights and their legitimate limitation. There may be scope for the Community interest, or at least Ireland's participation in the Community, to be considered an element of the common good. However this might lead the courts into questions of the effect of a putative breach of European Community law on the benefits Ireland receives from membership.

The right to private property has been raised by a European Parliament question to the Commission, asking what the Commission intends to do about the possibility in Ireland of farm tenants being able to extend their lease and buy land against the owner's will, in breach of the right of European Union citizens to safeguard their right to foreign property and land ownership in Ireland. The Commission's reply denied direct European Community competence because of Article 222 (EC) (an Article which has been virtually ignored by the Court of Justice) unless there is discrimination based on nationality.[11] However such discrimination could be shown if the provisions allowing for extension, conversion and purchase were in fact more to the detriment of non-Irish owners than to Irish owners. It is difficult to see how the European Community law concept of the public interest and the Irish constitutional law concept of the common good could be the same in such a case. For example, the latter might allow for variable limitation of the right to private property in pursuit of a policy of constitutional importance of land ownership and distribution itself based on the right to private property and a concept of personhood.

---

[11] Written Question E–337/95 [1995] O.J. C190/8, Reply by Fischler.

32. NATIONAL CONSTITUTIONAL LAW POLICY VERSUS EUROPEAN COMMUNITY POLICY / RIGHT / PRINCIPLE

32–1 By "constitutional law policy" is meant executive or legislative measures that implement constitutionally expressed goals. There may be a national constitutional law duty on agencies of government to act and a constitutional right to some form of implementation, but the specifics of a policy may not be constitutionally obligatory. Two examples are considered here.

Irish Constitutional Law v. European Community law

32–2 In Irish constitutional law, the promotion of the Irish language is a policy based on positive Irish constitutional law. Article 8 provides:

> "1. The Irish language as the national language is the first official language.
> 2. The English language is recognised as a second official language.
> 3. Provision may, however, be made by law for the exclusive use of either of the said languages for any one or more official purposes, either throughout the State or in any part thereof."

The status of Irish is reinforced by Article 25.5.6:

> "In case of conflict between the texts of any copy of this Constitution . . . the text in the national language shall prevail."

On the basis of these provisions the courts have found the following constitutional rights (although they could be cut down by law pursuant to Article 8.3[1]): the right to conduct a side of the case in Irish,[2] the right to be supplied with an official translation of official documents where relevant to a case (basing this right also on the right of access to the courts),[3] and the right to have

---

[1] There may be limitations to the exercise of this Article 8.3 power imposed by respect for Article 8.1.

[2] *An Stát (MacFhearraigh) v. MacGamhna, Cathaoirleach An Bhínse Achomhairc Fostsíochta*, unreported, High Court, O'Hanlon J., 1 June 1983.

[3] *Delap v. An tAire Dlí agus Cirt, Éire agus an tArd Aighne*, unreported, High Court, O'Hanlon J., 13 July 1990. Written Question E–1381/95 asked about the production of information on the European Union in Irish. The President of the Commission (J. Santer) replied that the Treaties and some brochures were written in Irish: [1995] O.J. C230/38. However, secondary legislation is not.

appropriate forms in Irish to incorporate and register an organisation with the Registrar of Companies.[4] Importantly, these last two rights were found to exist not primarily on the basis of Article 8 but on the right to equality before the law (Article 40.1), which is not potentially limited by Article 8.3. In *O'Murchú* O'Hanlon J. held that Article 8 of the Constitution gave stronger recognition to Irish as the first official language of the State than the Constitution of the Irish Free State, and quoted from Kennedy C.J. in *O'Foghludha v. McClean,*[5] a case decided under Article 4 of the Constitution of the Irish Free State:

> "The declaration by the Constitution that the national language of the Saorstát is the Irish language . . . did mean . . . by implication that the State is bound to do everything within it's sphere of action . . . to establish and maintain it in its status as the national language and to recognise it for all official purposes as the national language . . . None of the organs of the state, legislative, executive or judicial, may derogate from the pre-eminent status of the Irish language as the national language of the state without offending against the constitutional provisions of Article 4."

This strong constitutional promotion of Irish ("to establish and maintain") coupled with the right to equality may cause future problems for absence of Irish in the administration of European Community matters.

Case 378/87 *Groener v. Minister for Education*[6] illustrates the potential of conflict between constitutional policies and European Community law. The defendant Minister refused to appoint Groener as a teacher because she did not have the *Ceard-Teastas Gaeilge,* pursuant to a policy applying to teaching applicants of any nationality requiring them to have a certain proficiency in Irish. According to the Government, this requirement is part of a wider policy to promote the restoration and use of Irish as central to the identity of the State.[7] The education system plays a central role in that process and therefore it is a logical consequence that teachers should be capable of assisting persons educated by the system in both official languages.[8] Groener, a Dutch citizen, challenged this decision as being in contravention with the Council Regulation on the free movement of workers.[9]

What is at issue is the compatibility of a European Community law policy, right, and principle (the free movement of workers) and an Irish constitutional law policy, not an Irish constitutional law right (for example a student's right to be answered in Irish in any state-funded education).

---

4 *O'Murchú v. Cláraitheoir na gCuideachtaí agus an tAire Tionscoil agus Tráchtála,* unreported, High Court, O'Hanlon J., 20 June 1988. The forms were in a schedule to a statutory instrument which was in English, and printed copies of the forms were available in English.

5 [1934] I.R. 469.

6 Order of High Court making the Article 177 (EEC) reference of 17 November 1987, judgment in C–379/87 [1989] E.C.R. 3967, Order of High Court of 19 February 1990 dismissing the applicant's claim.

7 *ibid.* at 3971.

8 *ibid.* at 3972.

9 [1968] O.J. Spec. Ed. (II) 1612/475.

Advocate-General Darmon was of the opinion that the language requirement should be upheld on broad grounds. He stated:

> "The preservation of languages is one of those questions of principle which one cannot dismiss without striking at the very heart of cultural identity. Is it therefore for the Community to decide whether or not a particular language should survive?. . .
>
> . . .every *State has the right* to try to ensure the diversity of its cultural heritage and, consequently, to establish the means to carry out such a policy. . . ."[10]

The Court of Justice indicated that the particular policy adopted was compatible with European Community law on narrower grounds which did not mention States' rights. The Court of Justice held that European Community law:

> "does not prohibit the adoption of a policy for the protection and promotion of a language of a Member State which is both the national language and the first official language. However, the implementation of such a policy must not encroach upon a fundamental freedom such as that of the free movement of workers. Therefore, the requirements deriving from measures intended to implement such a policy must not in any circumstances be disproportionate in relation to the aim pursued and the manner in which they are applied must not bring about discrimination against nationals of other Member States."[11]

This potential conflict was therefore avoided by a Court of Justice decision which, in European Community law, is a landmark of cultural tolerance. It is clear however that even as regards this constitutional policy, the promotion of Irish, there remains potential for conflict. There is no reason why the Court of Justice position on proportionality should correspond to the Irish position, which has, as we have seen, a different notion of all the concepts which would go into a proportionate assessment, such as the common good.

It is not clear how such a conflict would be analysed in the Irish courts. A court might analyse the policy as of the same stature as positive Irish constitutional law, reasoning for example that the policy resulted from a constitutional duty on the minister which, within the limits of the Constitution, it was up to him to assess; or that students had a constitutional right to have such a policy implemented. Or the courts might regard the policy as having the status of the implementing instrument. If this instrument was legislation (not in this case), then there would be the question of how far that derogated from the European Communities Act. The potential for conflict with constitutional policies is there.

---

10 [1989] E.C.R. 3967, 3982 paras. 19 and 20 (emphasis added). The use of States' rights language here is noteworthy, and provides an indication of how the jurisprudence of the Court of Justice may develop particularly in this area of the protection of national culture and identity.

11 *ibid.* at 3993, para. 19. The Court of Justice replied to the High Court with very narrow wording: the language requirement was not illegal provided it was "imposed as part of a policy for the promotion of the national language which is, at the same time, the first official language and provided that requirement is applied in a proportionate and non-discriminatory manner."

French Constitutional Law versus European Community Law

32–3 France takes the promotion of its national language so earnestly that it has conflicted with the constitutional right of freedom of expression.[12]

In French constitutional law the safeguard of public order is a policy which may conflict with European Community law. It is an objective of constitutional value which implies that the protection of persons will be assured. The concept of public order has a meaning specific to French law.[13] This policy was considered by the *Conseil Constitutionnel* in the context of the Schengen Treaty,[14] but can equally arise in the context of European Community law.[15]

CONCLUSION

The potential exists for constitutional conflicts between the European Community and national legal orders occurring in concrete cases where both Community and national courts have their jurisdictions invoked. The scope of European Community law, the possibilities for judicial recourse, and the conflicting fundamentals of European Community law and national law are such that such conflicts are likely. When fifteen judges from 15 legal orders are obliged to decide cases in widely disparate fields under a new and complex legal order which each Member State, in addition to private parties, is trying to influence in its own favour,[16] it is not surprising that they should give general objectives such prominence.[17] It is not a question of conspira-

---

12 94–345 DC, 29 July 1994, J.O. 2 August 1994; [1994] Rec. Dalloz Sirey (Textes) 379, *Loi on the use of the French language.*

13 See above, para. 21–3, " Assuring the Guarantee of the Rights and Liberties of Citizens – As a Competence".

14 91–294 DC, 25 July 1991, Rec. p.91; (1991) *Revue de Droit Public* 1517, "Schengen Treaty".

15 Case 36/75 *Rutili v. French Minister of the Interior* [1975] E.C.R. 1219 is an early example of such a conflict.

16 See P.G. Cerny, "The Limits of deregulation: Transnational interpretation and policy change" (1991) 19 *European Journal of Political Research* 173 at p. 183: "[S]tates can seek to convince, or pressure, other states – and . . . international institutions – to adopt measures which shift the balance of competitive advantage. Such pressure will generally combine elements of a neo-mercantilist self-interest, of limited reciprocity, and of multilateral hard bargaining."

17 That there are proposals that courts dealing with economic matters should be staffed by economists (considered by G. Teubner and T. Daintith, "Contract and Organisation: Legal Analysis in the Light of Economic and Social Theory" in G. Farjat, *The Contribution of Economics to Legal Analysis: The Concept of the Firm* (1986)) is indicative of the difficulties facing the judges of the Court of Justice in their plurality of roles: as the arbiters of economic law, as members of an international tribunal, as labour law appeal judges in staff cases, as an advisor on the compatibility of international agreements with the constituent treaties, as the arbiter of inter-institutional disputes, and as judges in the evolved role of a Supreme Court of a federal legal order, who maintain a judicial policy with national courts.

cy. The Court of Justice employs the legal techniques discussed above as a response to the conflicts between competences which can only increase with increased integration. Case C–159/90 *S.P.U.C. v. Grogan* is the burial mound of the belief that the *approfondissement* of the normative structures of European Community law does not affect radically the protection of national constitutional law fundamental rights, and not just in one Member State. Ireland stands alone in elevating the right to life of the unborn to the status of a fundamental constitutional right. However the concept of the protection of fundamental rights in Irish constitutional law has characteristics in common with other Member States: the protection of fundamental rights forms part of the legitimation of constitutional law, is an end in itself, and helps achieve the realisation of an idea of the person which is one of the objectives of society. Fundamental rights and social goals are reconciled in national law by constitutional processes such as judicial review in order to achieve a national constitutional law harmony.

In European Community law by contrast, by the application of the techniques analysed above, where a human right and an economic objective conflict the human right is recognised only so far as it does not conflict with the attainment of objectives. In this way fundamental rights and Treaty objectives are also in harmony. The broadening of Treaty objectives to include more directly political and social objectives does not solve the problem because the relationship between fundamental rights and objectives differs to that in national constitutional law, because the meaning of the rights depends upon the order in which they are protected, and because the accompanying increase in competences increases the likely incidence of conflicts. The problem could be solved by a break making the European Community a federal state.[18] The conflicts between orders occurs through the effort to integrate two incompatible harmonies[19] where the incompatibilities go even to different legitimations

---

18 See above, para. 33–4, "Direction Three".

19 Stepping outside of the order approach here, R. Dworkin, *Taking Rights Seriously* (London: Duckworth, 1977) p. 171 is of interest:

> "Political theories will differ from one another, therefore, not simply in the particular goals, rights, and duties each sets out, but also in the way each connects the goals, rights, and duties it employs. In a well-formed theory some consistent set of these, internally ranked or weighted, will be taken as fundamental or ultimate within the theory. It seems reasonable to suppose that any particular theory will give ultimate pride of place to just one of these concepts; it will take some overriding goal, or some set of fundamental rights, or some set of transcendent duties, as fundamental, and show other goals, rights, and duties as subordinate and derivative."

Interestingly as regards what might be a political theory behind European Community law, Dworkin in general considers that goal-based theories "seem especially compatible with homogenous societies, or at least those temporarily united by an urgent, overriding goal, like self-defense or economic expansion" (p. 173). The European Community has both these goals. But Dworkin makes clear that a contract could never result in a goal based system because each party to the contract decides in the basis of

of constitutional law.[20] The current law of derogations cannot supply the solution because it is based on the functional balancing of incommensurables according to the calibration supplied by the socio-economic vision and development of European Community law to the attainment of the dynamic political goal of "European union".

The possibilities of conflicts have not been avoided by the references to fundamental rights introduced by the Treaty on European Union. The Member States are reiterating in that treaty what the Court of Justice has already decided – in the words of the Preamble "Confirming their attachment to the principles of liberty, democracy and respect for human rights and fundamental freedoms and the rule of law", concepts which are given meaning by the Court through the techniques discussed to achieve a European Community law harmony with its federal economic objectives.

The constitutional orders of European Community law and national law are such that a conflict may pose the dilemma of revolt or revolution.

---

his own self-interest (p. 174). This would imply that contracting states can never come together successfully in a goal based system based on international treaty unless they identified their self-interest with the common interest to an extent which would depend on greater homogeneity between the Member States. This identification is a possible future.

20 On the borders of the order approach here, there is a question whether the incompatibilities run even deeper. MacIntyre maintains that the process of rational enquiry is itself embedded in a tradition, and the standards of rational justification are part of a history of a tradition in which the standards are justified by improving on their predecessors. Diversity of traditions means diversity of rationalities means diversity of justice. The effect of trying to harmonise incompatible harmonies has implications beyond formal legalism: *Whose Justice? Which Rationality?* (London: Duckworth, 1988). As Pearse, who deliberately reconstructed and argued from the republican tradition, has put it:

> "Independence one must understand to include spiritual and intellectual independence as well as political independence; or rather, true political independence requires spiritual and intellectual independence as its basis, or it tends to become unstable, a thing resting merely on interests which change with time and circumstance."

"The Spiritual Nation", in *The Murder Machine and other Essays* (Dublin: Mercier, 1976) p. 62.

PART VI

FUTURE DIRECTIONS

THE PROBLEM

The problem is the resolution of conflicts between national and European Community legal orders which threaten their coherence. The focus remains throughout this work on this as a purely legal problem defined internally by the respective legal orders and by their interaction. This focus constitutes a specific way of looking at the tensions caused by the transformation of the originally international organisation of the European Economic Community (which now, as the European Community, comes under the European Union international organisation umbrella) towards "ever closer unity", an entity which legally at least tends to federation, and the problems of conflicts of identity and values, and of notions of constitutional law and political community. The legal problem runs deep, based as it is on the competing claims of incompatible constitutional orders with different legitimations and overlapping jurisdictions, and restricts the directions in which the European Community can develop.

33. AVAILABLE DIRECTIONS

33–1 The four available directions[1] in response to the problem are:

Direction One

33–2 A. European Community law continues to develop along current lines. There will be in national law either a revolt or a revolution.

The revolt may take many forms. For example:

- A national constitutional authority, the authority focused on in this work being a court, may refuse to apply European Community law which would cause a revolution in national law. The most likely scenario may be where European Community law demands that a national constitutional court not apply a fundamental right which is an essential commitment in national constitutional law the non-observance of which breaches the legitimation of national constitutional law. A national court refusal would put the Member State in breach of its European Community law obligations and result in a stand-off between the national court and the Court of Justice.
- The revolt could be the withdrawal of a Member State. For example, France might denounce the Treaty on a ground allowed by French constitutional law.
- Or there may be revolt by the invocation of the Luxembourg compromise within the Council of the European Union, or by members of the Council seeking to transform a meeting into a constitutive body.

If the national court does not revolt against the obligation European Community law imposes directly on it, but rather applies the European Community law rule or an implementing measure required by European Community law in conflict with a national constitutional law rule of such a fun-

---

[1] It is not accepted that the following hope of Frowein can be realised, although a legal revolution may occur, so-to-speak, *sub judice*:

> "It is hoped that a real test concerning the principle of harmony between the democratic structures of the member states and the fundamental principles of the Community can be avoided and that the slow harmonising influence of Community structures will lead to an increasing recognition of common fundamental standards within Europe."

J.A. Frowein, "The European Community and the Republican Form of Government" (1984) 82 *Michigan Law Review* 1311 at p. 1322.

damental nature that the legitimation of national constitutional law is broken, for example where a natural right is not vindicated, then there will be a revolution in national law. National courts must observe the national constitutional law order.[2]

B. There may be some reform in national law possible to postpone the day of reckoning for the mutually sustained pretence that the national and European Community legal orders are compatible. Perhaps the most effective way to try this would be to change the oath of office, to impose on a national judge the duty to uphold European Community law. This is a bit of a trick but no better trick occurs at present. However this may of itself cause a revolt or, if accepted, a legal revolution.

Direction Two

33–3 European Community law adopts the proposed direction below. European Community law remains integrated into national law, and applied by national jurisdictions, but at the same time national law retains its integrity. European Community law develops. The possibility of revolt by the Court of Justice or revolution in European Community law is raised, but this possibility probably can be discounted.[3]

Direction Three

33–4 This direction is to break with the past by the enactment of a European Union Constitution. The only two ways in which European Community law could be applied in the Member States the way European Community law wishes are (i) for a direct recognition of a direct duty to apply European Community law as the Court of Justice would apply it, or (ii) a separate system of Community courts, which would probably entail a separate executive to execute its orders, or the standoff would merely shift from court versus court to the far more explosive scenario of a divided executive. As regards (i), there is also the possibility that judges would recognise, in reaction, a direct natural law duty.[4] The present situation is one of permanent disobedience to European Community law because national courts do not accept the doctrine

---

[2] See Part III, "French Constitutional Law" and Part IV, "Irish Constitutional Law".

[3] This is analysed below in Chap. 37, "Resistance within European Community Law to the Proposed Direction".

[4] This would avoid the problem facing natural law doctrine in national constitutional law succinctly summarised by Duncan: "The Constitution cannot both be subject to the natural law and the legal justification for that subjection." – W. Duncan, "Can Natural Law be used in Constitutional Interpretation?" (1995) 45 *Doctrine & Life* 125 at p. 127. *Cf.* D.R. Phelan, "Two Hats, One Wig, No Halo" *ibid.* at p. 130.

of direct effect. Their reliance on national provisions to ground European Community law is not only contrary to European Community law's perception of direct effect and supremacy, national judicial duty and power, transfer of sovereignty, and the whole nature of the Community legal order, it is contrary to the principle enunciated in Case 39/72 *Commission v. Italy*[5] because the legal nature of the right is brought into doubt.[6]

The enactment of a Union constitution would certainly cause revolt and or revolution in national constitutional law, and possibly, depending on the Constitution and how it was enacted, in European Community law. There is a large question mark over whether it would be possible politically.

Direction Four

33–5 The proposed direction is based squarely on an order determined approach to the problem posed by the integration of legal orders. However it is worth noting another possibility which is based on a substantive distinction between various types of rights:

- classical liberal democratic rights, such as the right to property and to non-discrimination on grounds of gender or origin;
- rights born of the welfare state, such as the right to social security;
- rights necessitated by the conditions of post-industrial society and economic organisation, such as environmental rights and work relations.

The twin imperatives of society and economy require that the central organisation of the market through European Community law be accompanied by the definition and enforcement of these rights in European Community law, with suitable rules on parties, standing and remedies, and where necessary by placing the European Community in the framework of the international obligations such as the European Convention on Human Rights and Fundamental Freedoms.

However there is a set of basic principles in national constitutional law relating to life, liberty, religion and the family which are predicated on visions of personhood (not of the market or the proper distribution of goods) special to each Member State. The rights through which these principles find expression must be regarded as superior to European Community law within their sphere of application. These rights do not extend to encompass

---

5 [1973] ECR 101, paras. 17–18.

6 G.W. Hogan, and A. Whelan, *Ireland and the European Union: Constitutional and Statutory Texts and Commentary* (London: Sweet & Maxwell, 1995) have taken issue with this point. See above, nn.8–10 in Part I and Part II, para. 7–13, "Obligation is the result – non-transformation of Regulations – European Community Law Perception".

national liberal democratic rights which have as their object a person's relations to the economy or society at large – for example the right to property – which, where they conflict with European Community rules and rights, are subject to the principles of uniformity and supremacy.

The protection of these principles by the national courts is indispensable to the legitimacy of the national legal order (upon which European Community law ultimately rests), and the preservation of a national vision of personhood, morality, and identity. It is not possible to harmonise via Article 164 (EC) the unwritten law of Europe in a federation of States with such different histories and jurisprudential traditions.[7]

In this direction the Treaties would be amended to make explicit that the special type of rights embedded in national constitutions, which are considered by the national courts to express basic principles concerning life, liberty, religion, and the family, to have as their interpretive teleology a national vision of personhood and morality, and to be fundamental to the legitimacy of the national legal order and the preservation of its concept of law take precedence over European Community law within their field of application.[8]

---

7 This proposal was first made in D.R. Phelan, "The Right to Life of the Unborn v. the Promotion of Trade in Services – The European Court of Justice and the Normative Shaping of the European Union" (1992) 55 *Modern Law Review* 670. Finnis makes a distinction between rights on the basis of the goods on which they are based, for example the right to property (based on an instrumental good) and the right to life (based on a personal good) – "A Bill of Rights for Britain? The Moral of Contemporary Jurisprudence" (1985) LXXI *Proceedings of the British Academy* 303. This would fit with the approach suggested. *Cf.* M. Cappelletti, *The Judicial Process in Comparative Perspective* (Oxford: Clarendon Press, 1989) p. 316: "fundamental rights represents one area of the law which naturally favours integration." But Cappelletti was not advocating there the integration of fundamental rights on the basis adopted by the Court of Justice; as he states: "our epoch, if any, is *the* epoch of natural law" (p. 210). However the comparative strand of the approach of the Court of Justice would accord with his "comparative phenomenological approach".

8 See p. 417 opposite.

34. THE PROPOSED DIRECTION

34–1 The proposal is that a European Community law constitutional rule is adopted to the effect that the integration of European Community law into national law is limited to the extent necessary to avoid a legal revolution in national law. The extent to which such limitation is necessary is to be finally determined by national constitutional authorities (such as the Supreme Court or the *Conseil Constitutionnel*) in accordance with the essential commitments of the national legal order, not by the Court of Justice. The rule does not relieve Member States from the obligation to satisfy, short of causing a legal revolution European Community law demands.

European Community law should be explicit in the proposed direction that it lacks a basis for want of transfer to make demands which would necessitate, according to national constitutional authorities, a legal revolution, so as to avoid the risk of an interpretation similar to that given to Article 106 of the Australian Constitution,[1] by which the validity of the preservation of a

---

8 De Búrca has stated in response to this proposal that it is arguable that if states took seriously their commitments to the European Convention on Human Rights and Fundamental Freedoms there could be no objection to the Court of Justice reviewing national measures for compatibility with human rights if the same conclusion was reached as would be reached before the European Court of Human Rights. G. De Burca, "Fundamental Human Rights and the Reach of EC Law" (1993) 13 *Oxford Journal of Legal Studies* 283 at p. 317, n.138. However this misses the difference between the legal structures applicable. The government of Ireland decided to sign the Convention dedicated to the protection of human rights with the approval of *Dáil Eireann* but without the necessity to make any changes to domestic law, let alone to the Constitution. Dualist contracting states, of which Ireland is an example, may participate in the Convention system without making the Convention part of domestic law. The compatibility of Irish law can be questioned only if Ireland is sued as a state and after domestic remedies have been exhausted. The remedy is a declaration of non-compliance. It is not possible to derive, from a government commitment to such a system the waiver (on behalf, for example, of the people whom the Constitution protects from the government) of objection to a human rights jurisdiction in the Court of Justice on the basis of a treaty which made no reference to human rights over disputes (which could arise in disputes between private parties from any tribunal) the conclusion of which could have immediate non-discretionary effects in the domestic legal order)

Theoretical uniformity and normative hegemony are not the pillar values of the European Union. This proposal applies the principles of regional and cultural identity and subsidiarity and reflects the division of functions between national courts and the Court of Justice in the division of their competences, in order to promote judicial cooperation and legal cohesion.

1 Commonwealth of Australia Constitution Act 1900 (63 & 64 Victoria c.12):

"106. Saving of Constitutions. The Constitution of each State of the Commonwealth shall, subject to this Constitution, continue as at the establishment of the Commonwealth, or as at the admission or establishment of the State, as the case may be, until altered in accordance with the Constitution of the State."

core of the States' constitutions is said to derive from the federal constitution.

The proposed direction is narrower than national constitutional law courts would like since it does not aim to preserve national constitutional law in every aspect from European Community law, but only to preserve national constitutional law from revolution and restrain the national courts from revolt. The fact that the Court of Justice cannot test what the national courts determine to be necessary to avoid a national constitutional law revolution but must leave this determination to national courts should not of itself bother the Court of Justice because it has always maintained that it is for national courts to decide on the correct interpretation of national law.[2] The direction does not inhibit the development in national constitutional law of doctrines which increase respect for the European Communities, such as a doctrine extending national constitutional rights protection to all European Union citizens, or a doctrine which extends the national constitutional concepts of the common good, public interest, and general interest, to take cognizance of the Community interest.

It is a necessary inference from this work that the proposed direction benefits coherence of national law and European Community law and upholds the Rule of Law, but the Direction involves a rejection, as a matter of legal order determined necessity, of unlimited uniformity and perfect legal integration.[3] It is not argued that this is the best direction for the European Community to take because that would necessitate establishing what "best" is.[4]

---

[2] The case of unimplemented or improperly implemented Directives (where there is a European Community law duty on national courts to interpret national law as far as they can to give effect to the Directive: Case C–106/89 *Marleasing v. La Comercial Internacional de Alimentacion* [1990] E.C.R. 4135) appears to strain this principle but the interpretation is left ultimately to the national courts.

[3] The Treaty of Westphalia adopted the principle *cuius regio, euis religio.* In the era of the integration of the *Rechtsstaat,* a legal equivalent is necessary.

Joerges' third direction in response to the legitimacy problem of European economic law is in some ways related to the proposed direction: Joerges' direction accepts "imperfect legal integration":

> "the dichotomies between European law and national law – Community powers and national sovereignty, supremacy and national responsibility – would have to be replaced as coordinating principles. The Community would respect in principle the legitimacy of national law."

"European Economic Law, the Nation-State and the Maastricht Treaty" in Dehousse (ed.), *Europe after Maastricht: An Ever Closer Union?* (Munich: Beck, Law Books in Europe, 1994) p. 51.

[4] By way of comparison, it is worth noting the approach of the Charter of the United Nations, which provides in Article 2(7):

> "Nothing contained in the present Charter shall authorize the United Nations to intervene in matters which are essentially within the domestic jurisdiction of any state or shall require Members to submit such matters to settlement under the present Charter; but this principle shall not prejudice the application of enforcement

measures under Chapter VII [Action with respect to threats to the peace, breaches of the peace, and acts of aggression]"

The circumstances of adoption of the Charter differ from those of the European Community treaties: the Charter was instituted by the victors of the World War who were concerned with national independence as well as human rights (N. Valiticos, "Droits fondamenteaux de l'homme et compétence nationale des États" in J. O'Reilly (ed.), *Human Rights and Constitutional Law: Essays in Honour of Brian Walsh* (Dublin: Round Hall Press, 1992) p. 56). There is a trend in international law thinking to the effect that the protection of human rights is no longer essentially within the domestic legal order of the State (L'Institut de Droit international, "La protection des droits de l'homme et le principe de nonintervention dans les affaires intérieures des Etats" (1989)). In this work the order approach shows that the protection of human rights is essential to the coherence and legitimation of the domestic legal order of the state; the work argues for concern not about national independence as such but rather about the coherence and legitimation of the legal orders of the Member States and the autonomy essential to avoid a legal revolution.

35. HOW TO TAKE THE PROPOSED DIRECTION

35–1 This proposed direction falls within the bounds of existing European Community law, and may be achieved by two means.

First, by the Court of Justice. Given the basis for this step set out below, taking the step is certainly within the faculty to develop and interpret the law which this court appears to possess. For a court to which the grey line between *ius dicere* and *ius dare* is of little import, there should be no problem.

Secondly, by the Member States acting as the constituent power.

36. SUPPORT WITHIN EUROPEAN COMMUNITY LAW FOR THE PROPOSED DIRECTION

36–1 The proposed direction does not break the integrity of European Community law. European Community law encompasses both the notion of disuniformity and strands of doctrine which support the proposed direction.

Disuniformity[1]

36–2 There are very many limits to uniformity in European Community law, which indicates that there is no grave necessity to insist on uniformity as a constitutional principle not admitting of variation in the application of a European Community rule between the territories of Member States where the rule gives rise to a serious constitutional conflict. The most prominent limits to uniformity in the application of European Community law are the following[2]:

1. The Court of Justice in its early fundamental rights jurisprudence, such as Case 4/73 *Nold*[3] and Case 44/79 *Hauer*[4], recognised that it could not "uphold measures which are incompatible with fundamental rights recognized and protected by the Constitutions"[5] of the Member States. This statement was taken by some commentators and courts, such as by the German Federal Constitutional Court, to mean that the Court of Justice would not uphold a measure which was incompatible with a fundamental right protected by the constitution of a single Member State. However the phrase is admittedly ambiguous, since it possibly only applies where the Community rule conflicts with a fundamental right protected by all (or a majority of) the Member States, and the Court of Justice has not repeated the statement recently. Case C–159/90 *Grogan* is authority to the contrary.[6]

---

1 Or, to negative Dworkin's phrase, distributional inconsistency – *Taking Rights Seriously*, (Sixth impression, Dworkin ed., 1991) (London: Duckworth, 1977) p. 88.

2 For some other examples regarding the European Union in general, *see* O. Lhoest and P. Nihoul, "Le traité de Maastricht: vers l'Union européenne", *Journal des tribunaux*, 28 November 1992, No. 5652. The authors there state that "the application of particular regimes to certain Member States is, in effect, already admitted in principle."

3 [1974] E.C.R. 491.

4 [1979] E.C.R. 3727.

5 Case 4/73 *Nold* [1974] E.C.R. 491, para. 13.

6 [1991] E.C.R. 4685. See above, Part V, para. 30–2, "Irish Constitutional Law – Natural Right v. European Community Law Right".

2. Derogations are already provided for in European Community law (and are restrictively permitted by the Court of Justice[7]), for example to the free movement of goods (Article 36 (EC)), the right of establishment (Article 56 (EC)) and the free movement of services (Article 66 (EC)). Indeed the Court of Justice has itself evolved the category of derogations of imperative requirements of the public interest. As regards the free movement of capital, a Member State whose capital market is disturbed may take protective measures on its own initiative in cases of urgency (Article 73f (EC) and Article 73g (EC)). As regards the common commercial policy, the Commission may authorise a Member State to take protective measures where there are economic difficulties (Article 115 (EC)). As a matter of principle, disuniformity is not *per se* incompatible with the general tasks of the European Community or the specific objectives of its policies.[8]
3. Economic and Monetary Union, as provided for in Article 109j (EC), works on the assumption of a "two-speed Europe" since not all Member States will satisfy the prerequisites to participation.
4. Article 100a(4) (EC) allows for permanent derogation from the adoption of harmonisation measures which are not a means of arbitrary discrimination or a disguised restriction on trade.
5. Article 109i(1) (EC) provides for a suspension of European Community law obligations in the case of sudden crises.
6. Article 234 (EC) provides that the rights and obligations in international agreements concluded before the entry into force of the Treaty "shall not be affected by the provisions of this Treaty."[9]
7. Subsidiarity, which provides for the exercise by the Member States of competences jointly held with the Community (Article 3b (EC)). This concept should encompass judicial subsidiarity.[10] De Witte has suggested that the notion of subsidiarity is broad enough to encompass "the obligation for Community institutions to respect, whenever possible, common or specifically national constitutional values."[11]

---

[7] For an example of the Court's restrictive approach to the derogations to the free movement of services, and for an argument on their insufficiency as a mechanism to protect the fundamental constitutional rights of the Member States, *see* above Part V, para. 30–2.

[8] C.D. Ehlermann, *Increased Differentiation or Stronger Uniformity* (Florence: European University Institute Working Paper R.S.C. No. 95/21, 1995) p. 6.

[9] As regards Ireland, this Article is expressly stated to apply in Part One (principles) Article 5 of the Act Concerning the Conditions of Accession and the Adjustments to the Treaties (the "Accession Treaty").

[10] D.R. Phelan, "The Right to Life of the Unborn v. the Protection of Trade in Services – The European Court of Justice and the Normative Shaping of the European Union" (1992) *Modern Law Review* 670 at p. 688.

[11] B. de Witte, "Community Law and National Constitutional Values" (1991) *Legal Issues in European Integration* 1 at p. 20.

8. Protocols, of which there are many, provide for all kinds of exceptions. For example, as regards the third stage of Economic and Monetary Union, the United Kingdom has an opt-in and Denmark has an opt-out. These special rules allow a Member State not to participate in common institutional and substansive arrangements of constitutional importance for whatever reasons they think sufficient.[12] Another Protocol example, as regards the Free Movement of Persons and Freedom of Information, is the Protocol on the application of Article 40.3.3 of the Irish Constitution, which demonstrates that a Member State can obtain "a 'ring fence' of unlimited duration around, *inter alia*, specific *constitutional* provisions".[13] A final example is the Protocol (No. 2) concerning Article 119 (EC) (the "Barber Protocol") which limits in time the effect of the Court of Justice's rulings on a fundamental European Community law right based on an express Treaty article which is crucial to the attainment of the social objectives of the European Community.

9. The Social Chapter was not signed by the United Kingdom, but is annexed to the Treaty on European Union, and a Protocol allows the other eleven Member States use the institutions of the European Union to implement the Chapter.[14]

10. The purpose of the treaties of adhesion is in part to specify (temporary) derogations.

11. Disuniformity in the application of European Community law by national courts is tolerated in the differences in national remedies and procedural rules[15] and in the interpretation of national law in the light of unimplemented directives. The obligation imposed by Case C–106/89 *Marleasing* on national judges to interpret national law in conformity with European Community law "as far as possible" acknowledges that what may be possible for a national judge may vary.[16] Further, the *CILFIT* doc-

---

12 See F. Snyder, "EMU – Metaphor for European Union" in Dehousse (ed.), *Europe after Maastricht – an Ever Closer Union?* (Munich: Beck, Law Books in Europe, 1994) p. 63 at p. 98.

13 D. Curtin, "The Constitutional Structure of the Union: A Europe of Bits and Pieces" (1993) 30 *Common Market Law Review* 17 p. 49 (original emphasis). This Protocol is annexed both to the European Community and to the European Union treaties.

14 B. de Witte considers that this and other changes brought by the Treaty on European Union "should, if one takes the doctrine of the intangible core seriously, be considered unconstitutional revisions of the EEC Treaty." – "International Agreement of European Constitution", in *The Treaty on European Union: Suggestions for Revision* ('s-Gravenhage: Asser Instituut, 1995) p. 19.

15 The Commission had hoped for a Community competence in the Treaty on European Union to take harmonising measures in this area: [1991] 2 European Community Bull. Supp. 152.

16 [1990] E.C.R. 4135. But see F. Snyder, "The Effectiveness of European Community Law: Institutions, Processes, Tools and Techniques" (1993) 56 *Modern Law Review* 19 where *Marleasing* is put in the light of the principles of effective enjoyment of European

trine[17] allows national courts to refuse to make Article 177 (EC) references, although the doctrine is limited to questions of European Community law which are either irrelevant or the correct application of which is so obvious as to leave no scope for any reasonable doubt.[18]

12. In Opinion 1/76[19] the Court of Justice accepted (as a possibility but not in this case) a legal system where there are divergent interpretations and a consequent effect on legal certainty. The Court of Justice held that it was not feasible to give individuals legal protection in a system involving a third State without this problem.

Further Support from within European Community Law

36–3 The following further arguments can be made from within European Community law.

1. The attainment of "European unity" is dependent (according to European Community law) on the functioning of European Community law. To function in an executive sense European Community law requires an operational national legal order and the prevalence of the rule of law in national jurisdictions. Therefore the proposed direction assists the attainment of the overall objective of European unity, and the attainment of objectives is the most important ground given by the Court of Justice in its judgments, by the Member States in the Treaties, and by the institutions in legislation, for the development of European Community law. This is so unless one aspect of one interpretation of the goal of European unity, the executive uniformity of European Community law, is to be taken as an exceptionless *sine qua non*. It is not an exceptionless *sine qua non*, because there are many exceptions.

2. The proposed direction will be a matter of European Community law. Therefore disuniformity in the application of a particular substantive European Community law rule will be pursuant to the application of this European Community law rule so there will be no non-observance of European Community law. The logic of this argument receives some sup-

---

Community law rights and the Article 5 (EC) duty of solidarity. Curtin has stated that this phrase refers "to the nature of the judicial function *per se* – the Court of Justice naturally enough did not require national judges to assume the legislative task by rewriting the terms of their national law completely." – D. Curtin, "The Decentralised Enforcement of Community Law. Judicial Snakes and Ladders" in D. Curtin and D. O'Keeffe (eds.), *Constitutional Adjudication in European Community and National Law: Essays for the Hon. Mr. Justice T.F. O'Higgins* (Dublin: Butterworths Ireland, 1992) p. 40.

17 Case 283/81 [1982] E.C.R. 3415.

18 *ibid.*

19 [1977] E.C.R. 741 at 761, paras. 20–21.

port from authority from Case C–466/93 *Atlanta Fruchthandelsgesellschaft v. Bundesamt für Ernährung und Forstwirtschaft*: where the national jurisdiction feels that the validity of a European Community rule is seriously in doubt it may refuse to apply that rule as a matter of the European Community law right of litigants to jurisdictional protection.[20] So far as the observance of European Community law is the basis of European Community law (which the Court of Justice feared would be put into question by the suspension of European Community law if it conflicted with national constitutional law), the proposed direction protects that basis. Similarly, the autonomy of the European Community legal order would be protected by the fact that this is a European Community rule. It would not immediately matter to European Community law that the national constitutional court would have a different view of why the rule was non-applicable.

3. The security effect on national courts of the proposed direction may increase the executive uniformity of European Community law.

4. Article F(1) (EU) provides: "The Union shall respect the national identities of its Member States, whose systems of government are founded on the principles of democracy". Since the identities of the Member States differ this article supports a restriction (such as the Proposed Direction) on the current understanding of the uniform application of Community law. As de Witte states: "the fairly vague notion of 'national identity' might become legally relevant by referring to the constitutions as the main depositary of national identity."[21] However, Article F(1) (EU) is one of the Articles over which the Court of Justice is not given jurisdiction (Article L (EU)).

   An argument based on national identity is supported by the policy on culture.[22] Article 128 (EC) provides:

> "1. The Community shall contribute to the flowering of the cultures of the Member States, while respecting their national and regional diversity and at the same time bringing the common cultural heritage to the fore.
>
> . . .
>
> 4. The Community shall take cultural aspect into account in its action under other provisions of this Treaty."

The argument based on national identity is further supported by the objective of the European Union (Preamble (EU), Article A (EU)) and

---

20 [1995] ECR I–3799, para. 20.

21 B. de Witte, "Community Law and National Constitutional Values" (1991) *Legal Issues in European Integration* 20.

22 G.S. Karydis, "Le juge communautaire et la préservation de l'identité culturelle nationale" (1994) 30 *Revue Trimestrielle de Droit Européen* 551 at p. 560, favours a relaxation of the case law of the Court of Justice to accept limits to the principles of market integration necessary to protect national cultural diversity.

the European Community (Preamble (EC)) of "an ever closer union among the *peoples* of Europe" which confirms that these peoples are separate.[23]

5. Even if European Community law is viewed as federal law,[24] a federation does not suppose the degree of legal uniformity which European Community law aims to realise.[25]

6. Direct effect and supremacy have never been recognised as the Court of Justice would like them to be. Not only has the response in principle varied, but so also has the response in practice.[26] As regards uniformity in particular, not only is perfect uniformity not required as a matter of European Community law, even so far as it is required it often does not exist in practice.[27] Nor can it be compelled, since the ultimate legal sanction is penalty payment. Yet the basis of European Community law did not crumble as a result. The Court of Justice should be wary of those who wish to place the foundations of European Community law on federal conceit.

7. Application of European Community law and *effet utile*.[28] Strictly from the European Community law perspective, "The eye cannot say to the hand,

---

23 (Emphasis added.) While the Treaties establishing the European Communities and the Treaty on European Union recognise separate identities and cultures, the Statute of the International Court of Justice (which forms an integral part of the Charter of the United Nations – Article 92 (UN)) recognises different civilisations, albeit in an Article on the appointment of judges. Article 9 (Statute) provides: "in the body as a whole the representation of the main forms of civilisation and of the principal legal systems of the world should be ensured." The relevance of this Article may seem obscure. However, the argument behind this article, *viz.* there is a link between legal system and civilisation which should be respected, is very similar to the argument made here, *viz.* there is a link between legal order and culture and that respecting the one involves respecting the other.

24 See above, Chap. 13.

25 J. Boulouis, "Le droit des Communautés Européennes dans ses rapports avec le droit international général" (1992) Vol. 235 (IV) *Recueil des Cours de l'Academie de Droit International* 19 at p. 79. Federalism as a concept appears to depend much on the arts of the possible: "Identification and understanding of the possible forms of constitutional noncentralization in terms of what is possible and what actually exists is one of the major concerns of the study of federalism."– D.J. Eleizar, "International and Comparative Federalism" (1993) 26 *PS: Political Science and Politics* 190 at p. 192.

26 For example, not until 1989 did the *Conseil d'État* accept a jurisdiction to suspend the application of a *loi* which was posterior to and incompatible with the Community treaties, and the *Conseil d'État* still persists in refusing to accord full direct effect to provisions of directives. See above, Chap. 22, Annex to Part III. France has refused for years to comply with the ruling of the Court of Justice in an Article 169 (EEC) action: Case 167/73 *Commission v. France* [1974] E.C.R. 359, considered above, in para. 8–36.

27 The European Community writ does not run. A good example was given in Case C–466/93 *Atlanta Fruchthandelsgesellschaft v. Bundesamt für Ernährung und Forstwirtschaft*, 9 November 1995, para. 13, where the Administrative Court of Frankfurt Am Main ordered the German Federal authorities to provide certificates of additional banana import quotas contrary to European Community law.

28 Effectiveness of European Community law is a broad concept as F. Snyder points out in "The Effectiveness of European Community Law: Institutions, Processes, Tools and

'I do not need you', nor can the head say to the feet, 'I do not need you'".[29] As Advocate-General Roemer said in Case 26/62 *Van Gend en Loos*, unlimited direct effect would produce the consequences of an uneven development of the law "which consequences do not accord with the essential aim of the Community".[30] Revolution or revolt in national law would cause serious perturbations in national courts on which depends much of the effectiveness of European Community law. Pescatore's analysis, where he focuses on application in fact of European Community law rather than on distinct derivation of rules, would backfire.[31] In any event, Pescatore's version could not extend to a requirement that the rule be operative in all jurisdictions at all times, as the existence of disuniformity proves, unless one is to make the ludicrous claim that the non-application of an European Community law rule by one judge means that it is no longer a rule of law.

8. Judicial policy. If the Court of Justice took the proposed direction, judicial policy of cooperation with national courts would benefit.[32] The Court of Justice has shown itself willing in the past, particularly in the confrontation with the German Federal Constitutional Court, to adapt its jurisprudence to take account of national judicial concerns.[33] There is a lesson to be learned from the demand of Benhadad, king of Syria, on Ahab, king of Israel, to surrender as guarantees of obedience such family members and treasures as Benhadad chose. Ahab consented. But when the powerful Syrian overweeningly sought that his men should go into the Israelite capital to choose the guarantees, Ahab preferred war. This reaction, Daube has pointed out,[34] is to avoid the shame such a penetration would bring, and is related to the rule by which a creditor had to wait outside the poor

---

Techniques" (1993) 56 *Modern Law Review* 19: "it includes – but is not limited to – implementation, enforcement, impact and compliance." Professor Snyder calls "the notion of effective enjoyment" "the most important single principle" of European Community law (at p. 73).

29 The First Letter of St. Paul to the Corinthians, 1 Corinthians 12:21.

30 [1963] E.C.R. 1 at 24; See above, Part II, European Community law, para. 8–22, "Case 26/62 *Van Gend en Loos* – Uniformity".

31 P. Pescatore, "The Doctrine of 'Direct Effect': An Infant Disease of Community Law" (1983) 18 *European Law Review* 155: "If it is not operative, it is not a rule of law."

32 See, *e.g.* Costello J.'s veiled warning in *Attorney General v. X* [1991] 1 I.R. 1 at 15:

> "the attainment of the fundamental objectives of the Treaty is enhanced by laws which assist in the development of a Community in which legitimate differences on moral issues are recognised and which does not seek to impose a spurious and divisive uniformity on its members on such issues."

Pearse, in a different context, has used an interesting metaphor: "[L]ike the preposterous donkey in the pantomime whose head is in a perpetual state of strife with its heels because they belong to different individuals." – P.H. Pearse, "The Spiritual Nation" in *The Murder Machine and other Essays* (Dublin: Mercier, 1976) p. 24.

33 See, *e.g.* T.C. Hartley's account of the *Solange* cases: *Foundations of European Community Law* (2nd ed., Oxford: Clarendon Press 1988).

34 D. Daube, "Ahab and Benhadad: A Municipal Directive in International Relations" (1982) *Juridical Review* 62.

debtor's home until the debtor came out with the pawn. The Court of Justice would better succeed if it waited until the national courts produce the goods by recognising European Community law through national law if they so insist. Furthermore, so far as the Court of Justice has blurred the line between *ius dicere* and *ius dare* in the federalisation of European Community law it may appear unreasonable for it to expect rigid observance of legal obligation. Although the Court of Justice has led the process of legal integration, it has not been a missionary of the Rule of Law.

9. Limitations on transfers of sovereignty. There is an internal limit to European Community law's doctrinal claims. The constitutional character of European Community law is dependent in part on the limitation of sovereign rights in favour of European Community law. Such reasoning was relied on in Case 26/62 *van Gend en Loos* and in Opinion 1/91. However, when it comes to upholding the supremacy of European Community law over conflicting national constitutional law, the Court of Justice does not see itself obstructed by the fact that, as far as national constitutional law is concerned, the limitation of sovereign rights did not extend so far as to avoid all conflict with European Community law howsoever interpreted, and perhaps, depending on the national constitution, could not so extend. (Indeed, in order to establish the supremacy of European Community law in Case 6/64 *Costa v. ENEL* the Court of Justice relied in part on the fiction that there could be no conflict between European Community and national law because the Member States had limited their sovereign rights.) Yet this does seem to be a logical problem. Advocate-General Warner in Case 7/76 *IRCA*[35] believed that this meant the Community had no power to infringe the national constitutional law rights of any Member State. The Court of Justice in Opinion 2/94[36] has given prominence to the principle in Article 3b (EC) that the European Community must act within transferred powers and recognised that no specific competence in human rights has been transferred.

10. According to European Community law, if a national law is not observed in practice, then a restriction on a European Community law right on the basis of that national law is contrary to the principle of proportionality. If the Court of Justice applied the principle to those aspects of the doctrine of direct effect and supremacy which the national courts do not observe (and cannot under pain of legal revolution) then it may be better able to tailor its doctrines.

---

35 [1976] E.C.R. 1213 at 1237. In public international law the extent to which national constitutional law limitations on the treaty-making power can be invoked in public international law is controversial: I. Brownlie, *Principles of Public International Law* (4th ed., Oxford: Clarendon Press, 1990), p. 612. In any event, a strong argument on the intention of the contracting state can be made.

36 Opinion 2/94, *Accession by the European Community to the European Convention for the Protection of Human Rights and Fundamental Freedoms*, 28 March 1996.

37. RESISTANCE WITHIN EUROPEAN COMMUNITY LAW TO THE PROPOSED DIRECTION

Does this mean, as the Court of Justice indicated in Case 11/70 *Internationale Handelsgesellschaft*,[1] that the very basis of Community law is thereby put in doubt? The proposed direction only applies where the very basis of national law is put into question. One can argue, from within European Community law as above, that the answer to the question is no. However this answer is contrary to certain trends in the jurisprudence of the Court of Justice,[2] supported by doctrine. As Pescatore puts it: "Community law carries in itself an 'existential' requirement of primacy: if it is not capable of triumphing in all circumstances over national law, it is ineffective and thus, so far as that is the case [*pour autant*], inexistent." The authorities for and against Direction Two have now received treaty support in Article B of the Common Provisions which provides, as one of the objectives of the Union: "to maintain in full the '*acquis communautaire*' and build on it".

The Court of Justice has held that there are procedural and substantive limits to Treaty amendment.[3] However, even if argument was made on this, it is very difficult to see how such an amendment could fall foul of substantive limits given the existing support in European Community law: in Opinion 1/91, the Court of Justice was confronted by an attempt to institutionally undermine the obligatory character of its decisions, which attempt is very different from an amendment providing an additional exception to uniformity. If the Court of Justice maintained such a hard line whilst national constitutional courts came up against the limits of amendability of national constitutional law, the result could be a standoff closer to simultaneously posing the dilemma of revolt or revolution.

1 Case 11/70 [1970] ECR 1125.
2 See above, Part II, "European Community Law".
3 See above, Part II, Chap. 11, "Amendability".

CONCLUSION

This work has sought to establish the propositions set out in Part I. The importance of these propositions for the future legal shape of Europe will be evident without much ado in a conclusion. If those propositions can be refuted then the refutation must come from argument within the orders.

It is no refutation to state that legal revolutions occurred on the signing and/or the ratification of the Treaties. The legal development of Europe has reached constitutional boundaries which can only be overcome via one of the three directions set out above. The boundaries are drawn deeply across the legal face of Europe and depend not only on the fact that there are separate legal orders competing for a partly common jurisdiction but also because those legal orders have fundamentally different legitimations, yet make similar claims.

There is not only a fundamental conflict between national constitutional law and European Community law, there is also a conflict of fundamentals. Because of the nature of the problems, the competing claims of national and European Community legal orders will clash in the courts. It is extraordinary, both politically and legally, how an international organisation created to serve the needs of its Member States should now be threatening revolutions in the national constitutional law of those Member States. It is a revolution *sub judice* by a lawyer elite who are not even, as revolutionaries do, publicising and justifying the revolution.

The proposed direction presents an evolution from the dichotomous dilemma of revolt or revolution.[1] Extending the analogy of Frankenstein's monster,[2] will European Community law throw the Rule of Law into the Rubicon? This is the one truly shared legal value in the expanded Community, and the *sine qua non* of its legal success.[3] If there are legal revolutions in national

---

1 J.M. Kelly, *A Short History of Western Legal Theory* (Oxford: Clarendon Press, 1992) p. 409: "Just as the experience of the era which, in Western Europe, closed in 1945 led to a firmer entrenchment of constitutionalism and of human rights, as well as to a revival of interest in natural law, so the idea of legality (the rule of law, the *Rechtsstaat*) increased in value and acceptance."

2 B. Rudden, *Basic Community Cases* (Oxford: Oxford Unviversity Press, 1987) p. 52. See para. 8–16, "Case 6/64 *Costa v. ENEL* – The Text of the Judgment".

3 *Cf.* P. Pescatore: the first proposition establishing the essence of the Community is "the recognition of common values" (*The Law of Integration: Emergence of a New Phenomenon in International Relations Based on the Experience of the European Communities* (Leiden: Sitjhoff, 1974) p. 50.); "Les principles généraux du droit régissant la fonction publique internationale", in *Hacia un nuevo orden internacional y europeo*, p. 565 at p. 585, where he calls the Court of Justice a "*felix Curia*" because its control of secondary European Community law is established "on a clear perception of the hierarchy of legal norms and on the general principle of the respect of law".

constitutional law and European Community law holds sway, it will be a temporary victory, for it will have weakened the respect for the Rule of Law, and consequently the authority of the law[4] before all actors in the legal order and political actors, and judges' sense of duty to uphold the law. In attaining its objectives in this way, European Community law will weaken the means of the Rule of Law which enables it to attain them. A means is what law itself is, and as such is worth far more than the present vague notions of Europe, even if such could be identified.[5] The means is in many ways, certainly in permanence and positive contribution to world culture, more European than the end. The end is not worth the means.

4 Whatever the legitimation. What distinguishes legal justification from the open-ended dispute about the basic terms of social life is authority – J. Finnis, "On 'The Critical Legal Studies Movement'", (1973) in E. Eekelar and J. Bell *Oxford Essays in Jurisprudence* (third series, Oxford: Clarendon Press, 1987) p. 145.

5 The notion is debatable – P. Allott, "The European Community is not the True European Community" (1991) 100 *Yale Law Journal* 2485 – although it is a bit like debating the clouds. The overall objective identified by the Court of Justice, "European unity" (Opinion 1/91), appears to be more negative than positive in content. It is the negation of Member State control. The way the Court has, and to an extent must, develop its jurisprudence in response to Member State restrictions explains perhaps in part this negative European vision.

BIBLIOGRAPHY

Abraham, R., *Droit international, droit communautaire et droit français* (1st ed., Paris: Hachette, 1989, with Update, 1990)

Allott, P., "The European Community is Not the True European Community" (1991) 100 *Yale Law Journal* 2485

———, "Reconstituting Humanity – New International Law" (1992) 3 *European Journal of International Law* 219

Alphandery, E., *Observations et amendments présentes au nom de la commission des finances, de l'économie générale et du plan, saisie pour avis*, No. 2676 (Annexe) (Assemblée Nationale: 4 May 1992)

Andrews, J.A., and L.G. Henshaw, "The Irish and Welsh Languages in the Courts: A Comparative Study" (1983) XVIII *Irish Jurist* 1

Aquinas, Saint Thomas, *Summa Theologiae Ia 2ae*, Vol. 28 (ed. T. Gilby, London: Blackfriars, 1966)

Aristotle, *Nichomachean Ethics*, (trans. H. Rackham, Loeb Classical Library, Cambridge, Mass.: Harvard University Press, 1934)

Art, J.-Y., "Primacy and Direct Effect of Community Law: Presentation to the Maastricht Colloquium on EC Law" (Maastricht: Manuscript, 1991)

Bankowski, Z., "How does it feel to be on your own? The Person in the Sight of Autopoiesis" (1994) 7 *Ratio Juris* 254

———, "Social Justice and Equality" (Manuscript, 1992)

———, "Legalism and Legality" (Manuscript, 1992)

Barav, A., "State Liability in Damages for Breach of Community Law in the National Courts" in T. Heukels and A. McDonnell, *The Action for Damages in Community Law* (The Hague: Kluwer Law International, 1997)

Bravav, A., and Philip C. (eds.), *Dictionnaire Juridique des Communautés européennes* (Paris Universitaires de France, 1993)

Barnard, C., "An Irish Solution" (1992) *New Law Journal* 526

Barnes, I., "The Single European Market", in A. Griffiths, *European Community Survey* (Essex: Longman, 1992) p. 15

Barrington, D., "The North and the Constitution" in B. Farrell (ed.), *De Valera's Constitution and Ours* (Dublin: RTÉ, 1988)

———, "The Emergence of a Constitutional Court" in J. O'Reilly (ed.), *Human Rights and Constitutional Law: Essays in Honour of Brian Walsh* (Dublin: The Round Hall Press, 1992)

———, "Some Problems of Constitutional Interpretation" in D. Curtin and D. O'Keeffe (eds.), *Constitutional Adjudication in European Community and National Law: Essays for the Hon. Mr Justice T.F. O'Higgins* (Dublin: Butterworths, Ireland, 1992)

Bell, J., *French Constitutional Law* (Oxford: Clarendon Press, 1992)

Belloubet-Frier, N., "Droit Constitutionnel – France" (1991) 3 *Revue Européenne de Droit Public* 151

Bengoetxea, J., *The Justification of Decisions by the European Court of Justice* (Saarbrucken: Europainstitut der Universität des Saarlandes, 1989)

Bengoetxea, J., "Institutions, Legal Theory, and EC Law" (1991) *Archiv für Rechts und Sozial-philosophie* 195

———, *The Legal Reasoning of the European Court of Justice* (Oxford: Clarendon Press, 1993)

———, "L'État, c'est fini?" (1994) *Rechtstheorie: Zeitschrift für Logik, Methodenlehre, Kybernetik und Soziologie des Rechts* 93

Bieber, R., "Les limites matérielles et formelles à la revision des traités établissant la Communauté Européenne" (1993) 367 *Revue du Marché commun et de l'Union européenne* 343

Binchy, W., "Pluralism, Religious Freedom and Marriage Law" in Treacy B. and Whyte G., (eds.), *Religion, Morality and Public Policy* (Dublin: Dominican Publications, 1995)

Bishops' Conference, "The Value of Human Life" (1995) 262 Position Paper 181

Black, V., "The Confrontation Between Natural and Conventional Rights: A Semiotic Perspective" (1991) LXXVII Heft 1 *Archiv für Rechts und Sozial Politik* 17

Blaizot-Hazard, C., "Les contradictions des articles 54 et 55 de la Constitution face à la hiérarchie des normes" (1992) 5 *Revue du Droit Public* 1293

Boulouis, J., "Le droit des Communautés Européennes dans ses rapports avec le droit international général" (1992) Vol. 235 IV *Recueil des Cours de l'Académie de Droit Internationale* 19

Boyron, S., "The Conseil Constitutionnel and the European Union" (1993) *Public Law* 30

Brandt, W., "A New Europe in Global Perspective" (1991) 3 *Oxford International Review* 60

Brearly, M., and C. Quigley, *Completing the Internal Market of the European Community: 1992 Handbook* (2nd ed., London: Graham & Trotman, 1991)

Brennan, W.J. (Jr.), "The Ninth Amendment and Fundamental Rights" in J. O'Reilly (ed.), *Human Rights and Constitutional Law: Essays in Honour of Brian Walsh* (Dublin: The Round Hall Press, 1992)

Brittan, L., "Institutional Development of the European Community" (1992) *Public Law* 567

Brownlie, I. (ed.), *Basic Documents on Human Rights* (Oxford: Clarendon Press, 1981)

———, *Basic Documents in International Law* (3rd ed., Oxford: Clarendon Press, 1983)

———, *Principles of Public International Law* (4th ed., Oxford: Clarendon Press, 1990)

Buergenthal, T., and Maier, H. G., *Public International Law* (2nd ed., St. Paul, Minnesota, West Publishing Co., 1990)

Burke, Edmund, *Reflections on the Revolution in France* (ed. Conor Cruise O'Brien, Harmondsworth, Penguin, 1976)

Buxbaum, R., "The European Community: Federalism and Legitimacy"

———, and S. Riesenfeld, "Van Gend en Loos: A Pioneering Decision of the Court of Justice of the European Communities" (1964) 58 *American Journal of International Law* 152

Byrne, R., and P.J. McCutcheon, The Irish Legal System (2nd ed., Dublin: Butterworths, 1989)

Callan, P., "Citizens could lose the right of recourse to the Courts" (1992 May 10) The Sunday Tribune

Cappelletti, M., *Judicial Review in the Contemporary World* (Indianapolis: Bobbs-Merril Company, 1971)

——— (ed.), *New Perspectives for a Common Law of Europe* (Leiden: European University Institute, 1978)

———, *The Judicial Process in Comparative Perspective* (Oxford: Clarendon Press, 1989)

——— and W. Cohen, *Comparative Constitutional Law: Cases and Materials* (Indianapolis: Bobbs-Merril Company, 1979)

———, M. Secombe, and J. Weiler, *Integration Through Law: Europe and the American Federal Experience* (Leiden: European University Institute, 1986)

Caro, J.-M., *Observations et amendments présentés au nom de la commission des affaires étrangères, saisie pour avis*, No. 2676 (Annexe) (Assemblée Nationale: 4 May 1992)

Casey, J. P., "*Crotty v. An Taoiseach*: A Comparative Perspective", in J. O'Reilly (ed.), *Human Rights and Constitutional Law: Essays in Honour of Brian Walsh* (Dublin: Round Hall Press, 1992)

———, *Constitutional Law in Ireland* (2nd ed., London: Sweet & Maxwell, 1992)

Cassese, A., *International Law in a Divided World* (Oxford: Clarendon Press, 1986)

———, A., "Some Legal Observations on the Palestinians' Right to Self-Determination" (1993) 4 *Oxford International Review* 10

———, A., A. Clapham, and J. Weiler (eds.), *Human Rights and the European Community* (Baden-Baden: Nomos, 1991)

Cerny, P.G., "The Limits of Deregulation: Transnational Interpretation and Policy Change" (1991) 19 *European Journal of Political Research* 173

Clarke, D.M., "The Role of Natural Law in Irish Constitutional Law" (1982) XVII *Irish Jurist* 187 (N.S.)

———, D.M., "The Constitution and Natural Law: A Reply to Mr Justice O'Hanlon" (1993) 11 *Irish Law Times* 117 (N.S.)

———, D.M., "Natural Law and Constitutional Consistency" in G. Quinn, A. Ingram and S. Livingstone, *Justice and Legal Theory in Ireland* (Dublin: Oak Tree Press, 1995)

Cohen, H., "Current Survey II: Member State Ratification Process of the Treaty on European Union: France" (1993) *European Law Review* 233

Collins, A.M., "Administrative Law Remedies under Chief Justice O'Higgins", in D. Curtin and D. O'Keeffe (eds.), *Constitutional Adjudication in European Community and National Law: Essays for the Hon. Mr Justice T.F. O'Higgins* (Dublin: Butterworths Ireland, 1992)

———, A.M., "The Eleventh Amendment – Problems and Perspectives" (1992) 10 *Irish Law Times* 209 (N.S.)

———, A.M., and J. O'Reilly, *Civil Proceedings and the State in Ireland* (Dublin: Round Hall Press, 1990)

Commission of the European Communities, *Completing the Internal Market: White Paper from the Commission to the European Council* (Commission of the European Communities, June 1985)

Conlan, P. (ed.), *EC/EU Legislation in Ireland* (Dublin: Gill & MacMillan, 1994)

Coppel, J., and A. O'Neill, "The European Court of Justice: Taking Rights Seriously?" (1992) 12 *Legal Studies* 227

Costello, D., "Natural Law, the Constitution, and the Courts" in P. Lynch and J. Meenan, (eds.), *Essays in Memory of Alexis Fitzgerald* (Dublin: Incorporated Law Society of Ireland, 1987)

Council of Europe (ed.), *Universality of Human Rights in a Pluralistic World: Proceedings of the Colloquy organised by the Council of Europe in Cooperation with the International Institute of Human Rights, Strasbourg 17–19 April 1989* (Kehl: Council of Europe, 1989)

Court of First Instance of the European Communities, "Reflections on the Future Development of the Community Judicial System" (1991) 16 *European Law Review* 175

Cramton, R.C., "The Ordinary Religion of the Law School Classroom" (1978) 29 *Journal of Legal Education* 247

Cras, A., trans., Rivero, J., "The Constitutional Protection of Human Rights in French Law" (1977) XII *Irish Jurist* 1.

Craven, G., "Cracks in the Facade of Literalism: is there an Engineer in the House?" (1992) 3 *Melbourne University Law Review* 540

Curtin, D., "The Decentralised Enforcement of Community Law. Judicial Snakes and Ladders" in D. Curtin and D. O'Keeffe (eds.), *Constitutional Adjudication in European Community and National Law: Essays for the Hon. Mr. Justice T.F. O'Higgins* (Dublin: Butterworths, Ireland, 1992)

———, "The Constitutional Structure of the Union: A Europe of Bits and Pieces" (1994) 30 *Common Market Law Review* 17

——— and D. O'Keeffe (eds.), *Constitutional Adjudication in European Community and National Law: Essays for the Hon. Mr Justice T.F. O'Higgins*, (Dublin: Butterworths, Ireland, 1992)

Curzon, L.B., "Logic and Law" (1992) 7 *Student Law Review* 51

——— "Finnis and Natural Law" (1994) 13 *Student Law Review* 56

——— "Weber and the Legal Order" (1994) 12 *Student Law Review* 60

Dallen, R.M. (Jr.), "An Overview of European Community Protection of Human Rights with some special references to the U.K." (1990) 27 *Common Market Law Review* 761

Daly, C.B., *Law and Morals*, (Dublin: Four Courts Press, 1993)

Daube, D., "Intestatus" (1936) 15 *Revue historique de droit français et étranger* 341

———, "The Scales of Justice" (1951) 63 *Juridical Review* 109

———, "Ahab and Benhadad: A Municipal Directive in International Relations" (1982) *Juridical Review* 62

———, "Jehovah the Good" (1990) 1 A Journal of Philosophy and Judaism 17

———, "Addendum to God or Goddess" (1991)

———, "Judas" (1994) 82 California Law Review 95

Davis, M.H., "The Law/Politics Distinction, the French *Conseil Constitutionnel*, and the U.S. Supreme Court" (1986) 34 *American Journal of Comparative Law* 45

———, "A Government of Judges: A Historical Review" (1987) 35 *American Journal of Comparative Law* 559

de Burca, G., "Fundamental Human Rights and the Reach of EC Law" (1993) 13 *Oxford Journal of Legal Studies* 283

de Marnefe, P., "Popular Sovereignty and the *Griswold* Problematic" (1994) 13 *Law and Philosophy* 97

de Schoutheete, P., *Negotiating European Union: the Ambivalent Treaty* (European Studies Centre, Oxford: Lecture: 2 November 1992)

de Witte, B., "Retour à *Costa* La primauté du droit communautaire à la lumière du droit international" (1984) *Revue Trimestrielle de Droit Européen* 425

———, "Community Law and National Constitutional Values" (1991) *Legal Issues in European Integration* 1

———, "International Agreement or European Constitution" in *The Treaty on European Union: Suggestions for Revision* (Gravenhage: Asser Instituut, 1995)

———, "Sovereignty and European Integration: the Weight of Legal Tradition" (1995) 2 *Maastricht Journal of European and Comparative Law* 145

De Zayas, A.-M., "Westphalia, Peace of (1648)" in R. Bernhardt (ed.), *Encyclopedia of Public International Law* (Amsterdam – New York – Oxford: North Holland, 1984)

Debasch, C., and J.-M. Pontier, *Les Constitutions de la France* (2nd ed., Paris: Dalloz, 1989)

Dehousse, R., "1992 and Beyond: the Institutional Dimension of the Internal Market Programme" (1989) 1 *Legal Issues of European Integration* 109

Delacampagne, C., "Un entretien avec John Rawls" (30 November 1993) *Le Monde* 2

Delany, H., "The Scope of Judicial Review A Question of the Source of the Nature of Powers" (1993) 11 *Irish Law Times* 12 (N.S.)

Docksey, C., and K. Williams, "In Search of 1992 – Stroll Through the Law Books" (1992) 132 *Oxford Journal of Legal Studies* 99

Due, O., "Article 5 du traité CEE. Une disposition de caractère fédéral" in *Collected Courses of the Academy of European Law* (Dordrecht: Martinus Nijhoff, 1991) p. 15

———, "A Constitutional Court for the European Communities", in D. Curtin and D. O'Keeffe (eds.), *Constitutional Adjudication in European Community and National Law: Essays for the Hon. Mr Justice T.F. O'Higgins* (Dublin: Butterworths, Ireland, 1992)

Duncan, W., "The Divorce Referendum in the Republic of Ireland: Resisting the Tide" (1988) *International Journal of Law and the Family* 62

———, "Can Natural Law Be Used in Constitutional Interpretation?" (1995) 45 *Doctrine & Life* 125

Duncanson, I., "Legality in Perspectives" (1991) LXVII *Archiv für Rechts und Sozial-Philosophie* 28

Dworkin, R., *Taking Rights Seriously* (Sixth impression, 1991; London: Duckworth, 1977)

———, *Life's Dominion* (London: HarperCollins, 1993)

Edward, D., "Constitutional Rules of Community Law in EEC Competition Cases" in Fordham Corporate Law Institute, *1992 and EEC/U.S. Competition and Trade Law* (New York: Transnational Juris Publications, Inc., 1990).

———, "Is There a Place For Private Law Principles in Community Law?" in H.G. Schermers, T. Heukels and P. Mead (eds.), *Non-Contractual Liability of the European Communities* (Europa Instituut, Leiden: Martinus Nijhoff, 1991)

Ehlermann, C.-D., *Increased Differentiation or Stronger Uniformity* (E.U.I. Working Paper RSC No. 95/21, Florence: European University Institute, 1995)

Eleizar, D.J., "International and Comparative Federalism" (1993) 26 *PS: Political Science and Politics* 190

Elster, J., "Majority Rule and Individual Rights" in S. Schute and S. Hurley (eds.), *On Human Rights* (New York: HarperCollins, 1993)

European Council, "Birmingham Declaration" (1992) 12 (2) E.C. Bull. 9

European University Institute Law Department, *Roundtable on the Maastricht European Union Treaty* (Florence: European University Institute, 1992)

Farrell, B. (ed.), *De Valera's Constitution and Ours* (Dublin: RTÉ, 1988)

Favoreau, L., *Les Cours Constitutionnelles, Que sais-je?* (Paris: Presses universitaires de France, 1986)

Fidler, D.P., "Law, Democracy, and European Integration" (1991) 2 *Oxford International Review* 15

Finer, S.E., *Five Constitutions* (Harmondsworth, Penguin, 1979)

Finer, S.E., V. Bogdanor, and B. Rudden, *Comparing Constitutions* (Oxford: Clarendon Press, 1995)

Finnis, J., "India" (1967) *Annual Review of Commonwealth Law* 36

Finnis, J., "India" (1972) *Annual Review of Commonwealth Law* 39

———, "India" (1973) *Annual Review of Commonwealth Law* 30

———, "Revolutions and Continuity of Law" in A.W.B. Simpson (ed.), *Oxford Essays in Jurisprudence (Second Series)* (Oxford: Clarendon Press, 1973)

———, "The Rights and Wrongs of Abortion" in Dworkin, R.M. (ed.), *The Philosophy of Law* (Oxford: Oxford University Press, 1977)

———, *Natural Law and Natural Rights* (Oxford: Clarendon Press, 1980)

———, "A Bill of Rights for Britain? The Moral of Contemporary Jurisprudence" (1985) LXXI *Proceedings of the British Academy* 303

———, "On 'The Critical Legal Studies Movement'" in E. Eekelaar and J. Bell (eds.), *Oxford Essays in Jurisprudence (Third Series)* (Oxford: Clarendon Press, 1987)

———, *Moral Absolutes: Tradition, Revision, and Truth* (Washington D.C.: The Catholic University of America Press, 1991)

———, "Introduction" in J. Finnis, *Natural Law* (Aldershot: Dartmouth, 1992)

Forde, M., *Constitutional Law of Ireland* (Cork and Dublin: Mercier Press, 1987)

French Delegation to the Ninth Conference of European Constitutional Courts, "Protection constitutionnelle et protection internationale des Droits de l'Homme: concurrence ou complementarité" (1993) *Revue française de droit administratif* 849

Friendly, H.J., "Conference on the Public–Private Distinction" (1982) 130 *University of Pennsylvania Law Review* 1289

Frowein, J.A., "The European Community and the Republican Form of Government" (1984) 82 *Michigan Law Review* 1311

Gaja, G., "New Developments in a Continuing Story: the Relationship between EEC Law and Italian Law" (1990) 27 *Common Market Law Review* 83

Gallagher, P., "The Constitution and the Community" (1993) 2 *Irish Journal of European Law* 129

Gardner, J., "Moralizing the Law" (July 1992) *Times Literary Supplement*

Ghai Y., Luckham R. and Snyder F., *The Political Economy of Law, A Third World* (Delhi: Oxford University Press, 1987)

Gordon, R.W., "Critical legal histories" (1984) *Stanford Law Review* 57

Gouzes, G., *Rapport au nom de la commission des lois constitutionnelles, de la législation et de l'administration générale de la Republique sur le projet de loi constitutionnelle (no. 2623) ajoutant à la Constitution un titre: "De l'Union européenne"*, No. 2676 (Assemblée Nationale: 4 May 1992)

———, *Rapport au nom de la commission des lois constitutionnelles, de la législation et de l'administration générale de la Republique sur le projet de loi constitutionnelle, modifié par le Sénat, ajoutant à la Constitution un titre: "De l'Union européenne"*, No. 2803 (Assemblée Nationale: 18 June 1992)

———, *Rapport supplementaire au nom de la commission des lois constitutionnelles, de la législation et de l'administration générale de la Republique sur le projet de loi constitutionnelle (No. 2623) ajoutant a la Constitution un titre: "De l'Union européenne"*, No. 2684 (Assemblée Nationale: 11 May 1992)

Green, N., "Competition Law", in T.C. Hartley and J.A. Usher, *The Legal Foundations of the Single European Market* (Oxford: Oxford University Press, 1991)

Groux, J., and P. Manin, *Les Communautés européennes dans l'ordre international, Collection "Perspectives européennes"* (ed. Commission of the European Communities, Brussels: Office of Official Publications of the European Communities, 1984)

Guimezanes, N., "L'arret de l'immigration en France? Commentaire de la loi No. 931027 du 24 août 1993 sur la maitrise de l'immigration" (1994) *La Semaine Juridique* (Doctrine) 1

Handoll, J., "State Definition and Free Movement of Workers" (1987) 9 *Dublin University Law Journal* 73

———, *Free Movement of Persons in the EU* (Chichester: John Wiley & Sons, 1995)

Hannon, P., "Law and Morality in Ireland" (1992) Winter *Dlí* 26

Hartley, T.C., *The Foundations of European Community Law* (2nd ed., Oxford: Clarendon Press, 1988)

———, *The Foundations of European Community Law* (3rd ed., Oxford: Clarendon Press, 1994)

———, "The European Court, Judicial Objectivity and the Contribution of the European Union" (1996) 112 *Law Quarterly Review* 95

Heller, A., "The Limits to Natural Law and the Paradox of Evil", in S. Schute and S. Hurley (eds.) *On Human Rights: the Oxford Amnesty Lectures* (New York: HarperCollins, 1993)

Henchy, S., "Precedent in the Irish Supreme Court" (1962) 25 *Modern Law Review* 544

Hervouet, F., "Politique Jurisprudentielle de la Cour de Justice et des Juridictions Nationales: Reception du Droit Communautaire par le Droit Interne" (1992) *Revue de Droit Public* 1257

Hine, R.C., *The Political Economy of European Trade* (Brighton: Wheatsheaf, 1985)

Hogan, G.W., "Unenumerated Personal Rights: *Ryan's* Case Re-evaluated" (1990–1992) XXV–XXVII *Irish Jurist* (N.S.) 95.

———, "The Early Judgements of Mr Justice Brian Walsh" in J. O'Reilly (ed.), *Human Rights and Constitutional Law: Essays in Honour of Brian Walsh* (Dublin: The Round Hall Press, 1992)

———, "The Implementation of European Union law in Ireland: The *Meagher* case and the Democratic Deficit" (1994) 3 *Irish Journal of European Law* 190

———, "The *Meagher* Case and the Executive Implementation of European Directives in Ireland" (1995) 2 *Maastricht Journal of European and Comparative Law* 174

———, "McKinley v. Minister for Defence" (1992) Dublin University Law Journal 115

Hogan, G.W., "The Supreme Court and the Single European Act" (1987) XXII *Irish Jurist* 55

———, and D.G. Morgan, *Administrative Law in Ireland* (2nd ed., London: Sweet & Maxwell, 1992)

———, and Whelan, A., *Ireland and the European Union: Constitutional and Statutory Texts and Commentary* (London: Sweet and Maxwell, 1995)

———, and Whyte, G., *Supplement to the Second Edition of J.M. Kelly: The Irish Constitution* (Dublin: University College Dublin Press, 1988)

———, and Whyte, G., *J.M. Kelly: The Irish Constitution* (3rd ed., Dublin: Butterworths, Ireland, 1994)

Holland, S., *The European Imperative: Economic and Social Cohesion in the 1990's* (Nottingham: Spokesman, 1993)

Horwitz, M.J., "The History of the Public/Private Distinction" (1982) 130 *University of Pennsylvania Law Review* 1423

Hostert, J.M., "The Law of the European Communities and the Law of the Member States" (Oxford: Thesis, 1968)

Humphreys, R., "Constitutional Interpretation" (1993) 15 *Dublin University Law Journal* 59 (N.S.)

———, "Interpreting Natural Rights" (1993–1995) XXV–XXVIII *Irish Jurist* 221

———, "Sex, Dworkin and the Meaning of Life" in G. Quinn, A. Ingram and S. Livingstone (eds.), *Justice and Legal Theory in Ireland* (Dublin: Oak Tree Press, 1995)

Ingram, A., "Federalism in Theory" in G. Quinn, A. Ingram and S. Livingstone, (eds.) *Justice and Legal Theory in Ireland* (Dublin: Oak Tree Press, 1995)

Institut de Droit international, "La protection des droits de l'homme et le principe de non-intervention dans les affaires intérieures des États" (1989)

International Law Commission, "Report" (1967) *American Journal of International Law* 248

Jacobs, F.G., "Is the Court of Justice of the European Communities a Constitutional Court?" in D. Curtin and D. O'Keeffe (eds.), *Constitutional Adjudication in European Community and National Law: Essays for the Hon. Mr. Justice T.F. O'Higgins* (Dublin: Butterworths, Ireland, 1992)

Jacobs, F.G., "The Protection of Human Rights in the Member States of the European Community: the Impact of the Case Law of the Court of Justice", in J. O'Reilly, *Human Rights and Constitutional Law: Essays in Honour of Brian Walsh* (Dublin: The Round Hall Press, 1992)

Jacqué, J.-P., "Commentaire de la décision du Conseil Constitutionnel No. 92308 DC du 9 Avril 1992" (1992) 28 *Revue Trimestrielle de Droit Européen* 251

Jarvis, M., "Review of Bellamy *et al.*, Democracy and Constitutional Culture in the Union of Europe (London, 1995)" (1995) 59 *Modern Law Review* 315

Joerges, C., "European Economic Law, the Nation-State and the Maastricht Treaty", in R. Dehousse, *Europe After Maastricht: An Ever Closer Union?* (Munich: Beck (Law Books in Europe), 1994) 29

——— and Trubeck, (eds.), *Critical legal thought: an American-German Debate*, (Baden-Baden: Nomos, 1989)

Kakouris, C.N., "The position of constitutional rules in the hierarchy of rules of law and its importance for the protection of fundamental rights in the Community legal order", *Eighth Conference on European Constitutional Courts* (1990)

———, "La relation de l'ordre juridique communautaire avec les ordres juridiques des États membres (Quelques réflexions parfois peu conformistes)", in F. Capotorti and C-D Ehlermann *et al.*, *Du droit international au droit de l'intégration, Liber Amicorum Pierre Pescatore* (Baden-Baden: Nomos, 1987)

Karydis, G.S., "Le juge communautaire et la préservation de l'identité culturelle nationale" (1994) 30 *Revue Trimestrielle de Droit Européen* 551

Kelly, J.M., *Fundamental Rights in Irish Law and the Constitution* (1st ed., Dublin: Allen Figgis, 1961)

———, *Fundamental Rights in Irish Law and the Constitution* (2nd ed., Dublin: Allen Figgis, 1967)

———, "Grafting Judicial Review onto a System founded on Parliamentary Supremacy: the Irish Experience", *Human Rights Colloquium* (Florence: European University Institute Document 174/78, 14–17 June 1978)

———, *The Irish Constitution*, (2nd ed., Dublin: University College Dublin, 1984)

———, "Hidden Treasure and the Irish Constitution" (1988) 10 *Dublin University Law Journal* 5 (N.S.)

———, *Belling the Cats: Selected Speeches and Articles of John Kelly* (ed. J. Fanagan, Dublin: Moytura Press/Fine Gael, 1992)

———, *A Short History of Western Legal Theory* (Oxford: Clarendon Press, 1992)

———, G.W. Hogan, and G. Whyte, *Supplement to Second Edition of The Irish Constitution* (2nd ed., Dublin: University College Dublin, 1988)

Kennedy, David, *International Legal Structures* (Baden-Baden: Nomos, 1987)

Kennedy, Duncan, "The Stages of the Decline of the Public/Private Distinction" (1982) *University of Pennsylvania Law Review* 1349

Kingston, J., "Human Rights: The Solution to the Abortion Question" in C. Gearty and A. Tomkins (eds.), *Understanding Human Rights* (London and New York: Mansell, 1996)

———, and Whelan, A. with Bacik I., *Abortion and the Law*, (Dublin: Round Hall Sweet & Maxwell, 1997)

Laffan, B., "The European Community Dimension in Irish Government" in Chubb, B., *The Government and Politics of Ireland* (London and New York: Longman, 1992)

Lambert, E., *Le gouvernement des juges et la lutte contre la legislation sociale aux États-Unis,* (Paris: Giard, 1921)

Langenfeld, C., and A. Zimmermann, "The Interrelation between Domestic Constitutional Law, the European Convention on Human Rights and Community Law – Some Remarks on the Recent Decisions in Dublin, Strasbourg and Luxembourg Concerning the Distribution of Information about Abortions in Ireland (English Summary)" (1992) 52 2 *Zeitschrift für auslanisches ofentliches Recht und Volkerrecht* (Heidelberg Journal of International Law) 314

Larché, J., *Rapport fait au nom de la commission des Lois constitutionnelles, de législation, du suffrage universel, du Règlement et d'administration générale sur le projet de loi constitutionnelle adoptée par l'Assemblée Nationale ajoutant à la Constitution un titre: "Des Communautés européennes et de l'Union européenne",* No. 2676 (Annexe) (Sénat: 27 May 1992)

Lasok, D., "Part I: Towards a Political Union" (1992) 6 *Student Law Review* 36

———, "Part II: Towards an Economic and Monetary Union" (1992) 7 *Student Law Review* 33

———, *Lasok and Bridge's Law and Institutions of the European Union* (6th ed., London: Butterworths, 1994)

——— and J.W. Bridge, *Law and Institutions of the European Community* (5th ed., London: Butterworths, 1991)

Lasok, P., *Unwritten Principles of Community Law,* Nr. 8 (Europa-Institut der Universitat des Saarlandes: 10 December 1982)

Law Enforcement Commission, *Report to the Secretary of State for Northern Ireland and the Minister for Justice of Ireland, Cmnd. 5627* (London: HMSO, 1974)

Le Fur, L., *L'État fédéral et confédération des États* (Paris: 1896) pp. 540–589

Leben, C., "A propos de la nature juridique des Communautés européennes" (1991) *Droits – Revue française de Théorie juridique* 61

Lenaerts, K., *Le Juge et la Constitution aux Etats-Unis d'Amerique et dans l'Ordre Juridique Européen* (Brussels: Bruylant, 1988)

———, "Fundamental Rights to be Included in a Community Catalogue" (1991) 16 *European Law Review* 367

Lhoest, O., and P. Nihoul, "Le traité de Maastricht: vers l'Union Européenne" (1992, 28 November) 5652 *Journal des tribunaux*

Longo, G.E., "La jurisprudence la plus récente de la Cour de Cassation Italienne: en matière d'application de la Convention Européene des Droits de l'Homme", in J. O'Reilly (ed.), *Human Rights and Constitutional Law: Essays in Honour of Brian Walsh* (Dublin: The Round Hall Press, 1992)

Louis, J.-V., *The Community Legal Order, The European Perspectives Series* (ed. Commission of the European Communities, Brussels: Office for Official Publications of the European Communities, 1990)

———, and A. Alen, "La Constitution et la Participation à la Communauté Européenne" (1994) 27 *Revue belge de droit international* 81

Luchaire, F., "Le Conseil Constitutionnel et la Souveraineté Nationale" (1991) *Revue de Droit Public* 1499

———, "L'Union Européenne et la Constitution" (1992) *Revue de Droit Public* pp. 589–607, 933–955, 955–979, 1587–1624

Lukes, S., "Five Fables about Human Rights", in S. Schute and S. Hurley (eds.), *On Human Rights* (New York: HarperCollins, 1993)

Lysaght, C., "The Status of International Agreements in Irish Domestic Law" (1994) 12 *Irish Law Times* 171

MacCormick, N., "Beyond the Sovereign State" (1993) 56 *Modern Law Review* 1

MacIntyre, A., *Whose Justice? Which Rationality?* (London: Duckworth, 1988)

Lord Mackenzie Stuart, "Problems of the European Community – Transatlantic Parallels" (1987) 36 *International and Comparative Law Quarterly* 183

———, "Subsidiarity, A Busted Flush?" in D. Curtin and D. O'Keeffe (eds.), *Constitutional Adjudication in European Community and National Law: Essays for the Hon. Mr Justice T.F. O'Higgins* (Dublin: Butterworths, Ireland, 1992)

Maguire, J., and J. Noonan, *Maastricht and Neutrality* (Cork: People First/ Meitheal, 1992)

Mancini, F., *Safeguarding Human Rights: the Role of the Court of Justice of the European Communities* (Bologna: John Hopkins University Occasional Paper No. 62, 1990)

Mancini, G. F., "The Making of a Constitution for Europe" (1989) *Common Market Law Review* 595

March Hunnings, N., "The Stanley Adams Affair or the Biter Bit" (1987) *Common Market Law Review* 65

Marx, K. and Engels, F., *Selected Works* (Moscow: Progress Publishers, 1968) (Seventh Printing 1986)

Mathieu, B., "Note sur la décision du Conseil constitutionnel du 27 juillet 1994 relative au respect du corps humain" (1995) *Recueil Dalloz Sirey (Jurisprudence)* 238

McCarthy, N., "Observations on the Protection of Fundamental Rights in the Irish Constitution", in D. Curtin and D. O'Keeffe (eds.), *Constitutional Adjudication in European Community and National Law: Essays for the Hon. Mr Justice T.F. O'Higgins* (Dublin: Butterworths, Ireland, 1992)

McMahon, B. and Murphy, F., *European Community Law in Ireland* (Dublin: Butterworths, Ireland, 1989)

Moravcsik, A., "Preferences and Power in the European Community: a Liberal Intergovernmentalist Approach" (1993) 314 *Journal of Common Market Studies* 473

Morton, F.L., "Judicial Review in France: A Comparative Analysis" (1988) 36 *American Journal of Comparative Law* 89

Murphy, T., "Democracy, Natural Law, and the Irish Constitution" (1993) 11 *Irish Law Times* 81

Neill, P., "The European Court of Justice: a Case Study in Judicial Activism" (Oxford: Manuscript, 1995)

Nemeth, C.P., "A Commentary on the Natural Law, Moral Knowledge and Moral Application" (1992) 34 Catholic Lawyer 227

Newman, J., *Foundations of Justice: A Historico-Critical Study in Thomism* (Cork: Cork University Press, 1954)

Nicholas, B., "Fundamental Rights and Judicial Review in France" (1978) *Public Law* 82

Nixson, F.I., "Controlling the Transnationals? The UN Code of Conduct" in Ghai Y., Luckham R. and Snyder F., The Political Economy of Law: A Third World Reader (Delhi: Oxford University Press 1987)

O'Carroll, N., "The Right to Die: A Critique of the Supreme Court Judgment in 'the Ward' Case" (1995) 84 *Studies* 375

O'Dowd, "Dignity and Personhood in Irish Constitutional Law", in G. Quinn, A. Ingram and S. Livingstone (eds.), *Justice and Legal Theory in Ireland* (Dublin: Oak Tree Press, 1995)

O'Flaherty, H., "Opening Congress of the Trier Academy of European Law" (1992) 10 *Irish Law Times* 22

O'Hanlon, R., "*Attorney General v. X: R v. Dudley and Stephens* reconsidered" (1992) 10 *Irish Law Times* 86

———, "The Judiciary and the Moral Law" (1993) 11 *Irish Law Times* 129

———, "Natural Rights and the Irish Constitution" (1993) 11 *Irish Law Times* 8

O'Higgins, T.F., "The Constitution and the Communities' Scope for Stress?" in J. O'Reilly (ed.), *Human Rights and Constitutional Law, Essays in Honour of Brian Walsh* (Dublin: The Round Hall Press, 1992)

O'Keeffe, D., "Union Citizenship", in D. O'Keeffe and P.M. Twomey, *Legal Issues of the Maastricht Treaty* (London: Wiley Chancery Law, 1994)

O'Leary, S., "The Court of Justice as a Reluctant Constitutional Adjudicator: Note on Case 159/90 *S.P.U.C. v. Grogan*" (1992) *European Law Review* 139

———, "The Relationship Between Community Citizenship and the Protection of Fundamental Rights in Community Law" (1995) *Common Market Law Review* 519

O'Neill, A., "Proportionality and the Judicial Review of Legislation in the United Kingdom" (Manuscript, 1992)

O'Reilly, J., (ed.), *Human Rights and Constitutional Law: Essays in Honour of Brian Walsh* (Dublin: The Round Hall Press, 1992)

———, "Judicial Review and the Common Fisheries Policy in Community Law" in D. Curtin and D. O'Keeffe (eds.), *Constitutional Adjudication in European Community and National Law: Essays for the Hon. Mr Justice T.F. O'Higgins* (Dublin: Butterworths, Ireland, 1992)

Oliver, P., "The French Conseil Constitutionnel and the Treaty of Maastricht" (1994) *International and Comparative Law Quarterly* 1

Onestini, C., "Whose subsidiarity?" (1993) 4 *Oxford International Review* 29

Padoa-Schioppa, T., *Efficiency, Stability, and Equity: a Strategy for the Evolution of the Economic System of the European Community* (Oxford: 1987)

Pearse, Pádraig H., "Ghosts" in *The Murder Machine and Other Essays* (Dublin: Mercier, 1976)

———, "The Murder Machine" in *The Murder Machine and Other Essays* (Dublin: Mercier, 1976)

———, "The Separatist Idea" in *The Murder Machine and Other Essays* (Dublin: Mercier, 1976)

———, "The Sovereign People" in *The Murder Machine and Other Essays* (Dublin: Mercier, 1976)

———, "The Spiritual Nation" in *The Murder Machine and Other Essays* (Dublin: Mercier, 1976)

Pescatore P., "Les Principes Généraux du Droit Régissant la Fonction Publique Internationale", *Hacia un Nuevo Orden Internacional y Europeo* 565

———, *The Law of Integration – Emergence of a new phenomenon in international relations based on the experience of the European Communities* (Leiden: Sitjhoff, 1974)

———, *L'ordre juridique des Communautes Européennes: Etude des sources du droit communautaire* (Liège: 1975)

———, "The Doctrine of 'Direct Effect': An Infant Disease of Community Law" (1983) 18 *European Law Review* 155

Phelan, D.R., "The Right to Life of the Unborn v. the Promotion of Trade in Services – The European Court of Justice and the Normative Shaping of the European Union" (1992) 55 *Modern Law Review* 670

———, "Between the Single Market and the European Union" (1993) *PS: Political Science and Politics* 732

———, "'Necessitated' by the Obligations of Membership? Article 29.4.5 of the Constitution" (1993) 11 *Irish Law Times* 272

———, "The Concept of Social Rights" (1994) 16 *Dublin University Law Journal* 105

———, "Two Hats, One Wig, No Halo" (1995) 45 *Doctrine & Life* 130

Poiares Maduro, M., "*Keck*: The end? The beginning of the end? Or just the end of the beginning?" (1994) 3 *Irish Journal of European Law* 30

Pollard, D., "France's *Conseil Constitutionnel* – Not Yet a Constitutional Court?" (1988) XXIII *Irish Jurist* 2

Pope Jean Paul II, *Crossing the Threshold of Hope* (London: Jonathan Cape, trans. by Alfred A. Knopf Inc., 1994)

Quinn, G., "Reflections on the Legitimacy of Judicial Activism in the Field of Constitutional Law" (1991) Winter *Dlí* 29

———, "Book Review of J.M. Kelly, A Short History of Western Legal Theory" (1993–1995) XXVIII–XXX *Irish Jurist* 408

———, "Introduction", in G. Quinn, A. Ingram and S. Livingstone (eds.), *Justice and Legal Theory in Ireland* (Dublin: Oak Tree Press, 1995)

Quinn, G., A. Ingram, and S. Livingstone (eds.) *Justice and Legal Theory in Ireland* (Dublin: Oak Tree Press, 1995)

Rasmussen, H., *On Law and Policy in the European Court of Justice* (Dordrecht-Boston Martinus Nijhoff, 1986)

Rawls, J., "Justice as Fairness: Political not Metaphysical" (1985) *Philosophy and Public Affairs* 223

———, "The Law of Peoples", in S. Schute and S. Hurley (eds.), *On Human Rights: the Oxford Amnesty Lectures* (New York: HarperCollins, 1993)

Reid, M., *The Impact of European Community Law on Irish Constitutional Law* (Dublin: Irish Centre for European Law, 1991)

Renoux, T. S., "Le droit au recours juridictionnel" (1993) 3675 19 *La Semaine Juridique (Doctrine)* 211

Reuter, P., "Les recours de la Cour de Justice des Communautés Européennes à des principes généraux de droit", *Problèmes de droit des gens: Mélanges offerts à Henri Rolin* (Paris: Editions A. Pedone, 1964)

Rice, C.E., "Some Reasons for a Restoration of Natural Law Jurisprudence" (1989) 24 3 *Wake Forest Law Review* 539

Riesenfeld, S., "The Doctrine of Self-Executing Treaties and Community Law: A Pioneer Decision of the Court of Justice of the European Community" (1973) 67 *American Journal of International Law* 504

Riesenfeld, S., *Cases and Notes, Comparative Law Materials for Boalt Hall School of Law,* (Berkeley: Boalt Hall, 1990)

———, "Decisions of Foreign Courts – *In re Nicolo*" (1990) 84 *American Journal of International Law* 764

———, *Judicial Organization and Sources of Law, Comparative Law Materials for Boalt Hall School of Law* (1990)

———, *Judicial Review of the Constitutionality of Legislation in the Light of Comparative Law* (Berkeley: Boalt Hall, 1991)

———, "The Coming of Europe" (1993) 16 *Hastings International and Comparative Law Review* 461

———, "Review of J. Schwarze, Administrative Law (1992)" (1994) 42 *American Journal of Comparative Law* 449

———, and Buxbaum R., "*Van Gend en Loos*: A Pioneering Decision of the Court of Justice of the European Communities" (1964) 58 *American Journal of International Law* 152.

Rivero, J., "The Constitutional Protection of Human Rights in French Law" (1977) XII *Irish Jurist* 1 (trans. A. Cras)

Rodota, S., *Law and Moral Dilemmas Affecting Life and Death A General Presentation of the Issues, Law and moral dilemmas affecting life and death. Proceedings of the 20th Colloquy on European Law.* (Glasgow: Council of Europe, 1990)

Romeo-Casabona, C., *Human Life as Jurisdictional Value Protected by Criminal Law, Law and Moral Dilemmas Affecting Life and Death, Proceedings of the 20th Colloquy on European Law.* (Glasgow: Council of Europe, 1990)

Rorty, R., "Human Rights, Rationality, and Sentimentality" in S. Schute and S. Hurley, *On Human Rights: the Oxford Amnesty Lectures* (New York: HarperCollins, 1993)

Roseren, P., "The Application of Community Law by French Courts from 1982 to 1993" (1994) *Common Market Law Review* 315

Ross, M., "Beyond *Francovich*" (1993) 56 *Modern Law Review* 55

Rousseau, D., "Chronique de jurisprudence constitutionnelle 1992–1993" (1994) *Revue de Droit Public* 101

Rudden, B., *Basic Community Cases* (Oxford: Clarendon Press, 1987)

———, and L. Kahn-Freund, *A Source-Book on French Law* (ed. B. Rudden, Oxford: Clarendon Press, 1991)

——— and D. Wyatt, *Basic Community Laws* (Oxford: Clarendon Press, 1994)

———, and Frier S.E. and Bogdanor, Comparing Constitutions (Oxford: Clarendon Press, 1995)

Rullier, B., "L'application de l'article 884 de la Constitution au premier semestre, 1994" (1994) 19 *Revue française de Droit constitutionnel* 553

Ryssdal, R., "Brian Walsh and the European Court of Human Rights" in J. O'Reilly (ed.), *Human Rights and Constitutional Law: Essays in Honour of Brian Walsh* (Dublin: The Round Hall Press, 1992)

Schermers, H.G., "The European Communities Bound by Fundamental Human Rights" (1990) 27 *Common Market Law Review* 249

———, "The Scales in Balance: National Constitutional Courts v. Court of Justice" (1990) 27 *Common Market Law Review* 97

———, "Case note on Opinion 1/91 and Opinion 1/92" (1992) 29 *Common Market Law Review* 991

———, "Statement" (1992) *EuropaRecht* 49

Schrans, G., *The Morality and Instrumentality of European Economic Law,* (Gent: Rijksuniversiteit).

Sheehy, G., "The Right to Marry", in J. O'Reilly (ed.), *Human Rights and Constitutional Law: Essays in Honour of Brian Walsh* (Dublin: The Round Hall Press, 1992)

Sheridan, M., and J. Cameron, *EC Legal Systems: An Introductory Guide* (London: Butterworths, 1992)

Smyth, M., "The Relationship between Law and Morality in Irish Constitutional Law" (1992) Winter *Dlí* 28

Snyder, F., "Law and Development in the Light of Dependency Theory" (1980) 14 *Law and Society Review* 723

———, *New Directions in European Community Law* (London: Weidenfeld and Nicolson, 1991)

———, "The Effectiveness of European Community Law: Institutions, Processes, Tools and Techniques" (1993) 56 *Modern Law Review* 19

———, "Droit, Symboles et Politique Mediterranéenne: Réflexions sur Quelques Décisions Récentes de la Cour de Justice Européenne" in J.

Bourrinet, (ed.) *La Mediterrannée: Espace de Coopération – en l'honneur de Maurice Flory* (Paris: Economica, 1994)

Snyder, F., "EMU – Metaphor for European Union? Institutions, Rules and Types of Regulation", in Renaud Dehousse, (ed.) *Europe After Maastricht: An Ever Closer Union?* (Munich: Beck (Law Books in Europe), 1994)

——— and P. Slinn (eds.), *International Law of Development: Comparative Perspectives* (Abingdon Professional Books: 1987)

———, Ghai, Y., and Luckham R., The Political Economy of Law: A Third World Reader (Delhi: Oxford University Press, 1987)

Stein, E., "Toward Supremacy of Treaty – Constitution by Judicial Fiat in the European Economic Community" (1965) 48 *Rivista di Diritto Internazionale* 3

———, "Uniformity and Diversity in a Divided Power System: the United States' Experience" (1986) 61 *Washington Law Review* 1081

———, "External Relations of the European Community: Structure and Process" in *Collected Courses of the Academy of European Law* (Dordracht: Martinus Nijhoff, 1991)

Sandalow, T., and E. Stein, *Courts and Free Markets – Perspectives from the United States and Europe* (Oxford: Clarendon Press, 1982)

Strange, S., *States and Markets* (London: Pinter, 1988)

Sutherland, P., "Twin Perspectives: an Attorney General Views Political and European Dimensions" in B. Farrell (ed.), *De Valera's Constitution and Ours* (Dublin: RTÉ, 1988)

Symmons, C.R., "Ireland" in P.M. Eisemann, The Integration of International and European Community Law into the National Legal Order: A Study of the Practice in Europe (The Hague – London – Boston: Kluwer Law International 1996)

Szentes, T., *The Transformation of the World Economy* (London: ZED Books, 1988)

Tchakaloff, C., "Les mésures françaises d'application des normes communautaires" (1994) 10 *Revue française de droit administratif* 115

Temple-Lang, J., *European Community Law, Irish Law and the Irish Legal Profession – Protection and Cooperation between Member States and the Community* (Dublin: Trinity College Dublin, 1982)

———, "Constitution or Treaty", *1996 Inter-Governmental Conference: Issues, Options, Implications* (Dublin: Institute for European Affairs, 1995)

Lord Templeman, "The House of Lords: Supreme or Superfluous?" (Oxford: Unpublished Speech at University College, 1992)

Teubner, G., "How the Law Thinks: Toward a Constructivist Epistemology of Law" (1989) 23 *Law and Society Review* 727

———, "Global Bukinawa: the Politics of Lex Mercatoria" (First Draft, 1991)

———, "And God laughed . . . " (Florence: European University Institute Working Paper, 1989)

Teubner, G., and T. Daintith, "Contract and Organisation: Legal Analysis in the Light of Economics and Social Theory" in G. Farjat, *The contribution of economics to legal analysis: the concept of the firm* (1986)

Thomson, D., *Democracy in France since 1870* (5th ed., Oxford: Oxford University Press, 1969)

Thomson, J.J., "A Defence of Abortion" in R.M. Dworkin, *The Philosophy of Law* (Oxford: Oxford University Press, 1977)

Travers, N., "Current Survey: Member States: Ireland: the Implementation of Directives into Irish Law" (1995) 20 *European Law Review* 103

Treacy, B., and G. Whyte (eds.), *Religion, Morality and Public Policy* (Dublin: Dominican Publications, 1995)

Tribe, L.H., *Constitutional Choices* (Cambridge, Mass.: Harvard University Press, 1985)

Turley, J., "Introduction: the Hitchhiker's Guide to CLS, Unger, and Deep Thought" (1987) 81 *Northwestern University Law Review* 593

Usher, J., "Current Survey: Legal Order of the Communities: *Simmenthal*" (1978) *European Law Review* 214

Vaitsos, C., "Legal Issues in the Revision of the International Patent System" in Ghai Y., Luckham R. and Snyder F., The Political Economy of Law: A Third World Reader (Delhi: Oxford University Press, 1987)

Valiticos, N., "Droits fundamenteaux de l'homme et compétence nationale des États", in J. O'Reilly (ed.), *Human Rights and Constitutional Law: Essays in Honour of Brian Walsh* (Dublin: The Round Hall Press, 1992)

Van der Meersch, W.G., "L'Ordre juridique des Communautés européennes et le Droit internatonal" (1975) 148 (V) *Recueil des Cours de l'Academie de Droit International* 1

van Gerven, W., "Court Decisions, General Principles and Legal Concept: Ingredients of a Common Law of Europe", *Teaching the Common Law of Europe* (Maastricht: Maastricht Colloquium, 1991)

Vaughan, D. (ed.), *Law of the European Communities*, (London: Butterworths, 1990)

Vedel, G., "The *Conseil Constitutionnel*: Problems of Legitimization and Interpretation" in E. Smith (ed.), *Constitutional Justice under Old Constitutions* (The Hague: Kluwer Law International, 1995)

Ver Loren Van Themaat, P., "Some Preliminary Observations on the Intergovernmental Conferences: the Relations between the Concepts of a Common Market, a Monetary Union, an Economic Union, a Political Union, and Sovereignty" (1991) 28 *Common Market Law Review* 291

Verdier, M.–F., "La révision constitutionnelle du 25 juin 1992 nécessaire à la ratification du traité de Maastricht et à l'extension des provisions des assemblées parlementaires françaises" (1994) *Revue de Droit Public* 1137

Verzijl, J.H.W., *International Law in Historical Perspective – Part II: International Persons*, (Leiden: Sijthoff, 1969)

Walbroeck, M., "Contributions à l'étude de la nature juridique des Communautés Européennes", *Problèmes de droit des gens: Mélanges offerts à Henri Rolin* (Paris: Editions A. Pedone, 1964)

———, "The Emergent Doctrine of Federal Preemption" in T. Sandalow and E. Stein (eds.), *Courts and Free Markets* (Oxford: Clarendon Press 1982)

Waline, M., "Droit administratif" in B. Rudden, *A Source-Book on French Law* (Oxford: Clarendon Press, 1963)

Walsh, B., "The Origins of Human Rights", *Rett Og Rettsal (Festschrift für Rolv Ryssdal* (Oslo: 1984)

———, "Reflections on the Effects of Membership of the European Communities in Irish Law" in F. Capotorti, C.D. Ehlerman, et al. (eds.), *Du droit international au droit de l'intégration, Liber Amicorum Pierre Pescatore* (Baden–Baden: Nomos, 1987)

———, "The Constitution: a View from the Bench", in B. Farrell, (ed.), *De Valera's Constitution and Ours* (Dublin: RTÉ, 1988)

Ward, I., "In Search of a European Identity: Review of J. Derrida, The Other Heading: Reflections on Today's Europe" (1994) 57 *Modern Law Review* 315

Weber, L., "*Interhandel* Case" in R. Bernhardt (ed.), *Encyclopedia of Public International Law* (Amsterdam–New York: Holland, 1981)

Weiler, J., "The Community System: the Dual Character of Supranationalism" (1981) 1 *Yearbook of European Law* 267

———, "The Protection of Fundamental Rights within the Legal Order of the European Communities", in Bernhart and Jolowicz, *International Enforcement of Human Rights: reports submitted to the Colloquium of the International Association of Legal Science* (Heidelberg: 28–30 August 1985)

West, A. *et al.*, *The French Legal System, an introduction* (London: Fourmat Publishing, 1992)

Wheare, K.C., *Federal Government* (4th ed., Oxford: Oxford University Press, 1963)

Whelan, A., "Constitutional Law – *Meagher v. Minister for Agriculture*" (1993) 15 *Dublin University Law Journal* 152

———, "Constitutional Amendments in Ireland: The Competing Claims of Democracy" in G. Quinn, A. Ingram and S. Livingstone (eds.), *Justice and Legal Theory in Ireland* (Dublin: Oak Tree Press, 1995) 45

———, "Constitutional Democracy, Community and Corporatism in Ireland" in G. Quinn (ed.), *Irish Human Rights Yearbook 1995* (Dublin: Round Hall Sweet & Maxwell, 1995)

——— and Hogan, G.W., *Ireland and the European Union: Constitutional and Statutory Texts and Commentary* (London: Sweet & Maxwell, 1995)

——— and Kingston, J., "The Protection of the Unborn in Three Legal Orders [in three parts]" (1993) 10 *Irish Law Times* 93, 104, 166

———, and Kingston J., with Bacik I., *Abortion and the Law* (Dublin: Round Hall Sweet & Maxwell, 1997)

Whyte, G., "Education and the Constitution: Convergence of Paradigm and Praxis" (1990–1992) XXV–XXVII *Irish Jurist* 69

———, "Natural Law and the Constitution" (1995) 45 *Doctrine & Life* 481

——— and Hogan, G.W., *Kelly: The Irish Constitution* (3rd ed., Dublin: Butterworths, Ireland, 1994)

——— and B. Treacy (eds.), *Religion, Morality and Public Policy* (Dublin: Dominican Publications, 1995)

———, and Hogan, G.W., *Supplement to The Second Edition of J.M. Kelly: The Irish Constitution* (Dublin: University College Dublin Press, 1988)

Wieacker, F., "The Foundations of European Legal Culture" (1990) 38 *American Journal of Comparative Law* 1

Wilkinson, B., "Abortion, The Irish Constitution and the EEC" (1992) *Public Law* 19

Wright, G., and A.M. Soboul, "History of France", *Encyclopedia Britannica – Macropedia* (1982) p. 648

Wyatt, D., "New Legal Order or Old?" (1982) *European Law Review* 147

——— and A. Dashwood, *Wyatt and Dashwood's European Community Law* (London: Sweet & Maxwell, 1993)

INDEX

abortion, 282
  criminal offence in Irish law, 376–377
  information concerning, 372, 377, 379, 387–388, 397
  right to life of unborn in Irish constitutional law, 371–372, 397, 398–400
    European Community law right on services and, 372–391
  service, as, 376–381
    freedom to provide abortions for money, 396n
    prohibition on restrictions, 381–383
    rights in national courts, 382
  United Kingdom legislation, 379
Abraham, R., 175, 197, 259, 261n
administrative law, 314
  Irish law
    extension of constitutional justice into, 314–317
amendability of European Community law, 12, 16, 148–158
  appropriate measures, power of Council to take, 148–149
  automatic expiry
    exclusion of possibility of, 148
  general rules, 149–151
  limits to, 12–13, 16, 41
    procedural limits, 153–154
    substantive limits, 154–158
  unanimity, requirement of, 151–152
  unilateral change, 152
amendability of national constitutional law, 10
  French constitutional law, 199, 206–212
  Irish constitutional law, 357, 359–367, 368
amendability of treaties, 149–150, 152, 154
  restrictions on, 150
Aquinas, Thomas, 279, 280n, 281, 284n
Association Agreements, 35
  direct effect, 91
Australian Constitution, 417–418
autonomous law, 27
autonomous validity of European Community law, 11–13, 20, 22, 27, 28
  national courts, before, 55

Barnard, 392n
Belgium, 157n
Bell, J., 167n, 169, 250
Birmingham Declaration, 141
Bonaparte, Louis-Napoleon, 191
Brussels Convention on the Mutual Recognition of Judgments in Civil and Commercial Matters, 161

Cappelletti, M., 167, 295n, 416n
Caro's Report, 214n, 226
Casey, J., 278, 291n, 327n, 343
Cerny, P.G., 407n
Charles X (France), 191
Charter of the United Nations, 68, 126, 144, 418n–419n
Christianity
  recognition of, in Irish Constitution, 284–285
citizenship
  European Community law perception, 141–143
  European Union citizen, 8, 23, 141
    express rights of, 122, 142–143, 385n
  French constitutional law perception, 224–225
  national citizenship, 141–142
  public international law perception, 141
Codification of State Responsibility, 100

Collins, A., 346
commercial information
right to provide and receive, 394
Common Commercial Policy, 35
common defence, 149
common good
Irish constitutional law, 307–310
meaning of, 309–310, 402
moral aspect of society, 308
restriction of idea of people as unlimited sovereign, 308–309
Member States, 310
Commonwealth of Australia Constitution Act 1900, 417n
Community institutions, 23, 153, 161
Community law. *see* **European Community law**
compensation
breaches of Community law, 90
non-implementation of directive, 88–90
competences, 12, 32–37
Court of Justice interpretation, 34
European Community law perception, 33–35, 35–37
fundamental rights, 121–123
basis of extension of Community competence, 123–139
implied external competence, 36–37
public international law perception, 32, 35
sovereignty and
distinction between, 200–201
transfer of competence distinguished, 74
transfer of. *see* **transfer of competences**
Treaty establishing the European Community, 33
treaty-making powers, 35–37
express powers, 35
implied, 36–37
competition rules, 64
conflicts, 4, 369–370, 430
conflicting claims, 15
courts, between, 15
French constitutional law v. European Community law, 163–164, 172–173, 235, 254
domestic measures, 176–183
executive measures, 183–185
jurisdiction of *Conseil Constitutionnel,* 173–185
jurisdiction of *Conseil d'Etat,* 255, 256–265
jurisdiction of *Cour de Cassation,* 265–269
treaties, agreements and Council directives, 173–175
types of conflict, 172–173
fundamental commitments, between, 15, 164, 272, 299–302
fundamental rights, 15
conflict of fundamentals, 15, 388–391
derogations from European Community law economic principle, rights as, 392–400
different interpretations of a similarly named right, 401–403
national constitutional law natural right v. European Community law right, 371–391
Irish constitutional law v. European Community law, 326, 328–355. *see also* **Irish constitutional law**
coping with conflicts, 356–357
fundamental rights, 372–391
types of conflicts, 354–355
why conflicts can occur, 352–355
jurisdiction for, 159
French constitutional law, 173–185, 255–269
Irish constitutional law, 313–322
legal problem, 411
national and European Community legal orders, between, 13–14, 14–15
policy conflicts, 15, 404
French constitutional law v. European Community law, 407
Irish constitutional law v. European Community law, 404–406
proposals for resolution of, 16–17, 411; *see also* **future directions**

public international law rule v. national law rule, 100
revolt or revolution. *see* **revolt or revolution dilemma**
Conseil Constitutionnel, 166, 167–169
authority, 170
judicial acceptance of, 171
political acceptance of, 170
binding nature of constitutional decisions, 171
composition, 169, 170
European Community, interpretation of, 223–224
European Parliament, 224
right to vote in elections to European Parliament, 225–226
Union citizenship, 224–225
voting in Council, 226
independence, 169, 172
jurisdiction
advice to President in exercise of emergency functions, 170
confirmation of vacancy or incapacity of President, 170
constitutional legal order, control of, 172–185
electoral matters, 182–183
executive measures, control of, 183–185
heads of jurisdiction set out in Constitution, 172, 173–185
international treaties, agreements and Council directives, 173–175
Lois, control of, 176–183
organic *lois,* 181–182
parliamentary elections, supervision of, 170
political disputes, 170
regularity of referenda, supervision of, 170
suspension of Constitution, role during, 170
ultimate guardian of constitutional rights, 168
Parliament, and
relationship between, 168
reservation of interpretation, 238–239
supreme constitutional court, 166
Conseil d'Etat, 166, 183, 255, 256
direct effect and supremacy, interpretation of, 262–265
jurisdiction
application of public international law treaties, 256–257
control of *lois,* 257–261
control of *reglèments,* 261–262
loi ecran, doctrine of, 257n, 258
Constitution of Ireland 1937, 5n, 358n. *see also* **Irish constitutional law**
Constitution of Saorstát Eireann (Irish Free State) 1922, 5n, 303, 358n
constitutional boundaries, 7
constitutional conflicts. *see* **conflicts**
constitutional disobedience, 57
constitutional justice
Irish law, 314–315, 364
constitutional law. *see* **national constitutional law**
France. *see* **French constitutional law**
Ireland. *see* **Irish constitutional law**
constitutional law policy, 404
national constitutional law policy and EC policy conflicts between, 404–407
constitutional revolutions. *see* **revolt or revolution dilemma**
contraception
Irish law on, 281, 287
Costa v. ENEL, 48, 102–114
admissibility of Article 177 reference, 104–105
background to reference, 102–104
basis for supremacy, 107–114
integration and spirit, 109–110
rejection of public international law, 108–109
text of the judgment, 107–108
development and expansion of, 114–120
political backing, 114
role of Court of Justice, 105–107
Costello, D., 273n, 279, 290n, 3078
Council of Europe, 35

Cour de Cassation, 166, 255
decisions of *Conseil Constitutionnel* and, 171
jurisdiction, 265–269
Matter doctrine, 265n
Court of Justice, 8, 24–25, 31
autonomous validity of European Community law, 11, 20
binding nature of judgments, 24
competences of the Community, 34
constitutionalisation of European Community law, 24–25, 34–35, 36–37, 145–147
cooperation with national courts, 427–428
direct access of individuals to, 24
general public international law rules, application of, 46–61
exhaustion of domestic remedies, 51
interpretation, 57–59
obligation in the result, 52–57
pacta sunt servanda, 47
reciprocity, 48–49
implied external competence, doctrine of, 36–37
individual rights, doctrine of, 64–65
development of, 64–78
expansion of, 79–98
Van Gend en Loos judgment, 65–78
institutional role, 24
international treaties
interpretation of, 58–59, 60, 61
judicial review procedure, 40–41
precedence over secondary law, 41–42
international tribunals
status of decisions of, 45
interpretation
public international law influence in, 57–60
jurisdiction, 24, 64, 66–67, 105
application of European Community law, 106–107
fundamental rights, 120–40. *see also* **fundamental rights**
preliminary references (Article 177). *see* **preliminary reference procedure**
treaties, status of, 39–41
validity of national law, 105–106
role of, 105
self-perception, 24–25
sources of law, 61
supremacy
development of doctrine of, 100–120. *see also* **supremacy**
courts, 24. *see also* **Court of Justice; national courts**
conflicts between, 15
International Court of Justice, 45n, 61, 323, 346
cultural diversity, 425
Curtin, D., 155n–156n

Danube Commissioners, 52
De Burca, G., 392n, 396n, 417n
De Gaulle, C., 152, 360n
De Witte, B., 23n, 54, 108, 110, 113, 194, 422, 423n, 425
Debré, M., 167
Decisions
binding nature of, 88
individual rights resulting from, 88
Declaration of the Rights of Man and of the Citizen (1789), 163, 190, 223, 280, 402
natural, inalienable and sacred rights, 247, 248
Delaney, H., 315n
delegated sovereignty
French constitutional law, 209–210
democracy, promotion of, 121
democratic society, 137
public policy derogation
test of necessity, 395–396
Denmark, 152
Treaty on European Union, problems raised by, 74–75
denunciation of treaties, 220–221
French constitutional law, 217–218, 218–221
Irish constitutional law, 353
derogations, 15, 422
Court's control of, 393–395
fundamental rights as, 136–137, 392–400
permanent derogation, 422
test of necessity, 396

development cooperation, 35
diplomatic and consular authorities
right to protection by, 142
direct applicability, 113–114
European Community law perception, 52–57
Regulations, 52–57, 84–85
treaties, 83–84
direct effect, 12, 54, 56, 62, 426. *see also* **individual rights**
Association Agreements, 91
decisions, 88
development of doctrine of individual rights, 64–65
Van Gend en Loos, 65–78
directives, 85–86
European Community law perception, 64–65
expansion of doctrine, 79–98
French constitutional law interpretation
conflict with European Community law, 262–265
horizontal, 81, 318n
Irish constitutional law norms, 317–318
international treaties, 91–92
legitimacy, 91
independence from original legitimation, 91–92
national courts, problems before, 92–98
non-acceptance, 414–415
penetration of doctrine, 92–96
public international law perception, 63–64
regulations, 84–85
remedy in damages, 88–90
tests, 79–81
Treaty provisions, 81–83
Directives, 55
binding nature of, 85
relates only to Member States, 86
direct effect, 85–87; *see also* **direct effect**
French constitutional law interpretation, 263–265
individual rights resulting from, 85–88
remedies
damages, 87–88, 88–90
French constitutional law, 264
disuniformity, 45n, 73, 75, 76, 78, 103, 138, 139, 421–424, 424
provision for, 45n
divorce
Irish law, 286
dualist orders, 101
conflict of norms, 8
European Convention on Human Rights and Fundamental Freedoms and, 417n
Irish legal order, 100, 299, 323–324
public international law rules, status of, 100, 101
Dublin Convention, 196
Duncan, W., 280n, 281n, 311n, 313n, 414n
dwelling
non-violability of, 139
Dworkin, R., 354n, 383n, 408n, 421n

Economic and Monetary Union, 7n, 45n, 155, 161, 207, 211, 422
French constitutional law interpretation, 229–231
protocols, 423
economic objectives
human rights, conflict with, 374, 408–409
education policy, 58
Edward, D., 139n
EEC-Morocco Cooperation Agreement, 84n
EEC-Portuguese Association Agreement, 84n
EEC-Turkey Association Agreement, 84
effectiveness, 69, 75, 77–78, 95, 111–112, 119, 426n–427n
direct effect of Directives, 85. *see also* **direct effect**
proposed future direction and, 426–427
effet utile, 77
elections
European Parliament, 141, 142, 225–226, 227
municipal elections, 142, 225
French constitutional law interpretation, 231–233

Eleizar, D.J., 426n
England, 152. *see also* **United Kingdom**
ecclesiastical law, 284n
environmental rights, 415
equal pay, 82
establishment, right of, 64
Euratom, 5
European Atomic Energy Community, 5
European Central Bank, 23, 67
European Coal and Steel Community, 5
European Commission of Human Rights
Member State responsibility for acts of the EC, 43–44
European Community. *see also* **European Community law**
competences, 32–37; *see also* **competences**
implied exclusive external powers, 36–37
treaty-making powers, 35–37
essential scope or objectives of, 336
Irish constitutional law and, 337–338
French constitutional law interpretation of, 223–229
international organisation, as, 26, 44
legal personality, 35
meaning of term, 5
Member State responsibility for acts of, 42–45
treaty-making powers, 35–37
withdrawal from membership, 13, 335
Irish constitutional law, 335, 353
European Community law, 3, 20
amendability, 16, 148–158. *see also* **amendability of European Community law**
application of, 13, 24, 106–107
direct applicability of Regulations, 52–57
direct effect, doctrine of, 62–63; *see also* **direct effect**
autonomous legal order, as, 11–13, 20, 22, 27, 28, 31, 55, 109, 110
basis of, 10
breaches of
remedy in damages, 90
citizenship, 141–143
acquisition of, 141
express rights of Union citizen, 142
competences, 32–37; *see also* **competences**
treaty-making powers, 35–37
conflicts with national law. *see* **conflicts**
constitutionalisation, 24, 39, 146
constitutional characteristics, 20, 28, 65
federal state, 21, 145
meaning of "constitution" 21
Treaty as constitution, 34–35, 41, 144–147
Decisions, 88
derogations. *see* **derogations**
Directives. *see* **Directives**
disuniformity, 45n, 73, 421–424, 424
provision for, 45n
effectiveness. *see* **effectiveness**
enforceability
Irish constitutional law and, 349–352, 353
limits to, 13
essential characteristics, 62
ex proprio vigore legal order, 11–12, 21, 31, 75
executive uniformity, 56, 111–112, 424, 425. *see also* **uniformity**
federal legal order, as, 6n, 21, 426
European Community law perception, 160–162
federal characteristics, 161–162
public international law perception, 160
French constitutional law interpretation of, 222–36; *see also* **French constitutional law**
Conseil Constitutionnel's interpretation of European Community, 223–228
functioning of, 424
European unity dependent on, 424
fundamental rights, 120–140; *see also* **fundamental rights**
conflict between human right and economic objective, 408

conflict of fundamentals, 388–391
European Community law supremacy, 120
general principles, as, 123–126
future directions. *see* **future directions**
general principles of, 384–385
fundamental rights as, 123–126
textual basis for, 124–126
historical origin, 11, 29
indirect effect, 373n
individual rights, doctrine of
development of, 20, 62–78
expansion of, 79–98
public international law, 63–64
role of Court of Justice, 105–106
supremacy and, 98–120
innovative qualities, 26, 27, 52
integration into national law, 22, 48, 109–110, 116
limitation on, 16, 414, 417
international organisation, law of, 26, 44
international tribunals
status of decisions, 45
Irish constitutional law and, 328–355; *see also* **Irish constitutional law**
jurisdiction
conflicts, for, 159
extension of jurisdiction and demands, 121–139
legitimation, 10, 11–12, 20, 31, 62
monist system, 39
national constitutional law and, 10, 13–14, 22. *see also* **French constitutional law; Irish constitutional law**
autonomy from, 22
conflicts between, 4, 13, 14–15. *see also* **conflicts**
future directions, 16–17, 413–418. *see also* **future directions**
new constitution, 17, 414–415, 417
new legal order, as, 11, 49, 62, 71–72, 146
origin, 22, 29–31, 146
perceptions of, 21–28
European Community law perception, 22–25, 28, 31
French constitutional law, 198–199
national law perception, 22
public international law perception, 21, 26–27, 29–30
political theory, 408n
pre-Treaty rights and obligations, 422
primacy. *see* **supremacy**
proposed future direction as matter of European Community law, 424–425
protocols, 423
public international law and, 26–27. *see also* **public international law**
independence from, 11, 20, 21, 23, 27, 29, 31, 46
public international law nature of European Community law, 11, 23, 29
public international law principles and
exhaustion of domestic remedies, 50–57
pacta sunt servanda, 47
reciprocity, 47–50
source of European Community law, as, 60–61
status in European Community law, 46–61
reform in, 16, 414
Regulations
direct applicability, 52–57
remedies, 88–90
revolt or revolution. *see* **revolt or revolution dilemma**
secondary law
treaties and, 41–42
Social Chapter, 423
sovereignty, 29
"special and original nature" of, 109, 112
subsidiarity, 23, 422
sui generis legal order, as, 11, 12, 21, 22, 28
supremacy, doctrine of, 98–120; *see also* **supremacy**
suspension of obligations, provision for, 422

European Community law, *(Contd.)*
treaties establishing the European Community. *see* **Treaties establishing the European Communities**
treaties with third states
competence to conclude, 35–37
incompatibility, 39–41
Member State responsibility, 42–45
secondary law and, 41–42
status of, 38–45
Treaty establishing European Community and, 39–41
Treaty on European Union. *see* **Treaty on European Union**
uniformity. *see* **uniformity**
European Community law rights
conflicts. *see also* **conflicts**
Irish constitutional law natural rights, 372–391
enforcement of
direct applicability, 52–57
fundamental rights. *see* **fundamental rights**
individual rights, doctrine of. *see* **individual rights**
origin of, 55, 56
European Convention for the Protection of Human Rights and Fundamental Freedoms, 61, 120, 136, 395
dualist states, and, 417n
European Community accession to, 123
exhaustion of domestic remedies, rule as to, 50
infringement by Member State, 137
infringement of, 137
status of, in European Community law, 395n
status of, in Irish law, 324
European Council, 153
Declaration on human rights (1991), 122
Resolution on human rights (1991), 122
voting in Council, 226
European Court of Human Rights, 8, 24, 123
authority of judgments in Irish law, 324
European Economic Area, 156
European Economic Community, 5
European integration, 26n, 52, 58, 109–110
attainment of
dependent on functioning of European Community law, 424
European Community law based on, 10, 12
proposed future direction and, 424
constitutional boundaries, 7
direct applicability of Regulations, 52
limitation of, 16, 417
mirror image argument and, 55–56
objective of, 12, 13
reliance of Court of Justice on, 58
obstacles to, 28
European Parliament, 23, 31
elections to
direct election, 143, 199–200, 224
right to stand in, 142, 225
right to vote in, 141, 142, 225–226, 227
federal parliament, as, 143
French constitutional law interpretation of, 224
petition, rights of, 142
powers of, 143
rights of Union citizen, 142–143
European School, 43
European Union
citizenship, 122, 141–143, 224–225
Constitution, 17, 414–415
French constitutional law and, 228–229
European unity. *see* **European integration**
evidence on natural law
moral philosophers, 288–289
ex proprio vigore **legal order**
European Community law as, 11–12, 21, 31, 75
executive uniformity of European Community law, 56, 66, 111–112, 424, 425
exhaustion of domestic remedies, principle of
European Community law perception, 51

public international law perception, 50
external competence, 36, 162
implied, 36–37
external frontiers
control of
French constitutional law, 231

fair procedures, right to
Irish law, 315–316
family, rights of
Irish constitutional law, 275, 292, 312
Favoreau, L., 174, 204–205, 222, 226, 227
federal courts, 24
federal legal order, 20
European Community law as, 6n, 160–162
federal preemption, 118n
federalism, 426
federation, 37, 411
Finnis, J., 281n, 284n, 309n, 416n, 431n
Fitzpatrick, Barry, 81n
Food and Agriculture Organisation
accession of European Community to, 32, 33
constitution, 144
Forde, M., 280
foreign affairs. *see* **external competence**
foreigners, rights of
French constitutional law, 247–248
Irish constitutional law, 291
France, 152. *see also* **French constitutional law; French law; French Revolution**
free exercise of commerce, 139
free movement of capital
derogations, 422
free movement of persons, 58, 64, 123, 395
non-discrimination on grounds of nationality, 81
protocols, 423
Union citizens, 142
free movement of services. *see also* **services**
derogations, 422n
free movement of workers, 64, 380n, 405
agreements on, provision for, 35n–36n
Irish constitutional law policy on promotion of Irish language, and, 405–406
freedom of expression, 140, 373n, 394, 396
restrictions to, 394–395, 396
freedom of information, 373n, 423
freedom of work, 139
French Committee of National Liberation (C.F.N.L.), 215
French constitutional law, 5, 163–164
amendability
limits to, 199, 206–212
role of people, 192n
bloc de constitutionalité, 210
conflicts with European Community law, 163–164, 172–173, 235, 254, 369n, 371
constitutional control by courts, 165–185
direct effect and supremacy, 262–265
European Parliament and French Parliament, 369n
jurisdiction of *Conseil Constitutionnel*, 172–185
jurisdiction of *Conseil d'Etat*, 255, 256–265
jurisdiction of *Cour de Cassation*, 265–269
policy conflicts, 407
types of conflict, 172–173
Constitution of 1958, 167, 192, 193–194, 223
Conseil Constitutionnel, 169, 170, 171, 172, 173–185
international treaties and agreements, 196
limits on amendment, 206–208
constitutional control by courts, 165–166
Conseil Constitutionnel, 166, 167–185, 238–239. *see also* ***Conseil Constitutionnel***
Conseil d'Etat, 256–265
Cour de Cassation, 265–269
executive measures, 183–185, 256–262
international treaties and agreements, 173–174, 256–257

French Constitutional law *(Contd.)*
jurisdictional limits, 166–167, 172
lois, 176–183, 257–261
ordonnances, 258
règlements, 261–262
reservations of interpretation, 238–239
secondary EC legislation, 174–175
constitutionalisation of French law, 165
courts, 166
essential conditions for exercise of national sovereignty, 199, 204–206, 209–212
continuation of the life of the nation, 251–253
guarantee of rights and liberties, assuring, 240–250
institutions of the Republic, respect for, 250–251
substance of, 240–253
European Community law and
concepts involved, 198–216
conflicts. *see* **conflicts** *(above)*
Conseil Constitutionnel's interpretation, 222, 223–228
debates on ratification, 226–228
direct effect and supremacy, 262–265
elections, 231–233
EMU and control of external frontiers, 229–231
enforcement of European Community law, 255–256
European Communities and European Union, 228–229
European Parliament, 224
inalienability of sovereignty, 204
limitation and transfer distinguished, 199–204
perception of European Community law, 163–164, 198–216
ratification of Treaty on European Union, 222–235
reciprocity, condition of, 236
resolutions, 233–235
right to vote in European Parliament elections, 225–226
Union citizenship, 224–225
voting in Council, 226
fundamental commitments, 164, 193, 216, 223, 246–253
fundamental rights, 371
balancing of, 250
commitment to, 165, 193, 214
delegation of control of guarantee of, 240–243
foreigners' rights, 247–248
formal sources, 244
foundation of Constitution, 245–246
framework of independent concepts, 248–249
guarantee of rights and liberties, 240–250
liberty, 249
life, 168n, 371–372
limitations on rights, 248–249, 250
material sources, 244–245
natural rights, 247, 250
nature and legitimation, 245
non-positivist nature, 246–248
ordering of, 248–250
property, 402
recognition of, 247
sacred rights, 246–247
sources of rights and liberties of citizens, 243–250
human rights. *see* **fundamental rights** *(above)*
institutions of the Republic
respect for, 250–251
internal constitutional conflicts, 237–238
legal constitution, 165–167
nation
continuation of life of, 251–253
notion of, 252
national language, promotion of, 407
natural law, 246–250
natural rights, 247, 250
ordonnances, 183, 258
people, sovereignty of, 190, 191–194, 213, 252, 360n
public international law
constitutional basis of, 195–197
status of, 100
public order, safeguard of, 407
referenda, 192n–193n

règlements, 173n
control of, 261–262
republican form of government, 193, 202, 205, 208, 251
reservation of interpretation, 237, 238–239
separation of powers, 166, 265
sovereignty, 163, 190–216, 252
conceptual difficulties, 198–199
constitutional basis of public international law, 195–197
delegated sovereignty, 209–210
essential conditions for exercise of, 199, 204–206, 240–253
history of principle, 190–195
inalienability of, 199, 204, 214
limitation and transfer, distinction between, 199–204
limits on amendment, 206–212
popular sovereignty, 190, 191–194, 213, 252
recognition of legal effects, limits to, 212–216
superiority of constitutional law, 197
transfer of competences, 190
supreme courts, 166
treaties and agreements
control of, 173–174
denunciation and reversability, 217–221
future treaties, 218–219
interpretation of, 256–257
public international law, relevance of, 219–221
ratification requirement, 195–196
reciprocity, 236
status of, 195–197
Treaty on European Union
denunciation and reversability, 217–218
ratification of, 163, 186–189, 222–236
French language, promotion of
potential conflict with European Community law policy, 407
French law. *see also* **French constitutional law**
constitutionalisation, 165
French nation, 251–253
French Revolution, 166, 190, 191, 192, 214
sovereignty, 252
Frowein, J.A., 413n
fundamental commitments
conflicts between, 15, 164, 272, 299–302
French constitutional law, 164, 193, 216, 223
assuring continuation of the life of the nation, 251–253
assuring respect for the institutions of the Republic, 250–251
rights, 245, 246–250
Irish constitutional law, 272, 296, 297, 299
fundamental rights
citizens of European Union
express rights, 122–123, 142–143, 385n
conflicts. *see also* **conflicts**
economic objectives, with, 408–409
national constitutional law rights v. European Community law rights, 15, 371–391
Declaration of the Rights of Man and of the Citizen (1789), 163, 190, 223, 247, 248, 280, 402
derogations, as, 136–137, 392–400
economic objectives, and, 40–89
European Community law, 120–121
development of doctrine, 121–123
extension of jurisdiction and demands, 121–139
future development, 123
general principles of European Community law, rights as, 123–126
jurisprudential basis, 126–132
list of rights currently included, 139–140
political declarations, 122
sources independent from jurisprudential basis, 132–136
supremacy of European Community law, 120–121
textual basis, 124–126
Treaty establishing the European Community, 124–125

fundamental rights, *(Contd.)*
Treaty on European Union, 125, 126, 136, 409
French constitutional law. *see* **French constitutional law**
international sources, 136
Irish constitutional law. *see* **Irish constitutional law**
life, right to, 287
French constitutional law, 371–372
life of unborn, right to. *see* **unborn, right to life of**
market rights and human rights
confusion between, 395
meaning of "fundamental," 385–386
private property, 401–403
procedural rights, 139n
public international law perception, 120
services
right to information concerning, 372
right to receive, 372
future directions, 4, 16–17, 411
available directions, 413–416
European Union constitution, 414–415, 417
limitation on integration of European Community law, 16, 414, 417, 418
national constitutional law basic principles, precedence of, 415–416
proposed direction, 16, 17, 414, 415, 417–418, 430
methodology, 16, 420
resistance within European Community law to, 429
support within European Community law for, 421–428
reform
European Community law, 16, 414
national law, 414
revolt or revolution
Court of Justice, 414
European Community law, 414
national law, 413–414
rights
distinction between various types of, 415–416

General Agreement on Tariffs and Trade, 35
Geneva Convention (1951), 180n
German Constitution, 312n
German Empire, 30
Germany, 153n
God, 280n, 283, 308n
French constitutional law, 246–247, 250
Irish constitutional law, 282n–283n, 288, 289, 309
government intervention in private sphere, 140
Greek Constitution, 157n, 312n

Hannon, P., 281n–282n
Hartley, T.C., 41, 156n, 380n
Henchy, S., 287–288
Hogan, G., 278n, 290, 295, 296
Hogan, G., and Whelan, A., 5n–6n, 7n, 54–55, 297, 347, 355n, 363n, 366n, 415n
homosexuality, 285–286
horizontal direct effect, 81, 318n
Irish constitutional law norms, 317–318
Horwitz, M.J., 317n
human rights. *see* **fundamental rights**
Humphreys, R., 295n, 296n, 357n

implied external competence, doctrine of, 36–37
implied powers doctrine, 34n, 36
inadimplenti non est adimplendum, 47
individual rights, 20. *see also* **fundamental rights**
abortion as a service, 382
Decisions, 88
development of doctrine in European Community law
preliminary reference procedure (Article 177), 69–71
Van Gend en Loos, 62, 65–78
expansion of *Van Gend en Loos*, 79–98
international treaties, 63–64, 83–84
meaning of, 63
perceptions of
European Community law, 64–65
public international law, 63–64

Regulations, 84–85
remedy in damages, 88–90
supremacy, 98–110
tests, 79–81
Treaty provisions, 81–83

information, freedom of, 373n, 423
commercial information, 394

integration, *see* **European integration**

International Court of Justice, 45n, 61, 220, 323, 346

International Labour Organisation, 36

international law. *see* **public international law**

International Law Commission, 100

international organisation
European Community as, 26, 44

international responsibility of Member States, 42–45, 69

international treaties. *see* **treaties**

international tribunals
decisions of
Court of Justice and, 45
exhaustion of domestic remedies, rule as to, 50–51

interpretation
direct effect
French constitutional law interpretation, 262–265
European Community, of
French constitutional law, 223–226
European Community law, 269
role of Court of Justice, 105–106
fundamental rights
different interpretations of a similarly named right, 401–403
general rules and principles of public international law, 57–60
municipal elections
French constitutional law, 231–233
national law, 423
private property, right to, 402–403
reservation of
French constitutional law, 237, 238–239
supremacy, of
French constitutional law interpretation, 262–265
treaties, of. *see* **interpretation of treaties**

interpretation of treaties
decisions of international tribunals and, 45
public international law influence, 57–60
sources of law used as quarry, 60–61

Irish constitutional law, 5, 271–272
amendment, limits on, 357, 359–367, 368
Irish constitutional natural law limits, 365–367
manner of amendment, 360
popular sovereignty and natural law limits, 361–365
self-amendment, 361–365
Christianity, recognition of, 284–285
common good, 307–310, 402
meaning of, 309–310
concepts of, 303–312
conflicts with European Community law, 271–272, 328
amendment of national law to preempt conflict, 329–334
coping with conflicts, 356–357
different perspective of what constitutes European Community law, 352
duty of judges to give effect to Constitution, 318, 353–354, 399
essential scope or objectives of the Community, 337–338
fundamental conflict, 273–274
fundamental rights as derogations, 392
general principles of international law v. European Community law rule, 326–327
Grogan, 374–383
membership problems, 334–338
natural right v. European Community law right, 372–391
"necessitated by obligations of membership," 339–349
policy conflicts, 404–406
reasons for conflicts, 352–355
revolt or revolution dilemma, 356

Irish constitutional law, *(Contd.)*
types of conflict, 354–355
Constitution of Ireland 1937, 5n, 358n
Constitution of Saorstát Éireann 1922, 5n, 303, 358n
constitutional justice, 314–315, 364
extension into administrative and private law, 314–317
fair procedures, right to, 315–317
constitutional rights. *see* fundamental rights (*below*)
constitutionalisation of Irish law, 271, 313–322
courts, 313
Directive Principles of Social Policy, 312
dualist legal order, 100, 299, 323–324
European Community law in, 271–272, 328–355
bar to constitutional challenge, 331–332, 338–352, 339–349, 352
cessation of membership, 335, 353
conflicts. *see* **conflicts** (*above*)
constitutional amendments, 329–332
coping with conflicts, 356–357
Crotty v. An Taoiseach, 335–338
duty of judges, 353–354
enforceability of European Community law, 349–352, 353
history of membership, 328–329
limited recognition, 328
membership provisions, 334–338
mode of implementation, 339, 342, 344
options for government, 356–357
ratification of Treaty on European Union, 329, 335
references under Article 177, 339, 340–341, 347
Single European Act, 329, 335
status of European Community law, 333–334, 351, 352, 356
statutory amendments, 332–334
weak points, 352–353
external sovereignty, 303–306
family, 275, 292
fundamental unit group, as, 312
fundamental commitments, 272, 296, 297, 299
conflicts, 299–302
fundamental rights, 408
anti-majoritarian protection, 293, 363
changing concepts of prudence, justice and charity, 292–297
common good, restrictions based on, 309
conflict with European Community law rights, 274, 372–391, 397–400
conflicting constitutional rights, 299–302, 397, 398
contractarian legitimation, rejection of, 290–292
enforcement, 297–298, 398
equality before the law, 275, 291
European Convention on Human Rights and Fundamental Freedoms and, 278n
foreigners, rights of, 291
hierarchy of constitutional rights, 299, 300–302, 398
locus standi, 319–320
natural law basis, 273–274, 275, 276–277, 291
nature of the State, based on, 290
non-citizens, applicable to, 291–292
privacy, 312
private legal relations, extension into, 317–319, 319–320
private property, 402–403
procedural requirements, relaxation of, 321–322
remedies for breach of, 320–321
unborn, right to life of, 291n–292n, 372–391, 397, 398–400
waiver of constitutional rights, 298–299
God, references to, 282n–283n, 288, 309
internal sovereignty, 306
international relations, 304, 323
denunciation of treaties, 353

dualist nature of legal system, 100, 323–324
European Convention on Protection of Human Rights, 324
European Court of Human Rights, status of judgments of, 324
foundational principles, 323
general principles of public international law, status of, 100, 324–327
international agreements, 323–324
pacific settlement of disputes, 323
sovereignty of State, 303–306
Irish language, promotion of, 404–406
judges' duty to uphold Constitution, 353
conflict with European Community law duty, 353–354
jurisdiction in constitutional matters, 313–314
justice, concept of, 314–315
legal revolution, 358–359
legitimation of, 273–302, 368
immateriality of consequential difficulties, 297–298
natural law based on reason, 273–280
resolution of internal constitutional conflicts, 299–302
locus standi, 319
private parties, against, 319–320
State, against, 320
marriage, 286
natural law basis, 271, 365–367
jurisprudence, 276–277
meaning of "natural law," 277–278
popular sovereignty and natural law limits, 361–365
reason, based on, 273–280
role of reason, 277–280
text of the Constitution, 275
theology/religion basis: debunking the myth, 280–289
natural rights
overriding of, 366
people, sovereignty of. *see* sovereignty of the people (*below*)
perceptions of, 368
Preamble to the Constitution, 283, 292
amendment of, 360, 361
procedural requirements, relaxation of, 321–322
prudence, justice and charity
judges' changing concepts of, 292–297
public international law in, 323–327
religion, position of, 289
religion-based morality, role of, 281–287
religion-based natural law
debunking the myth, 280–289
remedies, provision of, 320–321
separation of powers, 313
society, 310–312
sovereignty of the people, 273, 306–307, 330, 368
common good and, 308
natural law limits, 307, 361–365
sovereignty of the State, 303–306, 330
limits on, 362
State, sovereignty of. see sovereignty of the State (*above*)
supremacy of Community law, 274
validity of statutes, 313–314
Irish language, promotion of
potential conflict with European Community law policy, 404–406

Joerges, C., 7n–8n, 391n, 418n
John Paul II, 283n, 287n
judges. *see* national judges
judicial policy
proposed direction and, 427–428
judicial review
preliminary reference procedure (Article 177). *see* **preliminary reference procedure**
treaties
compatibility with European Community law, 39–40
judicial subsidiarity, 422
jurisdiction
conflicts, for

jurisdiction, *(Contd.)*
European Community law, 159
French constitutional law, 173–185, 255, 256–269
Irish constitutional law, 313–322
preliminary reference procedure (Article 177). *see* **preliminary reference procedure**
Conseil Constitutionnel. see ***Conseil Constitutionnel***
Conseil d'Etat, 256–257
Cour de Cassation, 265–269
Court of Justice. *see* **Court of Justice**
European Community law fundamental rights
extension of jurisdiction and demands, 121–139
Irish constitutional law conflicts, 313–314
jurisprudential change, 16
justice
Irish constitutional law concept of, 314–317

Kakouris, C.N., 31, 380n–381n
Karydis, G.S., 425n
Kelly, J.M., 4n, 276n, 290, 296, 303, 304, 341n, 352, 430n

Lambert, E., 213n
language. *see* **national language**
legal heritage, 71, 75
legal orders, 3
conflicts between, 14
constitutional revolutions, 358
legal personality, 35
legal professional privilege, 140
legal revolution, 23, 368n, 414, 430. *see also* **revolt or revolution dilemma**
avoidance of, 16, 417–418
Irish law, 358–359
legitimate expectations, 123
legitimation, 10, 163
European Community law, 10, 11–12, 20, 31, 62
Irish constitutional law, 273–302, 368
immateriality of consequential difficulties, 297–298
natural law based on reason, 273–280
national constitutional law, 10, 14
Lhoest, O. and Nihoul, P., 421n
liberal democratic rights, 415
liberty of forms, 59
life, right to, 287, 318, 398
French constitutional law, 168n, 371–372
life of unborn. *see* **unborn, right to life of**
locus standi
assertion of constitutional rights
Irish law, 319–320
London Convention, 40n
Louis, J.V., 74
Louis, J.V., and Alen, A., 94n
Luchaire, F., 214, 217n, 229, 231, 239
Luxembourg Compromise, 60, 228, 413

Maastricht Treaty. *see* **Treaty on European Union**
McCarthy, N., 277n
Macintyre, A., 409n
MacMahon, B., 192
majority voting
Conseil Constitutionnel's interpretation of, 226
Mancini, F., 145
market rights
human rights, and
confusion between, 395
marriage
Irish law, 286
marry, right to, 401n
medical secrecy, right to, 140
Member States
amendment of European Community law. *see* **amendability of European Community law**
direct applicability of Regulations
failure to recognise, 52
national identity, 16, 425–426
nationality laws, 141–142
responsibility for acts of European Community, 42–45
transfer of sovereignty, 12–13
treaties with third states

binding nature of, 42, 45
power to make, 36
withdrawal from European Community, 13, 335
Mitterand, F., 163n
Montevideo Convention, 32n
morality
contraception, 281, 287
evidence of moral philosophers, 288–289
private morality
regulation by the State, 284–287
religion-based morality
role of, in Irish constitutional law, 281–287
sexual morality, 281, 285–286
move, right to. *see* **free movement**
municipal elections
right to vote and stand in, 142, 225, 232n
French constitutional law interpretation, 231–233
Murphy, T., 288

national citizenship
Union citizenship and, 141–142
national constitutional law, 3, 5. *see also* **French constitutional law; Irish constitutional law; national law**
amendability, 10
French constitutional law, 199, 206–212
Irish constitutional law, 357, 359–367, 368
basic principles, 415–416
precedence over European Community law proposed, 416
basis of, 10
breaking point, 10
European Community law and, 10
conflicts between, 4, 14–15, 20, 369–370. *see also* **conflicts**
relationship between, 13–14
legitimation of, 10, 14
meaning of term, 5
reconstruction of, 45
revision of, 14
revolt or revolution dilemma, 7, 8, 10, 13, 16, 370, 409, 413–414, 415. *see also* **revolt or revolution dilemma**
supremacy of, 6n
supremacy of European Community law, 114–120; *see also* **supremacy**
national courts. *see also* **national judges**
autonomous validity of European Community law, 55
constitutional disobedience, 57
duty to uphold Constitution, 10, 17
European Community law conditioning of, 97–98
European Community law constraints, 96–97
European Community law rights before
direct applicability of Regulations, 53, 54
interpretation of national law, 423
national cultural diversity
protection of, 425
national heritage, 311n
national identity, 16, 425–426
national judges
duty to uphold Constitution, 10, 17
conflict with European Community law duty, 353–354
Irish constitutional law, 318, 353–354
national language, promotion of
European Community law right and potential conflict between, 404–406
French language, 407
Irish language, 404–406
national law, 3, 5. *see also* **national constitutional law**
constitutionalisation, 15
demands of European Community law on, 10, 11, 13, 20, 78, 379–381
fundamental rights, 121–139
revolt against, 13
European Community law and, 13–14
conflicts between, 4, 10, 14–15; *see also* **conflicts**
direct applicability of Regulations, 52–57

national law, *(Contd.)*
implementation and transformation, distinction between, 52
limits to recognition, 57, 328
non-transformation of Regulations, 52–57
perception of European Community law, 22
state of constitutional disobedience, 57
integration of European Community law into, 22, 48, 109–110, 116
limitation on, 16, 414, 417
interpretation of
obligations of national judges, 423
meaning of term, 5
public international law rules and
conflict between, 100
validity of, 105–106
national partitioning, 76
nationality
non-discrimination on grounds of, 81–82
nationality of a Member State, 141–142
natural justice, principles of, 314
natural law, 14
evidence of moral philosophers, 288–289
French constitutional law, 246–250
Irish Constitutional law, basis of, 273–277
religion basis: debunking the myth, 280–289
role of reason, 277–280
universal application, 291–292
natural rights
common good, restrictions based on, 309–310
conflicts with European Community law rights, 371–372
Irish constitutional law, 372–391
French constitutional law, 247, 250
Irish constitutional law, 273–277, 280
waiver of, 298–299
New York Protocol (1967), 180n
Newman, J., 307n–308n
Nicholas, B., 168
non-discrimination
on grounds of nationality, 81–82
on grounds of sex, 139
non-violability of the dwelling, 139

obligation in the result, 51, 66
direct applicability, 52–57
O'Hanlon, R., 279, 281n, 282n
O'Leary, S., 391n
Oliver, P., 200n
Ombudsman
right to apply to, 142
right to petition, 143
omnis conventio intelligitur rebus sic stantibus, 220
order approach, 38
Organisation for Economic Cooperation and Development, 35
origin of European Community law
autonomous from national law, 22
European Community law perception, 31
historical origin, 11, 29
public international law perception, 29–30
Orwell, George, 71n

pacta sunt servanda, 109, 150, 154, 220
European Community law perception, 47
public international law perception, 47
patrimony, 75
Peace of Westphalia, 30n
Pearse, P.H., 401n, 409n, 427n
people, sovereignty of, 14
French constitutional law, 190, 191–194, 213, 252, 360n
Irish constitutional law, 306–307, 330, 361–365, 368
common good and, 308–309
perceptions of European Community law, 21–28
European Community law perception, 22–25, 28, 31
French constitutional law, 198–199
national law perception, 22
public international law perception, 21, 26–27, 29–30
Permanent Court of International Justice, 63

Pescatore, P., 28, 67, 69, 71n, 74, 77, 112, 427, 429, 430n
policy conflicts, 15, 404–407
political theory, 408n
popular sovereignty. *see* **people, sovereignty of**
Portugal, 84n
posterior lex derogat, 150
preemption, 118–119
preliminary reference procedure (Article 177), 24, 59, 101
 Costa v. ENEL, 102–114
 individual rights, ground for, 69–71
 Irish constitutional law and, 339, 340–341, 347
 public international law perception, 71
 right to make reference, 51
 role of Court of Justice, 105–108
  application of European Community law, 106–108
  validity of national law, 105–106
 uniformity object, 59, 69
 Van Gend en Loos, 65–78
primacy of European Community law, 98–120; *see also* **supremacy**
principe de l'acte contraire, 154
principe de l'attribution des compétences, 74
privacy, right to, 285, 312
private law
 Irish law
  extension of constitutional justice into, 315–317
private life
 right to respect for, 123, 140
private morality
 regulation by the State, 284–287
private property, right to, 401
 different interpretations
  Irish constitutional law v. European Community law, 402–403
 French constitutional law, 402
professional activities, right to, 139
property, right to, 139, 388, 401–403
proportionality, principle of, 393, 428
 conflicting rights, 396–398
protocols, 423
Provisional Government of the French Republic (G.P.R.F.), 215
public interest
 common European public interest, 401n
 European Community law concept
  Irish constitutional law concept of common good and, 403
public international law, 3
 amendability of treaties, 149–150, 154
  substantive limits, 154–155
 citizenship, 141
 competences, 32
  treaty-making powers, 35
 conflict with national law, 100
 direct applicability, 52
 European Community law and
  European Community law perception of public international law, 22–25
  perception of European Community law, 21, 26–27, 29–30, 32, 35, 160
  status of general public international law rules, 46–61
  status of treaties in European Community law, 38–45
 French constitutional law sovereignty, 195–197
 fundamental rights, 120
 general rules and principles, 46
  exhaustion of domestic remedies, 50–51
  interpretation, influence in, 57–60
  liberty of forms, 59
  obligation in the result, 51–57
  pacta sunt servanda, 47
  reciprocity, 47–50
  status in European Community law, 46–57, 46–61
  status in Irish law, 324–327
 quarry for unwritten European Community law rule, as, 60–61
 statehood, criteria for, 32, 160
 supremacy, perception of, 98–100
 treaties. *see also* **treaties**
  constitution, as, 144
  contractual model of treaty relations, 67
  violation of, 100

public policy, 392–393
derogations based on. *see* **derogations**
national constitutional law fundamental rights, 392–400

Quinn, G., 276n, 296n

reciprocity, 47
European Community law, status in, 47–50
French constitutional law, 236
Regulations
direct applicability, 52–57, 84–85, 113
Member State's failure to recognise, 52
individual rights arising from, 84–85
reproduction of, 53
transformation into national law, 52
Reid, M., 281, 282
religion-based natural law
Irish constitutional law
debunking the myth, 280–289
remedies
European Community law, 88–90
exhaustion of domestic remedies, 50–51
French constitutional law, 264
Irish constitutional law, 320–321
Republic of Tanzania, 30
research and technology, 35
reservation of interpretation
French constitutional law, 237, 238–239
reside, right to, 142
Reuter, P., 58
revolt or revolution dilemma, 7, 8, 10, 13, 16, 17, 370, 409, 413
European Community law, 16, 17, 414
European Union Constitution, 415
forms of revolt, 16, 413
future directions, 16–17, 413–418
proposed direction, 414, 415, 417–418, 420–429
Irish constitutional law, 356
legal revolution, 358–359, 414
avoidance of, 16, 417–418
reform of European Community law, 16, 414
reform of national law, 414
revolution. *see* **legal revolution; revolt or revolution dilemma**
rights. *see also* **fundamental rights; individual rights**
express rights of Union citizens, 142–143
market rights and human rights
confusion between, 395
Rivero, J., 166
Roman Catholic Church
natural law doctrine, exposition of, 281, 283–284
Roseren, P., 255n
Rudden, B., 108, 166
Rule of Law, 16, 17, 418, 428, 430–431

Schengen treaty, 196, 202, 218–219, 221, 242, 249
secondary Community law
French constitutional law, in, 174–175
individual rights, giving rise to, 84
precedence of treaties over, 41–42
self-financing, 23, 161
separation of powers
French constitutional law, 166, 265
services
abortion, 376–381, 382
information concerning, 372
European Community law right in conflict with Irish constitutional law right, 372–391
right to provision of
non-discrimination on grounds of nationality, 81
prohibition on restrictions, 381–382
right to receive, 372
scope of European Community law on, 376–383
sexual morality, 281, 285
homosexuality, 285–286
Sheehy, G., 281, 401n
Simmenthal, 119–120
single currency, 155, 230
Single European Act, 35, 143, 372n, 376n
fundamental rights, 126, 136
Ireland's ratification, 304–305, 310, 329, 335–336
Preamble, 121, 126, 136

Smyth, M., 282n
Snyder, F., 91, 423n–424n, 426n–427n
Social Chapter, 423
social security, 415
society
concept of, in Irish constitutional law, 310–312
sources of law, 61
public international law, 60–61
sovereignty, 16, 110–111, 163
competence and
distinction between, 200–201
divisibility of, 74
French constitutional law, 190–216
concepts involved, 198–216
essential conditions for exercise of national sovereignty, 204–206
history of principle, 190–195
inalienability of national sovereignty, 204
limitation and transfer, distinction between, 199–204
limits on amendment, 206–212
Irish constitutional law, 273, 306–307, 308, 330, 368
natural law limits, 307, 361–365
State sovereignty, 303–306, 330, 362
obstacle to integration, as, 194
popular sovereignty, 14
French constitutional law, 190, 191–194
Irish constitutional law, 306–307, 330, 361–365, 368
State sovereignty
Irish constitutional law, 303–306, 330
transfer of. *see* **transfer of sovereignty**
"spirit of the Treaties," 31, 60, 69, 110
state aids, 401n
statehood
public law criteria, 32, 160
Stein, E., 114
Stuart, Lord Mackenzie, 3n
subsidiarity, 23, 161, 422
sui generis **legal order**
European Community law as, 11, 12, 21, 22, 28
summary of argument, 10–17
supremacy, 6n, 12, 48, 56, 62–63, 98–120, 426, 428
basis for, 107–108
executive uniformity, 111–112
integration and spirit, 109–110
objectives of integration, 111–112
rejection of public international law, 108–109
sovereignty, 110–111
Treaty provisions, 113–114
Costa v. ENEL, 102–114
development and expansion of, 114–119
political backing, 114
development of *Costa v. ENEL*
abrogation of conflicting national law, 117–118
no power to strike down conflicting national law, 116–117
preemption, 118–119
supremacy over national law of whatever nature, 114–116
direct applicability, 113–114
dualist countries, 100, 101
European Community law perception, 48, 100–120
"existential" requirement, 429
French constitutional law interpretation of
Conseil Constitutionnel, 167
Conseil d'Etat, 262–265
fundamental rights, 120–121
national constitutional law, 6n
preemption, 118–119
public international law perception, 98–100
Simmenthal, 119–120
uniformity and effectiveness, 111

terminology, 56
transfer of competences, 26, 73, 74, 110, 156, 190
French constitutional law, 200–204, 205
reversibility, 156
transfer of sovereignty, 12–13, 16, 33, 72–75, 110
delegation of powers, 73

transfer of sovereignty, *(contd.)*
European Community law perception, 33–34
limitation and, distinction between, 199–204
limitations on, 428
public international law perception, 73–74
transfer of competences, 73, 74, 200–204, 205
transformation into national law, 52
treasure trove
royal prerogative, 311
treaties. *see also* **Treaties Establishing the European Communities; Treaty on European Union**
amendability, 149–150
modification by subsequent treaty, 154
restrictions on, 150
unilateral change, 152
compatibility with European Community law
judicial review procedure, 39–40
competence to enter into
European Community, 35–37
Member States, 36
denunciation, 220–221
French constitutional law, 217–218, 218–219
Irish constitutional law, 353
direct applicability, 83–84
individual rights resulting from, 63–64, 83–84
interpretation of
public international law influence, 57–60
invalidity in European Community law, 41
judicial review procedure, 39
Member State responsibility, 42–45
reciprocity, 47–50, 236
reversibility
French constitutional law, 218–219, 220
secondary law and, 41–42
status of
European Community law, in, 38–45
French constitutional law, in, 195–197
Irish constitutional law, in, 323–327
termination, 152
withdrawal from, 152, 220–221
Treaties establishing the European Communities, 5, 29, 31, 33–34
amendability. *see* **amendability of European Community law**
citation of articles, 5
competences of the Community, 33
constitution, as, 34–35, 39, 41, 144–147, 156
French ratification, 186n
fundamental principles, 95
fundamental rights, 124–126
general principles of European Community law, 124–126
"independent source of law", as, 109
individual rights, 63–64, 65–78, 81–83
nature of, 67–68, 69, 70
objectives, 67, 71, 77–78, 95, 145
obligations of
duty of Member States to ensure carrying out of, 89
Preambles, 125–126, 126
preliminary reference procedure (Article 177). *see* **preliminary reference procedure**
"spirit of the Treaties," 31, 60, 69, 110
supremacy, 113–114
treaties with Third States
competence to enter into, 35
status of, 38–39, 39–41
Treaty of Westphalia, 418n
Treaty on European Union, 5
citizenship, 141, 142, 224–225
Denmark's problems, 74–75
denunciation
French constitutional law, 217–218
European Parliament, 143, 224
French ratification, 163, 186–189, 222–236
European Parliament, 224–225
right to vote in European Parliament elections, 225–226
voting in Council, 226

fundamental rights, 125, 126, 136, 409
Irish ratification, 329, 335
Preamble, 126
protocols, 423
Tribunal des Conflits, 171
"two-speed Europe," 422

unanimity
amendment of treaties, 151–152
unborn, right to life of, 371–372. *see also* **life, right to; Irish constitutional law**, 291n–292n, 372n, 377, 389–390, 397n, 408
conflict with European Community law right, 372–391, 397, 398–400
uniformity, 54, 75–76, 78, 90, 95, 111–112, 417n. *see also* **disuniformity**
executive, 56, 66, 111–112, 424, 425
limits to, 421–424
obstacles to, 76
preliminary reference procedure (Article 177), 59, 69
proposed future direction and, 424–425
unilateral determination and, 137
unilateral change
treaties, 152
Union citizenship, 141–143
United Arab Republic, 30
United Kingdom, 40n, 83, 85, 157n
abortion legislation, 379
Sunday trading rules, 397n
United Nations, 35
Charter, 68, 126, 144, 418n–419n
Food and Agriculture Organisation
accession of EC to, 32n, 33
objectives, 68
United States
federal preemption, doctrine of, 118n
implied powers doctrine, 34n
United States Constitution, 3n
amendability, 151
supremacy, 101
Universal Postal Union, 144

Van der Meersch, W.G., 23n, 73
Van Gend en Loos, 65–78
basis of decision, 77–78
effectiveness and uniformity, 75–77
individual rights, doctrine of, 69–70, 78; *see also* **individual rights**
tests, 79–81
international responsibility, rejection of, 69
interpretation of Article 12, 68–69
jurisdiction, 66–67
legal heritage, 75
nature of legal order, 71–72
nature of the Treaties, 67–68
"new legal order," 71–72
sovereignty, 72–75
Vaughan, D., 106n
Vedel, G., 177n, 214, 219
Verdier, M.F., 235n
Verzijl, J.H.W., 30
Vichy Government (1940–1944), 215
Vienna Conventions, 27, 35, 38
amendment of treaties, 149–150
unilateral change, 152
interpretation of treaties, 59–60
vocational training, 58
voting
Council, in, 226
European Parliament elections, 142, 225–226, 227
municipal elections, 142, 225, 231–233

Walsh, B., 278, 280n, 318–319, 332n, 363, 400n
Ward, I., 391n
Weiler, J., 376n
welfare rights, 415
West, A., 251
Westphalia, Peace of, 30n
Westphalia, Treaty of, 418n
Whelan, A., 60n, 296n, 327n. *see also* Hogan and Whelan
Whyte, G., 282n
work relations, 415
workers. *see* **free movement of workers**
working conditions
equality, 81, 82, 86
World Trade Organisation, 45n
Wyatt, D., 23, 49, 60, 106

Yaoundé Convention, 83, 84n